W9-CFL-460

RUNNING

Microsoft® Excel 2000

Mark Dodge
Craig Stinson

PUBLISHED BY
Microsoft Press
A Division of Microsoft Corporation
One Microsoft Way
Redmond,Washington 98052-6399

Copyright © 1999 by Mark Dodge, Craig Stinson, and Chris Kinata

All rights reserved. No part of the contents of this book may be reproduced or transmitted in any form
or by any means without the written permission of the publisher.

Library of Congress Cataloging-in-Publication Data
Dodge, Mark.
    Running Microsoft Excel 2000 / Mark Dodge, Craig Stinson.
       p. cm.
    Includes index.
    ISBN 1-57231-935-6
    1. Microsoft Excel for Windows.   2. Business--Computer programs.
    3. Electronic spreadsheets.   I. Stinson, Craig, 1943-   .
    II. Title.
    HF5548.4.M523D629   1999
    005.369--dc21   98-52136
                                         CIP

Printed and bound in the United States of America.

8 9 QWTQWT 4 3 2 1

Distributed in Canada by Penguin Books Canada Limited.

A CIP catalogue record for this book is available from the British Library.

Microsoft Press books are available through booksellers and distributors worldwide. For further information
about international editions, contact your local Microsoft Corporation office or contact Microsoft Press
International directly at fax (425) 936-7329. Visit our Web site at mspress.microsoft.com.

Macintosh and TrueType fonts are registered trademarks of Apple Computer, Inc. FrontPage, IntelliMouse,
Microsoft, the Microsoft Excel logo, the Microsoft Internet Explorer logo, Microsoft Press, the Microsoft Press
logo, MS-DOS, NetMeeting, the Office logo, Outlook, PivotTable, PowerPoint, Visual Basic, the Visual Basic
logo, Windows, and Windows NT are either registered trademarks or trademarks of Microsoft Corporation in the
United States and/or other countries. Other product and company names mentioned herein may be the trademarks of their respective owners.

The example companies, organizations, products, people, and events depicted herein are fictitious. No association with any real company, organization, product, person, or event is intended or should be inferred.

For Microsoft Press
Acquisitions Editor: Christey Bahn
Project Editor: Sandra Haynes

for nSight, Inc.
Project Manager: Peter Whitmer
Manuscript Editor: Joanne Crerand
Technical Editor: Ronald Miller

Chapters at a Glance

Table of Contents

Acknowledgments

When I took over this book in 1990, I was sure that software would soon improve so that books like this would have become obsolete by now. The good news for you is that software does lots more cool stuff than ever. Which is also the bad news—it takes many lines of code to do all that cool stuff. Amazingly, brick-like books are still very much in demand to help sort it all out. While some might explain software "bloat" using chaos theory, we like to think of this phenomenon as "job security."

Many thanks to Kim Fryer, Sandra Haynes, Bill Teel, Kristen Weatherby, and all my Microsoft Press pals for doing that thing they continue to do so well. Equally important were the contributions of the ever-diligent Peter Whitmer and nSight, Inc. Special thanks to technical editor Ron Miller for finding all the right stuff. Thanks also to Microsoftees Eric Patterson and Gerry Lenocker for their kindly assistance in matters of miscellany. This edition's musical thanks go to the Amazing Rhythm Aces (*http://www.theaces.com*), creators of the world's deepest grooves, for coming back strong *Out of the Blue*.

Mark Dodge

I'd like to echo Mark's thanks to all the aforementioned 'Softees and nSighters. Your expertise is deeply appreciated. Thanks, too, to Jean, Russell, and Miranda for patience and support. And my deepest gratitude to Wagner, Sibelius, Elgar, and the gang.

C.S.

PART I

Getting Started with Microsoft Excel 2000

CHAPTER 1

Getting Your Bearings

When you start a new learning experience, the first task is to learn the language. You need to know what the basic elements are and where to find them. This chapter will help you learn the language of Microsoft Excel 2000.

Starting Microsoft Excel 2000

To start the program, from the Start menu, choose Programs, and then Microsoft Excel 2000. Excel opens and displays a blank workbook.

NOTE

> If you just installed Excel, you may see a prompt to register the product. This will continue to appear until you register.

Excel's on-screen appearance varies depending on the type of monitor you're using. Figure 1-1, for example, shows a blank Excel workbook on a 14-inch SVGA monitor (800 x 600 resolution). If you have another type of monitor, your screen might look slightly different.

SEE ALSO

For information about saving and renaming documents, see Chapter 4, "Managing Files."

When you start the Excel program, the first blank workbook Excel displays is called Book1. If you open another new workbook during the same work session, Excel names it Book2. You can have several workbooks open at the same time, and you can subsequently save each workbook under a different name.

FIGURE 1-1.

On a 14-inch SVGA monitor, your screen looks like this when you start Microsoft Excel 2000.

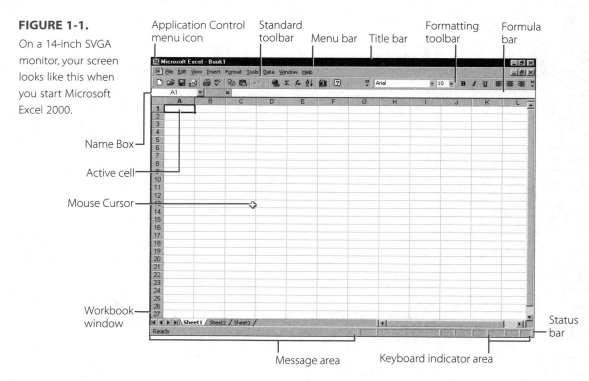

An Excel workbook can contain four types of sheets: worksheets, like the one visible in Figure 1-1; chart sheets; Microsoft Excel 5.0 dialog sheets; and Microsoft Excel 4.0 macro sheets. In Parts I and II of this book, you will work only with worksheets.

A Tour of the Excel Workspace

? SEE ALSO

For information about toolbars, see Chapter 3, "Toolbars and Menus."

When you start Excel, your screen consists of five areas: the workbook window, which occupies most of the screen; the menu bar; two or more toolbars; the formula bar; and the status bar. Collectively, these five areas are known as the Excel workspace.

The Workbook Window

? SEE ALSO

For information about the subtleties of workbooks, see Chapter 9, "Worksheets and Windows."

The workbook window dominates the Excel workspace. Navigational controls appear at the bottom of the workbook window, and a title bar is displayed at the top. The window also includes borders, worksheets, and scroll bars. A new workbook, shown in Figure 1-2, originally consists of three individual worksheets.

FIGURE 1-2.

An Excel workbook normally consists of three individual worksheets, but you can add more.

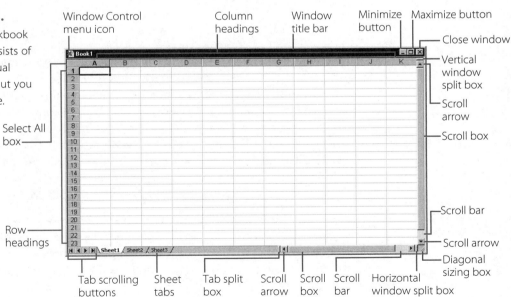

Workbooks are great organizational tools. For example, you can keep together in the same workbook all the documents that relate to a specific project or all the documents maintained by an individual. Workbooks can eliminate a considerable amount of clutter on your hard drive, as well as reduce the number of steps necessary to set up your workspace each day. The more documents you have to manage, the more valuable workbooks become.

You can use workbooks as a multiuser management tool. For example, you can organize worksheets in discrete groups for individual tasks or individual users.

You can also share a workbook so more than one person can work on it at the same time. *See Chapter 18, "Sharing Files with Others."*

Navigating in a Workbook

At the bottom of the workbook window are a number of controls you can use to move from worksheet to worksheet in a workbook. Figure 1-3 shows these navigational controls.

FIGURE 1-3.

The workbook navigational controls.

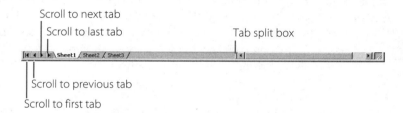

Scroll to next tab
Scroll to last tab
Tab split box
Scroll to previous tab
Scroll to first tab

Use the four tab scrolling buttons in the lower left corner only when you have more worksheets in the workbook than can be displayed at once. With the tab scrolling buttons you can scroll through the sheet tabs in your workbook and view the workbook's contents. The two tab scrolling buttons in the middle scroll the tabs one worksheet at a time in the indicated direction. The two outermost tab scrolling buttons scroll directly to the first or last tab in the workbook. You can drag the tab split box to change the number of sheet tabs displayed. To reset the tab display, simply double-click the tab split box.

These tab scrolling buttons and the tab split box do not activate the worksheets, however. To do so, you must click the tab of the worksheet you want to activate after you have scrolled to the worksheet using the tab scrolling buttons, as shown in Figure 1-4.

FIGURE 1-4.

When you click a tab, you activate the corresponding worksheet.

To activate Sheet 3, click the tab labeled Sheet 3.

TIP

You can use the keyboard to move from sheet to sheet in a workbook. Press Ctrl+Page Up to activate the previous sheet in the workbook and Ctrl+Page Down to activate the next sheet.

Resizing the Workbook Window

At the right end of the workbook window's title bar shown in Figure 1-2 on page 5, you'll notice three buttons; these are the Minimize, Maximize, and Close buttons. When your workbook window is maximized, the active window is displayed at full size in the Excel workspace, as shown in Figure 1-1 on page 4.

After you maximize the window, a button with two small boxes—the Restore button—appears to the right of the menu bar. When you click the Restore button, the window changes to a "floating" window, as shown in Figure 1-5.

FIGURE 1-5.

This workbook window is floating.

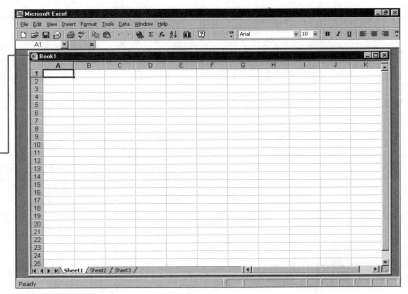

In a floating worksheet, the worksheet title appears at the top of the workbook window.

When you click the Minimize button (the one with a small line at the bottom), the workbook collapses to what looks like a small title bar, as shown in Figure 1-6 on the next page. Minimizing workbooks is a handy way to reduce workspace clutter when you have several workbooks open at the same time. Click the Restore button on the menu bar to redisplay the workbook at its former size.

Getting Started

FIGURE 1-6.

This workbook window is minimized.

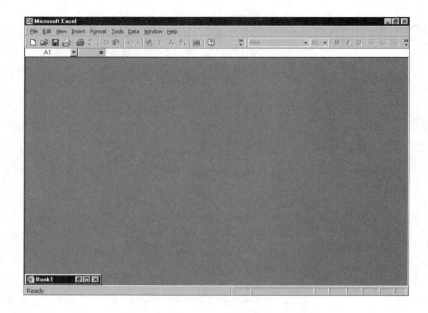

 SEE ALSO

For more information about using workbooks and windows, see Chapter 9, "Worksheets and Windows."

As you can see in Figure 1-1 on page 4, these three buttons also appear at the top of the screen in the Microsoft Excel title bar. They resize the Excel application window in similar ways, except that the application Minimize button collapses Excel to a button in the Windows taskbar.

You can also drag the borders of a floating window to control its size. The smaller the window, the less you see of the worksheet; however, because you can open multiple windows for the same workbook, you might find it more convenient to view different parts of the workbook, or even of an individual worksheet, side by side in two small windows rather than switch between sheets or scroll back and forth in one large window.

⭐ **TIP**

If you want to see more rows on your screen, the taskbar at the bottom of the screen can be set to automatically hide itself when not in use. Click the taskbar's Start button, and then choose Settings, Taskbar. On the Taskbar Options tab, click the Auto Hide check box, and then click OK. Now the taskbar stays hidden and pops up only when you move the mouse pointer to the bottom of the screen.

The Title Bar

At the top of the Excel workspace is the title bar, which displays the application name along with the name of the workbook in which you are currently working. If your worksheet is floating, as in Figure 1-5, the title (here, Book1) appears at the top of the workbook window. When you open additional windows and display workbooks in them, the names of the workbooks in those windows are displayed in their respective title bars.

The title bar of the window in which you are working is normally displayed in a different color than that of any inactive windows. You can reposition the active window on your screen by dragging its title bar.

The Worksheet

Like a traditional accounting ledger, a worksheet is divided into a grid of columns and rows. A letter is assigned to each column and appears as a column heading above the worksheet grid. The column letters range from A through IV. (After column Z comes column AA, after AZ comes BA, and so on, up to IV.) A number is assigned to each row and appears as a row heading to the left of the worksheet grid. The row numbers range from 1 through 65,536.

At the intersection of each column and row is a *cell*. Cells are the basic building blocks of every worksheet. Each cell occupies a unique location on the worksheet where you can store and display information, and each cell is assigned a unique set of coordinates, called the cell reference. For example, the cell at the intersection of column A and row 1 has the cell reference A1. The cell at the intersection of column Z and row 100 has the cell reference Z100.

The currently selected cell is referred to as the *active cell*. The cell reference for the active cell appears at the left end of the formula bar in the Name box. The headings for the column and row containing the active cell appear three-dimensional, making it easier to identify the location of the current cell, as shown in Figure 1-7.

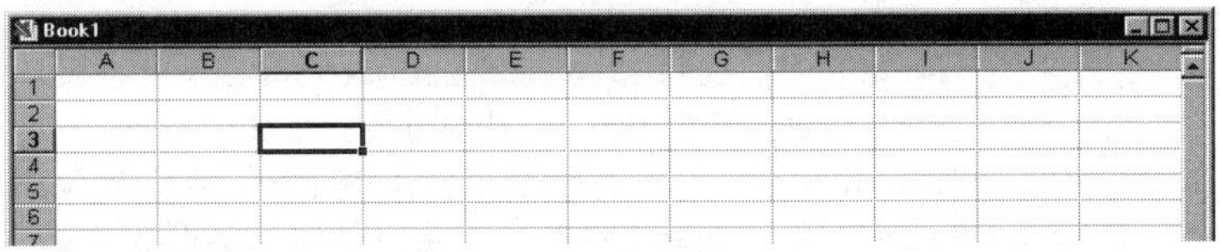

FIGURE 1-7.

The column and row headings for the active cell appear three-dimensional.

Looking at Your Data through Windows

The workbook window is like a porthole through which you can see only a portion of the worksheet. To illustrate, suppose you were to cut a small, square hole in a piece of cardboard and place the cardboard over this page. At any given time, you could see only a portion of the page through the hole. By moving the cardboard around on the page, however, you could eventually read the entire page through the "window" in your piece of cardboard. Viewing worksheets in Excel is much the same, except that you move around the worksheet to see different sections of it in the window. You can also open another window to view different sections of the same worksheet simultaneously.

 SEE ALSO

For more information about windows, see Chapter 9, "Worksheets and Windows."

With 256 columns and 65,536 rows, your worksheet contains more than 16 million individual cells. Before you try to unravel the mysteries of the universe on a single worksheet, however, remember that the number of cells you can use at any one time is limited by the amount of memory your computer has. Although Excel allocates memory only to cells containing data, you probably won't be able to use all the cells in one worksheet.

The Scroll Bars

To change your view of the worksheet, you can use the scroll bars along the right and bottom sides of the workbook window to move around the worksheet. Only the active workbook window—the one you are currently working in—has scroll bars.

The scroll arrows at either end of the scroll bars allow you to move through the worksheet one column or row at a time. Clicking the up or down arrow in the vertical scroll bar scrolls the sheet up or down one row at a time. Similarly, clicking the right or left arrow in the horizontal scroll bar scrolls the worksheet to the right or left one column at a time.

To move a long way through the worksheet, you can drag the scroll boxes in the scroll bars to positions that correspond to the position of the window over the worksheet. To move a new screen of information into view, click the shaded area of the scroll bar. Note that the Name box at the left end of the formula bar always displays the active cell reference, regardless of where you scroll in the window.

Talking Scroll Bars

The size of the scroll box (sometimes called the "thumb") changes depending on the size of the scrollable area. For example, the scroll boxes shown in Figure 1-2 on page 5 are nearly as large as the scroll bars themselves, indicating that there is little more to see in the active area of the workbook—nothing, in fact, because this is a blank workbook. As you add data to more columns and rows than can be displayed on a single screen, the scroll boxes get proportionally smaller, giving you immediate feedback about the size of the worksheet.

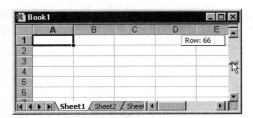

In addition, when you click a scroll box, a small screen tip box appears, as shown above. This box displays the name of the column or row that will appear in the upper right corner of the window when you release the mouse button. You can use these ScreenTips to help position the scroll box more precisely.

Scrolling Beyond the Active Area

The active area of a worksheet is the area that contains the data you've entered. In a new worksheet, Excel considers the default active area as roughly columns A through M and rows 1 through 26 (on an SVGA display) even before you enter any data. To move beyond the active area of a very large worksheet, you can quickly scroll distant columns or rows into view by pressing Shift while you drag. For example, by holding down Shift and dragging to the right end of the horizontal scroll bar, you can bring the last column of the worksheet—column IV—into view. Because this method scrolls through the worksheet quickly, keep a close eye on the column or row reference in the screen tip box as you scroll.

TIP

> As you scroll through the worksheet, you might lose sight of the active cell. To quickly bring the active cell back into view, press Ctrl+Backspace or type an entry for that cell. Alternatively, you can press one of the arrow keys to simultaneously move to an adjacent cell and bring the active cell into view.

Scrolling with the Keyboard

The arrow keys let you scroll up, down, left, and right, one column or row at a time; the Page Up and Page Down keys let you move a new screen of data into view. Scrolling with the keyboard relocates the active cell. To scroll through the worksheet without changing the active cell, press Scroll Lock and then press an arrow, Page Up, or Page Down key. For example, to scroll up or down one row at a time without moving the active cell, press Scroll Lock and then press the Up or Down arrow key. To scroll left or right one screen at a time, press Scroll Lock and then press Ctrl plus the appropriate arrow key.

If You Have an IntelliMouse

You can use the wheel on your IntelliMouse to scroll through your worksheet. Turn the wheel backward (toward your hand) to scroll down, or forward (away from your hand) to scroll up. You can change the default behavior of the wheel from scrolling to zooming—that is, displaying the active worksheet at a different magnification. To do so, choose Options from the Tools menu and, on the General tab, select the Zoom On Roll With IntelliMouse option. *For more information, see "Zooming Worksheets," page 322.* To pan (scroll through) the worksheet, press the wheel button down and drag the mouse in the direction you want to move. When you press the wheel button, a gray directional device appears, which is anchored to the spot where you first pressed the wheel button. As you hold the button down and drag, a black arrow appears, pointing in the direction you drag, as shown here.

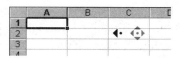

The speed of panning depends on how far you drag away from the anchored directional device.

Getting Started

The Menu Bar

At the top of the Excel workspace is the menu bar. Here, you select Excel commands to manipulate the information you have entered in your worksheet. Excel's menu bar has nine menus: File, Edit, View, Insert, Format, Tools, Data, Window, and Help. Display the contents of Excel's menus the same way you display those of any Windows-based program: point to the menu you want to use and click the mouse button.

When you display a menu, some commands appear more prominently, and others appear dimmed. Excel monitors the status of your worksheet and allows you to choose only those commands that are applicable at any given time. The black commands are available for use; the dimmed commands are unavailable.

 ## "Morphing" Menus

When you first display a menu in Excel 2000, the menu appears with a limited number of commands. After a few seconds, the menu automatically "grows" to include more commands, as shown in Figure 1-8. This feature is meant to help simplify the ever-increasing complement of commands Excel provides, by "hiding" some of them, at least for a while. When you first start Excel, the commands immediately visible are the ones that are historically the most often used, but as you work with Excel, the additional commands you choose will also appear on the shorter menus. This is referred to as the Recently Used Commands feature, which keeps track of your command-usage habits.

FIGURE 1-8.

The shorter menu on the left shows its most recently used commands. The full menu on the right shows all its commands.

You can click the double arrow to display the full menu.

If you find yourself distracted by the delayed unfurling of menus, you have a couple of options. First, choose the Customize command from the Tools menu, and then click the Options tab to display the Customize dialog box, shown in Figure 1-9 on the next page. If you clear the Menus Show Recently Used Commands First option, full menus are always displayed. If you clear the Show Full Menus After Short Delay option, short menus will stay short unless you click the double down-ward-pointing arrow visible at the bottom of shortened menus. Click the Reset My Usage Data button to return all menus to their original state. When you do this, the data collected about the commands you have used is discarded, and collection begins anew.

FIGURE 1-9.
You can choose to always display full menus, or turn off the delayed-display option.

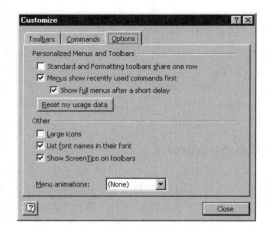

 TIP

To suit your personal work style, you can rearrange Excel's menus and commands and create your own menus. *For more information, see "Customizing Toolbars and Menus," page 43.*

Submenus

Some commands on the menus are followed by an arrow, indicating that a list of additional commands, called a submenu, is available for each of those commands, as shown in Figure 1-10.

FIGURE 1-10.
When you choose a command with an arrow next to it, a submenu is displayed.

Dialog Boxes and Tab Dialog Boxes

Some commands have an ellipsis (...) after them, indicating you must supply more information before Excel can carry out the command. You supply this information in a dialog box. For example, Figure 1-11 shows the dialog box that appears when you choose the Delete command from the Edit menu.

FIGURE 1-11.

Menu commands followed by an ellipsis (...) display a dialog box to prompt you for more information.

Some commands are more versatile. For these commands, Excel provides tab dialog boxes, which present several unique sets of options for the same command. Figure 1-12 shows the tab dialog box that appears when you choose the Options command from the Tools menu.

FIGURE 1-12.

Some commands display tab dialog boxes, which provide two or more sets of options for the corresponding command.

1 To activate a set of options, click the name of the tab you want to use. You can specify settings in one tab and then click another tab to set more options.

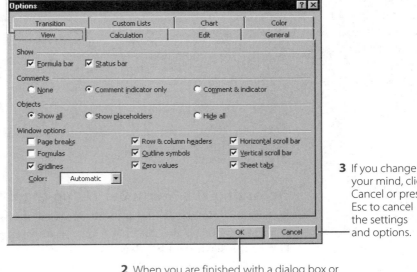

3 If you change your mind, click Cancel or press Esc to cancel the settings and options.

2 When you are finished with a dialog box or a tab dialog box, click OK or press Enter to activate the settings and options you specified.

The Options Dialog Box

The tab dialog box that appears when you choose the Options command from the Tools menu is probably the most important dialog box of all. As you can see in Figure 1-12 on the previous page, the Options dialog box contains tabs that control nearly every aspect of Excel, including general settings, such as how many worksheets appear in a default workbook and the name and point size of the default font. The Options dialog box also provides special settings for charts, Lotus 1-2-3 transition, and macro modules, among others. If you take a moment to click each tab and look through the options available in this dialog box, you'll get an idea of the scope of the program as well as the degree of control you have over your workspace. If you're unsure about what a particular setting or option does, simply click the Help button (the question mark) in the title bar, and then click the setting or option to display information about it.

Choosing Commands with the Keyboard

Some commands on Excel's menus are followed by their keyboard equivalents, as shown on the Edit menu in Figure 1-13. These key combinations allow you to choose a command without first displaying an Excel menu.

FIGURE 1-13.

Use the keyboard equivalents displayed to the right of command names to choose a command without displaying the menu.

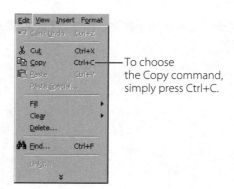

To choose the Copy command, simply press Ctrl+C.

Accessing the Menu Bar Using the Keyboard

Sometimes you might find it more convenient to choose commands from menus using the keyboard instead of the mouse. Pressing the Alt key or the slash (/) key lets you display the menus using the keyboard. When you press either key, Excel activates the menu bar. Pressing the Down arrow key or Enter displays the File menu. Pressing the Right arrow key highlights the next menu to the right, the Edit menu. Repeatedly pressing the Right or Left arrow key displays each menu in turn. When the menu you need is highlighted, press the Down arrow key to highlight the desired command, and then press Enter to choose the command.

For example, to use the keyboard to choose the Options command from the Tools menu, press the slash key, press the Right arrow key until the Tools menu is highlighted in the menu bar, press the Down arrow key to display the menu, and continue to press the Down arrow key until the Options command is highlighted. To choose the command and display the Options dialog box, press Enter.

The underlined letter in each of the menu names on the menu bar designates the letter key you can press to display that particular menu, as an alternative to using the arrow keys. For example, after you press the slash key to activate the menu bar, you can type *t* to display the Tools menu. Then, to choose a particular command, such as Options, type *O*—the underlined letter in Options—to display the Options dialog box.

 TIP

> Instead of pressing the slash key to activate the menu bar, you can press the Alt key along with the underlined letter to display a menu. Then, with the menu displayed, type the underlined letter of the command you want. For example, press Alt+T, and then type *O* to display the Options dialog box.

The Microsoft Excel Menu or Help Key Option

If you prefer, you can assign the slash key's menu-accessing function to another key. From the Tools menu, simply choose Options and click the Transition tab. Then type the key you want to use in the Microsoft Excel Menu Or Help Key edit box and click OK. (Don't use a key you will use in a worksheet, such as A or 2.) The new key allows you to access the menu bar, just as the slash key did.

Shortcut Menus

Shortcut menus contain only those commands that apply to the item indicated by the position of the mouse pointer when you activate the menu. Shortcut menus provide a handy way to access the commands you need with a minimum of mouse movement. Excel has many shortcut menus, each offering the commands most likely to be useful at the pointer's current location.

To access shortcut menus, click the right mouse button. The shortcut menu pops up adjacent to the mouse pointer, as you can see in Figure 1-14 on the next page. You choose the command you want with the mouse or keyboard just as you would choose a command from a regular menu.

FIGURE 1-14.

Clicking the right mouse button displays a shortcut menu.

This shortcut menu appears when you click a column heading with the right mouse button.

The shortcut menu can contain many combinations of commands, depending on the position of the pointer and the type of worksheet. For example, if you display a shortcut menu when the pointer is over a cell rather than a column heading, a menu like the one shown in Figure 1-15 appears.

 TIP

Press Shift+F10 to display a shortcut menu for the selected item. The shortcut menu appears adjacent to the active cell. For example, if you press Shift+F10 when a cell or range of cells is selected, the shortcut menu shown in Figure 1-15 appears. Note that if you have a "Windows 95" keyboard, you can access the shortcut menu by pressing the Shortcut key, which has an arrow pointing at a menu icon. This is usually located on the right side of the keyboard on the bottom row.

FIGURE 1-15.

This shortcut menu appears when you click the right mouse button while the pointer is over a cell.

TIP

> Many menu commands have corresponding toolbar buttons—an alternative, possibly easier, way to achieve the same result. An image that appears to the left of a menu command, such as the scissors next to the Cut command in Figure 1-15, indicates the toolbar button for that command. (Notice that the same scissors image appears on the Standard toolbar as the Cut button.) If one of these images is not currently visible on a toolbar, it is either located on a toolbar that is not displayed or is an optional button you can use in creating or modifying your own toolbars. *For more information about using, modifying, and creating toolbars, see Chapter 3, "Toolbars and Menus."*

The Formula Bar

We mentioned earlier that worksheet cells are Excel's building blocks. They store and display the information you enter in an Excel worksheet and allow you to perform worksheet calculations. You can enter information directly in a cell on the worksheet, or you can enter information through the formula bar. The contents of the active cell appear in the formula bar, as shown in Figure 1-16. The formula-editing buttons appear only when you enter or edit data in a cell.

FIGURE 1-16.

The formula bar displays the contents of the active cell.

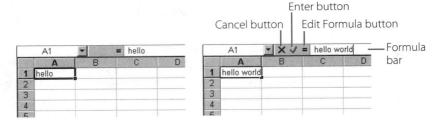

Enter button
Cancel button | Edit Formula button

Formula bar

Although you can enter information directly in a cell, using the formula bar has some advantages. If you move the pointer into the formula bar and click, three buttons appear in the formula bar, as shown in Figure 1-16. When you click the Enter button, Excel "locks in" the information you have typed in the formula bar and transfers that information to your worksheet. Clicking the Enter button is similar to pressing the Enter key except that pressing the Enter key normally activates the cell directly below the one in which you entered the data. If you make a mistake while typing, clicking the Cancel button tells Excel to delete what you have typed. Clicking the Cancel button is similar to pressing the Esc key.

When you click the Edit Formula button, the Formula Palette appears to help you construct a formula. *For information about names, creating formulas, and using the Formula Palette, see Chapter 6, "Building Formulas."*

By default, Excel displays the formula bar in your workspace. If you prefer to hide the formula bar, you can choose the Formula Bar command from the View menu. To redisplay the formula bar, simply repeat this process. (This command does not normally appear on shortened menus. Click the double arrow at the bottom of the View menu to display the Formula Bar command.)

The Status Bar

? SEE ALSO

For more information about keyboard modes, see the sidebar, "Keyboard Modes," page 95.

The status bar displays the condition of your workspace. For example, most of the time, Excel displays the word Ready at the left end of the status bar, meaning the worksheet is ready to accept new information. As you type new information, Excel displays the word Enter in the

Quick Totals in the Status Bar

When two or more cells are selected and at least one of them contains a value, Excel displays the total in the Status bar, as shown below. This is called the AutoCalculate feature. The AutoCalculate area of the status bar normally displays the sum of the selected values, but if you click the right mouse button over the area you get a shortcut menu from which you can select to get an average of the selected values, a count of the number of nonblank cells, a count of selected cells that contain only numbers, or the minimum or maximum values in the selection.

1 Click the AutoCalculate area of the status bar with the right mouse button to display the AutoCalculate menu.

2 Select a function from the menu to display its result in the status bar.

status bar. When you activate the formula bar or double-click a cell that already contains data, Excel displays the word Edit in the status bar. To return to Ready mode, you need to "lock in" the information you just typed by clicking the Enter button or pressing Enter on the keyboard, or you can discard the information by clicking the Cancel button or pressing the Esc key.

TIP

Excel displays the status bar by default. If you want to hide it, choose the Status Bar command from the View menu. To redisplay the status bar, simply choose this command again. (This command does not normally appear on shortened menus. Click the double arrow at the bottom of the View menu to display the Status Bar command.)

The boxes at the right end of the status bar display various keyboard modes that you can turn on or off. For example, CAPS appears in this area of the status bar when you activate the Caps Lock key. When you press the Num Lock key to activate the numeric keypad (to use it for numeric entry rather than navigation), NUM appears in this area of the status bar.

The Pointer

You should already be familiar with the basic technique of using the mouse to move the pointer around the screen. In Excel, the pointer serves different functions in different areas of the worksheet.

When you move the pointer to the menu bar, the pointer appears as an arrow so you can point to the command you want. When you move the pointer to the formula bar, the pointer's shape changes to an I-beam. When you see the I-beam, click to set an insertion point where you want to edit or enter information in your worksheet.

When you move your pointer over the worksheet grid, the pointer's shape changes to a plus sign. If you move the plus sign over cell C5 and click the mouse button, a border appears around the cell, and the Name box at the left end of the formula bar displays the cell reference C5, indicating that you have selected this cell.

You'll see the pointer take on other shapes as you begin using it to manipulate the worksheet and its window. We will explain the different functions of the pointer in subsequent chapters as we address various worksheet operations.

Exiting Microsoft Excel 2000

SEE ALSO

For more information about saving workbook files, see Chapter 4, "Managing Files."

When you are finished with your Excel session, choose the Exit command from the File menu or click the Close button. If you haven't already saved, Excel asks whether you want to save any changes you made to each open workbook. If you click Yes, you can specify a new filename for any unsaved workbook and then save it. If you click Yes To All, Excel saves changes made to all open workbooks. If you click No, any changes you've made are lost when you exit Excel. Clicking the Cancel button cancels the Exit command and returns you to the program.

Now that you're better acquainted with the Excel workspace, the next chapter shows you how to use the impressive online Help system to discover how to put the workspace to good use.

Getting Help

Microsoft Excel was a powerful program out of the starting gate way back in 1985. Over the years, Excel has developed into an extremely complex and sophisticated application. So complex, in fact, that most people need to learn only 20 percent or so of its capabilities. Many people turn to books like this one to help them make sense of it all. But almost every Excel user turns to the online Help system at one time or another. And in Microsoft Excel 2000, the Help system is *almost* impossible to ignore.

Meet the Assistant

When you start using Microsoft Excel 2000, you make the acquaintance of the Office Assistant, the Excel online Help "ambassador" and keeper of at least some of the keys to the online Help kingdom. The Office Assistant, shown in Figure 2-1, is more than happy to live in a corner of your screen, full time, ready to answer your every need. You might or might not welcome this obsequious little helper, but we'll show you how to make the best use of its talents or dismiss it permanently. The Help system in Excel 2000 is fully functional without the services of the Office Assistant.

The first time you meet the Office Assistant, its balloon offers three options, as shown in Figure 2-1. Clicking the first one displays a list of Help topics that explain how to get started using Excel, as well as what's new and improved in Microsoft Excel 2000. Clicking the second option displays some information about using the Office Assistant itself. The third option closes both the Office Assistant and the balloon and lets you get right to business working in Excel.

FIGURE 2-1.

The Office Assistant appears automatically when you first start Excel.

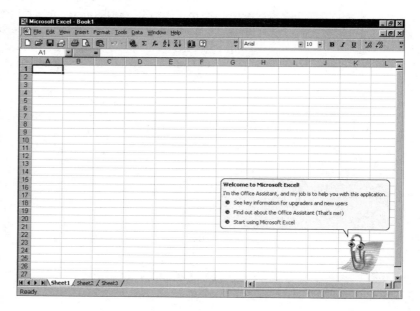

If you want to start using the Office Assistant immediately, click the Office Assistant itself (not the balloon) to display the Search balloon, shown in Figure 2-2.

FIGURE 2-2.

Click the Office Assistant to display the Search balloon.

When it first appears, the Search balloon asks *What would you like to do?* Your first and most likely choice is to type a question. For example, try typing *how do I change the color of text?* (You don't need to add the question mark, but it's OK if you do.) When you click Search or press Enter, the Office Assistant displays a set of Help topics that might address your query. If none of the topics seem to provide the help you're looking for, click the See More arrow at the bottom of the Search balloon to display another set of topics, as shown in Figure 2-3. (Not all questions you pose to the Office Assistant will return more than five topics, so the See More arrow might not always appear.) To redisplay the first set, click the See Previous arrow at the top of the screen.

FIGURE 2-3.

Ask a question in plain English, and the Office Assistant returns a list of Help topics that might address it. Click the See More arrow to go to page two, shown at the right.

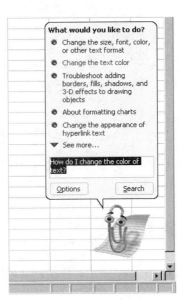

TIP

If the Office Assistant is not currently visible on your screen, you can summon it and the Search balloon by doing one of the following: pressing the F1 key, clicking the Help button on the Standard toolbar, or choosing the Microsoft Excel Help command on the Help menu.

Our sample question seems to be addressed by the second topic listed in the first set, "Change the text color." Click that item in the list to display the associated Help topic, shown in Figure 2-4.

FIGURE 2-4.

Click an item on the Office Assistant's list to display the associated Help topic.

Click the Show button to expand the Help window.

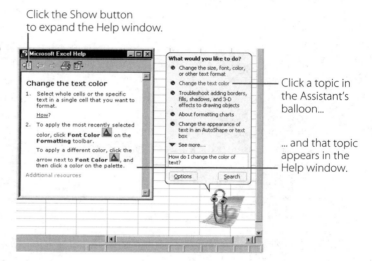

Click a topic in the Assistant's balloon...

... and that topic appears in the Help window.

The Office Assistant uses Microsoft's Answer Wizard technology, which allows you to enter questions in full or partial sentences, using natural language, just as if you were talking to the Excel guru down the hall. The Office Assistant then takes your question and, based on key words, juxtaposition of words, and verbs used, returns a list of topics that is generated by a sophisticated system of built-in probabilities. It is complicated, but only under the surface. When you ask a question, the Office Assistant finds up to ten likely topics. If the topic list doesn't address exactly what you're looking for, try rephrasing the question using a different word or two.

 TIP

To hide the Search balloon, click anywhere outside the balloon. To dismiss the Office Assistant entirely, click the Assistant using the right mouse button and choose the Hide Assistant command.

Firing the Assistant

Most folks either love or hate the Office Assistant. If you would be happier to see the Office Assistant never darken your desktop again, click the Assistant and then click the Options button at the bottom of the balloon. On the Options tab of the Office Assistant dialog box, clear the Use The Office Assistant check box. The next time you summon the Help system, the Help window appears, as shown in Figure 2-5. The Answer Wizard tab offers the same functionality as the Assistant balloon, sans cartoon.

FIGURE 2-5.

If you summon Help after giving the Assistant its walking papers, you get the Help window instead.

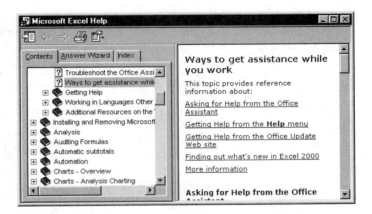

If you change your mind later, choose Show The Office Assistant on the Help menu. This command changes to Hide The Office Assistant when the Assistant is visible but does not hide it permanently. You still must use the Assistant Options dialog box if you want the Assistant to stay hidden.

Getting Answers to Unasked Questions

The Office Assistant also makes educated guesses about what you might be trying to do at any given moment. For example, if we select a few cells, and then move them to a new location by clicking and dragging the border of the selection with the mouse, a light bulb appears over the Assistant, as shown in Figure 2-6 on the next page. (The location of the light bulb may change depending on the current position of the Office Assistant.) When we click the Assistant or the light bulb, a tip appears in the Search balloon, based on the action we just performed, as shown on the right in Figure 2-6. We asked no specific question, yet the Office Assistant arrived at a tip that might be useful at the moment. As you work, the light bulb will keep popping up, indicating that another tip is available for you. You can ignore this, of course, but you might want to check periodically to see what you've missed. To do so, click the Assistant to display a list of unread tips. The Office Assistant stores tips for you as you work.

FIGURE 2-6.

Click the light bulb to display a tip about what you're currently doing.

Selecting Office Assistant Options

When you click the Options button at the bottom of the Office Assistant Search balloon, the Office Assistant dialog box appears. On the Gallery tab, shown in Figure 2-7, you can browse the characters available for the Office Assistant and select your favorite.

FIGURE 2-7.

On the Gallery tab, you can "interview" candidates for the Office Assistant position on your desktop.

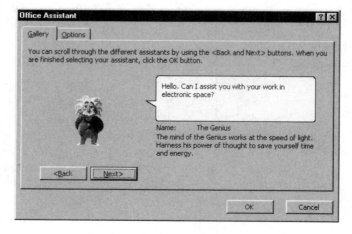

You access the many functions of the Office Assistant by using the Options tab shown in Figure 2-8. If you don't want the Assistant to appear ever again, clear the Use The Office Assistant option. If you do so, all the other options on the Options tab are deactivated. If you don't want the Assistant to appear when you press F1, remove the check from the Respond To F1 Key option. If you do this, the Help window appears instead. Even when this option is turned off, you can still display the Assistant by clicking the Help button or by choosing the Microsoft Excel Help command on the Help menu. *For more information about the Help window, see "Navigating through the Help System," page 31.* With the Help With Wizards option selected, whenever you start any of Excel's wizards the Office Assistant appears automatically to help you work through it.

FIGURE 2-8.

The Options tab gives you control over the Office Assistant's many features.

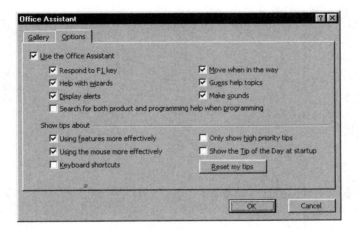

With the Display Alerts option selected, the standard Excel alert messages warning you of impending problems are displayed by the Office Assistant rather than in a normal alert box. For example, if you try to drag a cell over another cell that already contains data, an alert box warns, *Do you want to replace the contents of the destination cells?* With this option selected, you not only get the message, but you're also treated to a dramatic little dance by the Office Assistant.

With the Move When In The Way option selected, the Office Assistant automatically moves when something like a dialog box appears on the screen in the same location. The Guess Help Topics option controls whether the Office Assistant supplies Help topics based on what you're currently doing, as described in "Getting Answers to Unasked Questions," page 27. Clearing the Make Sounds option silences the Office Assistant. If you don't have a sound card, this option is irrelevant. The Search For Both Product And Programming Help When Programming option is somewhat self-explanatory. When this option is not selected and you are programming, the Office Assistant provides help on programming topics only.

The Show Tips About section lets you specify the kinds of tips you want to see, as described in "Getting Answers to Unasked Questions," page 27. The Office Assistant keeps track of the tips it has already displayed. Once a tip has been offered, the Office Assistant will not display it again, however, you can reset tips so that all tips appear. To do so, click the Reset My Tips button.

The Animated Assistant

The Animate! command on the Office Assistant's shortcut menu, shown at the top of the following illustration, is like no other command in Excel. Call it the comic relief feature. (To display the shortcut menu, click the right mouse button on the Assistant. We first selected the Assistant named Rocky before creating this montage.)

Each time you click the Animate! command, the Office Assistant performs a different quick cartoon-style vignette for you. The panels in the illustration above each show a moment from just a few of many different animation sequences for the Rocky assistant. Each character in the Office Assistant Gallery has its own unique, sometimes amusing routines. Take a break and tune in the Office Assistant show.

Using the Help System

The Help menu commands shown in Figure 2-9 include Microsoft Excel Help, which displays the Office Assistant; Hide The Office Assistant; What's This?, which displays a pop-up ScreenTip that describes any item you select on the screen; Office On The Web, which starts your Web browser and connects to Microsoft sites on the World Wide Web that are dedicated to providing additional assistance; and About Microsoft Excel, which displays information about the program. Two Help menu commands do not appear on shortened menus (click the downward-pointing double arrows at the bottom of the menu to display them). The Lotus 1-2-3 Help command displays the Help For Lotus 1-2-3 Users dialog box. The Detect And Repair command attempts to fix any errors that might have occurred in your Excel installation.

FIGURE 2-9.

The Help menu provides access to assistance, both built-in and on the Web.

Navigating through the Help System

When you click the Show button in the Microsoft Excel Help window, shown in Figure 2-4 on page 26, the window expands, offering three tabs: Contents, Answer Wizard, and Index, as shown in Figure 2-10.

FIGURE 2-10.

The Contents tab in the Help window reveals a wealth of information you can browse through.

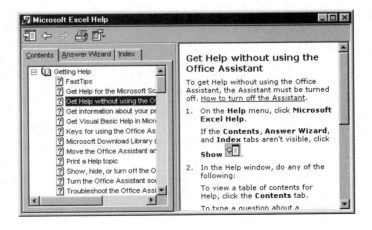

The Contents tab is similar to the table of contents in a book. When you activate the Contents tab, each "chapter" is represented by a title next to a small closed-book icon. Double-click one of the titles to display more detail under that heading (or click the plus [+] sign next to the book) as shown in Figure 2-10.

If you find a topic that interests you, double-click it to display it in the right pane of the Help window. Often, Help topics include pointers to other related Help topics. In Figure 2-10, the underlined text in the topic shown in the right pane of the Help window are hyperlinks to other Help topics. Clicking one of these hyperlinks activates the associated topic. If this seems a bit like a browser, you're right—it's very similar. In fact, the Back and Forward buttons at the top of the Help window function just like the ones in your browser: click the Back button to step back through the Help topics you have already displayed, one at a time.

If the Contents tab doesn't suit your fancy, try the Index tab. Type a keyword and click Search or select one from the keywords list by double-clicking, and the Choose A Topic list displays applicable Help topics, as shown in Figure 2-11. Click the topic name to display the corresponding Help topic.

Before You Call Product Support

We encourage you to use Excel documentation, online Help, the Microsoft Excel Web site (*http://www.microsoft.com/excel*), and this book to find answers to your questions before you reach for your telephone. When you have exhausted these resources, it's time to call Microsoft Product Support. But before you do, choose About Microsoft Excel from the Help menu and click the System Info button. Doing so displays a dialog box that lists your current system configuration, the applications running, display information, and much more. If you want, you can print the information in a report or save it as a file on disk. Then you can click the Tech Support button in the About Microsoft Excel dialog box to display a Help topic you can use to find telephone numbers for Microsoft Product Support Services around the world. When you talk to Product Support, having the System Info report at your fingertips will assist the representative in diagnosing your problem and will save you both some time.

FIGURE 2-11.

Type a keyword at the top of the Index tab or choose one from the keywords list to display a list of topics.

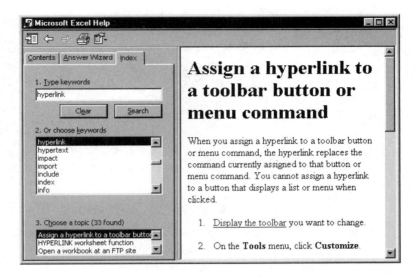

Getting Help on the World Wide Web

SEE ALSO

For information about additional Web features built into Excel, see Chapter 19, "Hyperlinks and the Internet."

If you have access to the World Wide Web, there is a wealth of additional resources available to you. Choose the Office On The Web command on the Help menu.

Using this command starts up your Web browser and connects to the Office Update page on Microsoft's Web site. This site is updated on an ongoing basis, so you will probably find new information each time you connect.

ON THE WEB

Throughout this book, look for this On the Web graphic, indicating where you can find a sample file available for you to download from the Web. You can refer to these sample files as you work through the examples in the book.

Help for Lotus 1-2-3 Users

The Lotus 1-2-3 Help command on the Help menu eases the transition of Lotus 1-2-3 users to Excel. (The Lotus 1-2-3 Help command does not normally appear on shortened menus. Click the double arrow at the bottom of the Help menu to display the Lotus 1-2-3 command.) When you choose this command, Excel displays a dialog box in which you can type the key sequence you would use to choose a particular command in Lotus 1-2-3, as shown in Figure 2-12 on the next page.

FIGURE 2-12.

The Lotus 1-2-3 Help command displays the Help For Lotus 1-2-3 Users dialog box.

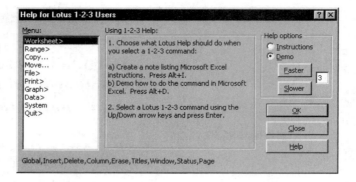

Getting Context-Sensitive Help

Excel also allows you to ask for information about a command without using the Help menu. Simply click the What's This? command on the Help menu and use the question mark pointer shown in Figure 2-13 to choose a command or click an object for which you want help. Excel then displays a pop-up Help topic that applies to the selected command or object.

FIGURE 2-13.

Click the What's This? command on the Help menu, and then click a command, button, or other item on the screen for more information.

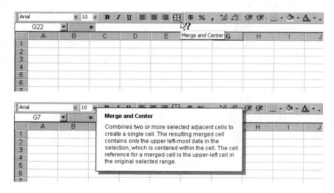

This type of help is called context-sensitive help because it relates to what you are doing in the worksheet.

For example, suppose you want to center a title above a range of cells. You think you need to use the Merge And Center button, but you're not sure. To display information about the Merge And Center button, click the What's This? command button on the Help menu, and then click the Merge And Center button, as shown in Figure 2-13.

Dialog Box Help

You can click the Question Mark button in most dialog boxes and tab dialog boxes to display a question-mark cursor similar to the one in Figure 2-13. Then click an option or area in the dialog box to display a tip for that item, as shown in Figure 2-14.

FIGURE 2-14.

Click the Question Mark button in the dialog box title bar, and then click the item you want help on.

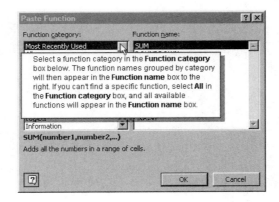

Identifying Toolbar Buttons with ScreenTips

? SEE ALSO

For more information about toolbars, see Chapter 3, "Toolbars and Menus."

For those who have trouble remembering what all those toolbar buttons do, Excel provides *ScreenTips*. With ScreenTips activated, a descriptive label appears when you move the mouse pointer over a toolbar button, as shown under the Merge And Center button in Figure 2-13 earlier.

ScreenTips are active by default. To deactivate them, choose Toolbars from the View menu, click the Customize command, and on the Options tab, clear the Show ScreenTips On Toolbars checkbox.

The next chapter takes you deep into Excel menus and toolbars, and shows you how to customize your workspace for utmost efficiency.

CHAPTER 3

Toolbars and Menus

When you first start Microsoft Excel 2000, two toolbars are visible on the screen: the Standard and the Formatting toolbars. These toolbars contain a lot of helpful buttons, but they are only the tip of the iceberg. Excel has many more toolbars, and you can place a staggering number of additional buttons on them. In this chapter, we'll show you how to use existing toolbars and how to create custom toolbars that fit your needs.

Introducing Toolbars

Microsoft Excel 2000 offers a smorgasbord of toolbars filled with buttons designed to simplify repetitive operations. You can build your own toolbars, choosing from over 500 predefined buttons, palettes, and drop-down list boxes, or using buttons that you create yourself. In this chapter, we'll describe some of these buttons, explore the existing toolbars, and show you how to create and customize toolbars to suit your needs. Even the Excel menu bar is a toolbar of sorts that you can customize and reposition on the screen. We'll explain how you can modify your commands and menus for optimum performance.

Excel gives you the option of displaying additional toolbars at the top of the window, along with the menu bar, or in other locations in the workspace. Excel includes a number of built-in toolbars that provide handy shortcuts for many common actions. Some of the other toolbars are displayed automatically when you need them. For example, Excel displays the Chart toolbar when you are working on a chart.

"Rafting" Toolbars

When you first start Excel, the Standard and Formatting toolbars are displayed in what the Excel developers refer to as the *rafting* configuration. This means that both toolbars share the same "row" in the workspace, as shown in Figure 3-1. You can change this, so that each toolbar occupies its own row, by choosing Customize from the Tools menu and, on the Options tab, clearing the Standard And Formatting Toolbars Share The Same Row check box. Your toolbars will appear as shown in Figure 3-2. (The Customize command does not normally appear on shortened menus. Click the downward-pointing double arrow at the bottom of the Options menu to display the Customize command.)

FIGURE 3-1.

The Standard and Formatting toolbars share the same row of space by default, displaying their most commonly used buttons.

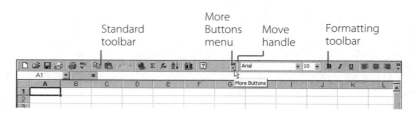

FIGURE 3-2.

You can specify that the Standard and Formatting toolbars appear in separate rows.

The advantage of having the Standard and Formatting toolbars occupy the same row is, of course, to make the greatest amount of screen space available to your worksheets. However, unless you have a very large monitor, some of the buttons in this configuration are hidden from immediate view. Still, you can get to the hidden buttons fairly easily by clicking the downward-pointing arrow—aka the More Buttons menu—at the right side of the toolbar, to display a drop-down menu similar to the one shown in Figure 3-3. Note that there is also a double "fast forward" arrow above the More Buttons menu. This arrow lets you know at a glance that there are more buttons on this toolbar than can be displayed in its current configuration.

FIGURE 3-3.

Click the down arrow to display more buttons.

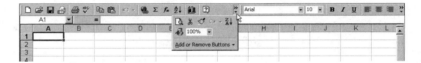

If you drag the *move handle* (shown in Figure 3-1) of the Formatting toolbar to the right or left while the toolbars are in the same row, each toolbar adjusts to fill the available space by adding or removing buttons. Buttons that don't fit as you shorten a toolbar are moved to the More Buttons menu. If you make a toolbar larger, buttons are moved back to the toolbar from the More Buttons menu. Which buttons move to and from the More Buttons menu, and in what order, are predetermined based on usage studies. The most-often-used buttons stay on the toolbar the longest. But you can help determine this yourself simply by using buttons. For example, if you click a toolbar's More Buttons menu and then click one of the buttons there, that button moves from the More Buttons menu to the toolbar. Excel keeps track of frequently used toolbar buttons, just as it does menu commands, and attempts to make sure that the ones you use are always available. *See "Morphing' Menus," page 13.*

Adding More Toolbars to Your Screen

? SEE ALSO

For information about the Formatting toolbar, see Chapter 7, "Formatting a Worksheet". For more information about the Chart toolbar, see "Working with the Chart Menu and Chart Toolbar," page 668.

You can display additional toolbars at any time. In fact, as Figure 3-4 illustrates, you can have as many toolbars active as you want—at the expense of your worksheet's window size, of course. To activate another toolbar, choose Toolbars from the View menu and select the desired toolbar from the submenu. You can also activate another toolbar using the toolbar shortcut menu. Position the mouse pointer over any displayed toolbar and click the right mouse button to display the shortcut menu, as shown in Figure 3-4.

The most useful toolbars are listed on the toolbar shortcut menu, along with the Customize command. Check marks indicate toolbars that are already active. To activate another toolbar, simply click its name. For example, click Drawing to display the Drawing toolbar.

You can hide a toolbar by opening the toolbar shortcut menu and reselecting the toolbar you want to hide. For example, open the toolbar shortcut menu and click Drawing (which now has a check mark next to it) to remove the Drawing toolbar from the workspace. Alternatively, you can deselect the name of the toolbar in the Toolbars submenu on the View menu.

FIGURE 3-4.

Click the right mouse button while the mouse pointer is over any toolbar to display the toolbar shortcut menu. Check marks indicate displayed toolbars.

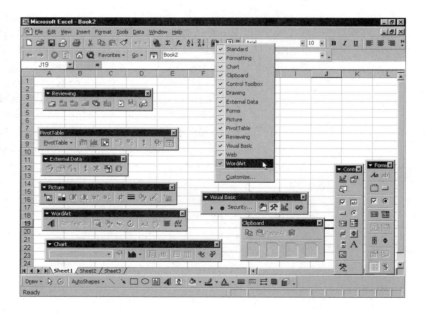

⭐ **TIP**

There are several toolbars that do not appear on either the Toolbars submenu of the View menu or the toolbars shortcut menu. Most of these toolbars appear automatically only when needed. However, you can activate any available toolbar by choosing the Customize command at the bottom of either the Toolbars submenu or the shortcut menu, clicking the Toolbars tab, and selecting the toolbar you want from the Toolbars tab. *For more information about the Customize command, see "Customizing Toolbars and Menus," page 43.*

Positioning Toolbars and Menu Bars on Your Screen

Excel allows you to relocate your toolbars and menu bars. When you first start Excel, the Main menu bar and the Standard and Formatting toolbars are located at the top of the screen, where they are said to be *docked.* You can undock a toolbar or menu bar by clicking the move handle and dragging it to another location. The move handle is the heavy vertical bar at the left end of a docked toolbar or menu bar, as indicated in Figure 3-1. (Be careful not to click one of the toolbar buttons by mistake.)

When you relocate a toolbar or menu bar, its appearance changes slightly. For example, if you drag the Standard toolbar from its default location to the middle of the screen, the toolbar looks like a miniature window, as shown in Figure 3-5, with a title bar and a Close button in

FIGURE 3-5.

You can change both the location and the shape of toolbars and menu bars.

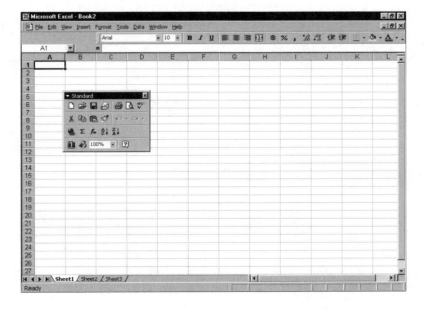

the upper right corner (which you click once to remove the toolbar from the screen). When you undock a toolbar or menu bar, you can change its shape by dragging its borders. Excel remembers the location and shape of the toolbar or menu bar. The next time you start Excel, the bar will appear as it did when you quit the program. You undock a docked bar by dragging it toward the middle of the screen. Similarly, you can dock an undocked bar by dragging it to any side of the screen or by double-clicking the title bar of an undocked bar. If you drag the toolbar shown in Figure 3-5 to the bottom of the screen, it reshapes itself into a single row, and the title bar and Close button disappear. The borders of the toolbar merge with those of the status bar, as shown in Figure 3-6. If you undock the toolbar again, it assumes the shape it had before you docked it.

Note that you can also dock a toolbar or menu bar on the right or left side of the screen, but some tools might not be visible if you do. For example, if you dock the Standard toolbar on the side of the screen, the Zoom Control box disappears because Excel cannot rotate drop-down list boxes. But you can safely dock the Reviewing toolbar on either side because it contains only buttons. Oddly enough, you can safely dock the Worksheet Menu Bar on the side of the screen if you so desire, and the menu names are rotated 90 degrees clockwise.

FIGURE 3-6.

You can dock a toolbar at the bottom of the screen.

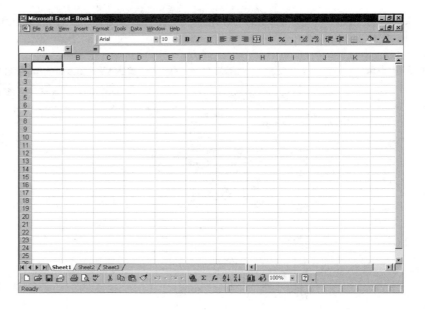

Getting Started

If Your Toolbar Looks Different from Those in This Book

Perhaps your computer was used previously by someone else or you share a computer with other people. Because Excel has so many toolbars that can be customized in so many ways, the copy of Excel you are using might already have been modified. You can use the toolbar shortcut menu to redisplay a toolbar that is not currently active. If any built-in toolbar has been modified, you can restore its default appearance by choosing the Customize command on the toolbar shortcut menu, selecting the toolbar in the list (if necessary), and then clicking Reset. (If the selected toolbar is not one of Excel's built-in toolbars, the Reset button is dimmed and the Delete button is enabled.) Alternatively, you can make some modifications of your own using the Customize command. *See the next section, "Customizing Toolbars and Menus."* You can completely reset all your toolbars' configurations by deleting a special file that keeps track of such things. First exit Excel, and then in the Windows Explorer, navigate to the C:\Windows\Application Data\Microsoft\Excel folder and delete the Excel.xlb file. The next time you start Excel, the toolbars appear in their default configuration.

NOTE

The downward-pointing arrow you click to display the More Buttons drop-down menu (see Figure 3-3 on page 39) is displayed on the right side of docked toolbars. When a toolbar is undocked, the More Buttons arrow appears as a downward-pointing arrow on the left side of the title bar (see Figure 3-5 on page 41).

In addition, some of the buttons on a vertically docked toolbar might not be visible, depending on the type of display you have. With longer vertically docked toolbars, additional buttons might be shifted to the More Buttons menu.

Customizing Toolbars and Menus

In Microsoft Excel 2000, the predefined toolbars and menu bars contain a wealth of buttons and commands. Many other buttons and commands, which are not on any of the predefined bars, are also available. In addition, you can create your own toolbar buttons and commands to add to the list. In this section, we'll tell you how to remove buttons and commands from bars, add buttons and commands to bars, rearrange toolbar buttons and menu commands, change the display format of bars, and create new toolbars and menus.

Removing and Adding Buttons and Commands

The easiest way to add buttons to toolbars is to use the More Buttons drop-down menu, which you can use to access hidden buttons or to add new buttons. We already showed you how to use additional buttons on the More Buttons menu. For additional buttons beyond the hidden ones, click the Add Or Remove Buttons command on the More Buttons menu, shown in Figure 3-7.

FIGURE 3-7.

The Add Or Remove Buttons command offers a quick and easy way to customize toolbars.

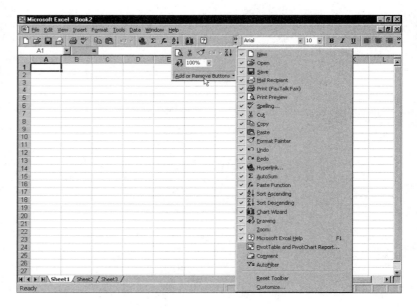

The Add Or Remove Buttons command displays a list of buttons currently installed on the corresponding toolbar. The check marks indicate installed buttons. For each toolbar, you'll notice a few unchecked buttons at the bottom of the list. These are optional buttons that have been identified as likely candidates for inclusion on that toolbar; each toolbar has different optional buttons available. For example, in Figure 3-7, the PivotTable And PivotChart Report, Comment, and AutoFilter buttons are not normally on the Standard toolbar, but you can add them by simply choosing them from the list.

Most of the time, a given toolbar will include several buttons you might never use. In the case of the Standard and Formatting toolbars, you might want to remove some of the buttons that normally appear to make room for others. To remove a button, simply choose it from the list to uncheck it. The removed button still appears on the Add Or Remove Buttons list, if you change your mind later.

If you want to restore a toolbar to its default state, choose the Reset Toolbar command on the Add Or Remove Buttons list. To effect more extensive changes on your toolbars, choose the Customize command.

Using the Customize Command

The Customize command displays the Customize dialog box and can be found in a number of places: on the Add Or Remove Buttons list; on the shortcut menu that appears when you click any toolbar or menu bar with the right mouse button; on the Toolbars submenu of the View menu; and on the Tools menu. (The Customize command is not normally visible on the shortened version of the Tools menu. To display the Customize command, click the downward-pointing double arrow at the bottom of the Tools menu.) Displaying the Customize dialog box is like flipping a switch that puts you into *modification mode*, allowing you to add and remove commands and buttons, as well as freely move them between toolbars and menu bars. Though you might not need to use the dialog box itself, it must be active before you can make changes.

You can remove a button or a command from a bar by taking the following steps:

1 From the View menu, choose Toolbars and click Customize (or choose Customize from the toolbar shortcut menu).

2 The Customize dialog box must be open, but you remove the button or command from the bar, not from the dialog box. Click the button or command that you want to remove, drag it anywhere outside the bar, and release the mouse button. (You click menus to open them as usual, and then click the menu command and drag to remove it.)

3 Click Close to close the dialog box.

For example, to remove the Cut button (the button with the scissors on it) from the Standard toolbar, first display the Customize dialog box and then drag the Cut button off the toolbar. When you click the command or button you want to remove, a heavy black border appears around it. As you drag, a small button icon appears next to the pointer. When you remove a command or button, an "X" icon also appears, as shown in Figure 3-8.

FIGURE 3-8.

Drag a button off the toolbar to remove it. We removed the Cut button from the Standard toolbar.

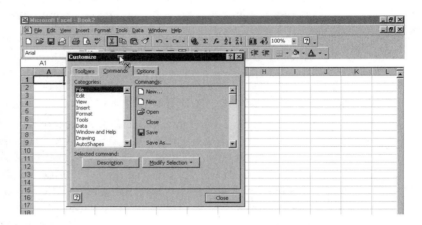

TIP

You can copy, move, or delete buttons from toolbars without opening the Customize dialog box. Hold down the Alt key and drag to remove buttons from toolbars or to relocate them to other toolbars. To copy buttons to other toolbars, hold down both the Ctrl and Alt keys while dragging.

To add a button or command, follow these steps:

1 From the View menu, choose Toolbars and click Customize (or choose Customize from the toolbar shortcut menu).

2 Click the Commands tab in the Customize dialog box and select the category of the command or button you want to add. Excel displays all the commands and buttons available in that category in the Commands window of the dialog box.

3 Click the command button you want to add and drag it to the position on the toolbar where you want it to appear. Any existing buttons move to the right to accommodate the new button.

Getting Started

It is possible to add more buttons to a toolbar than can be displayed while the toolbar is docked. Additional buttons appear on the toolbar's More Buttons menu.

To add the Clear Contents button to the newly modified Standard toolbar, follow these steps:

1 With the Customize dialog box open and the Commands tab visible, select the Edit category from the Categories list box.

2 Click the Clear Contents command button and drag it to the Standard toolbar, to the same location from which we removed the Cut button—to the left of the Copy button (the button with the two small pages on it), as shown in Figure 3-9. As you drag, the small button icon appears next to the pointer.

FIGURE 3-9.

Drag a button from the Customize dialog box to a toolbar to add it. We added the Clear Contents button to the left of the Copy button on the Standard toolbar.

When you drag a button onto a toolbar, a plus-sign icon appears and an "I-beam" insertion point indicates the destination.

Rearranging Buttons and Commands

You can also rearrange buttons on a toolbar or commands on a menu while the Customize dialog box is displayed. Using our Standard toolbar example, drag the Clear Contents button that we just added to the right until the insertion point indicator is to the right of the Format Painter button (the button with the paintbrush on it). The result looks something like Figure 3-10.

FIGURE 3-10.

We moved the Clear Contents button to the right of the Format Painter button.

Is There a Difference between Buttons and Commands?

In a word: no. The buttons that appear on toolbars are simply handy ways to issue commands. The commands that appear on menus are really no different from buttons, and in fact, many commands display corresponding button images on the menu. The portion of the File menu below shows three commands with familiar images to the left of the command names that also appear as buttons on the Standard toolbar.

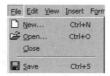

As you can see on the Commands tab of the Customize dialog box shown in Figure 3-8 on page 46 the list of commands shows button images next to the command name, just as they appear on menus (though not all commands have button images associated with them). *For more information, see "Controlling the Display of Buttons," page 52, and "Changing the Look of Buttons," page 56.*

In addition, you can add or remove lines between groups of buttons on toolbars or between groups of commands on menus. It takes a little practice, but the basic techniques are simple. To add a line to the left of a button, drag the toolbar button to the right, releasing the mouse button before the "I-beam" insertion point appears. To add a line above a menu command, drag the command down. Similarly, you can remove a line by dragging an adjacent button or command over the line until the button or command overlaps the line.

Another way to add and remove the lines between buttons and commands is to use the Modify Selection button on the Commands tab of the Customize dialog box. When you click the Begin A Group command, a new line appears to the left of or above the selected button or command. To remove an existing line, select the button or command to the right of or below the line and choose the Begin A Group command again to remove the check mark next to it.

You can also rearrange toolbars and menus by dragging buttons and commands between displayed toolbars or between menus. For example, with both the Standard and Formatting toolbars displayed, choose the Customize command from the toolbar shortcut menu. With the Customize dialog box displayed, drag any button from one toolbar to the other. The button disappears from its original location and reappears in the new location. To relocate a command, simply drag the command to the menu where you want it to appear.

TIP

You can also copy buttons and commands between toolbars and menus. With the Customize dialog box open, hold down Ctrl while you drag the button or command you want to copy to the new location. (A small plus sign appears next to the mouse pointer.) The button or command remains in the original location, and a duplicate appears in the new location.

Rearranging Menus and Submenus

You can customize your menus any way you like, using the same techniques as for customizing toolbars and commands. An additional technique for customizing menus is to use Built-In Menus. Built-In Menus is a category on the Commands tab of the Customize dialog box that contains all the predefined menus and submenus available in Excel. Just like with any command or button, you can place items from the Built-In Menus list on any toolbar, menu, or menu bar. For example, you can drag the Toolbars menu from the Built-In Menus list to the menu bar to create a separate menu for toolbars, as shown in Figure 3-11. Toolbars is normally a submenu of the View menu, so you could then drag Toolbars from the View menu to remove it.

FIGURE 3-11.

You can rearrange Built-In Menus to make frequently used commands more accessible.

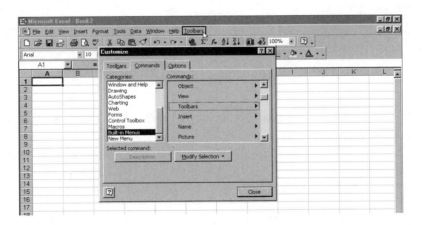

With the Customize dialog box open, you can drag entire menus to other menus, transforming them into submenus. For example, you could drag the Help menu to the bottom of the View menu to transform the Help menu into a submenu. You can even add menus to toolbars and add toolbar buttons to menu bars.

Restoring Default Toolbars

You can use the following procedure to remove all added buttons and return all deleted buttons to a toolbar:

1 From the View menu, choose Toolbars, and then choose Customize (or you can choose Customize from the toolbar shortcut menu).

2 Select the name of the toolbar you want to restore from the Toolbars list and then click the Reset button. Click OK to confirm the restoration. The toolbar returns to its default configuration. Click Close when you are finished.

Restoring Default Menus

You can return a modified menu to its original condition by taking the following steps:

1 From the View menu, choose Toolbars, and then choose Customize (or you can choose Customize from the toolbar shortcut menu).

2 With the right mouse button, click the menu you want to restore, and then choose the Reset command from the shortcut menu that appears.

To restore all menus, submenus, and commands at the same time, click the Toolbars tab in the Customize dialog box and select the Worksheet Menu Bar option (or the Chart Menu Bar option, if a chart is currently active). Then click the Reset button. Click Close when you are finished.

Restoring Personalized Menus and Toolbars

For information about personalized toolbars, see "'Rafting' Toolbars," page 38. For more information about personalized menus, see "'Morphing' Menus," page 13.

The preceding procedures reset toolbars and menus in terms of their inventory of commands and buttons, but they do not affect which commands and buttons are visible when personalization options are turned on. The personalization options are controlled by choosing the Options tab from the Customize dialog box, and selecting both the Standard And Formatting Toolbars Share One Row option and the Menus Show Recently Used Command First option. Figure 3-12 shows the Options tab.

FIGURE 3-12.

Click Reset My Usage Data to restore personalized menus and toolbars.

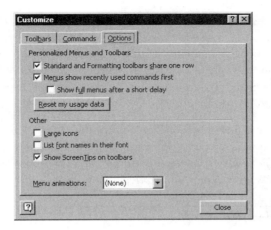

When you choose the Standard And Formatting Toolbars Share One Row option, you also activate the toolbar equivalent of the "recently used commands" option. Which buttons are visible on the Standard and Formatting toolbars (or any "rafting" toolbar) is partially determined by your usage habits, which are recorded by Excel as you work. Use the following procedure to return all menu commands and toolbar buttons to their original places—either on the visible portion of toolbars or on the More Buttons menu:

1   From the View menu, choose Toolbars, and then choose Customize (or you can choose Customize from the toolbar shortcut menu).

2   Click the Options tab (shown in Figure 3-12) and click the Reset My Usage Data button. Click Close when you are finished.

Restoring All Global Toolbar and Menu Settings

This procedure effectively comprises the three previous procedures. Follow these steps to reset all menus and toolbars and discard all personalization data:

1   Exit Excel by clicking the Close button at the right corner of the Excel window title bar or by choosing Exit from the File menu.

2   In the Windows Explorer, navigate to the C:\Windows\ Application Data\Microsoft\Excel folder.

3   Delete the Excel.xlb file.

SEE ALSO

For more information about changing a toolbar button's appearance, see "Changing the Look of Buttons," page 56.

Changing Other Toolbar Button Options

If you want, you can enlarge all the toolbar buttons for easy selection and improved legibility. Simply select the Large Icons option on the Options tab of the Customize dialog box shown in Figure 3-12. Note, however, that magnifying the buttons reduces the number of buttons visible on a docked toolbar.

When the Show ScreenTips On Toolbars option is selected, a small label appears when you move the mouse pointer over any toolbar button. *(For more information about ScreenTips, see "Identifying Toolbar Buttons with ScreenTips," page 35.)*

Animating Your Menus

The Options tab in the Customize dialog box also contains a drop-down list box labeled Menu Animations. This is another one of the "visceral" elements in Excel. Two other such elements are sound feedback and animated row and column insertion and deletion (both of which are controlled by the Options command on the Tools menu).

You can select one of the four options in the Menu Animations list box: Random, Unfold, Slide, and None (the default). When you click menus when animations are turned on, instead of simply appearing, they appear with a flourish! Try them out to see what you think.

Controlling the Display of Buttons

Many commands have associated buttons, the faces of which are normally displayed to the left of the commands on the menus. Many of the same button faces appear on toolbars as buttons that perform the same task as the equivalent menu command. On menus, you can choose to display or hide the button images.

If a command in the Customize dialog box has a button image next to it, you can use it as either a menu command or a button. If a command does not have a button image, you can simple create one from scratch.

You control the display of button faces using commands on the menu that appears when you click the Modify Selection button on the Commands tab of the Customize dialog box. Figure 3-13 shows the Modify Selection menu that appears when the Copy command on the Edit menu is selected.

Four commands on the Modify Selection menu, starting with Default Style, control the display of buttons. On toolbars, you can choose to

FIGURE 3-13.

Use the Modify Selection menu to change the way commands are represented on menus and toolbars.

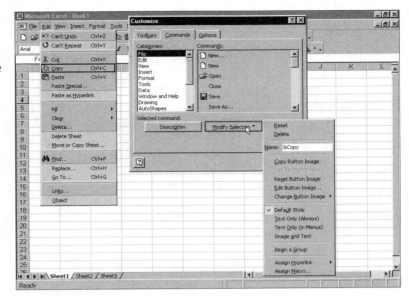

show command names or the button images, or both. If you choose the Text Only (In Menus) command, the button face disappears when the selected command is on a menu. If you subsequently drag the command from a menu to a toolbar, the button face appears and the text disappears. If you choose the Text Only (Always) command, the button face does not appear in either location. The Image And Text command causes both the button face and the command text to appear in any location. The Default Style command restores the command to its normal appearance, which for most commands is "image and text" in menus and "image only" on toolbars.

Creating New Toolbars

It's easy to create customized toolbars. To do so, follow these steps:

1 From the View menu, choose Toolbars, and then choose Customize (or you can choose Customize from the Toolbar shortcut menu).

2 On the Toolbars tab, click the New button.

3 The New Toolbar dialog box appears, as shown in Figure 3-14 on the next page. Type a name for your new toolbar. When you click OK, a small, empty, floating toolbar appears.

4 Add buttons to the empty toolbar by dragging buttons from the Commands tab of the Customize dialog box or by copying or moving buttons from other toolbars.

FIGURE 3-14.

Type a name for the new toolbar in the New Toolbar dialog box and click OK. The Customize dialog box remains open and an empty toolbar appears.

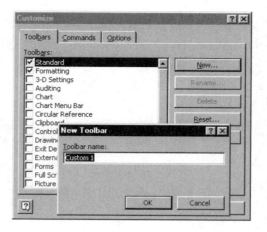

After you define a custom toolbar and close the Customize dialog box, its name appears on the Toolbars submenu of the View menu, on the toolbar shortcut menu, and in the Toolbars list in the Toolbars dialog box. You can choose to display, hide, and dock a custom toolbar just like any predefined toolbar.

Deleting Custom Toolbars

⊗ CAUTION

After you delete a toolbar, you cannot use the Undo command or button to restore it.

It's as easy to remove a custom toolbar as it is to create one. To remove a custom toolbar, follow these steps:

1 From the View menu, choose Toolbars, and then choose Customize (or you can choose Customize from the Toolbar shortcut menu).

2 On the Toolbars tab of the Customize dialog box, select the name of the custom toolbar you want to remove. You cannot remove any of Excel's built-in toolbars.

3 Click Delete and then click OK at the prompt.

Creating New Menus

The Categories list box on the Commands tab of the Customize dialog box contains a category called New Menu. This is a unique category that contains only one item: New Menu. When you drag the New Menu item to a menu bar, a menu, or a toolbar, a blank menu named, surprisingly enough, *New Menu*, appears. "New Menu" probably isn't a descriptive enough name, so you can rename the new menu: click New Menu with the right mouse button, type a name in the Name box, and press Enter. You can then populate the new menu with any commands, menus, or buttons on the Commands tab. You can even put drop-down list boxes on menus. For example, Figure 3-15 shows a new menu we created that contains three list boxes.

FIGURE 3-15.

Create your own menus for frequently used commands.

To remove new menus and return relocated menus and commands to their original positions, click the Worksheet Menu Bar option (or Chart Menu Bar, if a chart is selected) on the Toolbars tab of the Customize dialog box. Then click Reset.

Saving Toolbar and Menu Changes

When you exit Microsoft Excel, any predefined toolbars or menus you changed and any custom toolbars or menus you created are saved in the condition and position they were in when you quit. Each time you start Excel, your custom and modified toolbars and menus are ready for use. Excel saves your custom toolbar and menu settings in a special file named Excel.xlb. To create different combinations of toolbar or menu settings, you can save modified and custom toolbar and menu variations by renaming the .xlb file.

Whenever you quit Excel, the .xlb file saves any changes you have made to the toolbar or menu configuration. To save your current settings as well as another custom configuration, follow these steps:

1 Exit Excel by clicking the Close button at the right corner of the Excel window title bar or by choosing Exit from the File menu.

2 Start the Windows Explorer and navigate to the folder C:\Windows\Application Data\Microsoft\Excel.

3 Change the name of the Excel.xlb file by using the Rename command on the File menu. If you don't see file extensions in the Windows Explorer, choose Options from the View menu and clear the Hide MS-DOS File Extensions check box.

The settings that were active when you exited Excel are saved under the new filename, and any modifications you make during the next Excel session are saved in a new Excel.xlb file. You can subsequently

SEE ALSO

For more information about opening files, see "Opening Files," page 77.

rename this new .xlb file, if you like. In this way, you can create any number of toolbar and menu configurations, which you can access by opening the .xlb file using the Open command on Excel's File menu. Alternatively, you can double-click your custom .xlb file in the Windows Explorer when you want to start Excel with a particular configuration. You can even create a shortcut for it in the Windows Explorer or add it to the Windows taskbar Start menu.

Changing the Look of Buttons

There are several ways you can change the way a toolbar button looks:

- Change its face using the Change Button Image command.

- Change its face with Excel's Button Editor.

- Copy another face and paste it onto the button.

- Create your own button face from scratch.

With the Customize dialog box open, click the right mouse button on any toolbar button to display the shortcut menu. As shown in Figure 3-16, the Change Button Image command displays a palette of *button faces*—that is, buttons with images on them—that you can use to change the appearance of toolbar buttons.

FIGURE 3-16.

Change the face of any button with the Change Button Image command.

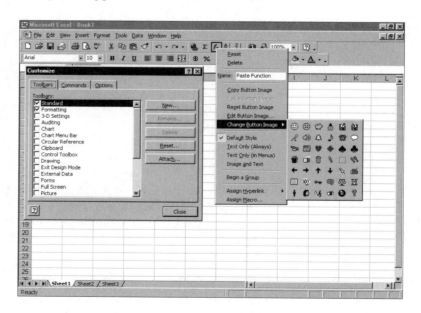

If the button face you want isn't on the Change Button Image palette, you can perform plastic surgery using the Edit Button Image command, which displays the Button Editor, shown in Figure 3-17.

FIGURE 3-17.

You can use the Button Editor to change the face of any toolbar button.

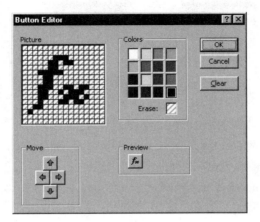

The small squares in the Picture section of the Button Editor dialog box correspond to *pixels,* which are the units of resolution on your computer screen. To erase only some of the existing pixels, click the Erase square in the Colors section and then click or drag through the pixels in the Picture section you want to remove.

Creating a Custom Button

To create a new button face from scratch, use the Edit Button Image command to open the Button Editor dialog box and then click Clear. Next, click a color square in the Color section and then click or drag through the pixel squares in the Picture section, as if you were dipping your "brush" in paint and then applying it to the canvas. Use the arrow buttons in the Move section to shift the image in the corresponding direction. The arrow buttons work only if there are blank pixels in the direction you want to shift, however. In Figure 3-17, for example, there is room to shift the image to the left one pixel by clicking the left arrow button. The Preview box shows the button as it will appear in its actual size.

NOTE

> When you create buttons with custom faces, those buttons are available on a toolbar or menu only. In other words, the buttons are not included in the Customize dialog box.

If you're not satisfied with your custom button face, restore the original button face using the Reset command on the button shortcut menu.

Copying Button Faces

To copy a button face from one button to another, follow these steps:

1   Open the Customize dialog box. If necessary, drag the button you want to copy to a toolbar or menu. You can copy a button only when it is on a toolbar or menu.

2   With the Customize dialog box still open, position the mouse pointer over the button you want to copy, and then click the right mouse button to display the button shortcut menu.

3   From the shortcut menu, choose Copy Button Image.

4   Position the mouse pointer over the button you want to change and display the shortcut menu.

5   Choose Paste Button Image. The face of the copied button image replaces the face on the current button.

6   If necessary, drag the button from which you copied the image off the toolbar to delete it. Click OK.

Editing and Button Size

The default dimensions of Excel's toolbar buttons are 16 pixels wide by 15 pixels high. These are also the dimensions of the pixel grid in the Picture section of the Button Editor dialog box shown in Figure 3-17 on the previous page. So what happens when you click the Options tab in the Customize dialog box and then select the Large Icons option? The buttons appear larger, but their actual pixel dimensions do not change. Instead, Excel displays a "zoomed-in" view of the buttons. When editing or creating a button face, you can check it with the Large Icons option to make sure it looks OK in this "zoomed-in" mode.

Attaching a Toolbar to a Workbook

Earlier in this chapter, we described how toolbar settings, including custom toolbars, are saved when you exit Microsoft Excel. Then, when you reload Excel, those settings are reactivated and ready for use. Excel also allows you to attach a custom toolbar to a workbook so that the toolbar is activated whenever the corresponding workbook is opened. That way, you can create many different toolbars for specific tasks in specific workbooks. Because the toolbars are attached to the workbooks, you can then eliminate them from the Toolbars list box in the Customize dialog box, thereby reserving the list for more "universal" toolbars.

To attach a custom toolbar to your workbook, select its name in the list on the Toolbars tab of the Customize dialog box and click the Attach button. The Attach Toolbars dialog box appears, as shown in Figure 3-18.

FIGURE 3-18.

Attach custom toolbars to workbooks using the Attach Toolbars dialog box.

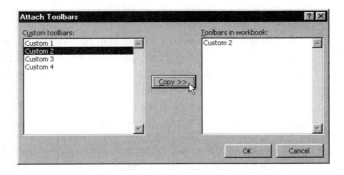

SEE ALSO

For more information about saving your toolbar settings, see "Saving Toolbar and Menu Changes," page 55.

In the Attach Toolbars dialog box, select the toolbar you want to attach to your workbook from the Custom Toolbars list. (Only custom toolbars can be attached to workbooks.) Click the Copy button to add the toolbar to the Toolbars In Workbook list box on the right.

SEE ALSO

For more information about creating macros, commands, and buttons, see Chapter 28, "Creating Macros." For more information about hyperlinks, see Chapter 19, "Hyperlinks and the Internet."

Creating Custom Commands and Buttons

There is one more special category—Macros—on the Commands tab of the Customize dialog box. Macros are sequences of commands you can create yourself to help perform repetitive tasks. The Macros category contains two items: Custom Menu Item and Custom Button. The only real difference between the two is that no button image is associated with the Custom Menu Item. But as we have seen, you could add one anyway, if you like. These two items are simply blank starting points you can use to create your own commands and buttons.

To use them, drag either one of these items to a menu, menu bar, or toolbar, click the right mouse button on the new command or button, and choose the Assign Macro command on the shortcut menu. All the macros available in the current workbook are listed in this dialog box. You can choose an existing macro and assign it to the selected command or button, or you can click the Record button to start recording a new macro. Similarly, you can assign a hyperlink rather than a macro to a command or button. Simply choose Assign Hyperlink on the shortcut menu and choose the Open command to display the Assign Hyperlink dialog box.

After you attach a custom toolbar to a workbook, you can delete the toolbar from the Toolbars list in the Toolbars tab of the Customize dialog box. Simply select the toolbar and click the Delete button. Then, whenever you open the workbook, the custom toolbar is automatically activated. When you close the workbook, the attached custom toolbar remains, allowing you to customize or remove it as needed.

To "unattach" a custom toolbar from a workbook, you must use the Attach Toolbars dialog box again, except this time, select the toolbar in the Toolbars In Workbook list, and then click the Delete button. (The Copy button changes to Delete when you select an attached toolbar.) If you do not "unattach" a toolbar in this way, it will reappear every time you open the workbook, even if you remove it from the Toolbars list.

The next chapter covers the essentials of file management. It covers everything from opening, saving, and creating new files, to taking advantage of Excel's file-searching capabilities (in case you have trouble remembering where you put one).

CHAPTER 4

Managing Files

O ne of the advantages of working with computers is that you can save your work on disk, in an electronic file. When your work is saved on disk, it's always at your fingertips, and with Microsoft Excel's Find File feature, you'll never have trouble locating your files. You can easily share work you've saved on disk with others, without having to produce paper copies. In this chapter, we describe all the ways you can save, open, and find your Excel files.

Working with Files

You use the File menu to save and retrieve your workbook files. Microsoft Excel 2000 "remembers" the files you worked on most recently and includes their names at the bottom of the menu so that you can open them quickly.

The File menu is shown in Figure 4-1.

FIGURE 4-1.

At the bottom of the File menu, Excel displays the files you worked on most recently so you can quickly open any one of them.

Creating a New File

You can create a new workbook quickly by clicking the New button on the Standard toolbar. Figure 4-2 shows the file-management buttons available on the Standard toolbar.

FIGURE 4-2.

Use the first three buttons on the Standard toolbar to help manage your files.

New   Save

Open

? SEE ALSO

For more information about switching from one workbook to another, see Chapter 9, "Worksheets and Windows."

If you create a new workbook when another workbook is already open, the new workbook window appears on top of the existing window. If the previous workbook was named Book1, the new workbook is named Book2. Later workbooks are numbered sequentially: Book3, Book4, and so on. You use the commands on the Window menu to switch from one workbook to another.

Creating a New File Based on an Existing File

When you use the New command on the File menu instead of the New button on the Standard toolbar, the New dialog box appears, as shown in Figure 4-3. Workbooks that appear in the New dialog box become the basis for your new workbooks. The General tab in the New dialog box contains a "Workbook" icon. Selecting the Workbook icon creates a new blank workbook, as if you had clicked the New toolbar button. The Spreadsheet Solutions tab contains several workbook template icons. These templates give you a head start on many common spreadsheet tasks. When you select one of these icons and click OK, Excel opens a *copy* of the workbook.

FIGURE 4-3.

You can open a copy of any file that appears in the New dialog box.

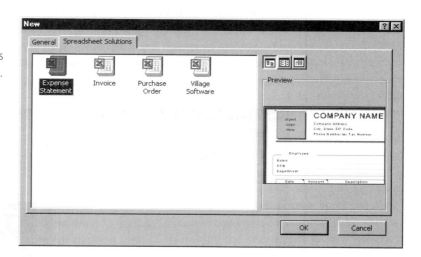

NOTE

To add all the available workbook templates, you must rerun setup. The Spreadsheet Solutions templates are not installed by default. When you click one of the icons on the Spreadsheet Solutions tab, the message *Click OK to install additional templates and create a new file.* appears in the Preview area. If you click OK, Excel asks if you want to install the selected template. However, the Spreadsheet Solutions templates depend upon several add-ins that also must be installed to ensure proper operation. So, although it's great that Excel 2000 makes it easier to install missing components, in this case it is best to rerun Setup to properly install the Spreadsheet Solutions templates.

When you save a workbook file with one of the Save commands, the workbook remains open. When you close a workbook file with the Close command or quit Excel with the Exit command, however, Excel removes the file from the screen.

Saving a File for the First Time

 SEE ALSO

For information about saving all the workbooks and settings you are currently working with, see "Saving the Entire Workspace," page 76.

Before you can save a workbook file for the first time, you must assign it a name and indicate where you want Excel to store the file. To name your document, choose either Save or Save As from the File menu, or click the Save button on the Standard toolbar.

When you save a file for the first time, the Save As dialog box appears, as shown in Figure 4-4.

FIGURE 4-4.

The Save As dialog box appears when you save a file for the first time.

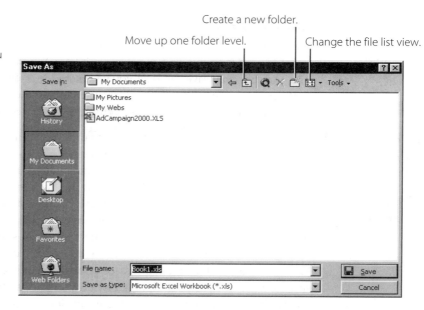

Create a new folder.

Move up one folder level.

Change the file list view.

NOTE

The Save As dialog box and the almost identical Open dialog box have been greatly enhanced in Microsoft Excel 2000. *For more information about the buttons and navigational controls in these dialog boxes, see "Opening Files," page 77.*

In Figure 4-4, the suggested filename, Book1, appears in the File Name edit box because you haven't yet assigned a new name to the document. To change the filename, simply type a new name. (You don't have to type the extension .xls; Excel adds that for you.) The original contents of the edit box disappear as soon as you begin typing. Click Save when you are finished entering the filename. After you save the file, the workbook window remains open on the workspace and Excel displays the workbook's new name in the title bar.

TIP

If you use the same folder for the majority of your file-management operations, you can designate that folder as the default folder. From the Tools menu, choose the Options command and then click the General tab. Click the Default File Location edit box and type the full pathname for the folder. The folder you specify in the Default File Location edit box is used as the default folder the first time you choose the Open, Save, or Save As command. Excel always displays the last folder you used during the current session. So if you switch to a folder other than the Default File Location when saving or opening a file, Excel returns to the new folder the next time you choose the Open, Save, or Save As commands, until you exit Excel. The next time you start Excel, the Default File Location is once again used.

How Much Disk Space Do You Need to Save?

To ensure that a new copy of a file is properly saved before the original is deleted, Excel makes a temporary file when it saves, and then deletes the original and renames the temporary file to the original name. This prevents loss of both the original and the version being saved if something goes wrong in midsave. Because of this you can never open, make changes to, and then save a file that is bigger than half the amount of available space on the disk being used. For example, if you have a 1.44-megabyte floppy disk, you cannot open, make changes to, and then save a file larger than approximately 720 KB from within Excel. In this case, you would need to make all your changes in a copy of the workbook located on your hard disk, and then save it to the floppy disk when you're finished.

Filename Rules

File naming in Microsoft Excel 2000 follows the same basic rules you use in other Microsoft Windows 95 and Windows 98 applications, with a few differences. Filenames in Excel can have up to 218 characters, rather than the 255 generally available in Windows. They can include any combination of alphanumeric characters, spaces, and the special characters, with the exception of the forward slash (/), backslash (\), greater than sign (>), less than sign (<), asterisk (*), question mark (?), quotation mark ("), pipe symbol (|), colon (:), and semicolon (;). Although you can use any combination of uppercase and lowercase letters, keep in mind that Excel does not distinguish case in filenames. For example, the names *MYFILE, MyFile,* and *myfile* are identical in Excel.

The familiar MS-DOS three-character file extension helps identify your Excel files, and it is added automatically when you save a file. Note, however, that file extensions may not appear with Windows filenames. The following table lists some of Excel's default extensions.

Document Type	Extension
Add-in	.xla
Backup	.xlk
Template	.xlt
Workbook	.xls
Workspace	.xlw

Depending on your Windows installation, the MS-DOS file extensions, such as .xls, might or might not appear. They are still there, but in Windows 95 and Windows 98 you can choose to display them or turn them off. From the Windows Explorer, choose the Options command on the View menu, and on the View tab, select or clear the Hide MS-DOS File Extensions For File Types That Are Registered check box. *For more information, see your Windows documentation.*

If you want to accept the program's default file extension, simply type the filename without a period or extension name. You might, however, find the Properties dialog box more helpful than using extensions. *For more information about recording details about a file, see "Adding Summary Information to Files," page 74.*

Unless you specify otherwise, Excel saves your file in the default folder. As shown in Figure 4-4 on page 66, the name of the current folder appears in the Save In box in the Save As dialog box. To save your file in a different folder, you can specify the path along with your filename in the File Name edit box (if you enjoy typing). Or you can select a different folder using the Save In drop-down list box, which you display by clicking the down arrow to the right of the box. Any folders or workbooks within the current folder are displayed in the list box that dominates the Save As dialog box. To select one of these folders, double-click the folder you want in the list box. The selected folder remains open until you make a new selection. You can also click the Up One Level button to move up the folder hierarchy one step at a time.

② SEE ALSO

For more information about saving files, see Chapter 18, "Sharing Files with Others," or Chapter 19, "Hyperlinks and the Internet."

If you want to save a file to another disk drive, click the down-arrow to the right of the Save In drop-down list box to display a list of all the disk drives connected to your system. Then select the desired drive from the list box. You can also save files on a network drive, if your computer is connected to a network, or to FTP sites on the Internet, if you have Internet access.

File Formats

In addition to providing the filename and location, you can specify a different file format in the Save As dialog box. Click the arrow to the right of the Save As Type drop-down list box. The list expands to reveal all the formats in which you can save your files.

② SEE ALSO

For more information about Excel's export formats, see "Importing and Exporting Files," page 86.

The default format is Microsoft Excel Workbook, and you'll almost always use this option. If you want to export an Excel file to another program, however, you can use one of the other options to convert the file to a format that is readable by that program.

The Template format allows you to save files to be used as the basis for multiple new files.

⊗ NOTE

> To open a template file in order to modify the original template, simply use the Open command.

Specifying a Default File Format

Normally when you save a new workbook, it is saved in the Microsoft Excel Workbook format. If you open a file that was saved in a different format, you are automatically asked when saving whether you want to use the original file format or change it to Excel 2000 format.

You can specify a format other than Microsoft Excel Workbook as the default format when saving. To do so, choose Options from the Tools menu and click the Transition tab, shown in Figure 4-5.

FIGURE 4-5.

You can specify the default format to use when saving.

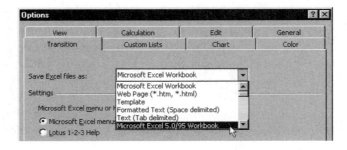

The Save Excel Files As list contains all the same file formats as the Save As Type list in the Save As dialog box. This feature is particularly useful if you normally share your workbooks with others who use different programs, such as previous versions of Excel.

Document Types in Previous Versions of Excel

In Microsoft Excel versions 5.0 through 2000, worksheets, chart sheets, Excel 5.0 dialog sheets, and Excel 4.0 macro sheets are all contained in workbooks. In previous versions of Excel, worksheets, chart sheets, and macro sheets were saved separately. When you open one of these earlier sheet types in Excel 2000, it is automatically converted to an Excel 2000 workbook, which you can then choose to save in the new Excel 2000 format or keep in its original format. You can also combine sheets from a previous version of Excel in a single Excel 2000 workbook. *For more information about working with workbooks, see Chapter 9, "Worksheets and Windows."*

Excel 5.0 workbooks were compatible with Excel 95, and vice versa. This compatibility meant you could save a workbook in Excel 95, and then open it in Excel 5.0 without problems. Excel 97 and Excel 2000 share a somewhat different file format than the one shared by Excel 95 and Excel 5.0. To accommodate situations where you must share files with others using different versions of Excel, the Save As Type list in the Save As dialog box includes a special format called Microsoft Excel 97-2000 & 5.0/95, which saves workbooks in these two formats simultaneously. Users of any of these versions of Excel can open a file saved in this format, but if someone using Excel 95 or Excel 5.0 saves changes to it, any Excel 2000 features and formatting it contains are lost.

Creating Backup Files Automatically

You can have Excel always create a duplicate copy of your file on the same disk and in the same directory as the original. Choose the Save As command from the File menu, click the Tools button at the top of the Save As dialog box, and then click the General Options command to display the Save Options dialog box shown in Figure 4-6. Then select the Always Create Backup option.

FIGURE 4-6.

The Save Options dialog box gives you control of various file-security features.

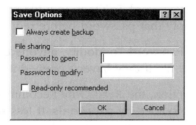

The backup file is a duplicate file that carries the same name as your original, but the name is preceded by "Backup of" and has the file extension .xlk. If this is the first time you've saved the file, the backup file and the workbook file are identical. If you saved the file previously with the Always Create Backup option selected, Excel renames the last saved version of your file, giving it a .xlk extension, and overwrites the existing .xlk file.

NOTE

Keep in mind that Excel always uses a .xlk extension when creating backup files, regardless of the file type. Suppose you work with a workbook named Myfile.xls as well as a template file on disk named Myfile.xlt, and you select the Always Create Backup option for both. Because only one Myfile.xlk can exist, the most recently saved file is saved as the .xlk file, and Excel overwrites the other file's backup, if one exists.

Protecting Files

You can password-protect your files with two types of passwords: Password To Open and Password To Modify. Passwords can have up to 15 characters, and capitalization matters. Thus, if you assign the password *Secret* to a file, you can't reopen that file by typing *SECRET* or *secret*. For added security, Excel does not display passwords on the screen when you type them to open a protected file.

Adding Summary Information to Files

When you choose the Properties command on the File menu, Excel displays a Properties dialog box that you use to record general information about the active workbook file. (The Properties command is not visible on shortened menus. Click the double arrow at the bottom of the File menu to display the Properties command.) The name of the active file appears in the title bar of the dialog box, as shown in Figure 4-7.

FIGURE 4-7.

The Properties dialog box lets you record information about your workbook.

? SEE ALSO

For more information about the Advanced Find dialog box, see "Adding Additional Search Criteria," page 84.

The information you enter in the Properties dialog box can be used later for file identification or clarification. For example, you can use properties as search criteria in the Advanced Find dialog box to search for files with a particular entry or combination of entries in any of the Properties edit boxes.

The Properties dialog box contains five tabs. The General tab displays information about the file, including size, location, attributes, creation date, and date of last modification. The Summary tab, shown in Figure 4-7, allows you to enter your own property values. The Author and Company values are filled in for you, based on the information you supplied when you first installed Excel.

 TIP

To change the default Author name shown on the Summary tab of the Properties dialog box, choose Options from the Tools menu, click the General tab, and type the new name in the User Name box.

Linking Custom Properties to Cells

You can link a custom property to a named cell in your worksheet. When you do, the value of the custom property becomes whatever the named cell contains and changes whenever the value in the cell changes. First you must name a cell *(see "Rules for Naming Cells and Ranges," page 138)*, which makes available the Link To Content check box on the Custom tab in the Properties dialog box. When the Link To Content box is checked, the workbook's defined names appear in a drop-down list in the Value edit box (whose name changes to Source when linking content), as shown here.

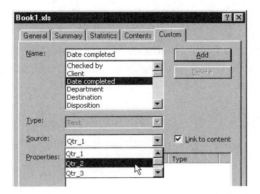

Select or create a name for the custom property in the Name box. (The Type box becomes inactive when linking to content.) When you've specified a Source (the named cell to which you want to link), click the Add button and the custom property appears in the Properties list box.

The Statistics tab lists helpful information, such as the name of the last person who made modifications to the file and total editing time, so you can see how much of your life went into a particular piece of work. The Statistics tab also includes a Revision Number field that indicates how many times the file has been saved while open for multi-user editing. *See Chapter 18, "Sharing Files with Others."*

The Contents tab lists the names of each worksheet that the workbook contains.

Use the Custom tab to create your own properties. You can create a property using a new name, or you can select one from a list of possibilities. Then you can assign it a data type: Text, Date, Number, or "Yes or No." Finally, assign a value to your custom property that is consistent with your data type. For example, you could create a custom text property called Client (which is one of the suggested possibilities) and type the client's name in the values field. Then, using the Find File features in the Open dialog box (*see "Opening Files," on the facing page*), you can locate all the files with a particular client name in this custom property field.

You can have Excel automatically display the Properties dialog box whenever you save a workbook for the first time by following the steps shown here:

1 Choose Options from the Tools menu and click the General tab.

2 Click the Prompt For Workbook Properties option to select it.

3 Click OK to return to the workbook window. The first time you save a file, the Properties dialog box will appear after you click the Save button in the Save As dialog box.

Saving the Entire Workspace

You can use the Save Workspace command on the File menu to save a snapshot of your current Excel environment. (The Save Workspace command is not visible on shortened menus. Click the double arrow at the bottom of the File menu to display the Save Workspace command.) When you choose the Save Workspace command, the dialog box in Figure 4-8 appears.

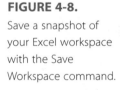

FIGURE 4-8.

Save a snapshot of your Excel workspace with the Save Workspace command.

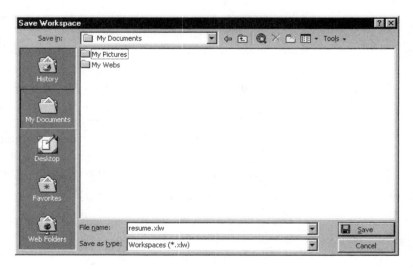

When you save a workspace, Excel notes the locations of all the workbooks that are currently open, as well as many of the workspace settings, so you can retrieve your workspace in the same condition it was in when you saved it. That is, all the workbooks that were open when you saved the workspace file will be opened, and all the applicable settings will be activated. Settings that are saved with workspaces include many of the display and calculation settings available in the Tab dialog box that appears when you choose the Options command from the Tools menu. The default filename suggested for a workspace file is "Resume. xlw," but you can use a different name as long as you follow the file naming rules (and you don't change the three-letter .xlw extension).

Opening Files

To retrieve a file from disk, choose the Open command from the File menu or click the Open button on the Standard toolbar. Excel displays a dialog box, like the one shown in Figure 4-9, that contains a list of the Excel files (files with the extension .xl*) stored in the current folder.

FIGURE 4-9.

Use the Open command to retrieve files stored on disk.

The Files Of Type list box near the bottom of the Open dialog box determines which files are available for selection. The default entry is All Microsoft Excel Files, which tells the program to display only Excel files in the Open dialog box—that is, only those files whose extensions begin with the characters *xl*. You can display specific types of files or display all files by selecting an option from the Files Of Type drop-down list box. For example, to show all files in the current directory, select All Files from the Files Of Type drop-down list box. To display only Lotus 1-2-3 files, select the Lotus 1-2-3 Files option.

The icons on the left side of the dialog box are navigational controls that change the view in the main window of the dialog box to show a list of files at the selected location. The My Documents icon is selected by default and displays the contents of the My Documents folder when you open the dialog box, unless you have changed the Default File Location (using the General tab of the Options command on the Tools menu).

Clicking the History icon displays a list of files you have opened and folders you have navigated to, in chronological order, with the latest first, as shown in Figure 4-10. This is a useful new feature if you work on a lot of files. This view actually displays the contents of a folder named Recent, which can be found in the C:\Windows\Application Data\Microsoft\Office folder. This folder is populated automatically whenever you use the Open or Save As dialog boxes, using shortcuts to the files and folders you use. It can store as many as 50 shortcuts.

FIGURE 4-10.

The History icon displays a chronological list of shortcuts to files and folders you have used.

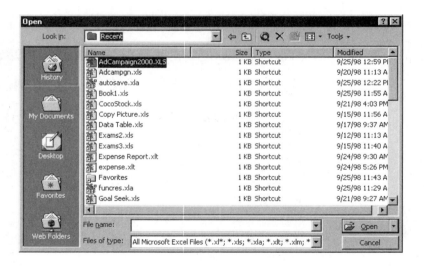

Clicking the Desktop icon is a quick way to jump to the very top level of your computer's file system so you can click your way down through the hierarchy. Click the Favorites icon to display the contents of the Favorites folder located in your Windows directory. The Favorites folder can be a useful tool for storage and organization. The Web Folders icon allows you to save files in any available locations on the Web. *For more information about Web folders, see Chapter 19, "Hyperlinks and the Internet."*

What's a "Favorites"?

Favorites is a concept originally used in Microsoft Internet Explorer in a manner similar to the way *bookmarks* are used in Netscape Navigator. Essentially, a "Favorites" is a file or folder you want to keep track of so you can easily return to it at a later time. The Favorites folder, which is created for you when you first install Excel, is located in your Windows folder. The Favorites icon, on the left side of the Open and Save As dialog boxes, immediately activates the Favorites folder, giving you easy access to files. The Favorites folder contains only shortcuts to files and folders—not the files and folders themselves—unless you move or save files there. You can create shortcuts to files located anywhere on your computer or on any computer to which you have a network or Internet connection.

When any folder other than Favorites is active in the Open or Save As dialog boxes, you can click the Tools button and choose the Add To Favorites command to create a shortcut to the currently selected file or folder and place it in the Favorites folder.

TIP

You can have as many files open at a time as your computer's memory allows. Each file you open occupies memory, however, regardless of the amount of data it contains. For that reason, you should limit the number of files you have open at any one time, especially if some of them contain large amounts of data (such as a workbook in which you have filled thousands of cells).

To open a file, double-click its icon in the list box, or select it and click Open. If you want to retrieve a file in another folder use the Look In list box and the Up One Level button to look through the available drives and folders.

TIP

You can open several files simultaneously using the Open dialog box. To open a group of consecutive files, click the first one, press the Shift key, and then click the last one. When you click Open, Excel opens all the selected files. Similarly, you can select a group of non-consecutive files by clicking on the first one, pressing the Ctrl key, and then clicking the names of any other files you want to open.

The Open dialog box includes a Views button similar to the one found in the Save As dialog box shown in Figure 4-4 on page 66. The Open dialog box shown in Figure 4-10 shows the file list displayed in Details view. Notice the headings that appear over each section of file information. When you click one of these headings, the files are sorted in order, based on that heading. For example, if you click the Modified heading, the files are sorted in date order. You can also change the width of the columns displayed in Details view by dragging the lines between headings, similar to the way you can drag to change column width in a worksheet.

 TIP

You can click the right mouse button on most files listed in the Open, New, or Save As dialog boxes to display a shortcut menu that contains commands you can use on the selected file. For example, you can delete a file displayed in the Open dialog box using this shortcut menu.

? SEE ALSO

For more information about Excel and the Web, see Chapter 19, "Hyperlinks and the Internet."

The Search The Web button activates your default browser, allowing you to use Web search engines to locate the information you're looking for. Click the Tools button to display a drop-down menu (shown in Figure 4-11) that contains additional commands you can use on selected files. When you choose the Print command from this location, Excel opens and prints the file without further actions on your part. This is equivalent to opening the file and then clicking the Print button on the Standard toolbar, which prints the active workbook using the default settings in the Print dialog box. The Properties command displays the Properties dialog box without closing the Open dialog box. The Map Network Drive command lets you connect to a remote drive on a network.

FIGURE 4-11.

Click the Tools button to display additional useful commands.

The Find command pertains to the file-finding features discussed in "Searching for Files," page 83. The Add To Favorites command creates a shortcut to the selected file and places it in your Favorites folder, which you can then access by clicking the Favorites icon on the left side of the dialog box.

The Open Options

The Open Options button shown in Figure 4-12 includes a small, downward-pointing arrow that provides access to the Open Options. The Open Options menu shown in Figure 4-12 displays commands you can use to open the selected file in special ways.

FIGURE 4-12.

The Open Options menu selections give you more control when opening documents.

The Open Read-Only command opens the file so that you cannot save any changes made to it without renaming it. The Open As Copy command goes one step further by opening a duplicate of the selected file and adding the words *Copy of* to the beginning of the file name, thereby allowing you to save but still protecting the original. The Open In Browser command applies only to HTML documents (a format you can use in Excel 2000, if you prefer) and opens the selected file in your default Web browser.

Opening Files as Read Only

Selecting the Open Read-Only command on the Open Options menu prevents changes to the saved version of the file on disk. If you have selected this command, you can view and even edit the file, but you can't save it under its current name. Instead, you must use the Save As command to save the edited file under a new filename. (If you choose the Save command, Excel displays a warning that the current file is read-only. Click OK to access the Save As dialog box where you can save the file under a different name.)

 SEE ALSO

For information about allowing more than one user to open a file at the same time, see "Sharing Workbooks on a Network," page 585.

The Open Read-Only command is most useful when you're working on a network. If you open a file without choosing the Open Read-Only command, others on the network must open the file as read only to view that file. Naturally, you can still save your changes, but the other users will have to use the Save As command and save their changes under a new filename. If other users try to open the same file without using the Read-Only command, they'll receive an error message unless the Allow Changes By More Than One User At The Same Time option is selected.

Reopening a Recently Opened File

Near the bottom of the File menu, you'll find the names of the files you've worked with most recently, even in previous sessions. To reopen one of these files, simply choose its name from this menu.

> You can increase (up to nine) or decrease the number of recently used files displayed on the File menu by choosing Options from the Tools menu and clicking the General tab. Select the Recently Used File List check box and choose the number of files you want to display. If you do not want any, clear the check box and no files will appear on the File menu.

To display even more recently opened files, click the Open button on the Standard toolbar and click the History icon to display as many as 50 of the last files and folders you have used.

Opening Files Automatically When You Start Excel

If you have a file or set of files you work with regularly, you can store them in a special folder called XLStart, which is located in the C:\Windows\Application Data\Microsoft\Excel folder. Microsoft Excel's Setup program automatically creates the XLStart folder for you when it installs Excel on your hard disk. When you start Excel, the files in the XLStart folder are automatically opened. You can use the Save As command to save files to the XLStart folder, or you can move the files to this folder with the Windows Explorer.

If you want to work with several workbooks for an extended period of time, you can save a workspace file in the XLStart folder so that the entire workspace is automatically loaded each time you start Excel.

The Alternate Startup Folder

If you want to start Excel and simultaneously open files that are located in a folder other than the XLStart folder, you can specify an alternate startup folder. Simply choose Options from the Tools menu, click the General tab, and type the full pathname of the folder you want in the Alternate Startup File Location edit box. This option is particularly useful if your computer is connected to a network and you want to open files from a shared folder.

Sometimes you can use a trick to recover data you thought was lost from a corrupted workbook. If you attempt to open a workbook without success, try the following: first open two new workbooks. Select cell A1 in one of the workbooks and then press Ctrl+C to copy. Activate the second workbook, choose Paste Special on the Edit menu, and then click Paste Link. Next, choose Links on the Edit menu, click Change Source, locate the corrupted workbook on your hard disk, select it, and click OK. Click OK again in the Links dialog box.

If luck is with you, data from cell A1 in the lost workbook appears in cell A1, thanks to the linking formula. If the data is there, press F2 to activate Edit mode and press F4 three times to change the absolute reference $A$1 to its relative form, A1.

Now you can copy the formula down and across until you can see all of the data you need to retrieve. Repeat for each sheet in the workbook.

Searching for Files

SEE ALSO

For more information about network issues, see Chapter 18, "Sharing Files with Others."

If you're unsure about the location of a particular file, you can use the file-finding features in the Open dialog box to search any location that is available to your system—and you can use a variety of search criteria to narrow your search. To access the file-finding features click the Tools button and choose the Find command. The Find dialog box is shown in Figure 4-13.

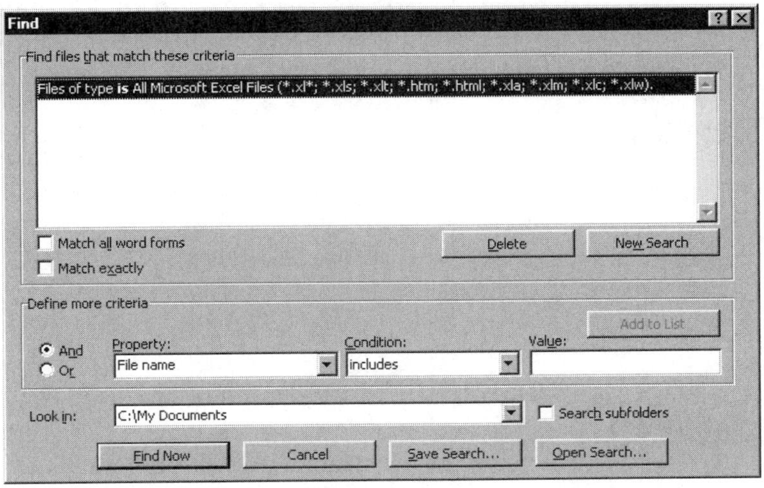

FIGURE 4-13.
Use the Find dialog box to search for files in any location available to your computer.

When you choose the Find command, the Find Files That Match These Criteria list in the Find dialog box displays the initial criteria specified in the File Name and Files Of Type edit boxes in the Open dialog box. For example, Figure 4-13 includes the criterion "Files Of Type Is All Microsoft Excel Files," which was specified in the Files Of Type edit box when we chose the Find command. If you also specify a filename (or partial file name) before choosing Find, that name will also appear in the criteria list.

TIP

If you know just part of a filename, you can use the Open dialog box to perform a "quick find" operation without using the Find command. Just type the filename or fragment thereof into the File Name edit box, select the appropriate File Type, and click the Open button. Now you can browse using the location icons and Look In list box, and only those files whose names contain the text you entered in the File Name edit box are displayed.

You can use the Look In box of the Find dialog box to specify the folder you want to search. The Search Subfolders check box extends the search to include any folders subordinate to the one you specify. When Search Subfolders is selected, the Find dialog box locates all files matching the specified criteria anywhere in the path you specify. For example, say you select Search Subfolders and "look in" the root of the C: drive using the default criterion at the bottom of the Open dialog box, which is "All Microsoft Excel Files." The dialog box displays all of the Excel files on your hard disk in one big list. If you're not sure what folder to look in, adding a few more criteria, such as a filename fragment, might be helpful.

TIP

When you use the Search Subfolders option, you might want to view files in the Open dialog box using the detail view by clicking the Details button. This displays all found files along with the folder structure, so you can easily tell where the files are stored. In List view, found files appear all together with no visible folder hierarchy.

Adding Additional Search Criteria

SEE ALSO

For more information about the Properties dialog box, see "Adding Summary Information to Files," page 74.

You use the Define More Criteria area of the Find dialog box to add criteria to the list. The Property list box lists most of the properties available in the Properties dialog box (on the File menu). If, for example, you enter "SUM Corporation" as the Company property in every workbook you create that relates to that company, select Company in the Property list box and type *SUM Corporation* in the Value box. Clicking the Add To List button adds the criterion to the list at the top of the dialog box and clears the Value box for the next criterion.

 TIP

> To get into the habit of entering properties to help identify groups of files, you can have the Properties dialog box appear automatically each time you save a file for the first time. On the Tools menu, choose Options, click the General tab, and click the Prompt For Workbook Properties option.

The Condition list box contains a number of text operators that change depending on the property you specify. For example, text properties such as Company have conditions such as "includes phrase," "begins with phrase," and even "is not." Conditions for date properties such as Last Printed include "last week" and "anytime between," and numeric conditions like Number of Characters include "equals," "at least," and "more than."

The And and Or buttons allow you to specify whether each criterion you add is "in addition to" or "instead of" the previous criterion. You can add quite a few criteria, but some property types allow only one "And." For example, if you attempt to add another Files Of Type criterion with the And button selected, a dialog box informs you that a file type already appears in the criteria list and asks if you want to change it to an "Or" criteria.

Use the Delete button to single out and remove individual criteria in the list. Click the New Search button to clear all the criteria from the list, except for the default Files Of Type criterion. The Find Now button dismisses the Find dialog box, carries out the search, and displays the results in the Open dialog box.

The Match All Word Forms option is a remarkable feature that finds variations of words in any text-based criterion *except* filenames. For example, entering *bite* as the value for the Contents property finds any files that contain the word bite, bites, biting, bit, or bitten. Excel normally ignores capitalization of criteria text, but selecting the Match Case option allows you to specify the case of text you're looking for.

Saving and Reusing Search Criteria

The Save Search button in the Find dialog box displays the Save Search dialog box, where you can type a name for the current search criteria. This name is displayed in the dialog box that appears when you click the Open Search button. These buttons make it easy to revisit a previous search.

Importing and Exporting Files

Microsoft Excel gracefully accepts data created in many other applications. If you're moving to Excel from Quattro Pro or Lotus 1-2-3, for example, you'll be glad to know that most of your existing worksheets and macros will work immediately when you bring them into Excel. Similarly, if you have database files created in dBase, you can import them into Excel without having to go through any kind of translation process. Your dBase fields will simply become column headings in Excel.

Excel also makes it easy to import data from text files and helps you parse the data into worksheet columns. Whether your text file is comma-delimited or set up as a columnar report, it's a simple matter to bring the data into Excel.

There is a lot of very specific, sleep-inducing technical detail available about importing and exporting non-native files. If you have need of such detail for conversion issues like transferring hundreds of macro-driven Lotus files into Excel, you should consult the *Microsoft Office Resource Kit*, available from Microsoft Press.

Using the Open and Save As Commands to Import Files

To import a file from another application or from an earlier version of Excel, choose the Open command from the File menu (or click the Open button on the Standard toolbar) and select the file you want to import from the list of files in the Open dialog box. You can use the Files Of Type drop-down list box in the lower left corner of the Open dialog box to display files with a particular extension, such as .wk* files. Keep in mind that it is not necessary to include a default filename extension when you import a file because Excel determines the format of the file by examining the file's contents, not its name.

To export a Microsoft Excel 2000 file to another application or to an earlier version of Excel, choose the Save As command from the File menu (or, if you're saving the file for the first time, click the Save button on the Standard toolbar). Then select the format of the application you're exporting to from the Save As Type drop-down list box. Note that when you select a format from the Save As Type drop-down list box, Excel automatically changes the .xls extension of the file you're exporting to the default filename extension of the application.

Importing and Exporting Text Files

To export an Excel file as a text file, choose Save As from the File menu and select one of the following seven text formats:

- Formatted Text (Space delimited) (*.prn)

- Text (Tab delimited) (*.txt)

- CSV (Comma delimited) (*.csv)

- Text (Macintosh) (*.txt)

- Text (MS-DOS) (*.txt)

- CSV (Macintosh) (*.csv)

- CSV (MS-DOS) (*.csv)

With all of these formats, Excel saves only the current sheet. Formatting assigned with the Number tab of the Format Cells dialog box is preserved, but all other formatting is removed.

Formatted Text (Space delimited) creates a file in which column alignment is preserved by means of space characters. You might want to use this kind of file when communicating via modem with a recipient who does not have Excel.

The Text (Tab delimited) format separates the cells of each row with tab characters. Any cell in which a comma appears is surrounded by quotation marks.

With the CSV (Comma delimited) format, Excel separates the cells of each row with commas. Comma-delimited text files are preferable to tab-delimited files for importing into database management programs. (Many database management programs can accept either form of text file, but some accept only .csv files.) Also, many word processing applications can use .csv files to store the information for form letters.

The differences between the normal, Macintosh, and MS-DOS variants of each file type have to do only with characters that lie outside the normal 7-bit ASCII range. The normal Text and CSV options use the ANSI character set. You should select one of these options if you intend to import your text file into a Windows-based application, such as Microsoft Word for Windows.

The Macintosh options use the Macintosh character set; select one of these options if you intend to transfer your file to a Macintosh application. The MS-DOS options use the IBM PC extended character set—the same character set your computer uses when it's not running Windows. (The documentation for some Windows-based programs or for Windows itself might refer to this character set as OEM text.) Select one of these options if you intend to import your text file into a non-Windows-based application, such as WordPerfect 5.1, or into an OS/2 application.

Exporting Files to Earlier Versions of Excel

Microsoft Excel 2000 shares a file format with its predecessor, Excel 97, that is incompatible with previous versions. You can use the Save As command, however, to export Excel 2000/97 workbooks to any earlier version of Excel.

If you regularly share files with colleagues who use Excel 5 or Excel 7, you might want to take advantage of the Microsoft Excel 97-2000 & 5.0/95 Workbook format. This saves your work in a format that can be read in Excel 97, Excel 5, or Excel 7 (Excel 7 for Windows 95).

Sharing Data with Microsoft Excel for the Macintosh

Microsoft Excel 98 for the Macintosh uses the same file format as Excel 2000 and Excel 97. You can share files with Macintosh users by simply transferring files from one computer to the other.

To share an Excel 2000 file with someone using the Macintosh version of Excel 5, use the Save As command and choose the Microsoft 5.0/95 Workbook option.

Importing Macintosh Files

To import Macintosh files to your PC, follow these steps:

1   Transfer the file to your PC (via a cable, modem, disk, or network).

2   Start the Windows version of Excel, choose Open from the File menu, and type the name of the document you want to open. Because Macintosh does not add filename extensions when you save a file, you can zero in on the Macintosh files by typing a wildcard and the null filename extension (*.) in the File Name edit box and then pressing Enter. Excel lists all the available files without extensions.

3   Select the file you want to import and click OK. Excel loads the selected file.

Exporting Microsoft Excel for Windows Files

Exporting files from a Windows version of Excel to the Macintosh version is just as easy as importing Macintosh files. First transfer the file from the PC to the Macintosh (via a cable, modem, disk, or network). Next start Excel on the Macintosh, and then use the Open command to load the file just as you would to load a file in Excel for Windows.

Adjusting Date Values

Although the Windows and Macintosh versions of Excel share many characteristics and capabilities, they do not use the same date system. In the Windows version of Excel, the base date is January 1, 1900. In the Macintosh version, the base date is January 2, 1904. When you transfer files either to or from the Macintosh, Excel maintains the date type by selecting or clearing the 1904 Date System option on the Calculation tab of the Options dialog box. This technique is usually acceptable, but it can cause problems when a date from a Macintosh file is compared with a date from a Windows file. For this reason, we suggest you use the same date setting on all your machines.

The remaining sections of the book focus on particular areas of Excel, starting with the most basic, essential, and all-encompassing area: the worksheet!

PART II

Worksheets

Worksheet Basics

Microsoft Excel 2000 gives you a lot of visual clues to help you as you work with your data. But Excel is an extremely powerful program and includes many ways to do things—even things that appear to be very simple. In this chapter, we'll first explain the basics of selection, navigation, data entry, and data protection. Then we'll show you some tricks that can make the simple stuff even simpler.

Moving Around the Worksheet

Before you can work with cells, you must select a cell or a group of cells. When you select a single cell, it becomes active, and its reference appears in the Name box at the left end of the formula bar. Although only one cell can be active at a time, you can often speed operations by selecting groups of cells called *ranges*. You can move among the cells in a selected range (but not those outside the range) without changing your range selection.

Selecting with the Mouse

To select a single cell, point to it and click the mouse button. The active cell border appears around the cell, and the cell reference appears in the Name box. Figure 5-1 shows how to select a range of cells.

FIGURE 5-1.

The selected cells are highlighted as you drag through a range. Excel describes the range in terms of the cells at the upper left and lower right corners.

The active cell always occupies one corner of the range.

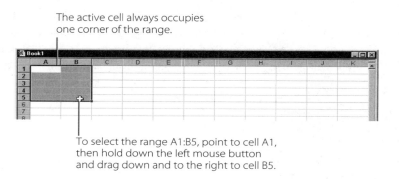

To select the range A1:B5, point to cell A1, then hold down the left mouse button and drag down and to the right to cell B5.

Extending a Selection

Instead of dragging through all the cells you want to work with, you can indicate any two diagonal corners of the range. This technique is known as *extending a selection*. For example, to extend the selection A1:B5 so that it becomes A1:C10, hold down the Shift key and then click cell C10. When you need to select a large range, you may find this technique more efficient than dragging the mouse across the entire selection.

Keyboard Modes

The right side of the status bar displays the following indicators when one of the corresponding modes is active:

EXT   Extend Mode. Press F8 to extend the current selection using the arrow keys. (Make sure Scroll Lock is turned off.) This is the keyboard equivalent of holding down Shift and selecting cells with the mouse.

ADD   Add mode. Press Shift+F8 to add more cells to the current selection using the keyboard. The cells need not be adjacent. This is the keyboard equivalent of holding down Ctrl and selecting cells with the mouse.

NUM   Num Lock mode. This mode is on by default and locks the keypad in numeric-entry mode. To turn off Num Lock, press the Num Lock key.

FIX   Fixed Decimal mode. Choosing the Options command from the Tools menu, clicking the Edit tab, and selecting the Fixed Decimal option adds a decimal point to numeric entries in the location you specify in the Places edit box. For example, if you turn on Fixed Decimal mode and specify two decimal places, the entry 12345 is entered in the cell as 123.45.

CAPS   Caps Lock mode. Pressing the Caps Lock key allows you to enter text in all capital letters. The number and symbol keys are not affected.

SCRL   Scroll Lock mode. Normally, when you use Page Up and Page Down, the active cell moves a page at a time as you scroll through the worksheet. Pressing Scroll Lock lets you use Page Up and Page Down without moving the active cell.

END   End mode. Pressing the End key and then pressing an arrow key moves the selection to the next region in the direction of the arrow on the key, or to the last worksheet cell in that direction.

This keyboard mode doesn't show an indicator in the status bar:

—   Overwrite mode. Normally, new characters you type in the formula bar are inserted between existing characters. With Overwrite mode turned on, the characters you type replace existing characters you type over. To activate Overwrite mode, press the Insert key while the Formula bar is active.

II

Worksheets

Selecting beyond the Window Borders

You cannot see the whole workbook in the window. How much of the workbook your window displays depends on the size and screen resolution of your monitor. To select a range that extends beyond your workbook window, you can simply drag the mouse pointer past the window border. For example, to select the range A14:A25, follow these steps:

1 Click cell A14.

2 Drag the mouse pointer down through cell A25. (When the pointer reaches the bottom of the window, the worksheet begins scrolling up.)

3 Release the mouse button. Figure 5-2 shows the result.

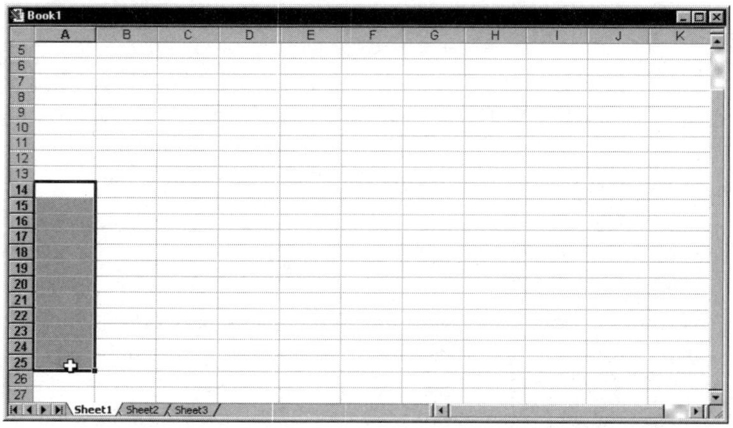

FIGURE 5-2.

You can drag past the window borders to bring additional cells into view as you make your selection.

Another way to select the range A14:A25 shown in Figure 5-2 is to click cell A25 and drag the mouse pointer up toward the title bar. When you reach cell A14, release the mouse button.

TIP

You can zoom out to see more of a worksheet that extends beyond the window borders. Choose the Zoom command from the View menu and select the magnification you want.

You can also drag past the left and right borders of the workbook window to bring additional columns into view as you make your selection.

When you need to select large ranges, the dragging technique can be too time-consuming. Here is an alternative for selecting A1:M38:

1 Click cell A1.

2 Use the scroll bars to bring cell M38 into view.

3 Hold down Shift or press F8.

4 Click cell M38.

 TIP

You can also use the Go To command on the Edit menu to select ranges. *For more information, see "Using the Go To Command," page 101.*

Selecting Multiple-Area Ranges

Multiple-area ranges (also known as nonadjacent or noncontiguous ranges) are cell ranges that do not encompass a single rectangular area. To select multiple-area ranges with the mouse, use the Ctrl key as shown in Figure 5-3.

FIGURE 5-3.

Hold down Ctrl to select multiple-area ranges with the mouse.

To add the range C7:E10 to the already selected range A1:B6, hold down Ctrl and drag through cells C7:E10. The first cell you click in the new range becomes the active cell.

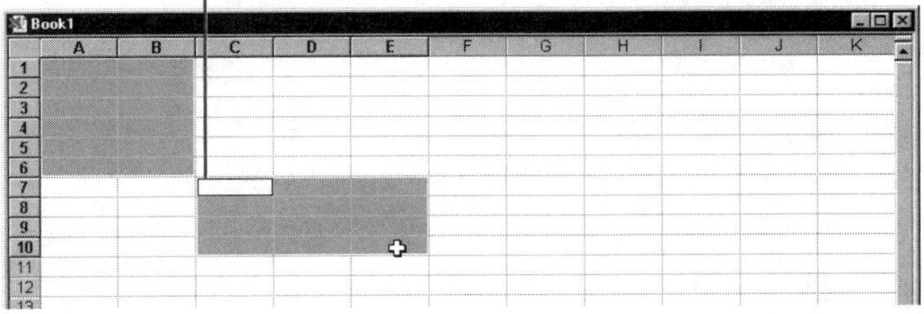

You can also use Add mode to select multiple-area ranges. After selecting the first area of your range, press Shift+F8 to turn on Add mode. When the ADD indicator appears at the right end of the status bar, drag through the cells of the new range. Press Esc or Shift+F8 to turn off Add mode.

II

Worksheets

Selecting Columns and Rows

To select an entire column or row, click the column or row heading. The first visible cell becomes the active cell. For example, to select B1 through B65536, click the heading for column B. The first visible cell in the column is the active cell. To select more than one adjacent column or row at a time, drag through the column or row headings, or click the heading at one edge of the range, press Shift or F8, and then click the heading at the opposite edge. To select nonadjacent columns or rows, use Ctrl or Shift+F8, as already described.

You can also select entire columns and rows at the same time, as shown in Figure 5-4.

FIGURE 5-4.

You can select entire columns and rows by clicking their headings.

1 To select column A and rows 1, 2, and 3, click row heading 1.

3 Press Ctrl and click column heading A.

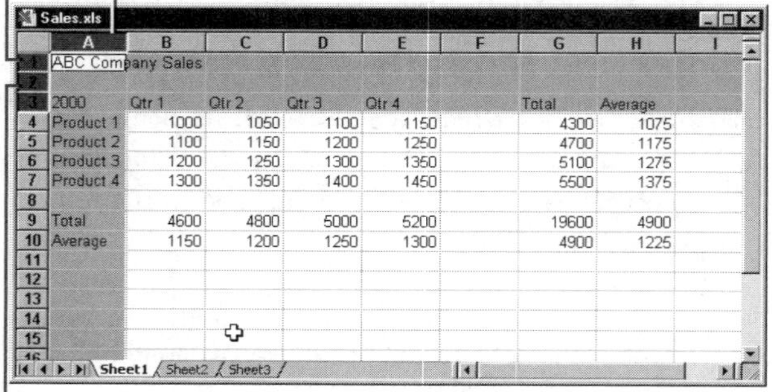

	A	B	C	D	E	F	G	H	I
1	ABC Company Sales								
2									
3	2000	Qtr 1	Qtr 2	Qtr 3	Qtr 4		Total	Average	
4	Product 1	1000	1050	1100	1150		4300	1075	
5	Product 2	1100	1150	1200	1250		4700	1175	
6	Product 3	1200	1250	1300	1350		5100	1275	
7	Product 4	1300	1350	1400	1450		5500	1375	
8									
9	Total	4600	4800	5000	5200		19600	4900	
10	Average	1150	1200	1250	1300		4900	1225	
11									
12									
13									
14									
15									

Sales.xls — Sheet1 / Sheet2 / Sheet3

2 Drag down to row heading 3.

The file ABC Sales.xls used in the example above can be found on the Microsoft Press World Wide Web site at *http://mspress.microsoft.com/mspress/products/2050/*.

At times you will want to select all the cells in a worksheet to change the format for the entire worksheet or to copy the contents of one worksheet to another. To select the entire worksheet at once, simply click the Select All box in the upper left corner of your workbook window, where the column and row headings intersect. The Select All box is labeled in Figure 1-2 on page 5.

Selecting and Moving within Regions

A *region* is a range of cell entries bounded by blank cells or column and row headings. For example, in Figure 5-5 the range A3:E7 is a region, as are the ranges G3:H7, A9:E10, and G9:H10.

TIP

> If the fill handle is not visible on your screen, it means that the Allow Cell Drag And Drop option is not turned on, which is necessary for region navigation to work. To turn on the Allow Cell Drag And Drop option, choose the Options command from the Tools menu and then click the Edit tab. Select the Allow Cell Drag And Drop option and then click OK.

When you move the mouse pointer over the edge of a cell border, the pointer changes from a plus sign to an arrow. With the arrow pointer visible, double-click the bottom edge of the cell border. Excel selects the cell at the bottom of the current region. If the active cell is already at the bottom of a region, double-clicking the bottom edge of the cell border selects the cell above the next region down. For example, if you double-click the bottom edge of the active cell in Figure 5-5, Excel selects cell A7. Double-clicking the top, bottom, left, or right edge of a cell border selects the next cell bordering a region in that direction.

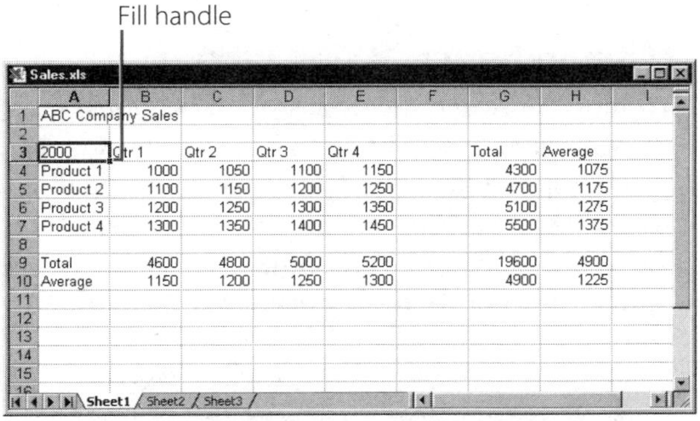

FIGURE 5-5.

The fill handle at the lower right corner of the cell border indicates that the Allow Cell Drag And Drop option is active.

Fill handle

If you hold down Shift as you double-click the edge of a cell border, Excel selects all cells from the current cell to the next edge of the region, as Figure 5-6 on the next page shows.

FIGURE 5-6.

Holding down Shift while double-clicking the edge of a range border extends the selection in that direction to the region's edge.

With cell A3 active, hold down the Shift key and then double-click the bottom edge of the cell border to select the range A3:A7.

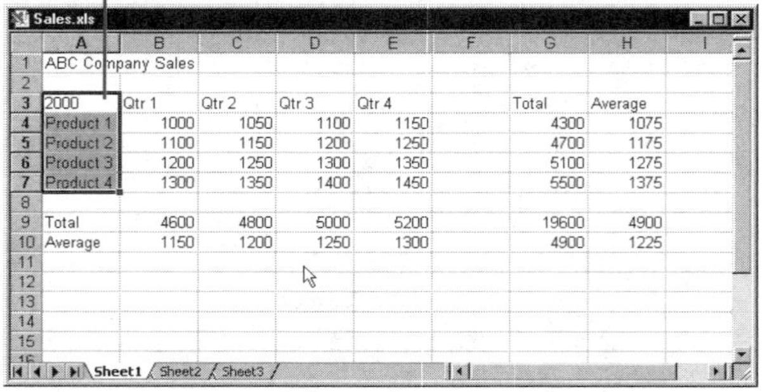

The cell from which you start the selection remains the active cell. If you double-click the right edge of the border around the range A3:A7 while holding down Shift, Excel then selects the range A3:E7.

Selecting with the Keyboard

You can also use the keyboard to select cells and move around your worksheet. To select a single cell, use the arrow keys. For example, if cell A1 is active, press the Down arrow key once to select cell A2. Press the Right or the Left arrow key to activate the cell to either side of the active cell.

Moving between Cell Regions

To move between the edges of cell regions, use Ctrl with the arrow keys. In Figure 5-7, for example, if cell A3 is the active cell, press Ctrl and the Right arrow key to activate cell E3. If a blank cell is active when you press Ctrl and an arrow key, Excel moves to the first cell in the corresponding direction that contains a cell entry, or to the last cell in that direction in the worksheet if there are no cells containing entries in that direction.

FIGURE 5-7.

You can use the Ctrl key and the arrow keys to move between the edges of cell regions.

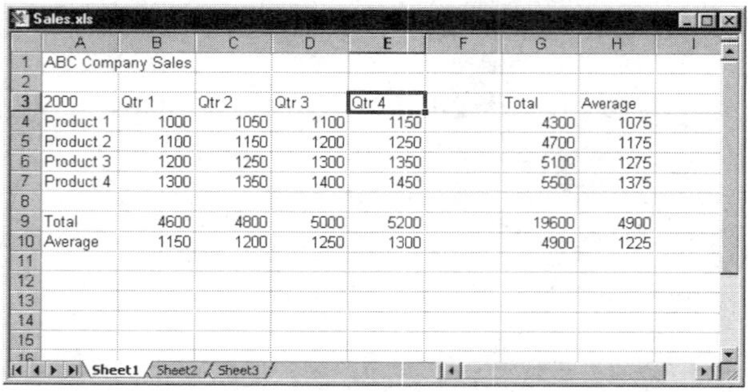

Using Home and End

The Home and End keys are valuable for selecting and moving around. The following table shows how you can use Home and End alone and in conjunction with other keys to make selections and move around a worksheet.

Press	To
Home	Move to the first cell in the current row.
Ctrl+Home	Move to cell A1.
Ctrl+End	Move to the last cell in the last column in the active area.
End	Activate End mode. Then use the direction keys to move between cell regions.
Scroll Lock+Home	Move to the first complete cell in the current window.
Scroll Lock+End	Move to the last cell entirely in the current window.

The *active area* referred to in the preceding table is a rectangle that encompasses all the rows and columns in a worksheet that contain entries. For example, in Figure 5-7, pressing Ctrl+End while any cell is active selects cell H10. Pressing Ctrl+Home selects cell A1.

To activate End mode, press End; to turn off End mode, press End again.

Using the Go To Command

? SEE ALSO

For more information about defined cell names, which can also be used with the Go To command, see "Naming Cells and Ranges," page 133. For more information about references, see "Using Cell References in Formulas," page 117.

To quickly move to and select a cell or a range of cells, choose the Go To command from the Edit menu (or press F5), enter the cell reference, range reference, or defined cell name in the Reference edit box, and click OK. You can also use the Go To command to extend a selection. For example, to select A1:Z100, you could click A1, choose the Go To command, type *Z100*, and then hold down the Shift key while pressing Enter.

To move to another worksheet in the same workbook, choose Go To and type the name of the worksheet, followed by an exclamation point and a cell name or reference. For example, to go to cell D5 in a worksheet called Sheet2, type *Sheet2!D5*.

When you use the Go To command, Excel lists in the Reference edit box the cell or range from which you just moved. This way, you can easily move back and forth between two locations by repeatedly pressing F5 and then Enter. Excel also keeps track of the last four locations from which you used the Go To command and lists them in the Go To dialog box. You can use this list to move among these locations in your worksheet. Figure 5-8 shows the Go To dialog box with four previous locations displayed.

FIGURE 5-8.

The Go To dialog box keeps track of the last four locations from which you used the Go To command.

Extending a Selection

Just as when you're using the mouse, you can extend a keyboard selection by using the arrow keys and either Shift or F8. (You cannot extend a selection with the Tab key.) *For more information, see the section on extending a selection under "Selecting with the Mouse," page 94.*

Selecting Multiple-Area Ranges

Just as when you're using the mouse, you can select multiple-area ranges using Shift+F8 to activate the Add mode. *For more information, see the section on selecting multiple-area ranges under "Selecting with the Mouse," page 94.*

Selecting Columns and Rows

You can select an entire column with the keyboard by selecting a cell in the column and pressing Ctrl+Spacebar. To select an entire row, select a cell in the row and press Shift+Spacebar.

To select several entire adjacent columns or rows, highlight a range that includes cells in each of the columns or rows and then press

Ctrl+Spacebar or Shift+Spacebar. For example, to select columns B, C, and D, select B4:D4 (or any range that includes cells in these three columns) and then press Ctrl+Spacebar.

TIP

To select the entire worksheet with the keyboard, press Ctrl+Shift+Spacebar.

Entering Data

SEE ALSO

For more information about formulas and error values, see Chapter 6, "Building Formulas," and for logical values, see Chapter 12, "Common Worksheet Functions."

Microsoft Excel 2000 accepts two basic types of cell entries: *constants* and *formulas*. Constants fall into three main categories: numeric values, text values (also called labels or strings), and date and time values. This section describes numeric and text values. (Date values are described in *Chapter 13, "Dates and Times."*)

Excel also recognizes two special types of constants called *logical values* and *error values*.

Simple Numeric and Text Values

An entry that includes only the numerals 0 through 9 and certain special characters such as + - E e ( ) . , $ % and /, is a numeric value. An entry that includes almost any other character is a text value. The following table lists some examples of numeric and text values.

Numeric Values	Text Values
123	Sales
345678	Hello
$9999.99	A Label
1%	123 Main Street
1.23E+12	No. 324

Entering Numeric Values

To enter a numeric value, select the cell and then type the number. As you type, the number appears in the formula bar and in the active cell. The flashing vertical bar that appears in the cell or in the formula bar is called the *insertion point*.

II

Worksheets

Locking In the Entry

When you finish typing, you must lock in the entry to store it permanently in the cell. The simplest way to lock in an entry is to press Enter after you type the entry. The insertion point disappears, and Excel stores the entry in the cell.

If you press the Tab key, Shift+Tab, Enter, Shift+Enter, or an arrow key after you type the entry, Excel locks in the entry and activates an adjacent cell.

 **TIP**

> Pressing Enter normally causes the active cell to move down one row. You can change this, however, so the active cell either stays the same or moves to an adjacent cell in another direction when you press Enter. To make the active cell stay the same, choose Options from the Tools menu, click the Edit tab, and deselect the Move Selection After Enter option. To change where the active cell moves, select a direction in the list box. For example, select Right if you normally want to activate the next cell to the right whenever you enter a value.

? SEE ALSO

For more information about editing formulas, see Chapter 6, "Building Formulas."

As mentioned in Chapter 1, "Getting Your Bearings," when you begin typing an entry, buttons appear on the formula bar: the Cancel button, the Enter button, and the Edit Formula button. If the entry begins with an equal sign (=), a plus sign (+), or a minus sign (-), a drop-down list of frequently used functions appears as well, shown in Figure 5-9.

FIGURE 5-9.

You can lock in a cell entry by clicking the Enter button or cancel a cell entry by clicking the Cancel button on the Formula bar.

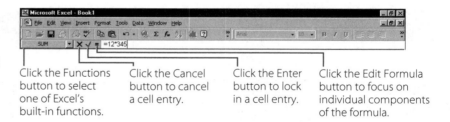

Click the Functions button to select one of Excel's built-in functions.

Click the Cancel button to cancel a cell entry.

Click the Enter button to lock in a cell entry.

Click the Edit Formula button to focus on individual components of the formula.

Special Characters

A number of characters mean something special to Excel. Here's a list of guidelines for special characters:

- If you begin a numeric entry with a plus sign (+), Excel drops the plus sign.

- If you begin a numeric entry with a minus sign (-), Excel interprets the entry as a negative number and retains the sign.

For more information about Excel's built-in Number formats, see "Assigning and Removing Formats," page 157.

- Excel interprets the character *E* or *e* as scientific notation. For example, it interprets 1E6 as 1,000,000 (1 times 10 to the sixth power).

- Excel interprets numeric constants enclosed in parentheses as negative numbers, which is a common accounting practice. For example, Excel interprets (100) as -100.

- You can use decimal points as you normally do. You can also use commas to separate hundreds from thousands, thousands from millions, and so on. When you enter numbers that include commas as separators, the numbers appear with commas in the cell but without them in the formula bar. For example, if you enter *1,234.56*, the formula bar displays 1234.56. Meanwhile, the cell displays the number with the comma in place, as if you had applied one of Excel's built-in Number formats.

- If you begin a numeric entry with a dollar sign, Excel assigns the Currency format to the cell. For example, if you enter *$123456*, Excel displays $123,456 in the cell, and the formula bar displays 123456. In this case, Excel adds the comma to the worksheet display because it is part of Excel's Currency format.

- If you end a numeric entry with a percent sign (%), Excel assigns the Percentage format to the cell. For example, if you enter *23%*, Excel displays 23% in the formula bar and assigns a percentage format to the cell, which displays 23%.

For more information about date and time formats, see Chapter 13, "Dates and Times."

- If you use a forward slash (/) in a numeric entry and the string cannot be interpreted as a date, Excel interprets the number as a fraction. For example, if you enter *11 5/8* (with a space between the number and the fraction), Excel displays 11.625 in the formula bar and assigns the Fraction format to the cell. The cell displays 11 5/8.

To make sure a fraction cannot be interpreted as a date, precede the fraction with a zero and a space. For example, to enter 1/2, type *0 1/2*.

Displayed Values Versus Underlying Values

Although you can type more than 16,000 characters in a cell, a numeric cell entry can contain a maximum of 15 digits. If you enter a number that is too long to appear in a cell, Excel converts it to

SEE ALSO

For more information about precision, see "Precision of Numeric Values," page 154.

scientific notation. Excel adjusts the precision of the scientific notation to display such an entry in a cell, as shown in Figure 5-10. However, if you enter a very large or a very small number, Excel also displays it in the formula bar using scientific notation with up to 15 digits of precision.

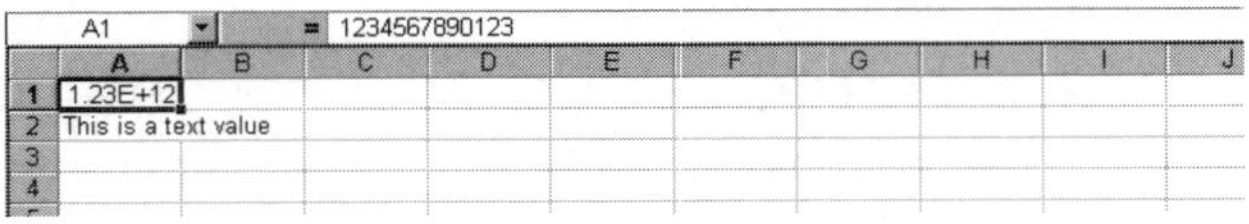

FIGURE 5-10.

Long numbers in narrow cells appear in scientific notation.

 SEE ALSO

For more information about increasing the width of a cell, see "Controlling Column Width," page 203.

The values that appear in cells are called *displayed values*; the values that are stored in cells and that appear in the formula bar are called *underlying values*. The number of digits that appears in a cell—its displayed value—depends on the width of the column. If you reduce the width of a column that contains a long entry, Excel might display either a rounded-off version of the number or a string of pound signs (#), depending on the display format you're using.

⭐ **TIP**

> If you see a series of pound signs (######) in a cell where you expect to see a number, simply increase the width of the cell in order to see the number.

Entering Text Values

Entering text is similar to entering numeric values. To enter text in a cell, select a cell, type the text, and then lock in the entry by pressing Enter or clicking the Enter button. To cancel an entry, press Esc or click the Cancel button.

Long Text Entries

If you enter text that is too long to be displayed in a single cell, Excel allows the text to overlap the adjacent cells. However, the text is stored in the single cell. If you then type text in a cell that is overlapped by another cell, the overlapping text appears truncated, as shown in cell A2 in Figure 5-11.

FIGURE 5-11.

Long text values overlap adjacent cells if they are empty.

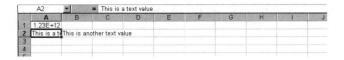

The easiest way to alleviate overlapping text is to widen the column by double-clicking the column border in the heading. For example, in Figure 5-11, when you double-click the line between the A and the B in the column heading, the width of column A adjusts to accommodate the longest entry in the column.

Using Wordwrap

SEE ALSO

For more information about wrapping text in cells, see "Aligning Cell Contents," page 179.

If you have long text entries, Wordwrap makes them easier to read. Select the cells, choose Cells from the Format menu, click the Alignment tab, and select the Wrap Text box; then click OK. The Wrap Text option lets you enter long strings of text that wrap onto two or more lines within the same cell rather than overlapping across adjacent cells. To accommodate the extra lines, Excel increases the height of the row that contains the formatted cell.

Numeric Text Entries

Sometimes you might want to make an entry that contains special characters that Excel would normally treat differently from plain text. You can force Excel to accept special characters as text by using numeric text entries. For example, you might want "+1" to appear in a cell. If you simply type *+1*, Excel interprets this as a numeric entry and drops the plus sign.

A numeric text entry may consist of text and numbers or all numbers. To enter text and numbers, select the cell, type the entry, and then press Enter. Because this entry includes nonnumeric characters, Excel interprets it as a text value.

To create a text entry that consists entirely of numbers, precede the entry with an apostrophe, or precede the entry with an equal sign and enclose it with quotation marks. For example, to enter the part number 1234, follow these steps:

1 Select the cell.

2 Type *'1234*.

3 Press Enter.

The apostrophe appears in the formula bar but not in the cell. Whereas numeric entries are normally right-aligned, the numeric text entry is left-aligned in the cell just like regular text, as illustrated in Figure 5-12 on the next page.

II

Worksheets

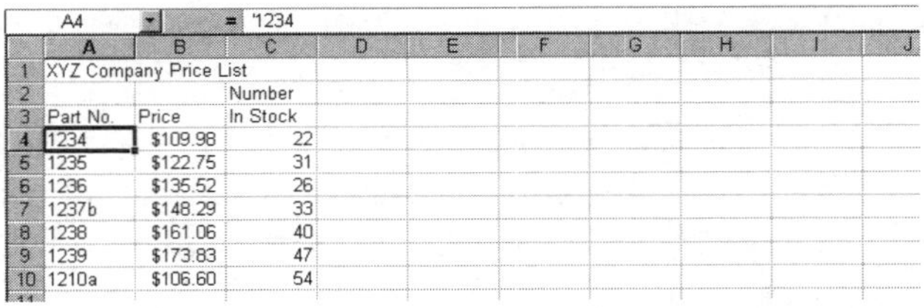

FIGURE 5-12.

The part numbers in column A were entered as text.

A4		=	1234							
	A	**B**	**C**	**D**	**E**	**F**	**G**	**H**	**I**	**J**
1	XYZ Company Price List									
2			Number							
3	Part No.	Price	In Stock							
4	1234	$109.98	22							
5	1235	$122.75	31							
6	1236	$135.52	26							
7	1237b	$148.29	33							
8	1238	$161.06	40							
9	1239	$173.83	47							
10	1210a	$106.60	54							

ON THE WEB

The file XYZ Prices.xls used in the example above can be found on the Microsoft Press Web site at *http://mspress.microsoft.com/mspress/products/2050/*.

Making Entries in Ranges

CAUTION

The behavior of the Enter key is controlled by an option on the General tab of the Options dialog box (Tools menu).

To make a number of entries in a range of adjacent cells, first select those cells. Then use Enter, Shift+Enter, Tab, and Shift+Tab to move the active cell within the range, as shown in the table below.

Press	To Activate
Enter	The cell below the active cell
Shift+Enter	The cell above the active cell
Tab	The cell one column to the right of the active cell
Shift+Tab	The cell one column to the left of the active cell

For example, to fill in a range of selected cells, you can take the following steps:

1 To make entries in the range B2:D4, select by dragging the mouse from cell B2 to cell D4 so that cell B2 is active.

2 Type *100* in cell B2 and then press Enter.

3 In cell B3 (now the active cell), simply type *200* and then press Enter.

4 In cell B4 (now the active cell), type *300* and then press Enter. Cell C2 becomes the active cell as shown in Figure 5-13. You can continue to make entries in this way until you fill the entire range.

FIGURE 5-13.

You can fill a range of selected cells by making entries and then pressing Enter.

 TIP

To enter the same value in several cells at once, first you must select the cells. Then type your entry and hold down Ctrl while you press Enter or click the Enter button.

Correcting Errors in Entries

You can correct typing mistakes before you lock in the entry, and you can change the contents of a cell after you lock in the entry.

Correcting Errors before You Lock In the Entry

To correct simple errors as you type, press Backspace, which erases the character to the left of the insertion point. To correct an earlier error, select the cell and then click the formula bar, or double-click the cell and position the insertion point at the error. Erase, insert, or replace characters. To delete several adjacent characters, select the characters by dragging across them in the formula bar and then press Backspace or Delete.

You can also correct typing errors using only the keyboard. To do so, select the cell you want to edit and press F2. The lower left corner of the status bar indicates that the mode has changed from Ready to Edit, and the insertion point appears at the end of the cell entry. Use the arrow keys to position the insertion point to the right of the character or characters you want to change, press Backspace, and then type any new characters.

To replace several characters, put the insertion point just before or just after the characters you want to replace, hold down the Shift key, and then press the Left or Right arrow key to extend your selection. To erase the characters, press Backspace or Delete; to replace them, type the new characters.

 TIP

To move from one end of a cell entry to the other, press Home or End. To move through an entry one word at a time, hold down Ctrl and press the Left or Right arrow key.

Entering Data in Tables Using Automatic Return

Here's a handy feature you can take advantage of while filling in tables of data, as shown in the following figure.

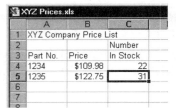

All you need to do is enter column headers or the first row of values to define the width of the table. Then, as long as you use the Tab key each time to activate the next cell to the right, you can press Enter after making the last entry in the row to automatically snap the selection to the first cell in the next row (as long as your Options are set so that Enter moves down).

Correcting Errors after You Lock In the Entry

To erase the entire contents of the active cell, press Delete, or press Backspace and then press Enter. Backspace lets you change your mind: if you press Backspace accidentally, click the Cancel button or press Esc to restore the contents of the cell before pressing Enter. You can also select the cell and type the new contents. Excel erases the previous entry as soon as you begin typing. To revert to the original entry, click the Cancel button or press Esc before you lock in the new entry by pressing Enter.

To restore an entry after you press Delete or after you have already locked in a new entry, choose the Undo command from the Edit menu or press Ctrl+Z.

The Undo command remembers the last 16 actions you performed. If you press Ctrl+Z repeatedly, each of the last 16 actions is undone, one after the other, in reverse order. You can also click the small arrow to the right of the Undo button to display a list of these actions. Drag the mouse to select one or more actions, as shown in Figure 5-14. When you release the mouse, all the selected actions are undone. The Redo button to the right of the Undo button works the same way, so you can quickly redo what you have just undone, if necessary. Note that you can't undo individual actions in the middle of the list. When you select an action, all actions up to and including that action are undone.

FIGURE 5-14.

Click the small arrow next to the Undo button to select any number of the last 16 actions to undo all at once.

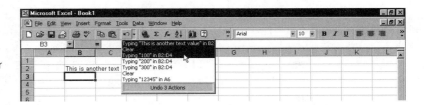

Protecting Your Data

In addition to password protection for your files, Excel offers several commands that let you protect workbooks, workbook structures, individual cells, graphic objects, charts, scenarios, and windows from access or modification by others.

By default, Excel "locks" (protects) cells, graphic objects, charts, scenarios, and windows, but the protection is not in effect until you choose Protection and then Protect Sheet from the Tools menu. Figure 5-15 shows the dialog box that appears when you choose this command. The protection status you specify applies to the current worksheet only.

FIGURE 5-15.

You can enable or disable protection for a particular worksheet in a workbook.

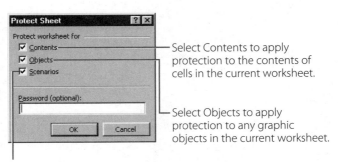

Select Contents to apply protection to the contents of cells in the current worksheet.

Select Objects to apply protection to any graphic objects in the current worksheet.

Select Scenarios to apply protection to any settings you have saved using the Scenario Manager.

II

Worksheets

After protection is enabled, you cannot change a locked item. If you try to change a locked cell, Excel displays the error message *Locked cells cannot be changed.*

Unlocking Individual Cells

⦿ SEE ALSO

For information about shared workbooks, see "Sharing Workbooks on a Network," page 585.

Every cell in a new worksheet is locked by default, ready for activation when you choose the Protect Sheet command. But most of the time you will not want to lock every cell. For example, in a worksheet you share with others, you might want to protect the formulas and formatting but leave particular cells unlocked so that necessary data may be entered without unlocking the entire sheet. Before you protect a worksheet, select the cells you want to keep unlocked, and then from the Format menu, choose the Cells command and click the Protection tab. Click the Locked check box to deselect it. Figure 5-16 shows the dialog box after you click the Protection tab of the Format Cells command.

FIGURE 5-16.

The Protection tab of the Format menu's Cells command lets you set the protection status for individual cells.

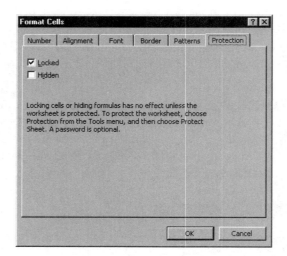

⭐ TIP

Keep in mind that Excel does not provide any indication of the protection status of individual cells on the screen. To distinguish unlocked cells from the protected cells in the worksheet, change their format; for example, you can change cell color or add borders. You can easily move between unprotected cells on a locked sheet by simply pressing the Tab key.

You can also use the Protect Workbook command on the Protection submenu of the Tools menu to prevent the alteration of a workbook's structure and to lock in the position of the workbook window itself. The dialog box that appears when you choose the Protect Workbook command is shown in Figure 5-17.

> **WARNING**
>
> When you select the Sharing With Track Changes option (Tools menu, Protection command, Protect And Share Workbook command) more than just protection is activated for a shared workbook. In addition, the Save As dialog box appears, and workbook sharing is turned on.

FIGURE 5-17.

The Protect Workbook dialog box lets you set the protection status for the workbook itself.

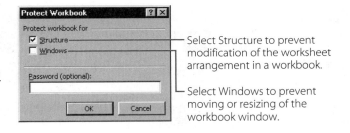

Select Structure to prevent modification of the worksheet arrangement in a workbook.

Select Windows to prevent moving or resizing of the workbook window.

Hiding Cells and Sheets

SEE ALSO

For more information about formatting numbers, see the sidebar, "The 'Hidden' Number Format," page 178.

If you apply the Hidden protection format to a cell that contains a formula, the formula remains hidden in the formula bar even when you select that cell. Formulas in these cells are still functional; they are simply hidden from view. Unless you also apply the "hidden" number format, however, the result of the formula is still visible. To apply the Hidden protection format and activate protection, follow these steps:

1 Select the cells you want to hide.

2 From the Format menu, choose the Protection tab of the Cells command.

3 Choose Hidden and click OK.

4 From the Tools menu, choose Protection and then Protect Sheet.

5 Make sure Contents is selected and click OK.

You can also hide entire worksheets in a workbook. Any data or calculations in a hidden worksheet are still available; the worksheet is simply hidden from view. To hide a worksheet in a workbook, follow these steps:

1 Click the tab of the worksheet you want to hide.

2 Choose Sheet and then Hide from the Format menu.

After a sheet is hidden, the Unhide command appears on the Sheet submenu of the Format menu, allowing you to restore the hidden sheet to view.

Entering Passwords

CAUTION

Password protection in Excel is serious business. Once you assign a password, there is no way to unprotect the sheet or workbook without it. Don't forget your passwords! And remember, capitalization matters!

In the dialog box that appears when you choose Protect Sheet or Protect Workbook from the Tools menu, you can assign a password that must be used in order to release Sheet or Workbook protection. (You can use a different password for each.) To assign a password, follow these steps:

1 Choose Protection and then Protect Sheet or Protect Workbook from the Tools menu.

2 Type a password and click OK.

3 When prompted, reenter the password and click OK to return to the worksheet or workbook.

Removing Protection

If protection is activated for a worksheet or a workbook, or both, the Protection command on the Tools menu changes to Unprotect Sheet or Unprotect Workbook, or both. To remove protection, choose the appropriate Unprotect command.

If you supplied a password when you protected the worksheet or workbook, you cannot remove protection until you type the password. Typing the wrong password generates the message

> The Password you supplied is not correct. Verify the CAPS lock key is off and that you used the correct capitalization.

The password you type must match the worksheet or workbook protection password in every detail, including capitalization.

Building Formulas

I f you didn't need formulas, you could use a word processor to build your spreadsheets. Formulas are the heart and soul of a spreadsheet, and Microsoft Excel 2000 offers a rich environment in which to build complex formulas. Armed with a few mathematical operators and rules for cell entry, you can turn your worksheet into a powerful calculator.

Creating Formulas

Let's walk through some rudimentary formulas to see how they work. First select blank cell A10 and type

=10+5

> Begin formulas in Microsoft Excel 2000 with an equal sign. The equal sign tells Excel that the succeeding characters constitute a formula. If you omit the equal sign, Excel may interpret the characters as text (even 10+5) unless the entry is a valid numeric value.

Now press Enter. The value 15 appears in cell A10, but when you select cell A10, the formula bar displays the formula you just entered. As mentioned in Chapter 4, "Managing Files," what appears in the cell is the displayed value; what appears in the formula bar is the underlying value. Now enter the following simple formulas and press Enter after you type each one:

=10-5

=10*5

=10/5

Each of the preceding formulas uses a mathematical operator: the plus sign (+), the minus sign (-), the multiplication sign (*), and the division sign (/).

Precedence of Operators

The term *precedence* refers to the order in which Excel performs calculations in a formula. Excel follows these rules:

- Expressions within parentheses are processed first.

- Multiplication and division are performed before addition and subtraction.

- Consecutive operators with the same level of precedence are calculated from left to right.

Let's enter some formulas to see how these rules apply. Select an empty cell and type

=4+12/6

Press Enter and you see the value 6. Excel first divides 12 by 6 and then adds the result (2) to 4. If Excel used a different order, the result would be different. Select another empty cell and type

=(4+12)/6

Press Enter and you see the value 2.666667. This example demonstrates how you can change the order of precedence using parentheses. The following formulas contain the same values and operators, but the placement of parentheses is different in each one, hence the results are also different.

Formula	Result
=3*6+12/4-2	19
=(3*6)+12/(4-2)	24
=3*(6+12)/4-2	11.5
=(3*6+12)/4-2	5.5
=3*(6+12/(4-2))	36

 TIP

If you are unsure of the order in which Excel will process a sequence of operators, use parentheses—even if the parentheses aren't actually necessary. Using parentheses will also make your formulas easier to read and interpret if you need to change them later.

Matching Parentheses

If you do not include a closing parenthesis for each opening parenthesis in a formula, Excel displays an error message and provides a suggested solution.

When you type a closing parenthesis, Excel briefly displays that pair of parentheses in bold. This feature is handy when you're entering a long formula and you're not sure which pairs of parentheses go together.

Using Cell References in Formulas

A *cell reference* identifies a cell or a group of cells in your workbook. When you create a formula that contains cell references, you link the formula to other cells in your workbook. The value of the formula is then dependent on the values in the referenced cells and changes when the values in the referenced cells change.

II

Worksheets

For practice, let's enter a formula that contains a cell reference. First select cell A1 and enter the formula

=10*2

Now select cell A2 and enter the formula

=A1

The value in both cells is 20. If at any time you change the value in cell A1, the value in cell A2 also changes. Now select cell A3 and type

=A1+A2

Excel returns the value 40. You'll find that cell references are extremely helpful as you create and use complex formulas.

Entering Cell References with the Mouse

SEE ALSO

For more on selecting cells or ranges, see "Selecting with the Mouse," page 94.

You can save time and increase accuracy when you enter cell references in a formula by selecting them with the mouse. For example, to enter references to cells A9 and A10 in a formula in cell B10:

1 Select cell B10 and type an equal sign.

2 Click cell A9 and type a plus sign.

3 Click cell A10 and press Enter.

When you click each cell, a flashing border called a *marquee* surrounds the cell, and a reference to the cell is inserted in cell B10. After you finish entering a formula, be sure to press Enter. If you do not press Enter and you select another cell, Excel assumes you want to include the cell reference in the formula.

The active cell does not have to be visible in the current window in order for you to enter a value in that cell. You can scroll through the worksheet without changing the active cell and click cells in remote areas of your worksheet as you build formulas. The formula bar displays the contents of the active cell, no matter what area of the worksheet is currently visible.

TIP

If you scroll through your worksheet and the active cell is no longer visible, you can redisplay the active cell by holding down Ctrl and pressing Backspace.

Relative, Absolute, and Mixed References

SEE ALSO

For information about copying cell references, see "Copying Relative, Absolute, and Mixed References," page 263.

Relative references (the type we've used so far in the sample formulas) refer to cells by their position in relation to the cell that contains the formula—for example, "the cell up two rows from this cell." *Absolute references* refer to cells by their fixed position in the worksheet—for example, "the cell located in column A and row 2." A *mixed reference* contains a relative reference and an absolute reference—for example, "the cell located in column A and up two rows." Absolute and mixed references are important when you begin copying formulas from one location to another in your worksheet.

The following is a relative reference to cell A1:

    =A1

An absolute reference to cell A1 looks like this:

    =$A$1

You can combine the relative and absolute references to cell A1 to create these mixed references:

    =$A1

    =A$1

If the dollar sign precedes the letter (A, for example), the column coordinate is absolute and the row is relative. If the dollar sign precedes the number (1, for example), the column coordinate is relative and the row is absolute.

When you are entering or editing a formula, press F4 to change reference types quickly. The following steps show how.

1　Select cell A1 and type

    =B1+B2

2　Press F4 to change the reference in the formula bar nearest the insertion point to absolute. The formula becomes

    =B1+$B$2

3　Press F4 again to change the reference to mixed (relative column coordinate and absolute row coordinate). The formula becomes

    =B1+B$2

II

Worksheets

4 Press F4 again to reverse the mixed reference (absolute column coordinate and relative row coordinate). The formula becomes

=B1+$B2

5 Press F4 again to return to the original relative reference.

What Are Mixed References Good For?

Sometimes you want to copy formulas across rows and down columns, but the formulas refer to other cells in the same rows or columns. Relative references automatically adjust when you copy them, and absolute references don't. Using relative or absolute references, you'd probably end up modifying each formula individually. But using mixed references, you can make the formula do the work for you. When you copy a mixed reference, the part of the reference preceded by a dollar sign does not adjust, while the other part adjusts to reflect the relative location of the copied formula.

The following sample from a worksheet displays formulas that calculate monthly payments for loan amounts specified in row 2, the fixed interest rates specified in column A, and the number of months specified in cell B1.

	A	B	C
1	Term in Months:	120	
2	Rate / Loan Amt.	10000	20000
3	0.07	=-PMT($A3/12,$B$1,B$2)	=-PMT($A3/12,$B$1,C$2)
4	0.08	=-PMT($A4/12,$B$1,B$2)	=-PMT($A4/12,$B$1,C$2)
5			

To create this worksheet, enter the formula shown in cell B3, and then copy it to the right and down as far as you need. The mixed references in the formula adjust to use the correct loan amount and interest rate for each cell. The absolute reference to the term in months in cell B1 does not change. The mixed reference to the annual interest rate, $A3/12, will always refer to a value in column A wherever you copy the formula (the interest rate is divided by 12 to represent a monthly rate). The row letter in this mixed reference will adjust so you can enter different interest rates in column A to see the effect of various rates. The absolute reference to the term of the loan, $B$1, will always refer to this exact cell wherever you copy the formula. The mixed reference to the loan amount, C$3, will always refer to a value in row 2 wherever you copy the formula, but the column number will adjust to refer to the loan amount in row 2 of the same column.

 **ON THE WEB** You can find the example file References.xls used in the previous sidebar on the Microsoft Press Web site at *http://mspress.microsoft.com/mspress/products/2050/*.

References to Other Worksheets in the Same Workbook

You can refer to cells in other worksheets within the same workbook just as easily as you refer to cells in the same worksheet. For example, to enter a reference to cell A9 in Sheet2 into cell B10 in Sheet1, do this:

1   Select cell B10 in Sheet1 and type an equal sign.

2   Click the Sheet2 tab at the bottom of the Book1 window.

3   Click cell A9 and then press Enter.

After you press Enter, Sheet1 is reactivated. Select cell B10 to see that it contains the formula

    =Sheet2!A9

Notice that the worksheet portion of the reference is separated from the cell portion by an exclamation point. Notice also that the cell reference is relative. When you select the cells to create references to other worksheets, the default cell reference is relative.

References to Worksheets in Other Workbooks

In the same way that you can refer to cells in other worksheets within the same workbook, you can also refer to cells in worksheets located in separate workbooks. These references are called *external references*. For example, to enter a reference to cell A2 in Sheet2 of Book2 into cell A1 in Sheet1 of Book1, follow these steps:

1   Create a new workbook by clicking the New button on the Standard toolbar (the first button on the left). In our example, the new workbook is named Book2.

2   Choose the Arrange command from the Window menu and then choose Vertical. Both workbooks appear, side by side, on your screen. (This command does not normally appear on shortened menus. Click the double arrow at the bottom of the Window menu to display the Vertical command.)

3   Select cell A1 in Sheet1 of Book1 and type an equal sign.

4   Click anywhere in the Book2 window to activate the workbook.

5   Click the Sheet2 tab at the bottom of the Book2 window.

6   Click cell A2.

II

Worksheets

Before pressing Enter to lock in the formula, your screen should look similar to Figure 6-1.

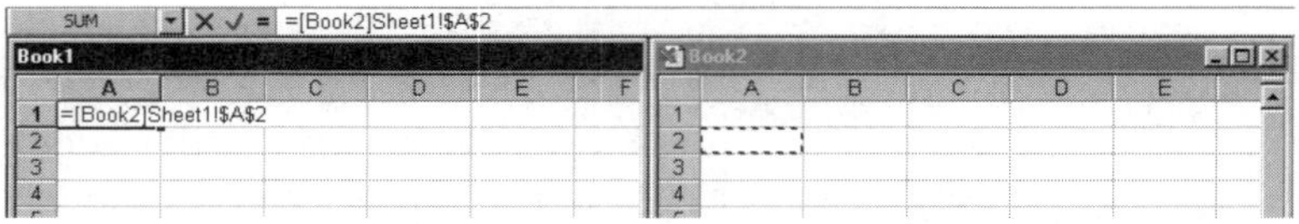

FIGURE 6-1.

Enter external references easily by clicking the cell to which you want to refer.

Notice that the workbook reference appears first in the formula and is enclosed in brackets. Notice also that external references entered in this fashion are absolute.

7 Press Enter to lock in the reference.

R1C1 Reference Style

Worksheet formulas usually refer to cells by a combination of column letter and row number, such as A1 or Z100. If you use R1C1 reference style, however, Excel refers to cells by row and column *number* instead. The cell reference R1C1 means row 1, column 1, so R1C1 refers to the same cell as A1. To activate R1C1 reference style, choose the Options command from the Tools menu, click the General tab, and select the R1C1 Reference Style option.

When you select the R1C1 Reference Style option, the cell references in your formulas change to R1C1 format. For example, cell M10 becomes R10C13, and cell IV65536, the last cell in your worksheet, becomes R65536C256.

When you use R1C1 notation, relative cell references are displayed in terms of their relationship to the cell that contains the formula rather than by their actual coordinates. This can be helpful when you are more interested in the relative positions of cells than in their absolute positions. For example, suppose you want to enter a formula in cell R10C2 (B10) that adds cells R1C1 (A1) and R1C2 (B1). After selecting cell R10C2, type an equal sign, select cell R1C1, type a plus sign, select cell R1C2, and then press Enter. With R10C2 selected, the formula bar displays

=R[-9]C[-1]+R[-9]C

Negative row and column numbers indicate that the referenced cell is above or to the left of the formula cell; positive numbers indicate that the referenced cell is below or to the right of the formula cell. The brackets indicate relative references. So, this formula reads "Add the cell nine rows up and one column to the left to the cell nine rows up in the same column."

A relative reference to another cell must include brackets around the numbers in the reference. Otherwise, Excel assumes you're using absolute references. For example, the formula

=R8C1+R9C1

uses absolute references to the cells in rows 8 and 9 of column 1.

Editing Formulas

You edit formulas the same way you edit text entries. To delete a cell reference or other character from a formula, drag through the reference or character in the cell or the formula bar and press Backspace or Delete. To replace a cell reference in a formula with another cell reference, highlight the cell reference you want to replace and click the new cell you want to reference and press Enter.

About Reference Syntax

So far, we've used Excel's default worksheet and workbook names for the examples in this book. When you save a workbook, you must specify a permanent name for it. If you create a formula first and then save the workbook with a new name, the formula is adjusted accordingly. For example, if you save Book2 as Mysales.xls, the reference

=[Book2]Sheet2!$A$2

automatically changes to

=[Mysales.xls]Sheet2!$A$2

And if you rename Sheet2 of Mysales.xls to February, the reference automatically changes to

=[Mysales.xls]February!$A$2

If the referenced workbook is closed, the full path to the folder where the workbook is stored appears in the reference, as shown in the example

='c:\Excel\[Mysales.xls]February'!$A$2

In the above example, notice that single quotation marks surround the workbook and worksheet portion of the reference. Excel automatically adds the quotation marks around the path when you close the workbook. Remember, if you type a new reference to a closed workbook, you must add the single quotation marks yourself. Obviously, it's better to avoid typing errors by opening the closed workbook and clicking cells with the mouse to enter references so that Excel inserts them in the correct syntax for you.

II

Worksheets

You can also insert additional cell references in a formula. For example, to insert a reference to cell B1 in the formula

> =A1+A3

simply move the insertion point between A1 and the plus sign and type

> +*B1*

or type a plus sign and click cell B1. The formula becomes

> =A1+B1+A3

⭐ TIP

To undo your changes if you have not locked them in, click the cancel button on the Formula bar or press Esc. If you already locked in the entry, use the Undo command on the Edit menu, press Ctrl+Z, or click the Undo button on the Standard toolbar.

Undo remembers the last 16 changes you made; repeatedly issuing the Undo command allows you to step back through them one by one. Similarly, the Redo command on the Edit menu or the Redo button on the Standard toolbar restores the last 16 actions undone. (The Redo button may be hidden on your screen. If so, click the double arrow on the right side of the Standard toolbar to display the More Buttons menu.)

Using Numeric Text in Formulas

❓ SEE ALSO

For information about entering numbers or text, see "Entering Data," page 103.

You can perform mathematical operations on numeric text values as long as the numeric string contains only the characters

> 0 1 2 3 4 5 6 7 8 9 . + - E e

In addition, you can use the / character in fractions. You can also use the five number-formatting characters

> $, % ( )

but you must enclose the numeric string in double quotation marks. For example, if you enter the formula

> =$1234+$123

Excel displays the message *Microsoft Excel found an error in the formula you entered*, and offers a proposed correction that essentially ignores the dollar signs. However, the formula

> ="$1234"+"$123"

produces the result 1357 with no dollar sign and no error message. Excel automatically translates numeric text entries into numeric values when it performs the addition.

Text Values

You manipulate most text values in the same way that you manipulate numeric values. For example, if cell A1 contains the text ABCDE and you enter the formula

=A1

in cell A10, cell A10 also displays ABCDE. Because this type of formula treats a string of text as a value, it is sometimes called a *string value* or *text value.*

You use the special operator & (ampersand) to *concatenate,* or join, several text values. For example, if cell A2 contains the text FGHIJ and you enter the formula

=A1&A2

in cell A3, cell A3 displays ABCDEFGHIJ. To include a space between the two strings, change the formula to

=A1&" "&A2

This formula uses two concatenation operators and a literal string, or *string constant*—a space enclosed in double quotation marks.

You can also use the & operator to concatenate strings of numeric values. For example, if cell A3 contains the numeric value 123 and cell A4 contains the numeric value 456, the formula

=A3&A4

produces the string 123456. This string is left-aligned in the cell because it is a text value. (Remember, you can use numeric text values to perform any mathematical operation as long as the numeric string contains only the numeric characters listed in *"Using Numeric Text in Formulas," page 124.*)

In addition, you can use the & operator to concatenate a text value and a numeric value. For example, if cell A1 contains the text ABCDE and cell A3 contains the numeric value 123, the formula

=A1&A3

produces the string ABCDE123.

II

Worksheets

Using Functions: A Preview

SEE ALSO

For more information about functions, see Chapter 12, "Common Worksheet Functions."

A *function* is a predefined formula that operates on a value or values and returns a value or values. Many Excel functions are shorthand versions of frequently used formulas. For example, the SUM function lets you add a series of cell values by simply selecting a range. Compare the formula

=A1+A2+A3+A4+A5+A6+A7+A8+A9+A10

with the formula

=SUM(A1:A10)

Obviously, the SUM function makes the formula a lot shorter and easier to create.

SEE ALSO

For more information, see "The PMT Function," page 483.

Some Excel functions perform extremely complex calculations. For example, using the PMT function, you can calculate the payment on a loan at a given interest rate and principal amount.

All functions consist of a function name followed by a set of *arguments* enclosed in parentheses. (In the previous example, A1:A10 is the argument in the SUM function.) If you omit a closing parenthesis when you enter a function, Excel will add the parenthesis after you press Enter, as long as it is obvious where the parenthesis is supposed to go. (Relying on this feature can produce unpredictable results; for accuracy, always double-check your parentheses.)

The AutoSum Button

The SUM function is used more often than any other function. To make this function more accessible, Excel includes an AutoSum button on the Standard toolbar. To insert the SUM function into a cell using the AutoSum button, see Figure 6-2 on the next page. *For more information about the AutoSum button, see "The SUM Function," page 420.*

TIP

Get a quick sum by selecting the cells you want to sum and looking at the AutoCalculate box in the status bar at the bottom of the screen, where the total of the selected range appears. Click the right mouse button on the AutoCalculate box to choose whether the range is summed, averaged, or counted, or whether the maximum or minimum value is displayed in the status bar. *See the sidebar "Quick Totals in the Status Bar," page 20.*

FIGURE 6-2.

To sum a column of numbers, select the cell below the numbers and click the AutoSum button.

1 Select the cell below the numbers in a column and click the AutoSum button to calculate the sum of the numbers in the column.

2 The AutoSum button inserts the entire formula for you and suggests a range to sum. If the suggested range is incorrect, simply drag through the correct range before you press Enter.

Accessing Built-In Functions with Paste Function

 SEE ALSO

For more on pasting functions, see "Entering Functions in a Worksheet," page 417.

When you want to use a built-in function, Excel's Paste Function is the best way. For example, to calculate the payment on a loan using the PMT function mentioned earlier, follow these steps:

1 Select a cell.

2 Click the Paste Function button on the Standard toolbar.

3 When the first Paste Function dialog box appears, as shown in Figure 6-3, select Financial from the Function Category list box.

4 Select PMT from the Function Name list box and click OK. When the *Formula Palette* appears, follow the steps shown in Figure 6-4 on the next page.

FIGURE 6-3.

When you click the Paste Function button, this dialog box appears.

II

Worksheets

FIGURE 6-4.

The Formula Palette appears when you click the OK button in the Paste Function dialog box.

1 In the Rate edit box, type *8%/12* (8% yearly interest, divided by 12 months).

2 In the Nper edit box, type *360* (30 years, in months).

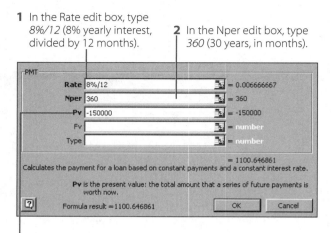

3 In the Pv edit box, type *-150000* (the loan amount, or present value, preceded by a minus sign) and then click the OK button.

> You can use the Formula Palette with existing formulas by clicking the equal sign button on the formula bar.

The formula is entered in the selected cell, and the resulting value is displayed on the worksheet.

> Drag the Formula Palette around on the screen if you need to see the cells under it. For the maximum view of the worksheet, shrink the dialog box by clicking one of the collapse buttons at the right side of the edit boxes. *For more information about the collapse buttons, see the sidebar "Selecting Cells While a Dialog Box Is Open," page 137.*

Using Functions to Create Three-Dimensional Formulas

For more on working with workbooks, see Chapter 9, "Worksheets and Windows."

You've seen how you can use references to cells in a worksheet and to cells in another worksheet within the same workbook. You can also use references to cells that span a range of worksheets in a workbook. These references are called *3-D references.* Suppose you set up 13 worksheets in the same workbook—one for each month—with a year-to-date summary sheet on top. If all the monthly worksheets are laid out identically, you could use 3-D reference formulas to summarize the monthly data on the summary sheet. For example, the formula

=SUM(Sheet2:Sheet13!B5)

adds all the values contained in cell B5 on all the worksheets between and including Sheet2 and Sheet13. To construct this three-dimensional formula, follow these steps:

1 Type *=SUM(* in cell B5 of Sheet1.

2 Click the Sheet2 tab and then click the tab scrolling button (located to the left of the worksheet tabs) until the Sheet13 tab is visible.

3 Hold down the Shift key and click the Sheet13 tab.

4 Select cell B5, type *)*, and press Enter.

Notice that when you hold down the Shift key and click the Sheet13 tab, all the tabs from Sheet2 through Sheet13 change to white, indicating that they are selected for inclusion in the reference you are constructing.

You can use the following functions with 3-D references:

SUM	MIN	VAR
COUNTA	PRODUCT	VARP
AVERAGE	STDEV	COUNT
MAX	STDEVP	

Formula Bar Formatting

You can enter spaces and line breaks in a formula to make it easier to read without affecting the calculation of the formula. To enter line breaks, press Alt+Enter. Figure 6-5 shows a formula that contains line breaks.

FIGURE 6-5.

You can enter line breaks in a formula to make it more readable.

Creating Formulas Using Plain Language

Microsoft Excel 2000 allows you to use labels instead of cell references when you create formulas in worksheet tables. Labels at the top of columns and to the left of rows identify the adjacent cells in the table when you use the labels in a formula. This is called a *natural language formula,* which is a fairly accurate description of the way it works, providing you use language that is, well, *natural.* The spreadsheet in Figure 6-6 on the next page shows a simple sales table as an example of how this works.

You can find Sales.xls used in the following example on the Microsoft Press Web site at *http://mspress.microsoft.com/mspress/products/2050/*.

FIGURE 6-6.

You can use the column and row labels in a table to refer to cells and ranges in formulas.

	B9		=	=SUM(Qtr 1)						
	A	B	C	D	E	F	G	H	I	J
1	ABC Company Sales									
2										
3	2000	Qtr 1	Qtr 2	Qtr 3	Qtr 4		Total	Average		
4	Product 1	1000	1050	1100	1150		4300	1075		
5	Product 2	1100	1150	1200	1250		4700	1175		
6	Product 3	1200	1250	1300	1350		5100	1275		
7	Product 4	1300	1350	1400	1450		5500	1375		
9	Total	4600	4800	5000	5200		19600	4900		
10	Average	1150	1200	1250	1300		4900	1225		
11										

TIP

When you use labels in formulas, leave a blank column and row between the worksheet table and the cells below and to the right that contain natural language formulas. Otherwise, results can be unpredictable, especially if you have more than one level of summary formulas, such as the two rows labeled Total and Average in Figure 6-6. Without a blank row separating the Total row from the table, the Average formulas below might attempt to include values in the Totals row as part of the Qtr 1 figures.

The formulas in rows 9 and 10 might normally contain formulas with range references, such as

=SUM(B4:B7)

But instead of a range reference, the natural language formula uses a column label from the table, such as

=SUM(Qtr 1)

as shown in Figure 6-6. When you use text in formulas instead of cell references, Excel automatically looks for column and row labels that match, and if it finds them, extrapolates what you're after, using a complex set of internal rules. For our purposes, we can say simply that:

- If a formula contains the label of the same column or row where the formula resides, Excel assumes you want to use the entire contiguous range of entries adjacent to the label (either below a column label or to the right of a row label).

- If a formula contains the label of a column or row other than the one where the formula resides, Excel assumes you want to act on a single intersecting cell at the intersection of the labeled column or row and the column or row containing the formula.

Finding the Right Intersection

In the worksheet in Figure 6-6, if at cell I4 you enter the formula

    =Qtr1*4

Excel assumes that you want to use only one value in the range B4:B7—the one that lies in the same row as the formula that contains the reference.

  This is called implicit intersection. Because the formula is in cell I4, Excel uses the value in B4. If you enter the same formula in cells I5, I6, and I7, each cell in that range contains the formula =Qtr 1*4, but at I5 the formula refers to cell B5, at I6 it refers to cell B6, and so on. You can also use implicit intersection to refer to individual cells in a row.

  Explicit intersection refers to a specific cell with the help of the intersection operator. The intersection operator is the space character that appears when you press the Spacebar. If, at any location on the same worksheet, you enter the formula

    =Qtr 1 Product 1*4

Excel knows that you want to refer to the value that lies at the intersection of the range labeled Qtr 1 and the range labeled Product 1—cell B4.

We use *intersection* to identify specific cells using natural language formulas. For example, we can refer to cell C5 in Figure 6-6 using the formula

    =Product 2 Qtr 2

which uses the column labels to pinpoint the cell located at the intersection of the row Product 2 and the column Qtr 2—cell C5. Note that you must enter a space between the row and column label in the formula.

You can copy and paste natural language formulas, and the columns and rows to which you refer will adjust accordingly. In Figure 6-6, the formula in cell B9 was copied to cells C9:G9. All the formulas in the range adjust automatically so that the label for the current column is used. For example, after copying the formula in cell B9 to the right, the formula in cell G9 becomes

    =SUM(Total)

Note that if you copy natural language formulas to places that don't make sense, Excel will alert you that something's wrong. For example, if you copy the formula in cell H9 to cell J9, Excel displays the error value NAME? because there is no label available in column J.

You can also change the column and row labels in tables, and the labels you typed into formulas will adjust automatically. For example, if the label "Total" in *Figure 6-6 on page 130* changed to "Year," the formula in cell G9 would adjust accordingly to read

=SUM(Year)

> You can use natural language formulas in the worksheet that contains the table, but you cannot use them to refer to cells located in other worksheets or in other workbooks; instead, use range names. You can turn off natural language formulas by choosing the Options command on the Tools menu, clicking the Calculation tab, and turning off the Accept Labels In Formulas workbook option. *For details about range names, see "Naming Cells and Ranges," page 133.*

Substituting Labels Automatically

You can also have Excel automatically substitute labels for cell references in formulas. To do so, you must first define the label ranges by choosing Name on the Insert menu, and then choosing Label. This displays the Label Ranges dialog box shown in Figure 6-7.

FIGURE 6-7.

You can use the Label Ranges dialog box to substitute labels for cell references in formulas.

1 Click here, drag on the worksheet to select the labels you want to define, and then click the Row Labels or Column Labels option.

2 Click the Add button to add the label range to the Existing Label Ranges list.

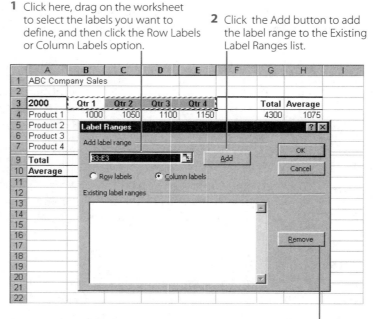

3 To remove a defined label range, select it here and click the Remove button.

After you define label ranges, any references to cells within the defined label ranges are automatically replaced by natural-language labels. For example, click cell I9 in Figure 6-7, type an equal sign and then click cell C4 to insert the cell reference. Normally, Excel would insert the cell reference "C4" in the formula, but instead label ranges are used and "Qtr 2 Product 1" appears in the formula.

Naming Cells and Ranges

? SEE ALSO

For more information about natural language formulas, see "Creating Formulas Using Plain Language," page 129.

? SEE ALSO

For more information about sheet-level names, see "Defining Sheet-Level Names," page 136.

You can assign names to cells and cell ranges and then use those names in your formulas. Using names instead of cell references is convenient because it eliminates the need to type complex cell references. Using names instead of the column and row labels used in natural language formulas allows you to refer to named cells from anywhere in the workbook, or even from another workbook.

After you define names in a worksheet, those names are made available to any other worksheets in the workbook. A name defining a cell range in Sheet6, for example, is available for use in formulas in Sheet1, Sheet2, and so on in the workbook. As a result, each workbook contains its own set of names. You can also define special "sheet-level" names that are available only on the worksheet in which they are defined.

Using Names in Formulas

You can use the name of a cell or range in a formula. The result is the same as it would be if you entered the reference of the cell or the range. For example, suppose you enter the formula

    =A1+A2

in cell A3. If you define the name Mark as cell A1 and the name Vicki as cell A2, the formula

    =Mark+Vicki

returns the same value.

Defining Names with the Name Box

The easiest way to define a name is to use the Name box in the formula bar as shown in Figure 6-8 on the next page.

FIGURE 6-8.

Use the Name box in the formula bar to define names in your worksheet.

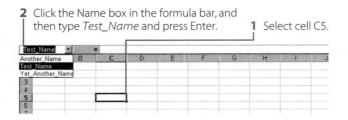

2 Click the Name box in the formula bar, and then type *Test_Name* and press Enter.   1 Select cell C5.

  SEE ALSO

For more information about naming cells and ranges, see "Rules for Naming Cells and Ranges," page 138.

If a selected cell or range is named, the name takes precedence over the cell reference and is displayed in the Name box. For example, the Name box displayed C5 at the beginning of the exercise, but now the Name box displays Test_Name when C5 is selected. Note that you cannot use spaces in a name.

When you define a name for a range of cells, the range name does not appear in the Name box unless the entire range is selected.

NOTE

> When you define a name, the worksheet name is part of the definition, and the cell reference is absolute. For example, when you define the name Test_Name for cell C5 in Sheet1, the actual name definition is recorded as Sheet1!$C$5. *For more information about absolute references, see "Relative, Absolute, and Mixed References," page 119.*

Moving to a Named Cell or Range

You can move to a named cell or range by clicking the arrow next to the Name box and selecting the cell or range name from the drop-down list. Also, if you type a name in the Name box that is already defined, Excel simply moves to the named cell or range in the worksheet rather than redefining it.

Defining Names with the Name Command

The Name command on the Insert menu lets you use the text in adjacent cells to define cell and range names, as seen in Figure 6-9. You can also use this command to redefine existing names.

TIP

> You can display the Define Name dialog box quickly by pressing Ctrl+F3.

FIGURE 6-9.

Excel inserts a text label in the Names In Workbook edit box if the selected cell or the cell immediately to the left or above the selected cell contains a text label that can serve as a cell name.

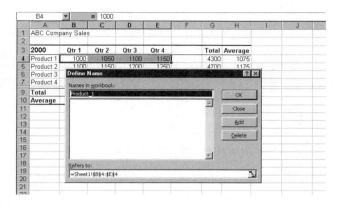

Suppose cell A4 contains the text Product 1 and you want to use this text as the name for the adjacent cells B4:E4. To define a name using the text in cell A4, follow these steps:

1 Select the range B4:E4.

2 From the Insert menu, choose Name and then Define to display the Define Name dialog box. Notice that Excel inserts the text Product_1 in the Names In Workbook edit box and inserts the cell reference Sheet1!$B$4:$E$4 in the Refers To edit box.

3 Press Enter.

The next time you open the Define Name dialog box, the name appears in the Names In Workbook list box, which displays all the defined names for the workbook.

You can also define a name without first selecting a cell or range in the worksheet. To define cell D20 with the name Test2, follow these steps:

1 From the Insert menu, choose Name and then Define.

2 Type *Test2* in the Names In Workbook edit box and then type *=D20* in the Refers To edit box.

3 Click the Add button.

The Define Name dialog box remains open, and the Refers To edit box displays the name definition =Sheet1!D20. Excel adds the worksheet reference for you, but note that the cell reference stays relative, just as you entered it. If you do not enter the equal sign preceding the reference, Excel interprets the definition as text. For example, if you entered *D20* instead of *=D20*, the Refers To edit box would display the text constant ="D20" as the definition of the name Test2.

II

Worksheets

When the Define Name dialog box is open, you can also insert references in the Refers To edit box by selecting cells in the worksheet. If you name several cells or ranges in the Define Name dialog box, be sure to click the Add button after entering each definition. (If you click OK, Excel closes the dialog box.)

Defining Sheet-Level Names

As mentioned earlier, names in Excel are normally "book-level"; that is, a name defined in one worksheet is available to other worksheets in the same workbook. But you can also create "sheet-level" names that are available only on the worksheet in which they are defined. To define a sheet-level name for a cell or range of cells, precede the name with the name of the worksheet, followed by an exclamation point. For example, to define TestSheetName as a sheet-level name in Sheet1, follow these steps:

1 Select the cell or range you want to name.

2 Choose Name and then Define from the Insert menu. Type *Sheet1!TestSheetName* in the Names In Workbook edit box.

3 Click OK.

When you select a cell or range that you have defined with a sheet-level name, the name of the cell or range (TestSheetName, for example) appears in the Name box on the formula bar, but the name of the worksheet (Sheet1!, for example) is hidden. If you want to see a sheet-level name in its entirety, activate the worksheet in which the name is defined and choose Name and then Define from the Insert menu.

When the Define Name dialog box appears, the sheet-level name is displayed in the Names In Workbook list box with the worksheet name (for example, Sheet1) at the right side of the list box. Because sheet-level names are available only in the worksheet in which they are defined, Excel displays the sheet-level names for only the active worksheet in the Define Name dialog box. Thus, in the example above, if you first select Sheet2 and choose Name and then Define from the Insert menu, TestSheetName no longer appears in the Define Name dialog box.

When a worksheet contains a duplicate book-level and sheet-level name, the sheet-level name takes precedence over the book-level name on the sheet where it lives. For example, suppose that on Sheet1 you define the name TestName (book-level) and on Sheet2, you define the name Sheet2!TestName (sheet-level), TestName is available on every worksheet in the workbook except Sheet2, where Sheet2!TestName takes precedence. Keep in mind that Excel does not allow you to use a duplicate book-level name in the worksheet where the sheet-level name is defined. Thus, in the example, you cannot use TestName in Sheet2. You can, however, refer to a sheet-level name in another worksheet by including the name, in its entirety, in a formula. For example, you could enter the formula *=Sheet2!TestName* in a cell in Sheet3.

Redefining Names in the Define Name Dialog Box

To redefine an existing cell or range name in the Define Name dialog box, first select the name in the Names In Workbook list box and then edit the cell or range reference in the Refers To edit box. You can either type a new reference or select a new cell or range directly in the worksheet while the Define Name dialog box is open.

Selecting Cells While a Dialog Box Is Open

The Define Name dialog box is one of the dialog boxes in Excel that allows you to select cells or worksheets while it is open. Click the Refers To box at the bottom of the dialog box, and then select the worksheet tab and cell range you want instead of typing the reference.

When a dialog box allows you to select directly in the worksheet, there is a button with an arrow in it, called a collapse dialog button, at the right end of the edit box. The Refers To box shown in *Figure 6-9 on page 135* shows a collapse dialog button. When you click the collapse dialog button, the dialog box collapses, allowing you to see more of your worksheet.

	A	B	C	D	E	F	G	H
1	ABC Company Sales							
2								
3	2000	Qtr 1	Qtr 2	Qtr 3	Qtr 4		Total	Average
4	Product 1	1000	1050	1100	1150		4300	1075
5	Product 2							
6	Product	Define Name - Refers to:						? X
7	Product	=Sheet1!$B$4:$E$4						
9	Total	4600	4800	5000	5200		19600	4900
10	Average	1150	1200	1250	1300		4900	1225

You can drag the collapsed dialog box around the screen using its title bar. When you finish, click the collapse button again, and the dialog box will return to its original size.

Rules for Naming Cells and Ranges

These rules will come in handy when you name cells and ranges in Excel.

- All names must begin with a letter, a backslash (\), or an underscore (_).

- Numbers can be used.

- Symbols other than backslash and underscore cannot be used.

- Blank spaces are indicated by an underscore.

- Names that resemble cell references cannot be used.

- Single letters, with the exception of the letters R and C, can be used as names.

Editing Names

You can use any of Excel's editing techniques to change the contents of the Refers To edit box in the Define Name dialog box. For example, to change the cells associated with a range name, follow these steps:

1 From the Insert menu, choose Name and then Define.

2 Select the name from the Names In Workbook list box.

3 In the Refers To edit box, drag through the cell references you want to change and type the new references.

4 Click OK.

You can also change the contents of the Refers To edit box by selecting cells in the worksheet while the Define Name dialog box is open.

To delete a name in the Define Name dialog box, select the name from the Names In Workbook list box and then click Delete. Keep in mind that when you delete a name, any formula in the worksheet that refers to that name returns the error value #NAME?.

Creating Names from Text Cells

You can also use the Name command on the Insert menu to name several individual cells or adjacent ranges at once. This is particularly useful when you need to define many names in a region on your worksheet. When you choose Name and then Create from the Insert menu, Excel displays the Create Names dialog box shown in Figure 6-10. Excel uses the labels in the column or row (or the column and row) adjacent to the range you want to define to name the other cells in the range.

FIGURE 6-10.

Use the Create Names dialog box to name several cells or ranges.

To assign names to the cell ranges in columns B through E that correspond to the labels in column A, follow these steps:

1   Select cells A4:E7.

2   From the Insert menu, choose Name and then Create to display the Create Names dialog box, shown in Figure 6-10. (You can also display the Create Names dialog box by pressing Ctrl+Shift+F3.)

3   The Left Column option is selected by default, so click OK.

Now when you click the arrow to the right of the Name box in the formula bar, you see the names Product_1, Product_2, Product_3, and Product_4 listed. (The name Product_1 is defined as the range =Sheet1!$B$4:$E$4, for example.)

If you select a range with labels for both rows and columns, the Top Row and Left Column options in the Create Names dialog box are selected, allowing you to create two sets of names at once. For example, in Figure 6-10, if you select the range A3:E7, you can create the names Qtr_1, Qtr_2, Qtr_3, and Qtr_4 at the same time. (The name Qtr_1, for instance, is defined as the range $B$4:$B$7.)

Naming Constants and Formulas

You can create names to define constants and formulas, even if the constants and formulas don't actually appear in any cell in your worksheet. For example, if you often use the value 5% to calculate sales tax, you can use the name Tax in your calculations. To do so, follow these steps:

1   From the Insert menu, choose Name and then Define.

2   When the Define Name dialog box appears, type *Tax* in the Names In Workbook edit box and type *5%* or *.05* in the Refers To edit box.

3   Click OK.

II

Worksheets

SEE ALSO

For more information about the Name box, see "Defining Names with the Name Box," page 133.

Now you can use the name Tax in a formula like =Price+(Price*Tax) to calculate the cost of items with a 5 percent sales tax. Note that named constants and formulas do not appear in the Name box in the formula bar, but they do appear in the Define Name dialog box.

You can also enter a formula as a name definition in the Refers To edit box. For example, you might want to define the name Tax with a formula like =Sheet1!$B$22+1.2%. If you enter a formula in the Refers To edit box that refers to a cell in a worksheet, Excel updates the formula whenever the value in the cell changes.

Using Relative References in Named Formulas

When you are creating a named formula that contains relative references, such as =Sheet1!B22+1.2%, Excel interprets the position of the cells referenced in the Refers To edit box as relative to the cell that is active. Later, when you use such a name in a formula, the reference is relative to the cell containing the formula that uses the name. For example, if cell B21 was the active cell when you defined the name Tax as =Sheet1!B22+1.2%, the name Tax will always refer to the cell one row below the cell in which the formula is currently located.

Three-Dimensional Names

You can create three-dimensional names, which use 3-D references as their definitions. For example, to define a three-dimensional name for the 3-D reference we created earlier in "Using Functions to Create Three-Dimensional Formulas" *(see page 128)*, follow these steps:

1   Select cell B5 in Sheet1.

2   Choose Name and then Define from the Insert menu.

3   Type *Three_D* (or any name you choose) in the Names In Workbook edit box and type *=Sheet2:Sheet13!B5* in the Refers To edit box.

4   Press Enter.

Now you can use the name Three_D in formulas that contain any of the functions listed on *page 129*. For example, the formula

    =SUM(Three_D)

totals the values in the three-dimensional range named Three_D. Because you used relative references in step 3, the definition of the range Three_D changes as you select different cells in the worksheet.

For example, if you select cell C3 and display the Define Name dialog box, you will see =Sheet2:Sheet13!C3 in the Refers To edit box.

Pasting Names into Formulas

After you define one or more names in your worksheet, you can use the Name and Paste commands on the Insert menu, or press F3, to insert the names in your formulas. For example, to paste the name Product_2 into a formula, follow the steps in Figure 6-11.

FIGURE 6-11.

Use the Paste Name dialog box to insert names in your formulas.

2 Choose Name and then Paste from the Insert menu, or press F3.

1 Begin entering a formula by typing an equal sign; then type the operators, functions, or constants of your formula.

4 Click OK to insert the name Product_2 in the formula, type any other operands and operators, and press Enter.

3 When the Paste Name dialog box appears, select Product_2.

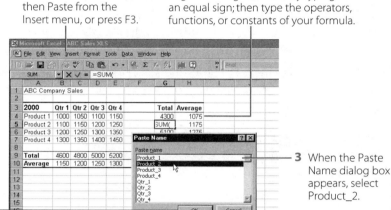

The Paste List Option

In large worksheet models, it's easy to accumulate a very long list of defined names. To keep track of all the names used, you can paste a list of defined names in your worksheet by clicking the Paste List option in the Paste Name dialog box. As shown in Figure 6-12, Excel pastes the list in your worksheet beginning at the active cell.

FIGURE 6-12.

Use the Paste List option to paste a list of the names and definitions in your worksheet.

When Excel pastes the list in your worksheet, it overwrites any existing data. If you inadvertently overwrite data, choose Undo List Names from the Edit menu.

If you want to locate a named cell reference in a workbook quickly, select the name in the Name box on the formula bar. Excel activates the corresponding worksheet and selects the named cell or range.

Applying Names to Formulas

To replace references in formulas with the corresponding names, choose Name and then Apply from the Insert menu. When you choose this command, Excel locates in formulas all the cell and range references for which you have defined names. If you select a single cell before you choose the Apply command, Excel applies names throughout the active worksheet; if you select a range of cells, Excel applies names only to the selected cells.

Figure 6-13 shows the Apply Names dialog box, which lists all the cell and range names you have defined. To apply more than one name, hold down Shift as you click each name.

FIGURE 6-13.

Use the Apply Names dialog box to substitute names for cell and range references in your formulas. Click the Options button to make additional choices available.

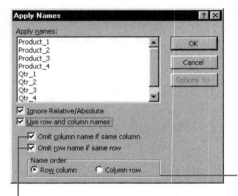

Use the Name Order options to control the order in which row and column components appear when Excel applies two names connected by an intersection operator.

When you apply names to formulas using the Apply Names dialog box, by default Excel does not apply the column or the row name if either is superfluous. To include the column or row name, clear the appropriate option.

Use the Ignore Relative/Absolute option to replace references with names regardless of the reference type. In general, leave this check box selected. Most name definitions use absolute references (the default when you define and create names), and most formulas use relative references (the default when you paste cell and range references in the formula bar). If you clear this option, Excel replaces absolute, relative, and mixed references only with name definitions that use the corresponding reference style.

SEE ALSO

For more information about the intersection operator, see the sidebar "Finding the Right Intersection," page 131.

If you find that typing range names (especially range names in formulas that require intersection operators) is tedious work, leave the Use Row And Column Names option selected (the default) in the Apply Names dialog box. Excel will then insert the range names for you. Referring back to *Figure 6-11, on page 141,* for example, if you enter the formula *=B4*4* (without names) in cell I4 and use the Apply Names dialog box with the Use Row And Column Names option selected, Excel changes the formula to read =Qtr_1*4. Without the Use Row And Column Names option, Excel does not apply names to the formula. Similarly, if you enter the formula *=B4*4* in cell I4 and then use the Apply Names dialog box, Excel changes the formula to read =Product_1 Qtr_1*4, but only if you leave the Use Row And Column Names option selected.

Using Range Names with the Go To Command

When you choose the Go To command from the Edit menu (or press F5), range names appear in the list box at the left side of the Go To dialog box, as shown in Figure 6-14.

FIGURE 6-14.
Use the Go To dialog box to select a cell or range name so you can move to that cell or range quickly.

TIP

The Go To dialog box remembers the last four places you "went to," as shown in Figure 6-14. The latest location is always in the Reference box when you display the dialog box, so you can jump back and forth between two locations by pressing F5 and then pressing Enter.

Understanding Error Values

An error value is the result of a formula that Excel cannot resolve. The seven error values are described in the table below.

Error Value	Means
#DIV/0!	You attempted to divide a number by zero. This error usually occurs when you create a formula with a divisor that refers to a blank cell.
#NAME?	You entered a name in a formula that is not in the Define Name dialog box list. You may have mistyped the name or typed a deleted name. Excel also displays this error value if you do not enclose a text string in double quotation marks.
#VALUE	You entered a mathematical formula that refers to a text entry.
#REF!	You deleted a range of cells whose references are included in a formula.
#N/A	No information is available for the calculation you want to perform. When building a model, you can enter #N/A in a cell to show that you are awaiting data. Any formulas that reference cells containing the #N/A value return #N/A.
#NUM!	You provided an invalid argument to a worksheet function. #NUM! can also indicate that the result of a formula is too large or too small to be represented in the worksheet.
#NULL!	You included a space between two ranges in a formula to indicate an intersection, but the ranges have no common cells.

Working with Arrays

Arrays are calculating tools you can use to build formulas that produce multiple results or to operate on groups of values rather than on single values. An *array formula* acts on two or more sets of values, called *array arguments,* to return either a single result or multiple results. An *array range* is a block of cells that share a common array formula. An *array constant* is a specially organized list of constant values that you can use as arguments in your array formulas.

Introducing Arrays

The easiest way to learn about arrays is to look at a few examples. For instance, using arrays, you can calculate the sum of the values in rows 1 and 2 for each column in Figure 6-15 by entering a single formula. Follow these steps:

1 Select the range A3:E3.

2 Type

   =A1:E1+A2:E2

3 Press Ctrl+Shift+Enter.

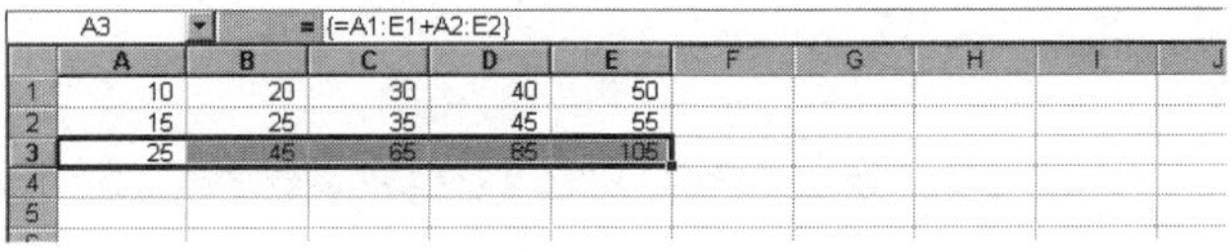

FIGURE 6-15.

An array formula totals the values in each column.

As you can see in Figure 6-15, a single array formula computes the sum of each group of values. This "single formula" exists in five cells at once. Although it seems to be five separate formulas, you cannot make any changes to it without selecting the entire formula—that is, the entire range A3:E3. Cells A3:E3 serve as the array range, and the array formula is stored in each cell of the array range. (Excel adds the "curly" braces, which are visible in the formula bar in Figure 6-15, when it distributes the array formula throughout the cells of the array range.) The array arguments are the range references A1:E1 and A2:E2.

The array formula in Figure 6-15 occupies a horizontal array range. The array formula in Figure 6-16 occupies a vertical array range.

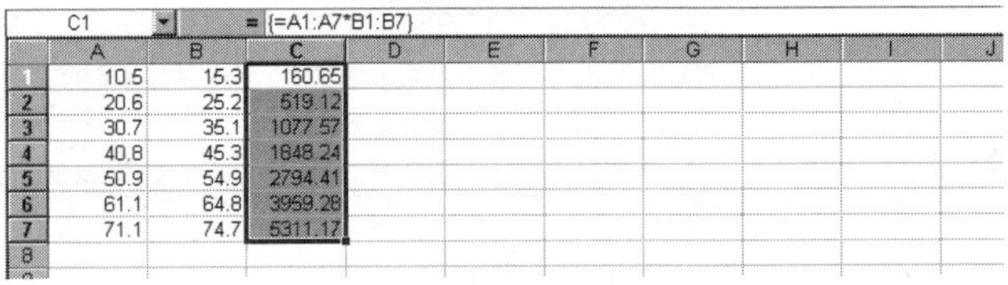

FIGURE 6-16.

In this worksheet, a vertical array formula calculates the products of the values in each row.

You can use an array formula and the AVERAGE function to compute the average of the products of each pair of values in the worksheet.

For example, to create the formula shown in Figure 6-17 and to average A1*B1, A2*B2, A3*B3, and so on, follow these steps:

1   Select any blank cell.

2   Type *=AVERAGE(A1:A7*B1:B7)*

3   Press Ctrl+Shift+Enter.

FIGURE 6-17.

The array formula in cell D1 returns the average of the products of the values in columns A and B.

	A	B	C	D	E	F	G	H	I	J
				=AVERAGE(A1:A7*B1:B7)						
1	10.5	15.3	160.65	2238.634						
2	20.6	25.2	519.12							
3	30.7	35.1	1077.57							
4	40.8	45.3	1848.24							
5	50.9	54.9	2794.41							
6	61.1	64.8	3959.28							
7	71.1	74.7	5311.17							
8										

Two-Dimensional Arrays

In the previous example, the array formulas resulted in horizontal and vertical one-dimensional arrays. You can also create arrays that include two or more columns and rows, otherwise known as two-dimensional arrays. For example, to calculate the integer values of each entry in cells A1:C7 of Figure 6-17, you can create a two-dimensional array range. The steps are shown in Figure 6-18.

FIGURE 6-18.

We used a two-dimensional array formula to compute the integer value of each of the entries in cells A1:C7, as displayed in the range E1:G7.

1   Select a range the same size and shape as the range you want to work with. (In this case, you would select a range with seven rows and three columns, such as E1:G7.)

	A	B	C	D	E	F	G	H	I	J
				=INT(A1:C7)						
1	10.5	15.3	160.65	2238.634	10	15	160			
2	20.6	25.2	519.12		20	25	519			
3	30.7	35.1	1077.57		30	35	1077			
4	40.8	45.3	1848.24		40	45	1848			
5	50.9	54.9	2794.41		50	54	2794			
6	61.1	64.8	3959.28		61	64	3959			
7	71.1	74.7	5311.17		71	74	5311			
8										

2   Type=*INT(A1:C7)*, and then press Ctrl+Shift+Enter.

 SEE ALSO

For more on the INT function, see Chapter 12, "Common Worksheet Functions."

Excel enters the array formula

{ =INT(A1:C7)}

in each cell in the range E1:G7. (The INT function simply changes a number to its integer value.)

NOTE

You cannot create three-dimensional arrays across multiple worksheets in workbooks.

Array Formula Rules

■ To enter array formulas, first select the cell or range that will contain the results. If the formula produces multiple results, you must select a range the same size and shape as the range or ranges on which you perform your calculations.

■ To lock in an array formula, press Ctrl+Shift+Enter. Excel will then place a set of braces around the formula in the formula bar to indicate that it is an array formula. Don't type the braces yourself; if you do, Excel will interpret your entry as a label.

■ To edit, clear, or move individual cells in an array range, you must treat them as a single unit and edit them all at once. You cannot edit, clear, or move individual cells in an array range, nor can you insert or delete cells.

■ To edit or clear an array, select the entire array and activate the formula bar. (The braces around the formula will disappear.) Edit or clear the formula and then press Ctrl+Shift+Enter.

⭐ **TIP**

To select an entire array, click any cell in the array and press Ctrl+slash (/).

❓ **SEE ALSO**

See "Moving and Copying with the Mouse," page 238, or for more information about the Cut and Paste commands, see Chapter 8, "Editing a Worksheet."

■ To move the contents of an array range, select the entire array and choose the Cut command from the Edit menu. Then select the new location and choose the Paste command from the Edit menu. You can also use the mouse to drag the selection to a new location.

■ You cannot cut, clear, or edit part of an array, but you can assign different formats to individual cells in the array. You can also copy cells from an array range and paste them in another area of your worksheet.

Using Array Constants

An array constant can consist of numbers, text, or logical values. You must enclose an array constant in braces ({ }) and separate its elements with commas and semicolons. Commas indicate values in separate columns, and semicolons indicate values in separate rows.

Suppose you want to compute the integer values of the three numbers 123.456, 1.234, and 12345.678. You can perform these three computations with a single array formula, as shown in Figure 6-19.

FIGURE 6-19.
An array constant is the argument for this array formula.

2 Type =INT({123.456,1.234,12345.678}). Be sure to type the braces yourself this time to indicate that the enclosed values make up an array constant. Then press Ctrl+Shift+Enter.
A1
{=INT({123.456,1.234,12345.678})}
123
1
12345
1 Select any horizontal three-cell range.

You can also create vertical array constants, in which elements are separated by semicolons.

SEE ALSO
For more information about the SQRT function, see Chapter 12, "Common Worksheet Functions."

In addition, you can create two-dimensional array constants. Commas place the elements in separate columns in the same row, and semicolons separate the rows. For example, to calculate the square roots of a series of 12 values and display them as a block, use the SQRT function with the following array formula:

=SQRT({4,9,16,25;36,49,64,81;100,121,144,169})

Figure 6-20 shows how to enter this formula.

FIGURE 6-20.
This array formula uses a four-column-by-three-row array constant.

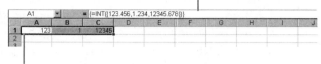

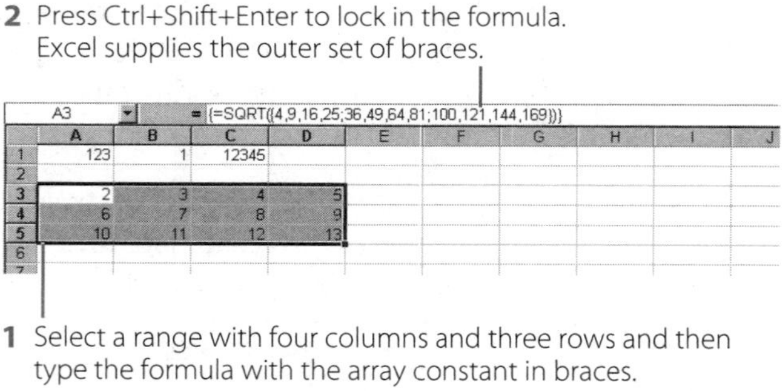
2 Press Ctrl+Shift+Enter to lock in the formula. Excel supplies the outer set of braces.
A3
{=SQRT({4,9,16,25;36,49,64,81;100,121,144,169})}
1 Select a range with four columns and three rows and then type the formula with the array constant in braces.

Array Expansion

When you use arrays as arguments in a formula, all your arrays should have the same dimensions. If the dimensions of your array arguments or array ranges don't match, Excel often expands the arguments. For example, to multiply all the values in cells A1:B5 by 10, Excel uses the following array formula:

{ =A1:B5*10}

To multiply these array constants, Excel uses this array formula:

{ ={1,2;3,4;5,6;7,8;9,10}*10}

Notice that these two formulas are not balanced; ten values are on the left side of the multiplication operator, and only one is on the right. Excel can expand the second argument to match the size and shape of the first. In the preceding example, the first formula is equivalent to

{ =A1:B5*{10,10;10,10;10,10;10,10;10,10}}

and the second is equivalent to

{={1,2;3,4;5,6;7,8;9,10}*{10,10;10,10;10,10;10,10;10,10}}

When you work with two or more sets of multivalue arrays, each set must have the same number of rows as the argument with the greatest number of rows, and the same number of columns as the argument with the greatest number of columns.

Calculating the Worksheet

Calculating is the process of computing formulas and then displaying the results as values in the cells containing the formulas. When you change the values in the cells to which these formulas refer, Microsoft Excel updates the values of the formulas as well. This updating process is called *recalculating,* and it affects only those cells containing references to the cells that have changed.

By default, Excel recalculates whenever you make changes that affect cell entries. If a large number of cells have to be recalculated, the words "Calculating Cells" and a number appear at the left end of the status bar. The number indicates the percentage of recalculation completed. During recalculation, the mouse pointer might assume the shape of an hourglass (or whatever shape indicates that the computer is busy). You can interrupt the recalculation process, however. Even if the mouse pointer indicates your system is busy (an hourglass by default), you can still use commands or make cell entries. Excel simply pauses in its recalculation and then resumes when you're done.

Manual Recalculation

To save time, particularly when you're entering changes in a large workbook with many formulas, you can switch from automatic to manual recalculation; that is, Excel will recalculate only when you tell it to. To set manual recalculation, choose Options from the Tools menu, and then follow the steps in Figure 6-21.

FIGURE 6-21.

The Calculation tab of the Options dialog box controls worksheet calculation and iteration.

1 Click the Calculation tab.

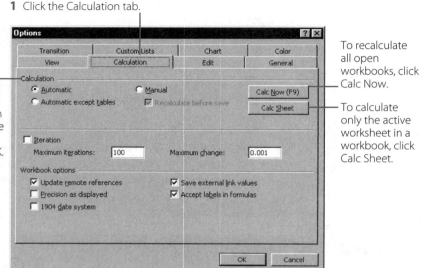

To recalculate all open workbooks, click Calc Now.

To calculate only the active worksheet in a workbook, click Calc Sheet.

2 In the Calculation section, select the Manual option and then click OK.

Now if you make a change that normally initiates recalculation, the status bar displays *Calculate* instead of recalculating automatically. To update your worksheet after making changes, press F9. Excel then calculates all the cells in all the worksheets that are affected by the changes you've made since the last recalculation.

TIP

If you want to calculate only the active worksheet, press Shift+F9.

You can also use the Calc Now or Calc Sheet buttons on the Calculation tab of the Options dialog box. In addition, you can recalculate all open workbooks by using the Calculate Now toolbar button, which you can add to a toolbar *(as described in Chapter 3, "Toolbars and Menus").*

SEE ALSO

For more information about data tables, see Chapter 16, "What-If Analysis."

Even if you have set recalculation to Manual, Excel normally recalculates your entire workbook when you save it to disk. To prevent this recalculation, clear the Recalculate Before Save option on the Calculation tab of the Options dialog box. If you select the Automatic Except Tables option, Excel automatically recalculates all the affected cells in your workbook except data tables.

Copying Formulas and Pasting Values

To copy a formula or a range of formulas and then paste only their resulting values, use the Paste Special command on the Edit menu. For example, suppose cell A1 contains the value 100, cell A2 contains the value 200, and cell A3 contains the value 300. If cell A6 contains the formula

    =A1+A2+A3

its resulting value is 600. If you want to eliminate the formula but retain the value 600 (or simply copy the resulting value and paste it elsewhere), follow these steps:

1 Select cell A6 and choose Copy from the Edit menu.

2 Choose Paste Special from the Edit menu.

3 When the Paste Special dialog box appears, select Values in the Paste box and press Enter twice.

The formula in cell A6 is replaced by the value 600.

To change part of a formula to a value, select the part you want to change and press F9. For example, let's modify the formula

    =A1+A2+A3

in cell A6 of the previous example. To replace the reference A1 with its value, highlight the cell reference in the formula bar and press F9. The formula then becomes

    =100+A2+A3

To replace individual cell references with their values, highlight each one and press F9. Then lock in the value by pressing Enter. To return the formula to its original state, click the Undo button on the Standard toolbar.

Circular References

A *circular reference* is a formula that depends on its own value. The most obvious type is a formula that contains a reference to the same cell in which it is entered. For example, if you enter the formula

    =C1-A1

in cell A1 (and this is the first time you have made a circular reference error), Excel displays the error message shown in Figure 6-22 on the next page.

FIGURE 6-22.

This error message appears when you attempt to enter a formula that contains a circular reference.

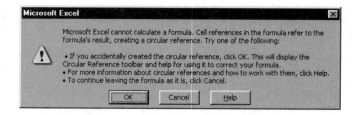

> NOTE

If the Office Assistant is active, the error message in Figure 6-22 is displayed in the Assistant's yellow text balloon rather than in a dialog box. *For more about the Office Assistant, see Chapter 2, "Getting Help."*

If a circular reference warning surprises you, this usually means that you made an error in a formula. Click OK and Excel displays a Help topic regarding circular references. Review this topic, then close Help by clicking the Close button. Next review the formula, and if the error is not obvious, check the cells that the formula references. Notice that Excel displays the Circular Reference toolbar to help you locate the error.

> NOTE

With subsequent circular reference errors, Excel displays a different error message that includes instructions on how to access the Circular Reference toolbar. If you click OK, no Help appears and you must select the Circular Reference toolbar yourself from the toolbars submenu on the View menu.

Sometimes you want to use circular references, as discussed in the next section. If this is the case, click Cancel.

? SEE ALSO

For more on Excel's auditing features, see "Auditing and Documenting a Worksheet," page 288.

Use the Circular Reference toolbar (View menu, Toolbars submenu) to help track down the problem reference with Excel's built-in auditing features. Click the Trace Precedents or Trace Dependents button to draw tracer arrows on the worksheet. These arrows show you a visual path to all the cells involved, as shown in Figure 6-23.

FIGURE 6-23.

If you click OK in the message box shown in Figure 6-22, Excel displays a large blue dot in the offending cell and displays the Circular Reference toolbar.

Click the Trace Precedents button, and Excel draws a line from the cell that contains the formula with the circular reference to cell C1, the only other cell involved.

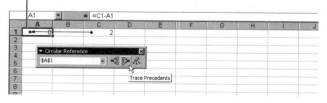

Intentional Circular References

Many circular references can be resolved. The worksheet in Figure 6-24 displays a set of circular formulas. Cells A1:A3 are formatted to show the underlying formula in each cell. This set of formulas is circular because the formula in A1 depends on the value in A3, and the formula in A3 depends on the value in A1.

FIGURE 6-24.

This worksheet contains a circular reference.

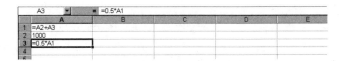

> To switch between displaying resulting values (the default) and displaying the underlying formulas on a worksheet, press Ctrl+` (backwards apostrophe on the tilde ~ key).

To resolve this kind of circular reference, select the Iteration option on the Calculation tab of the Options dialog box. Excel will recalculate, a specified number of times, all the cells in open worksheets that contain a circular reference. Each time Excel recalculates the formulas, the results in the cells get closer to the correct values.

When you select the Iteration option, Excel sets the Maximum Iterations option to 100 and the Maximum Change option to 0.001. Thus, Excel recalculates a maximum of 100 times or until the values change less than 0.001 between iterations, whichever comes first. For the formulas in Figure 6-24, we selected the Iteration option and accepted the default settings for Maximum Iterations and Maximum Change. As a result, the first iteration of the formula in cell A3 returns 999.9998, and the Calculate message in the status bar tells you that more iterations are possible. Pressing F9 recalculates the value, bringing it closer to 1000. The initial iteration returned 999.9995 because Excel calculated the value to within 0.001; each recalculation brings the value closer. If Maximum Change was set to 0.0001, the value would immediately appear as 1000.

Excel does not repeat the *Cannot resolve circular reference* message if it fails to resolve the reference. You must determine when the answer is close enough.

The process just described is called *convergence*: the difference between results becomes smaller with each iterative calculation. In the opposite process, *divergence,* the difference between results becomes larger with each calculation. Excel continues iterations until it completes

II

Worksheets

the number you specify. Excel can perform 100 iterations in seconds, but be sure the Calculation option is set to Manual; otherwise, Excel recalculates the circular references every time you make a cell entry.

Precision of Numeric Values

Excel stores numbers with as much as 15-digit accuracy and converts any digits after the fifteenth to zeros. Excel drops any digits after the fifteenth in a decimal fraction. In addition, Excel displays numbers that are too long for their cells in scientific notation. The following table lists some examples of how Excel treats integers and decimal fractions longer than 15 digits when they are entered in cells with the default column width of 8.43 characters:

Entry	Displayed Value	Underlying Value
123456789012345678	1.23457E+17	123456789012345000
1.23456789012345678	1.234568	1.23456789012345
1234567890.12345678	1234567890	1234567890.12345
123456789012345.678	1.23457E+14	123456789012345

Excel can calculate positive values approximately as large as 9.99E+307 and approximately as small as 1.00E-307. If a formula results in a value outside this range, Excel stores the number as text and assigns a #NUM! error value to the formula cell.

The Precision As Displayed Option

SEE ALSO

For more information about number formatting, see Chapter 7, "Formatting a Worksheet."

Your worksheet can appear erroneous if you use rounded values. For example, if you use cell formatting to display numbers in currency format with two decimal places, the value 10.006 is displayed as the rounded value $10.01. If you add 10.006 and 10.006, the correct result is 20.012. However, if all these numbers are formatted as currency, the worksheet displays $10.01 and $10.01, and the rounded result of $20.01. The result is correct, as far as rounding goes, but its appearance may be unacceptable for a particular purpose, such as a presentation.

You can correct this problem by selecting the Precision As Displayed option on the Calculation tab of the Options dialog box. However, you should exercise caution when you use this option, because the underlying values in your worksheet are actually changed to their displayed values. In other words, if a cell containing the value 10.006 is formatted as currency, selecting the Precision As Displayed option *permanently* changes this value to 10.01.

Formatting a Worksheet

I n this chapter, you'll learn how to assign and change the formats, alignments, and fonts of text and numeric cell entries. (We'll save the Format menu's Sheet command for Chapter 9, "Worksheets and Windows.") You'll also learn how to put template files to good use and how to change the way Microsoft Excel 2000 appears on your computer's screen. Later in the chapter, we'll explain Excel's outlining features.

Why use formats? Compare Figure 7-1 with Figure 7-2 and you'll have the answer. Although the information is basically the same in both worksheets, the worksheet in Figure 7-2 is formatted and therefore much easier to read and interpret.

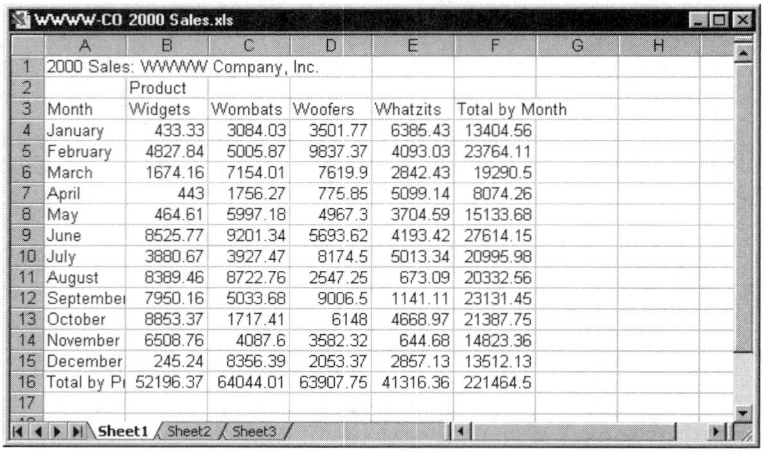

FIGURE 7-1.

All entries in this worksheet are displayed in their default formats.

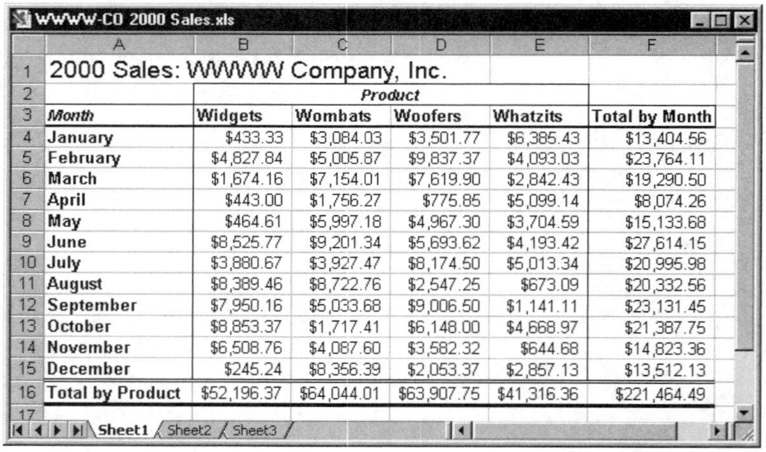

	A	B	C	D	E	F	G	H
1	2000 Sales: WWWW Company, Inc.							
2		Product						
3	Month	Widgets	Wombats	Woofers	Whatzits	Total by Month		
4	January	433.33	3084.03	3501.77	6385.43	13404.56		
5	February	4827.84	5005.87	9837.37	4093.03	23764.11		
6	March	1674.16	7154.01	7619.9	2842.43	19290.5		
7	April	443	1756.27	775.85	5099.14	8074.26		
8	May	464.61	5997.18	4967.3	3704.59	15133.68		
9	June	8525.77	9201.34	5693.62	4193.42	27614.15		
10	July	3880.67	3927.47	8174.5	5013.34	20995.98		
11	August	8389.46	8722.76	2547.25	673.09	20332.56		
12	September	7950.16	5033.68	9006.5	1141.11	23131.45		
13	October	8853.37	1717.41	6148	4668.97	21387.75		
14	November	6508.76	4087.6	3582.32	644.68	14823.36		
15	December	245.24	8356.39	2053.37	2857.13	13512.13		
16	Total by Pr	52196.37	64044.01	63907.75	41316.36	221464.5		
17								

FIGURE 7-2.

The formatted worksheet is easier to read.

	A	B	C	D	E	F
1	2000 Sales: WWWWW Company, Inc.					
2			Product			
3	*Month*	Widgets	Wombats	Woofers	Whatzits	Total by Month
4	January	$433.33	$3,084.03	$3,501.77	$6,385.43	$13,404.56
5	February	$4,827.84	$5,005.87	$9,837.37	$4,093.03	$23,764.11
6	March	$1,674.16	$7,154.01	$7,619.90	$2,842.43	$19,290.50
7	April	$443.00	$1,756.27	$775.85	$5,099.14	$8,074.26
8	May	$464.61	$5,997.18	$4,967.30	$3,704.59	$15,133.68
9	June	$8,525.77	$9,201.34	$5,693.62	$4,193.42	$27,614.15
10	July	$3,880.67	$3,927.47	$8,174.50	$5,013.34	$20,995.98
11	August	$8,389.46	$8,722.76	$2,547.25	$673.09	$20,332.56
12	September	$7,950.16	$5,033.68	$9,006.50	$1,141.11	$23,131.45
13	October	$8,853.37	$1,717.41	$6,148.00	$4,668.97	$21,387.75
14	November	$6,508.76	$4,087.60	$3,582.32	$644.68	$14,823.36
15	December	$245.24	$8,356.39	$2,053.37	$2,857.13	$13,512.13
16	Total by Product	$52,196.37	$64,044.01	$63,907.75	$41,316.36	$221,464.49
17						

We'll discuss the menu and toolbar methods of applying formats as we go through this chapter.

Assigning and Removing Formats

The Cells command on the Format menu controls most of the formatting you'll apply to the cells in your worksheets. Formatting is easy: simply select the cell or range and choose the appropriate Format menu commands. For example, to apply a number format to cells B4:F16 in Figure 7-1, follow these steps:

1 Select cells B4:F16.

2 From the Format menu, choose Cells.

3 Click the Number tab if it is not already active.

4 From the Category list box, select Currency.

5 Set the Decimal Places box to 2.

6 Click OK to return to the worksheet.

As you can see in Figure 7-2, Excel changes the numbers in selected cells to display currency values. (You might need to increase the column width to see the currency values.)

TIP

> If you want to quickly display the Format Cells dialog box, press Ctrl+1.

A formatted cell remains formatted until you remove the format or apply a new format. When you overwrite or edit an entry, you need not reformat the cell. To remove all assigned formats, follow these steps:

1 Select the cell or range.

2 From the Edit menu, choose Clear and then Formats.

SEE ALSO

For more information about the Clear command, see "Clearing Cell Contents and Formats," page 250.

To also remove the values in cells, select All from the Clear submenu.

> **Formatting before You Copy**
>
> When you copy a cell, you copy both its contents and its formats. If you then paste this information into another cell, the formats of the source cell replace the old formats. You can take advantage of this time-saver by formatting your source cell before you choose the Copy and Paste commands or buttons or the Fill command. *For more information about copying and pasting, see Chapter 8, "Editing a Worksheet."*

II

Worksheets

NOTE

> To format a common set of cells in two or more worksheets in the same work-book, you can use the group editing feature. *(See "Editing Groups of Sheets Simultaneously," page 326.)*

Formatting with Toolbars

Figure 7-3 shows the Standard toolbar, which contains the Format Painter button. This button lets you copy formats from selected cells to other cells and worksheets in the current workbook and even in other workbooks.

FIGURE 7-3.

Copy the formats of selected cells.

Format Painter

 **TIP**

> To see the entire Formatting toolbar, double-click the vertical bar on its left end, or click the vertical bar and drag the toolbar away from its "docked" loca-tion. *For more information about toolbars, see Chapter 3, "Toolbars and Menus."*

You can copy formats to another location by taking the following steps:

1 Select the cell or cells from which you want to copy formats.

2 Click the Format Painter button. (The pointer appears with a small paintbrush icon next to it.)

3 Select the cell or cells to which you want to copy formats.

If you copy formats from a range of cells and then select a single cell when you paste, the Format Painter pastes the entire range of formats, from the selected cell down and to the right. If, however, you select a range of cells when you paste formats, the Format Painter follows the shape of the copied range. If the range you want to format is a differ-ent shape from the copied range, the pattern is repeated or truncated as necessary.

As Figure 7-4 shows, Excel also provides the Formatting toolbar, which is, as its name suggests, designed specifically for formatting.

To apply a format with a toolbar button, select a cell or range and then click the button with the mouse. To remove the format, click the button again.

FIGURE 7-4.

The Formatting toolbar.

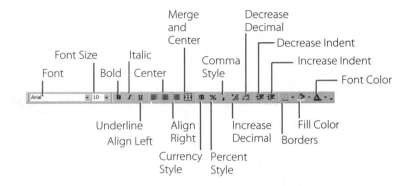

Formatting Individual Characters

? SEE ALSO

For more information about formatting individual characters, see "Selecting Font Styles and Effects," page 188.

You can apply formatting to the individual characters of a text entry in a cell as well as to the entire cell. Select the individual characters and then use toolbar buttons or choose the Cells command from the Format menu and apply the attributes you want. Press Enter to see the results of formatting individual characters. Figure 7-5 shows examples of formatted characters.

FIGURE 7-5.

You can format individual characters within a cell.

▷ NOTE

If you try to apply formats to the individual characters of a numeric entry, the formats disappear when you press Enter because they are overridden by the numeric format of the cell. To format digits within a number, you can convert a numeric entry to a text entry by preceding it with a single quotation mark.

Using AutoFormat

? SEE ALSO

For more information about font styles, see "Formatting Fonts," page 186.

You can save a lot of time by using the AutoFormat command on the Format menu. Excel's automatic formats are predefined combinations of formats: number, font, alignment, border, pattern, column width, and row height.

Build Your Own "Super Formatting" Toolbar

Using Microsoft Excel's toolbar customization features, you can create a toolbar for just about any purpose. After you get the hang of it, you'll want to create a few toolbars containing buttons for the commands you use most often. For example, we created this "Super Formatting" toolbar that contains a number of useful formatting buttons, including some that are not available on any other toolbar:

To construct the "Super Formatting" toolbar, follow these steps:

1 From the View menu, choose Toolbars and then Customize to display the Customize dialog box.

2 Click the New button on the Toolbars tab, type *Super Formatting* in the Toolbar Name box and click OK. (A small toolbar appears next to the Customize dialog box. If necessary, move it to a new location by dragging the title bar.)

3 Click the Commands tab.

4 Click Format in the Categories list.

5 Select a command button you want to add and drag it to the new toolbar. Repeat for each additional button. (We added the Style box; the Merge Cells and Unmerge Cells buttons; the Increase Font size, Decrease Font size, and Font color buttons; the Vertical Text, Rotate Text Up, Rotate Text Down, Angle Text Downward, and the Angle Text Upward buttons; the Cycle Font Color button; the two shading buttons; and the Auto Format button.) The new toolbar enlarges to hold each button you add.

6 Click Close when you finish adding buttons.

Now you can display the "Super Formatting" toolbar along with the regular Formatting toolbar whenever you are constructing a new worksheet. You can even put menus on toolbars: for example, you could move the Format menu from the main menu bar to the Super Formatting toolbar. *For more information about customizing toolbars, see Chapter 3, "Toolbars and Menus."*

NOTE

You can also use the AutoFormat button, which corresponds to the AutoFormat command, to apply the last format selected from the AutoFormat dialog box. You can add the AutoFormat button to a toolbar by selecting the Formatting category on the Commands tab in the Customize dialog box. *For information about customizing toolbars, see Chapter 3, "Toolbars and Menus."*

The AutoFormat command uses existing formulas and text labels to determine how to apply formatting. You can use other formatting commands after you use AutoFormat to adjust the overall appearance. If you don't like the way something looks, you can choose Undo AutoFormat from the Edit menu and then try adding blank columns or rows to set off areas you don't want AutoFormat to change. You can also select only those regions of a worksheet that you want AutoFormat to affect.

Automatic Format Extension

Automatic formatting became a little bit smarter in Excel 2000. Officially dubbed "extend list formatting," this new feature allows you to add data to a previously formatted table without having to format the new cells manually. For example, let's say you want to add another column for Dik-Diks to the existing table in the following figure.

	A	B	C	D	E	F	G
1	**Odd Pets With Short Names, Inc.**						
2			*2000 Sales*				
3		*Yaks*	*Emus*	*Eels*	*Ibises*	*Dik-Diks*	
4	*January*	$ 454.00	$ 752.00	$ 109.00	$ 234.00	$ 233.00	
5	*February*	$ 547.00	$ 884.00	$ 294.00	$ 935.00	$ 145.00	
6	*March*	$ 156.00	$ 552.00	$ 739.00	$ 477.00	$ 256.00	
7	*April*	$ 841.00	$ 315.00	$ 484.00	$ 845.00		
8	*May*	$ 645.00	$ 579.00	$ 274.00	$ 914.00		
9	*June*	$ 585.00	$ 788.00	$ 191.00	$ 250.00		
10	*July*	$ 954.00	$ 476.00	$ 839.00	$ 493.00		
11	*August*	$ 615.00	$ 432.00	$ 234.00	$ 358.00		
12	*September*	$ 187.00	$ 744.00	$ 912.00	$ 166.00		
13	*October*	$ 189.00	$ 802.00	$ 156.00	$ 772.00		
14	*November*	$ 354.00	$ 613.00	$ 898.00	$ 656.00		
15	*December*	$ 474.00	$ 345.00	$ 773.00	$ 837.00		
16	**TOTALS**	$6,001.00	$7,282.00	$5,903.00	$6,937.00		
17							
18							

Simply select cell F3 and type *Dik-Diks*. When you press Enter, Excel correctly surmises that you want the new entry to use the same formatting as the adjacent cell in column E. If you continue entering values in cells F4, F5, and F6, Excel extends the formats from the adjacent cells automatically.

II

Worksheets

To use AutoFormat, follow these steps:

1 Enter data in your worksheet, such as that shown earlier in Figure 7-1 on page 156.

2 Specify the *current region* by selecting any cell in the group of cells you want to format. (The current region is the contiguous block of cells that contains the active cell and is surrounded by blank columns, blank rows, or worksheet borders. AutoFormat automatically determines the current region and selects it.) Alternatively, you can select the specific range of cells you want to format.

3 From the Format menu, choose the AutoFormat command. The cell selection expands to include the entire current region, and a dialog box like the one in Figure 7-6 appears.

FIGURE 7-6.

The AutoFormat dialog box offers a selection of predefined formats you can apply to your worksheet data.

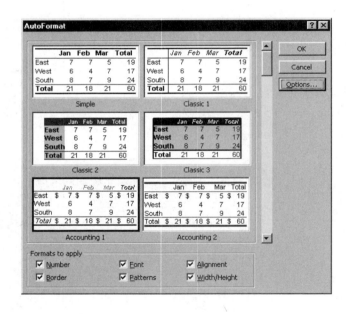

4 In the AutoFormat dialog box, click Options to display the Formats To Apply section, shown in Figure 7-6. (If you click an option to clear a format type, the Sample displays adjust accordingly.)

5 Select a format and then click OK. For example, if you entered the data as shown in Figure 7-1 and selected the Classic 2 table format, your worksheet would look like the one in Figure 7-7.

FIGURE 7-7.

In seconds, you can transform a raw worksheet into a presentation-quality table with the AutoFormat command.

	A	B	C	D	E	F	G
	WWWW-CO 2000 Sales.xls						
1	2000 Sales: WWWWW Company, Inc.						
2		Product					
3	Month	Widgets	Wombats	Woofers	Whatzits	Total by Month	
4	January	433.33	3084.03	3501.77	6385.43	13404.56	
5	February	4827.84	5005.87	9837.37	4093.03	23764.11	
6	March	1674.16	7154.01	7619.9	2842.43	19290.5	
7	April	443	1756.27	775.85	5099.14	8074.26	
8	May	464.61	5997.18	4967.3	3704.59	15133.68	
9	June	8525.77	9201.34	5693.62	4193.42	27614.15	
10	July	3880.67	3927.47	8174.5	5013.34	20995.98	
11	August	8389.46	8722.76	2547.25	673.09	20332.56	
12	September	7950.16	5033.68	9006.5	1141.11	23131.45	
13	October	8853.37	1717.41	6148	4668.97	21387.75	
14	November	6508.76	4087.6	3582.32	644.68	14823.36	
15	December	245.24	8356.39	2053.37	2857.13	13512.13	
16	Total by Product	52196.37	64044.01	63907.75	41316.36	221464.49	
17							

Sheet1 / Sheet2 / Sheet3 /

6 Select a cell outside the table to remove the highlight from the current region and see the effect of your changes.

Formatting Numbers and Text

Excel's Format commands let you control the display of numeric values and modify the display of text entries. From the Format menu, choose the Cells command (or simply press Ctrl+1) and then click the Number tab in the Format Cells dialog box, shown in Figure 7-8 on the next page.

TIP

Always select a cell that contains a number you want to format before opening the Format Cells dialog box. That way, you can see the results in the sample box.

SEE ALSO

For information about built-in date and time formats, see Chapter 13, "Dates and Times."

Keep in mind the difference between underlying and displayed worksheet values. Formats do not affect the underlying numeric or text values in cells. For example, if you enter a number with six decimal places in a cell that is formatted with two decimal places, the number is displayed with only two decimal places, but the underlying value is not changed. Excel uses the underlying value in calculations.

II

Worksheets

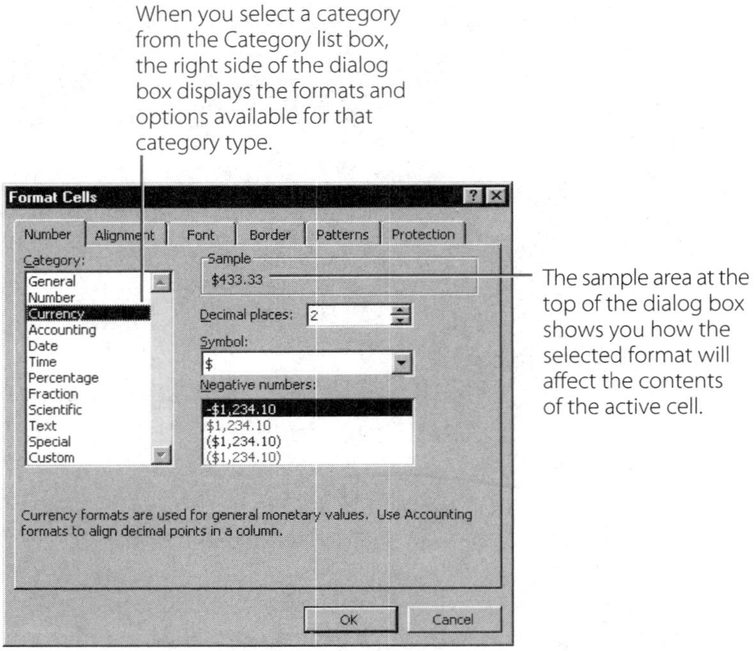

FIGURE 7-8.

The Format Cells dia-
log box includes the
Number tab, which
offers 12 built-in
numeric formats.

When you select a category
from the Category list box,
the right side of the dialog
box displays the formats and
options available for that
category type.

The sample area at the
top of the dialog box
shows you how the
selected format will
affect the contents
of the active cell.

The General Format

The General format is the first category in the Format Cells dialog
box. Unless you specifically change the format of a cell, Excel displays any text or numbers you enter in the General format. Except in
the three cases listed below, the General format displays exactly what
you type. For example, if you enter *123.45*, the cell displays 123.45.
Here are the three exceptions:

■ The General Format will abbreviate numbers too long to display
in a cell. For example, the number *12345678901234* (an integer) is displayed as 1.23457E+13 in a standard-width cell. Long
decimal values are rounded or displayed in scientific notation.
Thus, if you enter *123456.7812345* in a standard-width cell, the
General format displays the number as 123456.8. The actual
entered values are preserved and used in all calculations, regardless of the display format.

■ The General format does not display trailing zeros. For example,
the number *123.0* is displayed as 123.

■ A decimal fraction entered without a number to the left of the decimal point is displayed with a zero. For example, *.123* is displayed as 0.123.

The Number Formats

The Number category contains options that display numbers in integer, fixed-decimal, and punctuated formats, as shown in Figure 7-9. *For information about creating numeric formats, see "Creating Custom Numeric Formats," page 170.*

FIGURE 7-9.

Use the Number category for general purpose, noncurrency numeric formatting.

Select the number of decimal places to display (0 to 30) by typing or scrolling the value in the Decimal Places box. For example, selecting 2 decimal places displays 1234.567 as 1234.57, 1234.5 as 1234.50, and 1234 as 1234.00.

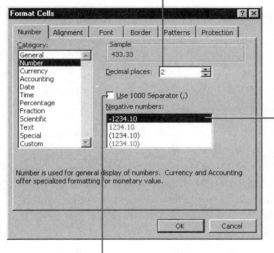

Select the Negative Numbers option to display negative numbers preceded by a minus sign, in red, in parentheses, or in both red and parentheses.

Select the Use 1000 Separator (,) option to add commas between hundreds and thousands, and so on. For example, with Use 1000 Separator, and 2 decimal places selected, Excel displays 1234.567 as 1,234.57.

The Currency Formats

The four Currency formats are similar to the formats in the Number category except that instead of selecting the thousand separator

II

Worksheets

(which accompanies all currency symbols by default), you can select which currency symbol, if any, precedes the number. Select the currency symbol from the drop-down list of worldwide currency symbols.

All of the Currency formats produce a blank space (the width of a close parenthesis) on the right side of positive values, ensuring that decimal points align in a column of similarly formatted positive and negative numbers.

TIP

> You apply a two-decimal-place Currency format when you click the Currency Style button on the Formatting toolbar. You apply a two-decimal-place Currency format *without currency symbols* when you click the Comma Style button on the Formatting toolbar.

The Accounting Formats

SEE ALSO

For more information about the accounting underline font formats, see "Formatting Fonts," page 186.

Excel provides special formats that address the needs of accounting professionals (and benefit the rest of us as well). When these formats are used with the accounting underline font formats, you can easily create P&L statements, balance sheets, and other schedules that conform to generally accepted accounting principles.

The Accounting format corresponds roughly to the Currency format—you can display numbers with and without your choice of currency symbols, and you can specify the number of decimal places. The big difference is that the Accounting format displays any currency symbol at the left of the cell, whereas the numbers are at the right as usual, as shown in Figure 7-10. The result is that both currency symbols and numbers are vertically aligned in the same column. Numbers with similar currency-symbol and noncurrency-symbol formats line up properly in a column.

FIGURE 7-10.

The Accounting format aligns currency symbols to the left of a cell and numbers to the right.

	A	B
1	accounting format	currency format
2	$ 123,456.78	$123,456.78
3	$ (123,456.78)	($123,456.78)
4		

Another way in which the Accounting format differs from the Currency format is that negative values are always displayed in black rather than in red (which is the more common format for currency). As shown in Figure 7-10, the red number appears as a light gray. Also, the Accounting format treats zero values as dashes. The spacing of the dashes depends on whether you select decimal places. If you include two decimal places, the dashes line up under the decimal point.

The Percentage Formats

The formats in the Percentage category display numbers as percentages. The decimal point of the formatted number shifts two places to the right, and a percent sign appears at the end of the number. For example, if you choose a percentage format without decimal places *0.1234* will be displayed as 12%; selecting two decimal places displays *0.1234* as 12.34%.

 TIP

You can also apply a percentage format without decimals by clicking the Percent Style button on the Formatting toolbar.

The Fraction Formats

The formats in the Fraction category shown in Figure 7-11 display fractional amounts as actual fractions rather than as decimal values. These formats are particularly useful for entering stock prices or measurements. The first three Fraction formats use single-digit, double-digit, and triple-digit numerators and denominators.

For example, the single-digit format displays *123.456* as 123 1/2, rounding the display to the nearest value that can be represented as a single-digit fraction. If you enter the same number in a cell to which the double-digit format has been applied, Excel uses the additional precision allowed by the format and displays 123 26/57. The underlying value does not change in either case.

The remaining six fraction formats allow you to specify the exact denominator you want, as shown in Figure 7-11 on the next page.

as shown in Figure 7-11 on the next page.

FIGURE 7-11.

Excel provides ample fraction formatting options.

If you enter 123.456 in a cell formatted using the As Sixteenths format, Excel displays 123 7/16. If you enter 123.5 into the same cell, Excel displays 123 8/16.

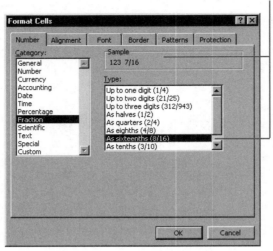

The Scientific (Exponential) Formats

The Scientific formats display numbers in exponential notation. For example, the two-decimal-place Scientific format displays the number *98765432198* as 9.88E+10.

The number 9.88E+10 is 9.88 times 10 to the tenth power. The symbol E stands for the word *exponent,* a synonym here for the words *10 to the nth power.* The expression *10 to the tenth power* means ten times itself ten times, or 10,000,000,000. Multiplying this value by 9.88 gives you 98800000000, an approximation of 98765432198. Increasing the decimal places allows you to increase the precision of the display, but at the possible cost of making the displayed number wider than the cell.

You can also use the Scientific format to display very small numbers. For example, this format displays *0.000000009* as 9.00E-09, which is 9 times 10 to the negative ninth power. The expression *10 to the negative ninth power* means 1 divided by 10 to the ninth power, 1 divided by 10 nine times, or 0.000000001. Multiplying this number by 9 gives our original number, 0.000000009.

The Text Format

? **SEE ALSO**

For more information about creating text formats, see "Formatting Positive, Negative, Zero, and Text Entries," page 175. For more information about creating custom formats, see "Creating Custom Numeric Formats," page 170.

Applying the Text format to a cell indicates that the entry in the cell is to be treated as text. For example, a numeric value is normally right-aligned in its cell. If you apply the Text format to the cell, however, the value is left-aligned as if it were a text entry.

For all practical purposes, a numeric constant formatted as text is still considered a number because of Excel's inherent ability to recognize numeric values. However, if you apply the Text format to a cell that contains a formula, the formula is considered text and is displayed as such in the cell. Any other formulas that refer to a formula formatted as text will either return the text value itself (as in a formula that is simply a direct reference to the text-formatted cell with no additional calculations) or the #VALUE error value.

★ **TIP**

> Formatting a formula as text is useful as a way of seeing the effects of "removing" a formula from a worksheet model without actually deleting it. You can format a formula as text so it is visible on the worksheet and then locate the other dependent formulas that produce error values. After you apply the Text format, however, you must click the formula bar and press Enter to "recalculate" the worksheet and change the formula to a displayed text value. To restore the formula to its original condition, apply the desired numeric format to the cell, click the formula bar again, and press Enter.

The Special Formats

The four Special formats are a result of many requests from users. These generally noncalculated numbers include two postal code formats, a phone number format (complete with the area code in parentheses), and a Social Security Number format. Each of these special formats lets you quickly type numbers without having to enter the punctuation characters.

If you choose the Phone Number format, shown in Figure 7-12 on the next page, Excel applies the parentheses and the dash for you in the format, which makes it much easier to enter a lot of numbers at once, since you don't have to move your hand from the keypad. In addition, the numbers you enter actually remain numbers instead of becoming text entries, which would be the case if you entered parentheses or dashes in the cell. Also, the leading zeros that often appear in postal codes are retained. Normally, if you enter *04321*, Excel drops the zero and displays 4321. But if you use the Zip Code format, Excel correctly displays the code as 04321.

FIGURE 7-12.

Excel provides several frequently requested number formats in the Special category.

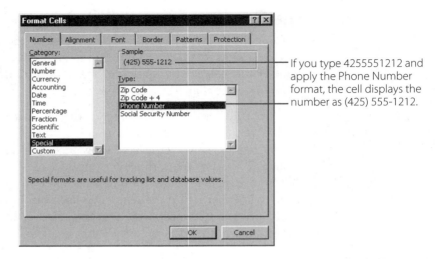

If you type 4255551212 and apply the Phone Number format, the cell displays the number as (425) 555-1212.

If you place a 1 in front of a phone number, Excel considers it part of the area code and includes it inside the parentheses.

Formatting Numbers as You Type

SEE ALSO

For information about entering dates and a complete listing of date and time formats, see Chapter 13, "Dates and Times."

You can include special formatting characters such as dollar signs, percent signs, commas, or fractions to format numbers as you enter them. When you type in numeric entry characters that represent a format Excel recognizes, Excel applies that format to the cell. For example, if you type *$45.00*, Excel interprets your entry as the value 45 formatted as currency with two decimal places. Only the value 45 appears in the formula bar, but the formatted value, $45.00, appears in the cell. If you type *1 3/8* (with a single space between the 1 and the 3), 1 3/8 appears in the cell and 1.375 appears in the formula bar. If you type *3/8*, however, 8-Mar appears in the cell. Assuming you make the entry in the year 2000, 3/8/2000 appears in the formula bar. To display 3/8 in the cell as a fraction, so that 0.375 appears in the formula bar, you must type *0 3/8* (with a space between the 0 and the 3).

Creating Custom Numeric Formats

You use the Number tab in the Format Cells dialog box to create custom formats by selecting the Custom category and typing special formatting symbols in the Type edit box. Excel adds your new format to the bottom of the list of formatting codes in the Custom category. Use the symbols in Table 7-1 on page 172 to create custom formats.

Creating New Formats

Often, you can use one of Excel's existing custom formats as a starting point for creating your own format. To build on an existing format, first select the cells you want to format. From the Format menu, choose the Cells command (or press Ctrl+1), click the Number tab, and click the Custom category. Select the format you want to change from the Type list box, and then edit the contents of the edit box. The original format is not affected, and the new format is added to the list in the Type list box.

To create a format to display a date with a long-format day of the week, month, day, and year, follow the steps illustrated in Figure 7-13:

FIGURE 7-13.

Create new custom formats based on existing ones.

FIGURE 7-13.

Create new custom formats based on existing ones.

1 Click Custom in the Category list box and then select the d-mmm-yy format.

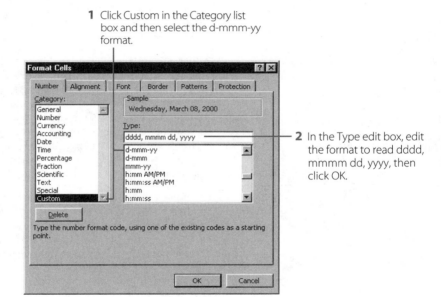

2 In the Type edit box, edit the format to read dddd, mmmm dd, yyyy, then click OK.

 TIP

Saving your workbook saves new formats, but to carry special formats from one workbook to another, you must copy and paste a cell with the Custom format. For easy access to special formats, consider saving them in one workbook.

TABLE 7-1. **Symbols Used to Create Custom Formats**

Symbol	Meaning
0	Digit placeholder. Ensures that a specified number of digits appear on each side of the decimal point. For example, if the format is 0.000, the value .987 is displayed as 0.987. If the format is 0.0000, the value .987 is displayed as 0.9870. If a number has more digits to the right of the decimal point than 0s specified in the format, the number is rounded. For example, if the format is 0.00, the value .987 is displayed as 0.99; if the format is 0.0, .987 is rounded to 1.0.
?	Digit placeholder. Follows the same rules as the 0 placeholder, except that space is left for insignificant zeros on either side of the decimal point. This placeholder allows you to align numbers on the decimal points. For example, 1.4 and 1.45 would line up on the decimal point if both were formatted as 0.??.
#	Digit placeholder. Works like 0, except that extra zeros do not appear if the number has fewer digits on either side of the decimal point than #s specified in the format. This symbol shows Excel where to display commas or other separating symbols. The format #,###, for example, tells Excel to display a comma after every third digit to the left of the decimal point. If you want Excel to include commas and display at least one digit to the left of the decimal point in all cases, specify the format #,##0.
.	Decimal point. Determines how many digits (0 or #) appear to the right and left of the decimal point. If the format contains only #s to the left of this symbol, Excel begins numbers smaller than 1 with a decimal point. To avoid this, use 0 as the first digit placeholder to the left of the decimal point instead of #.
%	Percentage indicator. Multiplies by 100 and inserts the % character.
/	Fraction format character. Displays the fractional part of a number in a nondecimal format. The number of digit placeholders that surround this character determines the accuracy of the display. For example, the decimal fraction 0.269 when formatted with # ?/? is displayed as 1/4, but when formatted with # ???/??? is displayed as 46/171.
$ - + / ( ) space	Standard formatting characters. Enter these characters directly into your format.

(continued)

TABLE 7-1.   *continued*

Symbol	Meaning
,	Thousands separator. Uses commas to separate hundreds from thousands, thousands from millions, and so on, if the format contains a comma surrounded by #s, 0s, or ?s. In addition, the comma acts as a rounding and scaling agent. One comma at the end of a format is used by Excel to tell it to round a number and display it in thousands; two commas tell Excel to round to the nearest million. For example, the format code #,###,###, would round 4567890 to 4,568, whereas the format code #,###,###,, would round it to 5.
E- E+ e- e+	Scientific format characters. Displays the number in scientific notation and inserts E or e in the displayed value if a format contains one 0 or # to the right of an E-, E+, e-, or e+. The number of 0s or #s to the right of the E or e determines the minimum number of digits in the exponent. Use E- or e- to place a negative sign by negative exponents; use E+ or e+ to place a negative sign by negative exponents and a positive sign by positive exponents.
\	Literal demarcation character. Precede each character you want to include in the format (except for : $ - + / ( ) and space) with a backslash. Excel does not display the backslash. For example, the format code #,##0" "\D;-#,##0" "\C displays positive numbers followed by a space and a D and negative numbers followed by a space and a C. To insert several characters, use the quotation-mark technique described in the "Text" table entry.
_	Underscore. Leaves space equal to the width of the next character. For example, _) leaves a space equal to the width of the close parenthesis. Use this formatting character for alignment purposes.
"Text"	Literal character string. Works like the backslash technique except that all text can be included within one set of double quotation marks without separate demarcation characters for each literal character.
*	Repetition initiator. Repeats the next character in the format enough times to fill the column width. Use only one asterisk in a format.
@	Text placeholder. If the cell contains text, the placeholder inserts that text in the format where the @ appears. For example, the format code "This is a "@"." displays *This is a debit.* in a cell containing the text debit.

The following table lists Excel's built-in codes for the Custom category and indicates how these codes relate to the other categories on the Number tab. (Note that Date and Time codes are covered in Chapter 13, "Dates and Times.")

Category	Format Codes
General	No specific format
Number	0
	0.00
	#,##0
	#,##0.00
	#,##0_);(#,##0)
	#,##0_);[Red](#,##0)
	#,##0.00_);(#,##0.00)
	#,##0.00_);[Red](#,##0.00)
Currency	$#,##0_);($#,##0)
	$#,##0_);[Red]($#,##0)
	$#,##0.00_);($#,##0.00)
	$#,##0.00_);[Red]($#,##0.00)
Percentage	0%
	0.00%
Scientific	.00E+00
	##0.0E+0
Fraction	# ?/?
	# ??/??
Date	See Chapter 13
Time	See Chapter 13
Text	@
Accounting	_($* #,##0_);_($* (#,##0);_($* "-"_);_(@_)
	_(* #,##0_);_(* (#,##0);_(* "-"_);_(@_)
	_($* #,##0.00_);_($* (#,##0.00);_($* "-"??_);_(@_)
	_(* #,##0.00_);_(* (#,##0.00);_(* "-"??_);_(@_)

Formatting Positive, Negative, Zero, and Text Entries

Excel assigns different formats to positive and negative currency values in your worksheet. You can also specify formats for positive and negative values when you create custom formats, and you can specify how you want zero and text values to appear.

You can create custom formats with as many as four parts, with the portions separated by semicolons, like this:

Positive format; Negative format; Zero format; Text-value format

If your custom format includes only one part, Excel applies that format to positive, negative, and zero values. If your custom format includes two parts, the first part applies to positive and zero values; the second part applies only to negative values. Text-value formatting instructions must be the last element in the format specification, and unless you include text-value formatting, your format has no effect on text entries.

For example, suppose you create a billing statement worksheet, and you want to format the entries in the Amount Due column so that they display differently depending on the value in each cell. You might create this format:

"Amount due: "$#,##0.00_);"Credit: "($#,##0.00);"Let's call it even.";"Please note: "@

Creating a Part-Number Format

Suppose you're creating an inventory worksheet and you want all the entries in the range A5:A100 to appear in the format Part XXX-XXXX. To create this format, follow these steps:

1 Select the range A5:A100.

2 From the Format menu, choose the Cells command and click the Number tab.

3 Click the Custom category, select the contents of the Type edit box, and type Part ###-####.

4 Click OK.

Now begin making entries in column A. (You might have to widen the column. After you make an entry or two, select the entire column. From the Format menu, choose Column and then AutoFit Selection.) Type the numbers for each part; Excel will add the word Part and the hyphen. For example, if you select cell A10 and enter 1234567, Excel displays the entry as Part 123-4567.

II

Worksheets

The following table shows the effects of this format on various worksheet entries.

Entry	Display
12.98	Amount due: $12.98
-12.98	Credit: ($12.98)
0	Let's call it even.
This is not a bill	Please note: This is not a bill

Again, you would probably need to widen the column to display the results.

TIP

The Sample box at the top of the Format Cells dialog box shows how the value in the active cell appears in each format.

Adding Color to Formats

SEE ALSO
For more information about Excel's color palette, see "Changing the Available Colors," page 222.

You can also use the Number formats to change the color of selected cell entries. For example, you might use color to distinguish categories of information or to make totals stand out. You can even assign colors to selected numeric ranges so that, for example, all values above or below a specified threshold appear in a contrasting color. Of course, colors don't appear on printed worksheets unless you have a color printer.

NOTE

You can also change the color of a cell entry with the Font tab in the Format Cells dialog box or with the Font Color button on the Formatting toolbar; however, the colors you specify with the Number tab take precedence over the colors you specify with the Font tab or Font Color button.

To change the color of an entry, type the name of the new color, in brackets, in front of the definition of the Custom format in the Type edit box. For example, if you want the totals in row 16 of the worksheet shown in Figure 7-2 on page 156 to appear in blue and in Currency format with two decimal places, edit the $#,##0.00_);($#,##0.00) format as follows:

    [Blue]$#,##0.00_);($#,##0.00)

When you apply this format to a worksheet, positive and zero values appear in blue, text and negative values appear in black (the default).

You can simply type the colors in the Type edit box. For example, the format

   [Blue];[Red];[Yellow];[Green]

displays positive values in blue, negative values in red, zero values in yellow, and text in green.

You can specify the following color names in your formats: Black, Blue, Cyan, Green, Magenta, Red, White, and Yellow. You can also specify a color as COLOR*n,* where *n* is a number in the range 1 through 16. Excel selects the corresponding color from your worksheet's current 16-color palette. If that color is *dithered* (combines dots of two or more solid colors), Excel uses the nearest solid color.

⭐ **TIP**

> You can suppress all zero values in a worksheet. From the Tools menu, choose Options and click the View tab. Then click the Zero Values option in the Window Options section to deselect it.

Using Custom Format Condition Operators

You can also display numbers that depend on comparison values. To do so, you add a condition operator to the first two parts of the standard four-part custom format, replacing the positive and negative formats. The third format becomes the default format for values that don't match the other two conditions. You can use the conditional operators <, >, =, <=, >=, or < > with any number to define a format.

⭐ **TIP**

> An easier and more powerful way to apply formatting that changes depending on the cell value is to use the Conditional Formatting command on the Format menu. *See "Applying Conditional Formatting," page 198.*

For example, suppose you are tracking accounts receivable balances. To display accounts with a balance of more than $50,000 in blue, negative values in parentheses and in red, and all other values in the default color, create this format:

   [Blue][>50000]$#,##0.00_);[Red][<0]($#,##0.00);$#,##0.00_)

Using these condition operators can also be a powerful aid if you need to scale numbers. For example, if your company produces a product that requires a few milliliters of a compound for each unit and you make thousands of units every day, you will need to convert from milliliters to liters and kiloliters when you budget the usage. Excel can make this conversion with the following numeric format:

[>999999]#,##0,,_m"kl";[<999]##,_k_m"L";#_k"ml"

The following table shows the effects of this format on various worksheet entries:

Entry	Display
72	72 ml
7286957	7 kl
7632	8 L

As you can see, using a combination of the conditional format, the thousand separator, and the proportional space indicator can improve both the readability and effectiveness of your worksheet, without increasing the number of formulas.

Deleting Custom Formats

To delete a custom format, select the format on the Number tab of the Format Cells dialog box and click Delete. You cannot delete built-in formats.

The "Hidden" Number Format

To hide values in a worksheet, assign a null format to them. To create a null format, enter only the semicolon separator for that portion of the format. For example, to hide negative and zero values only, use this format:
  $#,##0.00;;

To hide all entries in a cell, use this format:
  ;;;

The null format hides the cell contents in the worksheet, but the entry is still visible in the formula bar. To hide the cell contents so they don't appear in the worksheet or the formula bar, use Excel's protection features. *For more information about Excel's protection features, see "Protecting Your Data," page 111.*

Aligning Cell Contents

? SEE ALSO

For information about the Merge Cells option, see "Merging Cells," page 200.

FIGURE 7-14.

Excel offers many alignment options.

The Alignment tab in the Format Cells dialog box, shown in Figure 7-14, positions text and numbers in cells. It also lets you create multiline text labels, repeat a series of characters within one or more cells, and orient text vertically or at any angle in cells.

When you select General, the default Horizontal alignment option, numeric values are right-aligned and text values are left-aligned.

The vertical drop-down list controls vertical alignment within cells.

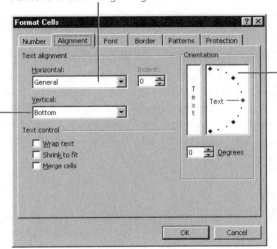

The Orientation controls allow you to align text at virtually any angle within a cell.

The Horizontal Text Alignment Options

The Left (Indent), Center, and Right options align the contents of the selected cells accordingly, overriding the default cell alignment. For example, in Figure 7-15, the entries in cells A1:B1 have the General alignment, so the number in cell B1 is right-aligned and the label in cell A1 is left-aligned. The entries in cells A5:B5 are right-aligned, and the entries in cells A6:B6 are centered.

FIGURE 7-15.

Use the Horizontal text alignment options to control placement of text from left to right.

	A	B	C	D
1	General		123	
2	Left (Indent) 0	123		
3	Left (Indent) 1	123		
4	Left (Indent) 2	123		
5	Right		123	
6	Center	123		
7	Center Across Selection			
8	Fill Fill Fill Fill Fill Fill Fill Fill Fill Fill Fill Fill Fill Fill Fill Fill			
9	The Wrap Text alignment format adjusts the row height to accommodate the entry within the current column width and makes the margins flush left and ragged right.	The Justify alignment format adjusts the row height to accommodate the entry within the current column width and makes the margins flush left and flush right.		
10				
11				
12				

Sheet1 / Sheet2 / Sheet3 /

Worksheets

II

The Left (Indent) option is linked to the Indent control, located next to the Horizontal drop-down list, as shown in Figure 7-14 on the previous page. Normally, when you apply Left (Indent), the value in the edit box of this control is zero—the standard left-alignment setting. Each time you increase this value by one, the entry in the cell begins one character width farther to the right. (One character width is approximately the width of the capital X in the Normal Style.) For example, in Figure 7-15 the entries in cells A2:B2 are left-aligned without indention. The entries in cells A3:B3 are indented by 1, and the entries in cells A4:B4 are indented by 2. The maximum indent value you can use is 15.

Centering Text across Columns

The Center Across Selection option in the Horizontal Text Alignment drop-down list centers text from one cell across all selected blank cells to the right, or to the next cell in the selection that contains text. For example, in Figure 7-15 the Center Across Selection format was applied to the range A7:B7. The centered text is in cell A7.

⭐ TIP

Although the results might look similar, the Center Across Selection alignment option works differently from the Merge And Center button on the Formatting toolbar. When you use the Merge And Center button, the cells you select are merged together—that is, they are actually replaced with a single cell. *For more information, see "Merging Cells," page 200.*

The Fill Option

The Fill option repeats your cell entry to fill the width of the column. For example, in Figure 7-16, on the next page, cell H10 contains a formula that averages the entries in cells H4 through H7. You can enter a row of greater-than signs to fill cells C10:G10 by following these steps:

1 Enter a single > (greater-than sign) in cell C10.

2 Select cells C10:G10.

3 From the Format menu, choose Cells and click the Alignment tab.

4 In the Horizontal Text Alignment drop-down list, select the Fill option and click OK.

Excel repeats the greater-than sign across cells C10:G10, as shown in Figure 7-16. Now, any character you type into any cell in this range will be filled across to the right. Although the cell range seems to contain many greater-than signs, the formula bar reveals that it actually contains a single greater-than sign. Like the other Format commands, the Fill option affects only the appearance, not the underlying contents, of the cell. Excel repeats the characters across the entire range, with no breaks between cells. Although they appear to contain entries, cells D10:G10 are empty.

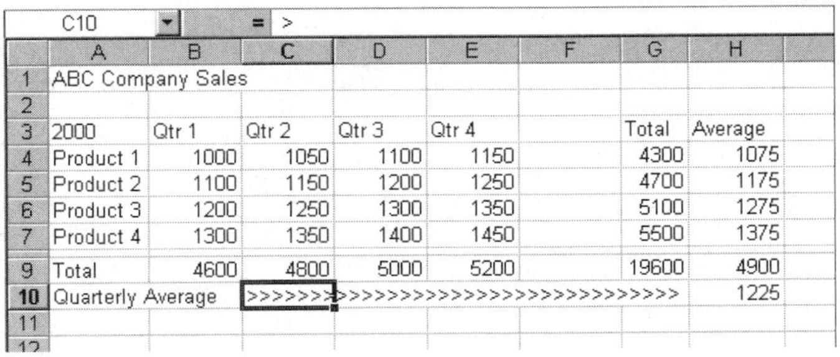

FIGURE 7-16.

Use the Fill option to repeat a character (or characters) across cells.

	A	B	C	D	E	F	G	H
1	ABC Company Sales							
2								
3	2000	Qtr 1	Qtr 2	Qtr 3	Qtr 4		Total	Average
4	Product 1	1000	1050	1100	1150		4300	1075
5	Product 2	1100	1150	1200	1250		4700	1175
6	Product 3	1200	1250	1300	1350		5100	1275
7	Product 4	1300	1350	1400	1450		5500	1375
9	Total	4600	4800	5000	5200		19600	4900
10	Quarterly Average	>>>>>>>>>>>>>>>>>>>>>>>>>>>>>>>>>>>>>>						1225
11								
12								

Usually the entries you repeat with the Fill alignment option are single characters, such as a hyphen (-), an asterisk (*), or an equal sign (=); however, you can also repeat multicharacter entries. For example, in Figure 7-15 on page 179, cell A8 contains the word *Fill* (followed by a space character), and the Fill option was applied to cells A8:B8.

Selecting Alignment from the Toolbars

You can select Left, Center, or Right alignment by clicking the corresponding buttons on the Formatting toolbar, shown in Figure 7-4 on page 159.

When you "turn on" one of the toolbar alignment options, its button appears as if it has been pressed to show that the option is activated. As a result, you can always glance at the toolbar to see if one of these alignment options has been applied to the active cell.

To turn an alignment option off (and return the active cell to General alignment), click the button a second time.

You can also apply the Left (Indent) alignment option using the Increase Indent button on the Standard toolbar. This button does not turn the alignment option off when clicked a second time, however. Instead, each click increases the indent by another character width. To reduce the indent, use the adjacent Decrease Indent button.

The Merge And Center button on the Formatting toolbar does two things: first, it merges the selected cells together to form a single cell, and then it applies center alignment to the cell. This button does not remove formatting or have any other effect when clicked a second time. *For more information about merged cells, see "Merging Cells," page 200.*

II

Worksheets

You might think it would be just as easy to type the repeating characters as it is to use Fill. However, the Fill option gives you two important advantages. First, if you adjust the column width, Excel increases or decreases the number of characters in the cell to accommodate the new column width. Second, you can repeat a single character or multiple characters across several adjacent cells.

NOTE

> Because the Fill option affects numeric values as well as text, it can cause a number to look like something it isn't. For example, if you apply the Fill option to a 10-character-wide cell that contains the number 3, the cell will appear to contain 3333333333, although the underlying value remains unchanged.

The Justify and Wrap Text Options

If you enter a label that's too wide for the active cell, Excel extends the label past the cell border and into adjacent cells—provided those cells are empty. If you then select the Wrap Text option in the Text Control area of the Alignment tab, however, Excel displays your label entirely within the active cell. To accommodate the entire label, Excel increases the height of the row in which the cell is located and then "wraps" the text onto additional lines within the same cell. As shown in Figure 7-15 on page 179, cell A9 contains a multiline label formatted with the Wrap Text option.

TIP

> You can select the Wrap Text option with any alignment option. However, if you use the Wrap Text option along with the Orientation controls, the row height might not adjust to accommodate angled text in quite the way you expect. If you want to wrap angled text, adjust the row height manually to achieve the effect you want.

The Alignment command provides two Justify options—one in the Horizontal drop-down list and one in the Vertical drop-down list of the Text Alignment section. The Horizontal Justify option wraps text in the active cell, adjusts the row height accordingly, and forces the text to align flush with the right margin, as shown in cell B9 in Figure 7-15 on page 179.

If you create a multiline label and subsequently clear the Wrap Text option or choose another Horizontal alignment format, Excel readjusts the row to its original height.

> **NOTE**

Do not confuse the Horizontal Justify alignment option with the Justify command on the Fill submenu of the Edit menu. The Horizontal Justify alignment option wraps text within a cell. In contrast, the Justify command on the Fill submenu redistributes a text entry in as many cells below it as necessary, actually dividing the text into separate chunks. *For more information about the Justify command on the Fill submenu, see "The Justify and Wrap Text Options," page 182.*

? **SEE ALSO**

For more information about adjusting row height manually, see "How Wrapping and Justifying Text Affects Row Height," page 208.

The Justify option in the Vertical section on the Alignment tab does essentially the same thing as its Horizontal counterpart, except that it adjusts cell entries relative to the top and bottom of the cell rather than the sides, as shown in cell E3 of Figure 7-17. For example, if a cell contains two lines of text and the current row height is greater than the two lines of text require, the Vertical Justify option forces the top line of text to the top of the cell and the bottom line of text to the bottom of the cell. This version of the Justify option is particularly useful for adjusting text that is oriented vertically.

The Vertical Text Alignment Options

The Vertical drop-down list includes four alignment options—Top, Center, Bottom, and Justify—which are similar to the horizontal alignment options. Cells B3:D3 in Figure 7-17 show examples of these alignment options.

FIGURE 7-17.

Use the Vertical text alignment options to control placement of text from top to bottom. The Orientation options let you rotate text to any angle.

The Vertical Text button in the Orientation area "stacks" the contents of the selected cell.

The Degrees spinner in the Orientation area rotates text to any angle.

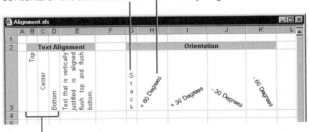

The Top, Center, and Bottom options force cell contents to align to each respective location within a cell.

W **ON THE WEB**

You can find Alignment.xls used in this example on the Microsoft Press Web site at *http://mspress.microsoft.com/mspress/products/2050/*.

II

Worksheets

A Cool Trick with Angled Text

Many times the label at the top of a column is much wider than the data stored below. You can use the Wrap Text option to make a multiple-word label narrower, but sometimes that's not enough. Vertical text is an option, but it can be difficult to read and takes a lot of vertical space. Excel offers a better solution using rotated text and cell borders.

	A	B	C	D	E	F	G
1	Publication	Cost per ad	Audience per ad (millions)	Number of ads placed	Total cost	Percent of total	Total audience (millions)
2	Pub1	$147,420	9.9	6.0	$884,520	26%	59
3	Pub2	$124,410	8.4	6.0	$746,460	22%	50
4	Pub3	$113,100	8.2	6.0	$678,600	20%	49
5	Pub4	$70,070	5.1	6.0	$420,420	13%	31
6	Pub5	$53,000	3.7	6.0	$318,000	9%	22
7	Pub6	$52,440	3.6	6.0	$314,640	9%	22
8	Total				$3,362,640		233
9							
10							

	A	B	C	D	E	F	G	H	I	J
1	Publication	Cost per ad	Audience per ad (millions)	Number of ads placed	Total cost	Percent of total	Total audience (millions)			
2	Pub1	$147,420	9.9	6.0	$884,520	26%	59			
3	Pub2	$124,410	8.4	6.0	$746,460	22%	50			
4	Pub3	$113,100	8.2	6.0	$678,600	20%	49			

Here's how to do it:

1 Select the cells you want to format and choose the Cells command on the Format menu.

2 On the Border tab, apply vertical borders to the left, right, and middle of the cell range.

3 On the Alignment tab, use the Orientation controls to select the angle you want. (It is usually best to choose a positive angle between 30 and 60 degrees.)

4 In the Horizontal Text Alignment drop-down list, select the Center option. When you click OK, Excel automatically rotates the left and right borders along with the text.

5 Select all the columns, choose the Column command on the Format menu, and then choose AutoFit Selection to shrink all the columns to their smallest possible width. Drag the bottom border of the Row 1 header down to make it deep enough to accommodate the labels.

② SEE ALSO

For more information about cell borders, see "Adding Custom Borders," page 190. For more information on selecting more than one border, see "Applying Two or More Borders at Once," page 191. For information about changing row heights, see "Controlling Row Height," page 206.

 **ON THE WEB** You can find Angled.xls used in the preceding sidebar at *http://mspress.microsoft.com/mspress/products/2050/*.

The Orientation Options

The Orientation section lets you change the angle of cell contents to read horizontally (the default), vertically from top to bottom (stacked), or at any angle from 90 degrees counterclockwise to 90 degrees clockwise. Excel automatically adjusts the height of the row to accommodate vertical orientation unless you previously or subsequently set the row height. If you want to return selected cells to their normal orientation, return the cell contents to the horizontal position.

Cell G3 in Figure 7-17 on page 183 shows what happens when you click the tall, skinny Text "button" at the top left of the Orientation section. Even though the button is labeled "Text," you can also apply this stacking effect to numbers and formulas.

The degree controls rotate text at any angle in a cell. You can either use the Degrees control box at the bottom or the large dial above it to adjust text rotation. Using the dial, click and drag the Text pointer to the desired angle, and the number of degrees appears in the spinner below. Or, click the small up and down arrow buttons in the Degrees spinner to increment the angle one degree at a time from horizontal (which is zero). You can also highlight the number displayed in the spinner box and type a number from -90 to 90. Cells H3:K3 in Figure 7-17 on page 183 show a few examples of rotated text.

The Shrink-To-Fit Option

The Shrink-To-Fit option in the Text Control section of the Alignment tab reduces the size of the font in the selected cell until the contents can be completely displayed in the cell. This is useful when you have a worksheet in which adjusting the column width to allow a particular cell entry to be visible has undesirable effects on the rest of the sheet, or where angled text, vertical text, and wrapped text aren't feasible solutions. In Figure 7-18, the same text was entered in cells A1 and A2, but the Shrink-To-Fit option was applied to cell A2. The Shrink-To-Fit format readjusts if you change the column width, either increasing or decreasing the font size as needed.

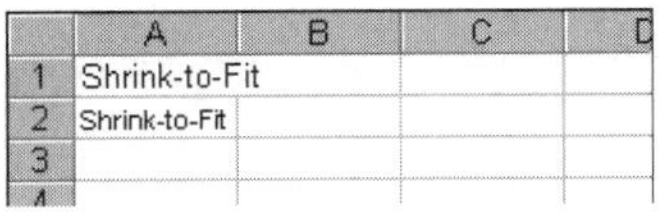

FIGURE 7-18.

Shrink-To-Fit reduces the font size until the cell contents fit.

	A	B	C	D
1	Shrink-to-Fit			
2	Shrink-to-Fit			
3				
4				

The assigned size of the font does not change in a cell with a Shrink-To-Fit-adjusted font size. The assigned font size is retained, so no matter how wide you make the column, the contents will expand only to the assigned size.

> **NOTE**
>
> The Shrink-To-Fit option can be a good way to solve a problem, but keep in mind that this option will reduce the font to as small a size as necessary. If the cell is narrow enough and the cell contents long enough, the result might be too small to read.

Text-Alignment Prefix Characters

You can use *text-alignment prefix characters* to assign alignment formats to text entries in your worksheet. To do so, you need to first choose Options from the Tools menu, click the Transition tab, and then turn on the Transition Navigation Keys option. This is called a "transition" feature to assist people who are familiar with Lotus 1-2-3 to continue using some of their hard-learned methods. *For more information about transition options, search for "Lotus 1-2-3" in the Excel Help system.*

To use a text-alignment prefix character, select a cell, type the desired prefix character, and then type the text entry and press Enter. The text-alignment character appears in the formula bar but not in the cell.

Character	Transition Navigation Keys Action
' (apostrophe)	Aligns data in the cell to the left
" (double quotation mark)	Aligns data in the cell to the right
^ (caret)	Centers data in the cell
\ (backslash)	Repeats characters across the cell

Formatting Fonts

The term *font* refers to a typeface (for example, Arial), along with its attributes (point size, color, etc.). In Excel, you use the Font tab in the Format Cells dialog box to select the font and color of your cell entries. You use fonts in a worksheet just as you do in printed text: to emphasize headings and to distinguish different kinds of information. To specify a font for a cell or for a range, first select the cell or range. From the Format menu, choose the Cells command (or press Ctrl+1) and click the Font tab, as shown in Figure 7-19.

FIGURE 7-19.

The Font tab in the Format Cells dialog box lets you assign typefaces, character styles, sizes, colors, and effects to your cell entries.

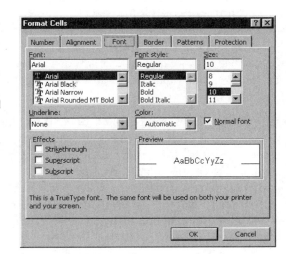

Fonts Forward

In Excel 2000, you can choose to have the appearance of fonts displayed in the Font drop-down list on the Formatting toolbar. To do so, choose Customize from the Tools menu, click the Options tab and in the "Other" section, select List Font Names In Their Font. (The Customize command does not normally appear on shortened menus. Click the double arrow at the bottom of the Tools menu to display this command.)

Selecting a Typeface and a Size

To select a typeface, click its name in the Font list box or type its name in the Font edit box. The numbers in the Size list box then change to show the sizes at which Excel can optimally print the selected typeface. You can use the Size list box scroll bar to see all the possible sizes. To specify a size, simply click it. When specifying a typeface size, keep in mind that these sizes are given in points, such as 10 point, and that one point is 1/72 of an inch. Unless you preset the row height, Excel automatically adjusts the height needed to accommodate larger point sizes.

To specify a typeface size not listed, select the contents of the Size edit box and type a new number. You will usually get the best output if you select from the sizes that Excel provides in the Size list box, but Excel will do its best to print at any size you specify. You will find that some combinations of typeface and size will be more satisfactory than others. You might want to experiment to see the results you get with your own printer and screen display.

Selecting Font Styles and Effects

The available font styles vary depending on the typeface you select in the Font list box. In addition to regular, most fonts offer italic, bold, and bold italic styles. For example, all these styles are available for the Arial font, but bold and bold italic are the only styles in which you can print Arial Rounded MT Bold. Simply select the style you want to use from the Font Style list box on the Font tab. You can see the effects of the options you select in the Preview section.

TIP

To return to the font and size defined by the Normal style, simply select the Normal style's Font option. *For more information about the Normal style, see "Formatting with Styles," page 208.*

The Font tab includes four Underline and three Effects options. Figure 7-20 shows examples of each of these options.

FIGURE 7-20.

You can apply Underline options, Strikethrough, Superscript, and Subscript to cells or to selected text in cells.

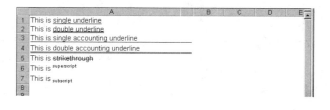

Applying Font Formats with Toolbars

You can apply the following font format options using boxes and buttons on the Formatting toolbar: Font, Font Size, Bold, Italic, Underline, and Font Color. (The Underline button applies the single underline style.) You can use the boxes and buttons individually or in combination. To remove a button-applied format from a cell or range, select the cell or range and then click the toolbar button again to turn the format off. Activate the Font and Font Size drop-down lists in the Formatting toolbar by clicking the downward-pointing arrow next to the box. *See Figure 7-4 on page 159 for an illustration of the Formatting toolbar.*

Accounting Underlines

The two Accounting underline formats differ from their normal counterparts in two ways. Accounting underlines are applied to the entire width of the cell, whereas regular underlines are applied only under characters in a cell. If the cell contains a text entry that extends beyond the cell border, the accounting underlines stop at the cell border. Also, the Accounting underline formats appear near the bottom of cells, unlike the Single and Double underlines, which are applied closer to the text or numbers and draw lines through the descenders of letters such as "g" and "p."

Selecting a Color

To see your color choices, click the downward-pointing arrow beside the Color drop-down list box on the Font tab of the Format Cells dialog box.

SEE ALSO

For more information about customizing the color palette, see "Changing the Available Colors," page 222. For more information about applying colors to cells, see "Adding Colors and Patterns," page 195.

If you select Automatic (the default color option), Excel displays the contents of your cell in black. (You might think that Automatic should select an appropriate color for text, based on the color you apply to the cell, but this is not the case. Automatic is always black unless you have selected another Window Font color in the Windows Properties dialog box.) The other 55 choices represent your current color palette. If you don't see the color you want there, you can customize the palette.

You can also apply font colors using the Font Color button on the Formatting toolbar. Clicking this button applies the color shown in the rectangle to your selection. When you click the arrow to the right of the Font Color button, a palette of colors drops down. Click one of the colored squares to apply the color to the contents of the selected cells. This button is a tear-off palette, which means that you can click and drag the button and the palette will float away from the toolbar.

II

Worksheets

After you select a color in the palette, the color in the Font Color button changes so you can apply the same color again by clicking the button itself, without using the palette.

Adding Custom Borders

Borders and shading can be effective devices for defining areas in your worksheet or for drawing attention to important cells.

> Borders often make a greater visual impact when worksheet gridlines are removed. From the Tools menu, choose the Options command and then click the View tab. Click the Gridlines option to remove gridlines from your worksheet. *For more information, see "Controlling the Display of Gridlines," page 219.*

Figure 7-21 shows the Format Cells dialog box after you click the Border tab. Here you specify the placement of the borders as well as the style and color of the lines.

FIGURE 7-21.

The Border tab in the Format Cells dialog box lets you assign 13 styles of borders in 56 colors.

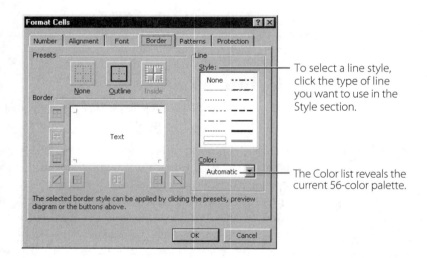

To select a line style, click the type of line you want to use in the Style section.

The Color list reveals the current 56-color palette.

Selecting a Line Style

Click any one of the 13 border styles, which include four solid lines in different weights, a double line, and eight kinds of broken lines. (The first finely dotted line is actually a solid hairline when printed.) The double line is particularly useful for underscoring columns of numbers above a total.

Selecting Line Color

The default color for borders is black, which appears as Automatic in the Color box on the View tab of the Options dialog box. (As mentioned in "Selecting a Color," page 189, the Automatic color is always black.)

To select a color other than black, click the downward-pointing arrow at the right end of the Color box. You can use one of the colors listed, or you can modify the palette to change these choices. Note that you must use the Color list in the Border tab to select border colors. If you try to use the Formatting toolbar, you will change the color of the text inside the cell, rather than the borders.

Selecting Border Placement

After you select a line style and color, you need to specify where you want to place the border in the cell. The Presets section contains the Outline preset, which places a line around the perimeter of the current selection, whether it is a single cell or a block of cells. The None preset removes all border formats from the selection. The Border section includes a preview area, which you can use to place borders. When you first open the dialog box with a single cell selected, the preview area looks like the one in Figure 7-21, with small tick marks indicating the corners of the cell. To apply borders, you can either click in the preview area where you want the border to appear, or you can click the buttons located below the preview area.

If you have more than one cell selected when you open the dialog box, the Border preview area includes tick marks in the middle as well as at the corners. An additional preset button, Inside, becomes active, which you can use to apply borders to all sides of all the selected cells. (If you click the Outline button, borders are applied only to the outside edge of the entire selection.) In addition, the preview area includes tick marks between the corners where the inside borders appear.

Change the border's style, color, and placement by clicking the option you want and then clicking the border you want to change in the preview area. If you want to start over, click the None preset button.

Applying Two or More Borders at Once

You can apply more than one kind of border to a cell selection. For example, you can apply a heavy outline border to a block of cells and, at the same time, apply a set of lightweight lines to the right border of each cell in the selection. The worksheet in Figure 7-22 on the next page shows another possible combination of border styles.

 **ON THE WEB**

You can find Borders.xls used in this example at *http://mspress.microsoft.com/mspress/products/2050/.*

FIGURE 7-22.

This budget worksheet makes use of several border styles.

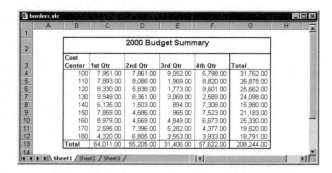

Changing or Removing Borders

If you change your mind about a border style, reselect the cell block and then redisplay the Border tab of the Format Cells dialog box. The Border tab then shows the border styles that have already been applied. To change an existing solid bottom border to a double line, for example, follow these steps:

1 Select the cells with the border you want to change.

2 From the Format menu, choose Cells and click the Border tab.

3 Select the double-line style and click the bottom border button or click near the bottom of the preview area, and then click OK.

To remove the solid bottom border, you can click the bottom border or button without selecting another style, which makes the solid line disappear from the box, and then click OK. Alternatively, you can select the None line style, click the bottom border or button, and click OK.

If a solid gray line appears in the preview area on the Border tab, the cells in your selection do not all share the same border style for the placement option in question. For example, if you select cells B2:G13 in the worksheet shown in Figure 7-22 and click the Border tab of the Format Cells dialog box, the dialog box shown in Figure 7-23 appears.

In this case, the cells in column B have a heavy border on their left. Those in columns C through E do not. Therefore, Excel displays gray instead of either line style for the inside lines in the preview area. If you click the inside borders, the selected line style is applied to all the inside cells, which might not be what you want to do. But by carefully selecting groups of cells, you can easily combine different border formats in the same worksheet.

II

Worksheets

FIGURE 7-23.

A solid gray line in the preview area means that the format applies to some, but not all, of the selected cells.

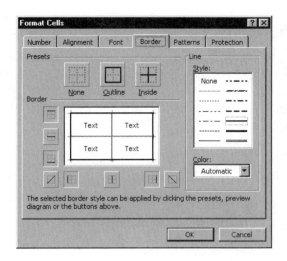

Applying Border Formats with the Borders Button

You can apply many combinations of border formats using the Borders button on the Formatting toolbar. When you click the small arrow on the Borders button, Excel displays a tear-off palette from which you can select a border style. If you click the arrow and then click the palette's border and drag away from the toolbar, the Borders palette "tears off" from the toolbar and floats independently, as shown in Figure 7-24.

FIGURE 7-24.

The Border palette can be undocked from the Formatting toolbar.

As you can see, the Borders palette offers 12 border options, including popular combinations such as single top border and double bottom border. The first option removes all border formats from a selected cell or range. The other options show, in miniature, the border combinations available when you select them. The last option you select subsequently appears on the face of the Borders button, which you can click to apply the last format you used without having to display the palette. To return the Borders palette to the Formatting toolbar, simply click the Close box in the upper right corner of the palette. Note that if you have applied a color to the borders, and then use the Borders button, the new borders will be black by default—regardless of the colors of the other borders in the cell or range.

A Cool Trick with Angled Borders

Sometimes you might wish you could use that cell in the upper left corner of a cell table a bit more effectively—for example, to provide information about the other labels in the same row or column. Now you can use the angled border options available on the Borders tab of the Format Cells dialog box to create dual-label corner cells like the one shown in the following example.

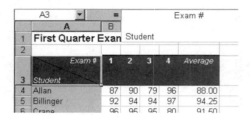

Here's how to do it:

1 Select the cell you want to format and type about ten space characters. Don't worry yet about the exact number to type; you can adjust this later (there are 20 spaces before the "Exam #" label in the above example).

2 Type the label you want to correspond to the column labels across the top of the table.

3 Hold down the Alt key and press Enter twice to create two line breaks in the cell.

4 Type the second label, which will correspond to the row labels down the left side of the table.

5 Press Enter.

6 Select the cell and then choose the Cells command on the Format menu and click the Border tab.

7 Select a line style and click the first angled border button.

8 Click the Alignment tab, click the Wrap Text option, then click OK.

You will probably need to fine-tune a bit by adjusting column width and row height and adding or removing space characters before the first label. In the example, we also selected cells B3:F3, and then selected the Top vertical text alignment option on the Alignment tab of the Format Cells dialog box so that all the labels line up across the top of the table.

? SEE ALSO

For more information about alignment, see "Aligning Cell Contents," page 179. For more about entering line breaks and tabs in cells, see "Formula Bar Formatting," page 129.

You can find Angled Borders.xls used in this sidebar at *http://mspress.microsoft.com/mspress/products/2050/*.

Adding Colors and Patterns

The Patterns tab of the Format Cells dialog box adds colors and shading to selected cells. The Patterns tab includes the current color palette (as specified on the Color tab of the Options dialog box) and a drop-down list box of colors and shading, as shown in Figure 7-25.

FIGURE 7-25.

The Patterns tab of the Format Cells dialog box lets you select colors and patterns for cell backgrounds.

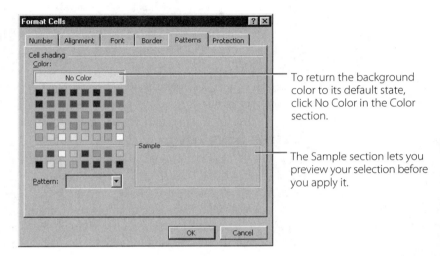

To return the background color to its default state, click No Color in the Color section.

The Sample section lets you preview your selection before you apply it.

The Color section on the Patterns tab controls the background of the selected cells. When you choose a color and do not select any pattern, a colored background appears in the selected cells.

> You can use the Fill Color button on the Formatting toolbar to apply a background color to a cell or range. When you click the arrow on the Fill Color button, a tear-off palette appears from which you can select a color.

If you pick a color from the Color section and then select a pattern from the Pattern drop-down list box, the pattern is overlaid on the solid background. For example, if you select red from the Color section and then click one of the dot patterns, the result is a cell that has a red background and black dots.

The color options in the Pattern drop-down list box control the color of the pattern itself. For example, if you leave the Color section set to No Color and select both red and the dot pattern from the Pattern drop-down list box, the cell will have a white background with red dots. Figure 7-26 on the next page shows different patterns assigned to cells in a worksheet.

FIGURE 7-26.

Using the Patterns tab, a different pattern has been assigned to each of these cells.

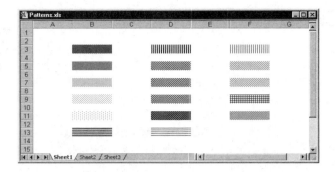

Of course, the way colors look when printed depends on the capabilities of your printer.

Using Shading

You can use the shading styles available on the Patterns tab to add emphasis to selected cells in your worksheet. For example, you might use shading to set apart worksheet totals or to draw attention to cells in which you want the user to make an entry in a worksheet template. Figure 7-27 shows how you can use shading to create a "banded" effect. In this case, the shading helps the reader follow a row of numbers while reading from left to right. Bands are particularly useful when you want to print wide reports without gridlines.

W ON THE WEB

You can find Borders.xls used in the following example at *http://mspress.microsoft.com/mspress/products/2050/.*

FIGURE 7-27.

Shading can be used for emphasis or, as in this example, to distinguish rows of numbers.

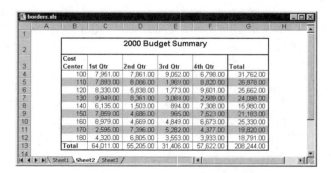

When selecting a color for the cell's background, you should pick one that allows you to easily read text and numbers in the default color, black. Another option is to select a complementary color for text and numbers by clicking the Font tab of the Format Cells dialog box or the

Font Color button on the Formatting toolbar. For example, yellow is an excellent background color for black text. Unless you have a color printer, however, you should test-print the worksheet to be sure the colors you select are acceptable when printed in black and white.

Adding Graphic Backgrounds to Your Worksheets

Excel allows you to add background images to worksheets by choosing the Sheet command from the Format menu and then choosing Background from the submenu. When you do so, Excel displays a dialog box, similar to that displayed by the Open command (File menu), that you use to open a graphic file stored on disk. The graphic image is then applied to the background of the active worksheet, much like a watermark might be used on a piece of paper.

The graphic image is "tiled" in the background of your worksheet, which means that the image is repeated as necessary to fill the worksheet. Be careful when using backgrounds behind data, however. It could be very difficult to read cell entries with the wrong background applied. You might want to turn off the display of gridlines, as we did in the figure above. To do so, choose Options from the Tools menu and, on the View tab, clear the Gridlines check box.

Cells to which you have assigned a color or pattern on the Patterns tab of the Format Cells dialog box display the color or pattern rather than the graphic background. You could, for example, apply a white or yellow solid color to cells containing data, allowing the text and numbers to stand out, while the background pattern decorates the rest of the worksheet.

Note that backgrounds you apply using the Background command are not used when you save the worksheet as a Web Page. *For more information, see Chapter 20, "Creating Web Pages with Excel."*

Applying Conditional Formatting

When is formatting like an alarm clock? When it's *conditional formatting*. Conditional formatting enables you to apply formats to individual cells that stay "asleep" until the values in those cells achieve a predetermined state. We call this *trapping* a value. For example, you could apply conditional formatting to a table, or a range of cells that contain sales totals, specifying that if any of the totals drops below $10,000, the format of the cell changes to stand out from the other cells. (Sometimes tables like these are referred to as *stoplight tables*.) Select the cells you want to format, then choose the Conditional Formatting command from the Format menu. The Conditional Formatting dialog box appears, as shown in Figure 7-28.

FIGURE 7-28.

You can create formatting "alarms" in cells using the Conditional Formatting command on the Format menu.

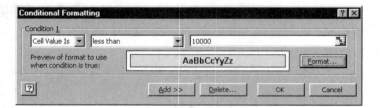

The first drop-down list of conditions in the Conditional Formatting dialog box allows you to choose whether you want to apply the condition to the cell value or to the formula itself. Normally, you want to use the Cell Value Is option, which applies the formatting based on the displayed value of the formula contained in the cell. (The only time it would make sense to use the Formula Is option is when you have a formula that changes itself, depending on other conditions in the worksheet. If this is the case, you would enter the exact formula you want to be alerted to into the second condition box.) The second condition list allows you to choose whether the cell value you want to trap is between, not between, equal to, not equal to, greater than, less than, greater than or equal to, or less than or equal to another value or range of values. The third (and fourth) boxes are where you enter the comparison value or values. If you choose Between or Not Between in the second condition list, two additional entry boxes appear, in which you provide two values: an upper and a lower limit; otherwise, only one box appears, as shown in Figure 7-28.

Once you establish the condition you want to apply, click the Format button. The Format Cells dialog box appears. Specify any combination of font, border, and pattern formats to be applied when your condition or conditions are met. For example, in Figure 7-28, if a sales total falls below $10,000, the cell background turns yellow, the font becomes bold, and a black border appears around the cell, as shown in Figure 7-29. Note that all the monthly totals in column F share the same conditional format, but only cell F7 displays it. If the sales figures change so that the total in cell F7 is above $10,000, the formatting disappears.

ON THE WEB

You can find WWW Company 2000.xls used in the following example at *http://mspress.microsoft.com/mspress/products/2050/*.

FIGURE 7-29.

The value in cell F7 falls below the threshold set in the Conditional Formatting dialog box.

	A	B	C	D	E	F	G
1	2000 Sales: WWWWW Company, Inc.						
2			*Product*				
3	*Month*	Widgets	Wombats	Woofers	Whatzits	Total by Month	
4	January	$433.33	$3,084.03	$3,501.77	$6,385.43	$13,404.56	
5	February	$4,827.84	$5,005.87	$9,837.37	$4,093.03	$23,764.11	
6	March	$1,674.16	$7,154.01	$7,619.90	$2,842.43	$19,290.50	
7	April	$443.00	$1,756.27	$775.85	$5,099.14	$8,074.26	
8	May	$464.61	$5,997.18	$4,967.30	$3,704.59	$15,133.68	
9	June	$8,525.77	$9,201.34	$5,693.62	$4,193.42	$27,614.15	

You can add up to three conditional formats at a time to a cell or range. To do so, click the Add button in the Conditional Formatting dialog box. For example, if you also want to be alerted on the occasion of good news—when sales rise above $25,000—click the Add button and apply another set of conditions to the same cell range, as shown in Figure 7-30.

FIGURE 7-30.

You can add up to three sets of conditions per cell.

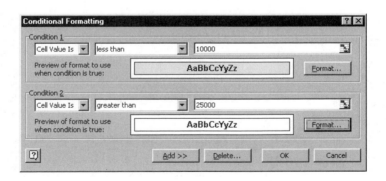

TIP

Sometimes it's hard to tell where you've applied conditional formatting. To select all cells on the current worksheet with conditional formats, choose Go To from the Edit menu, click the Special button, click the Conditional Formats button, and then click OK. (The Go To command does not normally appear on shortened menus. Click the double arrow at the bottom of the Edit menu to display this command.)

Worksheets

To remove conditional formatting, select the cell or range and choose Conditional Formatting from the Format menu. Then click the Delete button. The Delete Conditional Format dialog box appears, as shown in Figure 7-31. Select the condition(s) you want to delete and click OK. The condition disappears from the Conditional Formatting dialog box, but you can still change your mind by clicking the Cancel button, if necessary. The condition you deleted is not actually removed until you click OK in the Conditional Formatting dialog box.

FIGURE 7-31.

You can delete one or all of the conditions you applied.

Merging Cells

 SEE ALSO

For more information about border formats, see "Adding Custom Borders," page 190.

The spreadsheet grid is arguably the most versatile type of document. Still, sometimes it has been necessary to play formatting tricks with the grid to arrive at the effect you want, especially when creating forms. The merged cells feature gives the grid special powers you can use to create cleaner and more foolproof forms and reports.

For example, the spreadsheets shown in Figure 7-32 illustrate the difference between formatting cells and merging cells to accomplish a similar result.

FIGURE 7-32.

The sheet on the bottom uses merged cells to create a better-looking form.

In the top sheet, cells A1:A3 contain the three rows of address information, which spills over into column B. Row 2 has extra space because of the formatting in cell C2.

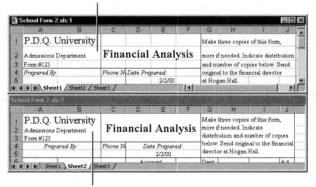

In the bottom sheet, cells A1:B3 are merged into one large cell.

When you merge selected cells, you start with two or more cells, and you end up with a single cell that comprises the original cells, as shown in Figure 7-32. For example, in the top sheet in Figure 7-32, text in the range A1:B3 is unevenly spaced due to the size of the text "Financial Analysis" in cell C2. In the bottom sheet, merging the range A1:B3 and moving all the rows of text into the merged cell eliminates this problem.

SEE ALSO

For more information about formulas and references, see Chapter 6, "Building Formulas."

When you merge cells, the new *big cell* uses the address of the cell in the upper left corner, as shown in Figure 7-33. The other merged cells, or *subsidiary cells*, are essentially nonexistent. A merged subsidiary cell acts like a blank cell when referred to in formulas, and returns zero (or an error value, depending on the type of formula).

FIGURE 7-33.

Cell A1 is a "big cell" created by merging cells A1:B3.

The big cell A1 is selected, as shown in the formula bar.

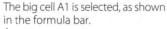
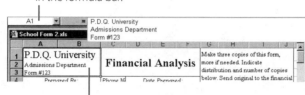

In the worksheet, the headings for rows 1, 2, and 3 and columns A and B are bold, which would normally indicate that the range A1:B3 is selected. For all practical purposes, however, cells A2:A3 and B1:B3 no longer exist.

TIP

In Figure 7-33, the information in the formula bar appears on three separate lines. To enter line breaks within a cell, press Alt+Enter. This is a technique that you will probably use often when working with merged cells. *For more information, see "Formula Bar Formatting," page 129.*

Merging and Unmerging Cells

CAUTION

When you merge several cells that contain data, only the data in the uppermost, left-most cell is preserved. Data in subsidiary cells is overwritten.

To merge cells, follow these steps:

1 Select the cells you want to merge.

2 From the Format menu, choose Cells and click the Alignment tab.

3 Click the Merge Cells option.

4 If the upper left cell contains a long string of text you want to have appear within the new big cell, click the Wrap Text option.

5 Click OK.

II

Worksheets

TIP

> The Merge And Center button on the Formatting toolbar applies a specialized version of merging to selected cells that is particularly useful for creating labels across multiple columns. This button merges the selected cells, then aligns the contents in the center (horizontally) of the newly merged cells.

You can also "explode" or *unmerge* a merged cell to return it to the original range of individual cells. To unmerge cells, follow these steps:

1 Select the big cell you want to unmerge.

2 From the Format menu, choose Cells and then click the Alignment tab.

3 Click the Merge Cells option to deselect it.

4 Click OK.

 TIP

> You can add the Merge Cells and Unmerge Cells buttons to your favorite toolbar. To do so, click the right mouse button on any visible toolbar and click the Customize command on the shortcut menu that appears. Click the Commands tab and click the Format category. Drag the Merge Cells and Unmerge Cells buttons from the Commands list to the toolbar where you want them to appear.

Guidelines for Merging Cells

Merging cells obviously has interesting implications, considering that it seems to violate the grid—one of the defining attributes of spreadsheet design. Actually, it's not as bad as you might think, but here are a few things to keep in mind:

- If you select a range of cells to merge, and any one cell contains text, a value, or a formula, the contents are relocated to the new big cell. For example, if you merge the range A1:C6 and cell B4 contains a value, that value is moved to the new big cell, located at A1.

- If you select a range of cells to merge and more than one cell contains text or values, only the contents of the uppermost, leftmost cell are relocated to the new big cell. Contents of subsidiary cells are deleted. If you want to preserve data in subsidiary cells, make sure that you add it to the upper left cell, or relocate it.

- Formulas adjust automatically. A formula that refers to a subsidiary cell in a merged range adjusts to refer to the address of the new big cell. If a merged range of cells contains a formula, relative references adjust automatically.

? SEE ALSO

For more information about copying, deleting, cutting, and pasting cells, see "Shortcuts for Entering and Editing," page 236. For more information about using the fill handle, see "Filling and Creating Series with the Mouse," page 241.

■ You can copy, delete, cut and paste, or click and drag big cells just as you would any other cell. When you copy or move a big cell, it replaces the same number of cells at the destination location. The original location of a cut or deleted big cell returns to individual cells.

■ You can use the fill handle of a big cell, just as you can with regular cells. When you do so, the big cell is replicated, replacing regular cells in its path, and the value it contains is copied or repeated as usual.

■ If you merge cells with border formatting other than along any side or sides of the selected range, the border formats are erased.

Controlling Column Width

Microsoft Excel's default column width is 8.43 characters. This does not mean that each cell in your worksheet can display 8.43 characters, however. Because Excel uses proportionally spaced fonts (such as Arial) as well as fixed-pitch fonts (such as Courier), different characters can take up different amounts of space. A default-width column, for example, can display about seven numerals in most 10-point fixed-pitch fonts.

Often, the standard column width is not wide enough to display the complete contents of a cell. As you have already seen, a label that is too long runs over into adjacent cells; if the adjacent cell contains an entry, the label is truncated. When you enter a long number in a narrow column that has the General numeric format, that number appears in scientific notation. If a cell's entry is too long to fit after you assign a numeric format, a series of pound signs (#) appears. To display the entire contents of the cell, you must change the width of the column or columns that contain the long entries. You can change column width in several ways.

Using the Mouse to Change Column Widths

To change column widths with the mouse, place the mouse pointer in the column-heading area on the line that divides the column you want to change from its neighbor to the right. For example, to widen or narrow column C, place the pointer in the column-heading area on the line separating column C from column D. Your mouse pointer changes to a double-headed arrow, as shown in Figure 7-34. Now hold down the mouse button and drag the column divider to the right or left. As you drag, the width of the column is displayed in a screen tips box, as shown in Figure 7-34. When the width is correct, release the mouse button.

FIGURE 7-34.

Use the double-headed arrow cursor to adjust column width and row height.

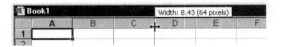

 TIP

To change the width of more than one column at a time, drag through the column headings of the columns you want to change. (You can select nonadjacent columns by holding down Ctrl as you click the column headings.) Next, change the width of one of the columns as we just described. When you release the mouse button, all of the columns change simultaneously, and they are all exactly the same width.

Automatically Fitting a Column to Its Widest Entry

You can change a column's width to accommodate its widest cell entry by double-clicking the column divider to the right of the column. To see how this works, enter the label *Total by Month* in cell A1 of a new worksheet. Next, move the mouse pointer to the column-headings area and double-click the divider line between column A and column B. The column snaps to the width necessary to accommodate your label.

If you add a longer entry to a column after automatically adjusting its width, you will need to use the automatic-adjustment feature again. Also, depending on the font you are using, characters that appear to fit within a column on your screen might not fit within a column when you print a worksheet. You can preview your output before printing by choosing the Print Preview command from the File menu. *For information about the Print Preview command, see Chapter 11, "Printing and Presenting."*

 TIP

You can also adjust a column's width to its widest entry by selecting the entry or the entire column and then using the AutoFit Selection command on the Column submenu of the Format menu.

Using the Column Commands

From the Format menu, choose Column to display a submenu that includes five commands—Width, AutoFit Selection, Hide, Unhide, and Standard Width. To assign a column width, simply select cells in each column you want to change (you need not select entire columns) and then choose the Width command.

TIP

To change the widths of all the columns in the current worksheet, click one of the row headings at the left edge of the worksheet (or select any cell and press Shift+Spacebar) and then choose the Width command to display the Column Width dialog box, shown in Figure 7-35.

FIGURE 7-35.

Use the Column Width dialog box to specify the widths of columns.

If all the columns you select are the same width, that width appears in the Column Width edit box; if the columns you select are of different widths, the edit box is blank. In either case, type a number from 0 through 255 in integer, decimal, or fraction form. (The old width setting is erased as soon as you begin typing.) When you click OK, Excel adjusts the widths of the selected columns.

To change the default width applied to columns in the current worksheet, choose the Standard Width command from the Column submenu of the Format menu. (The Standard Width command is not visible on shortened menus. Click the downward-pointing double arrow at the bottom of the Column submenu of the Format menu to display the Standard Width command.) As shown in Figure 7-36, the default column width of 8.43 appears in the Standard Column Width edit box. Simply enter a new width and click OK to change the width of all columns in the current sheet that have not been specifically resized.

FIGURE 7-36.

You can restore the default column width or change the standard width.

To change the standard width for all columns in the worksheet that are the default column width, choose Column from the Format menu and then choose Standard Width. Type the new value in the Standard Column Width edit box and then click OK. All columns currently set to the default width then adjust to the new setting. All columns become the new width, except those whose width you have changed.

Controlling Row Height

Microsoft Excel 2000 automatically adjusts the standard height of a row to accommodate the largest font used in that row. For example, when the largest font in row 1 is 10-point Arial, the standard height for that row is 12.75. If you apply 12-point Times New Roman to a cell in row 1, however, the standard height of the entire row automatically becomes 15.75. (Like font size, row height is measured in points. Remember that one point equals 1/72 of an inch, so a row with a height of 13 is a little over 1/6 of an inch.)

If you don't adjust any row heights yourself, Excel generally uses its standard row height. Thus, you don't usually need to worry about characters being too tall to fit in a row.

? SEE ALSO

For more information about the Protection command, see "Protecting Your Data," page 111.

Hiding a Column or Row

You might, on occasion, want to hide information in your worksheet—for example, employee salaries in a departmental budget worksheet. Fortunately, Excel allows you to hide entire columns or rows. (The Hidden option on the Protection tab of the Format Cells dialog box, when used in conjunction with the Protection command on the Tools menu, hides only formulas in the formula bar.)

To hide a column, first select a cell in the column you want to hide. From the Format menu, choose Column and then Hide. When you choose the Hide command, Excel sets the width of the selected column to 0. You can also hide a column by dragging the line between the column headings to the left until you have narrowed the column to nothing; or you can enter 0 in the Column Width dialog box. When a column's width is set to 0, Excel skips over that column when you move the active cell, and the column's letter disappears from the top of the worksheet. For example, if you hide column C, the column heading line reads A, B, D, and so on.

To redisplay a column, first drag across the column headings on both sides of the hidden column. Next, from the Format menu, choose Column and then click Unhide.

You can hide and redisplay rows in a similar manner, using the mouse or the equivalent Row submenu on the Format menu.

Using the Mouse to Change Row Heights

Adjusting the height of a row is similar to adjusting the width of a column. In the row-heading area, position the mouse pointer on the line under the number of the row you want to change. When the pointer takes on the double-headed arrow shape (see Figure 7-34 on page 204), hold down the mouse button, drag the line that divides the rows to the new position, and then release the mouse button.

To change the height of more than one row at a time, drag through the headings of the rows. (To select nonadjacent rows, hold down Ctrl as you click the row headings.) Next, change the height of one of the rows as described. When you release the mouse button, all the rows change simultaneously, and all are exactly the same height.

Automatically Adjusting Row Height

If you have changed a row's height, you can reset it to fit the tallest entry in the row by double-clicking the row divider below the row you want to change. To see how this works, click the bottom divider of row 1—the divider between row headings 1 and 2—and drag it down to make the row taller. Next, double-click the divider line you just dragged. The row snaps back to the standard height. If a row contains text that is larger than standard size, double-clicking the divider below the row adjusts the row height as necessary to fit the tallest entry.

Note that if you delete the text from the cell, the row height is still determined by the largest font size format applied to any cell in that row.

Using the Row Commands

Similar to the Column command, the Row command on the Format menu includes a submenu with four commands—Height, AutoFit, Hide, and Unhide. *For more information about the Hide and Unhide commands, see the sidebar, "Hiding a Column or Row."* You can use the Height command to change the heights of several rows at once. Simply select at least one cell in each row and choose the Height command to display the dialog box shown in Figure 7-37.

FIGURE 7-37.

Use the Row Height dialog box to change the height of selected worksheet rows.

Worksheets

To change the height of all the rows in the worksheet, click one of the column headings (or select any cell and press Ctrl+Spacebar) before you choose the Height command. If all the rows you select are the same height, that height appears in the Row Height edit box; if the rows are different heights, the edit box is blank. Either way, to change the height of all selected rows, simply enter a new row height and then click OK.

To reset a row's height to its tallest entry after you've changed it, choose the AutoFit command from the Row submenu.

How Wrapping and Justifying Text Affect Row Height

(?) SEE ALSO

For more information, see "The Justify and Wrap Text Options," page 182.

When you create a multiline text entry using the Wrap Text or the Justify option on the Alignment tab of the Format Cells dialog box, Excel automatically adjusts the row height to accommodate your multiline entry. If you subsequently add words to make that entry longer or increase the point size of the font you're using, Excel adjusts the row height again—so your text never spills out of the cell in which it's entered. Similarly, if you reduce the size of a multiline entry, Excel readjusts the row height accordingly.

Formatting with Styles

Microsoft Excel's Style feature allows you to assign names to combinations of formatting attributes. You can then apply those attributes by selecting the name from a list. Styles help you achieve consistency in formatting, both within a worksheet and across worksheets and workbooks. You can easily modify the formatting of many cells at once.

Every new workbook has six predefined styles: Comma, Comma [0], Currency, Currency [0], Normal, and Percent. (The Comma and Currency formats use two decimal places; the Comma [0] and Currency [0] formats round to the nearest integer value.) These six predefined styles have the same characteristics on each worksheet in a workbook and in each new workbook you create, but you can change them for any workbook, and you can add styles of your own. When you save a workbook, all its style definitions are saved along with the rest of your data.

(>) NOTE

If you have set up and used a Hyperlink, two other styles might already exist: Hyperlink and Followed Hyperlink. *For information about the Hyperlink styles, see Chapter 19, "Hyperlinks and the Internet."*

You define styles using the Style command on the Format menu. The Style dialog box in Figure 7-38 shows the attributes of the Normal style.

FIGURE 7-38.

Excel's predefined Normal style includes these attributes.

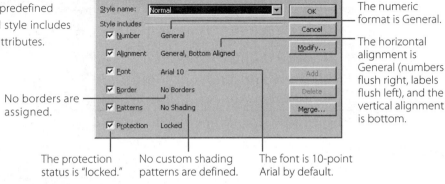

The numeric format is General.

The horizontal alignment is General (numbers flush right, labels flush left), and the vertical alignment is bottom.

No borders are assigned.

The protection status is "locked."

No custom shading patterns are defined.

The font is 10-point Arial by default.

(?) **SEE ALSO**

For information about redefining the Normal style, see "Modifying a Style," page 212.

Styles can have a minimum of one and a maximum of six attributes. All the predefined styles except Normal have only one attribute—a number format. The predefined Currency style, for example, has the Accounting number format with two decimal places.

The predefined Normal style has one important characteristic: it is automatically applied to every cell in every new workbook. Thus, if you want a cell to have the standard set of formatting attributes, you don't need to do anything. If, however, you want to change the default attributes, you can redefine the Normal style.

Applying a Style

To apply a style to a cell or a range, first select the cell or range and then follow the steps in Figure 7-39.

FIGURE 7-39.

You can apply styles to cells or ranges in your workbook with the Style dialog box.

1 From the Format menu, choose the Style command to display the Style dialog box.

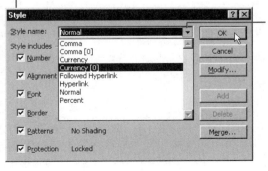

2 Click the downward-pointing arrow at the right end of the Style Name box, select a style, and then click OK.

> **Applying Styles with Toolbars**
>
> Excel includes a Style box, similar to the one in the Style dialog box, that you can place on a toolbar. You can add the Style box (in the Formatting category) to an existing toolbar or to a toolbar that you create using the methods described in Chapter 3, "Toolbars and Menus."
>
> When the Style box is available on a toolbar, you can use it to determine whether a style has been applied to any cell in your workbook. Simply select the cell and then check the name of the style that appears in the Style box on the toolbar.

 TIP

To quickly display the Style dialog box, press Alt+' (single quotation mark). If you have a toolbar that includes the style box, this key combination moves to the box instead of opening the dialog box.

Defining a Style

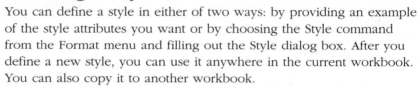 **SEE ALSO**

For more information about copying styles to other workbooks, see "Merging Styles from Different Workbooks," page 213.

You can define a style in either of two ways: by providing an example of the style attributes you want or by choosing the Style command from the Format menu and filling out the Style dialog box. After you define a new style, you can use it anywhere in the current workbook. You can also copy it to another workbook.

Defining Styles by Example

If you have already applied formatting attributes to a cell or a range, you can use the style-by-example procedure to encapsulate those commands in a new style. For example, suppose you format a cell with right alignment and 18-point Helvetica bold. To make this combination of attributes a new style—in this case called *MyStyle*—follow these steps:

1 Select the cell that contains the formatting you want. (In this case, right alignment and 18-point Helvetica bold.)

2 From the Format menu, choose the Style command.

3 When the Style dialog box appears, type *MyStyle* in the Style Name edit box.

4 Clear the Number, Border, Patterns, and Protection options in the Style Includes section and click OK.

The name of the new style will now appear in the Style dialog box and in the Style box's drop-down list.

The safest way to create a style by example is to select only one cell— one that you know has all the attributes you want to assign to the new style. If you select two or more cells that are not formatted identically, the new style assumes only those attributes that all cells in the selection have in common.

> You can also define a style by example with the Style box. First add the Style box to a toolbar as explained in Chapter 3, "Toolbars and Menus." Then, select a cell with the formats you want to name, click the name currently displayed in the Style box, and enter a name for the new style. Press Enter to save the custom style, which will appear in both the Style drop-down list box on your toolbar and in the Style Name drop-down list box in the Style dialog box.

Defining Styles from Scratch

To create a new style without first formatting a cell, you can take the following steps:

1 From the Format menu, choose the Style command.

2 In the Style Name edit box, type the name of the style you want to define.

3 Click the Modify button. The Format Cells dialog box appears, as shown in Figure 7-40. The changes you make in the Format Cells dialog box apply to your new style definition.

FIGURE 7-40.

Clicking the Modify button in the Style dialog box displays the Format Cells dialog box. Excel applies changes made here to the current style.

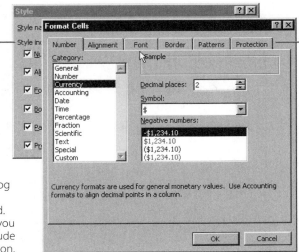

4 Select format options from the Number, Alignment, Font, Border, Patterns, and Protection tabs, and then click OK to return to the Style dialog box.

5 The Style Includes section of the dialog box reflects the formats you added. Clear the options you don't want to include in the style definition.

6 After you're satisfied with the formatting attributes you selected, click the Add button. Your new style appears among all the others defined for the current workbook, and you can apply it at any time from the Style Name drop-down list box (or the Style box if you add it to a toolbar).

7 Click OK to close the Style dialog box.

Modifying a Style

A major advantage to formatting with styles is that if you change your mind about the appearance of a particular element in your workbook, you can revise every instance of that element at once simply by redefining the style. For example, if you'd like the font in the MyStyle style—which is now 18-point Helvetica bold—to be italic as well as bold, you can simply redefine MyStyle.

To modify a style definition—to add italic to the definition of MyStyle, for example—follow these steps:

1 From the Format menu, choose the Style command.

2 Select the style—in this case MyStyle—from the Style Name drop-down list box and then click Modify to display the Format Cells dialog box.

3 Select the appropriate format options. For this example, click the Font tab and select the Bold Italic option in the Font Style list box.

4 Click OK to return to the Style dialog box and then click OK to confirm your changes.

Redefining a Style with Toolbars

You can also redefine a style using the toolbar Style box. *For more information about the Style box, see the sidebar "Applying Styles with Toolbars," page 210.* To redefine a style with the Style box, follow these steps:

1 Select a cell that is formatted with the style you want to redefine.

2 Make your formatting changes.

3 Click the name in the toolbar Style box and press Enter. Excel asks you to confirm that you want to redefine the existing style based on the style in the selected cell.

4 Click Yes. Excel then redefines the style and changes every instance of the style in the worksheet to match the new definition.

Overriding a Style with Direct Formatting Changes

You can change the appearance of any cell or range in your worksheet, whether or not you have applied a style to that cell or range, by using the Cells command on the Format menu to access the Number, Alignment, Font, Border, and Patterns tabs or by using the buttons on the Formatting toolbar.

Merging Styles from Different Workbooks

SEE ALSO

For more information about templates, see "Using Template Files," page 214.

To maintain formatting consistency across a group of worksheets, you can keep them all in the same workbook. If this is impractical but you still want to maintain stylistic consistency, you can copy style definitions between workbooks. (Another way to achieve consistency is with templates.)

To copy a style from one workbook to another, you can take the following steps:

1 Open both the source workbook (the one you're copying from) and the destination workbook (the one you're copying to).

SEE ALSO

For more information about opening multiple windows, see Chapter 9, "Worksheets and Windows."

2 Click the destination workbook to make it the active window.

3 Choose the Style command from the Format menu and click the Merge button. Excel displays a list of all other open workbooks, as shown in Figure 7-41.

FIGURE 7-41.

When you copy styles from one workbook to another, Excel displays a list of all other open workbooks.

4 Select the name of the workbook you want to copy styles from and click OK.

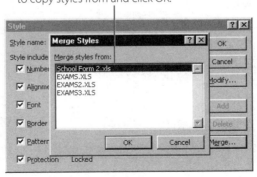

If a style in your source workbook has the same name as one already in your destination workbook, an alert box asks if you want to merge styles that have the same name from the source workbook. You will receive this warning only once, however, no matter how many duplicate style names exist. If you choose Yes, the styles from the source workbook override those with the same names in the destination workbook.

Deleting a Style

To delete a style's definition, choose the Style command from the Format menu, select the style in the Style Name drop-down list box, and then click Delete. Any cells that were formatted with the deleted style will revert to the Normal style. (You cannot delete the Normal style.) Any cell that was formatted with a deleted style and was then also formatted directly, however, retains all the direct formatting.

Using Template Files

A *template file* is a model that can serve as the basis for many worksheets. A template might include both data and formatting information. Template files are great time-savers. They're also an ideal way to ensure a consistent look among reports, invoices, and other documents you create. Figure 7-42 shows an example of a template file.

You can find Expenses.xlt used in the following example at *http://mspress.microsoft.com/mspress/products/2050/*.

FIGURE 7-42.

This template file serves as the basis for creating expense reports.

	A	B	C	D	E	F	G	H	I
	Expense Report						For period ending:		3/31/00
		Sun	*Mon*	*Tue*	*Wed*	*Thu*	*Fri*	*Sat*	*Total*
3	Date								0
4	Place								0
5	Air Fare								0
6	Meals								0
7	Taxi								0
8	Tips								0
9	Supplies								0
10	Car Rental								0
11	Parking								0
12	Tolls								0
13	Lodging								0
14	Telephone								0
15	Misc.								0
16	**Total**	0	0	0	0	0	0	0	0

Any Excel workbook can become a template. When you installed Excel, a folder named Templates was installed within the C:\Windows\ Application Data\Microsoft folder on your hard disk. Any workbook in the Templates folder, whether or not it was actually saved in the

Template format, can be used as the basis for new workbooks when you choose the New command from the File menu.

Workbooks you place in the Templates folder appear on the General tab of the New dialog box. This is important and a little confusing, so here it is again: any workbooks in the Templates folder will appear on the General tab of the New dialog box, whether or not you saved them in template format. When you use the New command to "open" any workbook that appears on the General tab (that is, in the Templates folder), rather than opening the workbook itself, a new copy of the workbook is created.

The advantages to using templates are standardization and protection. When you use the New command on the File menu to create a new workbook based on a template, it is difficult to accidentally save over the original. When you save the new template-based workbook for the first time, you must supply a new name for it. This way you can create new workbooks with the same appearance over and over again without worrying about overwriting the original file.

 TIP

If you only want to create a new blank workbook, simply click the New Workbook button on the Standard toolbar. This achieves the same result as clicking the Workbook icon on the General tab of the New dialog box.

To create a template file, follow these steps:

1 Create a workbook with all the data and formatting that is common to all the workbooks you will create, such as the information shown in Figure 7-42.

2 From the File menu, choose the Save As command and supply a filename.

3 Click the arrow to the right of the Save As Type drop-down list box and select Template, then click Save. Excel automatically switches to the Template folder so that your new template will always be available when you choose New from the File menu.

To use a template file, choose New from the File menu. Excel displays template files you save on the General tab of the New dialog box, as shown in Figure 7-43 on the next page.

When you create a new file from a template or workbook saved in the Templates folder, Excel opens a *working copy* of the file, leaving the original intact. The copy is given a temporary name made up of the original file name plus a number. If the template file is named

FIGURE 7-43.

Templates you save in
the Templates folder
appear in the New
dialog box (File menu).

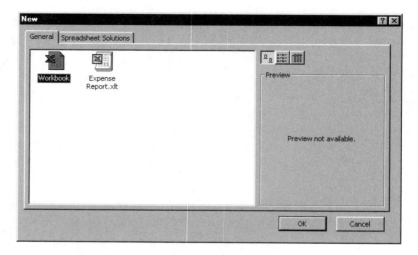

Expenses.xlt, for example, the working copy is named Expenses1.
When you save the file, Excel opens the Save As dialog box so you
can assign a different name to the template file. Excel then appends
the .xls extension to the name.

Adding Templates to the XLStart Folder

The XLStart folder was created when you installed Excel, and it is located in
the C:\Windows\Application Data\Microsoft\Excel\ folder. Regular workbooks
that you save in the XLStart folder (workbooks not saved in the Template format) are opened automatically when you start the Excel program. If you want
your template file to be displayed as an option whenever you create a new
workbook, you can also save templates in the XLStart folder, and they will
appear in the New dialog box, just as they do when you save them in the
Templates folder. Templates saved in the XLStart folder do not open automatically on startup, however. If any template files are present in the XLStart folder
when you choose the New command from the File menu, they appear on the
General tab of the New dialog box.

⭐ **TIP**

In Windows 95, you can show the old MS-DOS three-character extension so
you can tell at a glance if you intended a workbook to serve as a template
(.xlt) or a regular workbook (.xls). To do so, click the Start button, and under
Programs, click Windows Explorer. On the Explorer's View menu, choose
Options and make sure that the "Hide MS-DOS file extensions for file types
that are registered" option is not selected.

Modifying a Template File

To change a template file, follow these steps:

1 From the File menu, choose the Open command and select the template file in the File Name list box.

2 Make the desired changes to the template.

3 To resave the workbook as a template file, choose the Save command. To save it as a regular workbook, choose the Save As command, select Microsoft Excel Workbook in the Save As Type drop-down list box, and then click OK.

 NOTE

You no longer have to hold down the Shift key to open the template itself, as was the case in Excel versions 5.0 and earlier.

Controlling Display Options

In addition to the commands on the Format menu, there are three important tabs in the Options command on the Tools menu, described in Figure 7-44, that you can use to control the way your documents appear on screen: the View tab, the General tab, and the Color tab.

FIGURE 7-44.

The View tab, the General tab, and the Color tab in the Options dialog box control the appearance of your workbook.

SEE ALSO

For information about outlining and outline symbols, see "Outlining Your Worksheets," page 225. For information about automatic page breaks, see "Removing Manual Page Breaks," page 401. For information about graphic objects, see Chapter 10, "Graphics."

The View tab controls the display of the formula and status bars as well as the appearance of automatic page breaks, formulas, gridlines, column and row headings, outline symbols, zero values, and graphic objects, among other things.

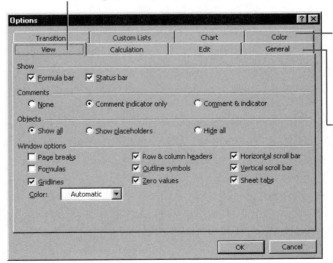

The Color tab allows you to modify the set of 56 colors available for any given workbook.

The General tab specifies the default font.

The commands on the Format menu affect only selected worksheet cells, while the tabs in the Options dialog box are global in scope.

Controlling the Display of the Formula Bar and Status Bar

You can use the Formula Bar and Status Bar options in the Show section of the View tab of the Options dialog box to suppress the display of the formula bar and status bar. (These options are the same as the Formula Bar and Status Bar commands on the View menu.)

Although you can function in Excel without the formula bar and status bar, you'll probably want to leave these options selected as a convenience. You can always hide them for display purposes when you complete a worksheet.

When the Windows In Taskbar option is selected, each window you have open in Excel appears as a separate icon in the Windows taskbar. This might create more clutter that it's worth when you have a lot of files and applications running at the same time.

The Window Options

SEE ALSO

For more information about using multiple windows, see Chapter 9, "Worksheets and Windows."

The options you select in the Window Options section on the View tab of the Options dialog box affect only the active workbook; they do not change the display of other workbooks. If you use the New Window command on the Window menu to create two or more windows in which to view the same workbook, you can even use different display options in each. For example, you can view formulas in one window and see the results of those formulas in another window.

Displaying the Underlying Formulas

Normally, when you enter a formula in a cell, you see the results of that formula, not the formula itself. Similarly, when you format a number, you no longer see the underlying (unformatted) value displayed in the cell. You can see the underlying values and formulas only by selecting individual cells and looking at the formula bar.

The Formulas option on the View tab of the Options dialog box lets you display all the underlying values and formulas in your worksheet. As you can see in Figure 7-45, the underlying contents of each cell appear, as in the sum formulas in row 16, and all cells are now left-aligned. (Excel ignores any alignment formatting when you select the Formulas option.) In addition, the width of each column in the worksheet approximately doubles to accommodate the underlying formulas. When you clear the Formulas option, Excel restores all columns to their former widths. (The actual width of the column remains unchanged; columns only appear wider on the screen.)

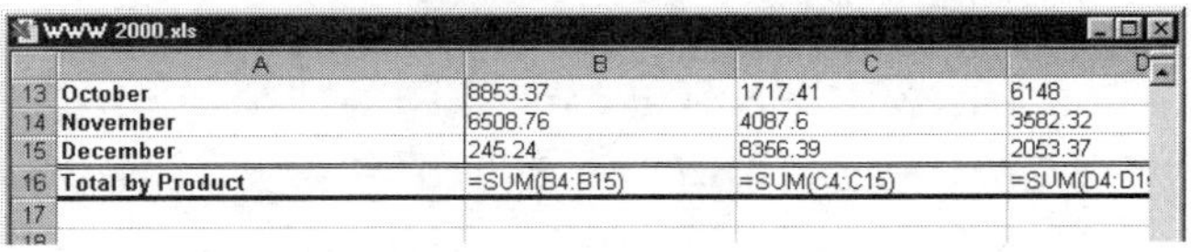

FIGURE 7-45.

Use the Formulas option to view underlying values and formulas.

	A	B	C	D
13	October	8853.37	1717.41	6148
14	November	6508.76	4087.6	3582.32
15	December	245.24	8356.39	2053.37
16	Total by Product	=SUM(B4:B15)	=SUM(C4:C15)	=SUM(D4:D1
17				

The Formulas option is particularly helpful when you need to edit a large worksheet. You can see your formulas without having to activate each cell and view its contents in the formula bar. You can also use the Formulas option to document your work: after you select Formulas, you can print your worksheet with the formulas displayed for archiving purposes.

You can quickly display formulas in your worksheet by pressing Ctrl+` (the single left quotation mark, which is usually located on the tilde key on most keyboards). To redisplay values, press Ctrl+` again. This keyboard shortcut is handy when you need to toggle the display back and forth for auditing purposes.

Controlling the Display of Gridlines

Typically, Excel displays a grid to mark the boundaries of each cell in the worksheet. Although this grid is usually helpful for selection and navigation, you might not want it displayed all the time. To suppress gridline display, clear the Gridlines option on the View tab of the Options dialog box.

You can increase the on-screen effectiveness of your border formats dramatically by eliminating the display of gridlines in your worksheet.

SEE ALSO

For more information about printing a document without gridlines, see Chapter 11, "Printing and Presenting."

Turning off the Gridlines option removes the gridlines from your screen and also suppresses them for printing. If you want gridlines printed but not displayed (or vice-versa), from the File menu, choose the Page Setup command, click the Sheet tab, and then select or clear the Gridlines option in the Print section.

Changing the Color of Gridlines

To change the color of the gridlines in your workbook, select a color from the Color drop-down list box on the View tab of the Options dialog box and click OK. Select the Automatic option to return to the default color.

Controlling the Display of Row and Column Headers, Scroll Bars, and Sheet Tabs

If you clear the Row & Column Headers option on the View tab of the Options dialog box, the row numbers and column letters disappear. Similarly, if you clear the Horizontal Scroll Bar, Vertical Scroll Bar, or Sheet Tabs options, those window items disappear from view for the current workbook. You can use these options to polish your finished workbooks for display purposes; they do not affect the way the worksheets in the current workbook will look when you print them. Figure 7-46 shows a worksheet without gridlines, column and row headings, scroll bars, or sheet tabs.

FIGURE 7-46.

You can suppress the display of column and row headings, horizontal and vertical scroll bars, and sheet tabs, as well as gridlines.

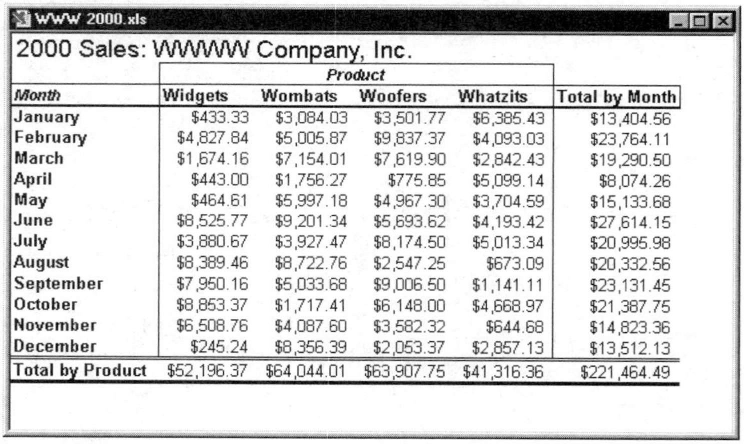

WWW 2000.xls					
2000 Sales: WWWWW Company, Inc.					
	Product				
Month	Widgets	Wombats	Woofers	Whatzits	Total by Month
January	$433.33	$3,084.03	$3,501.77	$6,385.43	$13,404.56
February	$4,827.84	$5,005.87	$9,837.37	$4,093.03	$23,764.11
March	$1,674.16	$7,154.01	$7,619.90	$2,842.43	$19,290.50
April	$443.00	$1,756.27	$775.85	$5,099.14	$8,074.26
May	$464.61	$5,997.18	$4,967.30	$3,704.59	$15,133.68
June	$8,525.77	$9,201.34	$5,693.62	$4,193.42	$27,614.15
July	$3,880.67	$3,927.47	$8,174.50	$5,013.34	$20,995.98
August	$8,389.46	$8,722.76	$2,547.25	$673.09	$20,332.56
September	$7,950.16	$5,033.68	$9,006.50	$1,141.11	$23,131.45
October	$8,853.37	$1,717.41	$6,148.00	$4,668.97	$21,387.75
November	$6,508.76	$4,087.60	$3,582.32	$644.68	$14,823.36
December	$245.24	$8,356.39	$2,053.37	$2,857.13	$13,512.13
Total by Product	$52,196.37	$64,044.01	$63,907.75	$41,316.36	$221,464.49

Spreadsheet Solutions Templates

The Spreadsheet Solutions tab of the New dialog box provides three predesigned templates for your number-crunching needs. These templates include Invoice, Expense Statement, and Purchase Order. These templates have associated database workbooks, located in the Library folder in your Excel folder. These templates work with the Template Wizard, allowing you to use these templates as forms to load data into databases.

ON THE WEB

Note that the Spreadsheet Solutions templates, as well as the Template Wizard, are options that might not be installed on your computer. If your Spreadsheet Solutions tab does not contain the templates listed, rerun the Setup program to install them. Additional Spreadsheet Solutions templates are available on the Microsoft Excel 2000 Web site. If you are connected to the Internet, choose the Office on the Web command from the Help menu to jump directly to the Office Web site. *For more information about the Office Web site, see Chapter 19, "Hyperlinks and the Internet."*

Navigating Without Headers or Scroll Bars

SEE ALSO

For information about the keyboard-naviga-tion options, see "Selecting with the Keyboard," page 100.

When Row & Column Headers is cleared, you must use the Format menu to change the height of a row or the width of a column. Also, to keep track of where you are on the current worksheet, you must rely on the cell reference display in the Name box at the left end of the formula bar. To scroll around the worksheet without scroll bars, you must use the keyboard-navigation options or choose the Go To command on the Edit menu (or press F5) and type the cell reference to which you want to move. To switch to another worksheet when the sheet tabs are hidden, press Ctrl+Page Up to move to the previous sheet or Ctrl+Page Down to move to the next sheet. You can also use the Go To command to move to other worksheets in a workbook. Simply type the worksheet name and a cell reference, such as *Sheet5!A1*, in the Reference edit box.

The Zero Values Option

Normally, zero values are displayed in your worksheet. To hide those values, clear the Zero Values option on the View tab of the Options dialog box. Any cells containing only zeros or formulas that result in zero values appear blank. The underlying entries are unaffected, how-ever. If you edit an entry or if the result of a formula changes so that the cell no longer contains a zero value, the value immediately becomes visible. If the Formulas option on the View tab is selected, clearing Zero Values has no effect on the display.

Changing the Standard Font

The General tab of the Options dialog box controls many aspects of your workspace, as you can see in Figure 7-47 on the next page. Most of these options are discussed elsewhere in this book: *For more infor-mation about other options in this dialog box, see "R1C1 Reference Style," page 122; "Adding Summary Information to Files," page 74; "If You Have an IntelliMouse," page 230; and "Working with Sheets," page 311.*

II

Worksheets

FIGURE 7-47.

The General tab of the Options dialog box controls the standard font used in new workbooks.

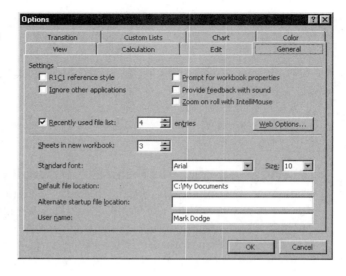

? SEE ALSO

For information about opening a file you have used recently, see "Reopening a Recently Opened File," page 82. For information about loading files automatically, see "Opening Files Automatically When You Start Excel," page 82.

You use the General tab to set the standard font, which Excel uses in several ways. All new workbooks are created with column and row headings displayed in the standard font, and any entries you make in a new workbook are displayed in this font. In addition, the standard font is used as the font definition in the Normal style.

To redefine the standard font, select the font name and size you want from the corresponding drop-down list boxes on the General tab of the Options dialog box. When you click OK, a dialog box informs you that the new standard font will not become active until you quit and restart Excel, enabling you to save changes to any open workbooks. The next time you start Excel, all new workbooks you create are displayed with the new standard font.

In the Style dialog box that appears when you choose Style from the Format menu, the Normal style now includes the new standard font as well. If you change the Font definition of the Normal style for a workbook, the worksheet display changes accordingly. However, each new workbook you open will continue to use the standard font defined on the General tab until you redefine it.

Changing the Available Colors

In Excel's Format Cells dialog box, the Font, Border, and Patterns tabs all offer a choice of 56 colors, which constitute your default color palette. This palette is also available for gridlines on the View tab of the Options dialog box and the tear-off palettes of the Fill Color and Font Color buttons on the Formatting toolbar. Using the Color tab in the Options dialog box, you can modify any color in the palette. The Color tab is shown in Figure 7-48.

FIGURE 7-48.

The Color tab in the Options dialog box controls the colors in the default color palette.

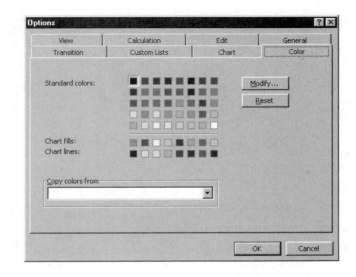

The Color tab presents samples of each solid color in the current palette in the Standard Colors section. The Chart Fills and Chart Lines sections reflect the default colors and order that Excel uses for chart elements.

To substitute a different color for one of the current colors, select the current color and then click Modify Color. You'll see the Colors dialog box. The Standard tab is shown in Figure 7-49.

FIGURE 7-49.

You can edit the colors in Excel's default color palette with the Colors dialog box.

The Standard tab displays a "color wheel" of sorts, with 127 colors and 15 shades of gray you can choose from.

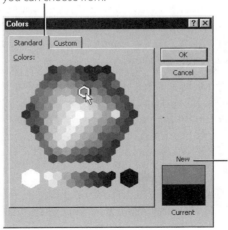

The New/Current box allows you to see the difference between the color you want to change (on the bottom) and the color you select (on the top).

The Custom tab, shown in Figure 7-50, gives you even more precise control over the color palette.

FIGURE 7-50.

The Custom tab in the Colors dialog box gives you more control of your colors.

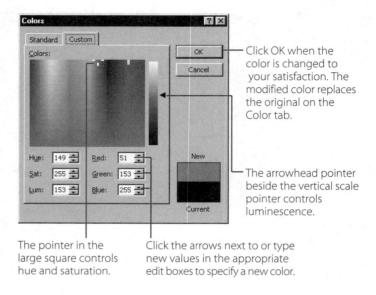

Click OK when the color is changed to your satisfaction. The modified color replaces the original on the Color tab.

The arrowhead pointer beside the vertical scale pointer controls luminescence.

The pointer in the large square controls hue and saturation.

Click the arrows next to or type new values in the appropriate edit boxes to specify a new color.

Colors displayed on your screen are defined by three parameters—their red, green, and blue values. An alternative system of specification uses three different parameters, called *hue, saturation,* and *luminescence* (labeled *Hue, Sat,* and *Lum* on the Custom tab). You can specify a new color by modifying the values of any of these parameters.

With the mouse, you can define a new color more directly by dragging either or both of the two pointers that control hue, saturation, and luminescence. By experimenting with these two pointers and looking at the samples that appear in the New/Current box, you can come up with new colors without having to know anything about the parameters that define them.

Any colors you define that are not among your system's repertoire of solids are achieved by a mixture of dots from solid colors. Such "blended" colors, which are said to be *dithered,* work well for shading. But for text and lines, Excel always uses the nearest solid color in preference to a dithered color.

After you edit the color palette, click OK to save it. Your customized palette then becomes an attribute of the current workbook. Click the Reset button on the Color tab to revert to the original color palette.

Copying Palettes from Other Workbooks

To achieve a consistent look among workbooks, you can copy your custom palette. To do so, follow these steps:

1 Open both the destination workbook (the one to which you're copying) and the source workbook (the one from which you're copying).

2 Make the destination workbook active.

3 From the Tools menu, choose the Options command and click the Color tab.

4 Click the arrow for the Copy Colors From drop-down list box to see a list of all other open workbooks.

5 Select your source workbook and then click OK.

Outlining Your Worksheets

Many typical spreadsheet models are built in a hierarchical fashion. For example, in a monthly budget worksheet, you might have a column for each month of the year, followed by a totals column. For each line item in your budget, the totals column adds the values in each month column. In this kind of structure, you can describe the month columns as subordinate to the totals column because their values contribute to the outcome of the totals column.

Similarly, the line items themselves can be set up in a hierarchy with groups of expense categories contributing to category totals. Microsoft Excel 2000 can turn worksheets of this kind into outlines.

Figure 7-51 on the next page shows a table of sales figures before and after outlining. Figure 7-52 on the next page shows how you can change the level of detail displayed after you outline a worksheet.

The difference between Figures 7-51 and 7-52 is that the columns and rows listing the months and individual team members are hidden in Figure 7-52. Without outlining, you would have to hide each group of columns and rows manually; with outlining, you can collapse the outline to change the level of detail instantly.

Outlining has two additional benefits. First, you can more easily reorganize an outlined worksheet than one that is not outlined. In Figure 7-52, for example, if you hold down the Shift key while clicking the

? SEE ALSO

For more information about creating charts and using the Chart Wizard, see Chapter 21, "Basic Charting Techniques."

FIGURE 7-51.

Here is a worksheet before and after outlining.

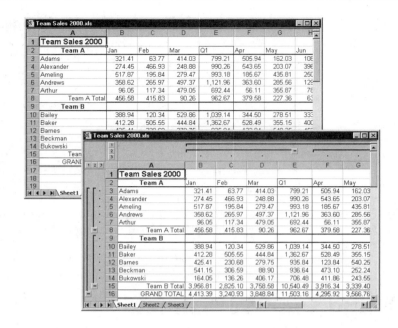

FIGURE 7-52.

Two clicks of the mouse button transformed the outlined worksheet in Figure 7-51 into this quarterly overview.

Row level bar

show detail symbol (the button with a plus sign) at the top of column E and use standard editing techniques to move that column, the subordinate columns B, C, and D automatically move as well.

ON THE WEB

You can find Team Sales 2000.xls used in this example at *http://mspress.microsoft.com/mspress/products/2050/*.

Second, in an outlined worksheet you can easily select only those cells that share a common hierarchical level. For example, to graph the quarterly sales totals in Figure 7-52 (omitting the monthly details), first collapse the outline as demonstrated in Figure 7-52, and select the range A2:Q15. Then use the Chart Wizard to build your graph.

The outline in Figure 7-52 is a simple one. It uses three levels each for columns and rows. You can create much more complex outlines—Excel can handle up to eight outline levels each for columns and rows.

Creating an Outline

To outline part of your worksheet automatically, first select the area to outline. From the Data menu, choose the Group And Outline command, and then choose Auto Outline. To outline your entire worksheet, select only one cell and then choose Auto Outline. In a moment or two, depending on the complexity of your worksheet, your outline appears. Generally, you'll need to make some adjustments to an auto-outline, but it usually helps to get you started. To make the adjustments faster and easier, we'll create a custom toolbar in the next section.

Outlining with Toolbar Buttons

The outlining buttons offer some shortcuts for working with an outline. Each corresponds to commands or dialog-box options available elsewhere, but the buttons help make fast work of this task. Figure 7-53 shows a custom toolbar containing the six outlining buttons.

FIGURE 7-53.

This custom toolbar has six buttons that can be used in outlining.

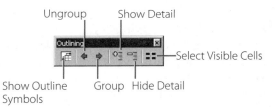

To create this custom toolbar, follow these steps:

1. From the View menu, choose Toolbars, and then choose Customize.

2. On the Toolbars tab of the Customize dialog box, click the New button, type *Outlining*, and then click OK.

3. Click the Commands tab and select Data in the Categories list.

4. From the Commands list, drag the Show Outline Symbols, Ungroup, Group, Show Detail, and Hide Detail buttons to the new toolbar.

5. Select Edit in the Categories list.

6. Drag the Select Visible Cells button to the new toolbar.

7. Click the Close button.

To create an outline using toolbar buttons, select the range to outline and then click the Show Outline Symbols button. An alert box asks if you want to create an outline, if none yet exists. Click OK. Excel creates your outline automatically. If you click the Show Outline Symbols button again, the outline symbols disappear from the screen. The outline is still there; it's just hidden. Click the button again and the outline reappears.

? SEE ALSO

For more information about creating custom toolbars, see "Creating New Toolbars," page 530.

The Ungroup and Group buttons allow you to modify the hierarchies in your outline. If you select entire columns or rows and click the Ungroup button, the outline level is removed. Similarly, if you select entire columns or rows, the Group button creates a new outline level; the selected columns and rows become the detail data.

The Show Detail and Hide Detail buttons operate when you select cells in summary columns or rows. The Show Detail button expands the outline level subordinate to the selected summary cell; the Hide Detail button does just the opposite.

Outlining a Worksheet with a Nonstandard Layout

The standard outline settings reflect the most common worksheet layout. To change these settings, choose Group And Outline from the Data menu and choose Settings to display the Settings dialog box shown in Figure 7-54. If your worksheet layout is not typical, such as a worksheet constructed with rows of SUM formulas (or other types of summarization formulas) in rows above the detail rows, or with columns of formulas to the left of detail columns, clear the appropriate Direction option—Summary Rows Below Detail or Summary Columns To Right Of Detail—before outlining. When you use nonstandard worksheet layouts, be sure that the area you want to outline is consistent to avoid unpredictable and possibly incorrect results; that is, be sure all summary formulas are located in the same direction relative to the detail data.

FIGURE 7-54.

Use the Settings dialog box to adjust for a nonstandard layout.

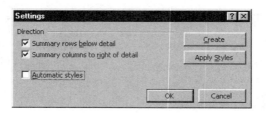

After you select or clear one or both Direction options, click the Create button to create the outline.

> The Automatic Styles option and Apply Styles button apply formats to your outline to distinguish different levels of data, such as totals and detail data. Automatic styles can produce unexpected results, however. To ensure that the outline is formatted the way you want, apply formats manually or use the AutoFormat command on the entire outline. *For more information about the AutoFormat command, see "Using AutoFormat," page 159.*

Extending the Outline to New Worksheet Areas

At times, you might create an outline and then add more data to your worksheet. You might also want to recreate an outline if you change the organization of a specific worksheet area. To include new columns and rows in your outline, simply repeat the procedure you followed to create the outline in the first place: select a cell in the new area, then from the Data menu choose Group And Outline and then Auto Outline. Excel asks you to confirm that you want to modify the existing outline; click OK.

Suppressing the Outline Display

When you outline a worksheet, Excel displays symbols, as shown in Figure 7-52 on page 226, above and to the left of the row and column headings. These symbols do take up screen space, so you can click the Show Outline Symbols button to suppress them if you created a custom Outlining toolbar such as the one described on page 227. Alternatively, you can choose the Options command from the Tools menu. Click the View tab and clear the Outline Symbols option. Click the button or select the option again to redisplay the outline symbols.

Collapsing and Expanding Outline Levels

When you create an outline, the areas above and to the left of your worksheet are marked by one or more brackets that terminate in *hide detail symbols,* which have minus signs on them. The brackets are called *level bars.* Each level bar indicates a range of cells that share a common outline level. The hide detail symbols appear above or to the left of each level's *summary* column or row.

To collapse an outline level so that only the summary cells show, click that level's hide detail symbol. For example, if you no longer need to see the sales numbers for January, February, and March in the outlined worksheet shown earlier in Figure 7-51, on page 226, click the hide detail symbol above column E. The worksheet then looks like Figure 7-55.

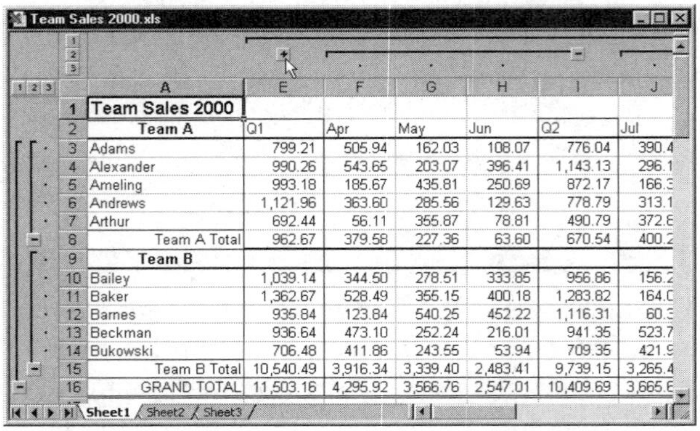

Team Sales 2000.xls

	A	E	F	G	H	I	J
1	Team Sales 2000						
2	Team A	Q1	Apr	May	Jun	Q2	Jul
3	Adams	799.21	505.94	162.03	108.07	776.04	390.4
4	Alexander	990.26	543.65	203.07	396.41	1,143.13	296.1
5	Ameling	993.18	185.67	435.81	250.69	872.17	166.3
6	Andrews	1,121.96	363.60	285.56	129.63	778.79	313.1
7	Arthur	692.44	56.11	355.87	78.81	490.79	372.8
8	Team A Total	962.67	379.58	227.36	63.60	670.54	400.2
9	Team B						
10	Bailey	1,039.14	344.50	278.51	333.85	956.86	156.2
11	Baker	1,362.67	528.49	355.15	400.18	1,283.82	164.0
12	Barnes	935.84	123.84	540.25	452.22	1,116.31	60.3
13	Beckman	936.64	473.10	252.24	216.01	941.35	523.7
14	Bukowski	706.48	411.86	243.55	53.94	709.35	421.9
15	Team B Total	10,540.49	3,916.34	3,339.40	2,483.41	9,739.15	3,265.4
16	GRAND TOTAL	11,503.16	4,295.92	3,566.76	2,547.01	10,409.69	3,665.6

Sheet1 / Sheet2 / Sheet3

FIGURE 7-55. We have hidden the details for January through March by clicking the hide detail symbol above Q1. Excel now displays a show detail symbol above Q1.

A *show detail symbol* with a plus sign on it now replaces the hide detail symbol above the Q1 column (column E). To redisplay the hidden monthly details, click the show detail symbol.

If You Have an IntelliMouse

You can use the wheel on your IntelliMouse to manipulate an outline without using the detail symbols or level symbols. This is helpful if you prefer to suppress the display of outline symbols in order to see more of the worksheet on the screen.

Hold the mouse pointer over the summary row or column you want to expand or collapse, then hold down the Shift key and turn the wheel backward (toward your hand) to collapse the outline, or forward (away from your hand) to expand it. For example, if you hold the mouse pointer over cell E1 in Figure 7-55, on the previous page, and turn the wheel forward, the detail columns for Q1 reappear. Or, if you hold the pointer over cell E8 in Figure 7-55 and turn the wheel backward, the detail rows for Team A collapse.

If you hold the pointer over a cell where a summary row and summary column intersect, the outline collapses or expands in both directions at once. For example, if you hold the pointer over cell I8 in Figure 7-55, hold down the Shift key, and turn the wheel backward, both the Team A detail rows and the Q2 detail columns collapse simultaneously.

Displaying a Specific Outline Level

To collapse each quarter so that only the quarterly totals and annual totals appear, you can click the hide detail symbols above Q1, Q2, Q3, and Q4. But the *level symbols*—the squares with numerals at the upper left corner of the worksheet—provide an easier way. An outline usually has two sets of level symbols, one for columns and one for rows. The *column level symbols* appear above the worksheet, and the *row level symbols* appear to the left of the worksheet.

You can use the level symbols to set an entire worksheet to a specific level of detail. The outlined worksheet shown in Figure 7-51 on page 226 has three levels each for both columns and rows. By clicking both of the number 2 level symbols in the upper left corner of the worksheet, you can transform the outline shown in Figure 7-51 to the one shown in Figure 7-52 on the same page. By clicking the number 1 level symbols, you can further reduce the level of detail displayed by the worksheet so that only the grand total sales figure for the year, in cell R16, is shown.

Selecting Only Visible Cells

When you collapse part of an outline, Excel hides the columns or rows that you don't want to see. In Figure 7-52 on page 226, for example, rows 2 through 7 and 9 through 14, as well as columns B through D, F through H, J through L, and N through P are hidden. Normally, when you select a range that includes hidden cells, those hidden cells are actually included in the selection. If you drag the mouse from E8 to Q8 in Figure 7-52, for example, Excel selects the entire range, including the hidden cells. Whatever you do with these cells also happens to the hidden cells. By clicking the Select Visible Cells button on our custom Outlining toolbar, however, you can restrict a selection to only the visible cells within a range.

The Select Visible Cells button is ideal for copying, charting, or performing calculations on only those cells that occupy a particular level of your outline. Select Visible Cells works the same way in worksheets that have not been outlined; it excludes any cells in hidden columns or rows from the current selection.

TIP

You can also use the Go To command on the Edit menu to restrict a selection to a range of visible cells. In the Go To dialog box, click the Special button to display the Go To Special dialog box, where you can select the Visible Cells Only option.

Ungrouping and Grouping Columns and Rows

If the default automatic outline doesn't give you the structure you expect, you can adjust it by ungrouping or grouping particular columns or rows.

You can easily change the hierarchy of outlined columns and rows using the Group and Ungroup commands on the Group And Outline submenu of the Data menu (or the buttons of the same name on our custom Outlining toolbar). Simply select the columns or rows you want to change and choose one of the commands. For example, you could select row 8 in the outlined worksheet shown in Figure 7-51 on page 226, choose the Ungroup command (or click the Ungroup button on our custom Outlining toolbar), and then click OK to change row 8 from level 2 to level 1. The outlining symbol to the left of the row moves to the left under the row level 1 button. To restore the row to its proper level, simply choose the Group command (or click the Group button). The outlining symbol then returns to its original level 2 position.

> **NOTE**
>
> You cannot ungroup or group a nonadjacent selection, and you cannot ungroup a selection that's already at the highest hierarchical level. If you want to ungroup a top-level column or row to a higher level so it is displayed separately from the remainder of the outline, you have to group all the other levels of the outline instead.

Removing an Outline

It's easy to remove an outline from a worksheet. From the Data menu, choose Group And Outline and then Clear Outline.

You can also remove either the column or row levels (or both) from an outline by ungrouping all of the outline's levels to the highest level. If your outline is many levels deep and your worksheet is large, this process can be laborious. Another way to make your worksheet behave as though it is not outlined is to display all the levels of detail (by clicking the highest numbered level button for both columns and rows) and then suppress the display of Excel's outline symbols. You can do this by clicking the Show Outline Symbols button on the custom Outlining toolbar described on page 227, or by choosing Options from the Tools menu and clearing Outline Symbols on the View tab.

Editing a Worksheet

The many editing features in Microsoft Excel 2000 take the place of old-fashioned erasers, scissors, and glue, so you can delete, copy, cut, and paste cells and ranges in your worksheets. Many editing operations can be performed using buttons on the Standard toolbar, shown in Figure 8-1 on the next page.

In this chapter we discuss how to use editing commands and features on a single worksheet. You can also edit two or more worksheets simultaneously. Chapter 9, "Worksheets and Windows," discusses the group editing feature.

FIGURE 8-1.

Buttons on the Standard toolbar make editing easier.

Spelling   Copy   Undo   Zoom Control

Cut   Paste   Redo

Setting Workspace Options for Editing

As you've already seen, the Options command on the Tools menu displays a stellar dialog box in the Microsoft Excel universe. The importance of the Options dialog box is further underscored by the Edit tab, which contains an assortment of options that allow you to control editing-related workspace settings, as shown in Figure 8-2. *For information about the Cut, Copy, And Sort Objects With Cells option, see Chapter 10, "Graphics."*

FIGURE 8-2.

From the Tools menu, choose the Options command and click the Edit tab to display a list of options that let you control editing-related workspace settings.

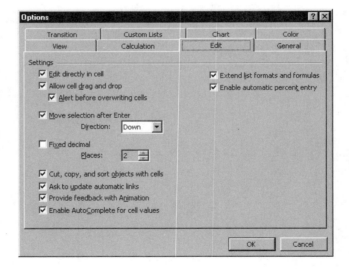

The Move Selection After Enter Option

When the Move Selection After Enter option is active and Down is displayed in the Direction drop-down list (the default setting), pressing Enter after typing a cell entry locks in the entry and activates the cell below. To change the direction of the selection after you press Enter, use the Direction drop-down list. The other options are for the cell to the right, above, or to the left. When you clear this option, pressing Enter simply locks in the entry and leaves the same cell active.

The Fixed Decimal Option

The Fixed Decimal option on the Edit tab of the Options dialog box is handy when you need to enter long lists of numeric values. (It's equivalent to the floating decimal feature available on most ten-key calculators.) For example, if you're entering multiple values that contain two decimal places, select the Fixed Decimal option and type *2*, if necessary, in the Places edit box. (The FIX indicator appears in the status bar after you close the Options dialog box.) After you type each numeric value, Excel adds a decimal point at the specified position. If the setting in the Places edit box is 2 and you enter the number *12345* in your worksheet, for example, your entry will be converted to 123.45; if you enter a single-digit value, such as *9,* it will be converted to 0.09. Whether it's called fixed or floating, what it boils down to is that you don't have to actually type the decimal points when entering numbers with the same number of decimal places.

The Fixed Decimal option does not affect existing entries in your worksheet; it applies only to entries you make after you select the option. Thus, you can select or clear the option or change the number of decimal places without altering your existing data. The Fixed Decimal option applies only when you do not type a decimal point. If you type a number with a decimal point, the option has no effect.

The Provide Feedback With Animation Option

When Provide Feedback With Animation is selected, the actions of using the arrows on the scroll bars and inserting or deleting entire rows or columns are animated on your screen. That is, the rows or columns appear to roll in the direction of the action. For example, when you delete, rows appear to roll upward and columns seem to roll to the left. When you insert, rows appear to roll down, and columns seem to roll to the right. When you click the down scroll arrow, the rows appear to roll upward. This movement offers a visual cue that confirms what you've done. With this option turned off, inserting and deleting rows or columns occurs instantaneously, making it difficult to tell if you did the right thing. If you keep an eye on the worksheet, you can watch the animation and tell immediately if you deleted when you meant to insert. Keep in mind, however, that this occurs only when working with entire rows and columns—inserting and deleting cells and other scrolling methods are not animated.

We'll discuss the other options available on the Edit tab throughout this chapter.

Shortcuts for Entering and Editing

In Excel, you can perform many of the most common editing tasks without using keyboard commands. Using the mouse in combination with the Shift and Ctrl keys to directly manipulate entire cells, you can cut, copy, paste, clear, insert, delete, and move cells. In addition, you can duplicate much of the functionality of the Fill commands with simple mouse movements.

You turn the direct cell-manipulation feature on and off by choosing the Options command from the Tools menu and selecting the Allow Cell Drag And Drop option on the Edit tab. (To guard against mistakes, be sure the Alert Before Overwriting Cells option is also selected.) When the direct cell-manipulation feature is turned on (the default condition), a small black square, called the *fill handle*, appears in the lower right corner of the selection rectangle, as shown in Figure 8-3.

FIGURE 8-3.

Fill handles appear in the lower right corner of selection rectangles.

Fill handle

With the Allow Cell Drag And Drop option selected, try moving the mouse pointer around the selection rectangle border. When you position the mouse pointer over the fill handle, it changes to a bold cross hair, as shown in Figure 8-4. When you position the pointer over the border, it changes to an arrow, as shown in Figure 8-5 on page 238.

FIGURE 8-4.

The pointer changes to a bold cross hair when you move it over a fill handle.

Automatic Extension

Officially dubbed "extend list formatting," this new feature allows you to add data to a previously constructed table without having to manually edit and format the new cells. For example, let's say you want to add another student to the existing table in the following figure. Just to make entry easier, we first selected A9:F9. Doing this allows you to press Enter instead of using arrow keys or the mouse to move to the next cell.

	A	B	C	D	E	F	
1	First Quarter Exam Scores						
2							
3	*Student*	Exam 1	Exam 2	Exam 3	Exam 4	*Average*	
4	Allan	87	90	79	96	88.00	
5	Billinger	92	94	94	97	94.25	
6	Crane	96	95	95	80	91.50	
7	Davis	85	87	87	88	86.75	
8	Evans	81	88	88	85	85.50	
9							
10							

Now enter the student's name and test scores in cells A9:E9. When you move to cell F9, which contains a formula, you'll notice that the correct formula pops in automatically. Excel also correctly surmises that you want the new entries to use the same formatting as the adjacent cells in row 8, as shown in the following figure.

F9	▼	=	=AVERAGE(B9:E9)				
	A	B	C	D	E	F	
1	First Quarter Exam Scores						
2							
3	*Student*	Exam 1	Exam 2	Exam 3	Exam 4	*Average*	
4	Allan	87	90	79	96	88.00	
5	Billinger	92	94	94	97	94.25	
6	Crane	96	95	95	80	91.50	
7	Davis	85	87	87	88	86.75	
8	Evans	81	88	88	85	85.50	
9	Gellert	88	84	96	91	89.75	
10							

If you continue adding students and scores, Excel extends the formats and formulas from the adjacent cells automatically. Automatic Extension works both horizontally and vertically.

 ON THE WEB

You can find the Operations tab in Editing.xls used to create the samples in this sidebar on the Microsoft Press Web site at *http://mspress.microsoft.com/ mspress/products/2050/*.

Moving and Copying with the Mouse

To quickly move a cell or range to a new location, select the cell or range and drag it to the new position. For example, on the left in Figure 8-5, the mouse pointer is positioned over the border that surrounds cells A1:A4. When the arrow pointer appears, click the border and drag it to column C. As you drag, an outline of the range appears. You can use this to help you position the range correctly. When the outline is over cells C1:C4, release the mouse button. The result is pasted in the new location, as shown on the right in Figure 8-5.

FIGURE 8-5.

Position the pointer over the selection's rectangle border to move these cells elsewhere by dragging.

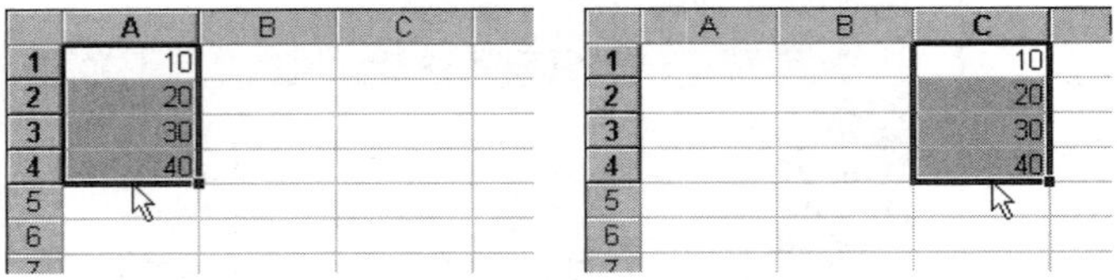

To copy the selection (copy and paste) rather than move it (cut and paste), press and hold down the Ctrl key before you release the mouse button. The mouse pointer then appears with a small plus sign next to it, as shown in Figure 8-6, which indicates you are copying rather than moving the selection.

FIGURE 8-6.

Before you finish dragging, press Ctrl to copy the selection.

? SEE ALSO

For information about using the keyboard for this task, see "Inserting Cut Cells," page 259.

You can also use direct cell manipulation to move cells in your worksheet and insert them in a new location. For example, at the top of Figure 8-7 on the next page, we first selected cells A1:A2 and then dragged the selection while holding down the Shift key. As you can see, a gray I-beam indicates where the selected cells will be inserted when you release the mouse button. In addition, the new address of the selected cells appears in a box adjacent to the mouse pointer. The I-beam appears whenever the arrow pointer passes over a horizontal or vertical cell border. In this case, the vertical border between cells C1:C2 and D1:D2 is indicated, but we could just as easily insert the cells horizontally, between cells C1 and C2. You'll see the I-beam insertion point flip between horizontal and vertical as you move the mouse around the worksheet. To insert the cells, release the mouse button while still pressing the Shift key. When you release the mouse button, the selected cells move to the new location, as shown at the bottom of Figure 8-7. In addition, the cells in columns B and C move to the left to fill the space vacated by A1:A2.

FIGURE 8-7.

The I-beam indicates where the selected cells will be inserted.

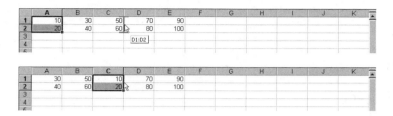

If you press Ctrl+Shift while dragging, the selected cells are copied instead of moved to the insertion point. Again, a small plus sign appears next to the arrow pointer, and a copy of the selected cells is inserted in the new location, while the original selected cells are left intact.

You can also use these techniques to select entire columns or rows and then move or copy them to new locations.

Inserting, Deleting, and Clearing Cells with the Mouse

To perform the next group of operations, you use the fill handle. If you select a cell or range, the fill handle appears in the lower right corner of the selection rectangle. If you select an entire column (or columns), the fill handle appears next to the column heading. If you select an entire row (or rows), the fill handle appears next to the row heading. Using the worksheet at the top of Figure 8-7, suppose you want to add some numbers between columns A and B. First select either cells A1:A2 or the entire column A. Next click the fill handle and drag one column to the right while holding down the Shift key. When you press the Shift key, the mouse pointer becomes a double line with a pair of outward-pointing arrows. Figure 8-8 shows the worksheet after you release the mouse button and Shift.

FIGURE 8-8.

Use the mouse to insert blank cells or columns.

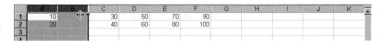

You can delete cells, columns, or rows just as easily using the same technique. For example, to delete the column we just inserted, select column B and then, while holding down the Shift key, drag the fill handle one column to the left. The selection turns a medium shade of gray, and the mouse pointer changes to a double line with a pair of inward-pointing arrows, as shown in Figure 8-9. When you release the mouse button, the selection is deleted. (This mouse action is equivalent to choosing the Delete command from the Edit menu.)

FIGURE 8-9.

You can use the mouse to delete cells or columns.

> **NOTE**
>
> If you don't hold down the Shift key while you drag back over the selected cells, you clear the cell contents instead of deleting the cells. This mouse action is equivalent to choosing the Contents command from the Clear submenu of the Edit menu, which clears formulas, text, and numbers only. If you hold down the Ctrl key while dragging back over the selection, you perform an operation that is equivalent to choosing the All command from the Clear submenu, which clears the entire contents of a cell, including formats and comments. *For more information about the Delete command, see "Deleting Cells, Columns, and Rows," page 251, and for more information about the Clear command, see "Clearing Cell Contents and Formats," page 250.*

Dragging with the Right Mouse Button

If you select cells and then drag any border of the selection rectangle (not the fill handle) using the right mouse button, a shortcut menu is displayed when you release the button, as shown in Figure 8-10. You can use the commands on the shortcut menu to manipulate your cell selection in a variety of ways.

FIGURE 8-10.

If you use the right mouse button to drag selected cells, this shortcut menu appears when you release the button.

The Move Here command moves the source cells from their original location to the destination cells. The Copy Here command copies the selected, or *source,* cells—both contents and formats—to the location, or *destination,* where you release the mouse button. The Copy Here As Values Only command copies the contents of the source cells to the destination cells but does not affect the formats of either. The

Copy Here As Formats Only command, on the other hand, copies to the destination cells all the formats that were applied to the source cells; without affecting the contents of either cell. The Link Here command creates a linking formula at the destination location that refers to the source cells. For example, choosing the Link Here command in Figure 8-10 would replace the contents of cell D1 with the formula =A1, while the contents of cell D2 would be replaced with the formula =A2.

SEE ALSO

For more information about Hyperlinks, see Chapter 19, "Hyperlinks and the Internet."

You use the Create Hyperlink Here command to create "jumps" to information stored in other documents or worksheets. For example, you can select a cell or range in one worksheet, then drag it with the right mouse button to another worksheet. Releasing the mouse button and choosing Insert or Create Hyperlink Here from the shortcut menu creates a hyperlink in the selected cell. The contents of that cell remain, but the formatting changes to indicate a hyperlink, which you can click to quickly jump to the destination.

The four Shift commands on the shortcut menu perform a variety of copying and moving functions. For example, if in Figure 8-10 we choose either of the Shift Down commands, cells D1:D2 and all the cells below them move down to accommodate the two cells we dragged (cells A1:A2). If we choose either of the Shift Right commands, cells D1:D2 and all the cells to their right move to the right to accommodate the two cells we dragged.

Filling and Creating Series with the Mouse

SEE ALSO

For more information about creating series, see "The Series Command," page 275.

You can use the fill handle to quickly and easily fill cells and create series using Excel's AutoFill feature. You can perform most of the functions available in the Series dialog box that appears when you choose the Series command from the Fill submenu.

When you select a single cell, click the fill handle, and then drag in any direction, the contents of that cell are copied to the selected range (with exceptions, which we'll discuss later). When you select a range of cells, either the range is copied in the direction you drag the mouse, or the series is extended in the direction you drag, depending on the cell contents, the shape of the selection, and whether you are holding down the Ctrl key. If a selected cell or range contains no formulas, a small yellow screen tip box appears next to the mouse pointer as you drag, showing the values to be entered into each cell along the way.

For example, using the worksheet shown earlier at the top of Figure 8-7, on page 239, if you select cell A2 and drag the fill handle down to

Worksheets

cell A5, the contents of cell A2 are copied to cells A3 through A5. Figure 8-11 shows the results.

FIGURE 8-11.

You can copy the contents of a cell to adjacent cells by dragging the fill handle.

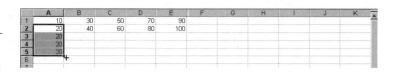

However, if you select the range A1:A2 and drag the fill handle down to cell A6, you create a series using the interval between the two selected values, as shown in column A of Figure 8-12. Alternatively, if you select cells C1:C2 and hold down the Ctrl key while you drag the fill handle down to cell C6, you copy the selected cells, repeating the pattern as necessary to fill the range, as shown in column C of Figure 8-12.

FIGURE 8-12.

We created a series in column A and copied a range in column C.

The small plus sign next to the mouse pointer indicates a copy operation.

⭐ **TIP**

Generally, when you create a series, you drag the fill handle down or to the right, and the values increase accordingly. You can also create a series of decreasing values, however, by simply dragging the fill handle either up or to the left. Enter the starting values in the cells at the bottom or to the right of the range you want to fill and then drag the fill handle back to the beginning of the range.

If you select a text value and drag the fill handle, the text is copied to the cells where you drag. If, however, the selection contains both text and numeric values, the AutoFill feature takes over and extends the numeric component while copying the text component. You can also extend dates in this way, using a number of date formats, including Qtr 1, Qtr 2, and so on. If you enter text that describes dates, even without numbers (such as months or days of the week), Excel treats the text as a series.

Figure 8-13 shows some examples of series created using the fill handle with various selected values. The values in column A were typed in, and the values to the right of column A were extended by AutoFill using the fill handle.

FIGURE 8-13.

The values in columns B through H were extended by selecting the values in column A and dragging the fill handle to the right.

	A	B	C	D	E	F	G	H	I	J
1	Selected Value	Resulting AutoFill Series								
2										
3	1/1/2000	1/2/2000	1/3/2000	1/4/2000	1/5/2000	1/6/2000	1/7/2000	1/8/2000		
4	19:00	20:00	21:00	22:00	23:00	0:00	1:00	2:00		
5	Qtr 1	Qtr 2	Qtr 3	Qtr 4	Qtr 1	Qtr 2	Qtr 3	Qtr 4		
6	Product1	Product2	Product3	Product4	Product5	Product6	Product7	Product8		
7	Mon	Tue	Wed	Thu	Fri	Sat	Sun	Mon		
8	Monday	Tuesday	Wednesday	Thursday	Friday	Saturday	Sunday	Monday		
9	Jan	Feb	Mar	Apr	May	Jun	Jul	Aug		
10	August	September	October	November	December	January	February	March		
11										

In Figure 8-14, columns A and B contain entries with different intervals, and columns C through H show how AutoFill can extrapolate a series based on a selected interval, even when text and numeric values are mixed in cells.

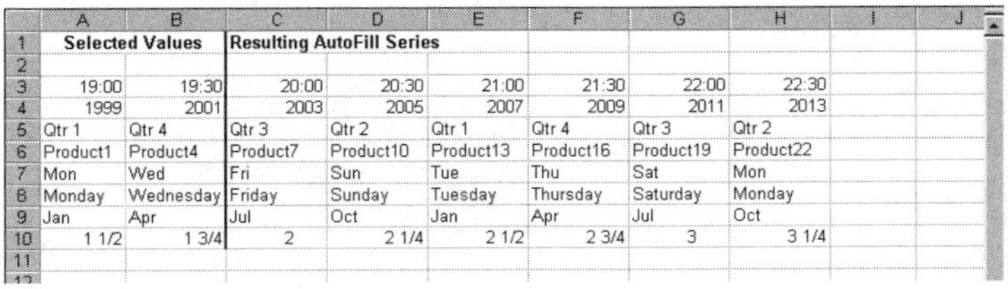

FIGURE 8-14.

The values in columns C through H were extended using the intervals between the starting values in columns A and B.

	A	B	C	D	E	F	G	H	I	J
1	Selected Values		Resulting AutoFill Series							
2										
3	19:00	19:30	20:00	20:30	21:00	21:30	22:00	22:30		
4	1999	2001	2003	2005	2007	2009	2011	2013		
5	Qtr 1	Qtr 4	Qtr 3	Qtr 2	Qtr 1	Qtr 4	Qtr 3	Qtr 2		
6	Product1	Product4	Product7	Product10	Product13	Product16	Product19	Product22		
7	Mon	Wed	Fri	Sun	Tue	Thu	Sat	Mon		
8	Monday	Wednesday	Friday	Sunday	Tuesday	Thursday	Saturday	Monday		
9	Jan	Apr	Jul	Oct	Jan	Apr	Jul	Oct		
10	1 1/2	1 3/4	2	2 1/4	2 1/2	2 3/4	3	3 1/4		
11										

(?) SEE ALSO

For more information about Date formats, see Chapter 13, "Dates and Times."

AutoFill normally increments various date and time values when you drag the fill handle, even if you initially select only one cell. For example, if you select a cell that contains Qtr 1 or 1/1/00 and drag the fill handle, AutoFill extends the series as Qtr 2, Qtr 3, or 1/2/00, 1/3/00, and so on. But if you hold down the Ctrl key while you drag, the AutoFill feature is suppressed, and the selected values are simply copied to the adjacent cells.

Conversely, Excel normally copies a single selected value like 100 to adjacent cells when you drag the fill handle. But if you hold down Ctrl while you drag, Excel extends the series to 100, 101, 102, and so on.

Sometimes you can double-click the fill handle to automatically extend a series from a selected range. AutoFill determines the size of the range by matching an adjacent range. For example, in Figure 8-12, we filled column A with a series of values. You can fill column B by simply entering series values in B1 and B2, and then selecting the range B1:B2 and then double-clicking the fill handle. The newly created series stops at cell B6 to match the filled cells in column A. The result is shown in Figure 8-15 on the next page.

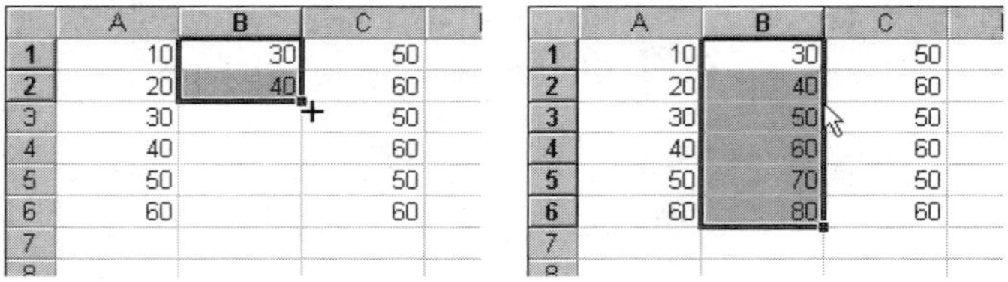

FIGURE 8-15.

We extended a series into B3:B6 by selecting B1:B2 and double-clicking the fill handle.

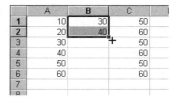

When the selected cells contain something other than a series, such as simple text entries, double-clicking the fill handle copies the selected cells to the adjacent range. For example, if the range D1:D2 contained text and you double-clicked the fill handle, the text entries would be copied down through cell D6.

Dragging the Fill Handle with the Right Mouse Button

When you use the right mouse button to fill a range or extend a series, a shortcut menu appears when you release the button, as shown in Figure 8-16. You can use the commands on the shortcut menu to control the way ranges are filled or the way series are extended.

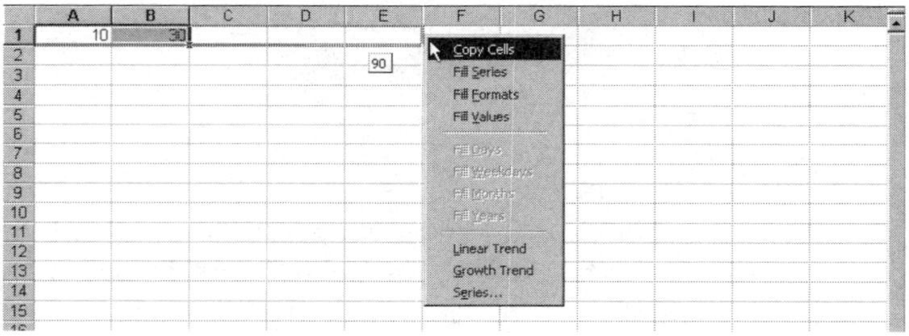

FIGURE 8-16.

If you use the right mouse button to drag the fill handle, this shortcut menu appears when you release the button.

The Copy Cells command on the shortcut menu simply copies the selected, or source, cells—both contents and formats—to the destination range where you drag, repeating the pattern of the source cells as necessary. If in Figure 8-16 we choose the Fill Series command, the sequence of selected numbers is extended as if we had used the fill handle normally with the left mouse button. In fact, the box that appears on the screen adjacent to the arrow pointer indicates what the last number of this sequence would be if we dragged the fill handle with the left mouse button (in this case, 90). If we choose the Fill Formats command, only the formatting of the source cells is copied—the contents of the cells are not affected. If we choose the Fill Values command, on the other hand, the contents of the source cells are copied (or a series is extended, depending on the contents), but the formats of the source cells and the destination cells remain intact.

If the source cells contain dates, the Fill Days, Fill Weekdays, Fill Months, and Fill Years commands on the shortcut menu are made available, allowing you to extend a series where only the corresponding component of the date is incremented.

The Linear Trend command creates a simple linear trend series similar to that which is created by dragging the fill handle with the left mouse button. The Growth Trend command creates a simple nonlinear growth series, using the selected cells to extrapolate points along an exponential growth curve. In Figure 8-17, rows 3 through 6 in column A contain a series created with the Linear Trend command, and the same rows in column B contain a series created with the Growth Trend command.

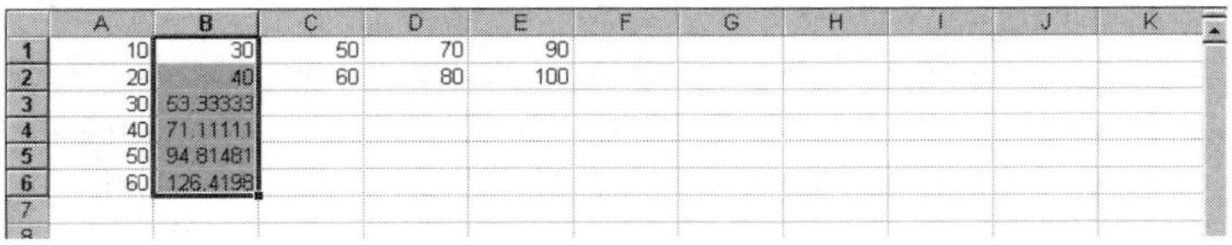

FIGURE 8-17.

We created a linear trend series in column A and a growth trend series in column B.

When you choose the Series command, the Series dialog box appears, allowing you to create custom incremental series. *The Series command is explained in more detail on page 275.*

Creating Custom Lists

If you find yourself repeatedly entering a particular sequence in your worksheets, such as a list of names, you can use Excel's Custom Lists feature to make entering that sequence as easy as dragging the mouse. After you've created the sequence, you can enter it in any range of cells by simply typing any item from the sequence in a cell and then dragging the fill handle.

For example, Figure 8-18 shows the single name we entered in cell A1 and the custom list we entered in cells A2:A5 by simply dragging the fill handle.

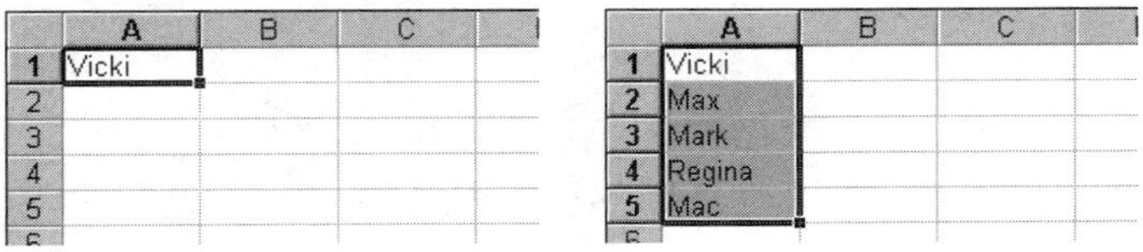

FIGURE 8-18.

You can create custom lists that you can enter automatically by dragging the fill handle.

To create a custom list, follow these steps:

1 From the Tools Menu, choose Options and then click the Custom Lists tab.

2 With NEW LIST selected in the Custom Lists list box, type the items you want to include in your list in the List Entries list box. Be sure to type the items in the order you want them to appear.

3 Click the Add button to add the list to the Custom Lists box.

4 Click OK to return to the worksheet.

Importing Custom Lists

You can also create a custom list by importing the entries in an existing cell range. To import the entries shown in Figure 8-18, we first selected the range A1:A5 and clicked the Custom Lists tab of the Options dialog box. Then we clicked the Import button to add the selected entries as a new list, as shown in Figure 8-19. Alternatively, you can click in the Import List from Cells edit box, which allows you to select cells directly on the worksheet. As soon as you begin to drag the mouse, the dialog box automatically "collapses" allowing you the maximum viewing area, then snaps back to full size when you're finished. You can also click the collapse dialog button—the small icon on the right side of the Import List from Cells edit box—to shrink the dialog before you select cells. We then clicked OK to close the dialog box. (To delete a custom list, click the list you wish to delete, and then click the Delete button.)

FIGURE 8-19.

Use the Import button on the Custom Lists tab to define existing selected cell entries as custom lists.

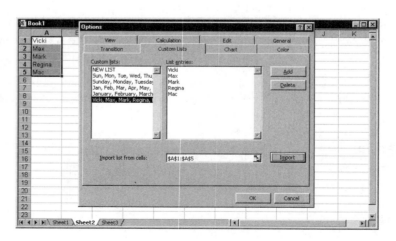

Editing Directly in Cells

You can edit the contents of cells without using the formula bar. By double-clicking a cell, you can perform any normal formula-bar editing procedure directly in the cell. Figure 8-20 shows a cell that is being edited in this fashion.

FIGURE 8-20.

You can edit a cell by double-clicking it.

> To edit directly in cells, the Edit Directly In Cell option must be selected. If this option, which is on by default, has been turned off, you can activate it by choosing the Options command from the Tools menu, clicking the Edit tab, and then selecting the Edit Directly In Cell option.

Undoing, Redoing, and Repeating Previous Actions

You can use the Undo command or button to recover from editing mistakes without having to reenter data or patch information back in place. Simply choose Undo from the Edit menu, click the Undo button on the Standard toolbar, or press Ctrl+Z to reverse the previous action. Repeated use of the command, button, or keyboard shortcut undoes the next-to-last action and allows you to undo up to the last 16 actions.

The Undo button includes a drop-down list of up to the last 16 actions you performed. You can then select and simultaneously undo any number of these actions at once. You display the drop-down list by clicking the small downward-pointing arrow next to the Undo button, as shown in Figure 8-21.

FIGURE 8-21.

Click the arrow next to the Undo button to select and simultaneously undo up to the last 16 actions.

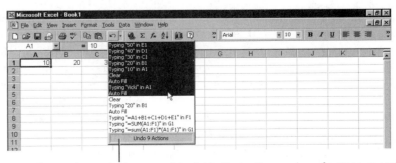

A small status bar at the bottom of the list indicates the number of actions you selected.

II

Worksheets

With the list visible, drag the mouse down the list and select the actions you want to undo. When you click the mouse, your worksheet reverts to the condition it was in previous to the selected actions.

Undo reverses the effect of most commands on the Edit menu and restores any entry in the formula bar. For example, if you accidentally delete a range of data, choose Undo to replace the entries. If you edit the contents of a cell and subsequently discover that your changes are incorrect, choose Undo to restore the original cell entry. In addition, you can use Undo to reverse formatting and many other types of commands.

 WARNING

> A few commands are irreversible. For example, you cannot reverse Delete Sheet on the Edit menu. If you aren't sure whether you need a worksheet, activate it and look at it before you delete it.
>
> Similarly, you cannot reverse the Worksheet command on the Insert menu. Be sure to save your workbook before you use either of these commands. If you later find that you deleted or inserted worksheets in error, you can always retrieve your original workbook.

The Undo command changes to indicate the action it's currently able to reverse. For example, suppose you choose the All command from the Clear submenu of the Edit menu to erase the contents of a range of cells and then discover that you have cleared the wrong range. The Undo command on the Edit menu changes to Undo Clear. Likewise, if you enter a formula in a cell, the Edit menu displays Undo Typing.

Unfortunately, Excel has many commands that Undo can't reverse. After you choose one of these commands, Can't Undo appears dimmed on the Edit menu. Predictably, actions that you cannot undo will not appear in the Undo button's drop-down list.

Actions That Don't Affect Undo

SEE ALSO

For more information about commands that move the cell pointer, see Chapter 5, "Worksheet Basics."

You can perform certain tasks in the worksheet without affecting Undo. For instance, you can use the cell pointer and scroll bars to move through your worksheet and activate other cells. Also, commands that move the cell pointer do not affect Undo. For instance, you can use Go To and Find on the Edit menu without affecting Undo. And you can move to other worksheets and workbooks using commands or the mouse without affecting Undo. Note that Excel does not keep separate Undo lists for each workbook, but rather keeps track of your edits in a linear fashion. Each action you take in any open workbook is recorded in sequence.

If you make changes in multiple workbooks, Undo will retrace your steps through those workbooks.

Redoing What You've Undone

After you use Undo, the command name changes to Redo. Redo reverses Undo, restoring the worksheet to its condition before you used Undo. For example, when you pull down the Edit menu after you use Undo Clear, the command appears as Redo Clear. If you choose this command, Microsoft Excel 2000 again clears the contents of the selected range and changes the name back to Undo Clear.

The Redo button on the Standard toolbar operates identically to the Undo button, as described above, allowing you to redo the last action by clicking the button itself, or to redo up to the last 16 undone actions. For example, when you undo a number of actions using the Undo drop-down list, these actions are transferred to the Redo button's own drop-down list. If you then redo the same actions, they are transferred back to the Undo drop-down list.

You can take advantage of the Undo/Redo command and buttons to see the effects of an editing change in your worksheet. Suppose you edit a cell that is referred to in several formulas. To see the effects of your change, scroll through the worksheet and view the other cells. If you don't remember what a cell looked like before the change, you can use Undo and Redo to get a "before and after" view.

Repeating Your Last Action

You can use the Repeat command to repeat an action—a great time-saver when you need to perform the same action in several areas. Repeat is particularly handy with commands such as Insert and Delete, which you cannot perform on nonadjacent multiple cell or range selections.

NOTE

> Microsoft Excel for Windows 95 included a Repeat button on the Standard toolbar that looked essentially the same as the current Redo button.

In some ways, Repeat is similar to Undo. The name of the command changes to reflect your most recent action. For example, suppose you choose the Formats command from the Clear submenu of the Edit menu. When you pull down the Edit menu a second time, the Repeat command appears as Repeat Clear. (This command does not normally appear on shortened menus. Click the double arrow at the bottom of

II

Worksheets

the Edit menu to display the Repeat command.) If you select another cell or range and choose Repeat Clear, Excel assumes that you want to perform the same action—clearing formats, in this case—on the new selection.

Unlike Undo, Repeat works with most commands. The only exceptions are those commands that can't logically be repeated. For example, if you save a file using the Save command on the File menu, you can't repeat the action. In this case, Repeat reflects the last repeatable command.

Using Editing Commands

While you can use direct cell manipulation, as described earlier in this chapter, to quickly and easily perform many common editing operations, menu commands sometimes offer advantages and additional functionality. This section describes Excel's editing commands and covers the rules and regulations that apply to editing operations.

Clearing Cell Contents and Formats

You can use the Clear commands on the Edit menu to erase the contents of a cell or range, the format assigned to that cell or range, or both. You can also use the Clear command with cell comments and charts.

?) SEE ALSO

For information about cell comments, see "Adding Comments to Cells," page 292. For information about Hyperlinks, see Chapter 19, "Hyperlinks and the Internet."

The Clear submenu offers five commands: All, Formats, Contents, Comments, and Hyperlinks. The All command erases the contents of the selected cells, any formats (other than column width and row height), and any comments attached to those cells. The Formats command removes the formats from the selected cells but leaves their contents and comments in place; the selected cells then revert to the General format and the Normal style. The Contents command erases the contents of the selected cells but leaves their formats and comments intact. The Comments command removes any comments from the selected cells but leaves their contents and formats in place. The Hyperlinks command removes any hyperlinks from selected cells, without affecting their contents, formats, or comments.

NOTE

If you're working in the formula bar or editing directly in a cell, pressing Delete erases the selected characters or the character to the right of the insertion point, while pressing Backspace erases the selected characters or the character to the left of the insertion point.

Deleting Cells, Columns, and Rows

You can use the Delete command to remove cells from your worksheet. Unlike Clear, which erases the formats, contents, or comments in a cell but leaves the cell in place, Delete removes the selected cell or range from the worksheet. In other words, Clear works like an eraser, and Delete works like a pair of scissors.

Deleting Entire Columns and Rows

You can use the Delete command to remove entire columns and rows from your worksheet and eliminate wasted space, as shown in Figure 8-22.

FIGURE 8-22.

The Delete command can remove the three extra rows that appear above the totals row in this worksheet.

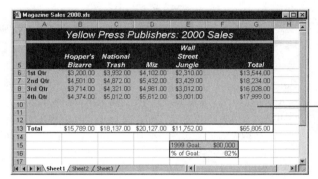

To delete these blank rows, drag through the row headings for rows 10, 11, and 12 and then choose Delete from the Edit menu.

As you can see in Figure 8-23, after you delete rows 10 through 12, every entry in the rows below the deleted rows is shifted upward so that the totals originally in row 13 now appear in row 10.

FIGURE 8-23.

When we deleted rows 10 through 12, the remaining rows in the worksheet moved up to fill the gap.

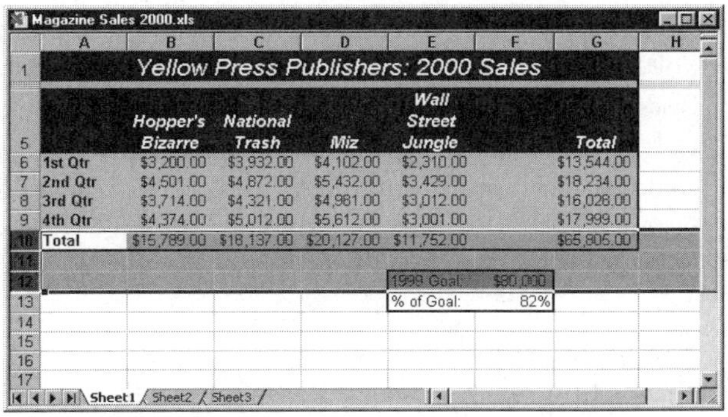

Worksheets

II

You can find the Columns And Rows tab from the file Editing.xls, used in Figures 8-22, 8-23, 8-25, and 8-27 on the Microsoft Press Web site at *http://mspress.microsoft.com/mspress/products/2050/*.

In addition, Excel adjusts the formulas in row 10 to account for the deleted rows. Before we deleted the extra rows, the formula in cell B13 (now in cell B10) was

=SUM(B6:B12)

However, cell B10 now contains the formula

=SUM(B6:B9)

You can also use Delete to remove columns. Simply select the column and choose Delete. Your column disappears from the worksheet, and all subsequent columns shift one column to the left. Again, Excel updates any formulas affected by the deletion.

You can delete multiple selections in one operation as long as you delete either entire rows or entire columns. For example, you can select columns A and F and choose Delete. If you select cell B6 and column C and choose Delete, however, you'll see the alert message *This command cannot be used with selections that contain entire rows or columns, and also other cells. Try selecting only entire rows, entire columns, or just groups of cells.*

Deleting Partial Columns and Rows

You can delete partial columns and rows—and even a single cell. Simply select the cell or cells and then choose Delete.

For example, to delete cells F6:F10 from the worksheet in Figure 8-23 without changing the remaining cells in column F, select cells F6:F10 and then choose Delete from the Edit menu. Excel displays the dialog box in Figure 8-24. As you can see, Excel needs more information before it can carry out the Delete command. You can use the Delete dialog box to shift remaining cells left or up to fill the gap or to delete entire rows and columns. For this example, leave Shift Cells Left selected and click OK. Excel deletes only the selected range—F6:F10. Excel then adjusts the worksheet so that the cells in G6:G10 move to F6:F10, those in H6:H10 move to G6:G10, and so on. Figure 8-25 shows how the worksheet looks after this deletion. Note that we widened column F to accommodate the totals.

FIGURE 8-24.

The Delete command deletes specific cells as well as entire rows and columns.

FIGURE 8-25.

The Shift Cells Left option deleted cells F6:F10.

	A	B	C	D	E	F	G	H
1	Yellow Press Publishers: 2000 Sales							
5		Hopper's Bizarre	National Trash	Miz	Wall Street Jungle		Total	
6	1st Qtr	$3,200.00	$3,932.00	$4,102.00	$2,310.00	$13,544.00		
7	2nd Qtr	$4,501.00	$4,872.00	$5,432.00	$3,429.00	$18,234.00		
8	3rd Qtr	$3,714.00	$4,321.00	$4,981.00	$3,012.00	$16,028.00		
9	4th Qtr	$4,374.00	$5,012.00	$5,612.00	$3,001.00	$17,999.00		
10	Total	$15,789.00	$18,137.00	$20,127.00	$11,752.00	$65,805.00		
11								
12					1999 Goal:	$80,000		
13					% of Goal:	82%		
14								
15								
16								
17								

Magazine Sales 2000.xls

Sheet1 / Sheet2 / Sheet3 /

If you select F6:F10, choose Delete, and then select Shift Cells Up, Excel still removes only the range F6:F10. It then moves the remainder of column F—the entire range F11:F65536—up five cells.

TIP

Although you can generally use Undo to cancel a deletion, you should take heed of the following:

- Before you delete an entire column or row, scroll through your worksheet to be sure you're not erasing important information that is not currently visible.

- If you delete a cell upon which formulas in other cells depend, a #REF! error message appears in those formulas. Deleting cells that are referred to by formulas can be disastrous.

- When you delete a column or row referred to by an argument of a function, Excel modifies the argument, if at all possible, to account for the deletion. This adaptability is a compelling reason to use functions where possible.

When you delete a partial row or column, it's easy to misalign data. For example, in Figure 8-25 the label *Total* in column G did not move left with the other data in that column. As a result, the heading for the data in column F now appears in the wrong column. We could have avoided this problem by deleting cells F1:F10 instead of F6:F10, as shown in Figure 8-26. (Again, you have to widen column F to see numbers. Otherwise, you see the #### symbol.)

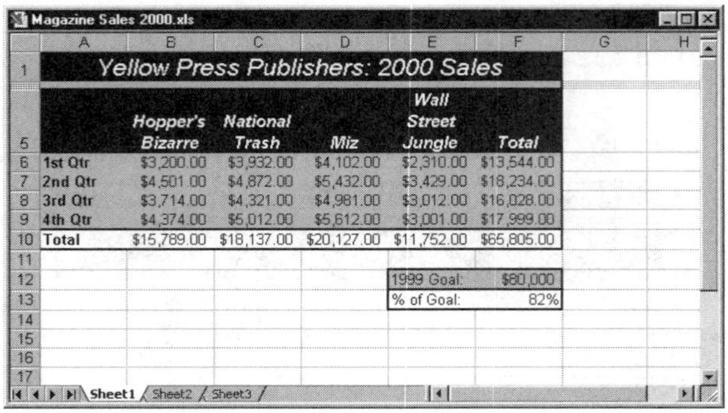

FIGURE 8-26.

We deleted cells F1:F5 to fix the column headings.

Inserting Columns and Rows

You can use the commands on the Insert menu to add cells, columns, and rows to a worksheet. For example, suppose that after you've made adjustments and put the finishing touches on the worksheet shown in Figure 8-26, you discover that the company has acquired another magazine whose sales figures are to be combined with the others. Fortunately, with the Columns command on the Insert menu, you can fix things up in a hurry without a lot of shuffling and recalculation.

To insert space for the new magazine, simply select a column heading, column F in this case, and choose the Columns command from the Insert menu. The contents of column F move to column G, leaving the inserted column F blank and ready for new information, as shown in Figure 8-27.

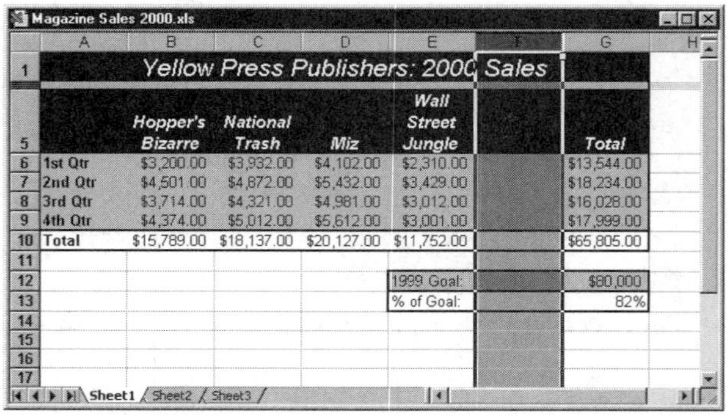

FIGURE 8-27.

The Columns command on the Insert menu added a column for a new magazine.

The newly inserted cells take on the same formats as the cells in the column to the left, and the formulas in cells G6:G13 are adjusted to account for the expanded range.

Similarly, to insert a row, select the row above which you want the new row inserted and choose the Rows command from the Insert menu. You can also insert cells rather than entire rows or columns by choosing the Cells command on the Insert menu, which displays the dialog box shown in Figure 8-28 on the next page.

Create a Custom Insert and Delete Toolbar

Excel provides six buttons for inserting and deleting rows and columns. These buttons are not located on any toolbar, so to use them you must either create a custom toolbar or modify an existing toolbar. If you do a lot of inserting and deleting, you might want to create an Insert/Delete custom toolbar, containing all six tools, like the one shown here.

The buttons are, from left to right: Insert Cells, Insert Rows, Insert Columns, Delete, Delete Row, and Delete Columns. Select Toolbars and Customize from the View menu. Choose the Toolbars tab, click the New button, and type a name for the toolbar. Then choose the Commands tab. The Insert buttons are in the Insert category, and the Delete buttons are in the Edit category. (For information about how to create *custom toolbars,* see Chapter 3, "Toolbars and Menus.")

You won't see the Insert or Delete dialog box when you use the Insert Cells or Delete button. Instead, Excel uses common-sense rules to determine the direction in which to shift the surrounding cells. If the selection is wider than it is tall, (2 cells wide by 1 cell high, for example), the Insert Cells button automatically shifts cells down, and the Delete button shifts cells up.

Using the Insert Rows, Insert Columns, Delete Rows, and Delete Columns buttons is equivalent to selecting the Entire Row or Entire Column options in the Insert and Delete dialog boxes. You need not first select entire rows or columns to use these buttons. Instead, simply select one or more cells below each row or to the right of each column where you want to insert, or select one or more cells in each row or column you want to delete.

II

Worksheets

FIGURE 8-28.

The Cells command on the Insert menu displays this dialog box.

For more information about the Cut and Copy commands, see "Cutting and Pasting," page 256. For more information about inserting cut cells, see "Inserting Cut Cells," page 259.

If you recently used the Cut or Copy command to transfer some information from your workbook to the Windows Clipboard (an area of memory that holds data temporarily), the Cells command on the Insert menu is replaced by the Cut Cells or the Copied Cells command. (This command does not normally appear on shortened menus. Click the double arrow at the bottom of the Insert menu to display the Cut Cells or Copied Cells command.) You can use either of these commands to simultaneously insert the necessary number of cells and paste the contents of the Clipboard into the new cells. To insert blank cells under these circumstances, first press Esc to clear the Clipboard's contents and then open the Insert menu. The Cells command reappears.

As with the Delete command, you can choose a multiple nonadjacent selection when you use the Insert command as long as you choose either entire rows or entire columns.

Cutting and Pasting

For information about using the mouse for cutting and pasting, see "Moving and Copying with the Mouse," page 238.

You can use the Cut and Paste commands on the Edit menu to move entries and formats from one place to another. Unlike Delete and Clear, which remove cells and cell entries, the Cut command puts a dotted-line marquee around the selected cells and places a copy of your selection on the Clipboard, which stores it so that you can paste it in another location.

When you select the range to which you want to move the cut cells, the Paste command places them in their new location, clears the contents of the cells within the marquee, and removes the marquee.

> Keyboard shortcuts are available for the Cut and Paste commands; they are the same ones used by almost all Windows programs. You can press Ctrl+X for the Cut command and Ctrl+V for the Paste command. Alternatively, you can click the Cut and Paste buttons on the Standard toolbar to execute these commands.

When you use the Cut and Paste commands to move a range of cells, Excel clears both the contents and the formats of the cut range and transfers them to the cells in the paste range. For example, to move the contents of the range A1:A5 on the top in Figure 8-29 to cells C1:C5, select cells A1:A5 and then choose Cut from the Edit menu. A marquee appears around the cells you selected. Next select cell C1 and choose Paste from the Edit menu. The bottom of Figure 8-29 shows the result: both the contents and the formats assigned to cells A1:A5 are transferred to cells C1:C5, and cells A1:A5 are blank. Now, if you enter values in cells A1:A5, those cells revert to their default formats.

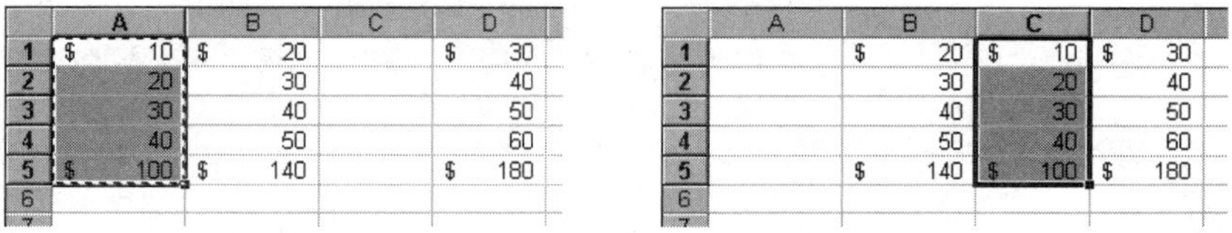

FIGURE 8-29.

Use the Cut and Paste commands to move the contents of the range A1:A5 to cells C1:C5.

	A	B	C	D
1	$ 10	$ 20		$ 30
2	20	30		40
3	30	40		50
4	40	50		60
5	$ 100	$ 140		$ 180
6				
7				

	A	B	C	D
1		$ 20	$ 10	$ 30
2		30	20	40
3		40	30	50
4		50	40	60
5		$ 140	$ 100	$ 180
6				
7				

Ⓦ **ON THE WEB**   You can find the Cut & Paste tab from the file Editing.xls used in Figures 8-29 and 8-30 at *http://mspress.microsoft.com/mspress/products/2050/*.

When you move a cell, Excel adjusts any formulas outside the cut area that refer to that cell. For example, in Figure 8-29, cell A5 contains the formula

    =SUM(A1:A4)

When we moved cells A1:A5 to cells C1:C5, the move had no apparent effect on the cell contents. However, the formula in cell C5 now reads

    =SUM(C1:C4)

Cut and Paste Rules

When you use the Cut and Paste commands, remember the following rules:

- The cut area you select must be a single rectangular block of cells. If you try to select more than one range, you'll see the message *Select only one range at a time, and then click the command again.*

- You can paste only once after you use Cut. To paste the selected data in two or more locations, use the Copy command. You can then use the commands on the Clear submenu to erase the contents of the original cell or range.

- You don't have to select the entire paste range before you choose Paste. When you select a single cell as your paste range, Excel extends the paste area to match the size and shape of the cut area. The cell you select becomes the upper-left corner of the paste area. If you do select the entire paste area, however, be sure the range you select is the same size and shape as the cut area. If the cut and paste areas are not identical in size and shape, an alert box appears, displaying the message *Cut and paste areas are not the same size and shape.* To correct the problem, click OK in the alert box and select a new paste area.

- Excel overwrites the contents and formats of any existing cells in the paste range when you use Paste. If you don't want to lose existing cell entries, be sure your worksheet has enough blank cells below and to the right of the cell you select as the upper-left corner of the paste area to hold the entire cut area.

Using Overlapping Cut and Paste Ranges

Suppose you want to move cells A1:B5 in the worksheet on the left in Figure 8-30 to cells B1:C5 to fill the empty column C. You could select cells A1:A5 and choose the Columns command from the Insert menu, but then all the cells in rows 1 through 5 would shift one column to the right and the blank column would still exist.

FIGURE 8-30.

You can use overlapping cut and paste areas when moving information.

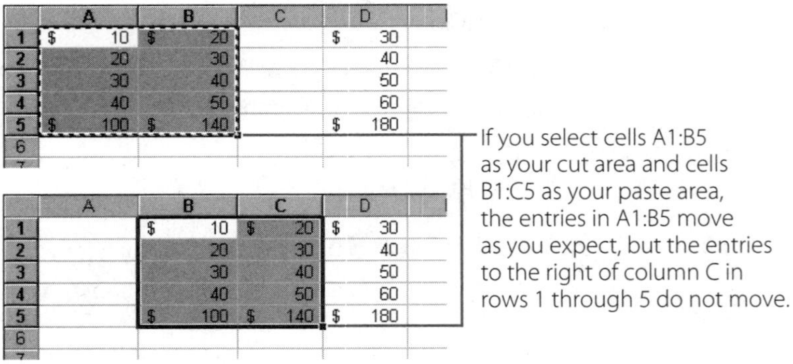

If you select cells A1:B5 as your cut area and cells B1:C5 as your paste area, the entries in A1:B5 move as you expect, but the entries to the right of column C in rows 1 through 5 do not move.

Fortunately, Excel offers a way around this problem. Because Excel transfers the contents of your cut area to your paste area before it erases them from the cut area, you can specify overlapping cut and paste areas without losing information in the overlapping cells.

Inserting Cut Cells

When you use the Paste command, Excel pastes cut cells into the selected area of your worksheet. If the selected area already contains data, that data is replaced by the data that you paste.

Under some circumstances, you can insert material from the Clipboard between existing worksheet cells instead of pasting it over existing cells. To do this, use the Insert menu's Cut Cells command instead of the Edit menu's Paste command. (The Cut Cells command does not normally appear on shortened menus. Click the double arrow at the bottom of the Insert menu to display the Cut Cells command.) The Cut Cells command replaces the Cells command and appears only after you have cut data to the Clipboard. (You can also use the mouse to perform this operation on cells and cell ranges directly. *See "Shortcuts for Entering and Editing," page 236.*)

For example, to rearrange the names of the months shown on the left in Figure 8-31 so that they start with September and end with August, follow these steps:

1   Select A10:A13 and then choose Cut from the Edit menu.

2   Make A2 the active cell.

3   From the Insert menu, choose Cut Cells.

Excel puts the data from A10:A13 in cells A2:A5 and then moves the rest of column A down to accommodate the insertion, as shown on the right in Figure 8-31.

FIGURE 8-31.

Using the Cut command on the Edit menu with the Cut Cells command on the Insert menu, we transferred four months from the bottom of the list without changing the rest.

	A	B	C
1		Jones	Smith
2	January		
3	February		
4	March		
5	April		
6	May		
7	June		
8	July		
9	August		
10	September		
11	October		
12	November		
13	December		
14			
15			

	A	B	C
1		Jones	Smith
2	September		
3	October		
4	November		
5	December		
6	January		
7	February		
8	March		
9	April		
10	May		
11	June		
12	July		
13	August		
14			
15			

 ON THE WEB

You can find the Insert Cells tab from the file Editing.xls used in the preceding example at *http://mspress.microsoft.com/mspress/products/2050/*.

Collect and Copy

In previous versions of Excel, you could only cut or copy one item at a time. But an exciting new feature in Excel 2000, called "Collect and Copy," allows you to cut or copy up to 12 separate items and then paste them where you want them, one at a time or all at once. You might have already seen the Clipboard toolbar, shown in the following figure, and wondered what it was all about.

When you copy an item (a cell, a range, some text, an object, and so forth), that item is saved in memory, in a temporary storage area called the Clipboard. In Excel 2000, the Clipboard is enhanced so that you can "graze" through one or more worksheets or workbooks, collecting up to 12 items that you need to copy elsewhere.

If you copy or cut one item, then copy or cut another, the Clipboard toolbar should appear automatically. (If the Clipboard toolbar does not appear, choose Toolbars on the View menu, then choose Clipboard.) Each time you copy or cut another item, another icon appears on the Clipboard toolbar. The above figure shows six different items on the Clipboard, which can be used like a palette, allowing you to paste any or all wherever you choose. The Clipboard toolbar expands to accommodate more icons as you cut or copy items, until all 12 slots are full.

To paste an item from the Clipboard toolbar, select the cell where you want to paste, then click the icon representing the item you want to paste. When you hover the mouse cursor over one of the icons, a tool tip appears, showing you what the item contains. In the above figure, the tool tip indicates that item three contains the word *February*.

You can easily build new lists using this feature. For example, you can copy items from various locations, then click the Paste All button on the Clipboard toolbar to paste all the items, in the order you collected them, into a single column. To empty the Clipboard for a new collection, click the Clear Clipboard button.

Copying and Pasting

? SEE ALSO

For more information about the Paste Special command, see "Selective Pasting," page 268.

You can use the Copy and Paste commands on the Edit menu to duplicate the contents and formats of selected cells in another area of your worksheet without disturbing the contents of the original cells. You use the Copy command (or the Copy button on the Standard toolbar) to indicate the range of cells you want to copy, and you use the Paste command (or the Paste button on the Standard toolbar) to indicate where you want the copies to be placed. You can also press the Enter key instead of choosing the Paste command, but only if you want to paste just a single copy. Pressing Enter after you choose Copy pastes one copy and then removes the copied cells from the Clipboard. (You can also use the mouse to copy and paste cells and cell ranges directly in your worksheet.)

The Paste command pastes everything from the copied cells—entries, formats, and comments. To paste only certain elements, use the Paste Special command.

Copying a Single Cell

Suppose cell A1 of your worksheet contains the value 100. To copy the contents of cell A1 to cell C1, simply select cell A1, choose Copy from the Edit menu, click cell C1, and then choose Paste from the Edit menu.

When you copy cell A1, a marquee appears around the cell, and does not disappear after you use Paste. This marquee indicates that the copy area is still active. As long as the marquee appears, you can continue to use Paste to create additional copies of the cell. You can even use the commands on the Window menu and the Open and New commands on the File menu to access other workbooks and windows without losing your copy area. For example, you might copy a cell to another area of your worksheet, use the Open command on the File menu to access a second workbook, and then paste the cell into the new workbook as well. To finish pasting and remove the contents of the copy area from the Clipboard, press Enter or press Esc.

By specifying paste areas of different sizes and shapes, you can create multiple copies of the contents of the copy area, as in Figure 8-32.

FIGURE 8-32.

You can create multiple copies of a single cell by selecting a range before you paste.

If you specify the range C1:E2 as the paste range, Excel copies the contents of cell A1 to all the cells in the range C1:E2.

You can also specify multiple nonadjacent paste areas. For example, to copy the contents of cell A1 to cells C1, C3, and D2, follow these steps:

1 Select cell A1.

2 Choose Copy from the Edit menu or click the Copy button.

3 Select cell C1 and then hold down the Ctrl key and click cells D2 and C3.

4 Choose Paste from the Edit menu or click the Paste button.

Your worksheet now looks like the one shown in Figure 8-33.

FIGURE 8-33.

You can copy one cell and paste many.

Copying Ranges

You can use the Copy command to copy ranges the same way you copy single cells.

As with the Cut and Paste commands, you don't have to select the entire paste area when you copy a range of cells. You need only indicate the upper left corner of the range by selecting a single cell.

The marquee remains active. You can continue to paste the contents of the copy area into new paste areas until you press Enter or Esc. Pressing Enter or Esc turns off the marquee and clears the contents of the copy area from the Clipboard.

You can also create multiple copies of the copy range. Not every paste range works when you're copying cell ranges, however. For example, if you copy cells A1:A3 and then designate a range, such as C1:C2, the alert message *Copy and paste areas are not the same size or shape* appears. In other words, you must either select only the first cell in each paste area or select one or more paste ranges of exactly the same size and shape as the copy area.

Inserting Copied Cells

For more information about inserting cut cells, see "Inserting Cut Cells," page 259.

When you use the Paste command, Excel pastes copied cells into the selected area of your worksheet. If the selected area already contains data, that data is replaced by the data that you paste.

With the help of the Copied Cells command on the Insert menu, you can insert material from the Clipboard between existing worksheet cells, instead of pasting it over existing cells. The Copied Cells command appears only after you have copied data to the Clipboard. (The Copied Cells command does not normally appear on shortened menus. Click the double arrow at the bottom of the Insert menu to display the Copied Cells command.)

The Copied Cells command works the same way as the Cut Cells command. If Excel needs more information about how to adjust the worksheet, it will present a dialog box similar to the one shown earlier in Figure 8-28 on page 256. Select either Shift Cells Right or Shift Cells Down and then click OK to finish the operation.

Copying Relative, Absolute, and Mixed References

As you learned in Chapter 6, "Building Formulas," Excel uses two types of cell references: relative and absolute. These two types of references behave very differently when you use the Copy command.

Relative References

When you copy a cell that contains relative cell references, the formula in the paste area doesn't refer to the same cells as the formula in the copy area. Instead, Excel changes the formula references in relation to the position of the pasted cell.

Returning to a worksheet like the one shown in Figure 8-26 on page 254, suppose you enter the formula

    =AVERAGE(B6:E6)

in cell G6. This formula averages the values in the four-cell range that begins five columns to the left of cell G6. Of course, you want to repeat this calculation for the remaining categories as well. Instead of typing a new formula in each cell in column G, select cell G6 and then choose Copy from the Edit menu. Next select cells G7:G10 and choose Paste from the Edit menu. The results are shown in Figure 8-34 on the next page. Because the formula in cell G6 contains a relative reference, Excel adjusts the references in each copy of the formula. As a result, each copy of the formula calculates the average of the cells in the corresponding row. For example, cell G7 contains the formula

    =AVERAGE(B7:E7)

II

Worksheets

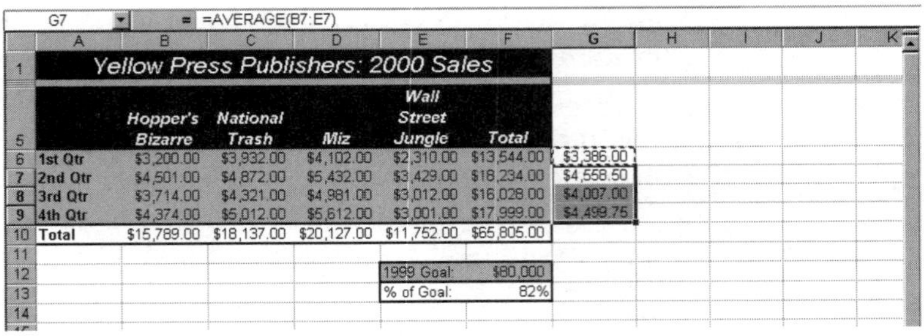

FIGURE 8-34.

We copied the relative references from cell G6 to cells G7:G10.

Absolute References

To ensure that cell references do not change when you copy them, use absolute references. For example, in the worksheet on the left in Figure 8-35, cell B2 contains the hourly rate at which employees are to be paid, and cell C5 contains the formula

=B2*B5

Suppose you want to copy the formula in C5 to the range C6:C8. The worksheet on the right in Figure 8-35 shows what happens if you copy the existing formula to this range. The formula in cell C6 returns the value 0, and cell C7 contains the #VALUE! error value. If you take a closer look at the formulas in cells C6:C8, you'll see that none of them refers to cell B2. For instance, the formula in cell C6 is

=B3*B6

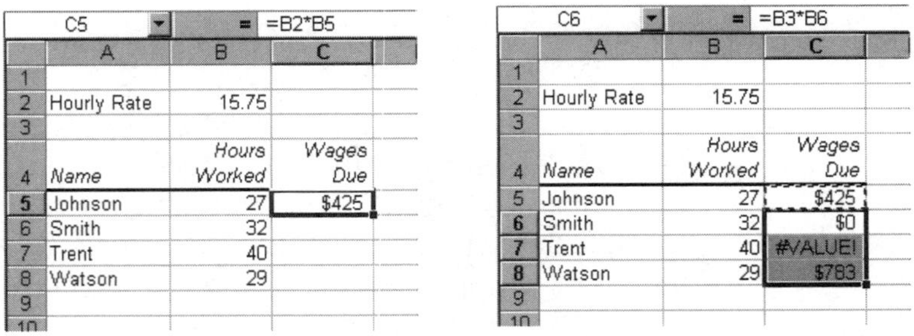

FIGURE 8-35.

The entry in cell C5 is a formula that contains relative references. We incorrectly copied the relative formula in cell C5 to cells C6:C8.

W ON THE WEB

You can find the Absolute Refs tab from the file Editing.xls used in Figures 8-35 and 8-36 at *http://mspress.microsoft.com/mspress/products/2050/*.

Because cell B3 is empty, the formula returns a 0 value. Similarly, cell C7 contains the formula

=B4*B7

Because cell B4 contains a label rather than a value, the formula in cell C7 returns an error value.

Because the reference to cell B2 in the original formula is relative, it changes as you copy the formula to other cells. To apply the wage rate in cell B2 to all the calculations, you must change the reference to cell B2 to an absolute reference before you copy the formula.

You can change the reference style by typing a dollar sign ($) in front of the column and row references. The $ symbol tells Excel to "lock in" the reference. For example, in the worksheet in Figure 8-35, you can select cell C5 and type dollar signs before the B and the 2. The formula becomes

=$B$2*B5

TIP

> You can adjust references in a formula by placing the insertion point any-where adjacent to the reference and pressing F4. Each time you press F4, Excel switches the nearest reference to the next type.

When you copy the modified formula to cells C6:C8, the second cell reference, but not the first, is adjusted within each formula. In Figure 8-36, cell C6 now contains the formula

=$B$2*B6

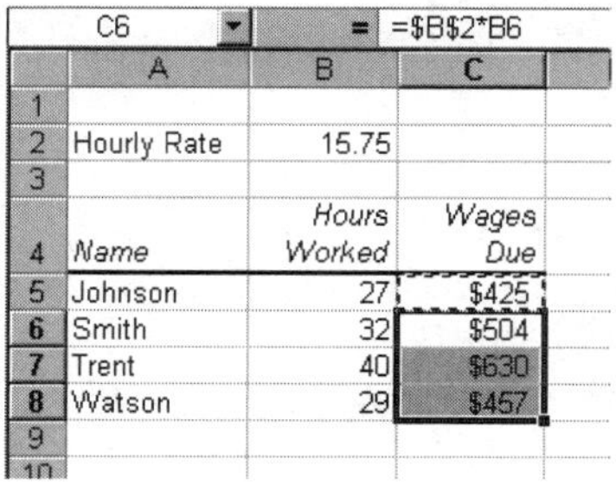

FIGURE 8-36.

We created an absolute reference to cell B2.

	C6	▼	=	=$B$2*B6
	A	B	C	
1				
2	Hourly Rate	15.75		
3				
4	Name	Hours Worked	Wages Due	
5	Johnson	27	$425	
6	Smith	32	$504	
7	Trent	40	$630	
8	Watson	29	$457	
9				
10				

Mixed References

In Microsoft Excel 2000, you can also use mixed references in your formulas to anchor only a portion of a cell reference. In a mixed refer-ence, one portion is absolute and the other is relative. When you copy a mixed reference, Excel anchors the absolute portion and adjusts the relative portion to reflect the location of the cell to which you copied the formula.

In a mixed reference, a dollar sign appears before the absolute portion. For example, $B2 and B$2 are mixed references. Whereas $B2 uses an absolute column reference and a relative row reference, B$2 uses a relative column reference and an absolute row reference.

To create a mixed reference, you can type the $ symbol in front of the column or row reference, or you can use the F4 key to cycle through the four combinations of absolute and relative references—from B2 to $B$2 to B$2 to $B2.

The loan payment table in Figure 8-37 shows a situation in which mixed references are convenient. Using mixed references, you need to enter only one formula in cell C5, and then you can copy it down and across to fill the table. Cell C5 uses the formula

=-PMT($B5,10,C$4)

to calculate the annual payments on a $10,000 loan over a period of 10 years at an interest rate of 7 percent. We copied this formula to cells C5:E8 to calculate payments on three loan amounts using four interest rates.

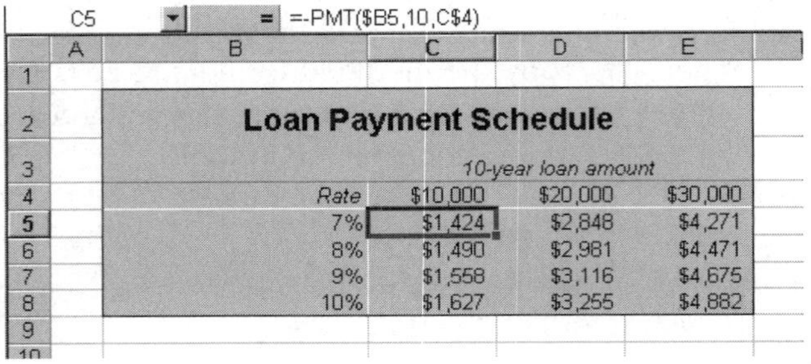

FIGURE 8-37.

This loan payment table uses formulas that contain mixed references.

W **ON THE WEB**   You can find the Mixed Refs tab from the file Editing.xls used in the preceding example at *http://mspress.microsoft.com/mspress/products/2050/*.

The first cell reference, $B5, indicates that we always want to refer to the values in column B. The row reference remains relative, however, so that the copied formulas in rows 6 through 8 refer to the appropriate interest rates in cells B6 through B8. Similarly, the second cell reference, C$4, indicates that we always want to refer to the loan amounts displayed in row 4. In this case, the column reference remains relative so that the copied formulas in columns C through E refer to the appropriate loan amounts in cells C4 through E4. For example, cell E8 contains the formula

=-PMT($B8,10,E$4)

Without mixed references, we would have to edit the formula manually for each column or row of the calculations in cells C5 through E8.

Using Cut, Copy, Paste, and Clear in the Formula Bar

You can also use Cut, Copy, Paste, and Clear to edit entries in the formula bar. Often, simply reentering a value or formula is easier, but the Edit menu commands are convenient when you're working with a long, complex formula or label. For example, to add another *very* to the label

> This is a very, very long label.

place the insertion point to the left of the space before the word *long*, type a comma and a space, and then type the word *very*. Alternatively, you can follow these steps:

1. Select the first instance of the word *very*, the comma, and the space after the comma in the formula bar.

2. Choose the Copy command from the Edit menu or click the Copy button on the Standard toolbar.

3. Place the insertion point in front of the *v* in the second *very*.

4. Choose the Paste command from the Edit menu or click the Paste button on the Standard toolbar.

5. Press Enter to lock in the revised entry.

Your label now reads

> This is a very, very, very long label.

You can also use this capability to copy all or part of a formula from one cell to another. For example, suppose cell A10 contains the formula

> =IF(NPV(.15,A1:A9)]0,A11,A12)

and you want to enter

> =NPV(.15,A1:A9)

in cell B10. Follow these steps:

1. Select cell A10.

2. In the formula bar, select the characters you want to copy—in this case, NPV(.15,A1:A9).

3. Choose Copy from the Edit menu (or click the Copy button) and then press Enter or Esc.

4. Select cell B10, type = to begin a formula, and choose Paste from the Edit menu (or click the Paste button).

The formula's cell references are not adjusted when you cut, copy, and paste in the formula bar.

Selective Pasting

At times, you might want to move or copy the value in a cell without carrying over the underlying formula on which the value is based. Or you might want to copy the formula but not the format of a cell. The Paste Special command on the Edit menu offers a convenient way to paste only certain elements of a copied cell.

For example, cell F4 in Figure 8-38 contains the formula

=AVERAGE(B4:E4)

FIGURE 8-38.
We want to use the value from cell F4 in cell G4.

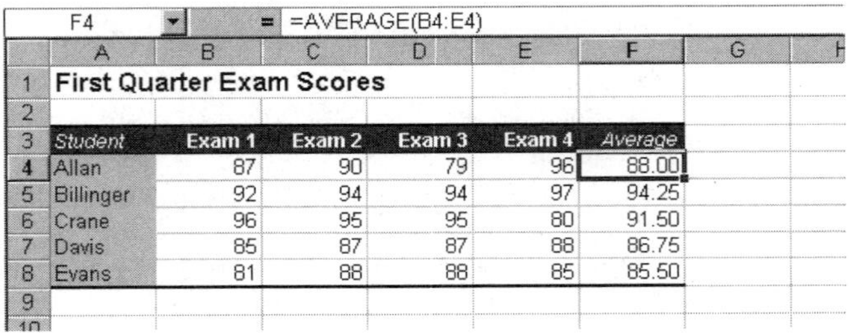
F4 =AVERAGE(B4:E4)

	A	B	C	D	E	F	G
1	First Quarter Exam Scores						
2							
3	*Student*	Exam 1	Exam 2	Exam 3	Exam 4	*Average*	
4	Allan	87	90	79	96	88.00	
5	Billinger	92	94	94	97	94.25	
6	Crane	96	95	95	80	91.50	
7	Davis	85	87	87	88	86.75	
8	Evans	81	88	88	85	85.50	
9							

ON THE WEB

You can find the Paste Special tab from the file Editing.xls used in Figures 8-38 and 8-40 at *http://mspress.microsoft.com/mspress/products/2050/*.

To use the value from cell F4 in cell G4 without copying the actual formula from cell F4 to the new location, follow these steps:

1. Select cell F4 and choose Copy from the Edit menu or click the Copy button on the Standard toolbar. (You must choose Copy to use Paste Special. When you choose Cut, Paste Special is unavailable.)
2. Select cell G4 and choose Paste Special from the Edit menu.
3. In the Paste Special dialog box, shown in Figure 8-39, select the Values option and click OK.
4. Press Esc to clear the marquee and clear the Clipboard.

TIP

After you copy a cell or range, here's a quicker way to display the Paste Special dialog box. Click the cell where you want to paste using the *right* mouse button. A shortcut menu appears containing the Paste Special command.

FIGURE 8-39.

The Paste Special dialog box lets you selectively paste various attributes of a cell or range.

When you select the Values option in the Paste Special dialog box, Excel pastes only the value of the formula in cell F4 into cell G4. After the operation is complete, cell G4 contains the number 88. Excel does not paste the formula or the format of the original cell, so if you later change any of the values in cells B4:E4, the value in cell G4 will remain unchanged.

The Formulas option transfers only the formulas from the cells in the copy range to the cells in the paste range. Any formats or comments in the paste range remain unaffected.

The Formats option transfers only the formats in the cells in the copy range to the paste range. This option has the same effect as selecting a range of cells and choosing the appropriate commands from the Format menu. For example, in Figure 8-38, cells F3:F8 are formatted with several border and font formats; cells H3:H8 are unformatted. If you copy cells F3:F7 and paste their formats into cells H3:H8 using the Formats option in the Paste Special dialog box, the worksheet looks like Figure 8-40. The formats in the copied cells have been pasted into cells H3:H8, but the contents have not.

FIGURE 8-40.

Only the formats of cells F3:F8 are pasted into cells H3:H8 using the Formats option in the Paste Special dialog box.

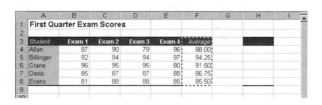

Sometimes you might want to copy cells from one place to another, but you don't want to disturb the borders you spent so much time applying. The All Except Borders option makes this easy.

You can quickly copy and paste formats from a single cell or from a range of cells using the Format Painter button on the Standard toolbar. *For more information about the Format Painter button, see "Formatting with Toolbars," page 158.*

The Validation option offers the capability of pasting only the Data Validation settings that have been applied to the selected cells. The All option pastes the formulas, values, formats, and cell comments from the copy range into the paste range. Because selecting All has the same effect as selecting Paste, you might wonder why Excel offers this option. That question brings us to our next topic—the Operation options.

The Operation Options

SEE ALSO

For more information about cell comments, see "Adding Comments to Cells," page 292. For more information about data validation, see "Validating Data Entry," page 785.

You use the options in the Operation section of the Paste Special dialog box to mathematically combine the contents of the copy area with the contents of the paste area. When you select any option other than None, Excel does not overwrite the paste range. Instead, it uses the specified operator to combine the copy and paste ranges. For example, say we want to calculate each student's final score. We'll need to add the average exam scores and bonus points in columns F and G at the top of Figure 8-41. To combine the contents of these two areas, follow these steps:

1   Select cells F4:F8 and choose Copy from the Edit menu.

2   Select cell H4 and choose Paste Special from the Edit menu.

3   Select the Values option and click OK in the Paste Special dialog box to paste only the values in cells F4:F8 into cells H4:H8. (Because the pasted cells are still selected, you can choose the Paste Special command again to paste only formats so that the numbers display correctly.)

4   Select the range G4:G8 and choose Copy again.

5   Select cell H4 and choose Paste Special.

6   In the Paste Special dialog box, select the Values option and the Add option and then click OK.

FIGURE 8-41.

We used the Values option of Paste Special to copy the averages to the Combined column, then used the Add operation to combine averages with bonus points.

	A	B	C	D	E	F	G	H
1	First Quarter Exam Scores							
2								
3	Student	Exam 1	Exam 2	Exam 3	Exam 4	Average	Bonus	Combined
4	Allan	87	90	79	96	88.00	2	88.00
5	Billinger	92	94	94	97	94.25	3	94.25
6	Crane	96	95	95	80	91.50	4	91.50
7	Davis	85	87	87	88	86.75	2	86.75
8	Evans	81	88	88	85	85.50	3	85.50
9								
10								

	A	B	C	D	E	F	G	H
1	First Quarter Exam Scores							
2								
3	Student	Exam 1	Exam 2	Exam 3	Exam 4	Average	Bonus	Combined
4	Allan	87	90	79	96	88.00	2	90.00
5	Billinger	92	94	94	97	94.25	3	97.25
6	Crane	96	95	95	80	91.50	4	95.50
7	Davis	85	87	87	88	86.75	2	88.75
8	Evans	81	88	88	85	85.50	3	88.50
9								
10								

 ON THE WEB

You can find the Operations tab from the file Editing.xls used in Figures 8-41 and 8-42 at *http://mspress.microsoft.com/mspress/products/2050/*.

As you can see in the worksheet at the bottom of Figure 8-41, Excel adds the values in cells G4:G8 to the values in cells H4:H8.

The other options in the Operation section of the Paste Special dialog box combine the contents of the copy and paste ranges using different operators. The Subtract option subtracts the contents of the copy range from the contents of the paste range, the Multiply option multiplies the contents of the ranges, and the Divide option divides the contents of the paste range by the contents of the copy range.

You'll usually select the Values option from the Paste section of the Paste Special dialog box when you take advantage of the Operation options. As long as the entries in the copy range are numbers, you can use the All option, instead of Values, to copy both the numbers and the formats of the copy range to the paste range. If the copy range contains formulas, however, you might get unexpected results using All.

TIP

As a rule, avoid using the All option with any of the Operation options in the Paste Special dialog box when the copy range includes formulas. In fact, you'll probably want to avoid the Operation options altogether if the paste range contains formulas.

SEE ALSO

For more information about Hyperlinks and the Web toolbar, see Chapter 19, "Hyperlinks and the Internet."

Pasting Hyperlinks

The Paste As Hyperlink command on the Edit menu is another kind of "paste special" command with a specific purpose: to paste a hyperlink to the copied data in the location you specify. When you create a hyperlink, Excel essentially draws an invisible box on top of the selected cell that acts like a button when you click it. (This command does not normally appear on shortened menus. Click the double arrow at the bottom of the Edit menu to display the Paste as Hyperlink command.)

If you are familiar with the World Wide Web, hyperlinks are closely related to the links you see on Web sites that, when clicked, launch a different Web page. The new Web page could be on the same computer or on a computer located halfway across the world. With a Web browser installed, you can add a hyperlink to a location on the World Wide Web. You can use hyperlinks to do a similar thing within your Excel worksheets, perhaps to provide a hyperlink to another workbook that contains additional information. You can also create hyperlinks to another Office document, such as a report created in Microsoft Word or a Microsoft PowerPoint presentation.

Within Excel, you create a hyperlink by copying a cell or range, navigating to the location where you want the hyperlink (on the same sheet, a different sheet, or a different workbook), then choosing Paste As Hyperlink.

When you move the mouse over the new hyperlink, the pointer changes to a little hand, indicating that something will happen when you click there, and a screen tip appears, showing you the name of the document to which the hyperlink is connected, as shown here.

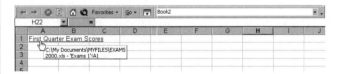

When you click a hyperlink, the document or location from which you copied appears on the screen. The data in the cell or range where you paste changes color and is underlined, indicating that it has been formatted as a link. In addition, the Web toolbar appears when you create a hyperlink to a separate document, as shown above. You can use the two Forward and Back buttons on the left side of the Web toolbar to move quickly back and forth between hyperlinked worksheets.

To edit or delete a hyperlink, move the mouse over it and click the right mouse button to display the shortcut menu. Then choose one of the commands on the Hyperlink submenu.

If the copy range contains text entries and you use Paste Special with an Operation option (other than None), Excel does not paste the text entries into the paste range. For example, if you copy cell A4 in Figure 8-41 and use Paste Special with both the Values and Multiply options selected to combine the text value with the numeric value in cell B4, nothing happens.

Blank spaces in the copy and paste ranges are assigned the value 0, regardless of which Operation option you select.

Pasting Links

The Paste Link button in the Paste Special dialog box (shown in Figure 8-39 on page 269) is a handy way to create references to cells or ranges. When you click the Paste Link button, an absolute reference to the copied cell is entered in the new location. For example, if you copy cell A3, then select cell B5, choose Paste Special from the Edit menu, and then click the Paste Link button, the formula

    =$A$3

is entered into cell B5. If you copy a range of cells, the Paste Link button enters a similar formula for each cell in the copied range to the same sized range in the new location.

Skipping Blank Cells

The Paste Special dialog box contains a Skip Blanks option that you use when you want Excel to ignore any blank cells in the copy range. Generally, if your copy range contains blank cells, Excel pastes those blank cells over the corresponding cells in the paste area. As a result, the contents, formats, and comments in the paste area are overwritten by the empty cells. When you use the Skip Blanks option, however, the corresponding cells in the paste area are unaffected.

Transposing Entries

You use the Transpose option in the Paste Special dialog box to reorient the contents of the copy range in the selected paste range: The entries in rows appear in columns, and the entries in columns appear in rows. To illustrate, use the Transpose option to reorient the contents of cells B3:E3 shown in Figure 8-38 on page 268. If you copy cells B3:E3, specify cell H3 as the beginning of the paste range, and use Paste Special with Transpose selected. The resulting worksheet looks like the one in Figure 8-42 on the next page.

II

Worksheets

FIGURE 8-42.
The Transpose option reorients a pasted selection.

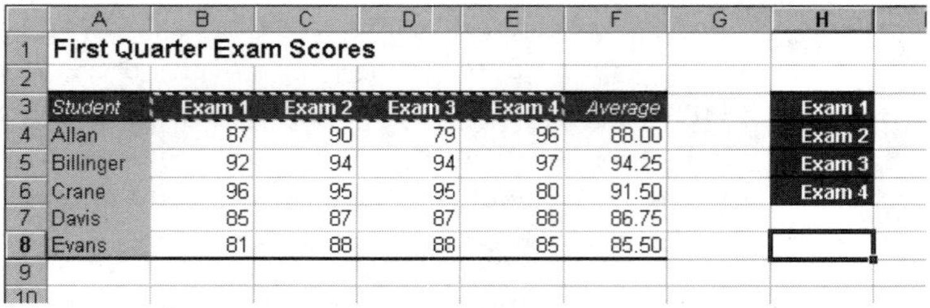

	A	B	C	D	E	F	G	H
1	First Quarter Exam Scores							
2								
3	Student	Exam 1	Exam 2	Exam 3	Exam 4	Average		Exam 1
4	Allan	87	90	79	96	88.00		Exam 2
5	Billinger	92	94	94	97	94.25		Exam 3
6	Crane	96	95	95	80	91.50		Exam 4
7	Davis	85	87	87	88	86.75		
8	Evans	81	88	88	85	85.50		
9								
10								

If the transposed cells contain formulas, Excel transposes the formulas as well as the values and adjusts cell references. To ensure that the transposed formulas refer to the correct cells, you can use absolute cell references. *For more information about absolute cell references, see "Using Cell References in Formulas," page 117.*

Using Paste Special with Arrays

As with any other formula, you can convert the results of an array formula to a series of constant values by selecting the entire array range, choosing Copy, and—without changing your selection—choosing Paste Special. If you select the Values option in the Paste Special dialog box, Excel overwrites the array formulas with constant values. Because the range now contains constant values rather than formulas, Excel no longer treats the selection as an array.

Filling Cell Ranges with Data

The Fill command on the Edit menu displays a submenu with several commands. The Down, Right, Up, and Left commands are handy when you want to copy one or more cells to an adjacent set of cells. Before choosing these commands, select the range you want to fill, including the cell or cells containing the formulas, values, and formats that you want to fill the selected range with. (Comments are not included when you use the Fill commands.)

TIP

> You can quickly fill a selected range of cells using keyboard shortcuts. Simply press Ctrl+D (down) to fill selected cells below, and press Ctrl+R (right) to fill selected cells to the right.

You can use the Right command on the Fill submenu to copy cells across your worksheet. In Figure 8-43, we copied the contents of cells A1:A4 to cells B1:C4 by selecting cells A1:C4 and choosing Fill and then Right from the Edit menu.

FIGURE 8-43.

FIGURE 8-43.

We chose Right from the Fill submenu of the Edit menu to copy data in cells A1:A4 to B1:C4.

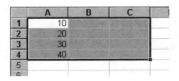

If any cells in the range B1:C4 contain entries, they are overwritten as a result of the Fill command. (You can also use the mouse to fill cell ranges directly in your worksheet by dragging the fill handle over the cells where you wish to copy the data. *See "Shortcuts for Entering and Editing," page 236.*)

The Across Worksheets Command

The Across Worksheets command on the Fill submenu allows you to copy cells from one worksheet in a workbook to other worksheets in the same workbook. *For more information about the Across Worksheets command, see "Editing Groups of Sheets Simultaneously," page 326.*

The Series Command

You can use the Series command on the Fill submenu to create quickly a regular series of numbers or dates. You supply a starting value, the range to be filled, an interval with which to increment the series (*step value*), and, if you want, a maximum value for the series (*stop value*).

Let's look at the Series command in action. Suppose cells A1 and A2 contain the values 10 and 20. If you select cells A1:A10 and choose Series from the Fill submenu of the Edit menu, Excel displays a dialog box like the one in Figure 8-44.

FIGURE 8-44.

Use the Series dialog box to create a regular series of numbers.

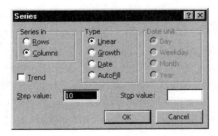

To create a series, first tell Excel whether you want to create the series in columns or in rows. The Rows option tells Excel to use the first value in each row to fill the cells to the right; the Columns option tells

Excel to use the first value in each column to fill the cells below. In this case, the selection is taller than it is wide, so the Columns option is selected automatically.

? SEE ALSO

For more information about creating series, see "Filling and Creating Series with the Mouse," page 241. For more information about Date series, see "Entering a Series of Dates," page 463.

Next select the type of data series you want to create. Excel uses the Type options in conjunction with the start values in cells A1:A2 and the value in the Step Value edit box to create your data series. The Linear option adds the value specified in the Step Value edit box to the values in your worksheet. The Growth option multiplies the first value in the selection by the step value. If you select the Date option, you can specify the type of date series from the options in the Date Unit section. For now, click OK to accept the suggested value of 10 in the Step Value edit box.

Now enter the same two starting values (10 and 20) in cells C1 and C2, select the range C1:C10, and then choose the Series command again. This time, use the Growth option with the suggested Step Value of 10. The resulting two series are shown in Figure 8-45.

FIGURE 8-45.

Starting with identical values in both columns, we created a linear series in column A and a growth series in column C.

	A	B	C	D	E	F	G	H	I	J	K
1	10		10								
2	20		100								
3	30		1000								
4	40		10000								
5	50		100000								
6	60		1000000								
7	70		10000000								
8	80		1E+08								
9	90		1E+09								
10	100		1E+10								
11											

? SEE ALSO

For more information about AutoFill, see "Filling and Creating Series with the Mouse," page 241.

The AutoFill option in the Series dialog box provides a powerful way to create data series. If you enter one or more values as an example, AutoFill will extend the series using the interval between the selected values.

The Justify Command

You can use the Justify command on the Fill submenu to split a cell entry and distribute it into two or more adjacent rows. Unlike other Fill commands, Justify affects the contents of the original cell. (The Justify command does not normally appear on shortened menus. Click the double arrow at the bottom of the Fill submenu of the Edit menu to display the Justify command.)

For example, cell A1 at the left side of Figure 8-46 contains a long label. To divide this label up into cell-sized parts, select cell A1 and choose Fill and then Justify from the Edit menu.

FIGURE 8-46.

The Justify command distributed the long label in cell A1 to cells A1:A7.

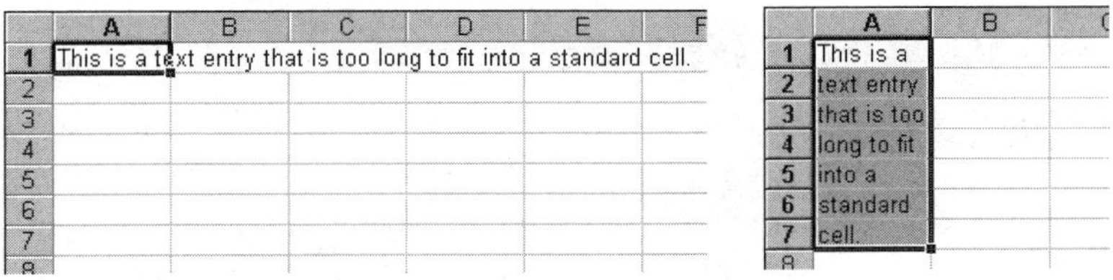

When you choose the Justify command, Excel displays the message *Text will extend below selected range.* Clicking OK in the alert box extends the length of the selected range to the length required for justification, overwriting the contents of any cells within the extended range in the process. The result is shown on the right side of Figure 8-46. To avoid overwriting, click Cancel in the alert box, widen the column that contains the range, and choose the Justify command again.

If you later decide to edit the entries in cells A1:A7 or to change the width of the column that contains those labels, you can use the Justify command again to redistribute the text. For example, you can widen column A in Figure 8-46. Select the range A1:A7 and choose Fill and then Justify. Figure 8-47 shows the result.

FIGURE 8-47.

After widening column A, use Justify to redistribute the text.

If you select a multicolumn range when you choose Justify, Excel justifies the entries in the leftmost column of the range, using the total width of the range you select as its guideline for determining the length of the justified labels. The cells in adjacent columns are not affected. As a result, some of your label displays might be truncated by the entries in subsequent columns.

⭐ **TIP**

> You can use the Text To Columns command on the Data menu to distribute cell entries horizontally. The Text To Columns command is located on the Data menu because you use it most often when you import database information into Excel from other programs.

Any blank cells within the leftmost column of the text you are justifying serve as "paragraph" separators; that is, Excel groups the labels above and below the blank cells when it justifies text entries.

II

Worksheets

Finding and Replacing Data

 SEE ALSO

For more information about linked formulas and error values, see Chapter 6, "Building Formulas."

Suppose you've built a large worksheet and you now need to find every occurrence of a particular character string or value in that worksheet. (A character string is defined as any series of characters you can type in a cell—text, numbers, math operators, or punctuation symbols.) You can use the Find command on the Edit menu to locate any string of characters, including cell references and range names, in the formulas or values in a worksheet.

This command is particularly useful when you want to find linked formulas or error values, such as #NAME? or #REF! What's more, you can use the Replace command to overwrite the strings you locate with new entries.

Using Find

If you want to search the entire worksheet to locate a string of characters, you select a single cell. Excel begins its search from that cell and travels through the entire worksheet. To search only a portion of the worksheet, select the appropriate range.

When you choose the Find command on the Edit menu or press Ctrl+F, you see a dialog box like the one in Figure 8-48. First specify the Find What string—the string of characters you want to search for.

FIGURE 8-48.

Use the Find dialog box to locate a character string.

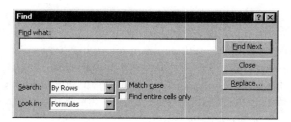

The Search Options

You can use the Search options in the Find dialog box to search by rows or by columns. When you select the By Rows option, Excel looks through the worksheet horizontally, row by row, starting with the currently selected cell. If it finds an occurrence of the string specified in the Find What entry box, Excel highlights the cell that contains that occurrence and stops searching. If it doesn't find an occurrence before it reaches the last cell in the active portion of the worksheet, Excel returns to cell A1 and continues to search through the worksheet until it either finds an occurrence or returns to the originally selected cell.

Select the By Rows option if you think the string is located to the right of the selected cell. The By Columns option searches through the worksheet column by column, beginning with the selected cell. Select the By Columns option if you think the string is below the selected cell.

The Look In Options

? SEE ALSO

For more information about comments, see "Adding Comments to Cells," page 292.

The Look In options in the Find dialog box tell Excel whether to search formulas, values, or comments for the string in the Find What entry box. When you select Formulas, Excel searches in the formulas contained in the worksheet cells. When you select Values, on the other hand, Excel searches in the displayed results of formulas in the worksheet. In either case, Excel searches in the constant values in the worksheet. When you select Comments, Excel examines any text attached as a comment to a cell.

The nuances of the Formulas and Values options can be confusing. Remember that the underlying contents of a cell and the displayed value of that cell are often not the same. When using the Formulas and Values options, you should keep in mind the following:

- If a cell contains a formula, the displayed value of the cell is usually the result of that formula (a number such as 100 or a character string if the formula involves text).

- If a cell contains a numeric value, the displayed value of the cell might or might not be the same as the cell's underlying contents.

- If a cell has the General format, the displayed value of the cell and the cell's contents are usually the same.

- If a cell contains a number that has a format other than General, the contents of the cell and its displayed value might be different.

- The underlying and displayed values of a cell that contains a text entry are usually the same.

In the simple worksheet in Figure 8-49 on the next page, cells B2 and B3 contain the number 1000. The entry in cell B2 has the General format, and the entry in cell B3 has a Currency format. Cell C2, which contains the value 600, has been assigned the name Test. Cell C3 contains the value 400. Cell C4 contains the formula

=Test+C3

which returns the value 1000. Cell E5 contains the label Test.

II

Worksheets

W ON THE WEB

You can find the file Find.xls used in this example on the Microsoft Press Web site at *http://mspress.microsoft.com/mspress/products/2050/*.

FIGURE 8-49.

Use this worksheet to test searching for a string in a value or formula.

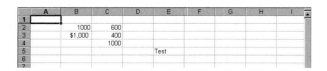

Suppose you select cell A1, choose Find from the Edit menu (or press Ctrl+F), and type *1000* in the Find What edit box. If you select Values as the Look In option and click Find Next, Excel looks at what is displayed in each cell; it first finds the occurrence of the string 1000 in cell B2. If you click Find Next or press Enter, Excel finds the next occurrence of the string in the displayed value of cell C4. Excel ignores the entry in cell B3 because the displayed value, $1,000, does not precisely match the Find What string, 1000. Because you're searching through values and not formulas, Excel ignores the fact that the underlying content of the cell is the number 1000.

TIP

If you close the Find dialog box and want to search for the next occurrence of the Find What string in your worksheet, you can press F4, the keyboard short-cut for repeating the last action.

Now suppose you select cell A1 again and repeat the search, this time selecting the Formulas option. As before, Excel first finds the occurrence of the Find What string in cell B2. If you click Find Next, Excel now highlights cell B3, which contains the number 1000 formatted as currency. Because you're searching through formulas and not displayed values, Excel ignores the format assigned to this cell. Instead it matches the Find What string to the underlying contents of the cell.

If you click Find Next again, Excel returns to cell B2. During this search, Excel ignored the value in cell C4. Even though this cell displays the value 1000, it actually contains the formula =Test+C3, which does not match the Find What string.

SEE ALSO

For more information about the Go To command, see "Using the Go To Command," page 101.

Let's look at one more example. If you specify *Test* as the Find What string and select Formulas as the Look In option, Excel first finds the string *Test* in the formula =Test+C3 and highlights the cell that contains that formula, C4. Notice that this search is not case sensitive. If you click Find Next, Excel highlights cell E5, which contains the label *Test*. If you repeat the search but this time select Values as the Look In option, Excel finds only the occurrence of the text entry *Test* in cell E5. To find the defined cell name *Test* in cell C2, you must use the Go To command on the Edit menu or select the name in the Name box on the formula bar.

The Match Case Option

If you select the Match Case option in the Find dialog box, Excel distinguishes capital letters from lowercase letters. It finds only those occurrences that match the uppercase and lowercase characters of the search string exactly. If you leave this box unselected, Excel disregards the differences between uppercase and lowercase letters.

The Find Entire Cells Only Option

You can use the Find Entire Cells Only option in the Find dialog box to specify a search for only complete and individual occurrences of the string. Normally, Find searches for any occurrence of a string, even if it is part of another string. For example, say a worksheet contains only two entries: the number 998 and the number 99. If you specify 99 as the Find What string, Excel finds the entry 99, which matches the Find What string exactly, and the entry 998, which contains a string that matches the Find What string. However, if you specify 99 as the Find What string and select the Find Entire Cells Only option, Excel finds only the entry 99.

Wildcard Characters

? SEE ALSO

For more information about wildcard characters, see "Using Wildcards in Custom Criteria," page 764.

You can use the wildcard characters ? and * to widen the scope of your searches. Wildcards are helpful when you're searching for a group of similar but not identical entries or when you're searching for an entry you don't quite remember.

The ? character takes the place of any single character in a Find What string. For example, the Find What string *100?* matches the values 1000, 1001, 1002, 1003, and so on up to 1009. (It also matches entries such as 100A, 100B, and so on.)

The * character takes the place of one or more characters in a Find What string. For example, the string *1** matches the entries 10, 15, 100, 1111, 10001, 123456789, 123 Maple Street, and 1-800-MSPRESS.

You can use the wildcard characters anywhere within a Find What string. For example, you can use the string **s* to find all entries that end with *s*. Or you can use the string **es** to find each cell that contains the string sequence *es* anywhere in its formula or value.

To search for a string that contains either ? or *, enter a tilde (~) before the character. For example, to find the string *Who?*—but not *Whom*—enter *Who~?* as your Find What text.

Using Replace

In addition to locating characters, you can replace a specified character string with a new string. The Replace command works much like the Find command. When you choose Replace from the Edit menu (or press Ctrl+H or click the Replace button in the Find dialog box), you see a dialog box like the one in Figure 8-50.

FIGURE 8-50.

Use the Replace command to replace a specified string with a new string.

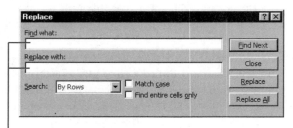

Type the character string you want to search for in the Find What edit box and the string you want to substitute in the Replace With edit box.

For example, to replace each occurrence of the name *Joan Smith* with *John Smith*, type *Joan Smith* in the Find What edit box and *John Smith* in the Replace With edit box. Click the Find Next button or press Enter to move from one occurrence of the Find What string to the next without changing the contents of the current cell. When you locate an occurrence you want to change, click the Replace button to substitute the Find What string with the Replace With string. After replacing the character string in the current cell, Excel moves to the next occurrence.

To replace every occurrence of the Find What string with the Replace With string, click the Replace All button. Instead of pausing at each occurrence to allow you to change or skip the current cell, Excel locates all the cells that contain the Find What string and replaces them.

You can also use wildcard characters (? and *) in the Find What string to broaden your search. For example, to change all occurrences of the names *Joan Smith* and *John Smith* to *John Smythe*, type *Jo?n Smith* in the Find What edit box and *John Smythe* in the Replace With edit box and then click the Replace All button. Excel changes all occurrences of both *Joan Smith* and *John Smith* to *John Smythe*.

Although you can use wildcards in the Find What edit box to aid in your search, if you enter wildcard characters in the Replace With edit box, Excel uses a literal ? or * symbol when it replaces each occurrence of your Find What text.

Getting the Words Right

Spreadsheets are not all numbers, of course, so Excel includes several features to help make entering and editing text easier. The new AutoCorrect command helps you fix common typing errors even before they become spelling problems. For the rest of the words in your worksheets, the Spelling command helps make sure you've entered your text according to Webster. Finally, you might be able to get the new AutoComplete feature to do some of the typing for you.

Fix Typing Errors on the Fly

Perhaps you always have to stop and think "i before e except after c" before you type "receive." Or perhaps you're such a fast typist that you're constantly typing the second letter of a capitalized word before the Shift key snaps back. Excel's AutoCorrect feature helps fix this kind of chronic problem for you as you type. AutoCorrect automatically recognizes and fixes many common typing and spelling errors. Choose the AutoCorrect command on the Tools menu to display the AutoCorrect dialog box shown in Figure 8-51. (The AutoCorrect command does not normally appear on shortened menus. Click the double arrow at the bottom of the Tools menu to display the AutoCorrect command.)

FIGURE 8-51.

You can add your most common typing errors to the AutoCorrect dialog box.

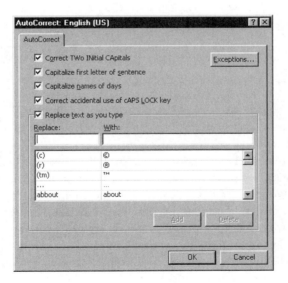

If the Correct TWo INitial CApitals check box is selected (as it normally is), you can't even type the name of the option as it appears in the dialog box. Most of the time, you wouldn't want to anyway, which is what makes this such a helpful feature. As you finish typing a word and press the Spacebar, Excel checks to see if the word contains capital letters. If the word is all caps, Excel leaves it alone (assuming that this was intentional), but if it contains both uppercase and lowercase characters, AutoCorrect makes sure that there's only one capital letter at the beginning of the word. If not, subsequent uppercase characters are changed to lowercase. Apparently, because of their increasing usage, AutoCorrect does not attempt to modify "mid-cap" words, such as AutoCorrect. Similarly, the Correct Accidental Use Of CAPS LOCK Key option automatically scans for this kind of Shift+key misuse. The Capitalize First Letter Of Sentence option, as you might suspect, automatically makes sure you use "sentence case," even if your sentences aren't grammatically correct.

All these capitalization options use very specific rules of order. For example, the TWo INitial CApitals option uses the following rules to determine likely candidates for auto-correction:

- The word starts with a capital letter.

- The second letter of the word is also capitalized.

- The entire word is not capitalized.

- The word is not indicated as an Exception.

- The word is more than two characters long.

- There is at least one vowel in the word.

- The word does not have more than two uppercase characters in a row.

AutoCorrect is smart enough to know the days of the week, and if it finds one, it makes sure it's capitalized, as long as the Capitalize Names Of Days option is selected. The Replace Text As You Type option turns on the replacement list at the bottom of the dialog box, where a number of common replacement items are listed. In addition to correcting common typing errors like replacing "adn" with "and," AutoCorrect also provides a few useful shorthand shortcuts in its replacement list. For example, instead of searching for the right font and symbol to add a copyright mark, you can simply type (c) and AutoCorrect automatically replaces it with ©.

If you have other Microsoft Office programs installed, anything you add to the AutoCorrect list will also appear in other Office programs' AutoCorrect lists.

AutoCorrect works when entering text in cells, formulas, text boxes, on-sheet controls, and chart labels. AutoCorrect does not work when entering text in dialog boxes.

Let Excel Help with the Typing

Often, when entering data in lists, you end up typing the same things over and over. For example, a worksheet that tracks sales transactions might contain columns for products and salespeople associated with each transaction. Usually, you'll have far more transactions than either products or salespeople, so inevitably you'll enter multiple transactions for each salesperson and each product. AutoComplete can help cut down the amount of typing you do, as well as help increase the accuracy of your entries, by at least partially automating them. You turn AutoComplete on by choosing Options from the Tools menu, clicking the Edit tab, and, if the feature is not already active, selecting the Enable AutoComplete For Cell Values option. (It is turned on by default.)

When you begin typing a cell entry, AutoComplete scans all the entries in the same column and, as each character is typed, determines whether there is a possible match in the column. For example, in Figure 8-52 on the next page, as soon as we typed "Wha" into cell B10, AutoComplete completed the entry with the unique match in the same column: "Whatsit."

Create Your Own Typing Shorthand

You can use AutoCorrect to add your own common typing errors and create your own "shorthand" typing shortcuts. Type the characters you want to use as the "code" into the Replace box, then enter the characters with which you want to replace them into the With box, and click the Add button. For example, you can type MS in the Replace box and then type Microsoft Corporation into the With box. Thereafter, each time you type "MS," Excel automatically replaces it with the words "Microsoft Corporation." Make sure you choose codes that are unique; otherwise Excel might apply AutoCorrect to entries you don't want changed. You can delete an item from this list by selecting it, then clicking on the Delete button.

II

Worksheets

You can find the file July Sales Log.xls used in this example on the Microsoft Press Web site at *http://mspress.microsoft.com/mspress/products/2050/*.

FIGURE 8-52.

AutoComplete finishes the entry "Whatsit" in cell B10.

	A	B	C	D	E	F	G	H	I	J
1	July Sales									
3	Date	Product	Salesperson	Units	Price	Total				
4	7/3/00	Widget	Max	2	799	1,598				
5	7/3/00	Wombat	Regina	5	599	2,995				
6	7/3/00	Woofer	Regina	1	199	199				
7	7/3/00	Woofer	Vicki	11	199	2,189				
8	7/3/00	Whatsit	Mac	4	399	1,596				
9	7/4/00	Whozit	Vicki	3	499	1,497				
10	7/4/00	Whatsit								
11										

The text added by AutoComplete is highlighted. You can either continue typing, press Backspace or Delete to delete the suggested completion, or press Enter or an arrow key to accept the completion and move to another cell.

AutoComplete matches only complete cell entries, not individual words in a cell, although an entry might consist of multiple words. For example, if you begin typing *A Whatsit* in column B of the worksheet, AutoCorrect doesn't find a match even after you get to the "Wha" in Whatsit, because the complete cell entry is not a match. As soon as it finds a unique match, AutoComplete suggests an entry. For example, in column C of the same worksheet, we could simply type V in cell C10, and AutoComplete would immediately suggest Vicki as the entry we were after, since it is the only entry beginning with the letter V in the column. AutoComplete does not work when editing formulas.

Instead of relying on automatic matching, you can use the Pick From List command to select an entry from the same column without typing. To do so, select a cell, click the right mouse button, and choose the Pick From List command at the bottom of the shortcut menu that appears, as shown in Figure 8-53. (If your shortcut menu looks different from the one shown in the figure, it's because you weren't already editing in the cell. It's OK. The Pick From List command appears near the bottom of the menu either way.) Once the pick list is displayed, simply click the entry you want, and Excel immediately enters it in the cell.

TIP

If you have activated a cell by double-clicking it or by clicking the formula bar, you can also display the pick list by pressing Alt+Down arrow key.

FIGURE 8-53.

Click the right mouse button and choose the Pick From List command to display a list of unique entries in the column.

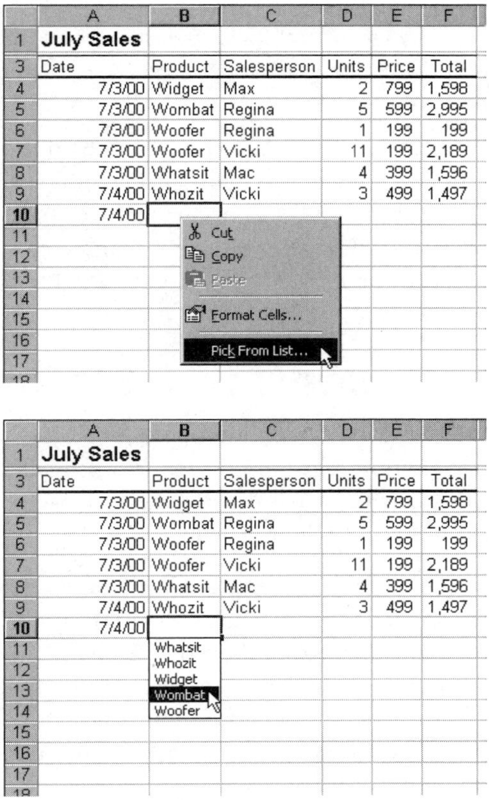

	A	B	C	D	E	F
1	July Sales					
3	Date	Product	Salesperson	Units	Price	Total
4	7/3/00	Widget	Max	2	799	1,598
5	7/3/00	Wombat	Regina	5	599	2,995
6	7/3/00	Woofer	Regina	1	199	199
7	7/3/00	Woofer	Vicki	11	199	2,189
8	7/3/00	Whatsit	Mac	4	399	1,596
9	7/4/00	Whozit	Vicki	3	499	1,497
10	7/4/00					
11		✂ Cut				
12		📋 Copy				
13		📋 Paste				
14						
15		📋 Format Cells...				
16						
17		Pick From List...				

	A	B	C	D	E	F
1	July Sales					
3	Date	Product	Salesperson	Units	Price	Total
4	7/3/00	Widget	Max	2	799	1,598
5	7/3/00	Wombat	Regina	5	599	2,995
6	7/3/00	Woofer	Regina	1	199	199
7	7/3/00	Woofer	Vicki	11	199	2,189
8	7/3/00	Whatsit	Mac	4	399	1,596
9	7/4/00	Whozit	Vicki	3	499	1,497
10	7/4/00					
11		Whatsit				
12		Whozit				
13		Widget				
13		Wombat				
14		Woofer				
15						
16						
17						

Check Your Spelling

? SEE ALSO

For more information about toolbars, see Chapter 3, "Toolbars and Menus." For information about headers and footers, see "Creating a Header and Footer," page 394.

If errors remain despite AutoCorrect and AutoComplete, you don't have to rely on your own proofreading skills when it comes to correct spelling. Instead, you can use the Spelling command on the Tools menu to check for typing errors. (You can also use the Spelling button on the Standard toolbar.)

Use the Spelling command to check the entire worksheet or any part of it. If you select a single cell, Excel checks the entire worksheet, including all cells, comments, Excel graphic objects, and page headers and footers. If you select more than one cell, Excel checks the selected cells only. If the formula bar is active, Excel checks only its contents, and if you select words that are within the formula bar, Excel checks the selected words only. If the range you select for spell checking contains hidden or outlined cells that are not visible, Excel checks these as well. Cells that contain formulas are not checked, however.

TIP

> You can press F7 to instantly begin a spell check. If Excel finds any unrecognized words, the Spelling dialog box appears.

If Excel finds a word that its dictionary does not recognize but is nonetheless correctly spelled, you can click Ignore or Ignore All to ignore the single instance or all the occurrences of the selected word and continue the spell check. If you use the unrecognized word often in your worksheets, you can click Add to add the word to your custom dictionary.

Auditing and Documenting a Worksheet

Microsoft Excel 2000 has a number of powerful and flexible features that help you audit and debug your worksheets and document your work. In this section, we'll discuss the cell tracers, the Comment command, and the Go To Special feature.

Most of Excel's auditing features can be accessed via the Auditing toolbar, which is shown in Figure 8-54. You display the Auditing toolbar by choosing Auditing on the Tools menu and then clicking the Show Auditing Toolbar command. The Auditing command does not normally appear on shortened menus. Click the double arrow at the bottom of the Tools menu to display the Auditing submenu.

FIGURE 8-54.

The Auditing toolbar contains buttons you can use to control the cell tracers and cell comments.

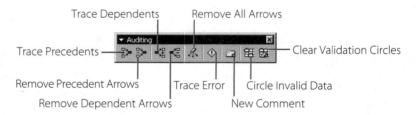

Tracing Cell References

If you've ever looked at a large worksheet and wondered how you could get an idea of the data flow—that is, how the formulas and values relate to one another—you'll appreciate the *cell tracers*. You can also use the cell tracers to help find the source of those pesky errors that occasionally appear in your worksheets.

The Auditing toolbar contains six buttons that control different functions of the cell tracers. To demonstrate how the cell tracers work, we'll use the Auditing toolbar. However, if you prefer, you can use the commands on the Auditing submenu of the Tools menu to control the cell tracers and to display the Auditing toolbar.

II

Worksheets

> ### Understanding Precedents and Dependents
>
> The terms *precedent* and *dependent* crop up quite often in this section. They refer to the relationships that cells containing formulas create with other cells. A lot of what a spreadsheet is all about is wrapped up in these concepts, so here's a brief description of each term.
>
> - **Precedents** are cells whose values are used by the formula in the selected cell. A cell that has precedents always contains a formula.
>
> - **Dependents** are cells that use the value in the selected cell. A cell that has dependents can contain either a formula or a constant value.

Tracing Dependent Cells

In the worksheet in Figure 8-55 we selected cell B2, which contains the hourly rate value. To find out which cells contain formulas that use this value, we clicked the Trace Dependents button on the Auditing toolbar (or you can choose the Trace Dependents command from the Auditing submenu of the Tools menu).

Although this worksheet is not too difficult to figure out, you should consider the ramifications of using the cell tracers in a large and complex worksheet.

ON THE WEB

You can find the file Audit.xls used in this example on the Microsoft Press Web site at *http://mspress.microsoft.com/mspress/products/2050/*.

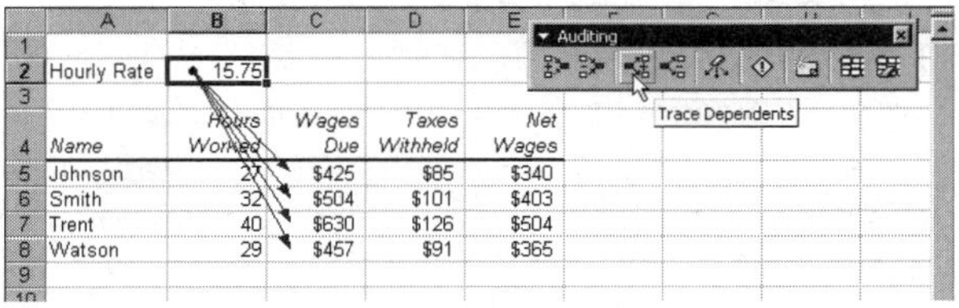

FIGURE 8-55.

When you trace dependents, arrows point to formulas that directly refer to the selected cell.

The *tracer arrows* indicate that cell B2 is directly referred to by the formulas in cells C5, C6, C7, and C8. A dot appears in cell B2, indicating that it is a precedent cell in the data flow. Now, if you click the Trace Dependents button again (or choose the Trace Dependents command), another set of arrows appears, indicating the next level of dependencies—or *indirect dependents*. Figure 8-56 on the next page shows the results.

FIGURE 8-56.

When you trace dependents again, arrows point to the next level of formulas.

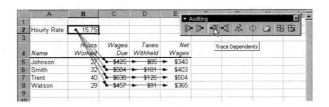

One handy feature of the tracer arrows is that you can use them to navigate, which can be a real advantage in a large worksheet. For example, in Figure 8-56, with cell B2 still selected, double-click the arrow pointing from cell B2 to cell C8. (When you move the mouse pointer over a tracer arrow, it becomes arrow-shaped.) The selection jumps to the other end of the arrow, and cell C8 becomes the active cell. Now, if you double-click the arrow pointing from cell C8 to cell E8, the selection jumps to cell E8. If you double-click the same arrow again, the selection jumps back to cell C8 at the other end. Double-click the arrow from cell C8 to cell B2, and you're back where you started.

If you double-click an arrow that extends beyond the screen, the window shifts to display the cell at the other end. You can use this feature to jump from cell to cell along a path of precedents and dependents.

Clearing Tracer Arrows

Each time you trace another cell's precedents or dependents, additional tracer arrows appear. You'll find, however, that your screen quickly becomes cluttered, making it difficult to discern the data flow for particular cells. It's a good idea to start fresh each time you want to trace cells. To remove all the tracer arrows from the screen, simply click the Remove All Arrows button on the Auditing Toolbar (or choose the Remove All Arrows command from the Auditing submenu).

Tracing Precedent Cells

You can also trace in the opposite direction by starting from a cell that contains a formula and tracing the cells that are referred to in the formula. In Figure 8-57, we selected cell E5, which contains one of the net wages formulas. To find out which cells this formula refers to, we clicked the Trace Precedents button. (You could also use the Trace Precedents command on the Auditing submenu.)

FIGURE 8-57.

When you trace precedents, arrows point from all cells that the selected cell's formula directly refers to.

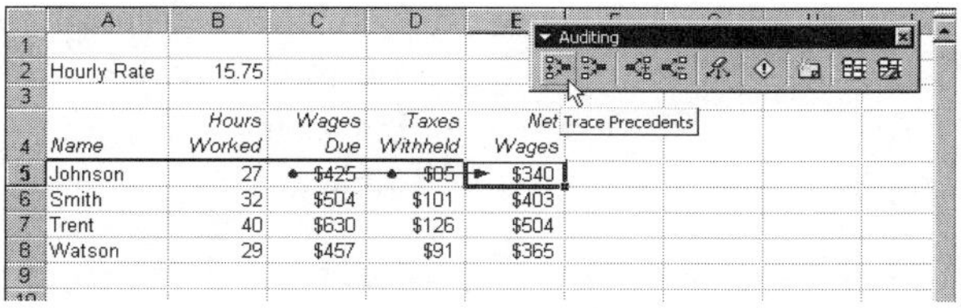

This time, an arrow appears with dots in cells C5 and D5. The dots identify these cells as precedents in the data flow. (The appearance of dots in both C5 and D5 indicates that both cells are equally precedent to the selected cell.) Notice that the arrow still points in the same direction—toward the formula and in the direction of the data flow—even though we started from the opposite end of the path. To continue the trace, click the Trace Precedents button again (or choose the Trace Precedents command). Figure 8-58 shows the results.

FIGURE 8-58.

Trace precedents again, and arrows point from the next (indirect) level of cells that the selected cell's formula refers to.

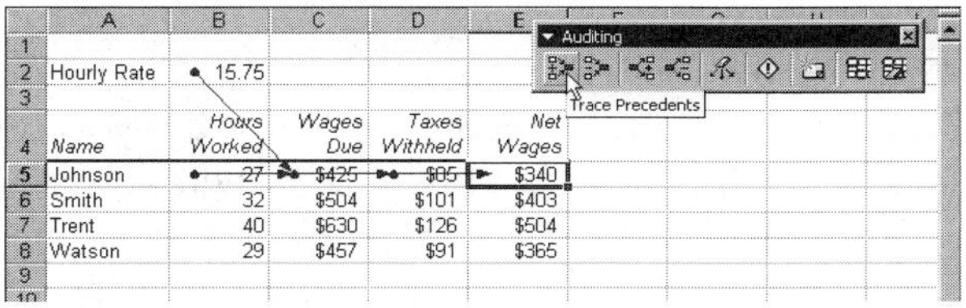

Tracing Errors

Suppose your worksheet displays error values, like the ones shown in Figure 8-59. To trace one of these errors back to its source, select the cell that contains the error and click the Trace Error button (or choose the Trace Error command from the Auditing submenu).

FIGURE 8-59.

Select a cell that contains an error value and click the Trace Error button to trace the error back to its source.

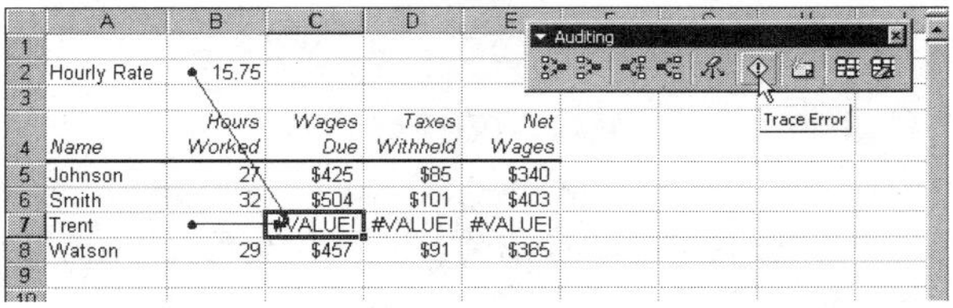

Excel selects the cell that contains the first formula in the error chain and draws arrows from that cell to the cell you selected. After you click OK, Excel draws arrows to the cell that contains the first erroneous formula from the values the formula uses. It's up to you to determine the reason for the error; Excel simply takes you to the source formula and shows you the precedents. In our example, the error is caused by a space character inadvertently entered in cell B7, replacing the hours worked figure.

Tracing References to Other Worksheets

If a cell contains a reference to a different worksheet or to a worksheet in another workbook, a dashed tracer arrow appears with a small icon attached, as shown in Figure 8-60.

FIGURE 8-60.

A special tracer arrow appears for a reference to another worksheet or workbook.

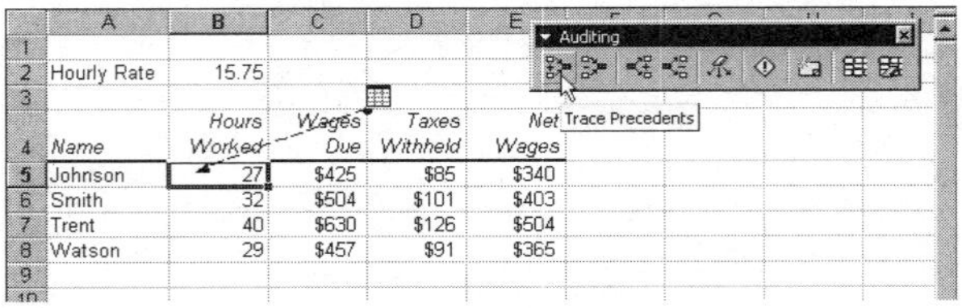

You cannot continue to trace precedents from the active cell when a dashed tracer arrow appears. If you want, you can activate the referenced worksheet or workbook and then start a new trace from the referenced cell. If you double-click a dashed tracer arrow, the Go To dialog box appears, with the reference displayed in the Go To list box. You can select the reference in the list box and click OK to activate the worksheet or workbook. However, if the reference is to another workbook that is not currently open, an error message appears.

? SEE ALSO

For more information about data validation, see "Validating Data Entry," page 785.

The Circle Invalid Data button on the Auditing toolbar draws a red circle around cells containing values that violate the specific parameters of the Data Validation command. The Clear Validation Circles button, as you might expect, removes these circles from the worksheet.

Adding Comments to Cells

You can attach comments to cells to document your work, explain calculations and assumptions, or provide reminders. Select the cell you want to annotate and then select the Comment command from the Insert menu. (You can also click the Insert Comment button on the Auditing toolbar.) Then type your message in the comment box that appears, as shown in Figure 8-61. (The Comment command does not normally appear on shortened menus. Click the double arrow at the bottom of the Insert menu to display the Comment command.)

FIGURE 8-61.

You can attach comments to cells to help document your worksheet.

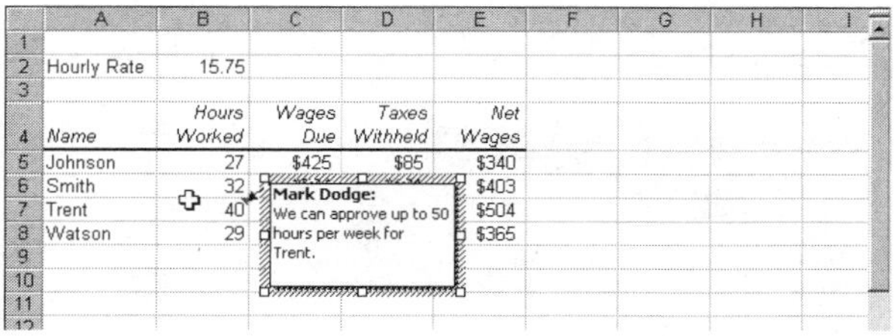

Although you can attach only one comment to a cell, you can make your message as long as you like. If you want to begin a new paragraph in the Text Note edit box, press Enter. When you're finished, you can drag the handles to resize the comment box.

When you add a comment to a cell, your name appears in bold at the top of the comment box. You can specify what appears here by choosing the Options command on the Tools menu, clicking the General tab, and then typing your name (or any other text) into the User Name edit box. Whatever you type here appears at the top of the comment box, followed by a colon.

Normally, a small red triangle appears in the upper right corner of a cell, indicating the presence of a comment. When you move the cursor over a cell displaying this comment indicator, the comment pops up automatically. You can suppress the display of this indicator by choosing the Options command from the Tools menu, clicking the View tab, and clicking the None option in the Comments group. Or you can display all the comments all of the time by clicking the Comment & Indicator option.

To edit a comment, select the cell containing the comment and choose Edit Comment from the Insert menu. The Insert Comment command changes to Edit Comment when you select a cell containing a comment. Similarly, the New Comment button, on the Auditing toolbar, changes to Edit Comment when you select a cell containing a comment (or you can right-click and select Edit Comment).

To delete a comment, click the hatched border of the comment after you activate it for editing and press the Delete key (or right-click and select Delete Comment).

You can work with comments a little more easily when you use the Reviewing toolbar shown in Figure 8-62 on the next page. To display the Reviewing toolbar, choose Toolbars from the View menu and then choose Reviewing.

Worksheets

FIGURE 8-62.
Use the Reviewing toolbar to work with comments.

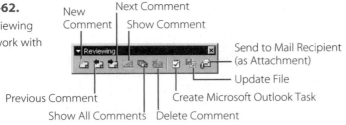

New Comment
Next Comment
Show Comment
Send to Mail Recipient (as Attachment)
Update File
Create Microsoft Outlook Task
Delete Comment
Show All Comments
Previous Comment

Use the Previous Comment and Next Comment buttons to activate each comment in the workbook for editing, one at a time. Even if your comments are located on several worksheets in the same workbook, these buttons allow you to jump directly to each one in succession without using the sheet tabs. The Show Comment button displays (rather than activates for editing) the comment in the selected cell. This button changes to Hide Comment if the comment is currently displayed. The Show All Comments button operates just like the Show Comment button, except that it operates on all the comments on the worksheet at once. The Delete comment button removes comments from all selected cells. (The last three buttons on the Reviewing toolbar relate to other features that are discussed in Chapter 18, "Sharing Files with Others.")

? SEE ALSO

For more information about printing, see Chapter 11, "Printing and Presenting."

To print comments, choose the Page Setup command from the File menu, click the Sheet tab, and select one of the options in the Comments drop-down list. The At End Of Sheet option prints all the comments in text form after the worksheet is printed. The As Displayed On Sheet option prints comments as they appear as text boxes if you display all the comments at once on the worksheet. Be careful, however, because comments printed this way can obscure some contents of the worksheet itself, or if your comments are clustered together, they might overlap.

Using the Go To Special Dialog Box

The options in the Go To Special dialog box provide powerful debugging tools that let you quickly find cells that meet certain specifications.

To access the Go To Special dialog box, shown in Figure 8-63, choose the Go To command from the Edit menu, or press F5, and then click the Special button. (The Go To command does not normally appear on shortened menus. Click the double arrow at the bottom of the Edit menu to display the Go To command.)

FIGURE 8-63.

Choose the Go To command from the Edit menu and click the Special button to display the Go To Special dialog box—a handy auditing and debugging tool.

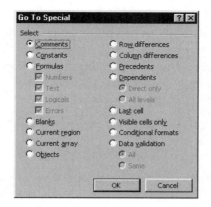

 SEE ALSO

For more information about working with graphic objects, see Chapter 10, "Graphics."

After you specify one of the Go To Special options and click OK, Excel highlights the cell or cells that match the criteria. With a few exceptions, if you select a range of cells before you open the Go To Special dialog box, Excel searches only the selected range; if the current selection is a single cell or one or more graphic objects, Excel searches the entire active worksheet.

Some of the Go To Special options, such as Comments, Precedents, and Dependents, might cause Excel to select multiple nonadjacent ranges. To navigate through these selections, you can use Enter to move down or to the right one cell at a time. Shift+Enter lets you move up or to the left one cell at a time.

The Constants, Formulas, and Blanks options locate cells that contain the specified type of entries. When you select the Constants or Formulas option, Excel activates the Numbers, Text, Logicals, and Errors options in addition to Constants and Formulas. Use these options to narrow your selection criteria.

The Current Region option is handy when you're working in a large, complex worksheet and need to select blocks of cells. (Recall that a region is defined as a continuous rectangular block of cells bounded by blank rows, blank columns, or worksheet borders.) When you choose Current Region, your selection is set to that area of the worksheet.

TIP

You can use the keyboard to quickly select the region to which the selected cell belongs. To select the current region, press Ctrl+Shift+*.

II

Worksheets

If the selected cell is part of an array range, you can use the Current Array option to select all the cells in that array. Note that when finding precedents and dependents, Go To Special simply selects cells, while using the Auditing features draws arrows on the worksheet between cells. *See "Tracing Cell References" earlier in the chapter.*

> You can also use a keyboard shortcut to select the array to which the selected cell belongs. To select the current array, press Ctrl+/.

Choose Row Differences or Column Differences to compare the entries in a range of cells to spot potential inconsistencies. To use these debugging options, select the range before displaying the Go To Special dialog box. The position of the active cell in your selection determines which cell or cells Excel uses to make its comparisons. When searching for row differences, Excel compares the cells in the selection with the cells in the same column as the active cell. When searching for column differences, Excel compares the cells in the selection with the cells in the same row as the active cell.

For example, you've selected the range B10:G20, and cell B10 is the active cell. If you select the Row Differences option, Excel compares the entries in cells C10:G10 with the entry in cell B10, the entries in cells C11:G11 with the entry in cell B11, and so on. If you use the Column Differences option, Excel compares the entries in cells B11:B20 with the entry in cell B10, the entries in cells C11:C20 with the entry in cell C10, and so on.

Among other things, Excel looks for differences in your cell and range references and selects those cells that don't conform to the comparison cell. Suppose cell B10 is your comparison cell and contains the formula

    =SUM(B1:B9)

If you select cells B10:G10 and then select the Row Differences option, Excel scans this range to check for any formulas that don't fit. For example, to follow the pattern in cell B10, the formula in cells C10 and D10 should be

    =SUM(C1:C9)

and

    =SUM(D1:D9)

If any of the formulas in row 10 don't match this pattern, Go To Special selects the cells containing those formulas. If they all match, Excel displays a *No cells found* message.

The Row Differences and Column Differences options also verify that all the cells in the selected range contain the same type of entries. For example, if the comparison cell contains a SUM function, Excel flags any cells that contain a function, formula, or value other than SUM. If the comparison cell contains a constant text or numeric value, Excel flags any cells in the selected range that don't exactly match the comparison value. The options, however, are not case sensitive.

TIP

You can also use keyboard shortcuts to select Column Differences or Row Differences. To search for column differences, select the range you want to search and press Ctrl+Shift+|. To quickly search for row differences, select the range you want to search and press Ctrl+\.

To use the Precedents and Dependents options, first select the cell whose precedents or dependents you want to trace, press F5, click the Special button, and select Precedents or Dependents. Excel then activates the Direct Only and All Levels options. Use these options to set the parameters of your search: Direct Only finds only those cells that directly refer to or that directly depend on the active cell; All Levels locates direct precedents and dependents plus those cells that are indirectly linked to the active cell. When searching for precedents or dependents, Excel always searches the entire worksheet.

TIP

You can also use these keyboard shortcuts to quickly select precedents and dependents of the active cell:

Ctrl+[	Selects direct precedents
Ctrl+Shift+{	Selects all precedents
Ctrl+]	Selects direct dependents
Ctrl+Shift+}	Selects all dependents

The Last Cell option in the Go To Special dialog box selects the cell in the lower right corner of the range that encompasses all cells that contain data, comments, or formats. When you select Last Cell, Excel finds the last cell in the active area of the worksheet, not the lower right corner of the current selection.

The Visible Cells Only option excludes from the current selection any cells in hidden rows or columns.

 TIP

> You can also press Alt+; to quickly select only the visible cells in the current selection.

The Objects option selects all graphic objects in your worksheet, regardless of the current selection.

SEE ALSO

For more information about conditional formatting, see "Applying Conditional Formatting," page 198. For more information about data validation, see "Validating Data Entry," page 785.

The Conditional Formats option selects only those cells that have conditional formatting applied. The Data Validation option selects all cells to which data validation has been applied.

Worksheets and Windows

I n Chapter 1, "Getting Your Bearings," we introduced you to both the workbook and the worksheet and showed you the basics of how to get around. In this chapter, we'll show you how to work with more than one workbook at a time. We'll also show you how to open multiple windows for the same workbook. (You'll find this useful when you want to see two widely separated regions of a worksheet at the same time.) Along the way, we'll survey the commands and shortcuts for opening, navigating, manipulating, hiding, saving, and closing multiple windows.

In addition, we'll show you how to add and remove worksheets, name them, and split them into windowpanes. We'll also examine Microsoft Excel 2000's powerful group editing feature, which allows you to format and edit two or more worksheets in the same workbook at once. We'll take a look at the Zoom command, with which you can reduce or enlarge the display of your workbooks, and custom views, which let you customize combinations of display, workspace, and print settings and save them for easy retrieval.

Working with Workbook Windows

In early versions of Microsoft Excel, worksheets, charts, and macro sheets were stored on disk as separate documents. Since Excel 5, however, all these types of data, and more, peacefully coexist in workbooks. You can keep as many sheets containing various types of data in a workbook as you want, you can have more than one workbook open at the same time, and you can have more than one window open for the same workbook. The only limitations to these capabilities are those imposed by your computer's memory and system resources.

Managing Multiple Workbooks

 SEE ALSO

For more information about the XLStart directory, see "Opening Files," page 77.

Generally, when you start Excel, a blank workbook opens with the provisional title Book1. The exception is when you load Excel and an existing file simultaneously. For example, if you start Excel by double-clicking a document icon—or if you have one or more worksheet files stored in the XLStart directory so that they open automatically—Excel does not start with a blank Book1.

To open an additional file, choose New or Open from the File menu or use the New Workbook or Open button on the Standard toolbar (the first two buttons on the left).

You can open as many workbooks as you like until your computer runs out of memory. The new workbook appears on top of the last active workbook window and becomes the active (or current) workbook window. The active window appears with scroll bars.

SEE ALSO

For more information about working with multiple windows, see "Opening Multiple Windows for the Same Workbook," page 306.

Note that if you use the Open command or the Open button to open a workbook that is already open, Excel displays a warning that the file is already open and that reopening a file will cause any changes you made to be discarded. It then asks if you want to open the file. Click Yes and the copy that is on your screen is replaced by the version last saved to disk.

Navigating Between Open Workbooks

To move from one open workbook window to another, you can click a window to activate it, and then shuffle through a "stack" of windows using a keyboard shortcut, or you can choose a window name from the Window menu.

In the example shown in Figure 9-1, three workbooks—Products, Expenses, and Sales—overlap. To switch from Products to Sales, click anywhere in the Sales workbook.

ON THE WEB

You can find Products.xls used in the following example on the Microsoft Press Web site at *http://mspress.microsoft.com/mspress/products/2050/.*

FIGURE 9-1.

To move to a window that's at least partially visible, position the mouse pointer anywhere in the window and click.

	A	B	C	D	E	F	G	H	I	J	K
1	2000 Product Sales Projections										
3		Jan	Feb	Mar	Apr	May	Jun	Jul	Aug	Sep	Oc
4	Product 1	$7,317	$6,329	$2,110	$1,710	$2,984	$1,100	$2,467	$9,954	$9,755	$6
5	Product 2	$2,814	$2,336	$9,199	$6,176	$2,842	$1,408	$3,737	$1,781	$5,377	$8
6	Product 3	$2,875	$4,107	$5,528	$8,599	$9,769	$5,557	$3,456	$4,692	$1,250	$4
7	Product 4	$4,365	$2,202	$5,607	$8,340	$5,832	$2,350	$1,669	$5,094	$9,658	$7
8	Product 5	$9,451	$3,398	$3,472	$4,585	$3,453	$8,476	$8,118	$5,796	$2,920	$4
9	Product 6	$7,810	$6,982	$7,018	$1,885	$4,336	$6,394	$6,989	$2,038	$8,336	$8
10	Product 7	$9,976	$7,267	$5,006	$6,692	$8,388	$9,072	$8,968	$5,923	$7,618	$1
11	Product 8	$2,536	$4,100	$6,328	$3,807	$7,850	$1,649	$5,253	$3,934	$4,261	$4
12	Product 9	$3,104	$2,467	$5,349	$7,142	$9,305	$2,712	$4,629	$3,961	$1,250	$6
13	Product 10	$5,442	$2,783	$1,642	$1,582	$2,456	$5,584	$9,140	$7,915	$2,343	$1
14	Product 11	$7,816	$8,626	$6,938	$5,200	$8,197	$7,728	$5,955	$1,775	$2,211	$4
15	Product 12	$2,786	$6,720	$4,754	$3,556	$2,535	$5,029	$4,740	$7,047	$9,284	$4
16	Product 13	$7,363	$3,248	$7,295	$9,822	$2,076	$8,372	$1,846	$1,264	$3,741	$7
17	Product 14	$9,917	$5,004	$6,873	$8,719	$8,399	$4,204	$8,290	$2,695	$1,417	$6
18	Product 15	$6,593	$8,499	$1,404	$1,749	$5,999	$4,398	$9,773	$1,167	$9,495	$4
19	Product 16	$2,036	$5,359	$8,656	$4,240	$2,690	$2,211	$4,893	$1,264	$7,469	$7
20	Product 17	$733	$5,814	$2,773	$4,464	$2,067	$8,424	$1,337	$1,404	$7,711	$5
21	Product 18	$1,831	$1,422	$1,572	$5,771	$6,611	$9,131	$9,121	$1,237	$9,969	$2
22	Product 19	$1,533	$2,938	$5,923	$9,180	$7,783	$1,542	$5,745	$5,953	$1,336	$4

TIP

If the workbook you want is open but not even partially visible on the screen, you can cycle through the open windows by pressing Ctrl+F6. To switch from workbook to workbook in the opposite direction, hold down the Shift key and then press Ctrl+F6.

If you have many windows open, the Window menu is the easiest route from one window to another. As shown in Figure 9-2, the bottom section of the Window menu lists the open workbooks by name. To move directly to a workbook, choose its name.

FIGURE 9-2.

The Window menu is your best navigational tool when you have many workbooks open.

The Window menu can list a maximum of nine workbooks. If you have more than nine open, the Window menu includes the More Windows command. When you choose this command, a dialog box appears, listing the names of all open workbooks. Simply select a name and then click OK.

Arranging Workbook Windows

In order to see two or more workbooks at once, simply choose the Arrange command from the Window menu. Excel displays the Arrange Windows dialog box, shown in Figure 9-3. The Arrange command arranges all open windows into one of four possible configurations: Tiled, in which the screen is divided among the open documents, as shown in Figure 9-4; Horizontal, as shown in Figure 9-5; Vertical, as shown in Figure 9-6; or Cascade, as shown in Figure 9-1 on the previous page.

FIGURE 9-3.

The Arrange command on the Window menu gives you a choice of four different configurations.

FIGURE 9-4.

These worksheets are tiled.

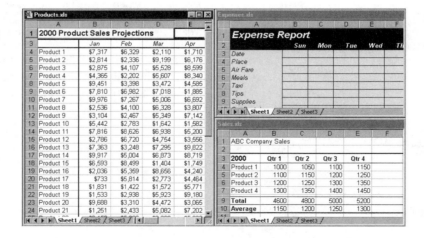

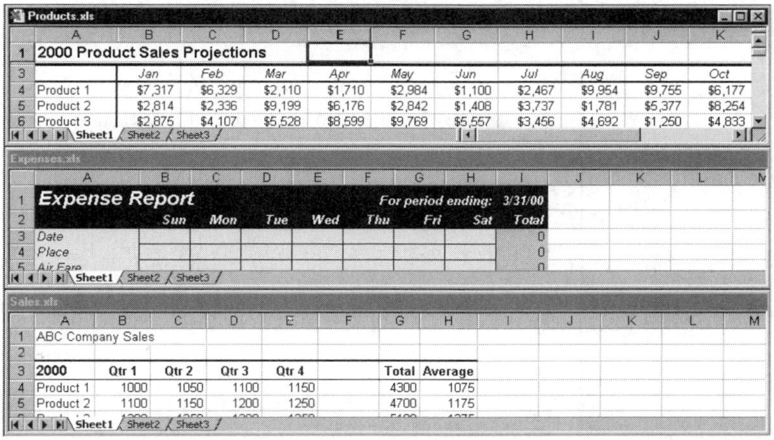

FIGURE 9-5.

These worksheets are arranged horizontally.

If you select the Windows Of Active Workbook option in the Arrange Windows dialog box, only the active window is affected. If more than one window is open for the active workbook, those windows are arranged according to the option set in the Arrange section of the dialog box. This is handy when you have several workbooks open, but you want to arrange only the active workbook's windows without closing the others. *For more information about working with multiple worksheets from one workbook, see "Opening Multiple Windows for the Same Workbook," page 306.*

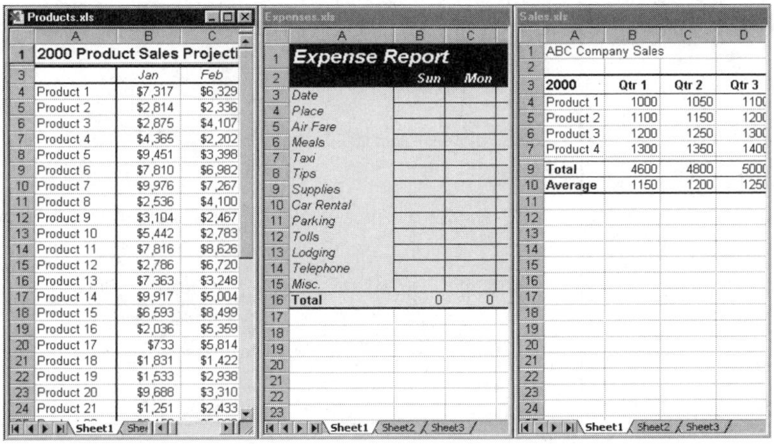

FIGURE 9-6.

These worksheets are arranged vertically.

II

Worksheets

Viewing the Whole Enchilada

You can maximize the workbook window if you need to see more of the active worksheet, but if that still isn't enough, you can use the Full Screen command on the View menu. (This command does not normally appear on shortened menus. Click the double arrow at the bottom of the View menu to display the Full Screen command.) When you choose this command, Excel removes the formula bar, status bar, toolbars, and title bars from your computer screen—everything except the menu bar, the Close Full Screen button, and the maximized workbook window—as shown in the following figure.

	A	B	C	D	E	F	G	H	I	J	K
1	2000 Product Sales Projections										
3		Jan	Feb	Mar	Apr	May	Jun	Jul	Aug	Sep	Oct
4	Product 1	$7,317	$6,329	$2,110	$1,710	$2,984	$1,100	$2,467	$9,954	$9,755	$6,177
5	Product 2	$2,814	$2,336	$9,199	$6,176	$2,842	$1,408	$3,737	$1,781	$5,377	$8,254
6	Product 3	$2,875	$4,107	$5,528	$8,599	$9,769	$5,557	$3,456	$4,692	$1,250	$4,833
7	Product 4	$4,365	$2,202	$5,607	$8,340	$5,832	$2,350	$1,669	$5,094	$9,658	$7,479
8	Product 5	$9,451	$3,398	$3,472	$4,585	$3,453	$8,476	$8,118	$5,796	$2,920	$4,840
9	Product 6	$7,810	$6,982	$7,018	$1,885	$4,336	$6,394	$6,989	$2,038	$8,336	$8,775
10	Product 7	$9,976	$7,267	$5,006	$6,692	$8,388	$9,072	$8,968	$5,923	$7,618	$1,683
11	Product 8	$2,536	$4,100	$6,328	$3,807	$7,850	$1,649	$5,253	$3,934	$4,261	$4,933
12	Product 9	$3,104	$2,467	$5,349			$2,712	$4,629	$3,961	$1,250	$6,166
13	Product 10	$5,442	$2,783	$1,642			$5,584	$9,140	$7,915	$2,343	$1,012
14	Product 11	$7,816	$8,626	$6,938			$7,728	$5,955	$1,775	$2,211	$4,688
15	Product 12	$2,786	$6,720	$4,754	$3,556		$5,029	$4,740	$7,047	$9,284	$4,445
16	Product 13	$7,363	$3,248	$7,295	$9,822	$2,076	$8,372	$1,846	$1,264	$3,741	$7,764
17	Product 14	$9,917	$5,004	$6,873	$8,719	$8,399	$4,204	$8,290	$2,695	$1,417	$6,003
18	Product 15	$6,593	$8,499	$1,404	$1,749	$5,999	$4,398	$9,773	$1,167	$9,495	$4,916
19	Product 16	$2,036	$5,359	$8,656	$4,240	$2,690	$2,211	$4,893	$1,264	$7,469	$7,903
20	Product 17	$733	$5,814	$2,773	$4,464	$2,067	$8,424	$1,337	$1,404	$7,711	$5,579
21	Product 18	$1,831	$1,422	$1,572	$5,771	$6,611	$9,131	$9,121	$1,237	$9,969	$2,604
22	Product 19	$1,533	$2,938	$5,923	$9,180	$7,783	$1,542	$5,745	$5,953	$1,336	$4,121
23	Product 20	$9,688	$3,310	$4,472	$3,065	$4,700	$6,384	$9,079	$6,995	$1,542	$6,603
24	Product 21	$1,251	$2,433	$5,082	$7,202	$1,237	$7,456	$9,631	$2,214	$1,542	$9,343
25	Product 22	$2,156	$5,623	$8,960	$5,829	$6,495	$4,953	$1,921	$2,956	$2,506	$1,542
26	Product 23	$7,412	$6,020	$7,572	$9,404	$6,670	$1,237	$4,160	$2,603	$2,501	$8,753
27	Product 24	$5,543	$6,617	$2,162	$5,924	$2,833	$3,214	$8,058	$5,130	$6,123	$6,827
28	Product 25	$5,573	$3,323	$7,267	$5,053	$7,493	$6,250	$6,249	$9,523	$6,319	$1,250
29	Product 26	$8,413	$2,571	$6,143	$7,898	$2,902	$9,117	$1,237	$8,783	$2,647	$4,293
30	Product 27	$3,684	$8,349	$1,237	$4,666	$7,075	$1,916	$5,163	$4,425	$4,209	$7,456
31	Product 28	$2,704	$8,279	$7,292	$6,997	$4,631	$7,928	$1,237	$1,727	$4,163	$1,542
32	Product 29	$7,546	$3,960	$7,582	$2,839	$7,823	$8,110	$2,778	$9,111	$8,539	$4,208

Sheet1 / Sheet2 / Sheet3 /

The Full Screen command provides a convenient way to display the most information on the screen without changing the magnification of the data. *For more information about changing the magnification, see "Zooming Worksheets," page 322.* To return the screen to its former configuration, simply click the Close Full Screen button that appears automatically, or choose the Full Screen command again.

Maximizing and Minimizing Workbook Windows

Even with your windows neatly arranged, as shown in Figure 9-6, you can still maximize a window by simply clicking its Maximize button at the right end of the window's title bar, shown in Figure 9-7. When you want the side-by-side view once more, simply click the Restore button (formerly the Maximize button), and Excel restores your screen to its former configuration. When a window is not maximized, it is floating.

FIGURE 9-7.

The Maximize button changes to the Restore button once a window is maximized.

Floating window buttons   Maximized window buttons   Minimized window icon

One other important point: when you maximize one window, you maximize all other open windows. If Products, Expenses, and Sales are open, for example, and you maximize Products, Excel also maximizes Expenses and Sales. You won't see these other windows because they lie behind Products, but you can move to them using Ctrl+F6 or the Window menu.

A window always includes a Minimize button. When you click the Minimize button, the window is reduced to an icon that resembles a short title bar. A minimized window contains both a Restore button, which restores the window to its most recent "floating" size, and a Maximize button.

 TIP

> If you're working with several workbooks in a particular arrangement that is often useful, choose the Save Workspace command on the File menu. You can save the current settings and set everything up the same way by simply opening one file. *For more information about saving a particular workspace, see "Saving the Entire Workspace," page 76.*

Moving and Sizing Workbook Windows

SEE ALSO

For more information about resizing windows, see "Resizing the Workbook Window," page 7.

To move a workbook window with the mouse, position the mouse pointer on the title bar of the window, hold down the mouse button, drag the window to a new position, and then release the mouse button. To change a window's size, drag the window borders.

Saving and Closing Workbooks

 SEE ALSO

For information about saving files and saving and opening groups of workbooks, see Chapter 4, "Managing Files."

When you save a workbook using the Save or Save As command on the File menu or the Save button on the Standard toolbar, characteristics such as the window's size, position on the screen, and display settings are also saved in the same file. The next time you open the file, the workbook window looks exactly the same as it did the last time you saved it. Even the same cells that were selected when you saved the file are selected when you open it.

To close an individual workbook window, choose the Close command from the File menu or click the Close box at the right end of the title bar (or to the right of the menu bar if the window is maximized). The Close box is the small button with the "x" on it. If you've made changes since the last time you saved your work, a dialog box asks whether you want to save the workbook before you close it. If you did not intend to close the workbook, simply click the Cancel button.

Opening Multiple Windows for the Same Workbook

Suppose you've created a workbook called Products, like the one shown in Figure 9-1 on page 301. Even if you maximize the workbook window, only cells A1:K26 are likely to be completely visible (this might vary depending on your monitor). If you need to see another area of the workbook simultaneously, open a second window for the workbook. To open another window, choose the New Window command from the Window menu. To view both windows together on your screen, choose the Arrange command from the Window menu and select one of the Arrange options. (The New Window command does not normally appear on shortened menus. Click the double arrow at the bottom of the Window menu to display the New Window command.) If you select the Vertical option, your screen then looks like the one in Figure 9-8.

You may notice that Excel assigns the name Products:2 to the new workbook window. In addition, it changes the name of the original workbook window to Products:1. Furthermore, Products:2 becomes the active window, as indicated by the color of its title bar and the presence of scroll bars.

FIGURE 9-8.

Use the New Window command to open a second window for the same workbook, and then use the Arrange command to view both windows simultaneously.

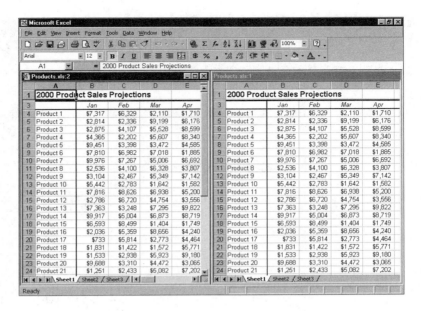

It's important for you to understand the difference between the File menu's New command and the Window menu's New Window command. The File menu's New command creates a new workbook that is displayed in a new window; you can save it as a separate file on disk. The workbook that results from the New command is completely separate from any preexisting workbooks. The New Window command, however, simply creates a new window for the active workbook.

Any work you do in a window affects the entire workbook, not just the portion of the workbook viewed in that window. For instance, when you make an entry in one workbook window, you can view that entry in any window associated with that workbook. By the same token, if you edit or erase the contents of a cell in one workbook window, you can see the change when you look at the same cell, or any cell dependent on that cell, in another window of the same workbook.

You can scroll through the new window to look at another section of the workbook. For example, if you click the down and right scroll arrows in Products:2 a few times, you can move cells L23:P45 into view, as shown in Figure 9-9 on the next page. In addition, you can also use Go To on the Edit menu (or press F5) to move to a different location in the new window. *For more information on moving in a workbook, see "Navigating in a Workbook," page 6, or "Using the Go To Command," page 101.*

TIP

> If other windows are open but you want to view only the windows on the active workbook, select the Windows Of Active Workbook box in the Arrange Windows dialog box.

FIGURE 9-9.

Cells L23:P45 now appear in the second window.

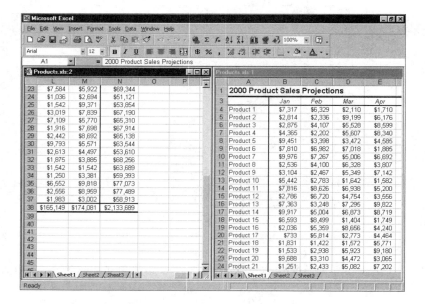

Hiding and Protecting Workbooks

Sometimes you might want to keep certain information out of sight or simply protect it from inadvertent modification. You can conceal and protect data by hiding workbook windows, workbooks, or individual worksheets from view. *For information about protecting individual cells, see "Protecting Your Data," page 111.*

Hiding Workbook Windows

At times, you might need to keep a workbook open so that you can use the information it contains, but you don't want it to take up room on your screen. When several open workbooks clutter your workspace, you can use the Hide command on the Window menu to conceal some of them. Excel can still work with the information in the hidden workbooks, but they don't take up space on your screen, nor do their filenames appear on the Window menu.

To hide a workbook, simply activate it and then choose Hide from the Window menu. Excel removes the workbook from your workspace, but the workbook remains open. To bring the hidden workbook into view, choose Unhide from the Window menu. (This command is unavailable unless a workbook is hidden.) A dialog box like the one shown in Figure 9-10 lists all the hidden workbooks.

FIGURE 9-10.

The Unhide dialog box lists all the workbooks that are currently hidden.

NOTE

The Hide command allows you to conceal any open window. If you have multiple windows open for the same workbook, choosing the Hide command hides only the active window. The entire workbook is not hidden; only the window is hidden. *For more information, see "Opening Multiple Windows for the Same Workbook," page 306.*

Select the workbook you want to view and click OK. The hidden workbook appears and becomes active.

SEE ALSO

For information about protecting the workbook file, see "Protecting Files," page 71.

If you've protected the hidden workbook by choosing the Protect Workbook command from the Protection submenu of the Tools menu and then selecting the Windows option, you must enter your password before you can hide or unhide the workbook.

Saving Workbooks or Windows as Hidden

Sometimes you might want to hide a particular workbook or window, perhaps to prevent others from opening and viewing its sensitive contents in your absence. If the workbook is saved as hidden, it will not be visible when it is opened. You can save a workbook or window as hidden by following these steps:

1 With the workbook or window you want to hide active, choose Hide from the Window menu.

2 While holding down the Shift key, choose Close All from the File menu.

II

Worksheets

3 When a message appears asking if you want to save changes to the workbook, click Yes.

The next time you open the workbook, the window is hidden when the workbook opens. To ensure that it cannot be unhidden by others, you might want to assign a password using the Protect Workbook command on the Protection submenu of the Tools menu before hiding and saving the workbook.

TIP

The opposite of hiding and protecting a workbook would be to make it available to others for editing. Excel's Share Workbook command on the Tools menu allows multiuser editing. *For more information, see Chapter 18, "Sharing Files with Others."*

SEE ALSO

For more information about hiding elements, see the sidebar, "The 'Hidden' Number Format," page 178. For more information about hiding entire columns and rows, see the sidebar, "Hiding a Column or Row," page 206.

Hiding Individual Worksheets

If you want to hide a particular worksheet in a workbook, you can use the Hide command on the Sheet submenu of the Format menu. When you choose the Hide command, the active worksheet no longer appears in the workbook.

To unhide a hidden worksheet, choose the Unhide command from the Sheet submenu. (The Unhide command appears dimmed when there are no hidden worksheets in the active workbook.) As shown in Figure 9-11, the Unhide dialog box for worksheets is similar to the Unhide dialog box for workbooks.

FIGURE 9-11.

Use the Unhide command on the Sheet submenu of the Format menu to unhide individual worksheets.

If the structure of your workbook is protected using the Protect Sheet command on the Protection submenu of the Tools menu, you cannot hide or unhide individual worksheets.

Working with Sheets

 SEE ALSO

For information about editing groups of worksheets, see "Editing Groups of Sheets Simultaneously," page 326.

The workbook is the binder for all your sheets, and like a binder, it can contain different kinds of sheets that you can insert, remove, or move anywhere you want. Unlike a binder, the workbook allows you to copy sheets as well as name and rename sheets. Finally, you can select groups of sheets and edit them together—that is, enter data and apply formats to all selected sheets at once.

NOTE

Up to now, we have discussed only worksheets; however, Excel actually has two different kinds of sheets: worksheets and chart sheets. For the purposes of this discussion, we will use the generic term "sheet" in this section, but we will return to the term "worksheet" for the more specific discussions later in this chapter and throughout the remainder of Part II.

Sheet Basics

A new workbook, by default, contains three worksheets, named Sheet1 through Sheet3. You can change the default number of sheets that appear in a new workbook by choosing the Options command from the Tools menu and clicking the General tab in the Options dialog box, shown in Figure 9-12.

FIGURE 9-12.

You can control the number of sheets that appear in a new workbook by using the General tab in the Options dialog box.

Change this number to determine how many sheets appear by default in a new workbook.

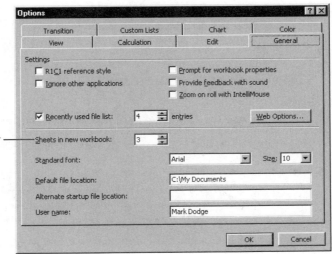

The General tab contains the Sheets In New Workbook edit box, where you can type the number or click the up and down arrows to indicate how many sheets you want all new workbooks to contain, up to a maximum of 255.

Each blank sheet in a workbook consumes additional disk space, so you might want to start with just one sheet and add new sheets only when necessary. Be sure to delete unused sheets in your workbooks to conserve disk space.

NOTE

Although the Options dialog box allows you to specify no more than 255 sheets for new workbooks, you can add as many sheets to an existing workbook as you want, subject only to the limitations of your computer's memory and system resources.

Inserting and Deleting Sheets in a Workbook

It's easy to change the number of sheets in a workbook. For example, to insert a new sheet in an existing workbook, follow these steps:

1 Select a sheet tab in the workbook before which you want to insert a new sheet, such as Sheet2 in Figure 9-13.

FIGURE 9-13.

You can use the Worksheet command on the Insert menu to add a new sheet before the selected sheet.

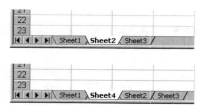

2 Choose the Worksheet command from the Insert menu.

Figure 9-13 shows Sheet4, the new sheet, inserted before Sheet2.

 **TIP**

To quickly insert, delete, move, or rename a sheet, click the right mouse button on the sheet tab to display a shortcut menu with applicable commands.

Using the same technique, you can also add several sheets to a workbook at the same time. To add more than one sheet, select a sheet tab, press the Shift key, and then select a range of sheets—the same number that you want to insert—before choosing the Worksheet command. (Notice that [Group] has been added to the workbook title in the window title bar, indicating that you have selected a group of sheets for editing.) Excel inserts the same number of new sheets before the first sheet in the selected range, as illustrated in Figure 9-14.

FIGURE 9-14.

To insert two new sheets at once, hold down Shift and select two existing sheets. Then choose Worksheet from the Insert menu.

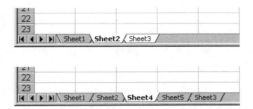

Notice that Excel numbers the new sheets based on the number of sheets in the workbook—in this case, 3. The first sheet you insert is Sheet4, the next is Sheet5, and so on. Keep in mind that you cannot undo the Worksheet command on the Insert menu.

> You can insert chart sheets in your workbooks using the Chart command on the Insert menu. *The Chart command is discussed in Chapter 21, "Basic Charting Techniques."*

To delete a sheet, you can use the Delete Sheet command on the Edit menu. Simply select the sheet you want to delete, choose Delete Sheet, and click OK at the prompt to permanently remove it from your workbook. If you want to delete more than one sheet, you can hold down the Shift key to select a range of sheets, or you can hold down Ctrl and select nonadjacent sheets before you choose the Delete Sheet command from the Edit menu. You cannot undo the Delete Sheet command. If you delete sheets and subsequently add new ones, Excel numbers the new sheets as though the original sheets still existed. For example if you delete Sheet4 and Sheet5 and later add two more sheets, Excel names the new sheets Sheet6 and Sheet7.

Naming and Renaming Sheets in a Workbook

If you grow weary of seeing Sheet1, Sheet2, and so on, in your workbooks, you can give your sheets more imaginative and helpful names by double-clicking the tab and typing a new name. You can also use the Rename command on the Sheet submenu of the Format menu.

You can use up to 31 characters in your sheet names. Remember, though, that the name you use determines the width of the corresponding tab at the bottom of the workbook window, as shown in Figure 9-15 on the next page.

II

Worksheets

FIGURE 9-15.

Double-click the sheet
tab to type a new name.

Therefore, you might still want to keep your sheet names concise so that you can see more than two or three tabs at a time.

Moving and Copying Sheets in a Workbook

As you might expect, Excel provides a very easy way to move a sheet from one place to another in the same workbook. In fact, all you have to do is click the sheet tab you want to move with the mouse and then drag the sheet to its new location. Figure 9-16 shows this process.

FIGURE 9-16.

To move a sheet, click a sheet tab and then drag it to the new location.

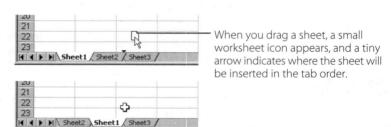

When you drag a sheet, a small worksheet icon appears, and a tiny arrow indicates where the sheet will be inserted in the tab order.

If you want to move the sheet to a new location that is not currently visible on your screen, simply drag past the visible tabs in either direction. The tabs scroll automatically in the direction you drag.

Using this technique, you can also move several sheets at the same time, as shown in Figure 9-17.

FIGURE 9-17.

You can select several adjacent sheets and move them together.

We selected Sheet1, and, while holding down Shift, we clicked Sheet2 to select the range Sheet1:Sheet2. We then dragged to the right to move the range of sheets to a new location.

In addition, you can copy sheets using similar mouse techniques. First, select the sheet or sheets you want to copy and then hold down Ctrl as you drag the sheet or sheets to the new location.

When you copy a sheet, the identical sheet appears in the new location; however, a number in parentheses is appended to the copy's name to distinguish it from the original sheet. For example, in Figure 9-18 the name of the Sheet1 copy is Sheet1 (2).

FIGURE 9-18.

When you hold down Ctrl and drag, Excel copies the selected sheet or sheets to the new location.

As you drag sheets, a plus sign appears in the small worksheet icon.

 TIP

You can move or copy several nonadjacent sheets at the same time by holding down Ctrl while you click the sheet tabs. Before dragging, release the Ctrl key to move the selected sheets, or keep holding it down to create copies. Notice that when you release the mouse button to drop the sheets in their new location, the formerly nonadjacent sheets are inserted together and become adjacent.

The Sheet Tab Shortcut Menu

If you position the mouse pointer over the sheet tabs in a workbook and click the right mouse button, the following menu appears.

In addition to providing a convenient method for inserting, deleting, renaming, moving, and copying sheets, this shortcut menu provides the Select All Sheets command. As its name indicates, you use this command to select all the sheets in a workbook. This comes in handy if you want to perform certain functions, such as copying or group formatting on all the sheets at once. Note that if you select a group of sheets, the Ungroup command appears at the top of the shortcut menu.

Another advantage of using this menu to insert sheets is that the Insert dialog box lets you choose the type of sheet you want to insert.

The View Code command launches the Microsoft Visual Basic authoring environment, giving you access to the underlying programming code for the current workbook. *For more information about Visual Basic, see Chapter 30, "A Sample Visual Basic Application."*

II

Worksheets

Excel also provides the Move Or Copy Sheet command on the Edit menu, which performs similar sheet-management functions, including moving and copying sheets between workbooks. When you choose this command from the Edit menu, the Move Or Copy dialog box in Figure 9-19 appears. (The Move Or Copy Sheet command does not normally appear on shortened menus. Click the double-arrow at the bottom of the Edit menu to display the Move Or Copy Sheet command.)

FIGURE 9-19.

Use the Move Or Copy dialog box to move or copy sheets in the same workbook or to other workbooks.

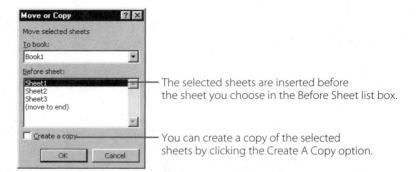

The selected sheets are inserted before the sheet you choose in the Before Sheet list box.

You can create a copy of the selected sheets by clicking the Create A Copy option.

This dialog box performs the same operations as the mouse methods already described. Select the sheet or sheets you want to move or copy, and then choose the Move Or Copy Sheet command from the Edit menu.

Moving and Copying Sheets Between Workbooks

One of the more exciting features of Excel is the ability to move and copy sheets between workbooks by dragging. You can use the same methods to move and copy that you use for worksheets in the same workbook.

For example, suppose you have two workbooks arranged horizontally in the workspace and you want to copy Sheet1 in Book1 to Book2. First rename Sheet1 in Book1 (because Book2 already has a "Sheet1") and then drag the renamed sheet to Book2. The Sheet from Book1 moves to Book2 without using a single command! (See Figure 9-20.) To copy rather than move sheets, press Ctrl while dragging.

You can also move or copy worksheets from one workbook to another simply by using the Move Or Copy Sheet command on the Edit menu, which displays the Move Or Copy dialog box shown in Figure 9-19. Just open the workbook to which you want to move sheets, and then select its name from the To Book drop-down list and select the location for the moved sheets in the Before Sheet list. Select the Create a Copy check box to copy the sheets or leave it unchecked to move the sheets and then click OK .

FIGURE 9-20.

You can drag a sheet or sheets directly to another visible workbook.

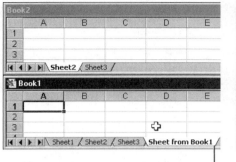
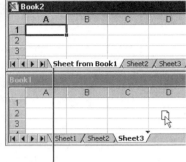

1 To move Sheet1 from Book1 to Book2, first rename Sheet1.

2 Then drag the renamed sheet to Book2.

You can simultaneously move the sheets and create a new workbook by simply selecting New Book from the To Book drop-down list.

Splitting Sheets into Panes

Windowpanes are another way to view different areas of your worksheet simultaneously. You can split any sheet in a workbook vertically, horizontally, or both vertically and horizontally.

The windowpane feature offers synchronized scrolling capability. We'll use the worksheet in Figure 9-21 to illustrate how this feature works.

FIGURE 9-21.

It will be easier to keep track of where you are in this worksheet when you split it into panes.

	A	B	C	D	E	F	G	H
1	2000 Product Sales Projections							
3		Jan	Feb	Mar	Apr	May	Jun	Jul
4	Product 1	$7,317	$6,329	$2,110	$1,710	$2,984	$1,100	$2,467
5	Product 2	$2,814	$2,336	$9,199	$6,176	$2,842	$1,408	$3,737
6	Product 3	$2,875	$4,107	$5,528	$8,599	$9,769	$5,557	$3,456
7	Product 4	$4,365	$2,202	$5,607	$8,340	$5,832	$2,350	$1,669
8	Product 5	$9,451	$3,398	$3,472	$4,585	$3,453	$8,476	$8,118
9	Product 6	$7,810	$6,982	$7,018	$1,885	$4,336	$6,394	$6,989
10	Product 7	$9,976	$7,267	$5,006	$6,692	$8,388	$9,072	$8,968
11	Product 8	$2,536	$4,100	$6,328	$3,807	$7,850	$1,649	$5,253
12	Product 9	$3,104	$2,467	$5,349	$7,142	$9,305	$2,712	$4,629
13	Product 10	$5,442	$2,783	$1,642	$1,582	$2,456	$5,584	$9,140
14	Product 11	$7,816	$8,626	$6,938	$5,200	$8,197	$7,728	$5,955
15	Product 12	$2,786	$6,720	$4,754	$3,556	$2,535	$5,029	$4,740
16	Product 13	$7,363	$3,248	$7,295	$9,822	$2,076	$8,372	$1,846

Horizontal split box

Vertical split box

In this worksheet, columns B through M and rows 4 through 37 contain data. Column N and row 38 contain totals.

II

Worksheets

There are several ways to split a sheet into panes:

- Drag either split box with the mouse to split the window vertically or horizontally.

- Double-click either split box to split the window vertically or horizontally.

- From the Window menu, choose the Split command to split the window into vertical and horizontal panes simultaneously. (The Split command does not normally appear on shortened menus. Click the double arrow at the bottom of the Window menu to display the Split command.)

In the worksheet in Figure 9-21, in order to keep an eye on the totals in column N as you work with the figures in columns B through M, you can split the window into two panes: one 7 columns wide and the other 1 column wide.

To create a vertical pane, simply click the vertical split box—the narrow box at the right end of the horizontal scroll bar (just to the right of the right scroll arrow)—and drag. When your mouse pointer is over the vertical split box, it changes to a double-headed arrow, as shown in Figure 9-22.

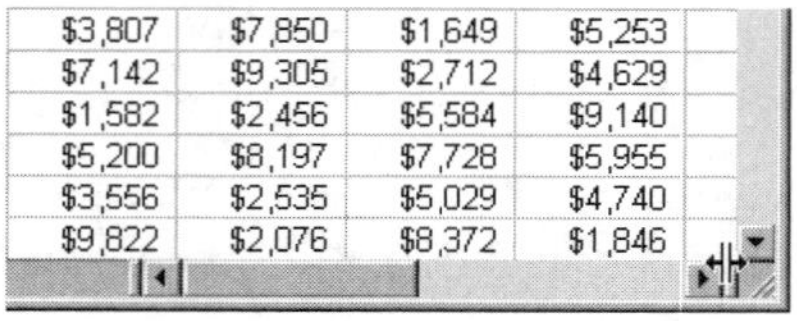

FIGURE 9-22.

When the mouse pointer is over a split box it becomes a double-headed arrow.

$3,807	$7,850	$1,649	$5,253
$7,142	$9,305	$2,712	$4,629
$1,582	$2,456	$5,584	$9,140
$5,200	$8,197	$7,728	$5,955
$3,556	$2,535	$5,029	$4,740
$9,822	$2,076	$8,372	$1,846

 TIP

Before choosing the Split command or double-clicking one of the split boxes, select a cell in the sheet where you want the split to occur. The sheet is split immediately to the left of or above the selected cell. For example, in Figure 9-21, cell B4 is selected. When you double-click the vertical split box, the split occurs between columns A and B—to the left of the selected cell. If cell A1 is active, the split occurs in the center of the sheet.

For example, if you select a cell in column G and double-click the vertical split bar, the worksheet looks like the one in Figure 9-23. Now the window displays two horizontal scroll bars—one for each pane. Next use the horizontal scroll bar below the right pane to scroll column N into view. Your worksheet now looks like the one in Figure 9-24.

FIGURE 9-23.

We split the window into two vertical panes.

	A	B	C	D	E	F	G	H
1	2000 Product Sales Projections							
3		Jan	Feb	Mar	Apr	May	Jun	Jul
4	Product 1	$7,317	$6,329	$2,110	$1,710	$2,984	$1,100	$2,467
5	Product 2	$2,814	$2,336	$9,199	$6,176	$2,842	$1,408	$3,737
6	Product 3	$2,875	$4,107	$5,528	$8,599	$9,769	$5,557	$3,456
7	Product 4	$4,365	$2,202	$5,607	$8,340	$5,832	$2,350	$1,669
8	Product 5	$9,451	$3,398	$3,472	$4,585	$3,453	$8,476	$8,118
9	Product 6	$7,810	$6,982	$7,018	$1,885	$4,336	$6,394	$6,989

Products.xls

FIGURE 9-24.

We scrolled column N into view in the right pane.

	A	B	C	D	E	F	N	O
1	2000 Product Sales Projections							
3		Jan	Feb	Mar	Apr	May	Total	
4	Product 1	$7,317	$6,329	$2,110	$1,710	$2,984	$68,007	
5	Product 2	$2,814	$2,336	$9,199	$6,176	$2,842	$55,038	
6	Product 3	$2,875	$4,107	$5,528	$8,599	$9,769	$64,558	
7	Product 4	$4,365	$2,202	$5,607	$8,340	$5,832	$62,438	
8	Product 5	$9,451	$3,398	$3,472	$4,585	$3,453	$61,437	
9	Product 6	$7,810	$6,982	$7,018	$1,885	$4,336	$71,618	

Products.xls

Now you can use the left pane's horizontal scroll bar to scroll between columns A and M without losing sight of the totals in column N. In addition, when you scroll vertically between rows 1 and 38, you'll always see the corresponding totals in column N. For example, if you scroll down to view rows 18 through 33 in the left pane, those same rows are visible in the right pane.

If you want to keep an eye on the monthly totals in row 38, you can create a horizontal pane. Simply select any cell in row 38 and double-click the horizontal split box. Your worksheet now looks similar to Figure 9-25.

FIGURE 9-25.

We created a horizontal pane so that we could keep an eye on the totals in row 38.

30	Product 27	$3,004	$6,345	$1,257	$4,000	$7,075	$63,544
31	Product 28	$2,704	$8,279	$7,292	$6,997	$4,631	$53,610
32	Product 29	$7,546	$3,960	$7,582	$2,839	$7,823	$68,256
33	Product 30	$8,589	$9,424	$3,965	$3,556	$3,610	$63,689
34	Product 31	$5,456	$8,638	$9,322	$7,071	$1,237	$59,393
35	Product 32	$9,648	$8,636	$6,259	$3,506	$4,668	$77,073
36	Product 33	$9,079	$2,357	$5,007	$2,205	$7,941	$77,489
37	Product 34	$2,312	$7,225	$2,423	$9,927	$1,067	$58,913
38	Total	$185,352	$176,366	$182,192	$188,361	$173,954	$2,133,689
39							

Sheet1 / Sheet2 / Sheet3 /

TIP

To create both vertical and horizontal windowpanes quickly, choose the Split command from the Window menu. For example, you can split the window as shown in Figure 9-25 by selecting cell N38 and choosing Split from the Window menu.

You can then reposition the split bars as you like simply by dragging them with the mouse. After you split a window, the Split command on the Window menu changes to Remove Split, which returns one or both split bars to their default "unsplit" position. You can also remove a split by double-clicking a split bar or by dragging the split bar back to the top or right side of the window.

To move from pane to pane using the keyboard, simply press F6. Each time you do so, the active cell moves to the next pane in a clockwise direction, activating the upper right cell in each pane unless you specifically select a cell in each pane. Alternatively, if you select a specific cell, pressing F6 moves to the last cell you selected in each pane. Pressing Shift+F6 moves you counterclockwise to the next pane.

Freezing Panes

After you've split a window into panes, you can freeze the left panes, the top panes, or both by choosing the Freeze Panes command from the Window menu.

For example, if you've split a window vertically, the Freeze Panes command "locks in" the columns that are in view in the left pane so that you can scroll through the worksheet without losing sight of these columns. Similarly, if you've split a window horizontally, the Freeze Panes command locks in the rows that are in view in the top pane. If you've split a window both vertically and horizontally, both the columns in the left panes and the rows in the top panes are frozen.

In Figure 9-26, we selected cell B4 and chose the Split command to split the window vertically and horizontally. We want to freeze the product entries in column A and the month entries in row 3. To keep this information in view as we enter and edit data in the worksheet, we chose the Freeze Panes command from the Window menu. Figure 9-27 shows the result, with the data scrolled to display the grand total in cell N38.

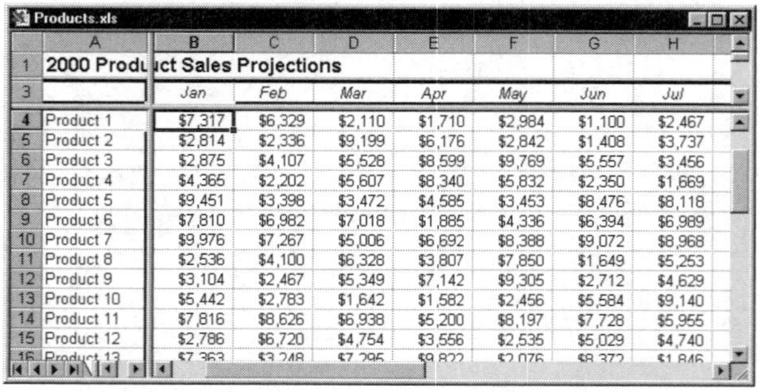

FIGURE 9-26.

Column A and row 3 are displayed in separate windowpanes.

FIGURE 9-27.

The Freeze Panes command locks in the data in the left and top panes.

	A	I	J	K	L	M	N	O
1	**2000 Produ**							
3		Aug	Sep	Oct	Nov	Dec	**Total**	
30	Product 27	$4,425	$4,209	$7,456	$9,793	$5,571	$63,544	
31	Product 28	$1,727	$4,163	$1,542	$2,613	$4,497	$53,610	
32	Product 29	$9,111	$8,539	$4,208	$1,875	$3,885	$68,256	
33	Product 30	$6,720	$8,134	$5,653	$1,542	$1,542	$63,689	
34	Product 31	$7,052	$7,731	$2,375	$1,250	$3,381	$59,393	
35	Product 32	$4,782	$4,114	$2,463	$6,552	$9,818	$77,073	
36	Product 33	$9,873	$9,457	$7,250	$2,556	$8,959	$77,489	
37	Product 34	$6,991	$6,162	$7,318	$1,983	$3,002	$58,913	
38	**Total**	$163,779	$181,090	$179,051	$165,149	$174,081	$2,133,689	
39								
40								
41								
42								

Notice that the double-line pane dividers have changed to single-line pane dividers. Now we can scroll through the remainder of the worksheet without losing sight of the entries in column A and row 3.

Notice also that in Figure 9-26 the sheet tabs are nearly invisible because the horizontal scroll bar for the lower left pane is so small. After freezing the panes in Figure 9-27, however, a single horizontal scroll bar appears, and the sheet tabs reappear.

TIP

To activate another sheet in the workbook if the sheet tabs are not visible, press Ctrl+Page Up to activate the previous sheet, or Ctrl+Page Down to activate the next sheet. You can also use the Go To command on the Edit menu or press F5. In the Go To dialog box, enter the sheet reference and any cell reference, using the following syntax:

= Sheet2!A1

When you press Enter or click OK, Sheet2 is activated, with cell A1 selected.

After you use the Freeze Panes command, it is replaced by the Unfreeze Panes command on the Window menu. Simply choose this command so that you can scroll all the windows again.

TIP

You can split and freeze panes simultaneously by choosing the Freeze Panes command directly, without first splitting the sheet into panes. For example, if you select cell B4 in the Sales Projections worksheet and then choose Freeze Panes, the window splits, and the panes above and to the left of the active cell freeze. When you use this method, subsequently choosing Unfreeze Panes both unfreezes and removes the panes.

II

Worksheets

After you choose Freeze Panes, you cannot scroll the upper left pane in any direction. You can scroll only the *columns* in the upper right pane and only the *rows* in the lower-left pane. You can scroll the lower right pane in either direction.

Zooming Worksheets

You can use the Zoom command on the View menu to change the size of your worksheet display. For example, to see the entire active worksheet area to check its overall appearance, use the Zoom command to reduce the on-screen display to the necessary size. When you choose Zoom from the View menu, the dialog box in Figure 9-28 appears. (This command does not normally appear on shortened menus. Click the double arrow at the bottom of the View menu to display the Zoom command.)

FIGURE 9-28.

The Zoom command gives you control over the size of your on-screen display.

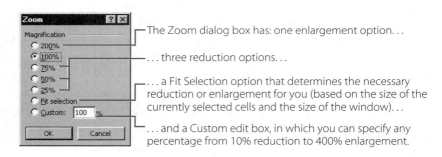

The Zoom dialog box has: one enlargement option. . .

. . . three reduction options. . .

. . . a Fit Selection option that determines the necessary reduction or enlargement for you (based on the size of the currently selected cells and the size of the window). . .

. . . and a Custom edit box, in which you can specify any percentage from 10% reduction to 400% enlargement.

The Zoom command affects only the selected sheets, so if you group several sheets together, they are all displayed at the selected Zoom percentage.

If You Have an IntelliMouse

You can use the wheel on the IntelliMouse to zoom. Simply hold down the Ctrl key and turn the wheel backward (toward your hand) to zoom out, or forward (away from your hand) to zoom in. Note, however, that you cannot zoom in larger than 100% using the IntelliMouse wheel.

If you want, you can make zooming the default behavior of the wheel, making it unnecessary to press the Ctrl key. To do so, choose Options from the Tools menu, click the General tab, and then select the Zoom On Roll With IntelliMouse option.

For example, to view the entire Sales Projections worksheet (shown in Figure 9-21 on page 317) on one screen, follow these steps:

1 Select the entire active area of the worksheet—in this case, cells A1:N38.

2 Choose the Zoom command from the View menu.

3 Select the Fit Selection option and click OK. Now the entire worksheet is displayed on the screen, as shown in Figure 9-29.

FIGURE 9-29.

Using the Zoom command, you can view the entire worksheet on one screen.

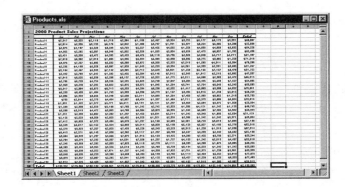

Of course, reading the numbers is a problem at this size, but you can select other reduction or enlargement sizes for that purpose. You can still select cells, format them, and enter formulas as you normally would. Choose the Zoom command again and notice that the Custom option, not the Fit Selection option, is activated, with a percentage entered in the edit box (in our case it was 48%, but the actual percentage depends on the size of the selection and the type of display your computer uses). When you select the Fit Selection option, Excel determines the proper reduction and displays it here. The next time you want to display the entire worksheet, you can simply type this number in the Custom edit box instead of preselecting the current region.

With the Zoom dialog box still open, select the 200% option and click OK. The worksheet changes to look like the one in Figure 9-30 on the next page.

The Zoom option that is in effect when you save the worksheet is active again when you reopen the worksheet.

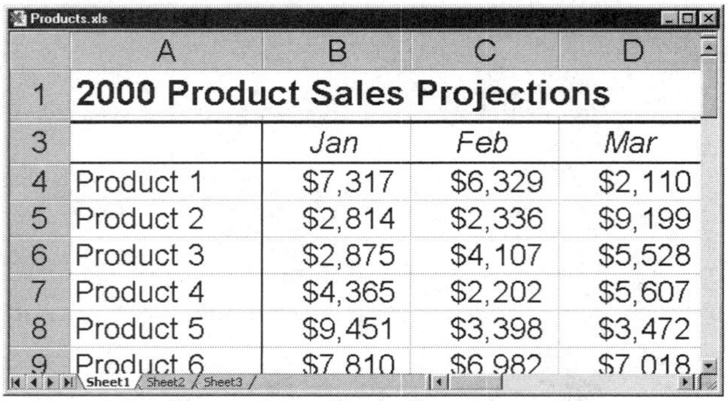

FIGURE 9-30.

You can enlarge your worksheets for easier viewing or presentation purposes.

	A	B	C	D
1	**2000 Product Sales Projections**			
3		*Jan*	*Feb*	*Mar*
4	Product 1	$7,317	$6,329	$2,110
5	Product 2	$2,814	$2,336	$9,199
6	Product 3	$2,875	$4,107	$5,528
7	Product 4	$4,365	$2,202	$5,607
8	Product 5	$9,451	$3,398	$3,472
9	Product 6	$7,810	$6,982	$7,018

Products.xls

Sheet1 / Sheet2 / Sheet3

Custom Views

SEE ALSO

For more information about print settings, see Chapter 11, "Printing and Presenting."

Suppose you want your sheet to have particular display characteristics and print settings for one purpose, such as editing, but different display characteristics and settings for another purpose, such as an on-screen presentation. Using the Custom Views command on the View menu, you can assign names to different sets of options. You can then save these options and select one by name when you need it, rather than implementing the changes in your sheet manually. (The Custom Views command does not normally appear on shertened

The Zoom Control Box and Buttons

You can use the Zoom Control box and the Zoom In and Zoom Out buttons to change the display size of your sheets quickly. The Zoom Control box appears on the Standard toolbar. Because the Zoom In and Zoom Out buttons are not on any toolbar, you must either add them to an existing toolbar or create a toolbar like the one shown in the next figure. The Zoom In and Zoom Out buttons appear in the View category on the Commands tab in the Customize dialog box.

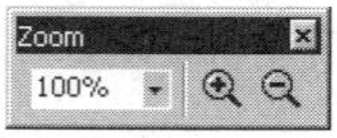

SEE ALSO

For more information about toolbars, see Chapter 3, "Toolbars and Menus."

When you click the arrow next to the Zoom Control box, a list with the default reduction and enlargement options appears. It includes the Selection option, which is the same as Fit Selection in the Zoom dialog box. When you click a Zoom button, the display changes to the next default reduction or enlargement option in that direction. For example, if you click the Zoom Out button when a sheet is at 100%, the display changes to 75% reduction.

menus. Click the double arrow at the bottom of the View menu to display the Custom Views command.)

When you choose the Custom Views command, the dialog box shown in Figure 9-31 appears, offering you instant access to these sets of options.

FIGURE 9-31.

The Custom Views dialog box lets you store different sets of display and print settings with your sheet.

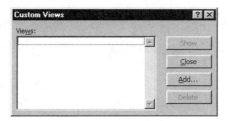

? SEE ALSO

For more information about filtering, see "Using Filters to Analyze a List," page 760.

The settings that are stored in custom views include column widths, row heights, display options, window size and position on the screen, windowpane settings, the cells that are selected at the time the view is created, and, optionally, the print and filter settings.

When you first choose the Custom Views command, the dialog box is empty. To define a custom view, follow these steps:

1 Set up your sheet with the display settings you want.

2 Choose the Custom Views command from the View menu and click Add. You'll see a dialog box like the one in Figure 9-32.

FIGURE 9-32.

You define a name for the current set of display and print settings with the Add View dialog box.

3 Type a name in the Name edit box, select the options you want, and then click OK.

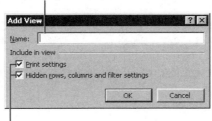

4 The Print Settings and Hidden Rows, Columns, and Filter Settings options let you include the corresponding settings in your custom view definition.

The next time you choose the Custom Views command, the name you entered in the Add View dialog box appears in the Views list box.

Editing Groups of Sheets Simultaneously

You can group together multiple sheets in a workbook and then add, edit, or format data in all the sheets in the group at the same time. You'll find this feature particularly useful when you're creating or modifying a set of worksheets that are similar in purpose and structure—a set of monthly reports or departmental budgets, for example.

You can select and group sheets using one of these methods:

- Select the tab of the first sheet in a range of adjacent sheets you want to group, hold down the Shift key, and click the tab of the last sheet in the range.
- Select the tab of the first sheet you want to group, hold down Ctrl, and then click the tabs of each sheet you want to include, whether or not the sheets are adjacent.
- Choose Select All Sheets from the sheet tab shortcut menu.

To see how the group editing feature works, imagine that you want to add the same set of formatting options to the worksheets Exams 1, Exams 2, Exams 3, and Exams 4, which are contained in the workbook Exams shown in Figure 9-33. (We entered data in the Exams 1 worksheet only—the other three worksheets are blank.) You can add formats to one worksheet and then use the Copy command to recreate them in the other worksheets. But a simpler approach is to group all four worksheets and then format all members of the group at the same time. As Figure 9-33 shows, we have already grouped the worksheets in the Exams workbook. (Excel indicates group editing mode by adding [Group] to the title bar of the workbook.)

ON THE WEB

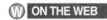

You can find Exams.xls used in the following example at *http://mspress.microsoft.com/mspress/products/2050/.*

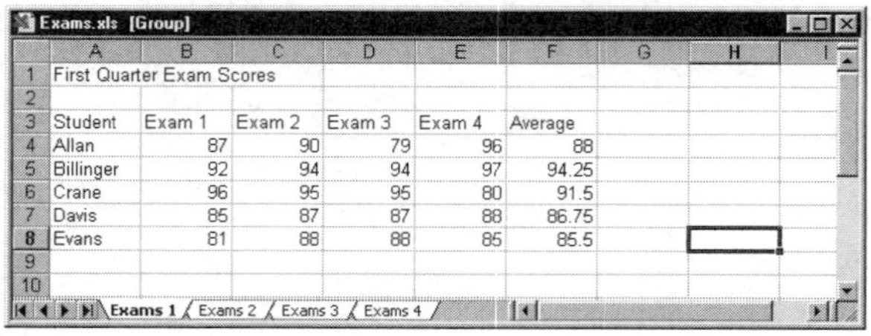

	A	B	C	D	E	F
1	First Quarter Exam Scores					
2						
3	Student	Exam 1	Exam 2	Exam 3	Exam 4	Average
4	Allan	87	90	79	96	88
5	Billinger	92	94	94	97	94.25
6	Crane	96	95	95	80	91.5
7	Davis	85	87	87	88	86.75
8	Evans	81	88	88	85	85.5

FIGURE 9-33.
We'll use this workbook as an example for group editing.

SEE ALSO
For more information about AutoFormat, see Chapter 7, "Formatting a Worksheet."

Now that we have a group of worksheets, we can add formatting, formulas, or any other data to the active worksheet, and all member worksheets will be modified simultaneously. For example, we applied formatting to the Exams 1 worksheet using the AutoFormat command. We also adjusted some font sizes and column widths to arrive at the worksheet in Figure 9-34.

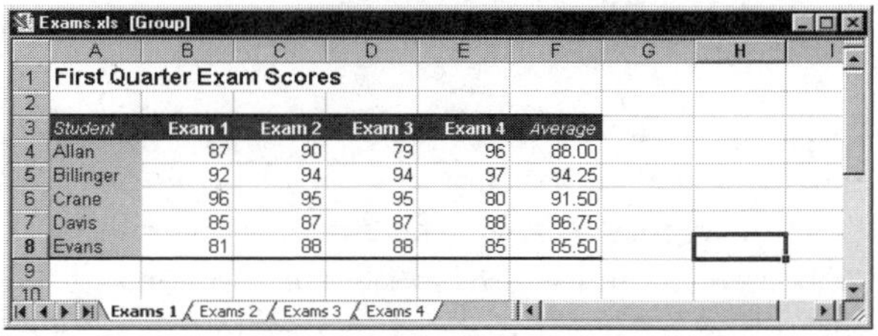

FIGURE 9-34.

Any formatting, formulas, or data you add to the active worksheet in a group is added to the other group members at the same time.

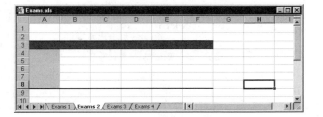

If we select the Exams 2 tab, as shown in Figure 9-35, we can see that all the formats we applied to the Exams 1 worksheet are also applied to the other worksheets in the group.

FIGURE 9-35.

The formats we applied to Exams 1 are also applied to the other worksheets in the group.

> **NOTE**
>
> You can select other sheets in the group without leaving group editing mode. If you click a worksheet tab outside the group, Excel leaves group editing mode and removes the [Group] indicator from the title bar of the workbook. If all sheets in the workbook are included in the group, clicking any sheet tab except that of the active sheet exits group editing mode.

Filling a Group

When you establish a group of sheets, the Across Worksheets command on the Fill submenu of the Edit menu becomes available. (This command does not normally appear on shortened menus. Click the double arrow at the bottom of the Fill submenu to display the Across Worksheets command.) The dialog box that appears when you choose this command is shown in Figure 9-36 on the next page.

II

Worksheets

FIGURE 9-36.

The Across Worksheets command lets you copy data to all the sheets in a group.

Using this command is similar to using the Copy and Paste commands, except that it's a lot simpler. For example, we can select the range A1:F8 in Figure 9-34 on the previous page and then choose the Across Worksheets command from the Fill submenu of the Edit menu. (Remember, this command is not available until you select a group of sheets.) We can then select the Contents option and click OK to copy the text and values entered in Exams 1 to Exams 2, Exams 3, and Exams 4. Now all we would have to do is edit the First Quarter Exam Scores headings in Exams 2, Exams 3, and Exams 4 to read Second Quarter, Third Quarter, and Fourth Quarter, and enter the proper scores for each student. Even the formulas in column F are copied correctly using the Across Worksheets command.

Other Group Editing Actions

Excel's group editing feature lets you perform a number of other actions on the same cells of all member sheets simultaneously.

- **Entering Text** Whatever you type in one sheet is duplicated in all sheets belonging to the group.

- **Printing** When editing a group, all printing commands on the File menu are applied to every sheet in your group at the same time.

- **Format Menu Commands** Any formatting changes you make with the Number, Alignment, Font, Border, Patterns, and Protection tabs in the Format Cells dialog box are applied to all group members at the same time. The results of the Row, Column, AutoFormat, Conditional Formatting, and Style commands are also applied across sheets in group editing mode.

  For example, if you assign the Number format to cells F4:F8 in the active worksheet, that format is also applied to cells F4:F8 in the other group worksheets, overriding any other numeric format you previously applied.

Similarly, if you assign a style to a range of cells in one worksheet, that style is assigned to the same range in the other worksheets.

- **Edit Menu Commands** All commands on the Edit menu except Find and Replace are applied to every sheet in the group at the same time.

- **Insert Menu Commands** You can use the Cells, Rows, Columns, and Function commands to insert the corresponding items in every sheet in the group at the same time.

Working with Linked Workbooks

? SEE ALSO

For information about linking workbooks, see Chapter 6, "Building Formulas."

Creating dynamic links between workbooks with external reference formulas provides a number of advantages. First, you can break large, complex models, such as all of your budget data, into more manageable portions, such as separate departmental budgets. You can then create links between a master budget workbook, known as the *dependent workbook*, and the individual departmental models, which are called *supporting workbooks*.

TIP

If you don't need to keep your files separate, creating links between different worksheets in the same workbook provides a flexible and easily manageable modeling system. *For more information about linking formulas, see "References to Other Worksheets in the Same Workbook," page 121.*

In addition to creating more manageable and flexible models, linked workbooks can save recalculation time and memory.

To establish links between workbooks, you build an external reference formula by typing, pointing with the mouse, or using Paste Special from the Edit menu and then clicking the Paste Link button. This section discusses some special considerations to be aware of when working with workbooks that are linked by external reference formulas.

TIP

You can use automatic consolidation to link two or more workbooks that contain worksheets that store the same kind of information and have a similar structure. Consolidation is particularly useful if you need to gather data from the same sources on a regular basis. *For more information, see "Consolidating Worksheets," page 337.*

II

Worksheets

Saving Linked Workbooks

? SEE ALSO

For more information about the Links command, see "Opening Supporting Workbooks" on the facing page.

As mentioned in Chapter 4, "Managing Files," you use the Save As command to give your workbooks descriptive names when you save them. When you create a set of linked workbooks, always save the supporting workbooks before you save the dependent workbooks. For example, suppose you're modeling your company's 2001 budget in a workbook called Book1. When you save the workbook, you can use the Save As command to give the workbook a name like Budget 2001.

Now suppose that you have another active workbook in which you plan to enter actual (as opposed to budgeted) expenditures, and you have already saved it with the name Actual 2001. This Actual workbook contains links to your Budget workbook and, therefore, is dependent on the Budget workbook for some of its information. When you created them, these links identified the Budget workbook as Book1. If you save Book1 as Budget 2001 while the Actual workbook is still open, all the references to Book1 in the Actual workbook change to Budget 2001. Thus, if the Actual workbook contains the reference

=[Book1]Sheet1!$A$1

the reference changes to

='[Budget2001.xls]Sheet1'!$A$1

? SEE ALSO

For more information about changing the source file, see "Redirecting Links," page 333.

If, on the other hand, you close the dependent Actual workbook before you save the supporting Book1 (Budget) workbook, you see the warning *Save 'Actual 2001' with references to unsaved documents?* If you click OK, Excel saves and closes Actual 2001. However, if you then save Book1 as Budget 2001, the references to Book1 in the Actual workbook are not updated, and the dependent formulas in the Actual workbook continue to assume that the name of the Budget workbook is Book1. When you reopen Actual 2001, Excel displays a message box notifying you that the workbook contains links to another workbook and prompting you to update the linked information. If you click Yes, Excel is unable to find Book1 and opens the File Not Found dialog box (similar to the Open dialog box), with which you can locate and open the workbook you want. Normally, you would select the file or insert the disk that contains the file for which Excel is searching. However, Book1 doesn't exist anymore (its new name is Budget 2001). To establish a link to the correct file, you must first clear the File Name box in the File Not Found dialog box, which contains the name Book1, and then click the Find Now button to refresh the file list display. Then locate the Budget 2001 workbook. When you click OK, the external reference formulas in Actual 2001 change from Book1 to Budget 2001.

You might or might not see the .xls filename extension on your computer. This is controlled in the Windows Explorer. To hide filename extensions, choose the Options command on the Explorer's View menu and click the "Hide MS-DOS File Extensions For File Types That Are Registered" option.

Opening a Dependent Workbook

When you save a workbook that contains dependent formulas, Excel stores the most recent results of those formulas. If you open and edit the supporting workbook after closing the dependent workbook, the values of some cells in the supporting workbook might be different. When you open the dependent workbook again, it contains the old values of the external references in the dependent formulas, but Excel displays an alert box with the message *The workbook you opened contains automatic links to information in another workbook. Do you want to update this workbook with changes made to the other workbook?* The alert box lets you tell Excel whether to read the current values from the closed workbook on the disk.

If you click No, Excel opens the dependent workbook without updating any references to the supporting workbook. All dependent formulas retain their last saved values.

If you click Yes, Excel searches for the supporting workbook. If found, Excel reads the supporting values and updates the dependent formulas in the dependent workbook. Excel does not open the supporting workbook; it merely reads the appropriate values from it.

If Excel can't find the supporting workbook, it displays the File Not Found dialog box, as described earlier. From this dialog box, you can cancel the update process, change the current directory, or identify the file.

Opening Supporting Workbooks

In addition to using the Open command on the File menu and the Open button on the Standard toolbar, you can open supporting workbooks by using the Links command on the Edit menu. The Links command becomes available only when an external or remote reference formula exists in the active worksheet. (This command does not normally appear on shortened menus. Click the double arrow at the bottom of the Edit menu to display the Links command.)

You can use the Links command to open the workbooks on which another workbook depends. The main difference between the Links and Open commands is that Open presents a list of all files in the current directory, whereas Links lists only those files that support the active workbook, regardless of the directory in which they are stored.

Using the Links command is a handy way to look up the names of all the supporting workbooks of a dependent workbook. The Links dialog box lists the links that exist for the entire workbook, not only for the active worksheet.

For example, to open a workbook that contains values that support Actual 2001, choose Links from the Edit menu. You'll see a dialog box like the one in Figure 9-37. Select the name of the workbook you want and then click Open Source.

NOTE

Be careful—the order in which you open files is important. For example, if you select Budget 2001 in the Links dialog box shown in Figure 9-37 and then click Open Source, Budget 2001 appears as the active document. If you then try to use the Links command to open another workbook that supports Actual 2001, you'll get a list of workbooks that support Budget 2001 instead, because it is now the active workbook. To see a list of the workbooks that support Actual 2001, you must reactivate that workbook after you open Budget 2001 and before you choose the Links command.

FIGURE 9-37.
Use the Links dialog box to quickly locate all your supporting workbooks.

An *A* in the Status column indicates a link that is updated automatically. An *M* in the Status column indicates a manual link that is not updated until you click the Update Now button.

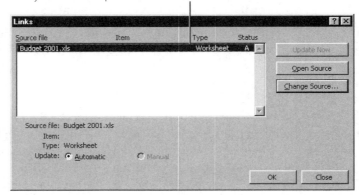

The list in the Links dialog box displays the name of the source file and the status of the link.

Updating Links Without Opening Supporting Workbooks

You can also use the Links command to update dependent formulas without opening the supporting workbooks. This is useful if you chose not to update links when you first opened a dependent workbook, or if you use Excel on a network and one of your colleagues is working with a supporting workbook. When you choose Links, select the workbook name in the Links dialog box and then click the Update Now button. Excel gets the necessary values from the last-saved version of the supporting workbook.

Redirecting Links

If you rename a supporting workbook or move it to another directory or disk, you must redirect your workbook links to let Excel know where to find the supporting data. To redirect your workbook links, select the original name of the supporting workbook or workbooks in the Links dialog box and then click the Change Source button. In the resulting dialog box, shown in Figure 9-38, type the name of the renamed or moved workbook referenced by your dependent formulas in the File Name edit box or select it from the list box. If necessary, you can select another directory or disk. When you click OK, Excel changes all references to the supporting workbook to reflect the new workbook name or location. Click OK in the Links dialog box to return to the worksheet.

FIGURE 9-38.

When you use the Change Source button to redirect your workbook links, you see a dialog box like this one.

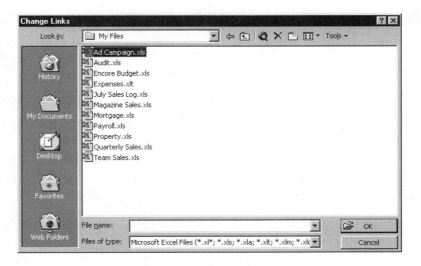

Linking Microsoft Excel 2000 to Another Application

The Links dialog box includes a Type field in the Source File list box. In Figure 9-37, on page 332, the Links dialog box displayed "Worksheet" as the Type; however, you can also link objects and documents created in other applications, such as Microsoft Word, to Excel worksheets and charts. When you use the Links command in an Excel document that has been linked to another application, the Type field displays the application name and the object type. For example, you might want to copy some text from a Word document and paste a link to it into Excel, so that if the text is changed in Word, it will also change in the Excel document. To do so, select the text in Word and choose Copy from the Edit menu. Then switch to Excel, choose Paste Special from the Edit menu, and then select the Paste Link button. Then when you choose the Links command, you'll see that the object is an OLE Link (OLE stands for Object Linking and Embedding, a Microsoft linking protocol), and the Type is "Word Document."

Copying, Cutting, and Pasting in Linked Workbooks

You can use relative or absolute references to cells in other workbooks the same way you use relative or absolute references within a single workbook. Relative and absolute references to cells in supporting workbooks respond to the Copy, Cut, and Paste commands and toolbar buttons in much the same way as references to cells in the same workbook.

For example, suppose you create the formula

> =[Form2]Sheet1!Z1

in cell A1 in Sheet1 of Form1 and use Copy and Paste to copy this formula to cell B1. The formula in cell B1 becomes

> =[Form2]Sheet1!AA1

The original formula changed when it was copied to cell B1 because the reference to cell Z1 in Form2 is relative. However, if the formula in cell A1 of Form1 contains an absolute reference to cell Z1 in Form2, as in

> =[Form2]Sheet1!$Z$1

the result of copying and pasting the formula in cell B1 would still be

> =[Form2]Sheet1!$Z$1

Copying and Pasting Between Workbooks

When you copy a dependent formula from one workbook to another and that formula includes a relative reference to a third workbook, the reference is adjusted to reflect the new position of the formula. For example, cell A1 in Form1 contains the formula

=[Form2]Sheet1!A1

If you copy and paste that formula from cell A1 in Form1 to cell B5 in Form3, the result is the formula

=[Form2]Sheet1!B5

The formula is adjusted to reflect its new relative position.

If you copy a formula that contains an absolute reference to another workbook, that formula remains the same. For example, cell A1 in Form1 contains the formula

=[Form2]Sheet1!$A$1

If you copy and paste that formula into cell B5 in Form3, the result is still

=[Form2]Sheet1!$A$1

Even if you copy a dependent formula to the workbook to which the formula refers, it is still a dependent formula. For example, if you copy the formula

=[Form2]Sheet1!$A$1

from cell A1 of Form1 to cell A3 on Sheet1 of Form2, the resulting formula is essentially the same, except that the book reference is not necessary because the formula is in the same workbook. As a result, the formula becomes

=Sheet1!$A$1

Cutting and Pasting Between Workbooks

You can cut a dependent formula and paste it in another workbook. Cutting and pasting dependent formulas is the same as cutting and pasting regular formulas.

Excel does not adjust the relative references in a formula when you cut it from one workbook and paste it in another, as it does when you copy a formula. For example, cell A1 in Sheet1 of Form1 contains the formula

=[Form2]Sheet1!A1

If you cut that formula and paste it in cell B5 of Form3, the result is still the formula

=[Form2]Sheet1!A1

Cutting and Pasting Cells Referred to by Dependent Formulas

As we mentioned in Chapter 8, "Editing a Worksheet," when you cut and paste cells, Excel adjusts any references to those cells in the formulas of the workbook. Dependent formulas do not follow the same rules. When you cut and paste a cell referred to by a dependent formula in a closed workbook, that formula is not adjusted to reflect the change.

For example, suppose you create the formula

=[Form2]Sheet1!A10

in cell A1 in Form1. If you close Form1 and use Cut and Paste to move the entry in cell A10 of Form2 to cell B10 of Form2, the formula in cell A1 of Form1 remains the same. You might expect the link to be broken because the worksheet containing the formula was closed when you modified the referenced cell. However, Excel manages to keep track of everything. When you open the workbook, the message *The workbook you opened contains automatic links to information in another workbook. Do you want to update this workbook with changes made to the other workbook?* This alerts you that data the workbook depended on has changed.

Severing Links Between Workbooks

 SEE ALSO

For more information about the Paste Special command, see "Selective Pasting," page 268.

To sever the links between workbooks, you use the Paste Special command on the Edit menu to change the external references in your dependent formulas to constant values. Then you won't be able to update the references because all ties to the supporting workbooks are removed.

To sever links using the Paste Special command, follow these steps:

1 Select the cell containing the dependent formula.

2 Choose Copy and then Paste Special from the Edit menu.

3 In the Paste Special dialog box, select the Values option, click OK, and then press Esc to clear the Clipboard.

? SEE ALSO

For more information about the Find command, see "Finding and Replacing Data," page 278.

4 As a precaution, use the Find command on the Edit menu to look for any dependent formulas you might have missed. Enter the exclamation point (!) required in all dependent formulas in the Find What edit box and then select Formulas from the Look In drop-down list box.

5 Click Find Next, and Excel searches your worksheet for any references to supporting workbooks.

You can change an external reference in a dependent formula to a constant value without eradicating the formula. To do this, select the cell and, in the formula bar, select the portion of the formula that contains the external reference, press F9, and then press Enter. Excel changes the external reference to a value without changing the rest of the formula.

Consolidating Worksheets

You can use the Consolidate command on the Data menu to combine the values from a set of worksheets in the same workbook or from different workbooks. The Consolidate command can assemble information from as many as 255 supporting worksheets into a single master worksheet. For example, if you have financial information for each of your company's divisions in separate workbooks, you can use the Consolidate command to create a master worksheet that totals the corresponding items in each divisional workbook. (The Consolidate command does not normally appear on shortened menus. Click the double arrow at the bottom of the Data menu to display the Consolidate command.)

You can use the Consolidate command in a number of ways. You can link the consolidated data to the supporting data so that subsequent changes in the supporting worksheets are reflected in the consolidation worksheet. Or you can simply consolidate the source data, without creating a link.

You can consolidate by position or by category. If you consolidate by position, Excel gathers information from the same cell location in each supporting worksheet. If you consolidate by category, Excel uses column or row labels as the basis for associating worksheets. Consolidating by category gives you more flexibility in the way you set up your supporting worksheets. For example, if your January column is

II

Worksheets

column B in one worksheet and column D in another, you can still gather the January numbers when you consolidate by category.

? SEE ALSO

For more information about functions, see Chapter 12, "Common Worksheet Functions."

You can consolidate worksheets using any of the functions listed in the Function drop-down list box in the Consolidate dialog box. As shown in Figure 9-39, the default function is Sum, which adds the data items from each supporting worksheet and places their totals in the consolidation worksheet. You can also use any of the following functions: Count (which corresponds to the COUNTA function), Average, Max, Min, Product, Count Nums (which corresponds to the COUNT function), StdDev, StdDevp, Var, and Varp.

You can consolidate worksheets in workbooks that are currently open or in workbooks that are stored on disk. The workbook containing the worksheet that receives the consolidated data must be open, but supporting workbooks can be closed—provided you give Excel the correct locations so it can find each workbook file. You must save all supporting workbooks before you begin consolidation.

FIGURE 9-39.

The default function in the Consolidate dialog box is Sum.

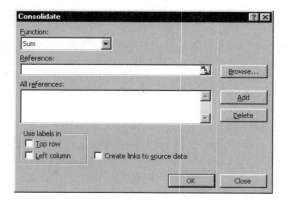

The following sections provide three examples of consolidation: consolidation by position, consolidation by category, and consolidation by category with links created to the source data. In these examples, we'll consolidate worksheets in the same workbook, but you can just as easily consolidate worksheets in separate workbooks.

Consolidating by Position

When you consolidate by position, Excel applies the consolidation function (Sum, Average, or whatever else you select) to the same cell references in each supporting worksheet. This is the simplest way to consolidate, but your supporting worksheets must have exactly the same layout.

Figure 9-40 shows a simple example of a workbook containing a master worksheet—Averages—that matches the layout of four supporting worksheets. These worksheets—Exams 1, Exams 2, Exams 3, and Exams 4—can be consolidated by position because each has five columns and five rows of identically structured data.

ON THE WEB

You can find Exams2.xls used in the following example at *http://mspress.microsoft.com/mspress/products/2050/*.

FIGURE 9-40.

We'll use the Consolidate command to add information from the worksheets named Exams 1, Exams 2, Exams 3, and Exams 4 to the worksheet named Averages.

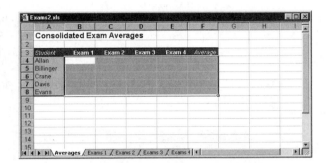

To consolidate the supporting worksheets into the worksheet named Averages, follow these steps:

1 Activate the consolidation worksheet and select the *destination area*—the block of cells that will receive the consolidated data. In Figure 9-40, the destination area is the range B4:F8 of Averages.

2 Choose the Consolidate command from the Data menu. (The Consolidate command does not normally appear on shortened menus. Click the double arrow at the bottom of the Data menu to display the Consolidate command.)

3 You will average values from each source worksheet, so select Average from the Function drop-down list in the Consolidate dialog box. Leave the options in the Use Labels In section unselected. Because you're not going to create a link with the source worksheets, leave the Create Links To Source Data option unselected as well.

4 Type a reference for each source range in the Reference edit box or select each range with the mouse.

Although using the mouse is easier, if you have any references to source worksheets that are not currently open, you will have to type them. (You can use the Browse button to locate and enter a filename and then manually enter the cell reference.)

If you type a reference, it must have the following form:

[Filename]Sheetname!Reference

If the reference is in the same workbook, the filename is unnecessary. If the source range has already been assigned a name, you can use this name in place of Reference.

If you use the mouse to select your source ranges, you can click the Collapse Dialog button to reduce the entire Consolidate dialog box to the size of the Reference edit box, as shown in Figure 9-41. You can activate a worksheet by clicking its tab. If a workbook is open but obscured by other workbooks on the screen, you can get to it by choosing its name from the Window menu. All of these window maneuvers can be performed while you make your selections in the Consolidate dialog box; the dialog box remains active until you close it.

FIGURE 9-41.

Click the Collapse Dialog button in the Reference edit box to collapse the Consolidate dialog box.

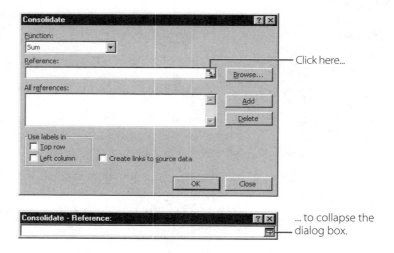

Click here...

... to collapse the dialog box.

5 Click the Add button on the Consolidate dialog box. Excel transfers the reference from the Reference edit box to the All References list box. Figure 9-42 shows the completed dialog box.

Notice that we selected B4:F8 in each of our source worksheets. Because we're consolidating by position and our consolidation worksheet has the appropriate column and row headings, our source references should include only the actual values we want to consolidate.

6 Click OK. Excel averages the source numbers in the destination area, as shown in Figure 9-43.

FIGURE 9-42.

The Consolidate command uses the references in the All References list box to create the consolidated averages.

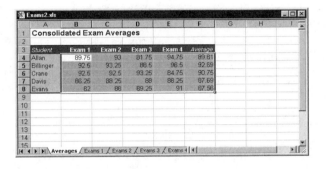

The averages in our example produced some noninteger results, as Figure 9-43 shows, so we might want to apply an appropriate Number format to the destination cells.

FIGURE 9-43.

Range B4:F8 in the Averages worksheet now contains the averages of the corresponding cells in the four supporting worksheets.

NOTE

After you perform a consolidation, the references you enter in the Consolidate dialog box are retained when you save the workbook. The next time you open the workbook and want to refresh the consolidated values, rather than entering the references again, simply choose the Consolidate command and then click OK. Note that you will have to select an appropriate number format each time you consolidate.

Consolidating by Category

Now let's look at a more complex example. We averaged grades from worksheets similar to those in our previous examples, except that this time each worksheet included a few different students and different numbers of students, as shown in Figure 9-44 on the next page.

II

Worksheets

 **ON THE WEB**

You can find Exams.xls used in the following example at *http://mspress.microsoft.com/mspress/products/2050/.*

FIGURE 9-44.

We'll use the categories (students) in the left column of each source worksheet as the basis for this consolidation.

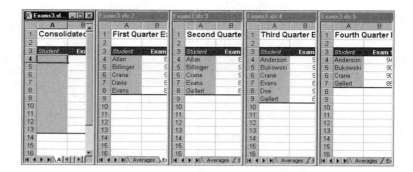

The consolidation worksheet has column headings for Exam 1 through Exam 4—each worksheet is the same in this respect. However, the consolidation worksheet has no row headings. We need to omit the row headings because they are not consistently arranged in the source worksheets. As you'll see, the Consolidate command enters the row headings for us.

To consolidate by category, follow these steps:

1 Select the destination area.

This time the destination area must include column A so Excel will have somewhere to enter the consolidated row headings. But how many rows should the destination area include? To answer that, we can look at each source worksheet and determine how many unique line items we have. An easier way, however, is to select cell A4 as the destination area. When you specify a single cell as your destination area, the Consolidate command fills out the area below and to the right of that cell as needed. In our example, we inserted more than enough rows to accommodate the data, in order to preserve the formatting. Alternatively, you could consolidate first and then use the AutoFormat command on the Format menu to quickly reformat the new data.

2 Choose the Consolidate command from the Data menu to open the Consolidate dialog box. (The Consolidate command does not normally appear on shortened menus. Click the double arrow at the bottom of the Data menu to display the Consolidate command.)

3 Select Average in the Function drop-down list box. To consolidate by row categories in this example, select the Left Column option in the Use Labels In section.

4 The consolidation worksheet already has column labels, so we can omit them from the source worksheet references. But our source references must include each row heading and extend from column A to column F (from the row headings column to the Average column). Therefore, in the Reference edit box, enter or select the following source references:

='Exams 1'!$A$4:$F$8

='Exams 2'!$A$4:$F$8

='Exams 3'!$A$4:$F$9

='Exams 4'!$A$4:$F$7

5 Click OK, and then Excel fills out the Averages worksheet, as shown in Figure 9-45. (The numbers in the figure were formatted as integers after consolidation.)

FIGURE 9-45.

The Consolidate command created a separate line item in the consolidation worksheet for each unique item in the source worksheets.

	A	B	C	D	E	F	G	H	I	J	K
1	Consolidated Exam Scores										
2											
3	Student	Exam 1	Exam 2	Exam 3	Exam 4	Average					
4	Allan	88	94	79	96	89					
5	Billinger	93	92	89	95	92					
6	Anderson	92	93	85	94	91					
7	Bukowski	93	95	88	98	93					
8	Crane	93	93	93	85	91					
9	Davis	85	87	87	88	87					
10	Evans	85	88	89	86	87					
11	Doe	90	88	94	97	92					
12	Gellert	84	89	88	94	89					
13											
14											
15											

SEE ALSO

For information about AutoFormat, see "Using AutoFormat," page 159.

The consolidation worksheet now includes a line item that corresponds to each unique line item in the source worksheets. If two or more worksheets have the same line item, the consolidation worksheet performs the selected mathematical operation on the corresponding figures for each column position. For this example, we applied Number formats to the destination cells after consolidation.

Creating Links to the Source Worksheets

In the previous examples, we simply consolidated numbers with the Average function. The result has been a series of constants in the consolidation worksheet. Subsequent changes to the source worksheets will not affect the consolidation worksheet until we repeat the consolidation.

You can also use the Consolidate command to permanently link between the consolidation and source worksheets. To create the link, select the Create Links To Source Data option in the Consolidate dialog box and then consolidate the same way you would without the links.

SEE ALSO

For more information about outlining worksheets, see "Outlining Your Worksheets," page 225.

When you consolidate with this option selected, Excel creates an outline in the consolidation worksheet, as shown in Figure 9-46. Each source item is linked separately to the consolidation worksheet, and Excel creates the appropriate summary items. You might have to adjust formatting after you perform a linking consolidation because additional columns and rows are created.

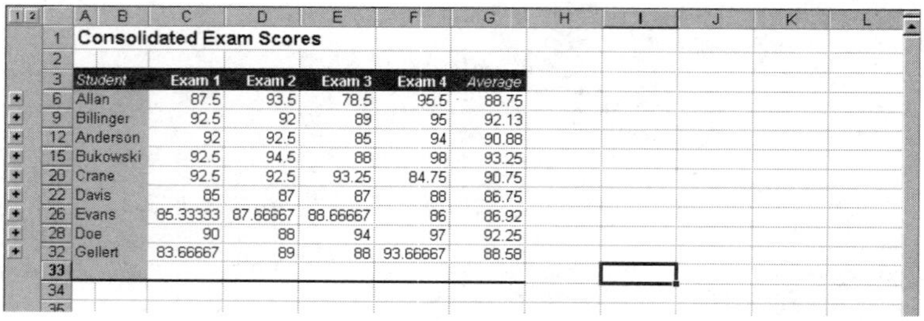

FIGURE 9-46.

When you create links to the source worksheets, your consolidation worksheet is outlined with linking formulas hidden in subordinate outline levels.

	Student	Exam 1	Exam 2	Exam 3	Exam 4	Average
6	Allan	87.5	93.5	78.5	95.5	88.75
9	Billinger	92.5	92	89	95	92.13
12	Anderson	92	92.5	85	94	90.88
15	Bukowski	92.5	94.5	88	98	93.25
20	Crane	92.5	92.5	93.25	84.75	90.75
22	Davis	85	87	87	88	86.75
26	Evans	85.33333	87.66667	88.66667	86	86.92
28	Doe	90	88	94	97	92.25
32	Gellert	83.66667	89	88	93.66667	88.58

Consolidated Exam Scores

Graphics

With Microsoft Excel 2000, you can create a variety of graphic objects—boxes, lines, circles, ovals, arcs, freeform polygons, text boxes, buttons, and a wide assortment of complex predefined objects called AutoShapes. You can specify font, pattern, color, and line formats, and you can position objects in relation to the worksheet or to other objects. You can also take pictures of your worksheets and use them in other Excel documents or in documents created in other applications. If you've already created graphics in other applications, Excel lets you import those graphics as well.

Throughout this chapter, we add graphics to worksheets, but you can also add many of the same kinds of graphics to chart sheets. In addition, you can apply the techniques discussed in this chapter to a variety of graphic objects called controls that you create using Microsoft Excel Visual Basic for Applications.

Creating Graphic Objects

? SEE ALSO

For more information about charts, see Part V, "Charts." For more information about Visual Basic for Applications, see Chapter 30, "A Sample Visual Basic Application."

Before we get started, you might want to display the Drawing toolbar, which contains all of the drawing buttons we describe in this chapter. The Drawing toolbar normally appears docked at the bottom of the Excel workspace. The easiest way to display the Drawing toolbar is to click the Drawing button on the Standard toolbar. You can also position the mouse pointer over any displayed toolbar, click the right mouse button, and then choose Drawing from the shortcut menu that appears. You might also want to hide the Standard and Formatting toolbars to free up as much screen space as possible. Use the shortcut menu to hide both the Standard and Formatting toolbars as well.

If you have ever used a drawing program, such as Microsoft Paint or CorelDRAW, you already know how to create lines, arrows, ovals, and rectangles. In Excel, as with those programs, you simply click the button you want on the Drawing toolbar and then drag the pointer to create the object. Figure 10-1 identifies the buttons on the Drawing toolbar.

FIGURE 10-1.

The buttons on the Drawing toolbar.

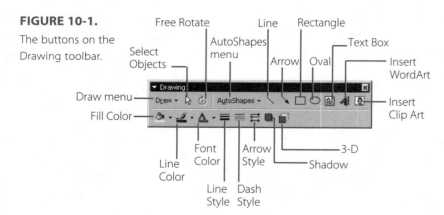

For example, you can select the Rectangle button and then drag the cross-hair pointer anywhere on the worksheet or chart to draw a simple box shape. The result looks something like Figure 10-2. Notice that Excel displays *Rectangle 1* at the left end of the formula bar. Excel refers to new graphic objects by category, in the order in which you create them.

FIGURE 10-2.

You can create a simple box using the Rectangle button.

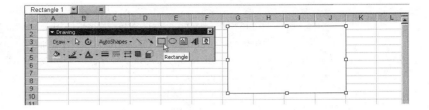

The Line, Arrow, and Oval buttons work essentially the same way: select the button, click and hold to position one corner of the intended shape, drag the mouse to the opposite corner of the intended shape, and then release the mouse button.

 TIP

> If you hold down Ctrl while creating an object, the object is drawn centered on the point at which you click the mouse button. As you draw by dragging away from the point where you clicked, a line or arrow is simultaneously drawn in the opposite direction at the same time, while two-dimensional objects "grow" out from the center point as you drag.

When you release the mouse button and move the mouse pointer away from the object you are drawing, Excel assumes you are finished and the pointer resumes its usual plus-sign shape, indicating that you are no longer in drawing mode. Excel automatically leaves drawing mode each time you finish drawing an object. You can also cancel drawing mode after you click a drawing button by simply clicking anywhere in the worksheet or chart without dragging.

 TIP

> To draw several objects one after the other, double-click the button when you first select it to lock Excel into drawing mode. The button you double-click then remains active until you cancel the drawing session or select another button. To cancel the drawing session, simply click the button again.

Assigning Macros to Objects

You can attach a macro to any object so you can activate the macro by simply clicking the object. To attach a macro to an object, first select the object and then choose the Assign Macro command from the shortcut menu (the menu that appears when you click the object with the right mouse button). When the Assign Macro dialog box appears, specify whether you want to record a new macro or assign an existing macro to the object.

Any objects you create appear to "float" over the worksheet or chart in a separate layer. Objects are separate from the worksheet or chart and can be grouped and formatted as discrete items. You can also click an object you have created, choose the AutoShape command from the Format menu, and then select an object positioning option on the Properties tab of the Format Objects dialog box to adjust the relationship of an object to a worksheet.

> NOTE

When you click an object created with the Line, Rectangle, and Oval buttons and then choose the Format menu, the first command on the menu is "AutoShape." These more ordinary objects, as well as objects created using the AutoShapes menu, are considered AutoShapes for formatting purposes.

? SEE ALSO

For information about macros, see Part VII, "Macros and Visual Basic." For more information about using the Object command, see "Positioning Objects," page 369.

After you've created a graphic, you can manipulate it in a variety of ways. When you move the mouse pointer over an object, the pointer changes to the standard arrow. You can then select the object or move it elsewhere by dragging. If you select the object and point to one of the handles that appears on its perimeter, the pointer changes to a double-headed arrow. You can use this pointer to stretch and resize the object. If you drag a center handle, you can change the object's height or width. If you hold down the Shift key while dragging a corner handle, you can resize the object both vertically and horizontally while retaining its shape.

Drawing Constrained Objects

You can hold down the Shift key while creating objects to *constrain* the objects, as Figure 10-3 illustrates. When you constrain objects, you can achieve the following effects:

- The Line and Arrow buttons draw perfectly horizontal or vertical lines, or diagonal lines constrained to exact 15-degree increments (0°, 15°, 30°, 45°, 90°, and so on).

- The Rectangle button draws perfect squares.

- The Oval button draws perfect circles.

- AutoShapes are drawn to predefined, roughly symmetrical constraints. AutoShapes are wildly different, so this means different things, depending on the shape.

FIGURE 10-3.

When you create or size objects, hold down the Shift key to constrain them along horizontal, vertical, or diagonal lines. (The labels at the right of the worksheet are text boxes created with the Text Box button.)

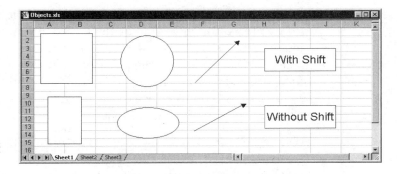

 TIP

Previous versions of Excel had an Arc button on the Drawing toolbar. You can find a more sophisticated incarnation of the Arc button on the Basic Shapes palette of the AutoShapes menu. When you draw an arc with this button, you can adjust its length by dragging the special yellow handle.

Using Cells as a Drawing Grid

You can hold down Alt while creating objects to use the gridlines on a worksheet as a drawing grid. The edges of your objects are then forced to follow the gridlines. If you use the Shift key and Alt together to draw a square or a circle aligned to the grid, Excel does its best, but the result might not be perfect. This is because the default height and width of the cells on a worksheet do not provide an ideal grid for perfect squares or circles.

 TIP

To make a copy of an object you have created, press Ctrl and then drag the object with the mouse. You can also use the Copy and Paste buttons on the Standard toolbar.

Types of Graphic Objects

Excel's drawing tool chest offers many of the same powerful capabilities as dedicated illustration programs. There is a Curve line tool you can use to create smooth curves. There are a variety of *connectors* you can use to link graphic objects together. There is a collection of "basic" shapes, including a few that fall decidedly beyond the basics, such as three-dimensional boxes and lightning bolts. You can draw a variety of straight, curved, and multiheaded arrows with a simple click and drag. A set of symbols designed specifically for creating flow charts is included. With a single click you can draw various stars, emblems, and banners. Finally, the drawing toolbox includes a collection of callouts you can use to add labels to your work—even a "thought balloon," or cloud callout.

The AutoShapes menu located on the Drawing toolbar is actually a palette of palettes. Each command on the AutoShapes menu displays a drop-down list or toolbar of buttons you can use to create AutoShapes. As you can see in Figure 10-4, you can create a toolbar from the AutoShapes menu simply by clicking the selection bar at the top of the menu and dragging it away from the Drawing toolbar. You can do the same with any of the commands on the AutoShapes menu (except the More AutoShapes command).

FIGURE 10-4.

The submenus of the AutoShape menu are palettes you can tear off by dragging.

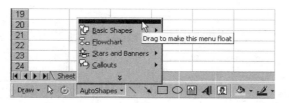

Drawing Freehand Lines and Polygons

To draw lines other than the straight lines and arrows available using the corresponding buttons on the Drawing toolbar, choose the Lines command on the AutoShapes menu and then click the button representing the type of line you want. (The Lines command does not normally appear on shortened menus. Click the double arrow at the bottom of the AutoShapes menu to display the Lines command.) The Scribble button lets you use your mouse to draw unconstrained lines. You can also combine freehand lines with straight lines using the Freeform button. The difference between the Scribble button and the Freeform and Curve buttons is that with either of those buttons, releasing the mouse button does not end the drawing. To leave drawing mode when you are using the Freeform or Curve button, you must click the beginning point of your drawing or double-click where you want to stop drawing.

For example, if you click the Freeform button and then click anywhere on the worksheet or chart to begin drawing, the line remains anchored to the point you clicked. If you release the mouse button, the line stretches from the anchor point to the cross-hair mouse pointer like a rubber band. If you stretch the line and click again, you create a straight line between the first anchor point and the second point you clicked. You can continue this as long as you want, creating lines between each anchor point. You can also hold down the mouse button while using the Freeform button to add a freehand line (and the mouse pointer becomes a pencil). In this way, you can create a hybrid object with both straight and curved lines. As mentioned, you complete the freeform polygon by clicking the point where you began drawing or by double-clicking to create an open shape.

The Edit Points Command

Drawing an attractive freehand line or polygon shape with a mouse can be challenging. For those times when you have difficulty creating the shape you want, Excel includes an Edit Points command that changes a line or polygon created with the Scribble, Curve, or Freeform button to a series of points, which you can drag to reshape the object. When you select a freehand line or a freeform polygon, eight handles appear around it, just as they do around objects drawn with the Rectangle or Oval button. To adjust the shape of a freehand line or a freeform polygon, select it and then choose Edit Points from the Draw menu (on the Drawing toolbar), or simply click the right mouse button and choose Edit Points from the shortcut menu that appears. (The Edit Points command does not normally appear on shortened menus. Click the double arrow at the bottom of the Draw menu to display the Edit Points command.) A new set of handles appears, following the curves and corners of the image; only two handles appear at the end points of straight lines. You can then drag as many of the handles as necessary to new positions.

TIP

After you choose the Edit Points command, you can add or delete handles on an object. If you want to clean up your drawing by eliminating some of the corners, press Ctrl and then click each handle you want to delete. If you want to add corners, press Ctrl and then click anywhere on a line where you want a handle to appear.

Worksheets

For example, we used the Freeform button to create the shape on the left in Figure 10-5, and then we selected the shape. The shape on the right is the same freeform polygon after we clicked the Edit Points command.

FIGURE 10-5.

When you click the Edit Points command, handles appear at each vertex, as in the image on the far right.

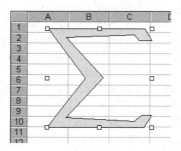 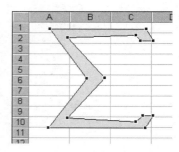

Working with Curves

When you use the Edit Points command to modify lines created with the Scribble, Curve, or Freeform buttons, you can fine-tune the curves using commands on the shortcut menu that appears when you click the right mouse button on one of the points. There are four types of points, each with a corresponding command on the shortcut menu:

- **Auto Point** Determined by the button used and the way the line was drawn. The Curve button always creates Auto Points.

Adding the Edit Points Button to the Lines Palette

The Edit Points command is so useful when drawing freeform curves and polygons that you'll want to keep it handy. Since you'll be editing points when drawing with three of the Line tools, it makes sense to add the Edit Points button to the Lines palette. Here's how:

1 First drag the Lines palette off of the AutoShapes menu by clicking AutoShapes, clicking the Lines command, and then dragging the selection bar at the top of the Lines palette away from the menu.

2 From the View menu, choose Toolbars, and then choose Customize.

3 With the Customize dialog box open, click the Draw menu, and then drag the Edit Points command from the menu to the floating Lines palette.

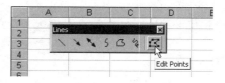

SEE ALSO

For more information about customizing toolbars, see "Customizing Toolbars and Menus," page 43.

- **Straight Point** Never produced automatically. Lines flowing out from either side of a straight point are equally curved and display vertex handles when selected. You can select any existing point and make it a straight point.

- **Smooth Point** Never produced automatically. Smooth points create gradual transitions between the lines flowing out from either side, displaying vertex handles when selected.

- **Corner Point** The opposite of a smooth point. Corner points can create abrupt transitions between the lines flowing out from either side, and display vertex handles when selected. The Scribble button always creates Corner Points.

All types of points except Auto Points display vertex handles when selected. These handles, shown in Figure 10-6, allow two-way control of the curve. You can change the angle of a curve by dragging a vertex handle perpendicular to the line, or you can change the slope of a curve by dragging a vertex handle parallel to the line. These are powerful controls that can be a little tricky to master at first. As you know, practice makes perfect.

FIGURE 10-6.

Edit points allow you to change the shape of freeform objects. Vertex handles appear when you click any type of edit point except an Auto Point.

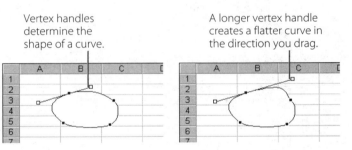

Vertex handles determine the shape of a curve.

A longer vertex handle creates a flatter curve in the direction you drag.

Working with Text Boxes

You can use the Text Box button on the Drawing toolbar to add notes, headings, legends, and other text to your worksheets and charts to give them more impact or to clarify them.

When you select the Text Box button and draw a box, a blinking insertion point appears in the box, indicating that you can begin typing. Text is left-aligned by default, but you can use the alignment tools on the Formatting toolbar or the Text Box command on the Format menu to realign the text. The worksheet in Figure 10-7 on the next page contains two text boxes.

FIGURE 10-7.

These two text boxes were created using the Text Box button.

Keep in mind that you can use the Spelling command on the Tools menu to check spelling in text boxes. When you use this command with a single cell selected, all the text in the current worksheet is checked, including text in text boxes. If you choose this command when a text box (or any object) is selected, only that text box (or object) is checked.

 TIP

You can link a text box or any other shape containing text to a cell. First, draw a text box. Next, with the text box selected, type an equal sign and then type a cell reference in the formula bar. For example, suppose cell D3 contains a formula that returns the value $123.45. When you type

=$D$3

in the formula bar while the text box is selected, the value $123.45 appears in the text box.

When you link a text box in this way, you cannot type additional text into it. To remove the link, select the text box and delete the reference formula in the formula bar.

Typing Text into Other Shapes

The Text Box button is quick and easy to use, but if you want to add a little graphic assistance to your message, you can type text into many of the shapes you create using the AutoShapes menu. You can add text to arrows, banners, boxes, and just about any shape except lines and connectors. To do so, just draw the shape you want and then start typing. Then use the AutoShape command on the Format menu to give the shape and its text the look you want.

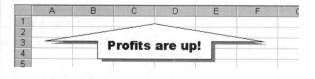

Working with AutoShapes

The AutoShapes menu on the Drawing toolbar offers dozens of predrawn shapes you can use to help speed the process of adding effective visual communication to your worksheets. Using AutoShapes with lines, connectors, and commands on the Draw menu, you can accomplish things you never would have thought possible in a spreadsheet program.

When you draw AutoShapes, you'll notice that most of them display a special yellow diamond-shaped handle somewhere on the perimeter. When you drag this special handle, you can control a specific dimension of the shape, as Figure 10-8 illustrates.

FIGURE 10-8.

You can modify most AutoShapes using special handles.

Many AutoShapes have special diamond-shaped handles you can drag . . .

. . . to control a specific dimension of the shape.

Most AutoShapes are easy to use and somewhat self-explanatory. Connectors and Callouts, however, have some special qualities that bear mentioning.

Using Connectors

If you've spent any time creating drawings using simple lines and boxes, only to find that you need to reposition everything later, you know what a problem this can be. Invariably, you end up spending as much time fine-tuning the drawing as you spent drawing it in the first place. Connectors can help. They are special kinds of lines that are "sticky" on both ends. You use them when you want to add lines to other lines or shapes that remain attached, allowing you to adjust positioning after you're done drawing.

After you click one of the buttons on the Connectors palette on the AutoShapes menu, special blue points appear when you hover the mouse pointer over any existing shapes. (The Connectors command does not normally appear on shortened menus. Click the double arrow at the bottom of the AutoShapes menu to display the Connectors command.) These blue points are *connector points,* and when you

Worksheets

click the mouse on one of them, the connector line attaches itself to the point. The second mouse click attaches the other end of the connector line to a blue point on another object and finishes the connector line. As Figure 10-9 shows, the resulting connector line stays attached to the two points, even when you move the shapes around.

FIGURE 10-9.

Connector lines are "sticky" on both ends so they can attach to two points.

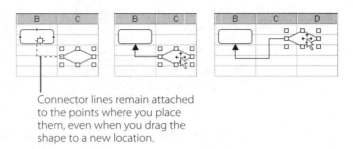

Connector lines remain attached to the points where you place them, even when you drag the shape to a new location.

Note that you don't have to attach connectors to anything. You can use them to create your own custom callouts, for example, by connecting one end to a shape and pointing the other end to a piece of information you want to describe.

Connectors are particularly useful for creating flow charts. First, sketch out your rough ideas using the Flowchart And Connectors palettes on the AutoShapes menu. You can move flow chart symbols around as you work, and the connector lines automatically reroute themselves as necessary.

Using Callouts

Callouts are special text boxes with connector lines attached. You use them to add labels to important information or to point out items in a complex worksheet model or graphic and describe each item individually. The most familiar types of callouts are the ones you see in comics. Excel includes several of this type, as shown in Figure 10-10.

FIGURE 10-10.

Use callouts to call attention to important messages.

After drawing a callout, you can begin typing the text you want to appear in the callout. Then you can drag the diamond-shaped handle to move the tip of the callout indicator to the desired location.

Shape Shifting

If you're unhappy with any of your shape selections, you needn't delete it and draw a new one. Just use the Change AutoShape command on the Draw menu. (The Change AutoShape command does not normally appear on shortened menus. Click the double arrow at the bottom of the AutoShapes menu to display the Change AutoShape command.) You can change most AutoShapes, with the exception of lines and connectors, whether or not the shape contains text. If the original shape does contain text, you might need to adjust its alignment within the new shape.

The More AutoShapes Command

The first time you choose More AutoShapes on the AutoShapes menu, Excel searches through your Clip Art Gallery to find images that will work as rudimentary AutoShapes. (The More AutoShapes command does not normally appear on shortened menus. Click the double arrow at the bottom of the AutoShapes menu to display the More AutoShape command.) This "indexing" process may take a few minutes. When it has finished, clip art that can be used as AutoShapes, such as WMF files, is displayed in the More AutoShapes dialog box, shown in Figure 10-11.

FIGURE 10-11.

The More AutoShapes command actually indexes simple clip art you can use as AutoShapes.

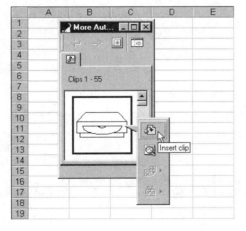

The clip art selected for use by the More AutoShapes command is somewhat rudimentary but can be manipulated using most of the normal AutoShape editing commands. To insert a shape, click it and then select the Insert Clip button on the palette that appears. The More AutoShapes dialog box is actually a variation on the Insert Clip Art dialog box, which is discussed in more detail later in this chapter.

Creating WordArt

The Insert WordArt button on the Drawing toolbar opens a palette of remarkable formatting styles you can employ to create impressive graphic objects using text. When you click the WordArt button, the WordArt Gallery dialog box opens, and you click the effect you want. When you click the OK button, the Edit WordArt Text dialog box opens and you choose the font and size and enter the text you want to use. Figure 10-12 illustrates this process.

FIGURE 10-12.
Create cool logos using the WordArt button.

1 Select the effect for the text.

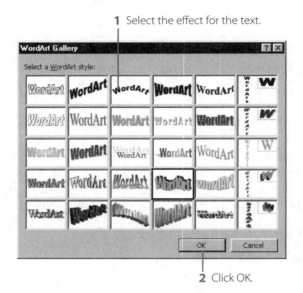

2 Click OK.

3 Select the font size to be used and type the text.

4 Click OK.

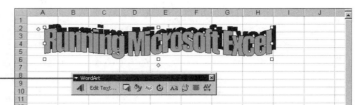

5 Use the WordArt toolbar to make changes.

 TIP

Notice in Figure 10-12 that WordArt objects display some of the same diamond-shaped handles as AutoShapes do. Try dragging these handles for additional interesting effects.

After you create your WordArt, and anytime you select the finished WordArt object, the WordArt toolbar appears, shown in Figure 10-13. With an existing WordArt object selected, clicking the WordArt Gallery button allows you to select a different effect in the WordArt Gallery dialog box. The Format AutoShape button opens the dialog box of the same name, where you can adjust fill and line styles, size, protection, and positioning properties. The WordArt Shape button displays a palette of additional shapes you can apply to an existing WordArt object. As you can see in Figure 10-14, not all shapes are always appropriate for the text you want to illustrate.

FIGURE 10-13.

Create and edit WordArt objects with the WordArt toolbar.

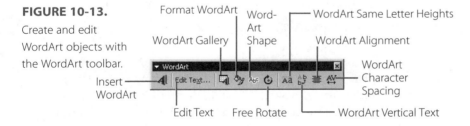

FIGURE 10-14.

The WordArt Shape button offers even more text-effect options.

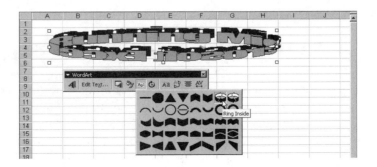

You can use the Free Rotate button, also available on the Drawing toolbar, to change the orientation of any graphic object. The WordArt Same Letter Heights button offers an interesting effect by making all letters fit into the same amount of vertical space. Lowercase letters are enlarged as necessary to be the same height as uppercase letters, and any letters with descenders (parts of letters that extend below the baseline, such as the tail on a "y") are moved up and fit into the same space. Figure 10-15 shows an example.

FIGURE 10-15.

The WordArt Same Letter Heights button fits all the letters into the same vertical space.

The WordArt Vertical Text button switches the orientation of the selected WordArt object to vertical, so the letters are stacked on top of one another. Use the WordArt Alignment button to change the alignment of WordArt objects (where alignment is applicable). This is a palette on which you'll see familiar options, such as Center and Left Align. There are also three Justify options, instead of the usual one that forces text to align to both the left and right margins. Word Justify behaves like normal justification, adding space between words. Letter Justify adds the space between letters as well as words. And Stretch Justify adds no space at all—instead it just stretches the letters to fit.

The WordArt Character Spacing button displays a palette of commands you use to control the amount of space between characters, sometimes called *tracking,* as well as the spacing of letter pairs, also known as *kerning.* The WordArt implementation of tracking isn't what you might expect, however. Instead of adding or removing space between characters, it makes the letters themselves wider or smaller, and the actual length of each word remains the same. The Kern Character Pairs command is either on or off and affects only pairs of letters that represent perennial spacing problems, such as *AV.*

Selecting and Grouping Objects

Sometimes you'll find it convenient to move, resize, or even reformat more than one object at a time. You might want to move several objects at once while preserving their positions relative to one another. For these purposes, Excel includes the Select Objects button on the Drawing toolbar, as well as the Group, Ungroup, and Regroup commands on the Draw menu (on the Drawing toolbar).

The Select Objects button has a few special properties that help you work with objects. After you click the button, the Drawing Selection arrow appears, with which you can select only objects, not cells. The Select Objects button remains active until you click it again. When you use the Select Objects button, your cell selections disappear on the worksheet, making it easier to distinguish the objects. Also, if an object has a macro assigned to it and the macro is normally activated when the object is clicked, you can use the Select Objects arrow to select the object without activating the macro. You can then edit the object itself. Finally, you can use the Drawing Selection arrow to select a group of objects by dragging a rectangle around them, as shown in Figure 10-16.

FIGURE 10-16.

Use the Select Objects button to drag a rectangle around the objects you want to select. Selection handles appear around each selected object.

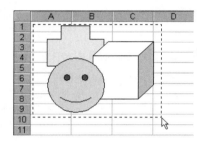 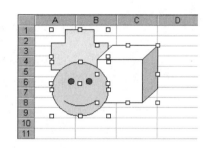

⭐ **TIP**

You can also select objects together by clicking each object while holding down the Shift key. In addition, you can select all the objects on the current worksheet or chart by choosing the Go To command from the Edit menu, clicking the Special button, and then selecting the Objects option.

After you select a group of objects, you can lock them together using the Group command on the Draw menu. (The Group command does not normally appear on shortened menus. Click the double arrow at the bottom of the Draw menu to display the Group command.) The sets of handles around each selected object are then replaced by a single set of handles for the entire group, as shown in Figure 10-17.

FIGURE 10-17.

These objects are grouped together.

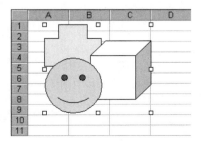

II

Worksheets

After you group a set of objects, you can manipulate them as if they were a single object. You can resize, move, and apply formatting to them as a group. When you apply formatting, however, the separate objects might behave differently, especially if you have grouped different kinds of objects with different formats. It is best to apply formatting before you group objects together, unless the objects are similar.

To ungroup a set of objects, select the group and then click the Ungroup command on the Draw menu. You can also use the handy Regroup command on the Draw menu to group the same objects you last ungrouped. For example, perhaps you ungrouped a set of objects to make changes to one or more of them. Rather than selecting them again and choosing the Group command, just choose the Regroup command.

Selecting Objects that Contain Text

Unlike other objects, when you first select a text box by clicking it, a gray border appears around the box to indicate that it is selected. You can then manipulate the text box as you would any other object. When you click the text box a second time, however, a flashing insertion point appears in the text area, giving you the opportunity to edit the text inside the box. If you want to move a text box while its text area is active, you must click and drag the text box's border; otherwise, you end up selecting the text inside the box instead. Any object into which you type text behaves in a similar manner when its text area is active.

Formatting Objects

In Chapter 7, "Formatting a Worksheet," we discussed using the Cells command on the Format menu to add patterns, colors, and shading to cells. You can apply these formats to objects using the same command, which always appears as the first command at the top of the Format menu. The command name that appears is dependent upon the type of object selected. For example, the first command on the Format menu can be AutoShape, Text Box, or Picture, when the corresponding object type is selected.

When you choose the AutoShape command from the Format menu or when you double-click the object, the Format AutoShape dialog box appears. The Colors And Lines tab of this dialog box gives you control over the style, color, and weight of the object's border, as well as over its fill color and pattern. Figure 10-18 shows the Format

AutoShape dialog box as it appeared after we double-clicked the cross-shaped object in Figure 10-17.

TIP

To display the Format AutoShape dialog box for a text box, double-click the text box's border. When you do, three additional tabs appear in the dialog box: Font, Alignment, and Margins. (The Margins tab controls the amount of space between the text and the object's borders.) These tabs also appear when you double-click any other object that contains text.

FIGURE 10-18.

The Format AutoShape dialog box appears when you double-click an object.

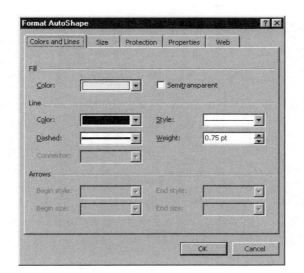

NOTE

If a chart sheet is active, the first command on the Format menu changes to the Selected Object command. The name of the actual command varies depending on which object is selected. Similarly, the name of the Format AutoShape dialog box changes. For example, if a chart's legend is selected, the command on the Format menu appears as Selected Legend and opens the Format Legend dialog box.

You can customize the lines of the selected object using the Color, Style, and Weight drop-down lists. The Dashed drop-down list offers different dashed line styles; the default is undashed. (The Line Style and Dash Style buttons on the Drawing toolbar make the corresponding formats more readily available.) You can select from 13 Style options, including three double-line styles and one triple-line style. The Weight drop-down list offers many of the same line thicknesses as the Style list but allows you the additional option of typing in any point size. The Color options include the 56 colors on the Color tab of the Options dialog box.

You can use the Fill section of the Colors And Lines tab to select a fill color and fill effects for the selected object. The Fill Effects option displays the Fill Effects dialog box, shown in Figure 10-19. You can add patterns and gradient fills to selected objects, as well as your choice of colors for each. In addition, you can apply textures such as wood, marble, canvas, and even paper bag to your objects.

FIGURE 10-19.

Use the Fill Effects dialog box to apply fancy fills to objects.

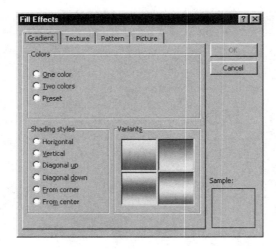

SEE ALSO

For more information about the Color tab or palette, see "Changing the Available Colors," page 222.

The Color Palette

The palette of colors available for use with objects is determined by the Color tab of the Options dialog box. To display the Options dialog box, choose the Options command from the Tools menu. You can then click the Color tab, click the Modify Color button, and change the selected color in the palette.

When you apply a pattern, the color you select for the background is assigned to the black areas of the pattern. The color you select for the foreground is assigned to the white areas. For example, if you select dark green as your foreground color and select any pattern, the object is filled with a dark green pattern. If, on the other hand, you select cyan as your foreground color, a dot pattern, and magenta as your background color, the object will be cyan with magenta dots.

The Semitransparent Option

When you click the Semitransparent check box in the Format Object, Format WordArt, or the Format AutoShape dialog box, the worksheet (or other object) behind the selected object shows through. This option essentially turns every other pixel in the object off, partially revealing whatever is behind it. Figure 10-20 shows two identical objects, but the one on the right has the Semitransparent option turned on.

FIGURE 10-20.

Semitransparent objects allow the background to show through.

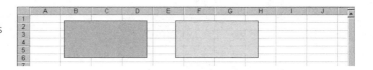

If you select a line or an arrow and then choose the Object command from the Format menu, or if you double-click a line or an arrow, the Arrows options on the Colors And Lines tab become available, as you can see in Figure 10-21. In addition to the Line options, you can change the style of each end of the selected line to include different types of arrowheads (or none). So, if you draw a line to which you want to add an arrowhead, you can add the arrowhead at either end of the line, regardless of which end was drawn first.

FIGURE 10-21.

When a line is selected, the Arrows options let you create custom arrows.

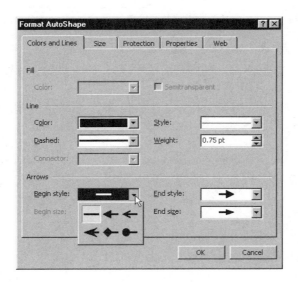

The Arrow Style button on the Drawing toolbar offers a selection of commonly used arrow styles. You can click the More Arrows option to display the Format Object dialog box.

The Color Buttons

The Fill Color, Line Color, and Font Color buttons on the Drawing toolbar are tear-off palettes. If you click and drag them away from the toolbar, they become little floating toolbars. The Fill Color and Font Color buttons can be used to format either cells or objects. These color buttons duplicate the palettes in the Format Object dialog box.

To hide a floating palette, click the tiny close box in the upper right corner.

Applying Shadows

You can use the Shadow button on the Drawing toolbar to add depth to any graphic object.

In Figure 10-22, we created the object with the Explosion 1 button from the Stars And Banners palette on the AutoShapes menu. Then we applied shadow effects with the palette of effects provided by the Shadow button on the Drawing toolbar. The Shadow Settings button on the Shadow palette displays the Shadow Settings toolbar, shown in Figure 10-23.

FIGURE 10-22.

You can create a variety of shadow effects using the Shadow button on the Drawing toolbar.

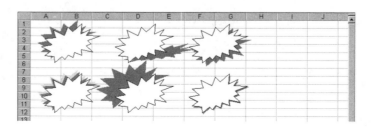

FIGURE 10-23.

The Shadow Settings toolbar.

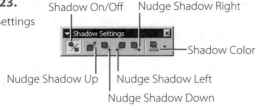

Shadow On/Off   Nudge Shadow Right

Shadow Color

Nudge Shadow Up | Nudge Shadow Left

Nudge Shadow Down

The Shadow Color button displays a familiar color palette and offers the interesting option of making the shadow semitransparent, as shadows actually are. Fine-tune the positioning of the shadow using the four Nudge buttons.

Applying 3-D Effects

When you click the 3-D button on the Drawing toolbar, a palette of predefined three-dimensional effects appears. You can apply 3-D effects to any object, including lines, arrows, and WordArt objects. When you apply a 3-D effect, several special formats are applied to the selected object: horizontal tilt, vertical tilt, depth, direction, lighting position, surface type, and color of the "extruded" 3-D area. In Figure 10-24, we started with three copies of the same object and applied 3-D effects using buttons on the 3-D palette. The object on the left has no effect, 3-D Style 1 was applied to the object in the middle, and 3-D Style 4 was applied to the object on the right.

FIGURE 10-24.

Start with a basic shape and give it depth using the 3-D button on the Drawing toolbar.

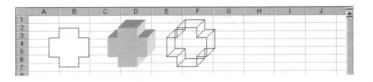

Once you apply a 3-D effect, click 3-D Settings to display the 3-D Settings toolbar shown in Figure 10-25. Use the 3-D Settings toolbar to modify the object to achieve the look you want.

FIGURE 10-25.

The 3-D Settings toolbar.

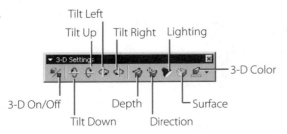

Tilt Left

Tilt Up   Tilt Right   Lighting

3-D Color

3-D On/Off   Depth   Surface

Tilt Down   Direction

The four Tilt buttons adjust the position of the selected object in three-dimensional space. You can use the Depth palette to change the depth of the selected object in points, from zero to infinity. The Direction palette lets you control the trajectory of the extruded portion of the selected object. Use the Perspective and Parallel options in the Direction palette to determine whether the sides of the extruded portion exhibit perspective—that is, appear to fade off into the distance. The Lighting palette controls the brightness and direction of the imaginary light source. The palette displays a small sample object surrounded by lamp buttons. Click a lamp button and the shading of the selected object changes, as if a light were shining on the object from that direction. The Surface palette allows you to choose the type of surface treatment: Matte, Plastic, Metal, or Wire Frame. Finally, the 3-D Color palette lets you control the color of the extruded area of the selected object.

Formatting Objects That Contain Text

There are two ways to select objects containing text: you select either the text area or the entire object. You can tell the difference by looking at the border, as Figure 10-26 shows.

Usually, when you first click an existing text object, the border is a gray dot pattern, indicating that the entire object is selected. Click the object again and the border changes to a hatched-line pattern, indicating that only the text area is selected.

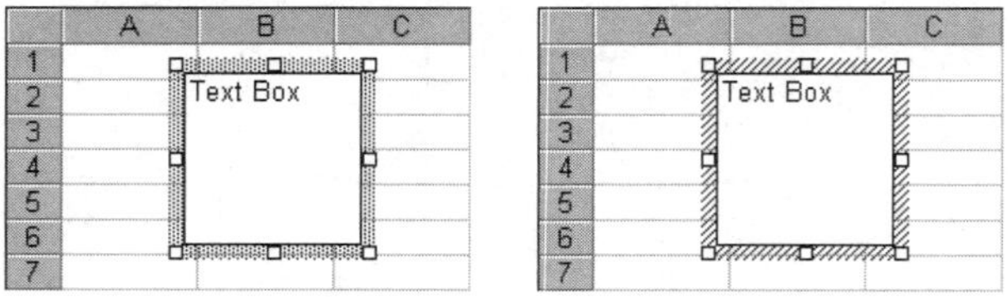

FIGURE 10-26.

The hatched border on the right means that only the text area is selected for editing.

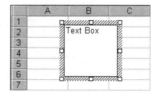

SEE ALSO

For more information about the Font tab, see "Formatting Fonts," page 186.

When you select a text object and display the Format Text Box dialog box, the tabs that appear in the dialog box differ, depending on how the object is selected. When only the text area is selected, only the Font tab appears; when the entire object is selected, eight tabs appear: Font, Alignment, Colors And Lines, Size, Protection, Properties, Margins, and Web.

NOTE

> When a text box is selected, the Format Text Box command appears on the Format menu. When any other type of object containing text is selected, the command is named Format AutoShape. The contents of the dialog box are otherwise identical.

SEE ALSO

For more information about the Alignment tab, see "Aligning Cell Contents," page 179. For more information about the Web tab, see Chapter 20 "Creating Web Pages with Excel."

The options on the Alignment tab of the Format Text Box dialog box control the alignment of text within the object. For example, we formatted the text boxes in Figure 10-27 with various alignment and orientation options. In addition, we selected the Automatic Size option on the Alignment tab for the two boxes containing the *Center Center* label. The Automatic Size option automatically adjusts the size of the text box to fit the text it contains.

FIGURE 10-27.

These alignment and orientation options are among those available on the Alignment tab. The two Center Center boxes were formatted with the Automatic Size option turned on.

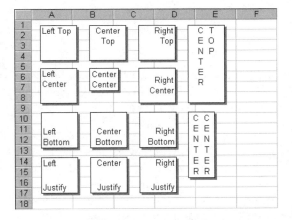

Setting the Default Format for Objects

If you find that you keep applying the same kinds of formatting to objects you create, you can easily make these hard-earned formats the default for all new objects you create. Simply select any object formatted the way you like, and then choose Set AutoShape Defaults from the Draw menu. The formats affected include fills, line styles, and even shadow and 3-D settings.

Positioning Objects

Think of the objects on a worksheet as stacked on top of each other. Each new object you draw is placed on top of the stack. You can

II

Worksheets

adjust the position of objects in relation to each other using the Order command on the Draw menu. The Order command displays a palette containing the Bring To Front, Send To Back, Bring Forward, and Send Backward commands.

Figure 10-28 shows two identical sets of ungrouped objects and the Order palette, which was "torn off" of the Draw menu. In the set on the right, we positioned the banner in front of the other objects using the Bring To Front button, and we positioned the star behind the other objects using the Send To Back button.

FIGURE 10-28.

You can reposition objects in relation to each other with the Order palette on the Draw menu.

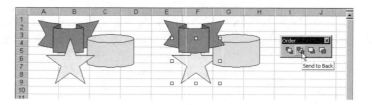

The Bring Forward and Send Backward buttons work in a similar manner, except that instead of moving the selected object all the way to the front or back of the stack, they move the object just one "layer" at a time in either direction.

You can change the way objects are attached to a worksheet by using the options on the Properties tab of the Format AutoShape dialog box, which is shown in Figure 10-29.

FIGURE 10-29.

You can use the Properties tab of the Format Object dialog box to control how cell changes affect graphics.

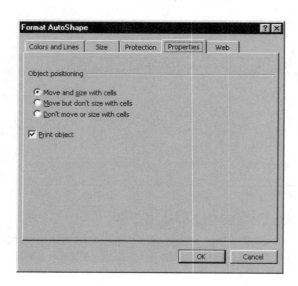

The default placement option is Move And Size With Cells, meaning that if you do anything to change the size or shape of the underlying cells, the object adjusts accordingly. For example, Figure 10-30 shows how the size and shape of three objects, which were originally identical to the fourth object on the worksheet, changed as we changed the width and height of the underlying cells.

An *underlying cell* is any cell whose right or bottom border is between the upper left corner and the lower right corner of the object. In Figure 10-30, notice that the object on the upper right is just touching the top border of cell F7, which is not an underlying cell, whereas the top of the object breaks across the bottom border of cell F1, which therefore qualifies as an underlying cell.

FIGURE 10-30.

When you select the Move And Size With Cells option, the object responds to any changes made to the underlying cells.

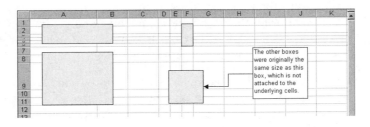

If you insert columns or rows before an object formatted with the Move And Size With Cells option, the object moves accordingly. If you insert columns or rows between the first and last underlying cells, the object stretches to accommodate the insertion. If you select the Move But Don't Size With Cells option and then insert or delete columns or rows, the object moves but retains its shape and proportion. If you select the Don't Move Or Size With Cells option, the object floats above the worksheet and is not affected by any changes you make to the underlying cells.

(?) SEE ALSO

For more information about printing, see Chapter 11, "Printing and Presenting."

The Print Object option on the Properties tab is normally turned on. If you turn off this option, the selected object is not printed when you print the worksheet.

Tools to Help You Position Objects on the Worksheet

It's great to be able to create cool graphics with Excel, but the free-floating nature of graphic objects sometimes makes it hard to maintain a semblance of order on your worksheet. The Draw menu on the Drawing toolbar contains several menus and tear-off palettes you can use to straighten things up.

The Snap command is a submenu that contains two commands you can use to get graphic objects lined up the way you want. (The Snap command does not normally appear on shortened menus. Click the double arrow at the bottom of the Draw menu to display the Snap command.) The To Grid command uses the columns and rows of the worksheet to align objects. Objects already created don't automatically line up with the grid when you choose this command, but as soon as you drag an existing object, it snaps to the nearest column and row borders. Any new objects you create will automatically align themselves to the nearest gridlines. The To Shape command operates in a similar fashion, except that the edges of any existing objects are used as part of the virtual grid as well, making it easy to align objects to one another. Both commands are *toggles*—that is, you click once to turn them on and click again to turn them off. Note, however, that choosing the To Shape command requires the To Grid command and automatically activates it. If you turn off the To Grid command, the To Shape command is turned off as well.

The Nudge, Align Or Distribute, and Rotate Or Flip commands on the Draw menu are tear-off palettes that offer a lot of help in getting graphic objects positioned just the way you want them. (Neither the Nudge command nor the Align Or Distribute command normally appear on shortened menus. Click the double arrow at the bottom of the Draw menu to display these commands.) These three palettes are shown in Figure 10-31.

FIGURE 10-31.

The Nudge, Align Or Distribute, and Rotate Or Flip palettes on the Draw menu.

If you select an object and click one of the Nudge tools, the object moves one pixel at a time in the direction you choose. These are handy tools to use when you want to position objects precisely but not necessarily align them to the grid or another object.

 TIP

You can also use the arrow keys on your keyboard—the functional equivalent of the Nudge buttons—to nudge objects one pixel at a time.

The Align Or Distribute tools can be a great help when you are working with multiple objects. Suppose you have a number of objects, such as the ones shown on the left in Figure 10-32, that you want to be evenly spaced.

FIGURE 10-32.

Use the Align Or Distribute palette on the Draw menu to create order out of chaos.

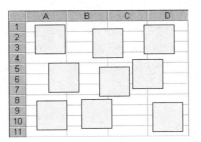 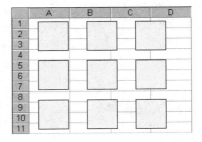

You could start by using the Align Top command to get one row of objects lined up and then choose Distribute Horizontally to get them evenly spaced. Then use the various Align Or Distribute commands to align the rest of the objects to the newly organized row.

The Align commands snap all the selected objects to the edge of the object that is in the direction you choose. For example, when you choose the Align Left command, the left edges of all selected objects line up with the leftmost edge of the leftmost object selected. The Align Center command lines up the centers of objects along a vertical axis and finds the average common centerline of all selected objects. The Align Middle command operates in a similar fashion along the horizontal axis.

The Distribute commands calculate the total amount of space between the selected objects and divide the space as equally as possible among them. The first and last objects (leftmost and rightmost, or top and bottom) do not move—all the objects in between are adjusted as necessary. More than two objects must be selected for the command to have an effect.

Cutting, Copying, and Sorting Objects with Cells

? SEE ALSO

For more information about the Sort command, see "Sorting Lists and Other Ranges," page 752.

In addition to moving and sizing objects with cells, Excel allows you to control what happens when you cut, copy, or sort objects that are attached to cells. Choose the Options command from the Tools menu, click the Edit tab, and then select or deselect the Cut, Copy, And Sort Objects With Cells option.

II

Worksheets

② SEE ALSO

For more information about importing objects from other applications, see "Using Graphics from Other Programs," page 379.

When Cut, Copy, And Sort Objects With Cells is turned on, you can easily construct "databases" of the objects that you create in Excel or that you import from other applications. For example, Figure 10-33 shows a rudimentary database of objects whose names are entered in the underlying cells. (Each corresponding object is drawn adjacent to the name so that the same cell becomes the underlying cell to which the object is attached.) In Figure 10-33, the window on the right shows what happens when you select any cell in the list, choose the Sort command from the Data menu, and click OK. The cells and attached objects are sorted according to the text in the cells.

Ⓦ ON THE WEB

You can find Sorting Objects.xls used in the following example on the Microsoft Press Web site at *http://mspress.microsoft.com/mspress/products/2050/*.

FIGURE 10-33.

You can sort objects along with cells, as shown in the window on the far right.

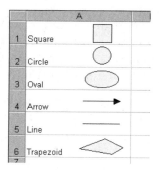

You can also use the Delete command on the Edit menu to simultaneously delete a cell and any objects attached to the cell. Similarly, if you copy a cell, any attached objects are also copied.

Controlling the Display of Objects

To speed up the scrolling of your worksheet, you can choose the Options command from the Tools menu and then click the View tab. In the Objects section of the View tab, the Show All option is normally active. Selecting the Show Placeholders option reduces text boxes, button objects, and embedded charts to simple patterns that indicate their locations on the worksheet. The Show Placeholders option increases your scrolling speed because Excel doesn't have to redraw the objects every time you scroll to a new screen. You must reactivate the Show All option before you print. The Hide All option suppresses the display of objects entirely, increasing screen redraw speed even more. Although you cannot directly modify objects when Hide All is activated, some actions will still change them. If anything other than Don't Move Or Size With Cells is selected on the Properties tab of the Format Object dialog box, the object will respond to adjustments made to the column width or row height of underlying cells.

Protecting Objects

? SEE ALSO

For more information about protecting worksheets, see "Protecting Your Data," page 111.

You can prevent objects from being selected, moved, formatted, or sized by choosing the AutoShapes command from the Format menu (or the Selected Object command, if the object is on a chart sheet), clicking the Protection tab, and selecting the Locked option, as shown in Figure 10-34.

You can also use the Lock Text option, which is visible only when a text box is selected, to protect the text contents of a text box. Newly drawn objects are automatically assigned Locked protection. However, to turn on worksheet security and activate protection for both text boxes and new objects, you must also choose the Protect Sheet command from the Protection submenu of the Tools menu.

FIGURE 10-34.

Choose the AutoShapes command from the Format menu, or double-click an object, and then click the Protection tab to check the object's protection status.

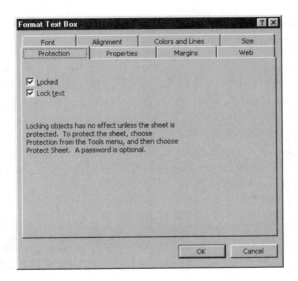

Taking Pictures of Your Worksheets

Microsoft Excel 2000 provides two techniques for taking "pictures" of your worksheets: the Camera button (which you can add to a toolbar) and the Copy Picture command (which appears on the Edit menu when you press the Shift key before you choose Edit).

Using the Camera Button

SEE ALSO

For more information about cell links, see "References to Worksheets in Other Workbooks," page 121.

With the Camera button, shown below in the margin, you can copy an image of a range of cells and paste the image anywhere in the same worksheet, another worksheet in the same workbook, or another workbook. Copying an image is not the same as copying the same range of cells with the Copy command on the Edit menu. When you use the Camera button, you copy a linked image of the cells, not their contents. The image floats over the sheet, just like a drawing object, yet behaves like a linked cell or range. As a result, the image changes dynamically as the contents of the original cells change.

To add the Camera button to a toolbar, choose the Toolbars command from the View menu and click the Customize button. In the Customize dialog box, click the Commands tab, select the Tools category, and drag the Camera button onto any toolbar. (If you don't drag the Camera button onto a toolbar, it creates its own toolbar.) Figure 10-35 shows the Camera button added to the end of the Picture toolbar.

Figure 10-35 shows two worksheets side by side. If you select the range A3:B6 in Exams3 and click the Camera button, the pointer changes from a plus sign to a cross hair. Click anywhere in Book2 to select it and then click the cross-hair pointer where you want the upper left corner of the picture to appear. Excel embeds the picture as shown on the right in Figure 10-35. Any graphic objects within the range A3:B6 or overlapping the range are also included in the embedded picture.

FIGURE 10-35.

The Camera button creates a linked image of a selected range.

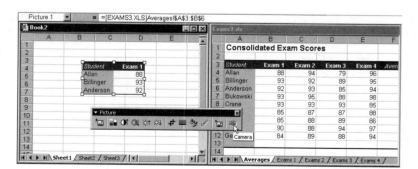

After you paste the picture, you can change its size and proportions by dragging its selection handles, and you can treat it just like any other graphic object. Changes in shape, size, or formatting do not affect the dynamic updating of the data displayed in the picture.

If you select the embedded picture in Figure 10-35, the formula bar displays a formula much like any other cell-linking formula. After you create the picture, you can change the formula in the formula bar, and the picture will change accordingly. You can even change the reference formula to link a completely different worksheet or workbook.

For example, if you select the embedded picture in Book2 in Figure 10-35, the Name box in the formula bar displays the name *Picture 1* and the formula shown for the object is

=[EXAMS.XLS]Averages!$A$3:$B$6

If you change the formula to

=[EXAMS.XLS]Averages!$A$3:$B$9

the picture adjusts to include the additional rows, as shown in Figure 10-36.

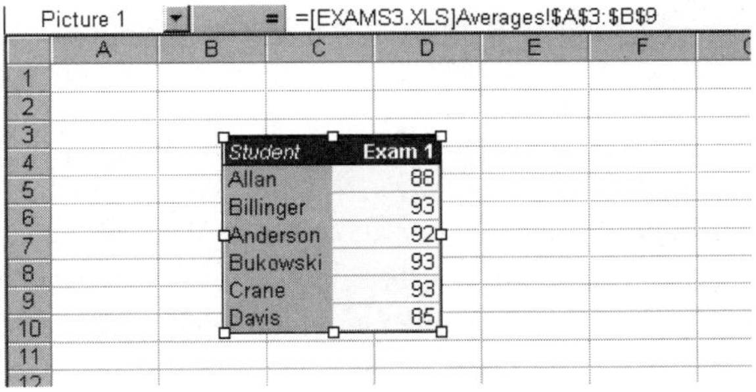

FIGURE 10-36.

If you change the cell references in a formula for a picture created with the Camera button, the picture changes accordingly.

The link between the source and destination documents has another distinctive and useful characteristic. Suppose you close the Exams3 worksheet in Figure 10-35 on the previous page. If you then double-click the embedded image in Book2, Exams3 opens automatically, with the pictured range selected.

Using the Copy Picture Command

The Copy Picture command creates an image just as the Camera button does, but with an important difference. The copied picture is static, with no links to any worksheet. Static pictures are useful when you don't need to update data or when the speed with which Excel recalculates the worksheet is more important than updating. You can use the Copy Picture command to add images of worksheets and charts to reports or other documents via the Clipboard. After you take the picture, you can paste it in another Excel document or in a document from any application that accepts Clipboard images.

To use the Copy Picture command, select the cells, object, or chart you want to copy, hold down the Shift key, and then choose Copy Picture from the Edit menu (where the Copy command has become the Copy Picture command and the Paste command has become the Paste Picture command). Excel displays the dialog box shown in Figure 10-37. (Neither the Copy Picture command nor the Paste Picture command normally appears on shortened menus. Continue to hold the Shift key while clicking the double arrow at the bottom of the Draw menu to display these commands.)

FIGURE 10-37.

The Copy Picture dialog box lets you control the appearance of the picture.

The default option, As Shown On Screen, reproduces the selection at the moment you take the picture. The As Shown When Printed option reproduces the selection according to the settings in the Page Setup dialog box that control the printing of gridlines and row and column headings. For example, the worksheet in Figure 10-38 contains two pictures of the same area. We created the top one with the As Shown On Screen option selected and the bottom one with the As Shown When Printed option selected, with the Page Setup options for printing gridlines turned off and the option for printing row and column headings turned on.

FIGURE 10-38.

The top picture was created with the As Shown On Screen option, and the bottom picture was created with the As Shown When Printed option.

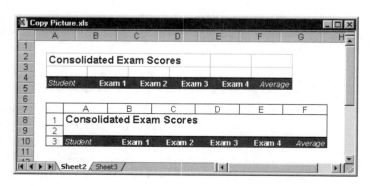

The Picture and Bitmap options are useful if your workbook will be viewed on different computers. The Picture option copies the picture in a format that can be displayed on monitors with different resolutions, whereas the Bitmap option copies the picture in a format that appears to be correct only when the display resolution is the same as the screen from which it was copied.

After you copy an image of the selection to the Clipboard, you can paste the image anywhere you want—in another location on the worksheet, in another worksheet, or even in a document from another application. You can paste the image into an Excel document with the Paste command, the Paste Picture command, or the Paste button on the Standard toolbar.

Using Graphics from Other Programs

You can import graphics into Microsoft Excel 2000 from other programs that produce files compatible with the Windows Clipboard, such as Windows Paint in Microsoft Windows 95 and 98.

? SEE ALSO

For more information about DDE and OLE, see Chapter 17, "Integrating Applications with OLE."

If the application used to create the graphic you want to import into Excel supports Dynamic Data Exchange (DDE) or OLE, you might be able to establish a link between the source file and the graphic. After you import the graphic into Excel, the link allows the graphic to be updated automatically if the source document changes.

To import a graphic from another application, begin by opening the file that contains the graphic in the source application and copying the image you want using the Copy command. Next, in Excel, open the workbook into which you want to paste the graphic and choose the Paste or Paste Special command (or click the Paste button on the Standard toolbar).

As with other graphic objects, you can size, position, and protect pasted-in images. You can also add borders with the Object command on the Format menu.

To export an image of an Excel worksheet or chart, use the Copy Picture command and then paste the image, via the Clipboard, into any other application that supports the Clipboard.

The Picture Command

The Picture command on the Insert menu allows you to embed in your workbooks graphics that have been saved in a variety of file formats. (The actual formats supported depend on your computer's configuration.) When you choose Picture on the Insert menu and then choose From File, a dialog box like the one in Figure 10-39 appears.

FIGURE 10-39.

Using the Insert Picture dialog box, you can insert graphic files from other applications into your workbook.

SEE ALSO

For more information about searching for files, see "Searching for Files," page 83.
For more information about the File Open dialog box, see "Opening Files," page 77.

The Insert Picture dialog box is functionally identical to the File Open dialog box. Use the Look In box or the Navigation bar icons to the left to locate a particular graphic. The Files Of Type drop-down list box allows you to zero in on a particular file type, but normally it displays All Pictures. A thumbnail representation of the selected file appears on the right side of the dialog box. When you find the file, click the Insert button to insert the graphic in the worksheet.

The Object Command

The Object command on the Insert menu gives you direct access to other applications you can use to create objects or edit existing objects that you will subsequently insert in your worksheet. The difference between inserting a picture and inserting an object is that a picture is always static and cannot be edited or updated, whereas an object retains a connection to its source application. You can open an embedded object for editing by double-clicking it, and you can choose to link an object to the source file so it is updated automatically if the source file changes.

When you choose the Object command from the Insert menu, a dialog box appears with two tabs—Create New and Create From File. The

Create New tab, shown in Figure 10-40, allows you to activate an application and then create the object directly in the selected application. (The Object command does not normally appear on shortened menus. Click the double arrow at the bottom of the Insert menu to display the Object command.)You select an application from the Object Type list box. The contents of this list box vary depending on the configuration of your system and the applications you have installed.

FIGURE 10-40.

You can use the Create New tab of the Object dialog box to simultaneously insert an object and activate the application to create it with.

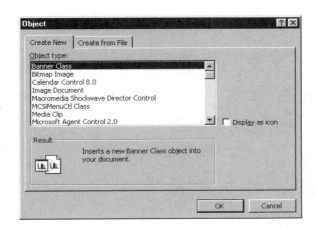

When you select an item from the Object Type list box, a small frame is inserted in the current worksheet at the location of the active cell, and the application needed to create or edit that object type is started. For example, if you select Paintbrush Picture from the Object Type list box, Microsoft Paint starts, and you can then create a new drawing or edit an existing one. When you are finished, click any cell in the worksheet. The object you created is inserted at the location of the active cell. (Note that you may have to drag the handles around the application box to view a larger area.)

The Object dialog box's Create From File tab is shown in Figure 10-41 on the next page. You can use this tab to insert an existing file as an object rather than create a new object with the Create New tab. (The object types you can actually embed depend on the applications installed in your computer.)

? SEE ALSO

For more information about linking objects, see Chapter 17, "Integrating Applications with OLE."

Although the Link To File option on the Create From File tab is not selected by default, you can still open the object in its source application by double-clicking it. If you select the Link To File option, the object is automatically updated when the source file changes. The Display As Icon option embeds the selected file in your workbook as an icon. This option is particularly convenient when an embedded object is very long or large and is more easily viewed in its source application. However, if you distribute the workbook to other users, be sure the same application is available on their computers, or they will not be able to open the embedded icon for viewing.

FIGURE 10-41.

With the Create From File tab of the Object dialog box, you can insert existing documents in your workbooks.

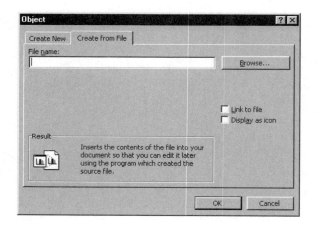

To make changes to any embedded object, simply double-click the object. The source application starts and the object file opens, allowing you to make modifications.

Using Clip Art

If you don't have the time or the inclination to create your own artwork using Excel's drawing tools, you can instantly call on the talents of numerous professional illustrators using the Insert ClipArt dialog box—the user interface of the Microsoft Clip Gallery. Art objects you add to your worksheets are essentially similar to objects you create using Excel's Drawing tools. You can resize, reposition, add borders, and sometimes even add fills and patterns to clip art objects. Besides art, the Clip Gallery also allows you to insert sounds and movies into your spreadsheets for that extra "wow" factor.

Choose Picture from the Insert menu, then choose ClipArt.

When you click the Insert ClipArt button or choose the Picture command on the Insert menu and then choose Clip Art, a dialog box similar to the one shown in Figure 10-42 appears.

FIGURE 10-42.

The Insert ClipArt dialog box offers a lot more than just clip art.

Use these buttons to move forward and backward, just like your Web browser.

Click to return to the main categories screen.

Click here to download additional clips from the Web.

To return to the main categories screen, click the Back arrow button.

Click here to make the dialog box smaller.

When you click a category icon, the main screen changes to display the clips in that category.

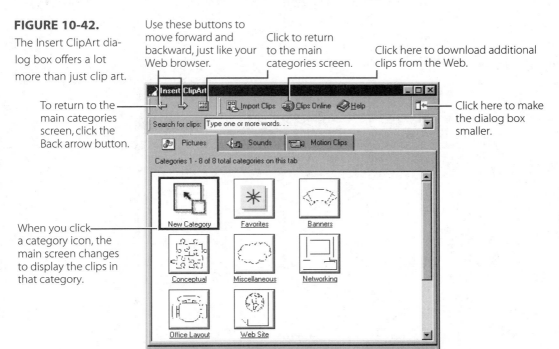

The Insert ClipArt dialog box operates in a similar way to a Web browser. When you click a tab or a category, the main window displays its contents. After you browse the tabs and categories of the dialog box, you can click the Back button at the upper-left of the dialog box to retrace your steps one at a time. You can also click the All Categories button to return to the main categories screen for the selected tab.

For example, when you click the Banners category on the Pictures tab, the dialog box changes to look similar to the one shown in Figure 10-43 on the next page.

When you click a clip, a small four-button toolbar appears, as shown in Figure 10-43. Clicking the first button—Insert Clip—places the clip on your worksheet. Clicking the Preview Clip button displays a

Preview window that shows you how the clip will look when you insert it. When you click the Add Clip To Favorites Or Other Category button, you can create a new category or choose from a list of current categories to which the selected clip will be added. Clicking the Find Similar Clips button allows you to select from a list of keywords associated with the selected clip to help find clips with similar keywords.

FIGURE 10-43.

Click a category to display clips.

When you hover the mouse cursor over a clip, a screen tip box pops up showing you its name and size.

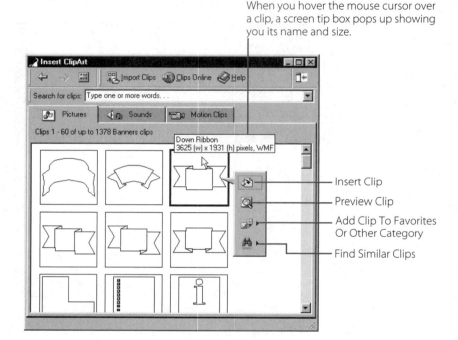

Insert Clip

Preview Clip

Add Clip To Favorites Or Other Category

Find Similar Clips

Some categories have more clips than can be displayed at once. For example, look just below the Pictures tab in Figure 10-43 and you'll see the message "Clips 1-60 of up to 1378 Banners clips." If you scroll to the bottom of the screen, you'll see a More Clips icon that, when clicked, displays the next 60 clips in the category.

You can type keywords into the Search For Clips edit box to help you find applicable clips more easily than browsing through thousands of clips. For example, typing *profit* into the Search For Clips edit box produced the set of clips shown in Figure 10-44.

FIGURE 10-44.

Type keywords into the Search For Clips edit box to help find the right clip for the job.

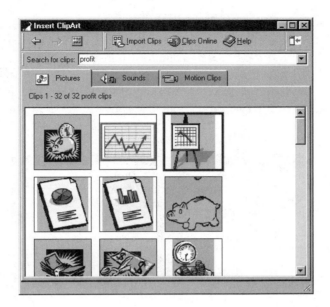

Importing Clips

Click the Import Clips button to add your own artwork, sounds, or movies to the Insert ClipArt dialog box. A dialog box appears that allows you to find the clip you want to import, then allows you to choose how you want to import it. You can simply copy the clip into the Clip Gallery, leaving the original untouched. You can move the selected clip into the Clip Gallery, removing it from its original location. Or you can choose to do neither and let the Clip Gallery find the selected clip and use it from its current location. If you choose this third option, make sure the clip is always available in the same location whenever you need it.

In the weeks and months following the release of Microsoft Excel 2000, more professionally created clips will be made available at a special location on the World Wide Web. If you have Web access, click the Clips Online button to automatically download these clips and import them into the Clip Gallery.

Organizing Clips

The New Category icon on the main screen allows you to create your own "buckets" for clips. For example, you could create a category for company logos or personal photographs that you can import using

II

Worksheets

the Import Clips button. You could also add existing clips to categories you create. Click the Add Clip To Favorites Or Other Category button on the toolbar that appears when you click a clip (shown in Figure 10-43). For example, we clicked the first clip in the Banners category and then clicked the Add Clip To Favorites Or Other Category button. Click the category where you want to add the clip, then click the Add button. Figure 10-45 shows the result.

FIGURE 10-45.

Use the Add Clip To Favorites Or Other Category button to populate your own clip categories.

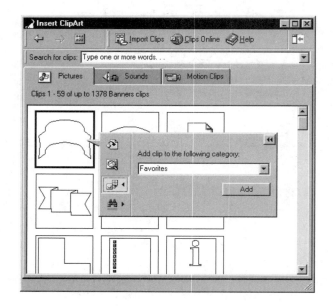

The Find Similar Clips button (shown in Figure 10-43) helps you find clips in the same vein as the one selected, in case it isn't quite what you're looking for. Each clip has several keywords that refer to actions or concepts associated with it. You can search for other clips with similar associations, or you can choose just one of the associated keywords, as shown in Figure 10-46.

You can edit the properties of any clip—that is, the associated keywords, the categories that include the clip, and the name of the clip. Click the clip using the right mouse button to display the shortcut menu, and then click Clip Properties to display the dialog box shown in Figure 10-47. The Description tab displays information about the clip, including its name, which you can edit. The Categories tab displays all the current clip categories and allows you to assign the selected clip to one or more of them. The Keywords tab lists all the keywords associated with the selected clip and allows you to add new keywords or delete existing keywords.

FIGURE 10-46.

Use the Find Similar Clips button to search for the perfect clip.

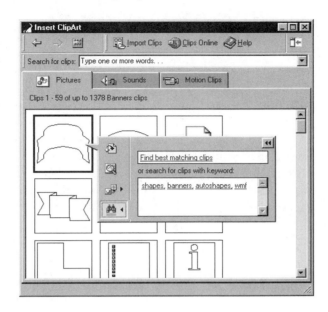

FIGURE 10-47.

Use the Clip Properties dialog box to edit a clip's description, categories, and keywords.

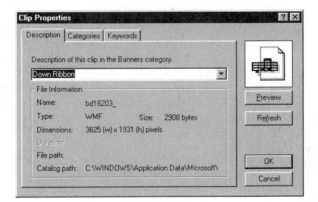

Restoring Defaults

If you edit or delete clips, categories, or properties for built-in clips, and then later wish you hadn't, you can easily restore the Clip Gallery to its original glory. Click the right mouse button anywhere in the display area of the Insert ClipArt dialog box and then choose the Recover command on the shortcut menu to display the Clip Gallery Database Recovery dialog box, shown in Figure 10-48.

II

Worksheets

FIGURE 10-48.

You can restore the default configuration of the Clip Gallery.

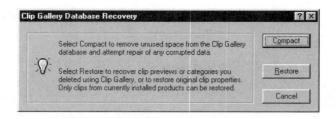

Click the Restore button to display the Clip Gallery Restore dialog box, which contains buttons you can use to restore categories, clips, or properties to their original state. The dialog box shown in Figure 10-48 also includes the Compact button, which helps you keep the size of the Clip Gallery under control by compacting the Clip Gallery on your hard disk. This feature is particularly useful when you've added clips of your own to the Clip Gallery.

Printing
and Presenting

Microsoft Excel 2000 makes it easy for you to produce polished, professional-looking reports from worksheets. In this chapter, we'll explain how to use the Page Setup command to define the layout of your printed pages. You'll also learn how to restrict your print range, define print titles, control page breaks, and use Excel's Print Preview feature. Here we concentrate on printing worksheets, but with a few of the refinements discussed in Chapter 21, you can apply the procedures covered in this chapter to printing charts.

This chapter also covers the Report Manager. You use the Report Manager to assign names to combinations of print areas and print settings, making it easy to recreate a printout at any time.

Specifying What to Print

Unless you tell Excel to do otherwise, choosing the Print command from the File menu and clicking OK prints one copy of the entire populated area of the current worksheet. You do not have to specify a print range as you do in some other spreadsheet programs. As you can see from the Print dialog box shown in Figure 11-1, however, you can specify what portion of your document Excel should print.

FIGURE 11-1.

Use the Print dialog box to tell Excel what you want to print and how many copies you want.

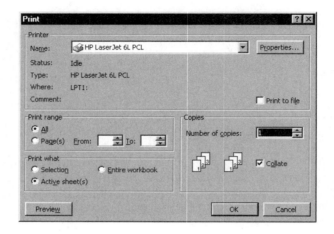

? SEE ALSO

For more information about selecting a group of worksheets, see "Working with Sheets," page 311.

- To print the entire workbook, not just the current worksheet, select Entire Workbook in the Print dialog box.

- To print a group of worksheets but not the entire workbook, select those worksheets as a group before choosing Print from the File menu. Then click the Active Sheet(s) option in the Print dialog box.

- To print part of a worksheet, first select what you want to print and then click the Selection option in the Print dialog box. (Alternatively, you can define an area on the Sheet tab of the Page Setup dialog box.)

- To print only a particular range of pages, enter the starting and ending page numbers in the From and To edit boxes.

The top line of the Print dialog box tells you which printer will handle your output. To use a different printer, click the down arrow to display the drop-down list and then select the printer you want from the list of those available.

Defining an Area to Print

? SEE ALSO

For more information about defining names, see "Naming Cells and Ranges," page 133.

When you choose the Active Sheet(s) option in the Print dialog box, Excel checks to see whether the range name *Print_Area* has been assigned on each worksheet. If this name has been assigned, Excel prints only the range to which you've assigned the name. Otherwise, it prints the entire populated area of the sheet. Thus, if you want to print the same area of a given sheet repeatedly, you can save yourself some steps by giving that area the name *Print_Area*. You can do that either by choosing Print Area and then Set Print Area from the File menu or by following these steps (Print Area does not normally appear on shortened menus. Click the double arrow at the bottom of the File menu to display the Print Area command.):

1   Choose Page Setup from the File menu and then click the Sheet tab. (Page Setup does not normally appear on shortened menus. Click the double arrow at the bottom of the File menu to display the Page Setup command.)

2   Specify the range you want to print in the Print Area edit box.

You can assign the name *Print_Area* on as many sheets as you like. If you select two or more sheets and print using the Active Sheet(s) option, Excel will print only the *Print_Area* range of any sheet where that name is defined and will print the entire populated area of any remaining selected sheets.

★ TIP

> To bypass the Print dialog box, click the Print button on the Standard toolbar, hold down Shift, and click the Print Preview button. Excel prints using the Active Sheet(s) option.

Printing Multiple Copies

Excel normally prints one copy of whatever you tell it to print. If you want more than one copy, enter the number of copies you want in the Number Of Copies edit box of the Print dialog box (shown in Figure 11-1).

If you want collated copies of your document, select the Collate option in the Print dialog box. Collated copies are more convenient but might take slightly longer to print.

Controlling the Appearance of Your Pages

For more information on Print Preview, see "Using Print Preview," page 402.

The various sections of the Page Setup dialog box let you specify factors that affect the appearance of your printed pages, such as orientation, scaling, paper size, print quality, and the number that prints on the first page of your document. Figure 11-2 shows the Page tab of the Page Setup dialog box, which you can display either by choosing the File menu's Page Setup command or by clicking the Setup button in Print Preview.

FIGURE 11-2.

The Page tab of the Page Setup dialog box lets you choose between portrait and landscape orientation, apply a scaling factor, select paper size and print quality, and specify a starting page number.

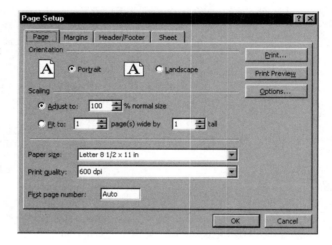

Printing Wide or Tall

The Orientation setting determines whether your worksheet prints vertically (tall) or horizontally (wide). When you select the Portrait option, pages are oriented so that they are taller than they are wide. As a result, you have more room to print rows but less room for columns. This setting is the default. With the Landscape option, pages are oriented so that they are wider than they are tall. In this case, you have room for more columns, but fewer rows will fit on a page.

Landscape orientation is useful for printing worksheet pages that are wider than they are long on 8 1/2-by-11-inch paper. For example, you could use this option to print on one sheet of paper a schedule that is 15 columns wide but only 8 rows deep.

Setting a Reduction Ratio

The Scaling setting lets you override the default size of your printouts in two ways: by specifying a scaling factor (from 10 percent through

400 percent) or by automatically fitting the report to a specified number of pages. These scaling options are available for any printer installed on your Windows system.

Be aware that Excel always applies a scaling factor in both the horizontal and vertical dimensions. For example, if your full-size printout is two pages deep by one page wide and you tell Excel to scale it to a single page, the resulting printout will be narrower as well as shallower.

If you want to return to a full-size printout after selecting a scaling option, you can choose the Page Setup command from the File menu, select the Adjust To option, and then type *100* in the % Normal Size edit box.

Specifying Paper Size and Print Quality

The Paper Size and Print Quality drop-down lists include the options available for your printer driver. Your laser printer, for example, may offer print-quality settings of 600 dpi, 300 dpi, and 150 dpi. The higher dpi settings look better but take longer to print.

The First Page Number Setting

The First Page Number edit box is meaningful only if you plan to include page numbers in your printout's header or footer. If you plan to print page numbers, you can start them at any number you want, including 0 or a negative number.

Setting Margins

The Margins tab of the Page Setup dialog box gives you control over the top, bottom, left, and right margins of your printed worksheets. As shown in Figure 11-3 on the next page, the default settings are 1 inch for the top and bottom margins and 0.75 inch for the left and right margins.

Centering Your Work on the Page

If you want your printout to be centered either vertically or horizontally on the page, you don't have to worry about margin settings. Simply tell Excel to center it automatically by selecting one or both of the Center On Page options at the bottom of the dialog box shown in Figure 11-3 on the next page.

II

Worksheets

FIGURE 11-3.

The Margins tab of the Page Setup dialog box lets you override the default margin settings by entering a new value in the corresponding edit box. You can also select centering options.

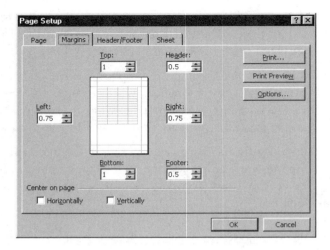

Creating a Header and Footer

A header is a line or block of text printed at the top of each page. A footer is a line or block of text printed at the bottom of each page. You can set the position of a header or footer by using the Margins tab of the Page Setup dialog box. By default, footers are printed .5 inch from the bottom edge, and headers are printed .5 inch from the top edge. When you change either of these values, Excel highlights the position of the header or footer on the preview page.

You can create a header or footer in the Header/Footer tab of the Page Setup dialog box, shown in Figure 11-4. Excel includes a number of predefined headers and footers, some of which automatically include your name or the name of your company.

FIGURE 11-4.

The Header/Footer tab of the Page Setup dialog box displays the text at the top and bottom of your printed pages and includes drop-down lists of existing items and buttons that allow you to create new headers and footers.

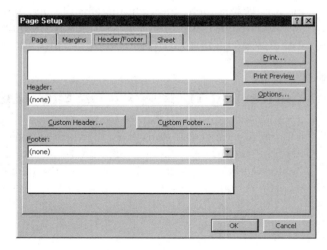

Initially, both drop-down lists include the same set of options. If you have created any custom headers or footers for the current workbook, they also appear in the drop-down lists. To see the list of predefined headers or footers and switch to a different one, follow these steps:

1 Click the down arrow next to the Header or Footer box.

2 Press Home to go to the top of the list.

3 Keep your eye on the corresponding example box as you press the Down arrow key to move through the list. (You will not see the previews if you move through the list using the scroll bar.)

4 Click the header or footer you want.

Creating Custom Headers and Footers

If you don't find exactly what you need in Excel's supply of predefined headers and footers, you can create your own or modify one of Excel's by clicking the Custom Header or Custom Footer button on the Header/Footer tab of the Page Setup dialog box. When you do this, you'll see the dialog box shown in Figure 11-5.

FIGURE 11-5.

Excel lets you create custom headers and footers by clicking the buttons on this dialog box.

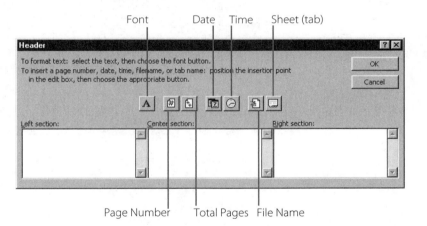

TIP

Create A Default Header and Footer

You can create a new workbook and set the header and footer as you want them. Then save the workbook as a template under the name Book.xlt. Store this template file in the XLStart folder of your Excel folder. *For more information on templates, see "Using Template Files," page 214.*

Excel uses various codes that begin with an ampersand and are enclosed in brackets to represent information that you might want to put in your headers and footers—such as the current time, current date, and current page number. Fortunately, you don't have to learn these codes to create headers and footers. Simply click the appropriate edit box (Left Section, Center Section, or Right Section), and then click the buttons above the section edit boxes.

To specify text in your header or footer, click the appropriate section edit box and then type your text. To divide the text between two or more lines, press Enter at the end of each line. To include an ampersand in your text, type two ampersands.

For example, to create a header that contains three elements—the text *Trey Research,* flush left; the current sheet name in the center of the page; and the current date flush right—follow the steps in Figure 11-6.

FIGURE 11-6.

This header prints *Trey Research* at the left, the current sheet name in the center, and the current date at the right.

2 Click the Center Section edit box and then click the SheetName button.

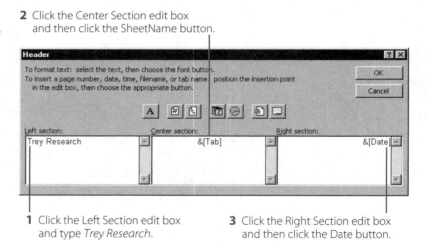

1 Click the Left Section edit box and type *Trey Research.*

3 Click the Right Section edit box and then click the Date button.

Changing Fonts

Excel's default font for headers and footers is 10-point Arial. To select a different typeface, point size, and style, click the Font button—the one with the capital A on it. The Font dialog box appears. (To assign a different font to text that you've already entered in one of the Section edit boxes, first select the text and then click the Font button.) Excel displays the header and footer text in the font and style you select. Note, however, that font options apply to the current section edit box only (so you must make a corresponding change to the other header or footer if you want them to have the same size font).

Setting Print Titles

On many worksheets, the column and row labels that identify information categories are located in only the leftmost columns and top few rows. When Excel breaks a large report into pages, those important column and row labels might appear only on the first page of the printout. You can use the Sheet tab of the Page Setup dialog box to print the contents of one or more columns, one or more rows, or a combination of columns and rows on every page of a report. The Sheet tab of the Page Setup dialog box is shown in Figure 11-7.

Suppose you want to print the contents of column A and rows 3 and 4 on all pages of a lengthy report. First, choose Page Setup from the File menu, and then follow the steps in Figure 11-7. (Page Setup does not normally appear on shortened menus. Click the double arrow at the bottom of the File menu to display the Page Setup command.)

FIGURE 11-7.

The sheet tab of the Page Setup dialog box lets you specify print titles and select various other printing options.

1 Click the Sheet tab.

2 Click the Rows To Repeat At Top edit box, then select the headings or any cells in rows 3 and 4 in the worksheet window. (Click the Collapse Dialog button at the right side of the edit box to see the worksheet.)

3 Click the Columns To Repeat At Left edit box, then select the heading or any cell in column A in the worksheet window.

4 Click OK.

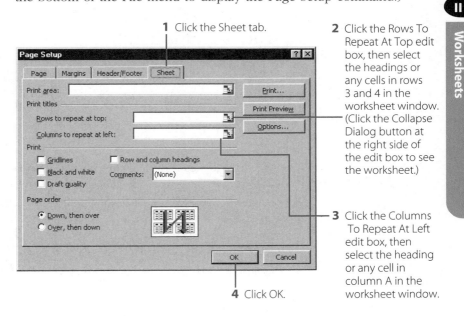

If you prefer to type your entries, you can simply enter the row numbers or column letters in the edit boxes. To specify rows 3 and 4, for example, type *3:4*. To specify column A, type *A:A*. Note that for a single row or column, you have to type the number or letter twice, with a colon in between. You can specify separate print titles for each worksheet in your workbook. Excel remembers the titles for each worksheet.

⭐ **TIP**

Deleting Print Titles

To remove print titles, you can go back to the Page Setup dialog box and delete the title specifications. But you might find it quicker to use the Define Name dialog box. Simply press Ctrl+F3 and then delete the name that ends in Print_Titles.

Printing Gridlines

By default, Excel does not print gridlines regardless of whether they're displayed. If you want gridlines printed, select the Gridlines option in the Page Setup dialog box's Sheet tab. *For information about displaying and suppressing gridlines, see "Controlling the Display of Gridlines," page 219.*

Translating Screen Colors to Black and White

If you've assigned background colors and patterns to your worksheet, but you're using a black-and-white printer, you'll probably want to select the Black And White option, which tells Excel to use only black and white when printing.

Draft Quality

If your printer offers a draft-quality mode, you can obtain a quicker, if less attractive, printout by selecting the Draft Quality option. This option has no effect if your printer has no draft-quality mode and is most useful for dot-matrix or other slow printers. (If you have a laser printer, you can affect print quality by making a selection from the Print Quality drop-down list on the Page tab. *For more information about print quality, see "Specifying Paper Size and Print Quality" on page 393.*)

Printing Row and Column Headings

If you select the Row And Column Headings option, Excel prints row letters to the left of and column numbers above worksheet data. This option is handy when you're using printouts to document the structure of a worksheet.

Printing Comments

? SEE ALSO

For information about creating cell notes, see "Adding Comments to Cells," page 292.

Comments are annotations created using the Comment command on the Insert menu. To include comments with your printout, select the Comments option. If you select At End Of Sheet from the drop-down list, Excel adds a page at the end of the printout and prints all your notes together starting on that new page. If you select As Displayed On Sheet, Excel prints the comments where they are located on a worksheet.

Setting the Printing Order of Large Print Ranges

When you print a large report, Excel breaks the report into page-size sections based on the current margin and page-size settings. If the print range is both too wide and too deep to fit on a single page, Excel normally works down, and then over. For example, if the print range measures 120 rows by 20 columns and Excel can fit 40 rows and 10 columns on a page, Excel prints the first 40 rows and first 10 columns on page 1, the second 40 rows and first 10 columns on page 2, and the third 40 rows and first 10 columns on page 3. On page 4, it prints the first 40 rows and second 10 columns, and so on.

If you prefer to have Excel print each horizontal chunk before moving down to the next vertical chunk, select the Over, Then Down option.

Setting Printer Driver Options

Occasionally while working in Excel 2000, you might need to set options that only your printer driver provides. You might, for example, need to switch from automatic to manual paper feed, or from one paper tray to another. You can do this by choosing Settings from the Start menu, and then opening your Printers folder, right-clicking the appropriate printer, and choosing Properties from the context menu. But you can use most options in the relevant dialog box from within Excel's own menu system by selecting the printer from the Printer drop-down list in the Print dialog box, which displays a list of your computer's installed printers. (Alternatively, click the Options button on the Sheet tab of the Page Setup dialog box.) Then click the Properties button to open the Properties dialog box for the selected printer. If you open the Printer Properties dialog box from within Excel, the General and Details tabs do not appear.

II

Worksheets

Adjusting Page Breaks with Page Break Preview

Excel makes it easy to adjust the positions of page breaks. You can do this using either the Print Preview command or the new Page Break Preview feature shown in Figure 11-8. Either way, you can move page breaks by dragging them with the mouse. In Page Break Preview (but not Print Preview), you can also edit your worksheet while you adjust its page breaks.

FIGURE 11-8.

Page Break Preview shows default page breaks with dashed lines. To reposition a page break, drag it with your mouse. You can toggle between Page Break Preview and Normal View using commands on the View menu.

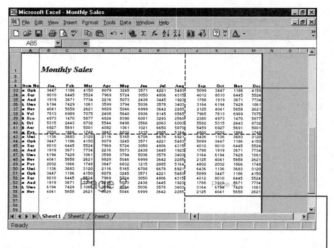

In this example, a horizontal page break occurs after row 42, and a vertical page break occurs after column I. The rows following row 42 will be on page 2, and the columns to the right of column I will appear on pages 3 and 4.

To use Page Break Preview, choose Page Break Preview from the View menu. As Figure 11-8 shows, Page Break Preview lets you see both the positions of your page breaks and the page numbers Excel will use when you print. (You can also access this command while in Page Preview mode by clicking the Page Break Preview button.)

Default page breaks—the ones that Excel proposes to use if you don't intervene—appear as dashed lines in Page Break Preview. If you're not happy with the position of a default break, simply use your mouse to drag the page break. Your page break will then become a manual page break, and Page Break Preview will display it as a solid line, as shown in Figure 11-9.

Notice that moving the default horizontal break in Figure 11-8 downward has caused the default vertical break to move to the right, to column L. That repositioning occurred because when you extend the dimensions of your printed page beyond their default values—by dragging a default page break downward or to the right—you cause Excel to apply a scaling factor to the page. The reduction allows more columns as well as more rows to fit on page 1. The vertical break is still shown as a dashed line, however, because only the horizontal break was repositioned manually.

FIGURE 11-9.

Dragging a default page break turns it into a manual page break, which Page Break Preview displays as a solid line.

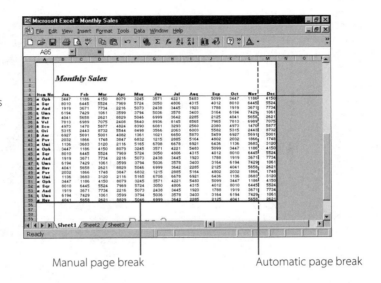

Manual page break   Automatic page break

To return from Page Break Preview to Normal view, choose Normal from the View menu.

Removing Manual Page Breaks

To remove a manual horizontal page break, select any cell of the row directly beneath the break. Then choose Remove Page Break from the Insert menu. To restore the horizontal break in Figure 11-9, for example, first position your mouse somewhere in row 56. To remove a manual vertical break, select any cell in the column directly to the right of the break, and choose Remove Page Break from the Insert menu.

NOTE

If you move a horizontal default page break downward or a vertical default page break to the right, Excel applies a scaling factor to your printout. If you subsequently remove the resulting manual page breaks, Excel does not remove the scaling factor. You have to do that yourself—by going to the Page tab of the Page Setup dialog box.

TIP

After the page breaks are set, Excel displays them in Normal view as dashed lines. If you'd rather not see these, choose Options from the Tools menu. Then, on the View tab, clear the Page Breaks check box.

Using Print Preview

Microsoft Excel's Print Preview lets you look at page breaks, margins, and the format of your printout before you begin printing. To get to Print Preview, use one of the following methods:

- Click the Print Preview button on the Standard toolbar.

- Hold down Shift and click the Print button on the Standard toolbar.

- Choose the Print Preview command from the File menu. (Print Preview does not normally appear on shortened menus. Click the double arrow at the bottom of the File menu to display the Print Preview command.)

- Click the Preview button on the Print dialog box or the Print Preview button on the Page Setup dialog box.

Figure 11-10 shows an example of a worksheet in Print Preview.

FIGURE 11-10.

A worksheet displayed in Print Preview.

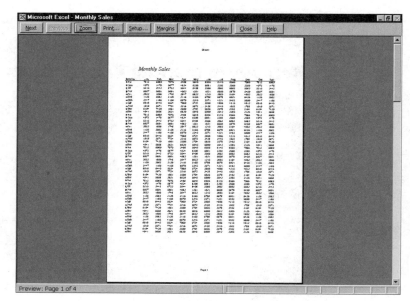

If you're not satisfied with the layout of your report, you can change the margins and column widths without leaving Print Preview. You can also click the Setup button to display the Page Setup dialog box and change any page settings. *For more information on Page Setup, see "Controlling the Appearance of Your Pages," page 392.*

> You can move forward or backward a page at a time by clicking the Next or Previous button or by pressing Page Up and Page Down. To move more quickly through a long document, drag the scroll box. As you drag, Excel displays the current page number in the lower left corner of the Print Preview screen.

After you're satisfied with the appearance of your document, you can click the Print button to print the document, or you can click Close to leave Print Preview and print using the File menu's Print command.

Zooming In or Out

Excel turns your mouse pointer into a magnifying glass while Print Preview is in effect so you can zoom in on any portion of the page. For example, to check the formatting of your header, point to the header and then click the mouse button. Your screen looks like the one shown in Figure 11-11. To return to the full-page preview, simply click anywhere on the page.

FIGURE 11-11.

Click the mouse button to magnify the Print Preview screen. Click the mouse button again to restore the normal display.

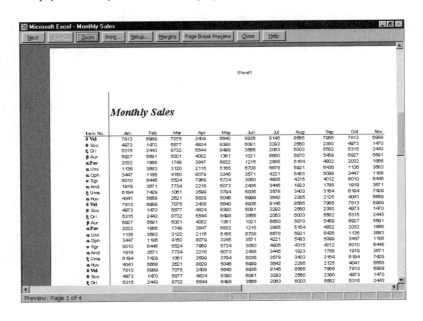

Adjusting Margins and Column Widths

If you have a mouse, you can use Print Preview to adjust any of the four margins, the width of any column, or the positions of your headers and footers. Start by clicking the Margins button. As Figure 11-12 shows, Excel displays dotted lines to represent your margins and header and footer placement. Handles at the top of the page mark the right boundary of each column.

To adjust a margin, drag the appropriate dotted line. As you drag, the page-number indicator in the lower left corner of the screen changes to display the name of the margin and its current setting.

To adjust a column width, click the column's handle and drag. Again, the indicator at the bottom of the screen assists you by reporting the current column width.

FIGURE 11-12.

Clicking the Margins button displays lines that let you change margins and handles that let you change column widths.

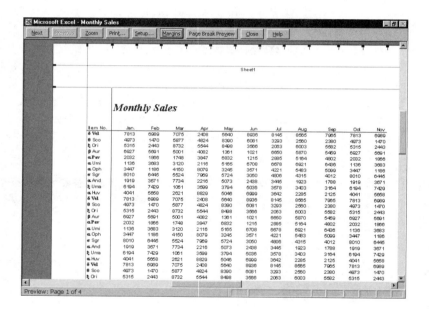

Using the Report Manager

The Report Manager lets you define a particular printout or collection of printouts as a named report. You can then recreate that report by selecting its name and clicking the Print button. You'll find the Report Manager invaluable when you need to create multiple reports from the same worksheet or when you have to create a particular report on a recurring basis. Instead of constantly switching print settings, you can define your report once and regenerate it at will.

? SEE ALSO

For more information about the Custom View command, see "Custom Views," page 324. For more information about the Scenarios command, see "The Scenario Manager," page 542.

The Report Manager is an add-in that works hand-in-hand with the Custom Views command (on the View menu) and the Scenarios command (on the Tools menu). If you have installed the Report Manager add-in, a Report Manager command appears on your View menu. If you do not see this command, you need to install the Report Manager add-in. Choose Add-ins from the Tools menu, select Report Manager from the list of available add-ins, and then click OK. If Report Manager does not appear in the list of available add-ins, rerun the Excel 2000 (or Office 2000) Setup program.

Defining the Report

A *report* consists of one or more elements, each of which can be a workbook page, a view created with the View Manager, or a scenario. Let's look at a simple example.

Suppose that from the worksheet shown in Figure 11-13 you want to print five separate printouts at the end of each month—one for each of your four divisions and one of the entire worksheet. To define each of your regular printouts as a named report, start by using normal Excel procedures to prepare the first printout. On the Sheet tab of the Page Setup dialog box, specify the area you want to print in the Print Area edit box. Also use Page Setup to specify your print titles, headers, footers, margins, and any other settings you want to use for this report.

When you have set up Excel to print your Division 1 sales figures, choose Custom Views from the View menu, click the Add button, and supply a name (such as *Division 1*). Be sure the Print Settings check box is selected. Note that it doesn't matter which part of your worksheet is visible when you create this named view; you'll (presumably) use the view only for the purpose of specifying a named report, so the current print settings are all that matter.

After you create a named view for your first divisional printout, repeat these steps for printouts of each of the remaining divisions and for a printout of the entire worksheet. When you finish, you have five named views, one for each combination of print settings that you commonly use.

II

Worksheets

FIGURE 11-13.

We'll use the Report Manager to define each of several divisional sales printouts as a named report.

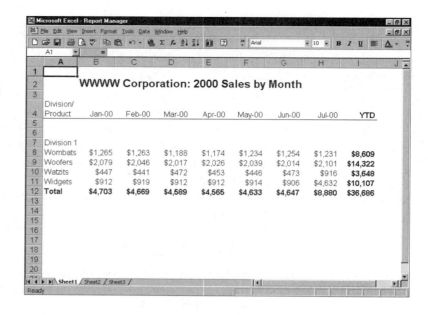

Now simply choose Report Manager from the View menu to invoke the Report Manager. The Report Manager dialog box, shown in Figure 11-14, appears.

FIGURE 11-14.

When you first invoke the Report Manager with a new worksheet, you see an empty Reports list box.

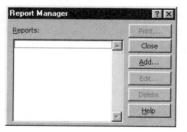

Because you haven't defined any reports yet, the Report Manager's initial dialog box presents an empty list. To define your first report, click the Add button to display the Add Report dialog box shown in Figure 11-15.

All you need to do is enter a name in the Report Name edit box at the top of the dialog box, open the View list box, and select the view that you want to include in your report. Then click Add to add the view as a section. Repeat these steps for each report you want to create. Now when you return to the Print Report dialog box, the list includes all your defined reports. To print one of them, simply select a report name and then click the Print button.

FIGURE 11-15.

To define a report, enter a name in the Report Name edit box and use the drop-down lists to indicate the named views and scenarios you want your report to include.

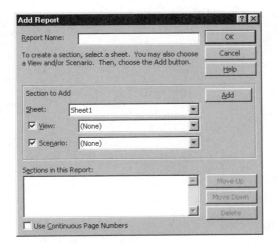

We've deliberately kept this example simple for illustrative purposes. Bear in mind, however, that you can define a report that consists of many pages, views, or scenarios, or a combination of any of these elements.

PART III

Analyzing Data

Common Worksheet Functions

Worksheet functions are special tools that perform complex calculations quickly and easily. They are like the special keys on sophisticated calculators that compute square roots, logarithms, and statistical evaluations.

The Analysis ToolPak

Most of the commonly used functions are built into Excel, but there are additional functions available in the Analysis ToolPak, a set of add-in tools and functions for data analysis. While this add-in includes a number of macro-based analysis tools, it also includes a number of worksheet functions that become available through the Paste Function dialog box.

To see if you have the Analysis ToolPak already installed, check the Tools menu. If the Data Analysis command is there (you might have to click the double arrow at the bottom of the menu to expand it to its full size), and then you're good to go. If you don't see the command, you may need to run Setup to install the Analysis ToolPak. *For more on the Analysis ToolPak add-in, see Chapter 15, "Statistical Analysis."*

Microsoft Excel 2000 has hundreds of built-in functions that perform a wide range of calculations. Some functions, such as SUM, SIN, and FACT, are the equivalent of lengthy mathematical formulas that you might create by hand. Other functions, such as IF and VLOOKUP, cannot be duplicated by formulas.

Excel offers several groups of functions not discussed in this chapter. We'll cover date and time functions in Chapter 13, financial functions in Chapter 14, statistical functions and the statistical tools available in the Analysis ToolPak in Chapter 15, and database statistical functions in Chapter 16.

When none of the built-in functions is quite what you need, you can create custom functions, as explained in Chapter 29.

Getting More Help with Worksheet Functions

? SEE ALSO

For more information about the Excel online Help system, see Chapter 2, "Getting Help."

While preparing this book, we had to make some tough choices. Fully describing each of the hundreds of worksheet functions would fill an entire book. To provide the greatest benefit, we had to judge which functions to focus on and which to mention only briefly. For those who want more information about the functions we do not cover in detail, the Excel online Help system includes a detailed description of each worksheet function.

You can also quickly get information about functions by using the Paste Function button, described on page 417.

The Power of Functions

Let's look at an example that demonstrates the power of Microsoft Excel functions. The worksheet in Figure 12-1 shows monthly pet sales for a 12-month period.

FIGURE 12-1.

The SUM function in cell B16 calculates yak sales for a 12-month period.

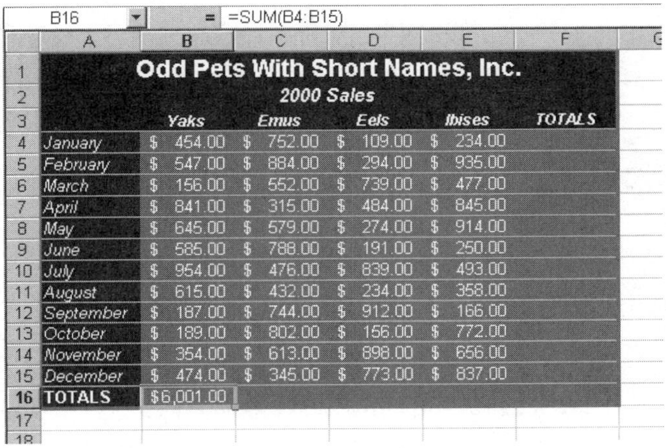

	Yaks	Emus	Eels	Ibises	TOTALS
	Odd Pets With Short Names, Inc.				
	2000 Sales				
January	$ 454.00	$ 752.00	$ 109.00	$ 234.00	
February	$ 547.00	$ 884.00	$ 294.00	$ 935.00	
March	$ 156.00	$ 552.00	$ 739.00	$ 477.00	
April	$ 841.00	$ 315.00	$ 484.00	$ 845.00	
May	$ 645.00	$ 579.00	$ 274.00	$ 914.00	
June	$ 585.00	$ 788.00	$ 191.00	$ 250.00	
July	$ 954.00	$ 476.00	$ 839.00	$ 493.00	
August	$ 615.00	$ 432.00	$ 234.00	$ 358.00	
September	$ 187.00	$ 744.00	$ 912.00	$ 166.00	
October	$ 189.00	$ 802.00	$ 156.00	$ 772.00	
November	$ 354.00	$ 613.00	$ 898.00	$ 656.00	
December	$ 474.00	$ 345.00	$ 773.00	$ 837.00	
TOTALS	$6,001.00				

W **ON THE WEB**
You can find Pet Sales 2000.xls found in the example above on the Microsoft Press Web site at *http://mspress.microsoft.com/mspress/products/2050/*.

To find the total yak sales for the year, you could enter the formula

    =B4+B5+B6+B7+B8+B9+B10+B11+B12+B13+B14+B15

in cell B16, but this formula is very cumbersome. You can use the SUM function to create

    =SUM(B4:B15)

which tells Excel to add the numbers stored in the range B4 through B15. The result of this formula and that of the longer version are identical: $6,001.

Formulas can contain more than one function, and you can nest functions within formulas. For example, the formula

    =AVERAGE(SUM(B4:E4),SUM(B5:E5))

returns the overall average combined pet sales for January and February.

III

Analyzing Data

The Syntax of Functions

Worksheet functions have two parts: the name of the function followed by one or more *arguments*. Function names—such as SUM and AVERAGE—describe the operation the function performs. Arguments specify the values or cells to be used by the function. For example, in the formula

=SUM(C3:C5)

SUM is the function's name, and C3:C5 is its single argument. This formula sums, or totals, the numbers in cells C3, C4, and C5.

> The equal sign (=) at the beginning of the formula indicates that the entry is a formula, not text (such as a comment or table heading). If you leave out the equal sign, Excel interprets the entry as text, and no calculation is performed.

Notice that parentheses surround the function's argument. The opening parenthesis marks the beginning of the argument and must appear immediately after the name of the function. If you enter a space or some other character between the name and the opening parenthesis, Excel displays the error message *Microsoft Excel found an error in the formula you entered. Do you want to accept the correction proposed below?* If you click Yes, Excel corrects the formula automatically. If you click No, the error value #NAME? appears in the cell.

A few functions, such as PI and TRUE, have no arguments. (As you'll see, these functions are usually nested in other formulas or functions.) Even though they have no arguments, they must be followed by an empty set of parentheses, as in

=A1*PI( )

Using Arguments

When you use more than one argument in a function, you separate the arguments with commas. For example, the formula

=PRODUCT(C1,C2,C5)

tells Excel to multiply the numbers in cells C1, C2, and C5.

You can use as many as 30 arguments in a function, as long as the total length of the formula does not exceed 1024 characters. However, a single argument can be a range that refers to any number of cells in your worksheet. For example, the function

=SUM(A1:A5,C2:C10,D3:D17)

has three arguments but totals the numbers in 29 cells. (The first argument, A1:A5, refers to the range of five cells from A1 through A5, and so on.) The referenced cells can, in turn, contain formulas that refer to more cells or ranges. Using arguments, you can easily create complex chains of formulas to perform powerful worksheet operations.

Expressions as Arguments

You can use combinations of functions to create an *expression* that Excel evaluates to a single value and interprets as an argument. For example, in the formula

=SUM(SIN(A1*PI( )),2*COS(A2*PI( )))

the SIN(A1*PI( )) and 2*COS(A2*PI( )) are expressions that are evaluated and used as the arguments to the SUM function.

Types of Arguments

In the examples presented so far, all the arguments have been cell or range references. You can also use numbers, text, logical values, range names, arrays, and error values as arguments. Some functions return values in these data types, and you can then use these values as arguments to other functions.

Numeric Values

The arguments to a function can be numeric. For example, the SUM function in the formula

=SUM(327,209,176)

totals the numbers 327, 209, and 176. Usually, however, you enter the numbers you want to use in cells of a worksheet and then use references to those cells as arguments to your functions.

Text Values

You can use text as an argument to a function. For example, in the formula

=TEXT(NOW( ),"MMM D, YYYY")

in the second argument to the TEXT function, *"MMM D, YYYY"*, is a text argument that specifies a pattern for converting the serial date value returned by NOW into a text string. Text arguments can be text strings enclosed in double quotation marks or references to cells that contain text.

Logical Values

? SEE ALSO

For more information about logical functions, see "Logical Functions," page 439.

The arguments to a few functions specify only that an option is either set or not set; you can use the logical values TRUE to set an option and FALSE to specify that the option isn't set. A logical expression returns the value TRUE or FALSE to the worksheet or the formula containing the expression. For example, the first argument to the IF function in the formula

=IF(A1=TRUE,"Future ", "Past ")&"History"

is a logical expression that uses the value in cell A1; if the value in A1 is TRUE, the expression A1=TRUE evaluates to TRUE, the IF function returns Future, and the formula returns the text *Future History* to the worksheet.

Named References

? SEE ALSO

For more information about names, see "Naming Cells and Ranges," page 133.

You can use a range name as an argument to a function. For example, if you use the Define command from the Name submenu of the Insert menu to assign the name *QtrlyIncome* to the range C3:C6, you can use the formula

=SUM(QtrlyIncome)

to total the numbers in cells C3, C4, C5, and C6.

Arrays

? SEE ALSO

For more information about arrays, see "Working With Arrays," page 144.

You can use an array as an argument in a function. Some functions, such as TREND and TRANSPOSE, require array arguments; other functions don't require array arguments but will accept them. Arrays can be composed of numbers, text, or logical values.

Error Values

Excel accepts error values as arguments to a few functions. *For more information about error values as arguments, see "Conditional Tests," page 439.*

Mixed Argument Types

You can mix argument types within a function. For example, the formula

=AVERAGE(Group1,A3,5*3)

uses a range name (*Group1*), a cell reference (A3), and a numeric expression (5*3) to arrive at a single value. All three are acceptable.

Entering Functions in a Worksheet

You can enter functions in a worksheet by typing the function from the keyboard or by choosing the Function command from the Insert menu. If you type the function, use lowercase letters. When you finish typing the function and press Enter or select another cell, Excel changes the name of the function to uppercase letters if you entered it correctly. If the letters don't change, you probably entered the name of the function incorrectly.

Using the Insert Function Command

When you select a cell and choose Function from the Insert menu, Excel displays the first Paste Function dialog box, as shown in Figure 12-2. (To have the Assistant offer advice along the way, press the Help button in the lower left corner of the Paste Function dialog box.) You can also click the Paste Function button on the Standard toolbar to display the Paste Function dialog box.

To select a function, first select a category from the Function Category list (or select All) and then scroll through the alphabetic Function Name list and select the function. Alternatively, you can press the first letter of the function name you want until the name is highlighted in the Function Name list. To enter the function, click OK or press Enter.

FIGURE 12-2.

Select the function you want to use from the first Paste Function dialog box.

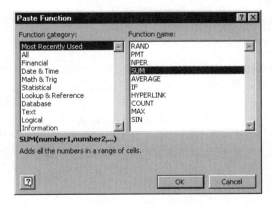

Excel enters an equal sign (if you're inserting the function at the beginning of a formula), the function name, and a set of

III

Analyzing Data

parentheses. Excel then moves to the second Paste Function dialog box, shown in Figure 12-3.

FIGURE 12-3.

The second Paste Function dialog box helps you enter the arguments to the function.

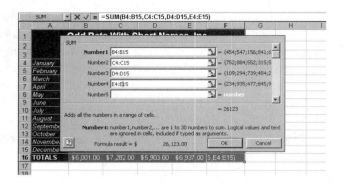

The second Paste Function dialog box contains one edit box for each argument of the function you selected. If the function accepts a variable number of arguments, the dialog box grows as you enter optional arguments. A description of the argument whose edit box currently contains the insertion point appears near the bottom of the dialog box.

To the right of each argument edit box, a display area shows the current value of the argument. This display is very handy when you are using references or defined names. The current value of the function (Formula result) appears at the bottom of the dialog box.

When you click OK or press Enter, the completed function appears in the formula bar.

Some functions, such as INDEX, have more than one form. When you select a function with more than one form from the Function Name list, Excel presents an additional Paste Function dialog box, like the one shown in Figure 12-4, in which you select the form you want to use.

FIGURE 12-4.

If a function has more than one form, the Select Arguments dialog box lets you choose the one you want.

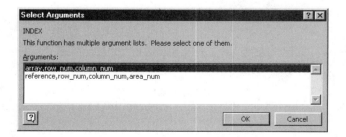

Inserting Arguments with the Keyboard

If you know the name of the function you want to use but you can't remember all its arguments, you can use a keyboard shortcut to paste the argument names in the formula bar. Type an equal sign followed by the function's name in the formula bar and then press Ctrl+A. Excel jumps directly to the second Paste Function dialog box. This feature is particularly useful when you're working with functions that have easy-to-remember names and long strings of arguments.

Inserting References

As with any other formula, you can insert cell references and defined names into your functions. For example, to enter a function in cell C11 that averages the cells in the range C2:C10, first select cell C11 and type *=average(*. Next, select the range C2:C10. A marquee appears around the selected cells, and a reference to the selected range appears in the formula bar. When you press Enter to lock in the formula, the marquee disappears and Excel supplies a closing parenthesis for you. (When you type the function name rather than use Insert Function, you must add the closing parenthesis only if you nest the function within a formula. However, Excel's parentheses can sometimes cause unexpected results; always double-check them.)

If you define named ranges, constants, or formulas in your worksheets, you can insert them into your formulas by choosing the Paste command from the Name submenu of the Insert menu and then selecting the name from the list in the Paste Name dialog box. When you click OK, the name appears at the insertion point in the formula.

Selected Mathematical Functions

This section describes some of the more useful functions Excel has to offer. It is by no means comprehensive, so for details on functions not discussed here, please take advantage of the descriptive information presented in the Paste Function dialog box, as well as the online Help system.

SEE ALSO

For more information about the Analysis ToolPak, see Chapter 15, "Statistical Analysis."

Several Microsoft Excel 2000 mathematical functions are available for carrying out specialized calculations quickly and easily. Other mathematical functions are available in the Analysis ToolPak add-in.

III

Analyzing Data

The SUM Function

The SUM function totals a series of numbers. It takes the form

=SUM(numbers)

The *numbers* argument is a series of as many as 30 entries that can be numbers, formulas, ranges, or cell references that result in numbers. SUM ignores arguments that reference text values, logical values, or blank cells.

Because SUM is such a commonly used function, Excel provides a special button on the Standard toolbar for entering it. If you select a cell and click the AutoSum button, which is labeled Σ, Excel creates a=SUM( ) formula and guesses which cells you want to total. For example, if you select cell C16 in Figure 12-1 (shown on page 413) and then click the AutoSum button, Excel proposes the formula =SUM(C4:C15) and draws a marquee around the cells used as the argument in the formula.

If the proposed SUM function argument is correct, you can click the AutoSum button a second time or press Enter to lock in the formula and remove the marquee. If the argument is not correct, you can edit it by selecting the correct range of cells while the argument is still highlighted and the marquee is still present. Excel then replaces the argument with the selected range and redraws the marquee.

Automatic Range Expansion

One of the most common spreadsheet auditing problems used to occur when cells were inserted at the bottom or to the right of a range of cells referenced in a formula. For example, if we enter the formula =SUM(A1:A4) in cell A5, and then select row 5 and insert a new row (which is inserted above the selected row, thus pushing the SUM formula down to cell A6), any numbers in the new inserted cell A5 would not have been included in the sum. Until Excel 2000, that is.

Now you can insert one or more cells at the bottom or to the right of a cell range referenced in a formula, and Excel automatically adjusts formulas for you as soon as you enter values in the new inserted cells.

This automatic expansion only works when you insert cells immediately to the right or below a referenced range. Inserting cells at the top or to the left of a referenced range still involves editing the referencing formulas manually.

You can use the AutoSum button to enter several SUM functions at one time. For example, if we selected cells C16:E16 in Figure 12-1 and then clicked the AutoSum button, Excel enters a SUM formula for C16 using arguments similar to those of the formula in B16 and replicates it across the row in D16 and E16. (You can also use this technique to replicate a SUM formula up or down a column.)

Expanding a SUM range to include a new value is much easier than expanding a range totaled with ordinary addition operators. Suppose cell F4 in Figure 12-5 contains the formula

=B4+C4+D4+E4

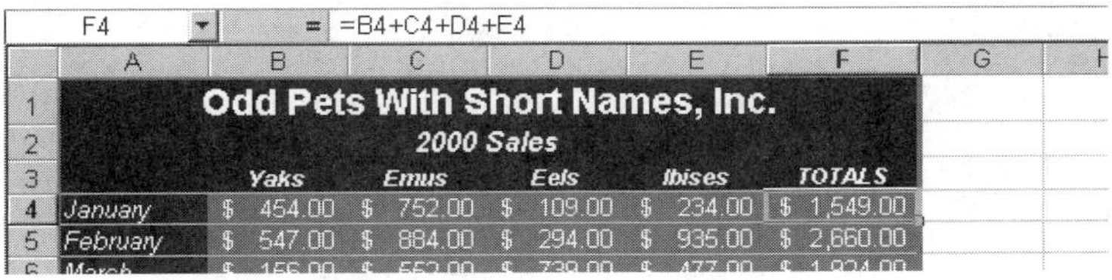

FIGURE 12-5.

The formula =B4+C4+D4+E4 calculates total sales for January.

If, after entering this formula, you discover that you omitted the Bats category, you can select column C and then choose the Columns command from the Insert menu to insert a column of cells for the new category. Excel adjusts the TOTALS formulas, which now appear in column G, to account for the shift of the columns, but it won't include the new column in the formulas. As Figure 12-6 shows, the formula in cell G4 now reads

=B4+D4+E4+F4

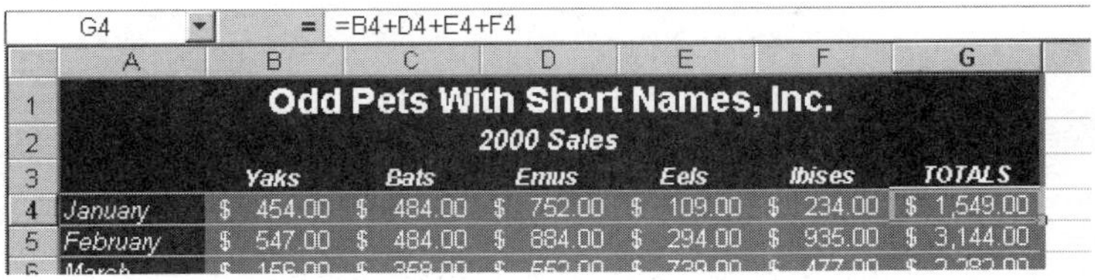

FIGURE 12-6.

Although a new category was added, the totals do not change because the formula references the individual cells.

If, instead of using addition operators, you had used the SUM function to create the formula

=SUM(B4:E4)

in cell F4 of Figure 12-5, Excel would have expanded the range of the numbers argument to include the inserted column. Because Excel always adjusts cell ranges when you insert or delete rows and columns within the range, the formula would have been updated to read

=SUM(B4:F4)

Keep in mind that arguments do not have to consist of continuous ranges of cells. For example, to total the numbers in cells A3, B12, and G13 through H15, you enter each reference as a separate argument, like this:

=SUM(A3,B12,G13:H15)

The ROUND, ROUNDDOWN, and ROUNDUP Functions

The ROUND function rounds the number referred to by its argument to a specified number of decimal places. Round takes the form

=ROUND(number,num_digits)

The *number* argument can be a number, a reference to a cell that contains a number, or a formula that results in a number. The *num_digits* argument, which can be any positive or negative integer, determines how many places will be rounded. Specifying a negative *num_digits* argument rounds that number of places to the left of the decimal; specifying a *num_digits* argument of 0 rounds to the nearest integer. Excel rounds digits less than 5 down and digits greater than or equal to 5 up. The following table shows examples of the ROUND function:

Entry	Returns
=ROUND(123.4567,-2)	100
=ROUND(123.4567,-1)	120
=ROUND(123.4567,0)	123
=ROUND(123.4567,1)	123.5
=ROUND(123.4567,2)	123.46
=ROUND(123.4567,3)	123.457

 TIP

Rounding vs. Formatting

Don't confuse the ROUND function with fixed formats such as 0 and 0.00, which are available when you choose Cells from the Format menu and then click the Number tab. When you use Number to round the contents of a cell to a specified number of decimal places, you change only the display of the number in the cell; you don't change the value. When performing calculations, Excel always uses the underlying value, not the displayed value.

The ROUNDDOWN and ROUNDUP functions take the same form as ROUND. As their names imply, they always round down or up.

Rounding with the EVEN and ODD Functions

You can use the EVEN and ODD functions to perform rounding operations. The EVEN function rounds a number up to the nearest even integer. The ODD function rounds a number up to the nearest odd integer. Negative numbers are correspondingly rounded down. These functions take the forms

>=EVEN(*number*)

and

>=ODD(*number*)

The following table shows some examples of these functions in action:

Entry	Returns
=EVEN(23.4)	24
=EVEN(2)	2
=EVEN(3)	4
=EVEN(-3)	-4
=ODD(23.4)	25
=ODD(3)	3
=ODD(4)	5
=ODD(-4)	-5

Rounding with the FLOOR and CEILING Functions

The FLOOR and CEILING functions can be used to carry out rounding operations. The FLOOR function rounds a number down to the nearest given multiple, and the CEILING function rounds a number up to the nearest given multiple. These functions take the forms

>=FLOOR(number,multiple)

and

>=CEILING(number,multiple)

In both cases, the values of *number* and *multiple* must be numeric and have the same sign. If they have different signs, Excel returns the #NUM! error value. The table on the following page shows some examples of rounding operations performed with these functions.

III

Analyzing Data

Entry	Returns
=FLOOR(23.4,0.5)	23
=FLOOR(5,3)	3
=FLOOR(5,-1)	#NUM!
=FLOOR(5,1.5)	4.5
=CEILING(23.4,5)	25
=CEILING(5,3)	6
=CEILING(-5,1)	#NUM!
=CEILING(5,1.5)	6

The INT and TRUNC Functions

The INT function rounds numbers down to the nearest integer and takes the form

=INT(*number*)

The *number* argument is the number for which you want to find the next lowest integer. For example, the formula

=INT(100.01)

returns the value 100, as does the formula

=INT(100.99999999)

even though the number 100.99999999 is essentially equal to 101.

When *number* is negative, INT also rounds that number down to the nearest integer. For example, the formula

=INT(-100.99999999)

results in the value -101.

The TRUNC function truncates everything to the right of the decimal point in a number, regardless of its sign. The optional *num_digits* argument truncates everything after the digit position specified. It takes the form

=TRUNC(number,num_digits)

If it is not specified, *num_digits* is set to zero. For example, the function

=TRUNC(13.978)

returns the value 13.

NOTE

> ROUND, INT, and TRUNC all eliminate unwanted decimals, but the three functions work differently. ROUND rounds up or down to the number of decimal places you specify; INT rounds down to the nearest integer; TRUNC truncates decimal places with no rounding. The primary difference between INT and TRUNC is in the treatment of negative values. If you use the value -100.99999999 in an INT function, the result is -101, but using the same value in a TRUNC function results in -100.

The RAND and RANDBETWEEN Functions

The RAND function generates a random number between 0 and 1 and takes the form =RAND( ).

The RAND function is one of the few Excel functions that doesn't take an argument. As with all functions that take no arguments, you must still enter the parentheses after the function name.

The result of a RAND function changes each time you recalculate your worksheet. If you use automatic recalculation, the value of the RAND function changes each time you make a worksheet entry.

SEE ALSO

For more information about the Analysis ToolPak add-in, see Chapter 15, "Statistical Analysis."

The RANDBETWEEN function, which is available when you install the Analysis ToolPak add-in, provides more control than RAND. With RANDBETWEEN you can specify a range of numbers within which to generate random integer values.

This function takes the form

=RANDBETWEEN(*bottom*,*top*)

The *bottom* argument represents the smallest integer, and the *top* argument represents the largest integer the function should use. The values you use for these arguments are inclusive; that is, they are values that the function might return. For example, the formula

=RANDBETWEEN(123,456)

can return any integer from 123 up to and including 456.

The PRODUCT Function

The PRODUCT function multiplies all the numbers referenced by its arguments and takes the form

=PRODUCT(number1,number2,…)

The PRODUCT function can take as many as 30 arguments. Excel ignores any arguments that are text, logical values, or blank cells.

III

Analyzing Data

The MOD Function

The MOD function returns the remainder of a division operation (modulus) and takes the form

=MOD(number,divisor)

The result of the MOD function is the remainder produced when *number* is divided by *divisor*. For example, the function

=MOD(9,4)

returns 1, the remainder that results from dividing 9 by 4.

If *number* is smaller than *divisor*, the result of the function equals *number*. For example, the function

=MOD(5,11)

returns 5. If *number* is exactly divisible by *divisor*, the function returns 0. If *divisor* is 0, MOD returns the #DIV/0! error value.

The SQRT Function

The SQRT function returns the positive square root of a number and takes the form

=SQRT(*number*)

The *number* argument must evaluate to a positive number. For example, the function

=SQRT(4)

returns the value 2.

If *number* is negative, SQRT returns the #NUM! error value.

The COMBIN Function

The COMBIN function determines the number of possible combinations, or groups, that can be taken from a pool of items. It takes the form

=COMBIN(number,number_chosen)

The *number* argument is the total number of items in the pool, and the *number_chosen* argument is the number of items you want to group in each combination. For example, to determine how many 12-player football teams can be created with 17 players, use the formula

=COMBIN(17,12)

The result, 6188, indicates that 6,188 teams could be created.

The ISNUMBER Function

? SEE ALSO

For more information about this and other IS functions, see "The ISTEXT and ISNONTEXT Functions," page 434; and "The ISBLANK Function," page 443.

The ISNUMBER function determines whether a value is a number and takes the form

=ISNUMBER(value)

Suppose you want to know if the entry in cell A5 is a number. The formula

=ISNUMBER(A5)

returns TRUE if cell A5 contains a number or a formula that results in a number; otherwise, it returns FALSE.

Logarithmic Functions

Excel's five logarithmic functions are LOG10, LOG, LN, EXP, and POWER. We'll discuss only the LOG, LN, and EXP functions in this section. The Analysis ToolPak add-in provides several other advanced logarithmic functions and is discussed in Chapter 15.

The LOG Function

The LOG function returns the logarithm of a positive number using a specified base. This function takes the form

=LOG(number,base)

For example, the formula

=LOG(5,2)

returns the value 2.321928095, or the base 2 logarithm of 5. If you don't include the *base* argument, Excel assumes the base is 10.

The LN Function

The LN function returns the natural (base *e*) logarithm of the positive number referred to by its argument. This function takes the form

=LN(number)

For example, the formula

=LN(2)

returns the value 0.693147181.

The EXP Function

The EXP function computes the value of the constant *e* (approximately 2.71828183) raised to the power specified by its argument. It takes the form

=EXP(*number*)

III

Analyzing Data

For example, the formula

=EXP(2)

returns 7.389056099 (2.718281828*2.718281828).

The EXP function is the inverse of the LN function. For example, if cell A1 contains the formula

=LN(8)

then the formula

=EXP(A1)

returns 8.

Trigonometric Functions

? SEE ALSO

For more information about the Analysis ToolPak, see Chapter 15, "Statistical Analysis."

Excel lists more than 50 functions in the Math & Trig category in the Function Wizard dialog box, but we'll cover only a few of the most common functions in this section. The Analysis ToolPak contains additional functions.

The PI Function

The PI function returns the value of the constant *pi* (π) accurate to 14 decimal places: 3.14159265358979. This function takes the form

=PI( )

PI has no arguments, but you must still enter the empty parentheses after the function name.

Usually the PI function is nested within a formula or function. For example, to calculate the area of a circle, you multiply π by the square of the circle's radius. The formula

=PI( )*(5^2)

computes the area of a circle with a radius of 5. The result of this formula rounded to two decimal places is 78.54.

The RADIANS and DEGREES Functions

The trigonometric functions measure angles in radians rather than in degrees. Radians measure the size of an angle based on the constant π, where a 180-degree angle is defined as π radians. Excel provides two functions, RADIANS and DEGREES, that make trigonometric life easier for you.

You can convert radians to degrees using the DEGREES function, which takes the form

=DEGREES(*angle*)

where *angle* is a number that represents an angle measured in radians. You can convert degrees to radians using the RADIANS function, which takes the form

=RADIANS(*angle*)

where *angle* is a number that represents an angle measured in degrees. For example, the formula

=DEGREES(3.1415927)

returns 180, whereas the formula

=RADIANS(180)

returns 3.1415927.

The SIN Function

The SIN function returns the sine of an angle and takes the form

=SIN(*number*)

where *number* is the angle in radians. For example, the formula

=SIN(1.5)

returns the value 0.997494987.

The COS Function

The COS function, the complement of the SIN function, calculates the cosine of an angle and takes the form

=COS(*number*)

where *number* is the angle in radians. For example, the formula

=COS(1.5)

returns the value 0.070737202.

The TAN Function

The TAN function computes the tangent of an angle and takes the form

=TAN(*number*)

where *number* is the angle in radians. For example, the formula

=TAN(1.5)

returns the tangent of an angle of 1.5 radians: 14.10141995.

III

Analyzing Data

Engineering Functions

? SEE ALSO

For more information about the Analysis ToolPak, see Chapter 15, "Statistical Analysis."

The Analysis ToolPak contains dozens of functions that are of interest mostly to engineers and scientists. These functions fall into three main groups: functions for working with complex numbers (also called *imaginary numbers*); functions for converting between the decimal, hexadecimal, octal, and binary numbering systems and between systems of measurement; and various forms of the Bessel function.

Text Functions

Text functions convert numeric text entries into numbers and number entries into text strings and let you manipulate the text strings themselves.

The TEXT Function

The TEXT function converts a number into a text string with a specified format. This function takes the form

    =TEXT(value,format_text)

The *value* argument can be any number, formula, or cell reference. The *format_text* argument designates how the resulting string is displayed. You can use any of Excel's formatting symbols ($, #, 0, and so on) except the asterisk (*) to specify the format you want; you cannot use the General format.

For example, the formula

    =TEXT(98/4,"0.00")

returns the text string *24.50*.

The DOLLAR Function

Like the TEXT function, the DOLLAR function converts a number into a string. However, DOLLAR formats the resulting string as currency with the number of decimal places you specify. This function takes the form

    =DOLLAR(number,decimals)

For example, the formula

    =DOLLAR(45.899,2)

returns the text string *$45.90* and the formula

    =DOLLAR(45.899,0)

returns the text string *$46*. Notice that Excel rounds the number when necessary. If you omit the *decimals* argument for the DOLLAR function, Excel uses two decimal places. If you use a negative number for the *decimals* argument, Excel rounds to the left of the decimal point.

The LEN Function

The LEN function returns the number of characters in an entry and takes the form

=LEN(*text*)

The *text* argument can be a literal number, a literal string enclosed in double quotation marks, or a reference to a cell. For example, the formula

=LEN("Test")

returns 4. If cell A1 contains the label *Test*, the formula

=LEN(A1)

also returns 4.

The LEN function returns the length of the displayed text or value, not the length of the underlying cell contents. For example, suppose cell A10 contains the formula

=A1+A2+A3+A4+A5+A6+A7+A8

and its result is the value 25. Then the formula

=LEN(A10)

returns the value 2, the length of the value 25. The LEN function ignores trailing zeros.

The cell referenced as the argument of the LEN function can contain another string function. For example, if cell A1 contains the function

=REPT("-*",75)

then the formula

=LEN(A1)

returns the value 150.

The ASCII Functions: CHAR and CODE

Every computer uses numeric codes to represent characters. The most prevalent system of numeric codes is called *ASCII,* or *American Standard Code for Information Interchange*. ASCII uses a number from 0 to 127 (in some systems, to 255) to represent each number, letter, and symbol.

The CHAR and CODE functions deal with these ASCII codes. The CHAR function returns the character that corresponds to an ASCII code number; the CODE function returns the ASCII code number for the first character of its argument. These functions take the forms

=CHAR(*number*)

and

=CODE(*text*)

For example, the formula

=CHAR(83)

returns the text *S*. (Note that you can enter the argument with a leading zero.) The formula

=CODE("S")

returns the ASCII code 83. Similarly, if cell A1 contains the text *S*, the formula

=CODE(A1)

also returns the code 83.

Because numerals are also characters, the argument for CODE can be a numeral. For example, the formula

=CODE(8)

results in 56, the ASCII code for the character *8*.

If you type a literal character as the *text* argument, be sure to enclose the character in double quotation marks; otherwise, Excel returns the #NAME? error value.

The Clean-Up Functions: TRIM and CLEAN

Leading and trailing blank characters often prevent you from correctly sorting entries in a worksheet or database. If you use string functions to manipulate text in your worksheet, extra spaces can prevent your formulas from working correctly. The TRIM function eliminates leading, trailing, and extra blank characters from a string, leaving only a single space between words. This function takes the form

=TRIM(*text*)

For example, if cell A1 of your worksheet contains the string *Fuzzy   Wuzzy   Was   A Bear*, the formula

=TRIM(A1)

returns *Fuzzy Wuzzy Was A Bear* as its result.

The CLEAN function is similar to TRIM, except that it operates only on nonprintable characters, such as tabs and program-specific codes. CLEAN is especially useful if you import data from another program and some entries contain nonprintable characters. (These characters might appear in your worksheet as bold vertical bars or small boxes.) You can use CLEAN to remove these characters from the data. This function takes the form

=CLEAN(*text*)

The EXACT Function

? SEE ALSO

For more information about comparing two strings while ignoring case differences, see "Conditional Tests," page 439.

The EXACT function is a conditional function that determines whether two strings match exactly, including uppercase and lowercase letters. Formatting differences are ignored. This function takes the form

=EXACT(text1,text2)

If *text1* and *text2* are identical, including uppercase and lowercase letters, EXACT returns TRUE; otherwise, EXACT returns FALSE. The *text1* and *text2* arguments must be either literal strings enclosed in double quotation marks or references to cells that contain text. For example, if cell A5 and cell A6 of your worksheet both contain the text *Totals*, the formula

=EXACT(A5,A6)

returns TRUE.

The Case Functions: UPPER, LOWER, and PROPER

Three functions manipulate the case of characters in text strings: UPPER, LOWER, and PROPER. The UPPER function converts a text string to all uppercase letters. The LOWER function converts a text string to all lowercase letters. The PROPER function capitalizes the first letter in each word and any other letters in the text string that do not follow another letter; all other letters are converted to lowercase. These functions take the forms

=UPPER(*text*)

and

=LOWER(*text*)

and

=PROPER(*text*)

III

Analyzing Data

Suppose you enter a series of names in a worksheet and you want all the names to appear in capital letters. If cell A1 contains the text *john Johnson* you can use the formula

=UPPER(A1)

to return *JOHN JOHNSON*. Similarly, the formula

=LOWER(A1)

returns *john johnson*, and

=PROPER(A1)

returns John Johnson.

Unexpected results can occur when the text contains punctuation, however. For example, if cell A1 contains *a two-thirds majority wasn't possible*, the previous formula produces *A Two-Thirds Majority Wasn'T Possible*.

TIP

When using text functions on existing lists of data, you often want to modify the very text to which you apply the functions. Of course, you can't enter a function in the same cell as the text you're working on, since that would over-write the text. Instead, create temporary text function formulas in unused cells in the same row, and then copy the results. To replace the original text with the modified text, select the cells containing the original text, choose Paste Special from the Edit menu, select the Values option, and click OK. Then you can delete the temporary formulas.

The ISTEXT and ISNONTEXT Functions

SEE ALSO

For more information about this and other IS functions, see "The ISNUMBER Function," page 427 and "The ISBLANK Function," page 443.

The ISTEXT and ISNONTEXT functions test whether an entry is text. These functions take the forms

=ISTEXT(*value*)

and

=ISNONTEXT(*value*)

Suppose you want to determine whether the entry in cell C5 is text. If you use the formula

=ISTEXT(C5)

and the entry in C5 is text or a formula that returns text, Excel returns the logical value TRUE. If you test the same cell using the formula

=ISNONTEXT(C5)

Excel returns the logical value FALSE.

The Substring Functions

The following functions locate and return portions of a text string, or assemble larger strings from smaller ones: FIND, SEARCH, RIGHT, LEFT, MID, SEARCH, SUBSTITUTE, REPT, REPLACE, and CONCATENATE.

The FIND and SEARCH Functions

You use the FIND and SEARCH functions to locate the position of a substring within a string. Both functions return the number of the character where Excel first finds the text. (Excel counts blank spaces and punctuation marks as characters.)

These two functions work the same way, except that FIND is case-sensitive and SEARCH allows wildcards. The functions take the forms

    =FIND(find_text,within_text,start_num)

and

    =SEARCH(find_text,within_text,start_num)

The *find_text* argument identifies the text sought, and the *within_text* argument indicates where to look for it. You can use either literal text enclosed in double quotation marks or a cell reference for either argument. The optional *start_num* argument specifies the character position in *within_text* where you want to begin the search. The *start_num* argument is helpful when *within_text* contains more than one occurrence of *find_text*. If you omit *start_num*, Excel reports the first match it locates.

You get a #VALUE! error value if *find_text* isn't contained in *within_text*, if *start_num* isn't greater than zero, or if *start_num* is greater than the number of characters in *within_text* or greater than the position of the last occurrence of *find_text*.

For example, to locate the *p* in the string *A Night At The Opera*, use the formula

    =FIND("p","A Night At The Opera")

This formula returns 17, because *p* is the seventeenth character in the string.

If you're not sure of the character sequence you're searching for, you can use the SEARCH function and include wildcards in your *find_text* string. To search for a single character that occupies a specific position, use a question-mark character (?); to search for any sequence of characters that occupies a specific position, use an asterisk (*).

Suppose you've used the names Smith and Smyth in your worksheet. To determine whether either name is in cell A1, use the formula

    =SEARCH("Sm?th",A1)

If cell A1 contains the text *John Smith* or *John Smyth,* the SEARCH function returns the value 6—the starting point for the string *Sm?th.* If you're not sure of the number of characters, use the * wildcard. For example, to find the position of *Allan* or *Alan* within the text stored in cell A1 (if any), use the formula

    =SEARCH("A*an",A1)

The RIGHT and LEFT Functions

The RIGHT function returns the rightmost series of characters from a string argument, whereas the LEFT function returns the leftmost series of characters from a string argument. These functions take the forms

    =RIGHT(text,num_chars)

and

    =LEFT(text,num_chars)

The *num_chars* argument indicates the number of characters to extract from the text argument. These functions count blank spaces in the text argument as characters; if text contains leading or trailing blank characters, you might want to use a TRIM function within the RIGHT or LEFT function to ensure the expected result.

The *num_chars* argument must be greater than or equal to zero. If you omit *num_chars,* Excel assumes it is 1. If *num_chars* is greater than the number of characters in text, RIGHT and LEFT return the entire text argument.

For example, suppose you enter *This is a test* in cell A1 of your worksheet. The formula

    =RIGHT(A1,4)

returns the word *test.*

The MID Function

You can use the MID function to extract a series of characters from a text string. This function takes the form

    =MID(text,start_num,num_chars)

The *text* argument is the string from which you want to extract the substring, *start_num* is the place in the string where the substring begins (relative to the left end of the string), and *num_chars* is the number of characters you want to extract. For example, if cell A1 contains the text *This Is A Long Text Entry*, you can use the formula

=MID(A1,11,10)

to extract the characters *Long Text* from the entry in cell A1.

The REPLACE and SUBSTITUTE Functions

These two functions substitute new text for old text. The REPLACE function replaces one string of characters with another string of characters and takes the form

=REPLACE(old_text,start_num,num_chars,new_text)

The *old_text* argument is the text string in which you want to replace characters. The next two arguments, *start_num* and *num_chars*, specify which characters to replace (relative to the left end of the string). The *new_text* argument specifies the text string to insert.

Suppose cell A3 contains *Millie Potter, Psychic*. To place this text in cell A6, replacing the first six characters with the string *Mildred*, select A6 and use the formula

=REPLACE(A3,1,6,"Mildred")

The new text is *Mildred Potter, Psychic*. The label in A3 remains unchanged, and the new label appears only in cell A6, where you entered the formula.

With the SUBSTITUTE function, you don't specify the starting number and number of characters to replace; instead, you simply specify the text to replace. The SUBSTITUTE function takes the form

=SUBSTITUTE(text,old_text,new_text,instance_num)

Suppose cell A4 contains the text *candy* and you want to place it in cell D6 and change it to *dandy*. Use the formula

=SUBSTITUTE(A4,"c","d")

When you enter this formula in cell D6, the text in cell A4 remains the same. The new text appears only in D6, the cell that contains the formula.

The *instance_num* argument is optional. It tells Excel to replace only the specified occurrence of *old_text*. For example, if cell A1 contains the text *through the hoop* and you want to substitute *loop* for *hoop*, the 4 in the formula

=SUBSTITUTE(A1,"h","l",4)

III

Analyzing Data

tells Excel to substitute an *l* for the fourth *h* in the text in cell A1. If you don't include *instance_num,* Excel changes all occurrences of *old_text* to *new_text*.

The REPT Function

? SEE ALSO

For information about filling a cell by repeating its contents, see "The Fill Option," page 180.

The REPT function lets you fill a cell with a string of characters repeated a specified number of times. This function takes the form

=REPT(text,number_times)

The *text* argument specifies the string in quotation marks to be repeated. The *number_times* argument specifies how many times to repeat the text string; it can be any positive number, but the result of the REPT function is limited to 255 characters. If you enter 0 for the *number_times* argument, REPT leaves the cell blank; if *number_times* is not an integer, REPT ignores the decimal portion of the number.

Suppose you want to create a row of asterisks 150 characters wide. Enter the formula

=REPT("*",150)

The result is a string of 150 asterisks.

The *text* argument can be more than one character. For example, the formula

=REPT("-*",75)

results in a row of asterisks and hyphens 150 characters wide. The *number_times* argument specifies the number of times you want *text* repeated, not the total number of characters you want to create. If the text string has two characters, the length of the resulting string is two times the *number_times* argument.

The CONCATENATE Function

Using the CONCATENATE function is the equivalent of using the "&" character to assemble larger strings from smaller strings. This function takes the form

=CONCATENATE(*text1,text2*, ...)

You can use up to 30 *text* arguments, which are the pieces of text you want to assemble.

For example, if cell B4 contains the text *strained*, the formula

=CONCATENATE("The Koala Tea of Mercy, Australia, is not ",B4,".")

returns *The Koala Tea of Mercy, Australia, is not strained.*

Logical Functions

? SEE ALSO

For more information about the Analysis ToolPak, see Chapter 15, "Statistical Analysis."

Microsoft Excel 2000 has a rich set of logical functions, including some that are included in the Analysis ToolPak add-in. Most logical functions use conditional tests to determine whether a specified condition is true or false.

Conditional Tests

A conditional test is an equation that compares two numbers, functions, formulas, labels, or logical values. For example, each of these formulas performs a conditional test:

    =A1>A2

    =5-3<5*2

    =AVERAGE(B1:B6)=SUM(6,7,8)

    =C2="Female"

    =COUNT(A1:A10)=COUNT(B1:B10)

    =LEN(A1)=10

Every conditional test must include at least one logical operator. Logical operators define the test relationship between elements of the conditional test. For example, in the conditional test A1>A2, the greater-than (>) logical operator compares the values in cells A1 and A2. The table below lists Excel's six logical operators.

The result of a conditional test is either the logical value TRUE (1) or the logical value FALSE (0). For example, the conditional test

    =Z1=10

returns TRUE if the value in Z1 equals 10 and FALSE if Z1 contains any other value.

Operator	Definition
=	Equal to
>	Greater than
<	Less than
> =	Greater than or equal to
< =	Less than or equal to
< >	Not equal to

III

Analyzing Data

The IF Function

The IF conditional function takes the form

=IF(logical_test,value_if_true,value_if_false)

For example, the formula

=IF(A6<22,5,10)

returns 5 if the value in cell A6 is less than 22; otherwise, it returns 10.

You can nest other functions within an IF function. For example, the formula

=IF(SUM(A1:A10)>0,SUM(A1:A10),0)

returns the sum of A1 through A10 if it is greater than 0; otherwise, it returns 0.

You can use text arguments in IF functions. For example, the worksheet which appears in Figure 12-7 lists exam scores for a group of students. The formula

=IF(F4>75,"Pass","Fail")

entered in cell G4 tells Excel to test whether the average test score contained in cell F4 is greater than 75. If it is, the function returns the text *Pass*; if the average is less than or equal to 75, the function returns text *Fail*.

W | ON THE WEB

You can find Test Scores.xls used in the following example at *http:// mspress.microsoft.com/mspress/products/2050/.*

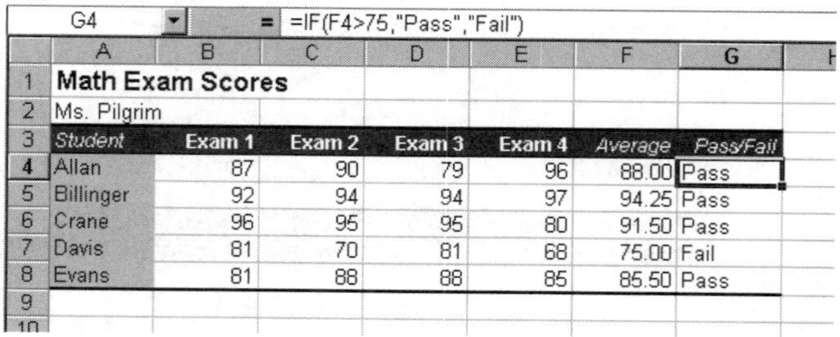

FIGURE 12-7.

You can use the IF function to return a text string.

	A	B	C	D	E	F	G	H
1	Math Exam Scores							
2	Ms. Pilgrim							
3	*Student*	Exam 1	Exam 2	Exam 3	Exam 4	*Average*	*Pass/Fail*	
4	Allan	87	90	79	96	88.00	Pass	
5	Billinger	92	94	94	97	94.25	Pass	
6	Crane	96	95	95	80	91.50	Pass	
7	Davis	81	70	81	68	75.00	Fail	
8	Evans	81	88	88	85	85.50	Pass	
9								
10								

G4 = =IF(F4>75,"Pass","Fail")

You can use text arguments in IF functions to return nothing, instead of 0, if the result is false. For example, the formula

=IF(SUM(A1:A10)>0,SUM(A1:A10),"")

returns a null string ("") if the conditional test is false.

The *logical_test* argument of an IF function can also consist of text. For example, the formula

=IF(A1="Test",100,200)

returns the value 100 if cell A1 contains the string *Test* and 200 if it contains any other entry. The match between the two text entries must be exact except for case.

The AND, OR, and NOT Functions

Three additional functions help you develop compound conditional tests: AND, OR, and NOT. These functions work in conjunction with the simple logical operators =, >, <, >=, <=, and <>. The AND and OR functions can have as many as 30 logical arguments each and take the forms

=AND(logical1,logical2,...,logical30)

=OR(logical1,logical2,...,logical30)

The NOT function has only one argument and takes the form

=NOT(logical)

Arguments for AND, OR, and NOT can be conditional tests, or they can be arrays or references to cells that contain logical values.

Suppose you want Excel to return the text *Pass* only if the student has an average score above 75 and fewer than 5 unexcused absences. In Figure 12-8, we use the formula

=IF(AND(G4<5,F4>75),"Pass","Fail")

Although the OR function takes the same arguments as AND, the results are radically different. For example, the formula

=IF(OR(G4<5,F4>75),"Pass","Fail")

returns the text *Pass* if the student's average test score is greater than 75 *or* if the student has fewer than 5 absences. Thus, the OR

III

Analyzing Data

FIGURE 12-8.

You can create complex conditional tests using the AND function.

	H4	▼		=	=IF(AND(G4<5,F4>75),"Pass","Fail")		
	A	B	C	D	E	F	G	H
1	**Math Exam Scores**							
2	Ms. Pilgrim							
3	*Student*	**Exam 1**	**Exam 2**	**Exam 3**	**Exam 4**	*Average*	*Absences*	*Pass/Fail*
4	Allan	87	90	79	96	88.00	2	Pass
5	Billinger	92	94	94	97	94.25	5	Fail
6	Crane	96	95	95	80	91.50	0	Pass
7	Davis	85	87	87	88	86.75	4	Pass
8	Evans	81	88	88	85	85.50	1	Pass
9								
10								

function returns the logical value TRUE if any one of the conditional tests is true; the AND function returns the logical value TRUE only if *all* the conditional tests are true.

The NOT function negates a condition, so it is usually used in conjunction with other functions. NOT instructs Excel to return the logical value TRUE if the argument is false and the logical value FALSE if the argument is true. For example, the formula

=IF(NOT(A1=2),"Go","NoGo")

tells Excel to return the text *Go* if the value of cell A1 is not 2.

Nested IF Functions

At times, you cannot resolve a logical problem using only logical operators and the AND, OR, and NOT functions. In these cases, you can nest IF functions to create a hierarchy of tests. For example, the formula

=IF(A1=100,"Always",IF(AND(A1>=80,A1<100),"Usually",
IF(AND(A1>=60,A1<80),"Sometimes","Who cares?")))

uses three separate IF functions. If the value in cell A1 is always an integer, the formula can be read: If the value in cell A1 is 100, return the string *Always*; otherwise, if the value in cell A1 falls between 80 and 100 (that is, 80 through 99), return the string *Usually*; otherwise, if the value in cell A1 falls between 60 and 80 (60 through 79), return the string *Sometimes*; and, finally, if none of these conditions is true, return the string *Who cares?*

You can nest as many as seven IF functions, as long as you don't exceed the character limit for single-cell entries.

Other Uses for Conditional Functions

You can use all the conditional functions described in this section as stand-alone formulas. Although you usually use functions such as AND, OR, NOT, ISERROR, ISNA, and ISREF within an IF function, you can also use formulas such as

=AND(A1>A2,A2<A3)

to perform simple conditional tests. This formula returns the logical value TRUE if the value in A1 is greater than the value in A2 *and* the value in A2 is less than the value in A3. You might use this type of formula to assign TRUE and FALSE values to a range of numeric database cells and then use the TRUE and FALSE conditions as selection criteria for printing a specialized report.

The TRUE and FALSE Functions

The TRUE and FALSE functions offer alternative ways to represent the logical conditions TRUE and FALSE. Neither of these functions accepts arguments. They take the forms

=TRUE( )

and

=FALSE( )

For example, suppose cell B5 contains a conditional test formula. The formula

=IF(B5=FALSE( ),"Warning!","OK")

returns *Warning!* if the result of the conditional test formula in cell B5 is FALSE. It returns *OK* if the result of the formula in cell B5 is TRUE.

The ISBLANK Function

You can use the ISBLANK function to determine whether a referenced cell is blank. ISBLANK takes the form

=ISBLANK(*value*)

The *value* argument is a reference to a cell or range. If *value* refers to a blank cell or range, the function returns the logical value TRUE; otherwise, it returns FALSE.

Lookup and Reference Functions

Several functions "look up" information stored in a list or a table, or manipulate references.

The ADDRESS Function

The Address function provides a handy way to build a reference from numbers. ADDRESS takes the form

=ADDRESS(row_num,column_num_num,abs,a1,sheet_text)

The *row_num* and *column_num* arguments designate the row and column values for the address. The *abs_num* argument determines if the resulting address uses absolute references: for absolute, use 1; for mixed, use 2 (absolute row, relative column) or 3 (relative row, absolute column); for relative, use 4. The *a1* argument is also a logical value. If *a1* is TRUE, the resulting address will be in A1 format; if *a1* is FALSE, the resulting address will be in R1C1 format. The *sheet_text* argument allows you to specify the name of the sheet for the beginning of the address. Excel places single quotation marks around the sheet text in the resulting reference if the sheet text isn't one word. For example, the formula

    =ADDRESS (1,1,1,TRUE,'Data Sheet')

results in the reference 'Data Sheet'!$A$1.

The CHOOSE Function

You use the CHOOSE function to retrieve an item from a list of values stored as the arguments to the function. CHOOSE takes the form

    =CHOOSE(index_num,value 1,value 2,...,value 29)

The *index_num* argument is the position in the list of the item you want to look up, and *value 1, value 2,* and so on are the elements of the list. The *index_num* value must always be positive and cannot exceed the number of elements in the list. If you use an *index_num* value less than 1 or greater than the number of values in the list, Excel returns the #VALUE! error value.

The CHOOSE function returns the value of the element of the list that occupies the position indicated by *index_num*. For example, the function

    =CHOOSE(2,6,1,8,9,3)

returns the value 1, because 1 is the second item in the list. (The *index_num* value itself is not counted as part of the list.)

The arguments of CHOOSE can be cell references. If you use a cell reference for *index_num*, Excel selects an item from the list according to the value stored in that cell. Suppose cell A11 contains the formula

    =CHOOSE(A10,0.15,0.22,0.21,0.21,0.26)

If cell A10 contains the value 5, the CHOOSE function returns the value 0.26; if cell A10 contains the value 1, the function returns the value 0.15.

Similarly, if cell C1 contains the value 0.15, cell C2 contains the value 0.22, and cells C3, C4, and C5 all contain the value 0.21, the formula

    =CHOOSE(A10,C1,C2,C3,C4,C5)

returns 0.15 if cell A10 contains the value 1 and returns 0.21 if cell A10 contains the value 3, 4, or 5.

You cannot specify a range as a single item in the list. You might be tempted to create a function such as

    =CHOOSE(A10,C1:C5)

to take the place of the longer function in the previous example. If you do, however, the result is a #VALUE! error value.

The elements in the list can be text strings. For example, the function

=CHOOSE(3,"First","Second","Third")

selects the third item from the list and returns the string *Third*.

The MATCH Function

The MATCH function is closely related to the CHOOSE function. However, where CHOOSE returns the item that occupies the position in a list specified by the *index_num* argument, MATCH returns the position of the item in the list that most closely matches a lookup value. This function takes the form

=MATCH(lookup_value,lookup_array,match_type)

The *lookup_value* argument is the value or string to look up, and the *lookup_array* is the range that contains the values with which to compare the *lookup_value*.

In the worksheet in Figure 12-9, if you enter the formula

=MATCH(10,A1:D1,0)

in cell E1, the result is 1, because the cell in the first position of the *lookup_array* contains a value that matches the *lookup_value*.

The *match_type* argument defines the rules for the search and must be 1, 0, or -1. If the *match_type* is 1 or is omitted altogether, the MATCH function looks for the largest value in the range that is less than or equal to the *lookup_value*. The *lookup_array* must be sorted in ascending order. For example, in the worksheet in Figure 12-9, the formula

=MATCH(19,A1:D1,1)

would return the value 1, because 10, the first item in the range, is the largest value in the range that doesn't exceed the *lookup_value* 19. If no items in the range are less than or equal to the *lookup_value*, the function returns the #N/A error value.

FIGURE 12-9.

The MATCH function locates the position of a value in a list.

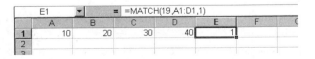

III

Analyzing Data

To see what happens if you do not sort the *lookup_array* in ascending order, look at Figure 12-10. The formula

=MATCH(20,A1:D1,1)

incorrectly returns the value 1.

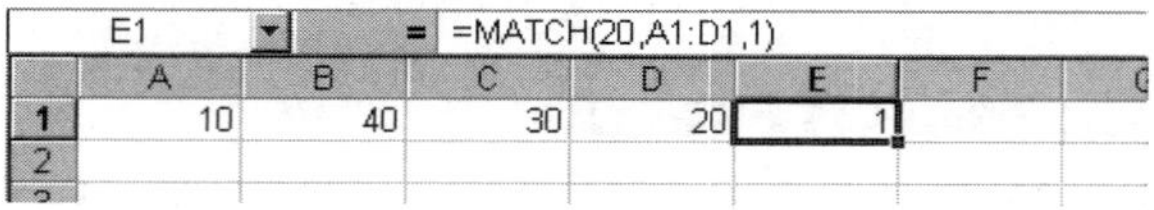

FIGURE 12-10.

The MATCH function requires the *lookup_array* to be in ascending order.

E1	▼	=	=MATCH(20,A1:D1,1)			
	A	B	C	D	E	F
1	10	40	30	20	1	
2						

If the *match_type* is 0, the MATCH function finds the first value in the range that exactly matches the *lookup_value*. The *lookup_array* does not need to be sorted. If no items in the range exactly match the *lookup_value*, the function returns #N/A.

If the *match_type* is -1, MATCH looks for the smallest value in the range that is greater than or equal to the *lookup_value*. When the *match_type* is -1, the items in the list must be sorted in descending order. If no items in the range are greater than or equal to the *lookup_value*, the function returns the #N/A error value.

The *lookup_value* argument and the items in the range can also be text strings. For example, if cells A1:D1 contain the text entries shown in Figure 12-11, the formula

=MATCH("Twenty",A1:D1,0)

returns the value 2. When you use MATCH to locate text strings, you should specify a *match_type* argument of 0 (an exact match). You can then use the wildcards * and ? in the *lookup_value* argument.

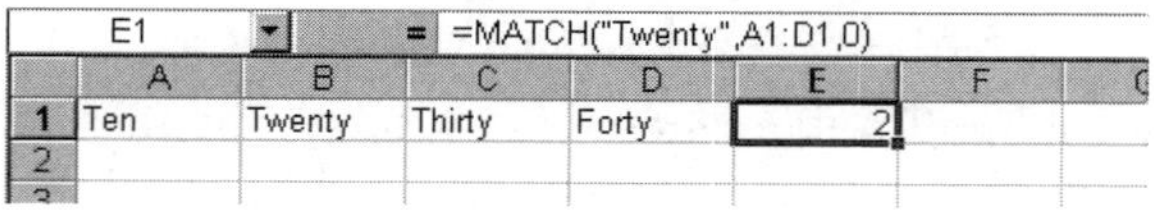

FIGURE 12-11.

You can use MATCH to locate the position of a text string.

E1	▼	=	=MATCH("Twenty",A1:D1,0)			
	A	B	C	D	E	F
1	Ten	Twenty	Thirty	Forty	2	
2						

The VLOOKUP and HLOOKUP Functions

VLOOKUP and HLOOKUP are nearly identical functions that look up information stored in tables you've constructed. When you look up information in a table, you normally use a row index and a column index to locate a particular cell. Excel uses this method with a slight variation: it derives the first index by finding the largest value in the first column or row that is less than or equal to a *lookup_value* argument you supply and then uses a *row_index_num* or *col_index_num* argument as the other index. This method allows you to look up a value based on information in the table, rather than having to know exactly where the value is.

These functions take the forms

=VLOOKUP(lookup_value,table_array,col_index_num,range_lookup)

and

=HLOOKUP(lookup_value,table_array,row_index_num,range_lookup)

The *lookup_value* argument is a value to look up in the table to find the first index, *table_array* is an array or range name that defines the table, and *row_* or *col_index_num* designates the row or column of the table (the second index) from which to select the result. Because the *lookup_value* is compared to the first column or row of data to determine the first index, we call the data in that first column or row the comparison values. The *range_lookup* argument is a logical value that determines whether the function matches the *lookup_value* exactly or approximately. Use FALSE for the *range_lookup* argument to match the *lookup_value* exactly.

The difference between VLOOKUP and HLOOKUP is the type of table each function uses: VLOOKUP works with vertical tables (tables arranged in columns); HLOOKUP works with horizontal tables (tables arranged in rows).

Whether a table is considered vertical or horizontal depends on where the comparison values are located. If they are in the leftmost column of the table, the table is vertical; if they are in the first row of the table, the table is horizontal. The comparison values can be numbers or text. In either case, they must be arranged in ascending order. In addition, no comparison value should be used more than once in a table.

The *index_num* argument (sometimes called the *offset*) provides the second table index and tells the lookup function which column or row of the table to look in for the function's result. The first column or row in the table has an index number of 1, so if the index number is 1, the result of the function is one of the comparison values. The *index_num* argument must be greater than or equal to 1 and must never be greater than the number of rows or columns in the table; that is, if a vertical table is three columns wide, the index number cannot be greater than 3. If any value does not meet these rules, the function returns an error value.

The VLOOKUP Function

You can use the VLOOKUP function to retrieve information from the table in Figure 12-12. The formula

=VLOOKUP(41,A3:C7,3)

returns the value 14.

You can find LookupPlus.xls, used in all the following LOOKUP examples, at *http://mspress.microsoft.com/mspress/products/2050/*.

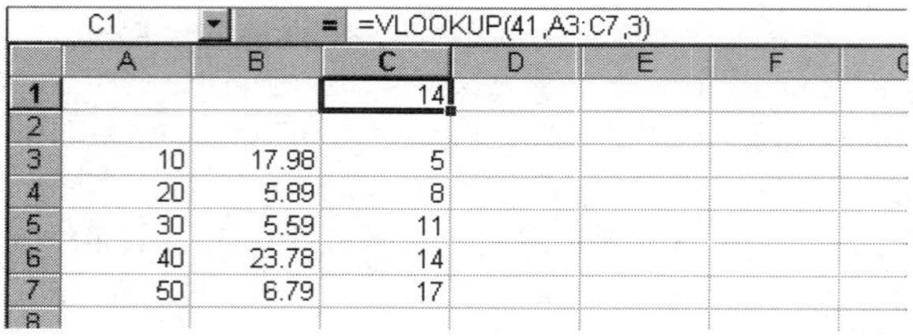

FIGURE 12-12.

You can use the VLOOKUP function to retrieve information from a vertical table like this one.

C1		=	=VLOOKUP(41,A3:C7,3)			
	A	B	C	D	E	F
1			14			
2						
3	10	17.98	5			
4	20	5.89	8			
5	30	5.59	11			
6	40	23.78	14			
7	50	6.79	17			
8						

Let's see how Excel came up with this result. The function first locates the column that contains the comparison values—in this case, column A. Next it scans the comparison values to find the largest value that is less than or equal to the *lookup_value*. Because the fourth comparison value, 40, is less than the *lookup_value* of 41, and the fifth comparison value, 50, is greater than the *lookup_value*, Excel uses the row containing 40 (row number 6) as the row index. The column index is the *col_index_num* argument; in this example, *col_index_num* is 3, so column C contains the data you want. The function, therefore, returns the value from cell C6, which is 14.

The *lookup_value* argument in a lookup function can be a value, a cell reference, or text enclosed in double quotation marks. The *lookup_array* can be indicated by cell references or a range name. If we assign the name *Table* to the range A3:C7 in Figure 12-12 and enter the number 41 in cell A1, the formula

=VLOOKUP(A1,Table,3)

returns the same result as the previous example.

Remember that these lookup functions search for the greatest comparison value that is less than or equal to the lookup value (unless you use FALSE as the *range_lookup* argument), not for an exact match between the comparison values and the lookup value. If all the comparison values in the first row or column of the table range are greater than the lookup value, the function returns the #N/A error value. If, however, all the comparison values are less than the lookup value, the function returns the value that corresponds to the last (largest) comparison value in the table.

You can also use the lookup functions to look up text. For example, the formula

=VLOOKUP(8,B2:E6,4)

returns the string *Barb* from the table in Figure 12-13.

The *lookup_value* and comparison values can also be text strings. Figure 12-14 shows a lookup table that uses text comparison values. For example, the formula

=VLOOKUP("doug",B2:C6,2)

returns the value 46000. (If you use a text string as the lookup value, you must enclose it in double quotation marks.)

FIGURE 12-13.

You can use VLOOKUP with text comparison values.

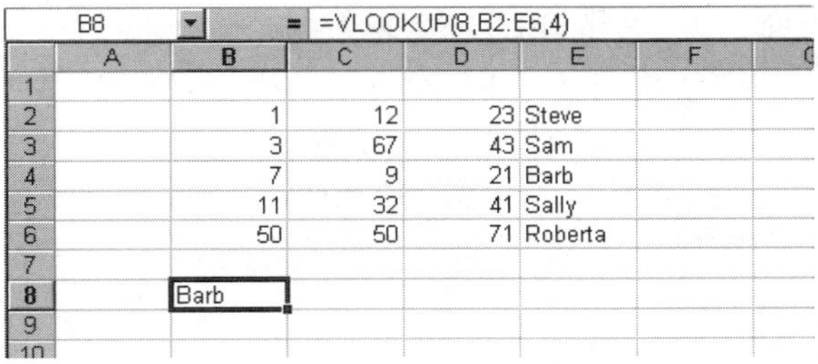

	B8			=	=VLOOKUP(8,B2:E6,4)		
	A	B	C	D	E	F	
1							
2		1	12	23	Steve		
3		3	67	43	Sam		
4		7	9	21	Barb		
5		11	32	41	Sally		
6		50	50	71	Roberta		
7							
8		Barb					
9							
10							

FIGURE 12-14.

This vertical lookup table uses text comparison values.

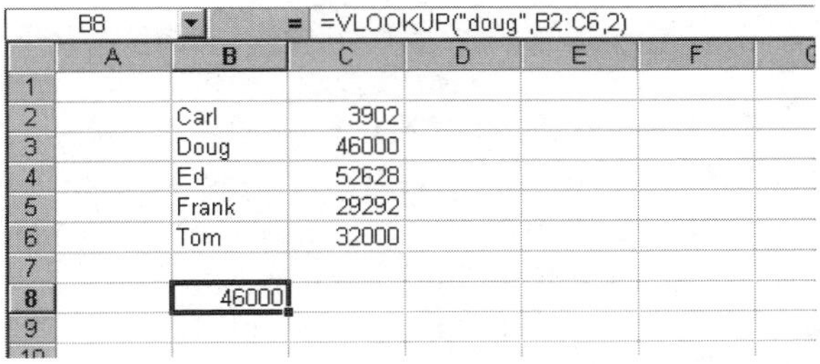

	B8			=	=VLOOKUP("doug",B2:C6,2)		
	A	B	C	D	E	F	
1							
2		Carl	3902				
3		Doug	46000				
4		Ed	52628				
5		Frank	29292				
6		Tom	32000				
7							
8		46000					
9							
10							

> **NOTE**
>
> In versions prior to Excel 97, it was necessary to sort the comparison values in ascending numeric or alphabetic order for the LOOKUP functions to work properly. This is no longer necessary.

III

Analyzing Data

Unless you include the *range_lookup* argument of FALSE to specify an exact match, Excel finds the comparison value that is less than or equal to the *lookup_value*, rather than an absolute match. Thus, the formula

> =VLOOKUP("Steve",B2:C6,2)

returns the value 29292 from Figure 12-14. This value corresponds to the comparison value *Frank*, which is the "greatest" comparison value that is "less than" the lookup value *Steve*. Although this method is consistent, it does not yield the expected result.

The HLOOKUP Function

The HLOOKUP function is identical to the VLOOKUP function except that it works with horizontal tables. The worksheet in Figure 12-15 shows an example of a horizontal lookup table. The formula

> =HLOOKUP(6,B2:E7,3)

returns the value 101 because the lookup value, 6, equals the comparison value in column C, and the index number, 3, tells the function to look in the third row of the table (row 4) for the correct item.

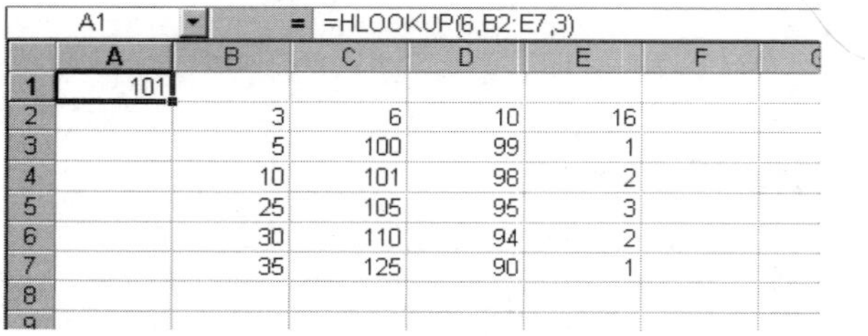

FIGURE 12-15.

You can use the HLOOKUP function to retrieve information from a horizontal table like this one.

	A	B	C	D	E	F	
1	101						
2		3	6	10	16		
3		5	100	99	1		
4		10	101	98	2		
5		25	105	95	3		
6		30	110	94	2		
7		35	125	90	1		
8							

A1 = =HLOOKUP(6,B2:E7,3)

The LOOKUP Function

The LOOKUP function has two forms. In both forms, it is similar to VLOOKUP and HLOOKUP, and follows the same rules. When you select LOOKUP from the Function Name list in the first Paste Function dialog box, a second dialog box appears. Select the form of the LOOKUP function you want to use.

The First Form

The first form (or vector form) of LOOKUP is

> =LOOKUP(lookup_value,lookup_vector,result_vector)

The *lookup_value* argument is a value to find in the comparison values given by *lookup_vector*, and *result_vector* contains the possible results. Each range consists of a single row or column.

Like HLOOKUP and VLOOKUP, LOOKUP searches *lookup_vector* for the largest comparison value that is not greater than *lookup_value*. It then selects the result from the corresponding position in *result_vector*. Although *lookup_vector* and *result_vector* are often parallel in the worksheet, they don't have to be. They can be located in separate areas of the worksheet, and one range can be horizontal and the other vertical. The only requirement is that they must have exactly the same number of elements.

For example, consider the worksheet in Figure 12-16. The formula

=LOOKUP(3,B3:B7,E3:E7)

compares the *lookup_value*, 3, with the values in the *lookup_vector*, B3:B7. The third cell of the *lookup_vector*, B5, contains the largest value that is not greater than the *lookup_value*, so the function returns the contents of the third cell of the result range, E5, as the result 300.

Now consider Figure 12-17 below, where the ranges are not parallel. The formula

=LOOKUP(3,A1:A5,D6:H6)

returns 300. Both the *lookup_vector*, A1:A5, and the *result_vector*, D6:H6, have five elements. The *lookup_value*, 3, matches the entry in the third cell of the *lookup_vector*, so the result of the formula is the entry in the third cell of the result range: 300.

FIGURE 12-16.

You can use the LOOKUP function to retrieve information from a range.

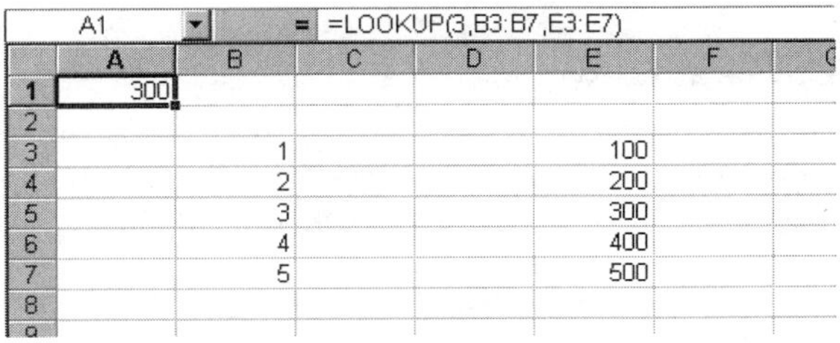

FIGURE 12-17.

The LOOKUP function can retrieve information from a nonparallel cell range.

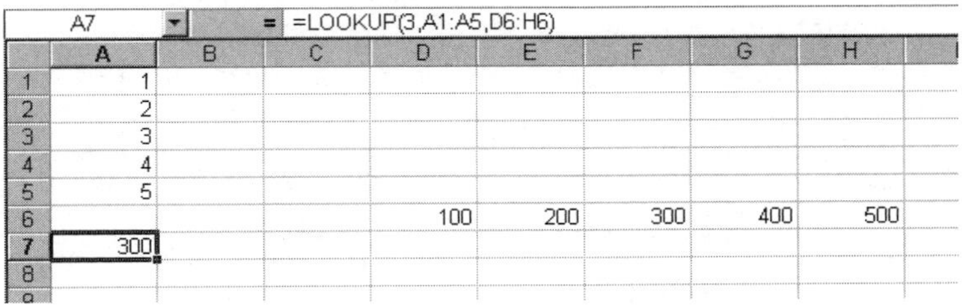

III

Analyzing Data

The Second Form

The second form (or array form) of LOOKUP is

=LOOKUP(lookup_value,array)

The *lookup_value* argument is a value to find in the table defined by *array*. This form of the LOOKUP function has no *index_num* or *result_vector* argument. The result is always taken from the last column or row of *array*.

You can use this form of LOOKUP with either a horizontal or a vertical table. LOOKUP uses the dimensions of the table to figure out where the comparison values are. If the table is taller than it is wide, or if the table is square, the function treats it as a vertical table and assumes that the comparison values are in the leftmost column. If the table is wider than it is tall, the function views the table as horizontal and assumes the comparison values are in the first row of the table.

Because HLOOKUP and VLOOKUP are more predictable and controllable, you'll generally find using them preferable to using LOOKUP.

The INDEX Function

Like CHOOSE and LOOKUP, INDEX is a lookup function. It has two forms: an array form, which returns the value or values in those cells, and a reference form, which returns an address, or reference (not a value) to a cell or range of cells in the worksheet. We'll discuss the array form first.

The First Form

The first form (or array form) of the INDEX function works only with array arguments and it returns the values of the results, not their cell references. This form of the function is

=INDEX(array,row_num,column_num)

The result is the value at the position in the array argument indicated by the *row_num* and *column_num* arguments.

For example, the formula

=INDEX({10,20,30;40,50,60},1,2)

returns the value 20, because 20 is the value in the cell in the second column and first row of the array.

The Second Form

The second form (or reference form) of INDEX returns a cell address and is useful when you want to perform operations on a cell (such as changing the cell width), rather than on its value. This function can be confusing, however, because if an INDEX function is nested in another function, that function can use the value in the cell whose address is returned by INDEX. Furthermore, the reference form of INDEX doesn't display its result as an address; it displays the value(s) in that address. The important thing to remember is that the result is actually an address, even if it doesn't look like one.

The INDEX function has two advantages: you can give it multiple, noncontiguous areas of the worksheet as a lookup range argument, which in this case is called the index range argument; and it can return a range (more than one cell) as a result. The reference form of this function is

=INDEX(reference,row_num,column_num,area_num)

The *reference* argument can be one or more ranges, which are called *areas*. Each area must be rectangular and can contain numbers, text, or formulas. If the areas are not adjacent, the *reference* argument must be enclosed in parentheses.

The *row_num* and *column_num* arguments must be positive numbers (or references to cells that contain numbers) that designate a cell in the *reference* argument. If the *row_num* argument is greater than the number of rows in the table or if the *column_num* argument is greater than the number of columns, the INDEX function returns the #REF! error value.

If every area in *reference* consists of only one row, the *row_num* argument is optional. Similarly, the *column_num* argument is optional if every area consists of only one column. If you enter 0 as the *row_num* or *column_num* argument, INDEX returns a reference for the entire row or column, respectively.

The *area_num* argument is needed only if more than one area is included in *reference*. It identifies which area in *reference* the *row_num* and *column_num* arguments are to be used with. The first area specified in *reference* is designated area 1, the second area 2, and so on. If the *area_num* argument is omitted, it is assumed to be 1. The *area_num* argument must always be a positive integer. If *area_num* is less than 1, the function returns the #REF! error value.

Let's consider some examples to see how all this works. Figure 12-18 on the next page shows an example of an INDEX function. The formula in cell A1

=INDEX(C3:E6,A2,A3)

uses the row coordinate in cell A2,*3*, and the column coordinate in cell A3,*2*, to return the address of the cell in the third row and the second column of the range C3:E6, which is D5. However, because Excel displays the value of the result—the number 700—the contents of cell D5 are displayed in cell A1.

 ON THE WEB

You can find LookupPlus.xls used in the following example at *http://mspress.microsoft.com/mspress/products/2050/.*

FIGURE 12-18.

You can use the INDEX function to retrieve the address of the cell where information is located.

A1		=	=INDEX(C3:E6,A2,A3)			
	A	B	C	D	E	F
1	700					
2	3					
3	2		100	500	9000	
4			200	600	1100	
5			300	700	1200	
6			400	800	1300	
7						

Here's another example that's a bit more tricky. Using the worksheet in Figure 12-18, the formula

=INDEX(C3:E6,0,2)

displays the #VALUE! error value because the *row_num* argument of 0 causes INDEX to return a reference to the entire column specified by the *column_num* argument of 2, which is the range D3:D6. You see the #VALUE! error value because Excel can't display the value as a range result. However, if we nest this formula in another function, as follows

=SUM(INDEX(C3:E6,0,2))

the result is 2600, the sum of the values in D3:D6. Now you can see the utility of obtaining a reference result with INDEX.

If the *reference* argument is only one row deep or one column wide, you can use only one index to select a value. Using Figure 12-18 again, the formula

=INDEX(C3:C6,2)

returns the value 200. Similarly, the formula

=INDEX(C3:E3,2)

returns the value 500. (The INDEX function is similar to the CHOOSE function when used with a one-dimensional table.)

? SEE ALSO

For information on the CHOOSE function, see "The CHOOSE Function," page 444.

Now let's see how the INDEX function works with multiple ranges in the reference argument. (Remember, when more than one range is used, you must enclose the argument in parentheses.) For example, in the formula

=INDEX((A1:C5,D6:F10),1,1,2)

the reference range is composed of two areas: A1:C5 and D6:F10. The *area_num* argument, 2, tells INDEX to work on the second of these areas. This formula returns the address D6 (800), which is the cell in the first column and first row of the range D6:F10. The displayed result is the value in that cell.

The OFFSET Function

The OFFSET function returns a reference of a specified height and width, located at a specified position relative to another reference. This function takes the form

=OFFSET(reference,rows,cols,height,width)

The *reference* argument specifies the position from which the offset is calculated. The *rows* and *cols* arguments specify the vertical and horizontal distances between the *reference* argument and the reference returned by the function. Positive values for *rows* and *cols* specify offsets below and to the right of *reference,* respectively. Negative values specify offsets above and to the left of *reference,* respectively. The *height* and *width* arguments specify the shape of the reference returned by the function. The *height* and *width* arguments are optional. If you omit them, the function returns a reference of the same dimensions as *reference*. If you include them, *height* and *width* must be positive.

The INDIRECT Function

You can use the INDIRECT function to find out the contents of a cell from its reference. INDIRECT takes the form

=INDIRECT(*ref_text,a1*)

The *ref_text* argument is an A1 reference, an R1C1 reference, or a cell name, and *a1* is a logical value that indicates which of these types of reference you're using. If *a1* is FALSE, Excel interprets *ref_text* as the R1C1 format; if *a1* is TRUE or is omitted, Excel interprets *ref_text* as the A1 format. If your entry for *ref_text* isn't valid, INDIRECT returns the #REF! error value.

For example, if cell C6 of your worksheet contains the text value B3, and cell B3 contains the value 2.888, the formula

=INDIRECT(C6)

returns the value 2.888. If your worksheet is set to display R1C1-style references, cell R6C3 contains a text reference to cell R3C2, and cell R3C2 contains the value 2.888, and then the formula

=INDIRECT(R6C3,FALSE)

also returns the value 2.888.

The ROW and COLUMN Functions

Although the names of the ROW and COLUMN functions are nearly the same as the names of the ROWS and COLUMNS array functions, the functions are quite different. These functions take the forms

=ROW(reference)

and

=COLUMN(*reference*)

The result of these functions is the row or column number of the cell or range referred to by the function's argument. For example, the formula

=ROW(H5)

returns the result 5. The formula

=COLUMN(C5)

returns the result 3 because column C is the third column on the worksheet.

If the *reference* argument is omitted, the result is the row or column number of the cell that contains the function.

If the *reference* argument is a range or a range name and the function is entered as an array, the result of the function is an array that consists of the row or column numbers of each of the rows or columns in the range. For example, if you select cells B1:B10, type the formula

=ROW(A1:A10)

and then press Ctrl+Shift+Enter to enter the formula in all of the cells of the range B1:B10, that range will contain the array result {1;2;3;4;5;6;7;8;9;10}, the row numbers of each cell in the argument.

The ROWS and COLUMNS Functions

The ROWS function returns the number of rows in a reference or an array and takes the form

ROWS(*array*)

The *array* argument is an array constant, a range reference, or a range name.

For example, the result of the formula

=ROWS({100,200,300;1000,2000,3000})

is 2, because *array* consists of two "rows." The formula

=ROWS(A1:A10)

returns 10, because the range A1:A10 contains ten rows.

The COLUMNS function is identical to the ROWS function except that it returns the number of columns in the *array* argument. For example, the formula

=COLUMNS(A1:C10)

returns 3, because the range A1:C10 contains three columns.

The AREAS Function

An area is a single cell or a rectangular block of cells. You can use the AREAS function to determine the number of areas in a range. This function takes the form

=AREAS(reference)

The *reference* argument can be a cell reference, a range reference, or several range references. (If you use several range references, you must enclose them in a set of parentheses so that Excel doesn't interpret the commas that separate the ranges as argument separators.) The result of the function is the number of areas referred to by the argument.

For example, suppose you assign the name *Test* to the group of ranges A1:C5,D6,E7:G10. The function

=AREAS(Test)

returns the number 3, the number of areas in the group.

The TRANSPOSE Function

The TRANSPOSE function changes the horizontal or vertical orientation of an array. This function has the form

=TRANSPOSE(*array*)

If the *array* argument is vertical, the resulting array is horizontal. If *array* is horizontal, the resulting array is vertical. The first row of a horizontal array becomes the first column of the vertical array result, and vice versa. The TRANSPOSE function must be entered as an array formula in a range that has the same number of rows and columns as the *array* argument has columns and rows, respectively.

> For quick and easy transposition, select the range you want to transpose, press Ctrl+C to copy the range, and then choose Paste Special from the Edit menu. Select the Transpose check box, and then click OK.

The COUNTBLANK Function

The COUNTBLANK function simply counts the number of empty cells in the specified range and takes the form

=COUNTBLANK*(range)*

The *range* argument is the range you want to check. This function is a little tricky, because formulas that evaluate to null text strings, such as =""or =" ", or formulas that evaluate to zero, such as

=100-A1

where A1 contains the number 100, might seem empty but they really aren't empty.

The TYPE Function

The TYPE function determines whether a cell contains text, a number, a logical value, an array, or an error value. This function takes the form

=TYPE(*value*)

The result of the TYPE function is a code for the type of entry in the referenced cell: 1 for a number, 2 for text, 4 for a logical value (TRUE or FALSE), 16 for an error value, and 64 for an array.

For example, if cell A1 contains the number 100, the formula

=TYPE(A1)

returns 1. If A1 contains the text *Microsoft Excel*, the formula returns 2.

CHAPTER 13

Dates and Times

With Microsoft Excel 2000, you can enter date values and time values in your worksheet to date stamp documents or to perform date and time arithmetic. As a result, creating a production schedule or a monthly billing system is relatively easy. Although Excel uses numeric values to count each nanosecond, starting from the turn of the century, you can use formatting to display those numbers in forms you can more easily recognize.

Yes, Excel 2000 is Y2K Friendly, But Are You?

No need to worry about Excel's ability to deal with the much-feared year 2000 phenomenon, affectionately known as the "Millennium Bug." Just try typing *1/1/00* into Excel, and then select the cell you just typed in and look at the formula bar. You'll see that Excel evaluates your entry as *1/1/2000,* as you had probably hoped.

However, if you routinely deal with dates that span several decades (or centuries!), you should develop the habit of entering years in four digits. In Excel 2000, December 31, 2029 is the "magic date"—that is, the last day that Excel assumes is in the future if you enter only *00* as the year component. For example, if you type *12/31/29* into a cell, Excel assumes that you mean the year 2029. If, however, you type *1/1/30* into a cell, you'll see that Excel evaluates this entry as January 1, 1930. So if you need to enter dates that occur in the year 2030 and later (or in 1929 and earlier), you should get into the habit of typing the full four-digit year to avoid surprises.

How Excel Records Dates and Times

The basic unit of time in Excel is the day. Each day is represented by a serial date value from 1 through 65380. The base date, represented by the serial value 1, is Sunday, January 1, 1900. When you enter a date in your worksheet, Excel records the date as a serial value that represents the number of days between the base date and the specified date. For example, the date January 1, 2000, is represented by the serial value 36526, because there are 36526 days between the base date—January 1, 1900—and January 1, 2000.

The time of day is a decimal value that represents the portion of a day between its beginning—12:00 midnight—and the specified time. The time 12:00 noon, for example, is represented by the value 0.5, because the difference between midnight and noon is exactly half a day. The time/date combination 2:09:03 PM, October 23, 2000, is represented by the serial value 36822.589618056.

By assigning serial values to days, hours, minutes, and seconds, Excel enables you to perform sophisticated date and time arithmetic. You can manipulate dates and times in your worksheet formulas just as you manipulate other types of values.

> You can use the Cells command on the Format menu to see the serial value Excel assigns to a date or time. Simply select the Number tab of the Format Cells dialog box and highlight General. You can quickly apply the general format with the keyboard by pressing Ctrl+Shift+Tilde (~). Press Ctrl+Z if you want to undo the formatting change.

Entering Dates and Times

Although Excel records dates and times as serial date values, you don't have to enter them that way. In Chapter 7, you learned that you can enter a number in a cell and format that number in one step by typing the number "in format." Generally, you use this "in format" technique to enter dates and times. Simply select the cell in which you want to make the entry and type the date in one of the following formats: m/d/yy, d-mmm-yy, d-mmm, or mmm-yy. There are many more built-in time and date formats, but these are the only ones that Excel will apply as you type.

For example, to enter December 1, 2000, select the cell and type *12/1/00* or *12-1-00*. (You can use either forward slashes or hyphens as separators.) Excel does not display the date's serial value in the formula bar; instead, it assigns the m/d/yy format to the cell (if the cell isn't already formatted differently) and displays 12/1/00 in the formula bar. If you want, you can change default date, time, currency, and numbering settings through the Regional Settings dialog box, available on the Control Panel.

> Although you can (and probably should) enter dates using four-digit years, the formats that Excel assigns on the fly use two-digit years. For example, if you type *1/1/2247* into a cell, Excel displays this as 1/1/47, but if you click the cell and look in the formula bar, you'll see that the year in the underlying date is really 2247.

If your entry doesn't exactly match an on-the-fly format, Excel picks the format that is most similar to your entry. For example, if you enter *1 Dec*, you see the formatted entry *1-Dec* in the cell. In the formula bar, the entry appears as 12/1/2000 (if the current year is 2000) so you can edit the date more easily.

III

Analyzing Data

The 1904 Date System Option

You can change the base date (the date that corresponds to the serial value 1) from January 1, 1900—used by Microsoft Excel for Windows—to January 2, 1904—used by Microsoft Excel for the Macintosh. Choose Options from the Tools menu, click the Calculation tab, and then select the 1904 Date System option. When you turn on the option, the serial date values in your worksheet remain the same, but the display of all dates changes, and the serial values of any dates you enter in your Excel for Windows worksheets match corresponding serial values from Excel for the Macintosh worksheets. If you transfer information into Excel for Windows from a worksheet created in Excel for the Macintosh, turning on this option ensures that the serial date values are evaluated correctly. In this book, we use the 1900 date system, which is the standard for Microsoft Windows and MS-DOS programs.

If you transfer documents between Excel for the Macintosh and Excel for Windows, the proper date system for the worksheet is automatically set for you. When the date system changes, existing serial date values display different dates, but the underlying values do not change. As a result, if you change date systems after you have begun entering dates in a worksheet, all your dates will be off by four years.

(?) SEE ALSO

For more information about the [h]:mm:ss format, see "Measuring Elapsed Time," page 471.

You can also enter times "in format." Select the cell in which you want to make the entry and type the time in one of the following forms: h:mm AM/PM, h:mm:ss AM/PM, h:mm, h:mm:ss, or the combined date and time format, m/d/yy h:mm. Notice that the hours, minutes, and seconds of the time entries must be separated by colons. (You cannot enter minutes "in format.")

(?) SEE ALSO

For more information about custom formats, see "Creating Your Own Date and Time Formats," page 469.

For example, to enter the time 2:15 PM in a cell, select the cell and then type *2:15 PM* or *14:15*. Either way, Excel recognizes the time as the decimal value equivalent of 0.59375 and displays it on the worksheet in the Time format you used for the entry. (If you don't include AM, PM, am, or pm with the time, Excel uses the 24-hour, or military, time convention. On the 24-hour clock, 3:00 AM is 300 hours, 2:00 PM is 1400 hours, and 11:00 PM is 2300 hours.)

(★) TIP

You can enter the current time in a cell or formula by holding down Ctrl and Shift together and pressing the colon (:) key. The time is entered in h:mm AM/PM format. You can enter the current date in a cell or formula by holding down Ctrl and pressing the semicolon (;) key. The date is entered in m/d/yy format.

Entering a Series of Dates

You can create an evenly spaced series of dates in a row or column in several ways, but the job is especially easy when you use the Series command on the Fill submenu of the Edit menu. With this command, you can build a series of dates that are days, weeks, months, or years apart.

Suppose you want to create a series of dates in cells A1 through A16. The series begins with March 1, 2000, and the dates must be exactly one month apart. Follow these steps:

1 Type the starting date in the first cell of the range in which you want the series to appear—in this case, type *3/1/00* in cell A1.

2 Select the range—in this case, A1:A16—and choose Fill and then Series from the Edit menu. The Series dialog box appears, as shown in Figure 13-1.

FIGURE 13-1.

Use the Series dialog box to create date series.

3 Accept the default options in the Series In and Type sections. (Columns creates a columnar series, and Date creates a date series.)

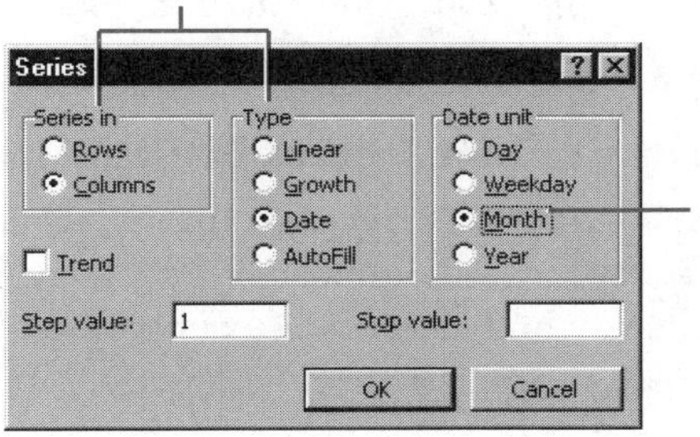

4 In the Date Unit section, select Month to specify the interval. Check that the Step Value is 1, and click OK.

Figure 13-2 on the next page shows the result. The range A1:A16 contains a series of dates exactly one month apart.

The other options in the Date Unit section of the Series dialog box let you specify different intervals for your date series. The Day option builds a series of dates one or more days apart (depending on the step value); the Weekday option creates a series of dates using only the five working days of the week. The Year option builds an annual date series.

The Step Value option lets you specify the interval between cells. For example, by typing *2* in the Step Value edit box and selecting Date in the Type section and Month in the Date Unit section, you can create a series of dates for every other month. By typing a negative number in the Step Value edit box, you can create a series that goes backward (decreases) in time.

III

Analyzing Data

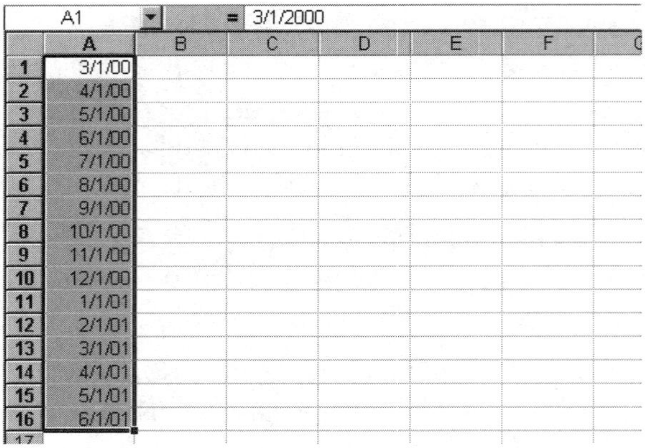

FIGURE 13-2.

Using the Series command on the Fill submenu of the Edit menu, we created a series of dates one month apart.

	A	B	C	D	E	F	G
	A1			=	3/1/2000		
1	3/1/00						
2	4/1/00						
3	5/1/00						
4	6/1/00						
5	7/1/00						
6	8/1/00						
7	9/1/00						
8	10/1/00						
9	11/1/00						
10	12/1/00						
11	1/1/01						
12	2/1/01						
13	3/1/01						
14	4/1/01						
15	5/1/01						
16	6/1/01						
17							

? SEE ALSO

For more information about the Series command, see "Filling Cell Ranges with Data," page 274.

To set an ending date for the series, you can enter a date in the Stop Value edit box. For example, to enter a series of dates that extends from 1/1/00 through 12/31/01, type *1/1/00* in a cell. Then select that cell, display the Series dialog box, select the Columns option, and type *12/31/01* in the Stop Value edit box. Excel extends a series of dates from 1/2/00 to 12/31/01 below the original cell.

Entering a Date Series Using AutoFill

In Chapter 8, we introduced you to AutoFill, which lets you create a series of data with the mouse. This feature also lets you create date series quickly and easily. For example, to quickly create the same one-month date series shown in Figure 13-2, follow these steps:

1 Enter the starting date—in this case, *3/1/00*—in A1 (the first cell of the range) and the second date in the series, *4/1/00,* in A2 (the second cell).

2 With the mouse, select the two cells.

3 Move the mouse pointer over the small black fill handle in the lower right corner of the selection. (If the fill handle is not visible, choose Options from the Tools menu, click the Edit tab, and then select the Allow Cell Drag And Drop option.) The mouse pointer changes to a bold cross hair when it is over the fill handle.

4 Drag the fill handle until the range you want to fill with dates— in this case, cells A1:A16—is selected.

5 Release the mouse button. AutoFill analyzes the two selected cells, determines that their entries are one month apart, and then creates the same one-month data series shown in Figure 13-2.

AutoFill uses the selected cells to determine the type of series you intend to create with the fill handle. As described in Chapter 8, it copies text and nonsequential values and automatically increments sequential numeric values. Because dates are stored as serial values, AutoFill extends them sequentially, as illustrated in Figure 13-3.

FIGURE 13-3.

Using AutoFill, we started with the values in the Selected Value(s) section of the worksheet and created the values to the right.

	A	B	C	D	E	F	G	H	I	J	K
1	Selected Value(s)		Resulting AutoFill Series								
2											
3	1/1/00	2/1/00	3/1/00	4/1/00	5/1/00	6/1/00	7/1/00				
4	1/1/00	3/1/00	5/1/00	7/1/00	9/1/00	11/1/00	1/1/01				
5	1-Jan	2-Jan	3-Jan	4-Jan	5-Jan	6-Jan	7-Jan				
6	Dec-00	Dec-01	Dec-02	Dec-03	Dec-04	Dec-05	Dec-06				
7	Dec-00	Dec-02	Dec-04	Dec-06	Dec-08	Dec-10	Dec-12				
8											
9											
10	1/1/2000	1/2/2000	1/3/2000	1/4/2000	1/5/2000	1/6/2000	1/7/2000				
11	Qtr 1	Qtr 2	Qtr 3	Qtr 4	Qtr 1	Qtr 2	Qtr 3				
12	Jan	Feb	Mar	Apr	May	Jun	Jul				
13	January	February	March	April	May	June	July				
14	Day 1	Day 2	Day 3	Day 4	Day 5	Day 6	Day 7				
15	Mon	Tue	Wed	Thu	Fri	Sat	Sun				
16											

Row 3 contains a common one-month date series, and row 4 contains a bimonthly series created using 1/1/00 and 3/1/00 as starting values. Rows 5 and 6 illustrate different formats and increments, and row 7 contains an every-other-year series.

? SEE ALSO

For more information about AutoFill, see "Filling and Creating Series with the Mouse," page 241.

The examples in rows 10 through 15 in Figure 13-3 show how even a single cell can provide enough information for AutoFill to determine a series. When you use the fill handle on single-cell values like the ones in rows 10 through 15, Excel assumes you want to increment the numeric value in each cell. (If you want to copy the cell instead, hold down Ctrl while dragging the fill handle.) Notice, however, that the entries in rows 11 through 15 contain text values. AutoFill recognizes text entries for days and months and extends them as if they were numeric values. In addition, when a cell contains a mixed text and numeric entry, AutoFill automatically copies the text portion (if it is not the name of a month or day). AutoFill also increments the numeric portion if it occurs at either end of the entry (but not in the middle). The results are shown in rows 11 and 14 of Figure 13-3.

As you drag the fill handle, notice the small yellow screen tip box that appears near the cursor (as shown in Figure 13-4 on the next page) displaying the values that each cell will contain when you release the mouse button.

There is one more timesaving AutoFill trick you'll want to know: drag the fill handle by clicking the *right* mouse button. When you do this, a shortcut menu appears when you release the mouse button, as shown in Figure 13-4.

III

Analyzing Data

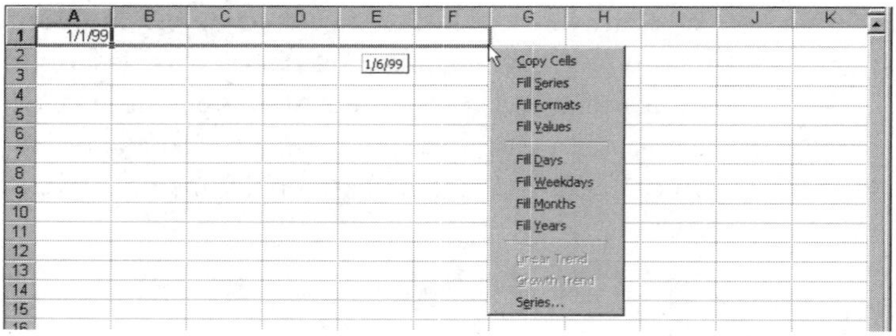

FIGURE 13-4.

Drag the fill handle by clicking the right mouse button to display a shortcut menu.

The shortcut menu appears before any fill action is consummated, allowing you to select one of the commands that will then be applied to your fill operation. If what you want to do is not represented on the menu, this right-drag technique also happens to be the easiest way to display the Fill Series dialog box—just click the Series command at the bottom of the shortcut menu.

Formatting Dates and Times

After you enter a date, you can use the Cells command on the Format menu to change its format. The following table shows how the date February 24, 2000, looks in the first five built-in Date formats:

Format	Display
m/d	2/24
m/d/yy	2/24/00
mm/dd/yy	02/24/00
d-mmm	24-Feb
d-mmm-yy	24-Feb-00

To assign a Date format to a cell, follow these steps:

1 Select the cell you want to format.

2 From the Format menu, choose Cells (or press Ctrl+1) and then click the Number tab of the Format Cells dialog box shown in Figure 13-5.

FIGURE 13-5.

Use the Number tab of the Format Cells dialog box to apply Date formats to cells.

3 Select the Date category.

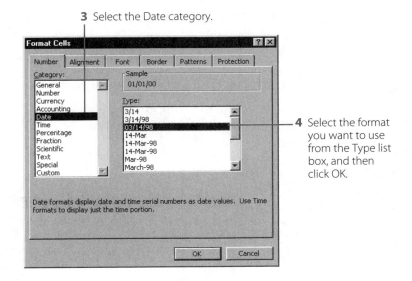

4 Select the format you want to use from the Type list box, and then click OK.

Similarly, you can change the format of a time entry. The following table shows the results of formatting the entry 13:52:32.44 using the first eight Time formats:

Format	Display
h:mm	13:52
h:mm PM	1:52 PM
h:mm:ss	13:52:32
h:mm:ss PM	1:52:32 PM
mm:ss.0	52:32.4
[h]:mm:ss	13:52:32
m/d/yy h:mm PM	1/0/00 1:52 PM
m/d/yy h:mm	1/0/00 13:52

 SEE ALSO

For more information about the [h]:mm:ss format, see "Measuring Elapsed Time," page 471.

Notice that some formats use the traditional 12-hour time convention and other formats use the 24-hour time convention. In addition, the last two formats display the date as 1/0/00 because the entry does not include a date.

III

Analyzing Data

The fifth format (mm:ss.0) displays only minutes and seconds, allowing you to measure times to a decimal fraction of a second.

To assign a Time format to a cell, follow these steps:

1 Select the cell you want to format.

2 From the Format menu, choose Cells (or press Ctrl+1) and then click the Number tab in the Format Cells dialog box shown in Figure 13-6.

FIGURE 13-6.

Use the Cells command on the Format menu to apply Time formats to cells.

3 Select the Time category.

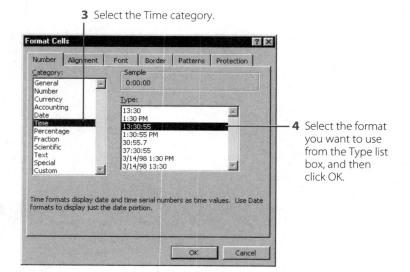

4 Select the format you want to use from the Type list box, and then click OK.

Combining Date and Time Formats

In addition to the built-in formats that display dates and times, the combined format—m/d/yy h:mm—displays the date and time in one cell. For example, if a cell contains the serial value 36355.625 and you apply the m/d/yy h:mm PM format to that entry, the date and time display as 7/14/99 3:00 PM.

When you enter a combination date and time in format, you can type either *7/14/99 3:00* or *3:00 7-14-99*. In the formula bar, 7/14/99 3:00 is displayed as 7/14/1999 3:00:00 AM because the value for seconds and the AM or PM designation are part of the underlying value of dates and times.

Creating Your Own Date and Time Formats

To supplement the standard Date and Time formats, you can create custom formats. The general technique is the same as the technique for creating custom numeric formats.

For example, to create a format that displays a date in the most complete form, so that the date entry July 14, 2000, appears as Monday, July 14, 2000, follow these steps:

1 Select the cell that contains the date.

2 From the Format menu, choose Cells (or press Ctrl+1) and then click the Number tab.

3 Select the Custom category.

4 Highlight the entry in the Type edit box and then type your custom format—in this case, *dddd mmmm d, yyyy*.

5 Click OK. Excel stores the new format in the Type list box for the Custom category and then displays the date with the new format in the selected cell.

You can use the same technique to display only a portion of a date or a time. For example, if you enter the format *mmmm*, Excel displays the date July 14, 2000, as the word *July*.

? SEE ALSO

For more information about custom formats, see "Creating Custom Numeric Formats," page 170.

After you add a custom date or time format to the Type list box, you can apply it to any date or time entry. Simply select the cell that contains the entry, choose the Cells command from the Format menu (or press Ctrl+1), click the Number tab, select the Custom category, select the format from the Type list box, and then click OK to apply the format.

The table on the next page shows the formatting codes you can use to create custom date and time formats. Keep in mind two points. First, when you enter the code *m* immediately after an *h* or the code *mm* immediately after an *hh*, Excel displays minutes instead of months; otherwise, Excel assumes that *m* means months. Second, if you include one of the codes AM/PM, am/pm, A/P, or a/p in a time format, Excel uses the 12-hour time convention; if you omit these codes, Excel uses the 24-hour time convention.

III

Analyzing Data

Code	Display
General	Number in General (serial value) format
d	Day number without leading zero (1–31)
dd	Day number with leading zero (01–31)
ddd	Day-of-week abbreviation (Sun–Sat)
dddd	Day-of-week name (Sunday–Saturday)
m	Month number without leading zero (1–12)
mm	Month number with leading zero (01–12)
mmm	Month name abbreviation (Jan–Dec)
mmmm	Complete month name (January–December)
yy	Last two digits of year number (00–99)
yyyy	Entire year number (1900–2078)
h	Hour without leading zero (0–23)
hh	Hour with leading zero (00–23)
m	Minute without leading zero (0–59)
mm	Minute with leading zero (00–59)
s	Second without leading zero (0–59)
ss	Second with leading zero (00–59)
s.0	Second and tenth of second without leading zero
s.00	Second and hundredth of second without leading zero
ss.0	Second and tenth of second with leading zero
ss.00	Second and hundredth of second with leading zero
AM/PM	Time in AM/PM notation
am/pm	Time in am/pm notation
A/P	Time in A/P notation
a/p	Time in a/p notation
[ ]	When used to enclose a time code, as in [h], displays the absolute elapsed time; allows you to display more than 24 hours, 60 minutes, or 60 seconds.

Measuring Elapsed Time

The brackets listed at the bottom of the table deserve some special discussion. You can enclose time codes in brackets to display more than 24 hours, more than 60 minutes, or more than 60 seconds in a time value. The brackets must always appear around the first code in the format. Excel provides one built-in elapsed time code, [h]:mm:ss, in the Custom category of the Format Cells dialog box. Other valid bracketed time codes are

[mm]:ss

[ss]

Bracketed codes have no effect if used in any other position than first. For example, the code h:[mm]:ss simply indicates the normal h:mm:ss format.

Suppose you want to determine the elapsed time between two dates and you enter the following in cells A1, A2, and A3, respectively:

11/23/00 13:32

11/25/00 23:59

=A2-A1

If you apply the built-in format [h]:mm:ss (found on the Number tab Custom list) to cell A3, the result of the formula in that cell is 58:27:00, the elapsed time between the two dates. If you apply the standard h:mm:ss format to cell A3 instead, the result is 10:27:00, the difference in the times, without regard to the difference in dates. The [h]:mm:ss format is also available in the Time category.

Using Date and Time Arithmetic

After you enter a date, you can use it in formulas and functions as you would any other value. Suppose you want to calculate the date 200 days after July 4, 2000. If cell A1 contains the entry 7/4/00, you can use the formula

=A1+200

to compute the date 200 days later, which is 36911, or 1/20/01.

As another example, suppose you want to find the number of weeks between October 31, 1999, and May 13, 2000. Use the formula

=(("5/13/00")-("10/31/99"))/7

which results in approximately 27.9 (weeks).

You can use times in formulas and functions just as you can use dates. However, the results of time arithmetic are not as easy to understand as the results of date arithmetic. For example, you can determine how much time has elapsed between 8:22 AM and 10:45 PM with this formula

="22:45"-"8:22"

The result is .599306, which can be formatted as 2:23 PM. Excel displays the result in relation to 12 midnight; therefore, 2:23 PM indicates that there are 14 hours and 23 minutes between the two times.

Suppose you want to determine the time that is 2 hours, 23 minutes, and 17 seconds after 12:35:23 PM. The formula

=("12:35:23 PM")+("2:23:17")

returns the correct answer: .624074, which can be formatted as 2:58 PM. In this formula, 2:23:17 represents not an absolute time (2:23:17 AM) but an interval of time (2 hours, 23 minutes, and 17 seconds). This format is perfectly acceptable to Excel.

> Excel's default format doesn't display the seconds, but the time's full value—
> 0.624074074074074—includes them.

Date and Time Functions

For more information about using dates and times in formulas and functions, see "Using Date and Time Arithmetic," page 471.

Excel's date and time functions let you perform worksheet calculations quickly and accurately. For example, if you use your worksheet to calculate your company's monthly payroll, you might use the HOUR function to determine the number of hours worked each day and the WEEKDAY function to determine whether employees should be paid at the standard rate (for Monday through Friday) or at the overtime rate (for Saturdays and Sundays). In this section we'll discuss in detail a few (but not all) of Excel's date and time functions.

The TODAY Function

The TODAY function always returns the serial value of the current date. The TODAY function takes the form

=TODAY( )

Although this function takes no argument, you must remember to include the empty parentheses.

Use this function when you want a cell on your worksheet to always reflect the current date.

The NOW Function

You can use the NOW function to enter the current date and time in a cell. This function takes the form

=NOW( )

Like the TODAY function, the NOW function has no argument. The result of the function is a serial date and time value that includes an integer (the date) and a decimal value (the time). For example, if today is July 21, 2000, and the time is 11:45 AM, the NOW function returns the value 36728.48958.

Excel doesn't update the value of NOW continuously. If the value of a cell that contains the NOW function is not current, you can update the value by recalculating the worksheet. (You calculate the worksheet by making an entry, by clicking the Calc Now button on the Calculation tab of the Options dialog box on the Tools menu, or by pressing F9 or Ctrl+=.) Excel also updates the NOW function whenever you open the worksheet.

⊘ SEE ALSO

For more information about the RAND function, see "The RAND and RANDBETWEEN Functions," page 425.

The NOW function is an example of a *volatile* function; that is, a function whose calculated value is subject to change. If you open a worksheet that contains one or more NOW functions and then immediately close the worksheet, Excel prompts you to save your changes even though you haven't made any, because the current value of NOW has changed since the last time you used the worksheet. (Another example of a volatile function is RAND.)

The WEEKDAY Function

The WEEKDAY function returns the day of the week for a specific date and takes the form

=WEEKDAY(serial_number,return_type)

The *serial_number* argument can be a serial date value, a reference to a cell that contains either a date function or a serial date value, or text, such as 1/27/00 or January 27, 2000. If you use text, be sure to enclose it in quotation marks.

The WEEKDAY function returns a number that represents the day of the week that the specified date falls on. The optional *return_type* argument determines the way the result is represented. If *return_type* is 1 or omitted, the function returns a number from 1 through 7 where 1 is Sunday and 7 is Saturday. If *return_type* is 2, the function returns a number from 1 through 7 where 1 is Monday and 7 is Sunday. If *return_type* is 3, the function returns a number from 0 through 6 where 0 is Monday and 6 is Sunday.

TIP

You might want to format a cell containing the WEEKDAY function with a custom day-of-week format, such as dddd. This formatting lets you use the result of the WEEKDAY function in other functions and still have a meaningful display on the screen.

The YEAR, MONTH, and DAY Functions

The YEAR, MONTH, and DAY functions return the value of the year, month, and day portions of a serial date/time value. These functions take the form

    =YEAR(serial_number)

and

    =MONTH(serial_number)

and

    =DAY(serial_number)

The *serial_number* argument can be a serial date value, a reference to a cell that contains either a date function or a serial date value, or a text date enclosed in quotation marks.

The result of these functions is the value of the corresponding part of the specified *serial_number* argument. For example, if cell A1 contains the date

    3/25/2000

the formula

    =YEAR(A1)

returns the value 2000, the formula

    =MONTH(A1)

returns the value 3, and the formula

    =DAY(A1)

returns the value 25.

The HOUR, MINUTE, and SECOND Functions

Just as the YEAR, MONTH, and DAY functions let you extract the year, month, and day portions of a serial date/time value, the HOUR,

MINUTE, and SECOND functions extract the hour, minute, and second portions of a serial date/time value. These functions take the form

=HOUR(serial_number)

and

=MINUTE(serial_number)

and

=SECOND(serial_number)

The result of these functions is the value of the corresponding part of the specified *serial_number* argument. For example, if cell B1 contains the time

12:15:35 PM

the formula

=HOUR(B1)

returns the value 12, the formula

=MINUTE(B1)

returns the value 15, and the formula

=SECOND(B1)

returns the value 35.

The DATEVALUE and TIMEVALUE Functions

Excel's DATEVALUE function translates a date into a serial value. It is similar to the DATE function, except that you must enter a text argument. The DATEVALUE function takes the form

=DATEVALUE(*date_text*)

The *date_text* argument represents any date from January 1, 1900 on, in any of Excel's built-in Date formats. (You must add quotation marks around the text.) For example, the formula

=DATEVALUE("December 31, 2345")

returns the serial value 162899. If you enter *date_text* without a year, Excel uses the current year from your computer's internal clock.

The TIMEVALUE function translates a time into a decimal value. It is similar to the TIME function, except that you must enter a text argument. The TIMEVALUE function takes the form

=TIMEVALUE(*time_text*)

III

Analyzing Data

The *time_text* argument represents a time in any of Excel's built-in Time formats. (You must add quotation marks around the text.) For example, if you enter

=TIMEVALUE("4:30 PM")

the function returns the decimal value 0.6875.

Specialized Date Functions

? SEE ALSO

For more information about the Analysis ToolPak, see "Accessing the Analysis ToolPak," page 502.

A set of specialized date functions performs such operations as calculations for the maturity dates of securities, for payroll, and for work schedules. The functions described in this section are available only when you install the Analysis ToolPak add-in.

The EDATE and EOMONTH Functions

You use the EDATE function to calculate the exact date that falls an indicated number of months before or after a given date. This function takes the form

=EDATE(start_date,months)

The *start_date* argument is the date you want to calculate from, and *months* is an integer value that indicates the number of months before or after the start date. If the *months* argument is positive, the EDATE function returns a date after the start date; if the *months* argument is negative, the function returns a date before the start date.

For example, to find the date that falls exactly 23 months after June 12, 1999, enter the formula

=EDATE("6/12/99", 23)

which returns the value 37023, or May 12, 2001.

The EOMONTH function returns a date that is an indicated number of months before or after a given date. EOMONTH is similar to EDATE, except that the value returned is always the last day of the month. The EOMONTH function takes the form

=EOMONTH(start_date,months)

For example, to calculate the serial date value that is the last day of the month and 23 months after June 12, 1999, enter the formula

=EOMONTH("6/12/99", 23)

which returns 36311, or May 31, 2001.

The YEARFRAC Function

The YEARFRAC function calculates a decimal number that represents the portion of a year that falls between two given dates. This function takes the form

=YEARFRAC(start_date,end_date,basis)

The *start_date* and *end_date* arguments specify the period of time you want to convert to a fractional year. *Basis* is the type of day count you want to use. A *basis* argument of 0 (or omitted) indicates a basis of 30/360, or 30 days per month and 360 days per year, as established in the United States by the National Association of Security Dealers (NASD). A basis of 1 indicates actual/actual, or the actual number of days in the month(s)/actual days in the year. Similarly, a basis of 2 indicates actual/360, and a basis of 3 indicates actual/365. A basis of 4 indicates the European method of determining the basis, which also uses 30 days per month/360 days per year.

For example, to determine the fraction of a year that falls between 4/12/00 and 12/15/00, enter the formula

=YEARFRAC("4/12/00", "12/15/00")

which returns 0.675, based on the default 30-day month and 360-day year.

The WORKDAY and NETWORKDAYS Functions

The WORKDAY and NETWORKDAYS functions are invaluable for anyone who calculates payroll and benefits or determines work schedules. Both functions return values that are based on working days only, excluding weekend days. In addition, you can choose whether to include holidays and specify the exact dates.

The WORKDAY function returns the date that is exactly the indicated number of working days before or after a given date. This function takes the form

=WORKDAY(start_date,days,holidays)

The *start_date* argument is the date you want the function to count from, and *days* is the number of workdays before or after the start date, excluding weekends and holidays. Use a positive value for days to count forward from the start date; use a negative value to count backward. For example, to determine the date that is 100 working days from the current date, use the formula

=WORKDAY(NOW( ),100)

The optional *holidays* argument can be an array or a reference to a cell range that contains the dates you want to exclude from the calculation. Simply enter any dates that you want to exclude in the array or range specified as this argument. If you leave *holidays* blank, the function counts all weekdays from the start date.

Similarly, the NETWORKDAYS function calculates the number of working days between two given dates. This function takes the form

=NETWORKDAYS(start_date,end_date,holidays)

The *end_date* argument is the last date you want to include in the range. Again, you can choose to exclude *holidays*. For example, to determine the number of working days (*holidays* included) between January 15, 2000, and June 30, 2000, use the formula

=NETWORKDAYS("1/15/00", "6/30/00")

which results in a value of 120.

Financial Analysis

T he Microsoft Excel 2000 financial functions allow you to perform common business calculations, such as net present value and future value, without building long and complex formulas. For example, suppose you're considering a real estate purchase and want to calculate the net present value of the purchase price to determine whether the investment is worthwhile. You've already entered the payment amounts into the cells in the range A1:D1. To find this value without using functions, you would have to build a formula similar to this one:

=(A1/(1+.08))+(B1/(1+.08)^2)+(C1/(1+.08)^3)+ (D1/(1+.08)^4)

Using the NPV function, you can perform the same calculation with only 15 keystrokes:

=NPV(.08,A1:D1)

> Many of the financial functions discussed in this chapter are supplied with the Analysis ToolPak add-in. *For information about accessing the Analysis ToolPak add-in, see "Accessing the Analysis ToolPak," page 502.*

Functions for Calculating Investments

Most financial functions accept similar arguments. To streamline this section, we'll define the common arguments in the following table and explain any differences in how they are used in the individual function descriptions. Another list of common arguments accompanies the section on depreciation, on page 488.

Argument	Description
future value	Value of investment at end of term (0 if omitted)
inflow 1, inflow 2, ..., inflow n	Periodic payments when individual amounts differ
number of periods	Term of investment
payment	Periodic payments when individual amounts are the same
type	When payment is to be made (0 if omitted) 0 = at end of period 1 = at beginning of period
period	Number of an individual periodic payment
present value	Value of investment today
rate	Discount rate or interest rate

The PV Function

Present value is one of the most common methods for measuring the attractiveness of a long-term investment. Basically, Present Value is today's value of the investment. It is determined by discounting the inflows (payments received) from the investment back to the present time. If the present value of the inflows is greater than the cost of the investment, the investment is a good one.

The PV function computes the present value of a series of equal periodic payments or of a lump-sum payment. (A stream of constant payments is often called an ordinary annuity.) This function takes the form

=PV(rate,number of periods,payment,future value,type)

For definitions of these arguments, see the preceding table. To compute the present value of a series of payments, use *payment*, and to compute the present value of a lump-sum payment, use *future value*. For an investment with both a series of payments and a lump-sum payment, you use both arguments.

Suppose you are presented with an investment opportunity that returns $1,000 each year over the next five years. To receive this annuity, you must invest $4,000. Are you willing to pay $4,000 today to earn $5,000 over the next five years? To decide whether this investment is acceptable, you need to determine the present value of the stream of $1,000 payments you will receive.

Assuming that you could invest your money in a money-market account at 4.5 percent, we'll use 4.5 percent as the discount rate of the investment. (Because this discount rate is a sort of "hurdle" over which an investment must leap before it becomes attractive to you, it is often called the *hurdle rate*.) To determine the present value of this investment, use the formula

=PV(4.5%,5,1000)

This formula uses a *payment* argument, has no *future value* argument, and has no *type* argument, indicating that payments occur at the end of the period (the default). This formula returns the value -4389.98, meaning that you should be willing to spend $4,389.98 now to receive $5,000 over the next five years. Because your investment is only $4,000, you decide that this is an acceptable investment.

Now suppose you're offered $5,000 at the end of five years, rather than $1,000 for each of the next five years. Is the investment still as attractive? To find out, use the formula

=PV(4.5%,5,,5000)

You must include a comma as a placeholder for the unused *payment* argument so Excel knows that 5000 is a *future value* argument. Again, no *type* argument is used. This formula returns the present value -4012.26, which means that, at a hurdle rate of 4.5 percent, you should be willing to spend $4,012.26 to receive $5,000 in five years. Although the proposal is not as attractive under these terms, it is still acceptable because your investment is only $4,000.

III

Analyzing Data

The NPV Function

Net present value is another common method for determining the profitability of an investment. In general, any investment that yields a net present value greater than zero is considered profitable. This function takes the form

=NPV(rate,inflow 1,inflow 2,...,inflow 29)

For definitions of these arguments, see the table on page 480. As many as 29 *inflow* values are allowed as arguments. (Any number of values can be plugged into the formula by using an array as an argument.)

NPV differs from PV in two important respects. Whereas PV assumes constant *inflow* values, NPV allows variable payments. The other major difference is that PV allows payments and receipts to occur at either the beginning or end of the period, whereas NPV assumes that all payments and receipts are evenly distributed and occur at the end of the period. If the cost of the investment must be paid up front, you should not include the cost as one of the function's *inflow* arguments but should subtract it from the result of the function. On the other hand, if the cost must be paid at the end of the first period, you should include it as a negative first inflow argument. Let's consider an example to help clarify this distinction.

Suppose you are contemplating an investment on which you expect to incur a loss of $55,000 at the end of the first year, followed by gains of $95,000, $140,000, and $185,000 at the ends of the second, third, and fourth years. You will invest $250,000 up front, and the hurdle rate is 12 percent. To evaluate this investment, use the formula

=NPV(12.,-55000,95000,140000,185000) - 250000

 SEE ALSO

For more information about the Goal Seek command, see "The Goal Seek Command," page 556.

The result, -6153.65, tells you not to expect a net profit from this investment. Note that the negative values in this formula indicate the money you spend on your investment. (To determine what initial cost or interest rate would justify the investment, you can use the Goal Seek command.)

This formula does not include the up-front cost of the investment as an argument for the NPV function. However, if you make the initial $250,000 investment at the end of the first year, the formula is

=NPV(12%,(-250000-55000),95000,140000,185000)

The result, $20,632.07, would suggest that this might be a profitable investment.

The FV Function

Future value is essentially the opposite of present value, and the FV function computes the value at some future date of an investment that makes payments as a lump sum or as a series of equal periodic payments. This function takes the form

=FV(rate,number of periods,payment,present value,type)

For definitions of these arguments, see the table on page 480. You use *payment* to compute the future value of a series of payments and *present value* to compute the future value of a lump-sum payment.

Suppose you're thinking about starting an IRA. You plan to deposit $2,000 in the IRA at the beginning of each year, and you expect the average rate of return to be 11 percent per year for the entire term. Assuming you're now 30 years old, how much money will your account accumulate by the time you're 65? Use the formula

=FV(11%,35,-2000,,1)

to learn that your IRA balance will be $758,328.81 at the end of 35 years.

Now assume that you started an IRA account three years ago and have already accumulated $7,500 in your account. Use the formula

=FV(11%,35,-2000,-7500,1)

to learn that your IRA will grow to $1,047,640.19 at the end of 35 years.

In both of these examples, the *type* argument is 1 because payments occur at the beginning of the period. Including this argument is particularly important in financial calculations that span many years. If you omit the *type* argument in the formula above, Excel assumes that you add money to your account at the end of each year and returns the value $972,490.49—a difference of more than $75,000!

The PMT Function

The PMT function computes the periodic payment required to amortize a loan over a specified number of periods. This function takes the form

=PMT(rate,number of periods,present value,future value,type)

Suppose you want to take out a 25-year mortgage for $100,000. Assuming an interest rate of 8 percent, what will your monthly

 SEE ALSO

For definitions of these arguments, see the table on page 480.

III

Analyzing Data

payments be? First divide the 8-percent interest rate by 12 to arrive at a monthly rate (approximately 0.67 percent). Next convert the number of periods into months by multiplying 25 by 12 (300). Now plug the monthly rate, number of periods, and loan amount into the PMT formula

=PMT(0.67%,300,100000)

to compute the monthly mortgage payment, which turns out to be -$774.47. (The result is negative because it is a cost to you.)

Because 0.67 percent is an approximation, you could use the formula

=PMT((8/12)%,300,100000)

for a more accurate result. This formula returns -$771.82.

The IPMT Function

The IPMT function computes the interest part of the payment required to repay an amount over a specified time period, with constant periodic payments and a constant interest rate. This function takes the form

=IPMT(rate,period,number of periods,present value,future value,type)

For definitions of these arguments, see the table on page 480.

As in the previous example, suppose you borrow $100,000 for 25 years at 8 percent interest. The formula

=IPMT((8/12)%,1,300,100000)

tells you that the interest component of the payment due for the first month is -$666.67. The formula

=IPMT((8/12)%,300,300,100000)

tells you that the interest component of the final payment of the same loan is -$5.11.

The PPMT Function

The PPMT function is similar to the IPMT function, except that it computes the principal component of the payment when a loan is repaid over a specified time period with constant periodic payments and a constant interest rate. If you compute both IPMT and PPMT for the same period, you can add the results to obtain the total payment. The PPMT function takes the form

=PPMT(rate,period,number of periods,present value,future value,type)

For definitions of these arguments, see the table on page 480.

Again suppose you borrow $100,000 for 25 years at 8 percent interest. The formula

=PPMT((8/12)%,1,300,100000)

tells you that the principal component of the payment for the first month of the loan is -$105.15. The formula

=PPMT((8/12)%,300,300,100000)

tells you that the principal component of the final payment of the same loan is -$766.70.

The NPER Function

The NPER function computes the number of periods required to amortize a loan, given a specified periodic payment. This function takes the form

=NPER(rate,payment,present value,future value,type)

For definitions of these arguments, see the table on page 480.

Suppose you can afford mortgage payments of $1,000 per month and you want to know how long it will take to pay off a $100,000 loan at 8 percent interest. The formula

=NPER((8/12)%,-1000,100000)

tells you that your mortgage payments will extend over 165.34 months.

If the payment argument is too small to amortize the loan at the indicated rate of interest, the function returns an error value. The monthly payment must at least be equal to the period interest rate times the principal amount; otherwise, the loan will never be amortized. For example, the formula

=NPER((8/12)%,-600,100000)

returns the #NUM! error value. In this case, the monthly payment must be at least $666.67 (or $100,000 * (8/12)%) to amortize the loan.

Functions for Calculating the Rate of Return

The RATE, IRR, and MIRR functions compute the continuously paid rates of return on investments.

The RATE Function

The RATE function lets you determine the rate of return of an investment that generates a series of equal periodic payments or a single lump-sum payment. This function takes the form

    =RATE(number of periods,payment,present value,future
    value,type,guess)

For definitions of these arguments, see the table on page 480. You use *payment* to compute the rate for a series of equal periodic payments and *future value* to compute the rate of a lump-sum payment. The *guess* argument, which like *type* is optional, gives Excel a starting place for calculating the rate. If you omit the *guess* argument, Excel begins with a guess of 0.1 (10 percent).

Suppose you're considering an investment that will pay you five annual $1,000 payments. The investment costs $3,000. To determine the actual annual rate of return on your investment, use the formula

    =RATE(5,1000,-3000)

This formula returns 20 percent, the rate of return on this investment. The exact value returned is 0.198577098, but because the answer is a percent, Excel formats the cell as a percent.

The RATE function uses an iterative process to compute the rate of return. The function begins by computing the net present value of the investment at the *guess* rate. If that first net present value is greater than zero, the function selects a higher rate and repeats the net present value calculation; if the first net present value is less than zero, the function selects a lower rate for the second iteration. RATE continues this process until it arrives at the correct rate of return or until it has gone through 20 iterations.

If you receive the #NUM! error value when you enter the RATE function, Excel probably cannot calculate the rate within 20 iterations. Try entering a different *guess* rate to give the function a running start. A rate between 10 percent and 100 percent usually works.

The IRR Function

The internal rate of return of an investment is the rate that causes the net present value of the investment to equal zero. In other words, the internal rate of return is the rate that causes the present value of the inflows from an investment to exactly equal the cost of the investment.

Internal rate of return, like net present value, is used to compare one investment opportunity with another. An attractive investment is one whose net present value, discounted at the appropriate hurdle rate, is greater than zero. Turn that equation around and you can see that the discount rate required to generate a net present value of zero must be greater than the hurdle rate. Thus, an attractive investment is one for which the discount rate required to yield a net present value of zero—that is, the internal rate of return—is greater than the hurdle rate.

The IRR function is closely related to the RATE function. The difference between RATE and IRR is similar to the difference between the PV and NPV functions. Like NPV, IRR accounts for investment costs and unequal payments. The IRR function takes the form

=IRR(values,guess)

The *values* argument is an array or a reference to a range of cells that contain numbers. Only one *values* argument is allowed, and it must include at least one positive and one negative value. IRR ignores text, logical values, and blank cells. IRR assumes that transactions occur at the end of a period and returns the equivalent interest rate for that period's length.

As with RATE, the *guess* argument gives Excel a starting place for its calculations and is optional. If you receive the #NUM! error value when you enter an IRR function, include a *guess* argument in the function to help Excel reach the answer.

Suppose you agree to buy a condominium for $120,000. Over the next five years, you expect to receive $25,000, $27,000, $35,000, $38,000, and $40,000 in net rental income. You can set up a simple worksheet that contains your investment and income information. Enter the six values into cells A1:A6 of the worksheet. (Be sure to enter the initial $120,000 investment as a negative value.) Then the formula

=IRR(A1:A6)

returns the internal rate of return of 11 percent. If the hurdle rate is 10 percent, you can consider this condominium purchase a good investment.

III

Analyzing Data

The MIRR Function

The MIRR function is similar to IRR in that it calculates the rate of return of an investment: the modified internal rate of return. The difference is that MIRR takes into account the cost of the money you borrow to finance the investment and assumes that you'll reinvest the cash it generates. MIRR assumes that transactions occur at the end of a period and returns the equivalent interest rate for that period's length. The MIRR function takes the form

=MIRR(values,finance rate,reinvestment rate)

The *values* argument must be an array or a reference to a range of cells that contain numbers, and it represents a series of payments and income occurring at regular periods. You must include at least one positive and one negative value in the values argument. The *finance rate* argument is the rate at which you borrow the money you need for the investment. The *reinvestment rate* argument is the rate at which you reinvest the cash.

Continuing with the example from the IRR function, use the formula

=MIRR(A1:A6,10%,8%)

to calculate a modified internal rate of return of 10 percent, assuming a cost of funds rate of 10 percent and a reinvestment rate of 8 percent.

Functions for Calculating Depreciation

Five functions help you determine the depreciation of an asset for a specific period: the SLN, DDB, DB, VDB, and SYD functions. The following table lists four arguments commonly used in these functions:

Argument	Description
cost	Initial cost of asset
life	Length of time asset will be depreciated
period	Individual time period to be computed
salvage	Asset's remaining value after it has been fully depreciated

The SLN Function

The SLN function lets you determine the straight-line depreciation for an asset for a single period. The straight-line depreciation method assumes that depreciation is uniform throughout the useful life of the asset. The cost or basis of the asset, less its estimated salvage value, is deductible in equal amounts over the life of the asset. This function takes the form

=SLN(cost,salvage,life)

Suppose you want to depreciate a machine that costs $8,000 new and has a life of ten years and a salvage value of $500. The formula

=SLN(8000,500,10)

tells you that each year's straight-line depreciation is $750.

The DDB and DB Functions

The DDB function computes an asset's depreciation using the double-declining balance method, which returns depreciation at an accelerated rate—more in the early periods and less later. Using this method, depreciation is computed as a percentage of the net book value of the asset (the cost of the asset less any prior years' depreciation). The function takes the form

=DDB(cost,salvage,life,period, factor)

For definitions of the first four arguments, see the table on page 488. All DDB arguments must be positive numbers, and you must use the same time units for *life* and *period*; that is, if you express *life* in months, *period* must also be in months. The *factor* argument is optional and has a default value of 2, which indicates the normal double-declining balance method. Using 3 for the *factor* argument specifies the triple-declining balance method.

Suppose you want to depreciate a machine that costs $5,000 new and that has a life of five years (60 months) and a salvage value of $100. The formula

=DDB(5000,100,60,1)

tells you that the double-declining balance depreciation for the first month is $166.67. The formula

=DDB(5000,100,5,1)

tells you that the double-declining balance depreciation for the first year is $2,000.00. The formula

=DDB(5000,100,5,5)

computes the double-declining balance depreciation for the last year as $259.20.

The DB function is similar to the DDB function except it uses the fixed declining balance method of depreciation and can calculate depreciation for a particular period in the asset's life. It takes the form

=DB(cost,salvage,life,period,month)

For definitions of the first four arguments, see the table on page 488. The *life* and *period* arguments must use the same units. The *month* argument is the number of months in the first year. If you omit this argument, Excel assumes *month* to be 12, a full year. For example, to calculate the real depreciation for the first period on a $1,000,000 item with a salvage value of $100,000, a life of six years, and seven months in the first year, use the formula

=DB(1000000,100000,6,1,7)

which returns $186,083.33.

The VDB Function

The VDB function calculates the depreciation of an asset for any complete or partial period, using either the double-declining balance or another accelerated-depreciation factor that you specify. (VDB stands for *variable declining balance*.) This function takes the form

=VDB(cost,salvage,life,start,end,factor,no switch)

For definitions of the first three arguments, see the table on page 488. The *start* argument is the period after which depreciation will be calculated, and *end* is the last period for which depreciation will be calculated. These arguments let you determine the depreciation for any length of time during the life of the asset. The *life*, *start*, and *end* arguments must all use the same units (days, months, years, and so on). The *factor* argument is the rate at which the balance declines. The *no switch* argument is a value that specifies whether to switch to straight-line depreciation when the straight-line depreciation is greater than the declining balance.

The last two arguments are optional. If you omit *factor*, Excel assumes that the argument is 2 and uses the double-declining balance method. If you omit *no switch* or set it to 0 (FALSE), Excel switches to straight-line depreciation when the depreciation is greater than the declining balance. To prevent Excel from making this switch, specify a *no switch* value of 1 (TRUE).

Suppose you purchased a $15,000 asset at the end of the first quarter of the current year and that this asset will have a salvage value of $2,000 after five years. To determine the depreciation of this asset next year (the fourth to seventh quarters of its use), use the formula

>   =VDB(15000,2000,20,3,7)

The depreciation for this period is $3,760.55. The units used here are quarters. Notice that the *start* argument is 3, not 4, since we are jumping over the first three periods to start in the fourth. This formula does not include a *factor* argument, so Excel calculates the depreciation using the double-declining balance method. To determine the depreciation for the same period using a factor of 1.5, use the formula

>   =VDB(15000,2000,20,3,7,1.5)

With this rate, the depreciation for the same period is $3,180.52.

The SYD Function

The SYD function computes an asset's depreciation for a specific time period with the sum-of-the-years'-digits method. Using the sum-of-the-years'-digits method, depreciation is calculated on the cost of the item less its salvage value. Like the double-declining balance method, the sum-of-the-years'-digits method is an accelerated depreciation method. The SYD function takes the form

>   =SYD(cost,salvage,life,period)

For definitions of these arguments, see the table on page 488. You must use the same units for *life* and *period*.

Suppose you want to depreciate a machine that costs $15,000 and has a life of three years and a salvage value of $1,250. The formula

>   =SYD(15000,1250,3,1)

tells you that the sum-of-the-years'-digits depreciation for the first year is $6,875. The formula

>   =SYD(15000,1250,3,3)

tells you that the sum-of-the-years'-digits depreciation for the third year is $2,291.67.

Functions for Analyzing Securities

Excel offers a group of functions designed for specific tasks relating to the computation and analysis of various types of securities. All of these functions are part of the Analysis ToolPak. If these functions are not available, you have not installed the Analysis ToolPak add-in. To install this add-in, choose the Add-Ins command from the Tools menu, select Analysis ToolPak from the Add-Ins Available list box, and then click OK. If this option is not listed, you will need to run the Microsoft Excel Setup program again to add the ToolPak.

III

Analyzing Data

Many of these functions share similar arguments. We'll describe the most common ones in the table below, to avoid revisiting the same information in the function discussions that follow.

Argument	Description
basis	Day count basis of the security. If omitted, defaults to 0, indicating US (NASD) 30/360 basis. Other basis values: 1 = actual/actual 2 = actual/360 3 = actual/365 4 = European 30/360
frequency	Number of coupon payments made per year: 1 = annual 2 = semiannual 4 = quarterly
investment	Amount of investment in the security
issue	Issue date of the security
maturity	Maturity date of the security
par	Par value of the security; $1000 if omitted
price	Security's price
rate	Interest rate of the security at the issue date
redemption	Value of the security at redemption
settlement	Settlement date of the security (the day you have to pay for it)
yield	Annual yield of the security

Excel calculates functions using serial date values. You can enter dates in a function in three ways: by entering the serial number, by entering the date enclosed in quotation marks, or by entering a reference to a cell that contains a date. For example, June 30, 2000, can be entered as the serial date value 36707, or as "6/30/00." If you enter the date in a cell as 6/30/00 and then reference that cell in the function rather than entering the date itself, Excel uses the serial date value. (To find a date's serial value, you can press Ctrl+Shift+~ to apply the General format to the cell.) If the security-analysis function results in a #NUM! error value, check that the dates are in the correct form.

The maturity date value must be greater than the settlement date value, which must be greater than the issue date value. Also, the yield and rate arguments must be greater than or equal to zero, and the *redemption* argument must be greater than zero. If any of these conditions is not met, the #NUM! error value is displayed in the cell containing the function.

The DOLLARDE and DOLLARFR Functions

One of this pair of functions converts the familiar fractional pricing of securities to decimals, and the other converts decimals to fractions. These functions take the forms

=DOLLARDE(fractional dollar, fraction)

and

=DOLLARFR(decimal dollar, fraction)

The *fractional dollar* argument is the value you want to convert expressed as an integer, followed by a decimal point and then the numerator of the fraction. *Decimal dollar* is the value you want to convert expressed as a decimal fraction, and *fraction* is an integer indicating the denominator to be used as a rounding unit. For the DOLLARDE function, *fraction* is the actual denominator of the fraction you are converting. For the DOLLARFR function, *fraction* is the unit the function is to use when converting the decimal value, which effectively rounds the decimal number to the nearest half, quarter, eighth, sixteenth, thirty-second, or whatever the value specified by *fraction*.

For example, the formula

=DOLLARDE(1.03,32)

translates as 1+3/32, which is equivalent to 1.09375. The formula

=DOLLARFR(1.09375,32)

returns the result 1.03.

The ACCRINT and ACCRINTM Functions

The ACCRINT function returns the interest accrued by a security that pays interest on a periodic basis. This function takes the form

=ACCRINT(issue,first interest,settlement,rate,par, frequency,basis)

For definitions of these arguments, see the table on page 492.

III

Analyzing Data

For example, suppose a Treasury bond has an issue date of March 1, 2000, a settlement date of April 1, 2000, a first interest date of September 1, 2000, a 7-percent coupon rate with semiannual frequency, a par value of $1,000, and a basis of 30/360. The accrued interest formula is

=ACCRINT("3/1/00","9/1/00","4/1/00",0.07,1000,2,0)

which returns 5.833333, indicating that $5.83 accrues between March 1, 2000, and April 1, 2000.

Similarly, the ACCRINTM function returns the interest accrued by a maturity security that pays interest on a periodic basis. This function takes the form

=ACCRINTM(issue,settlement,rate,par,basis)

Using the previous example with a maturity date of July 31, 2004, the accrued interest formula is

=ACCRINTM("3/1/00","7/31/04",0.07,1000,0)

which returns 309.1667, indicating that the $1,000 bond will pay $309.17 interest on July 31, 2004.

The INTRATE and RECEIVED Functions

The INTRATE function calculates the rate of interest, or discount rate, for a fully invested security. This function takes the form

=INTRATE(settlement,maturity,investment,redemption,basis)

For definitions of these arguments, see the table on page 492. For example, suppose a bond has a settlement date of March 31, 2000, and a maturity date of September 30, 2000. The $1,000,000 investment will have a redemption value of $1,032,324, using the default 30/360 basis. The bond's discount rate formula is

=INTRATE("3/31/00","9/30/00",1000000,1032324,0)

which returns 0.064648, or 6.46 percent.

Similarly, the RECEIVED function calculates the amount received at maturity for a fully invested security. The form of this function is

=RECEIVED(settlement,maturity,investment,discount,basis)

Using the previous example with a 5.5 percent discount rate, the formula is

=RECEIVED("3/31/00","9/30/00",1000000,0.055,0)

which returns 1028277.63.

The PRICE, PRICEDISC, and PRICEMAT Functions

The PRICE function calculates the price per $100 of face value of a security that pays interest on a periodic basis. This function takes the form

=PRICE(settlement,maturity,rate,yield,redemption,frequency,basis)

For definitions of these arguments, see the table on page 492. For example, suppose a bond's settlement date is March 31, 2000, and its maturity date is July 31, 2000. The interest rate is 5.75 percent, with semiannual frequency. The security's annual yield is 6.50 percent, its redemption value is $100, and it is calculated using the standard 30/360 basis. The bond price formula is

=PRICE("3/31/00","7/31/00",0.0575,0.065,100,2,0)

which returns $99.73498.

Similarly, the PRICEDISC function returns the price per $100 of face value of a security that is discounted instead of paying periodic interest. This function takes the form

=PRICEDISC(settlement,maturity,discount,redemption,basis)

Using the preceding example with the addition of a discount amount of 7.5 percent, the formula is

=PRICEDISC("3/31/00","7/31/00",0.075,100,0)

which returns 97.5.

Finally, the PRICEMAT function returns the price per $100 of face value of a security that pays its interest at the maturity date. This function takes the form

=PRICEMAT(settlement,maturity,issue,rate,yield,basis)

Using the previous example with an issue date of March 1, 2000, and the maturity date changed to July 31, 2001, the formula is

=PRICEMAT("7/31/00","7/31/01","3/31/00",0.0575,0.065,0)

which returns $99.17879.

The DISC Function

The DISC function calculates the discount rate for a security and takes the form

=DISC(settlement,maturity,price,redemption,basis)

See the table on page 492 for the definitions of these arguments.

III

Analyzing Data

For example, suppose a bond has a settlement date of June 15, 2000, a maturity date of December 31, 2000, a price of $96.875, and a $100 redemption value, and uses the standard 30/360 basis. The bond discount rate formula is

=DISC("6/15/00","12/31/00",96.875,100,0)

which returns 0.057398, or 5.74 percent.

The YIELD, YIELDDISC, and YIELDMAT Functions

The YIELD function determines the annual yield for a security that pays interest on a periodic basis. It takes the form

=YIELD(settlement,maturity,rate,price,redemption,frequency,basis)

For definitions of these arguments, see the table on page 492. For example, suppose a bond has a settlement date of February 15, 2000, a maturity date of December 1, 2000, a coupon rate of 5.75 percent with semiannual frequency, a price of $99.2345, and a $100 redemption value, and uses the standard 30/360 basis. The annual bond yield formula is

=YIELD("2/15/00","12/1/00",0.0575,99.2345,100,2,0)

which returns 0.067399, or 6.74 percent.

The YIELDDISC function, on the other hand, calculates the annual yield for a discounted security. It takes the form

=YIELDDISC(settlement,maturity,price,redemption,basis)

Using the preceding example but changing the price to $96.00, the bond yield formula is

=YIELDDISC("2/15/00","12/1/00",96,100,0)

which returns 0.052448, or 5.245 percent.

The YIELDMAT function calculates the annual yield for a security that pays its interest at maturity. This function takes the form

=YIELDMAT(settlement,maturity,issue,rate,price,basis)

Using the arguments from the YIELD example but adding an issue date of January 1, 2000, and changing the price to $99.2345, the yield-at-maturity formula is

=YIELDMAT("2/15/00","12/1/00","1/1/00",0.0575,99.2345,0)

which returns 0.067178, or 6.718 percent.

The TBILLEQ, TBILLPRICE, and TBILLYIELD Functions

The TBILLEQ function calculates the bond-equivalent yield for a Treasury bill. It takes the form

    =TBILLEQ(settlement,maturity,discount)

See the table on page 492 for definitions of these arguments. For example, suppose a Treasury bill has a settlement date of February 1, 2000, a maturity date of July 1, 2000, and a percent discount rate of 8.65. The formula for calculating the Treasury bill yield that is equivalent to the yield of a bond is

    =TBILLEQ("2/1/00","7/1/00",0.0865)

which returns 0.091, or 9.1 percent.

You use the TBILLPRICE function to calculate the price per $100 of face value for a Treasury bill. This function takes the form

    =TBILLPRICE(settlement,maturity,discount)

Using the previous example, the formula to calculate the price per $100 of face value is

    =TBILLPRICE("2/1/00","7/1/00",0.0865)

which returns 96.3718, or $96.37.

Finally, the TBILLYIELD function calculates a Treasury bill's yield. It takes the form

    =TBILLYIELD(settlement,maturity,price)

Using the previous example with its result, a price of $96.40, the yield formula is

    =TBILLYIELD("2/1/00, 7/1/00",96.40)

which returns the yield 0.0890, or 8.9 percent.

The COUPDAYBS, COUPDAYS, COUPDAYSNC, COUPNCD, COUPNUM, and COUPPCD Functions

The following group of functions performs calculations relating to bond coupons. For all the sample formulas in this section, we'll use as our example a bond with a settlement date of March 1, 2000, and a maturity date of December 1, 2000. Its coupons are payable semiannually, using the actual/actual basis (that is, a basis argument of 1).

The COUPDAYBS function calculates the number of days from the beginning of the coupon period to the settlement date. This function takes the form

=COUPDAYBS(settlement,maturity,frequency,basis)

For definitions of these arguments, see the table on page 492.

Using our sample data, the formula looks like this:

=COUPDAYBS("3/1/00","12/1/00",2,1)

and returns 91.

The COUPDAYS function calculates the number of days in the coupon period that contains the settlement date. This function takes the form

=COUPDAYS(settlement,maturity,frequency,basis)

Using our sample data, the formula looks like this:

=COUPDAYS("3/1/00","12/1/00",2,1)

and returns 183.

The COUPDAYSNC function calculates the number of days from the settlement date to the next coupon date. This function takes the form

=COUPDAYSNC(settlement,maturity,frequency,basis)

Using our sample data, the formula looks like this:

=COUPDAYSNC("3/1/00","12/1/00",2,1)

and returns 92.

The COUPNCD function calculates the next coupon date after the settlement date. This function takes the form

=COUPNCD(settlement,maturity,frequency,basis)

Using our sample data, the formula looks like this:

=COUPNCD("3/1/00","12/1/00",2,1)

and returns 36678, or June 1, 2000.

The COUPNUM function calculates the number of coupons payable between the settlement date and the maturity date and rounds the result to the nearest whole coupon. This function takes the form

=COUPNUM(settlement,maturity,frequency,basis)

Using our sample data, the formula looks like this:

=COUPNUM("3/1/00","12/1/00",2,1)

and returns 2.

The COUPPCD function calculates the coupon date previous to the settlement date. It takes the form

=COUPPCD(settlement,maturity,frequency,basis)

Using our sample data, the formula looks like this:

=COUPPCD("3/1/00","12/1/00",2,1)

and returns 36495, or December 1, 1999.

The DURATION and MDURATION Functions

The DURATION function calculates the annual duration for a security whose interest payments are made on a periodic basis. Duration is the weighted average of the present value of the bond's cash flows and is used as a measure of how a bond's price responds to changes in yield. This function takes the form

=DURATION(settlement,maturity,coupon,yield,frequency,basis)

See the table on page 492 for definitions of these arguments.

For example, suppose a bond has a settlement date of January 1, 1999, a maturity date of December 31, 2004, a semiannual coupon rate of 8.5 percent, a yield of 9.5 percent, and uses the default 30/360 basis. The resulting formula is

=DURATION("1/1/99","12/31/04",0.085,0.095,2,0)

which returns a duration of 4.78708.

The MDURATION function calculates the annual modified duration for a security with interest payments made on a periodic basis, adjusted for market yield per number of coupon payments per year. This function takes the form

=MDURATION(settlement,maturity,coupon,yield,frequency,basis)

Using the values from the DURATION formula, the modified duration formula looks like this:

=MDURATION("1/1/99","12/31/04",0.085,0.095,2,0)

and returns a value of 4.570005.

III

Analyzing Data

The ODDFPRICE, ODDFYIELD, ODDLPRICE, and ODDLYIELD Functions

This group of functions is used to improve the accuracy of formulas that determine price and yield for securities whose first or last period is unusual. These functions use two arguments in addition to those listed in the table on page 492. The *first coupon* argument is the security's first coupon due date as a serial date value, and the *last interest* argument is the security's last coupon due date as a serial date value.

The ODDFPRICE function returns the price per $100 of face value for a security having an odd (short or long) first period. This function takes the form

=ODDFPRICE(settlement,maturity,issue,first coupon,rate,yield, redemption,frequency,basis)

The ODDFYIELD function calculates the yield of a security that has an odd (short or long) first period and takes the form

=ODDFYIELD(settlement,maturity,issue,first coupon,rate,price, redemption,frequency,basis)

The ODDLPRICE function calculates the price per $100 face value of a security having an odd (short or long) last coupon period. This function takes the form

=ODDLPRICE(settlement,maturity,last interest,rate,yield, redemption,frequency,basis)

The ODDLYIELD function calculates the yield of a security that has an odd (short or long) last period and takes the form

=ODDLYIELD(settlement,maturity,last interest,rate,price, redemption,frequency,basis)

For example, the following formula calculates the price of a security with $100 redemption value that settles on 3/15/99, was issued on 1/1/99, whose first 5.94 percent semiannual coupon is due 1/1/2000, has a 5.26 percent yield, and reaches maturity on 12/31/2011.

=ODDFPRICE("3/15/99","12/31/11","1/1/99","1/1/00",   0.0594, 0.0526,100,2)

which returns a price of 106.19.

Statistical Analysis

Microsoft Excel 2000 provides a wide range of features that can help you analyze statistical data. Built into the program are a number of functions, such as AVERAGE, MEDIAN, and MODE, that assist in simple analysis tasks. When the built-in statistical functions aren't enough, you can turn to the Analysis ToolPak.

The Analysis ToolPak, an add-in module, provides a collection of functions and tools to augment Excel's built-in analytic capabilities. You can use the ToolPak to create histograms, produce rank-and-percentile tables, extract random or periodic samples from a data set, perform regression analysis, derive statistical measures of a data sample, generate random-number sets that are not uniformly distributed, apply Fourier and other transformations to your data, and more.

Accessing the Analysis ToolPak

For details about specific commands and functions not covered here, consult Excel's excellent online Help system.

The capabilities of the Analysis ToolPak are broad enough to warrant a book of their own. In this chapter, we'll focus on the capabilities that apply to the analysis of statistical data.

If you performed a complete installation of Excel, the Analysis ToolPak is available each time you start Excel. You can use the ToolPak functions just as you would other Excel functions, and you can access the ToolPak tools by following these steps:

1 Choose Data Analysis from the Tools menu. The first time you choose this command, you'll have to wait a moment while Excel reads a file from disk, and then you'll see the dialog box shown in Figure 15-1.

FIGURE 15-1.

The Data Analysis dialog box presents a list of tools.

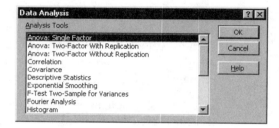

2 To use an analysis tool, select its name from the list box and then click OK.

3 Complete the dialog box that appears. In most cases, this means identifying the data you want to analyze by specifying the input range, telling Excel where you want it to put its analysis by specifying the output range, and selecting the options you want.

If the Data Analysis command does not appear on the Tools menu or if a formula that uses a ToolPak function returns a #NAME? error value, choose Add-Ins from the Tools menu and then select Analysis ToolPak from the Add-Ins Available list and then click OK. If Analysis ToolPak is not listed in the Add-Ins Available list, you must install it by running Setup.

Analyzing Distributions of Data

In statistics, a collection of measurements is called a *distribution*. With Microsoft Excel 2000, you can analyze distributions using several tools: the built-in statistical functions; the sample and population statistical functions; the Descriptive Statistics tool, which automates the reporting of Descriptive Statistics functions; the Histogram tool; and the rank and percentile functions together with the Rank and Percentile tool.

Built-In Statistical Functions

? SEE ALSO

For information about LINEST, LOGEST, TREND, and GROWTH, see "Linear and Exponential Regression," page 526.

You use Microsoft Excel's built-in statistical functions to analyze a group (or *population*) of measurements. In this section, we limit the discussion to the most commonly used statistical functions. Excel also offers the advanced statistical functions LINEST, LOGEST, TREND, and GROWTH, which operate on arrays of numbers.

The "A" Functions

Excel includes a set of functions that give you more flexibility when calculating data sets that include text or logical values. These functions are AVERAGEA, COUNTA, MAXA, MINA, STDEVA, STDEVPA, VARA, and VARPA.

Normally, the "non-A" versions of these functions ignore cells containing text values. For example, if a range of 10 cells contains one text value, AVERAGE ignores that cell and divides by 9 to arrive at the average, while AVERAGEA considers the text value part of the range and divides by 10.

For example, if cell B7 in the spreadsheet in Figure 15-2 contained the word "none" instead of a numeric value, the AVERAGE function would return $469.09, indicating that the cell was simply skipped, which might be what you want. However, using the AVERAGEA function, the result would be $430.00, as if the cell contained a zero instead of a text value. This is helpful when you always want to include all referenced cells in your calculations, especially if you use formulas that return text flags such as "none" when a certain condition is met.

The AVERAGE Function

The AVERAGE function computes the arithmetic mean, or average, of the numbers in a range by summing a series of numeric values and then dividing the result by the number of values.

This function takes the form

=AVERAGE(number1,number2,...)

AVERAGE ignores blank, logical, and text cells and can be used instead of long formulas. For example, to calculate the average of the sales figures in cells B4 through B15 of Figure 15-2, you could use the formula

=(B4+B5+B6+B7+B8+B9+B10+B11+B12+B13+B14+B15)/12

to arrive at the result $500.08. This method has the same drawbacks as using the + operator instead of a cell range with the SUM function: you must edit the cell references and the divisor each time you change the range to be averaged. It's obviously more efficient to enter

=AVERAGE(B4:B15)

W ON THE WEB

You can find Pets2000.xls used in the following example on the Microsoft Press Web site at *http://mspress.microsoft.com/mspress/products/2050/*.

FIGURE 15-2.

We'll use this worksheet to demonstrate some of Excel's built-in statistical functions.

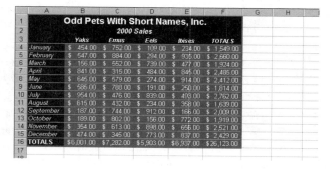

The MEDIAN, MODE, MAX, MIN, COUNT, and COUNTA Functions

These functions all take the same arguments: essentially just a cell range or a list of numbers separated by commas. These functions take the following forms:

=MEDIAN(number1,number2,...)

=MODE(number1,number2,...)

=MAX(number1,number2,...)

=MIN(number1,number2,...)

=COUNT(value1,value2,...)

=COUNTA(value1,value2,...)

The MEDIAN function computes the median of a set of numbers. The median is the number in the middle of the set; that is, an equal number of values is higher and lower than the median. If the numbers specified include an even number of values, the value returned is the average of the two that lie in the middle of the set. For example, the formula

=MEDIAN(1,3,4,6,8,13,35)

returns 7.

The MODE function determines which value occurs most frequently in a set of numbers. For example, the formula

=MODE(1,3,3,6,7)

returns 3. If no number occurs more than once, MODE returns the #N/A error value.

The MAX function returns the largest value in a range. For example, in the worksheet shown in Figure 15-2, you can use the formula

=MAX(B4:B15)

to determine the highest monthly yak sales: $954.

The MIN function returns the smallest value in a range. For example, in the worksheet shown in Figure 15-2, you can determine the lowest monthly yak sales—$156—by using the formula

=MIN(B4:B15)

The COUNT function tells you how many cells in a given range contain numbers, including dates and formulas that evaluate to numbers. For example, in the worksheet in Figure 15-2, the formula

=COUNT(F3:F16)

returns the value 13—the number of cells in the range F3:F16 that contain numbers.

The COUNT function counts only the numbers in a range and ignores blank cells and cells that contain text, logical, or error values. To count all nonblank cells (regardless of what they contain), you can use the COUNTA function. Using the worksheet in Figure 15-2, the formula

=COUNTA(F3:F16)

returns the value 14 because the COUNTA function includes the text value in cell F3. (See the sidebar entitled "The 'A' Functions," page 503.)

III

Analyzing Data

The SUMIF and COUNTIF Functions

The SUMIF function is similar to SUM but tests each cell in a range before adding it to the total. This function takes the form

=SUMIF(range,criteria,sum_range)

The *range* argument specifies the range you want to test, *criteria* specifies the test to be performed on each cell in the range, and *sum_range* specifies the corresponding numbers to be totaled. For example, in Figure 15-2 on page 504, if the column containing the names of the months has the defined name *monthNames,* and the column containing yak sales has the defined name *yakSales,* you can find the sales for June with the formula

=SUMIF(monthNames,"June",yakSales)

which returns the number 585.

Similarly, COUNTIF counts the cells that match the specified criteria and takes the form

=COUNTIF(range,criteria)

For example, you can find the number of months in which yak sales fell below $600 with the formula

=COUNTIF(yakSales,"<600")

which returns the number 8. Notice that you can use relational operators in the *criteria* argument to test for complex conditions.

The SUMPRODUCT and SUMSQ Functions

The SUMPRODUCT function multiplies the corresponding members of each of two or more arrays (sets of numbers), totals the products, and then returns the sum of the products. Nonnumeric values in the arguments are treated as zeros. This function takes the form

=SUMPRODUCT(array1,array2,array3,...)

Figure 15-3 shows a worksheet that uses SUMPRODUCT. The formula in F6

=SUMPRODUCT(B2:G2,B3:G3)

determines the total number of sprockets needed to produce the desired number of all six widget types. It does this by multiplying B2*B3, C2*C3, and so on through G2*G3, and then totaling the six products.

The SUMPRODUCT function can accept as many as 30 array arguments. Each array must have the same dimensions; otherwise, SUMPRODUCT returns the #VALUE! error value.

ON THE WEB   You can find Analysis.xls used in Figures 15-3 and 15-4 at *http://mspress.microsoft.com/mspress/products/2050/.*

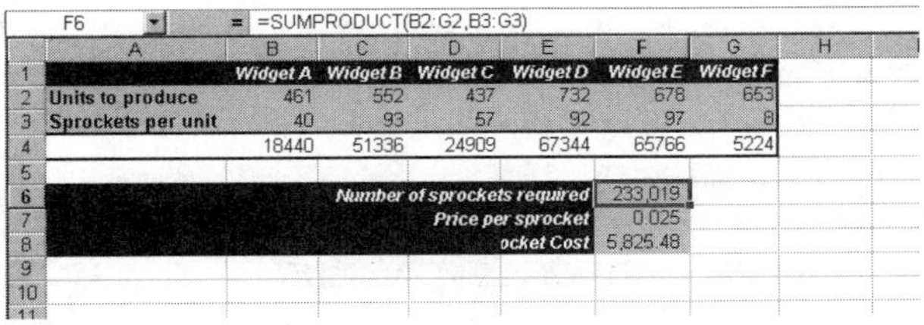

FIGURE 15-3.

This worksheet uses SUMPRODUCT to calculate the sprockets needed to produce the desired numbers of all six types of widgets.

F6		= =SUMPRODUCT(B2:G2,B3:G3)							
	A	B	C	D	E	F	G	H	I
1		Widget A	Widget B	Widget C	Widget D	Widget E	Widget F		
2	Units to produce	461	552	437	732	678	653		
3	Sprockets per unit	40	93	57	92	97	8		
4		18440	51336	24909	67344	65766	5224		
5									
6				Number of sprockets required		233,019			
7				Price per sprocket		0.025			
8				ocket Cost		5,825.48			
9									
10									
11									

The SUMSQ function is similar to the SUMPRODUCT function, except that it squares the numbers in the arguments and returns the sum of the squares, rather than the products. This function takes the form

=SUMSQ(number1,number2,...)

For example, the formula

=SUMSQ(5,6)

returns the value 61 (25+36).

Sample and Population Statistical Functions

Variance and standard deviation are statistical measurements of the dispersion of a group, or population, of numbers. The standard deviation is the square root of the variance. As a rule, about 68 percent of a normally distributed population falls within one standard deviation of the mean, and about 95 percent falls within two standard deviations. A large standard deviation indicates that the population is widely dispersed from the mean; a small standard deviation indicates that the population is tightly packed around the mean.

Four statistical functions—VAR, VARP, STDEV, and STDEVP—compute the variance and standard deviation of the numbers in a range of cells. Before you calculate the variance and standard deviation of a group of values, you must determine whether those values represent the total population or only a representative sample of that population. The VAR and STDEV functions assume that the values represent only a sample of the total population; the VARP and STDEVP functions assume that the values represent the total population.

Calculating Sample Statistics: VAR and STDEV

The VAR and STDEV functions take the forms

=VAR(number1,number2,...)

and

=STDEV(number1,number2,...)

III

Analyzing Data

Figure 15-4 shows exam scores for five students and assumes that the scores in cells B4:E8 represent only a part of the total population.

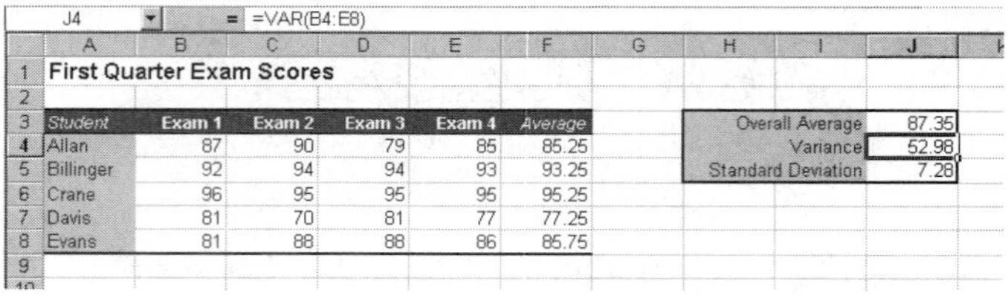

J4 = =VAR(B4:E8)

First Quarter Exam Scores

Student	Exam 1	Exam 2	Exam 3	Exam 4	Average		
Allan	87	90	79	85	85.25	Overall Average	87.35
Billinger	92	94	94	93	93.25	Variance	52.98
Crane	96	95	95	95	95.25	Standard Deviation	7.28
Davis	81	70	81	77	77.25		
Evans	81	88	88	86	85.75		

FIGURE 15-4.
The VAR and STDEV functions measure the dispersion of sample exam scores.

Cell C13 uses the VAR function to calculate the variance for this sample group of test scores:

=VAR(B4:E8)

Cell C14 uses the STDEV function to calculate the standard deviation:

=STDEV(B4:E8)

As displayed, the VAR function returns 52.98, and the STDEV function returns 7.28. Assuming that the test scores in the example are normally distributed, we can deduce that about 68 percent of the students achieved scores between 80.07 (87.35-7.28) and 94.63 (87.35+7.28).

Calculating Total Population Statistics: VARP and STDEVP

If the numbers you're analyzing represent an entire population rather than a sample, you use the VARP and STDEVP functions to calculate variance and standard deviation. To compute the variance for the total population, use the formula

=VARP(number1, number2,...)

To find the standard deviation, use the formula

=STDEVP(number1, number2,...)

Assuming that cells B4:E8 in the worksheet shown in Figure 15-4 represent the total population, you can calculate the variance and standard deviation with the formulas

=VARP(B4:E8)

and

=STDEVP(B4:E8)

The VARP function returns 50.33, and the STDEVP function returns 7.09.

The SUMX2PY2, SUMX2MY2, and SUMXMY2 Functions

? SEE ALSO

For more information about using arrays, see "Working with Arrays," page 144.

The SUMX2PY2, SUMX2MY2, and SUMXMY2 functions let you perform three variations on sum-of-the-sum-of-the-squares operations, which are used in many statistical calculations. The SUMX2PY2 function calculates the sum of the sum of the squares of the corresponding values in X and Y, where X and Y are arrays that contain the same number of elements. The SUMX2MY2 function calculates the sum of the differences of the squares of the corresponding values in X and Y. And finally, the SUMXMY2 function calculates the sum of the squares of the differences of the corresponding values in X and Y. These functions take the forms

=SUMX2PY2(array_x,array_y)

and

=SUMX2MY2(array_x,array_y)

and

=SUMXMY2(array_x,array_y)

For example, using the same two arrays for all three functions, you can build the following formulas:

=SUMX2PY2({ 1,2,3,4} ,{ 2,4,6,8})

which returns 150;

=SUMX2MY2({ 1,2,3,4} ,{ 2,4,6,8})

which returns -90; and

=SUMXMY2({ 1,2,3,4} ,{ 2,4,6,8})

which returns 30.

The Descriptive Statistics Tool

The Descriptive Statistics tool provides a table of descriptive statistics for one or more sets of input values. As shown in Figure 15-5 on the next page, for each variable in the input range, this tool's output range includes the following information: the mean, standard error, median, mode, standard deviation, sample variance, kurtosis, skewness, range, minimum, maximum, sum, count, k^{th} largest and smallest values (for any value of k you specify), and the confidence level for the mean.

W ON THE WEB

You can find Analysis.xls used in the following example at *http://mspress.microsoft.com/mspress/products/2050/*.

III

Analyzing Data

FIGURE 15-5.

We generated 1000 normally distributed random numbers, using 100 as the mean and 2 as the standard deviation, and then verified their "normalcy" with the Descriptive Statistics tool.

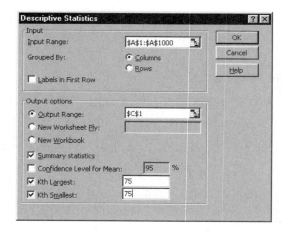

	A	B	C	D	E	F	G	H	I
1	99.39954			Column1					
2	97.44463								
3	100.4885		Mean	100.0501282					
4	102.5529		Standard Error	0.064578902					
5	102.3967		Median	100.034272					
6	103.4663		Mode	103.4662662					
7	95.63282		Standard Deviation	2.042164194					
8	99.53164		Sample Variance	4.170434595					
9	102.19		Kurtosis	-0.388877776					
10	97.8266		Skewness	0.048003657					
11	98.61959		Range	11.57037332					
12	96.61914		Minimum	94.46110451					
13	96.30618		Maximum	106.0314778					
14	98.04474		Sum	100050.1282					
15	98.45299		Count	1000					
16	95.76414		Largest(75)	103.0917454					
17	98.86415		Smallest(75)	97.10988959					
18	99.1919								
19	100.2697								

To use the Descriptive Statistics tool, choose Data Analysis from the Tools menu, select the Descriptive Statistics option from the Data Analysis dialog box, and then click OK. The dialog box shown in Figure 15-6 appears.

FIGURE 15-6.

Use the Descriptive Statistics tool to create a table of descriptive statistics.

The Descriptive Statistics tool requires an input range that consists of one or more variables and an output range. You must also indicate whether the variables are to be arranged by column or by row. If you include a row of labels, be sure to select the Labels In First Row option. Excel then uses the labels to identify the variables in its output table.

Select the Summary Statistics option only if you want a detailed output table as shown in Figure 15-5; otherwise, leave this check box empty and then select the check boxes of individual items to tell Excel which information you want.

SEE ALSO

For information about
random number
generation, see
"Generating Random
Numbers," page 519.

Like the other tools in the Analysis ToolPak, Descriptive Statistics creates
a table of constants. If a table of constants doesn't suit your needs, you
can get most of the same statistical data from other Analysis ToolPak
tools or from formulas that use Excel's worksheet functions. The statistics and formulas are listed in the table below.

Statistic	Formula
Mean	=AVERAGE(number1,number2,...)
Standard error	Similar to STEYX (*Known_y's, Known_x's*) but uses the ±-distribution rather than the standard normal distribution.
Median	=MEDIAN(number1,number2,...)
Mode	=MODE(number1,number2,...)
Standard deviation (sample)	=STDEV(number1,number2,...)
Standard deviation (population)	=STDEVP(number1,number2,...)
Variance (sample)	=VAR(number1,number2,...)
Variance (population)	=VARP(number1,number2,...)
Kurtosis	=KURT(number1,number2,...)
Skewness	=SKEW(number1,number2,...)
Range	=MAX(number1,number2)—MIN (number1,number2,...)
Minimum	=MIN(number1,number2,...)
Maximum	=MAX(number1,number2,...)
Sum	=SUM(number1,number2,...)
Count	=COUNT(value1,value2,...)
K^{th} largest	=LARGE(array,k)
K^{th} smallest	=SMALL(array,k)
Confidence	Similar to CONFIDENCE (*alpha, standard_dev, size*) but uses a different algorithm.

III

Analyzing Data

The Histogram Tool

A histogram is a chart (usually a simple column chart) that takes a collection of measurements and plots the number of measurements (called the *frequency*) that fall within each of several intervals (called *bins*).

To see how Microsoft Excel's Histogram tool works, we'll use a table of SAT test scores which consists of 1000 scores. (The input range must contain numeric data only.) To see a breakdown of the total scores at 50-point intervals, start by setting up the distribution "bins" shown in column F of Figure 15-7.

You can find SAT Scores.xls used in the following two examples at *http://mspress.microsoft.com/mspress/products/2050/*.

FIGURE 15-7.

Column F contains the distribution bins.

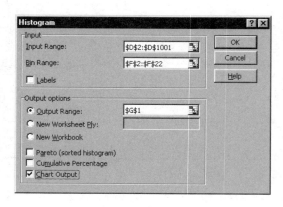

The bins don't have be equally spaced, these are, but they must be in ascendir order. If they are equally spaced, you can create the bins easily by using the AutoFill feature or b choosing Fill and th Series from the Edit menu.

Next choose Data Analysis from the Tools menu, select the Histogram tool, and then click OK. The Histogram dialog box appears, as shown in Figure 15-8.

FIGURE 15-8.

This dialog box appears when you select the Histogram tool from the Data Analysis dialog box.

The Histogram tool can take three items of information: the location of the data (in this case, D2:D1001), the location of the bins (F2:F20), and the upper left cell of the range where you want the analysis to appear (G1).

> **NOTE**
>
> If you want, leave the Bin Range edit box blank. Excel then creates evenly distributed bin intervals using the minimum and maximum values in the input range as beginning and end points. The number of intervals is equal to the square root of the number of input values.

Optionally, the Histogram tool can create a pareto (sorted) analysis, include cumulative percentages, and generate a chart. For now, select the Chart Output option and skip the other options. (We'll come back to them in a moment.) When you click OK, Excel creates a chart and writes its analysis in columns G and H, as shown in Figure 15-9.

FIGURE 15-9.

This analysis tells us that 3 scores were at least 900 but less than 950, 48 are at least 950 but less than 1000, and so on.

	A	B	C	D	E	F	G	H	I	J	
1	Student ID	Verbal	Math	Total			Bin	Frequency			
2	172-24-4999	418	518	936		600	600	0			
3	360-53-4755	465	557	1022		650	650	0			
4	354-63-5005	463	549	1012		700	700	0			
5	365-58-5506	466	587	1053		750	750	0			
6	581-26-4480	520	544	1064		800	800	0			
7	381-46-5039	470	537	1007		850	850	0			
8	633-23-4537	533	549	1082		900	900	3			
9	405-50-4764	476	570	1046		950	950	48			
10	374-50-5399	468	548	1016		1000	1000	155			
11	267-51-5445	441	562	1003		1050	1050	329			
12	783-66-5139	570	560	1130		1100	1100	291			
13	514-64-5099	503	554	1057		1150	1150	150			
14	704-59-4501	551	556	1107		1200	1200	23			
15	492-43-5382	498	562	1060		1250	1250	1			
16	366-49-5592	466	525	991		1300	1300	0			
17	159-65-4256	414	549	963		1350	1350	0			
18	491-41-4839	497	545	1042		1400	1400	0			
19	976-63-4600	581	519	1100		1450	1450	0			

In the Frequency column, the Histogram tool reports the number of input values that are equal to or greater than the bin value but less than the next bin value. The last value in the table reports the number of input values equal to or greater than the last bin value.

> **SEE ALSO**
>
> For more information about direct cell manipulation, see "Shortcuts for Entering and Editing," page 236.

Notice that the Histogram tool duplicates your column of bin values in the Bin column, which is convenient if you place the output somewhere other than next to the bin values. Unfortunately, you'll get an error message if you try to overwrite the bin-value range with the output range. If you're placing the output right next to the bins, as we did in Figure 15-9, you might want to delete the original bin values.

Because the Histogram tool copies the bin-value range, it's best to fill the range with numeric constants rather than formulas. If you do use formulas, be sure they don't include relative references; otherwise, when Histogram copies the range, the formulas might produce unwanted results.

Charting a Distribution Analysis

 SEE ALSO

For more information about formatting, saving, embedding, printing, and editing Excel charts, see Part V, "Charts."

Because you selected the Chart Output option in the Histogram dialog box, the Histogram tool generated a chart (shown in Figure 15-10) at the same time it performed its analysis. The chart was created from the data shown in Figure 15-7 on page 512. (We enlarged the chart to make it easier to see.) This standard Excel column chart can be manipulated just like any other chart.

FIGURE 15-10.

The Histogram tool can automatically create a column chart like this one.

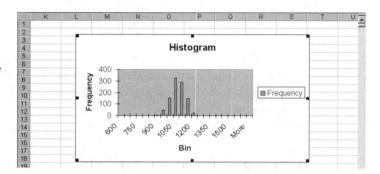

The Pareto and Cumulative Percentage Options

You use the Pareto option in the Histogram dialog box to sort the output (in descending order) and the Cumulative Percentage option to create a table that lists the cumulative percentages of each bin level. For example, creating a table of cumulative percentages with the data shown in Figure 15-7 on page 512 tells you that 82.6 percent of the student population scored below 1100.

Analyzing Distribution with the FREQUENCY Function

 SEE ALSO

For more information about using formulas that work with arrays, see "Array Formula Rules," page 147.

The Histogram tool generates a set of numeric constants. If you'd rather create formulas linked to the input values, you can use the Analysis ToolPak's FREQUENCY array function, which takes the form

=FREQUENCY(data_array,bins_array)

To use the FREQUENCY function, follow these steps:

1 Set up a column of bin values, just as you would with the Histogram tool.

2 Select the entire range where you want the output to appear. This range must be a column of cells; the FREQUENCY function can't use a row or multicolumn range as its output range.

3 Enter the formula, specifying the input range as the first argument and the bin range as the second. Press Ctrl+Shift+Enter to lock in the array formula.

Figure 15-11 shows the FREQUENCY function applied to the data shown in Figure 15-7 on page 512.

W **ON THE WEB**

You can find SAT Scores.xls used in the following two examples at *http://mspress.microsoft.com/mspress/products/2050/*.

FIGURE 15-11.

Use the FREQUENCY function to link the distribution analysis to the input data.

	G2		▼		= {=FREQUENCY(D2:D1001,F2:F20)}			
	A	B	C	D	E	F	G	H
1	Student ID	Verbal	Math	Total				
2	172-24-4999	418	518	936		600	0	
3	360-53-4755	465	557	1022		650	0	
4	354-63-5005	463	549	1012		700	0	
5	365-58-5506	466	587	1053		750	0	
6	581-26-4480	520	544	1064		800	0	
7	381-46-5039	470	537	1007		850	0	
8	633-23-4537	533	549	1082		900	3	
9	405-50-4764	476	570	1046		950	48	
10	374-50-5399	468	548	1016		1000	155	
11	267-51-5445	441	562	1003		1050	329	
12	783-66-5139	570	560	1130		1100	291	
13	514-64-5099	503	554	1057		1150	150	
14	704-59-4501	551	556	1107		1200	23	
15	492-43-5382	498	562	1060		1250	1	
16	366-49-5592	466	525	991		1300	0	
17	159-65-4256	414	549	963		1350	0	
18	491-41-4839	497	545	1042		1400	0	

Functions That Analyze Rank and Percentile

The Analysis ToolPak includes several functions that extract rank and percentile information from a set of input values: PERCENTRANK, PERCENTILE, QUARTILE, SMALL, LARGE, and RANK.

The PERCENTRANK Function

The PERCENTRANK function returns a percentile ranking for any member of a data set. You can use this function to create a percentile table that's linked to the input range so that the percentile figures are updated if the input values change. We used this function to create the percentile ranking in column E of Figure 15-12, on the next page.

The PERCENTRANK function takes the form

=PERCENTRANK(array,x,significance)

FIGURE 15-12.

PERCENTRANK links percentile figures to input values.

E2 = =PERCENTRANK(D2:D1001,D2,4)

	A	B	C	D	E
1	**Student ID**	**Verbal**	**Math**	**Total**	**Percentile**
2	172-24-4999	418	518	936	3%
3	360-53-4755	465	557	1022	34%
4	354-63-5005	463	549	1012	27%
5	365-58-5506	466	587	1053	55%
6	581-26-4480	520	544	1064	62%
7	381-46-5039	470	537	1007	24%
8	633-23-4537	533	549	1082	73%
9	405-50-4764	476	570	1046	49%
10	374-50-5399	468	548	1016	30%
11	267-51-5445	441	562	1003	21%
12	783-66-5139	570	560	1130	94%
13	514-64-5099	503	554	1057	57%
14	704-59-4501	551	556	1107	86%
15	492-43-5382	498	562	1060	59%
16	366-49-5592	466	525	991	17%
17	159-65-4256	414	549	963	8%
18	[illegible]	[illegible]	[illegible]	[illegible]	[illegible]

The *array* argument specifies the input range (which is D2:D1001, in our example), and *x* specifies the value whose rank you want to obtain. The *significance* argument, which is optional, indicates the number of digits of precision you want; if omitted, results are rounded to three digits (0.*xxx* or *xx.x*%).

The PERCENTILE and QUARTILE Functions

You use the PERCENTILE function to determine which member of an input range stands at a specified percentile ranking. It takes the form

=PERCENTILE(*array,k)*

For example, to find out which score in Figure 15-12 represents the 87th percentile, you can use the formula

=PERCENTILE(D2:D1001,0.87)

resulting in 1110.13—the SAT score representing the 87th percentile in this sampling.

You must express the percentile as a decimal fraction between 0 and 1.

The QUARTILE function, which takes the form

=QUARTILE(*array,quart*)

works much like the PERCENTILE function, except that it returns only the lowest, the 25th percentile, the median, the 75th percentile, or the highest value in the input set. The first argument specifies the input range. The second argument, which must be 0, 1, 2, 3, or 4, specifies the value to be returned, as shown in the table at the top of the next page.

Argument	Returns
0	Lowest value
1	25th percentile value
2	Median (50th percentile) value
3	75th percentile value
4	Highest value

Note that you can use the MIN function instead of the UARTILE(*range*,0) function, the MEDIAN function instead of the QUARTILE(*range*,2) function, and the MAX function instead of the QUARTILE(*range*,4) function. These functions are faster than QUARTILE, particularly with large data sets.

The SMALL and LARGE Functions

The SMALL and LARGE functions return the kth smallest and k^{th} largest values in an input range and take the forms

=SMALL(*array*,*k*)

and

=LARGE(*array*,*k*)

To find the 15th highest score in Figure 15-12 on the previous page, you can use the formula

=LARGE(D2:D1001,15)

resulting in 1158—the 15th highest SAT score in this sampling.

The RANK Function

The RANK function, which takes the form

=RANK(number,ref,order)

returns the ranked position of a particular number within a set of numbers. For example, to find out which ranking the score 1200 has in the data set in Figure 15-12, you can use the formula

=RANK(1100,D2:D1001)

to determine that the score 1100 is the 175th highest score in this sampling. By default, the highest value is ranked 1, the second highest is ranked 2, and so on. If you want the values ranked from the bottom instead of the top, add a third argument that is any number other than 0.

III

Analyzing Data

If RANK can't find an exact match between its first argument and an input value, it returns the #N/A error value.

The Rank and Percentile Tool

Suppose you want to rank the scores shown in Figure 15-7 on page 512. You could rank the scores by sorting the data in descending order, with the best score at the top and the worst score at the bottom of the column. To find the rank of any score, you might want to create an ascending series of numbers beside the sorted scores, with 1 beside the best score and 1000 beside the worst.

The Analysis ToolPak includes a Rank and Percentile tool that not only performs these tasks for you but also creates percentile figures for each value in your input range. To use this tool, choose Data Analysis from the Tools menu, select the Rank And Percentile option, and then click OK. The dialog box that appears asks for input and output ranges. As with the Histogram tool, the input range must contain numeric data only.

Columns E through H in Figure 15-13 show the result of using the Rank and Percentile tool to analyze column D of the test-score data in Figure 15-7 on page 512.

? **SEE ALSO**

For more information about using INDEX, see "The INDEX Function," page 452.

Suppose you want to know the student ID number of the person whose total test score was the 421st item in the input range, the ID number of the student whose score was the 600th item, and so on. One easy way to obtain this information is to insert a new column next to the Rank column, add the heading Student ID, and then use the INDEX function to get the ID numbers from the table shown in Figure 15-7. Figure 15-14 shows the result.

W **ON THE WEB**

You can find SAT Scores.xls used in the following two examples at *http://mspress.microsoft.com/mspress/products/2050/*.

FIGURE 15-13.

Use the Rank and Percentile tool to analyze the totals in column D.

The second row of this report tells us that the 285th item in the input range is a score of 1206, which ranks first and is better than 100 percent of the other scores.

	Point	Column1	Rank	Percent
1	Point	Column1	Rank	Percent
2	285	1206	1	100.00%
3	213	1198	2	99.80%
4	295	1191	3	99.70%
5	449	1190	4	99.60%
6	344	1179	5	99.50%
7	406	1178	6	99.30%
8	448	1178	6	99.30%
9	270	1175	8	98.90%
10	682	1175	9	98.90%

The third row of the report indicates that the second-best score is 1198, it is the 213th item in the input range, and it is better than 99.80 percent of the competition—and so on.

FIGURE 15-14.

Use the INDEX function to match student ID numbers with the ranked scores.

	G2	▼	=	=INDEX($A$2:$A$1001,E2,0)						
	A	B	C	D	E	F	G	H	I	J
1	Student ID	Verbal	Math	Total	Point	Column1	Student ID	Rank	Percent	
2	172-24-4999	418	518	936	285	1206	344-47-4055	1	100.00%	
3	360-53-4755	465	557	1022	213	1198	909-62-5620	2	99.80%	
4	354-63-5005	463	549	1012	295	1191	119-47-5900	3	99.70%	
5	365-58-5506	466	587	1053	449	1190	140-50-5377	4	99.60%	
6	581-26-4480	520	544	1064	344	1179	883-38-5042	5	99.50%	
7	381-46-5039	470	537	1007	406	1178	959-66-4808	6	99.30%	
8	633-23-4537	533	549	1082	448	1178	968-48-5093	6	99.30%	
9	405-50-4764	476	570	1046	270	1175	965-54-4300	8	98.90%	
10	374-60-5399	468	548	1016	682	1175	180-46-4941	8	98.90%	

In this example, we used the Rank and Percentile tool to analyze a single column of data. We could also use this tool to analyze all three scores—verbal, math, and total. In that case, we would specify the range B1:D1001 as the input range, and the tool would generate 12 columns of output, 4 for each input column.

 NOTE

> Be sure that the data you analyze consists only of numeric constants or formulas that use absolute references. If the input cells contain formulas with relative references, these references might become scrambled in the output range when they're sorted.

Generating Random Numbers

Microsoft Excel's built-in random-number function, RAND, generates a uniform distribution of random real numbers between 0 and 1. In other words, all values between 0 and 1 share the same probability of being returned by a set of formulas based on the RAND function. Because the sample is relatively small, the distribution is by no means perfectly uniform. Nevertheless, repeated tests of this kind demonstrate that the RAND function doesn't favor any position within its spectrum of distribution.

You can use the random-number component of the Analysis ToolPak to create sets of random numbers that are not uniformly distributed, then use the Histogram tool to sort and plot the results. These random-number sets are useful for Monte Carlo decision analysis and other kinds of simulations. Six distribution types are available: Uniform, Normal, Bernoulli, Binomial, Poisson, and Discrete (user-defined). In addition, you can use the Patterned Distribution option to create non-random numbers at specified intervals. (The Patterned Distribution option can serve as an alternative to Excel's Series command from the Fill submenu of the Edit menu.)

To use the Random Number Generation tool, choose Data Analysis from the Tools menu, select the Random Number Generation option in the

Data Analysis dialog box, and then click OK. Excel presents a dialog box like the one shown in Figure 15-15.

FIGURE 15-15.

The Parameters section of the Random Number Generation dialog box changes to reflect the distribution type you select.

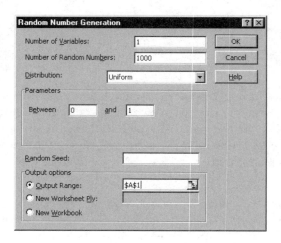

In the Number Of Variables and Number Of Random Numbers boxes, you indicate how many columns of numbers you want and how many numbers you want in each column. For example, if you want 10 columns of 100 numbers each, specify 10 in the Number Of Variables edit box and 100 in the Number Of Random Numbers edit box.

The Parameters section of this dialog box changes, depending on the type of distribution you select. As Figure 15-15 shows, when you select the Uniform Distribution option, you can specify the end points of the distribution.

You can also specify a seed value. However, each time you generate a random-number set with a particular distribution type using the same seed value, you get exactly the same sequence of numbers, so you should specify a seed value only if you need to be able to reproduce a random-number sequence.

For all distribution types, you use the Output Range edit box to tell Excel where you want the random numbers to go. If the range you specify already contains data, you'll see a warning message before the data is overwritten.

The Uniform Distribution Option

The Uniform Distribution option works much the same way as the RANDBETWEEN function, generating an evenly distributed set of real numbers between specified beginning and end points.

SEE ALSO

For more information about RAND and RANDBETWEEN, see "The RAND and RANDBETWEEN Functions," page 425.

You can use this option as a more convenient alternative to RAND when you want end points other than 0 and 1 or when you want sets of numbers to be based on the same seed value.

The Normal Distribution Option

A normal distribution has the following characteristics:

- One particular value, the mean, is more likely to occur than any other value.

- Values above the mean are as likely to occur as values below it.

- Values close to the mean are more likely to occur than values distant from the mean.

To generate normally distributed random numbers, you specify two parameters: the mean and the standard deviation. The standard deviation is the average absolute difference between the random numbers and the mean. Approximately 68 percent of the values in a normal distribution will fall within one standard deviation of the mean.

 SEE ALSO

For more information about the Descriptive Statistics tool, see "The Descriptive Statistics Tool," page 509.

You can use the Descriptive Statistics tool to verify the "normalcy" of a normally distributed set of random numbers. For example, Figure 15-5 on page 510 shows a table of descriptive statistics for a set of 1000 random numbers generated with the Normal Distribution option, using a mean of 100 and a standard deviation of 2. Because the sample is small, the output does not accord perfectly with statistical theory.

The Bernoulli Distribution Option

The Bernoulli Distribution option simulates the probability of success of a number of trials, given that all trials have an equal probability of succeeding and that the success of one trial has no impact on the success of subsequent trials. (Note that "succeed" in this context has no value implication. In other words, you can use this distribution to simulate failure as readily as success.) All values in the Bernoulli distribution's output are either 0 or 1.

The probability that each cell will return a 1 is given by the distribution's sole parameter, p, which must be a number from 0 to 1. For example, if you want a sequence of 100 random Bernoulli values whose most likely sum is 27, you define a 100-cell output range and specify a p value of 0.27.

III

Analyzing Data

The Binomial Distribution Option

The Binomial Distribution option simulates the number of successes in a fixed number of trials, given a specified probability rate. As with the Bernoulli Distribution option, the trials are assumed to be independent; that is, the outcome of one has no effect on any other.

To generate binomially distributed numbers, you specify the probability—the *p* argument—that any trial will succeed and the number of trials. (Again, "succeed" in this context has no value implication. In other words, you can use this distribution to simulate failure as readily as success.)

For example, suppose you make 10 sales presentations a week; you close the sale 20 percent of the time; and you would like to know what your success rate might be over the next year. You enter *50* (for 50 working weeks in the year) in the Number Of Random Numbers edit box, *0.2* in the P Value box, and *10* in the Number Of Trials edit box to learn that you can expect to make no sales four weeks in the coming year.

The Poisson Distribution Option

The Poisson Distribution option simulates the number of times an event occurs within a particular time span, given a certain probability of occurrence. The occurrences are assumed to be independent; that is, each occurrence has no effect on the likelihood of others.

The Poisson Distribution option takes a single parameter, λ, *lambda*, which represents the expected outcome of an individual occurrence. For example, suppose you expect to receive an average of 10 service calls a day. You want to know how often you can expect to get 18 or more service calls in a day over a year. To get this information, you enter *260* (52 weeks times 5 days) in the Number Of Random Numbers edit box and *10* in the Lambda edit box. The result is that you'll have about 3 days on which you can expect 18 or more service calls.

The Discrete Distribution Option

The Discrete Distribution option creates a custom distribution pattern by specifying a table of possible outcomes along with the probability associated with each outcome. The probability values must be between 0 and 1, and the sum of the probabilities in the table must equal 1. To use the Discrete Distribution option, you specify the possible outcomes and their probabilities as a two-column range whose reference is the only parameter used by this option.

The Patterned Distribution Option

The Patterned Distribution option in the Random Number Generation dialog box generates nonrandom numbers. Selecting the Patterned Distribution option displays the dialog box shown in Figure 15-16.

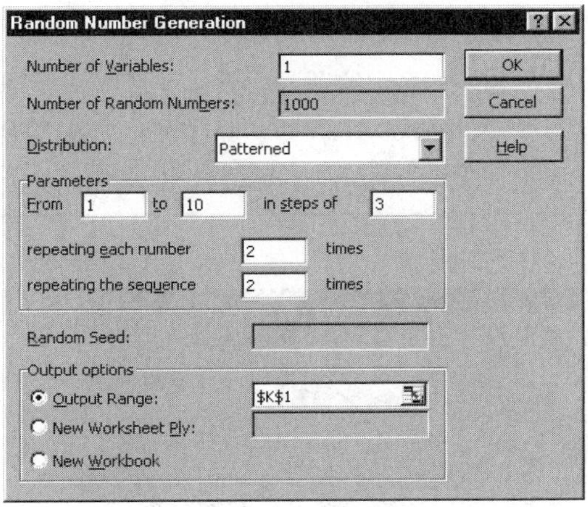

FIGURE 15-16.

The Patterned Distribution option lets you create an arithmetic series with operational repetitions.

You can think of the Patterned Distribution option as a fancy Series command. It lets you create one or more arithmetic series with optional internal repetitions.

For example, to create the series 1, 1, 4, 4, 7, 7, 10, 10, 1, 1, 4, 4, 7, 7, 10, complete the dialog box as shown in Figure 15-16, requesting two sequences of the numbers 1 through 10, using a step interval of 3, and repeating each number twice within each cycle.

If the step interval takes the series beyond the specified upper value, the Patterned Distribution option includes the upper value by truncating the last interval. For example, if you specify a step interval of 4 and the numbers 1 through 10, Excel creates the series 1, 5, 9, and 10.

Sampling a Population of Numbers

The Sampling tool extracts a subset of numbers from a larger group (or *population*) of numbers. From an input range, you can sample a specified number of values at random or at every *n*th value. The Sampling tool copies the extracted numbers to an output range you specify.

To use the Sampling tool, choose Data Analysis from the Tools menu, select the Sampling option in the Data Analysis dialog box, and then click OK. Figure 15-17 on the next page shows the dialog box that appears.

Sampling Text Values

To perform the equivalent of sampling from a range containing text values, follow these steps:

1 Set up a series of ascending integers beginning at 1 in a column alongside the text values.

2 Use the Sampling tool to extract numbers from this series.

3 Extract the text values by using the resulting numbers as arguments to the INDEX function. *See "The INDEX Function," page 452.*

FIGURE 15-17.

The Sampling tool lets you extract a random or periodic subset of a numeric population.

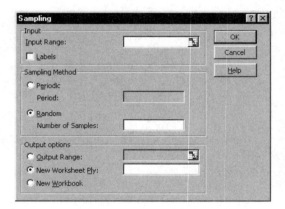

The values in the input range must be numeric. They can include blank values and dates, provided the dates are entered as numbers, not text. For example, to simplify a chart of daily commodity prices, you can use the Sampling tool to extract every *n*th data point and then create a new plot from the extracted data.

Calculating Moving Averages

A moving average is a forecasting technique that simplifies trend analysis by smoothing fluctuations that occur in measurements taken over time. These fluctuations can be caused by random "noise" that is often a by-product of the measurement technique. For example, measurements of the height of a growing child will vary with the accuracy of the ruler and whether the child is standing straight or slouching. You can take a series of measurements, however, and smooth them over time, resulting in a curve that reflects the child's actual growth rate.

Fluctuations in measurements can result from other temporary conditions that introduce bias. Monthly sales, for example, might vary with the number of working days in the month or the absence of a star salesperson who takes a vacation.

Suppose you have created the 18-month demand curve shown in Figure 15-18. To generate a less "noisy" trend line from this data, you can plot a six-month moving average. The first point in the moving average line is the average of the first six monthly figures (January through June 2000). The next point averages the second-through-seventh monthly figures (February through July 2000), and so on. You can use the Moving Average tool to perform this analysis for you.

FIGURE 15-18.

We'll use this 18-month demand curve to demonstrate Excel's Moving Average tool.

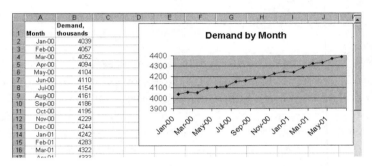

To use the Moving Average tool, choose Data Analysis from the Tools menu, select the Moving Average option in the Data Analysis dialog box, and then click OK.

The Moving Average tool requires three pieces of information: the range that contains the data you want to analyze, the range where the averaged data will appear, and the interval over which the data is averaged. To determine a three-month moving average, for example, specify an interval of 3.

Figure 15-19 on the next page shows a six-month moving average superimposed over the original demand curve in Figure 15-18. The Moving Average tool produced the data in column C, which was used to create the straighter plot line in the chart. Notice that the first five cells in the tool's output range contain #N/A error values. Where the interval is n, you will always have $n-1$ #N/A error values at the beginning of the output. Including those values in a chart presents no problem, because Excel simply leaves the first area of the plot line blank.

 You can find Analysis.xls used in the following example at *http:// mspress.microsoft.com/mspress/products/2050/.*

FIGURE 15-19.

The Moving Average tool provides a better perspective of the overall trend.

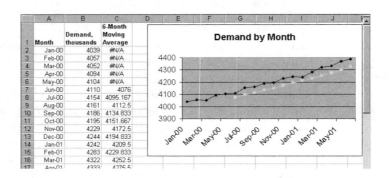

Linear and Exponential Regression

Excel includes several array functions for performing linear regression—LINEST, TREND, FORECAST, SLOPE, and STEYX—and exponential regression—LOGEST and GROWTH. These functions are entered as array formulas and produce array results. You can use each of these functions with one or several independent variables.

The term *regression*, as it is used here, might be confusing to some people because regression is commonly associated with a movement backward, whereas in the world of statistics, regression is often used to predict the future. To better understand the concept, we advise you to erase the dictionary definition from your mind and start fresh with the following definition: *Regression is a statistical technique that lets you find the equation that best describes a set of data.*

Often businesses try to predict the future by using sales and percent-of-sales projections based on history. A simple percent-of-sales technique identifies assets and liabilities that vary along with sales, determines the proportion of each, and assigns them percentages. Although using percent-of-sales forecasting is often sufficient for slow or steady short-term growth, the technique loses accuracy as growth accelerates.

Regression analysis uses more sophisticated equations to analyze larger sets of data and translate them into coordinates on a line or curve. In the past, regression analysis was not widely used because of the large numbers of calculations involved. Since spreadsheet applications such as Excel began offering built-in regression functions, the use of regression analysis has become much more widespread.

Linear regression produces the slope of a line that best fits a single set of data. Based on a year's worth of sales figures, linear regression can tell you the projected sales for March of the following year by giving you the slope and *y*-intercept (that is, the point where the line crosses the *y* axis) of the line that best fits the sales data. By following the line forward in time, you can estimate future sales, assuming linear growth.

Exponential regression produces an exponential curve that best fits a set of data that you suspect does not change linearly with time. For example, a series of measurements of population growth will nearly always be better represented by an exponential curve than by a line.

Multiple regression is the analysis of more than one set of data, which often produces a more realistic projection. You can perform both linear and exponential multiple regression analyses. For example, suppose you want to project the appropriate price for a house in your area based on square footage, number of bathrooms, lot size, and age. Using a multiple regression formula, you can estimate a price, based on a database of information gathered from existing houses.

Calculating Linear Regression Statistics

The following equation algebraically describes a straight line for a set of data with one independent variable:

$$y = mx + b$$

where x is the independent variable, y is the dependent variable, m represents the slope of the line, and b represents the y-intercept.

When a line represents the contribution of a number of independent variables in a multiple regression analysis to an expected result, the equation of the regression line takes the form

$$y = m_1 x_1 + m_2 x_2 + \ldots + m_n x_n + b$$

where y is the dependent variable, x_1 through x_n are n independent variables, m_1 through m_n are the coefficients of each independent variable, and b is a constant.

The LINEST Function

The LINEST function uses this more general equation to return the values of m_1 through m_n and the value of b, given a known set of values for y and a known set of values for each independent variable. This function takes the form

LINEST(known_y's,known_x's,const,stats)

The *known_y's* argument is the set of y values you already know. This argument can be a single column, a single row, or a rectangular range of cells. If *known_y's* is a single column, each column in the *known_x's* argument is considered an independent variable. Similarly, if *known_y's* is a single row, each row in the *known_x's* argument is considered an independent variable. If *known_y's* is a rectangular range, you can use only one independent variable; *known_x's* in this case should be a range of the same size and shape as *known_y's*.

If you omit *known_x's*, Excel uses the sequence 1, 2, 3, 4, and so on.

The *const* and *stats* arguments are optional. If either is included, it must be a logical constant—either TRUE or FALSE. (You can substitute 1 for TRUE and 0 for FALSE.) The default settings for *const* and *stats* are TRUE and FALSE, respectively. If you set *const* to FALSE, Excel forces b (the last term in the straight-line equation) to be 0. If you set *stats* to TRUE, the array returned by LINEST includes the following validation statistics:

se_1 through se_n	Standard error values for each coefficient
se_b	Standard error value for the constant b
r^2	Coefficient of determination
se_y	Standard error value for y
F	F statistic
df	Degrees of freedom
ss_{reg}	Regression sum of squares
ss_{resid}	Residual sum of squares

Before creating a formula using LINEST, you must select a range large enough to hold the result array returned by the function.

If you omit the *stats* argument (or set it explicitly to FALSE), the result array encompasses one cell for each of your independent variables and one cell for b. If you include the validation statistics, the result array looks like this:

m_n m_n	m_{n-1}	...	m_2	m_1	b
se_n	se_{n-1}	...	se_2	se_1	se_b
r^2	se_y				
F	df				
ss_{reg}	ss_{resid}				

After selecting a range to contain the results array, type the function and then press Ctrl+Enter to enter the function in each cell of the result array.

Note that, with or without validation statistics, the coefficients and standard error values for your independent variables are returned in the opposite order from your input data. For example, if you have four independent variables organized in four columns, LINEST evaluates the leftmost column as x_1, but it returns m_1 in the fourth column of the result array.

Figure 15-20 shows a simple example of the use of LINEST with one independent variable. The entries in column B of this worksheet represent monthly product demand for a small business. The numbers in column A represent the months in the period. Suppose you want to compute the slope and y-intercept of the regression line that best describes the relationship between the demand and the months. In other words, you want to describe the trend of the data. To do this, select the range F6:G6, type the formula

=LINEST(B2:B19,A2:A19)

and then press Ctrl+Shift+Enter. The resulting number in cell F6, 20.613, is the slope of the regression line; the number in cell G6, 4002.065, is the y-intercept of the line.

W ON THE WEB You can find Analysis.xls used in the following three examples at *http://mspress.microsoft.com/mspress/products/2050/*.

FIGURE 15-20.
The LINEST function computes the slope and y-intercept of a regression line.

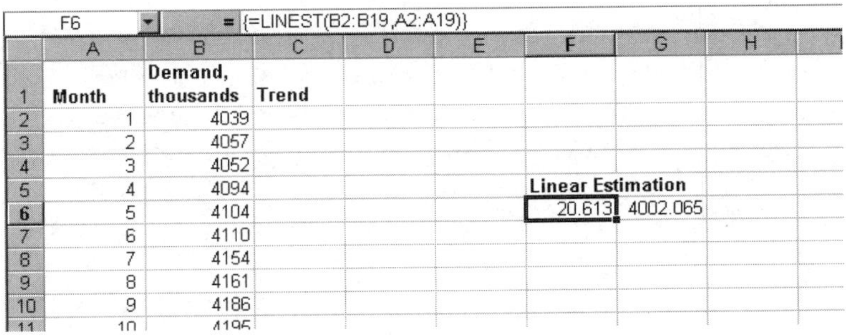

	A	B	C	D	E	F	G	H	
	Month	Demand, thousands	Trend						
1									
2	1	4039							
3	2	4057							
4	3	4052							
5	4	4094				Linear Estimation			
6	5	4104				20.613	4002.065		
7	6	4110							
8	7	4154							
9	8	4161							
10	9	4186							
11	10	4195							

The TREND Function

LINEST returns a mathematical description of the straight line that best fits known data. TREND enables you to find points that lie along that line. You can use the numbers returned by TREND to plot a trend line— a straight line that helps make sense of actual data. You can also use TREND to extrapolate, or make intelligent guesses about, future data based on the tendencies exhibited by known data. (Be careful. Although you can use TREND to plot the straight line that best fits the known data, it can't tell you if that line is a good predictor of the future. Validation statistics returned by LINEST can help you make that assessment.)

The TREND function accepts four arguments:

=TREND(known_y's,known_x's,new_x's,const)

The first two arguments represent the known values of your dependent and independent variables, respectively. As in LINEST, the *known_y's* argument is a single column, a single row, or a rectangular range. The *known_x's* argument also follows the pattern described for LINEST on page 527.

The third and fourth arguments are optional. If you omit *new_x's*, the TREND function considers *new_x's* to be identical to *known_x's*. If you include *const*, the value of that argument must be TRUE or FALSE (or 1 or 0). If *const* is TRUE, TREND forces b to be 0.

To calculate the trend-line data points that best fit your known data, simply omit the third and fourth arguments from this function. The results array will be the same size as the *known_x's* range. In Figure 15-21, we used TREND to find the value of each point on the regression line that describes the data set from the example in Figure 15-20. To create these values, we selected the range C2:C19 and entered the following as an array formula using Ctrl+Shift+Enter:

=TREND(B2:B19,A2:A19)

To extrapolate from existing data, you must supply a range for *new_x's*. You can supply as many or as few cells for *new_x's* as you want. The result array will be the same size as the *new_x's* range. In Figure 15-22 we used TREND to calculate demand for the 19th, 20th, and 21st months. To arrive at these values, we entered the numbers 19 through 21 in A21:A23, selected C21:C23, and then entered the following as an array formula:

=TREND(B2:B19,A2:A19,A21:A23)

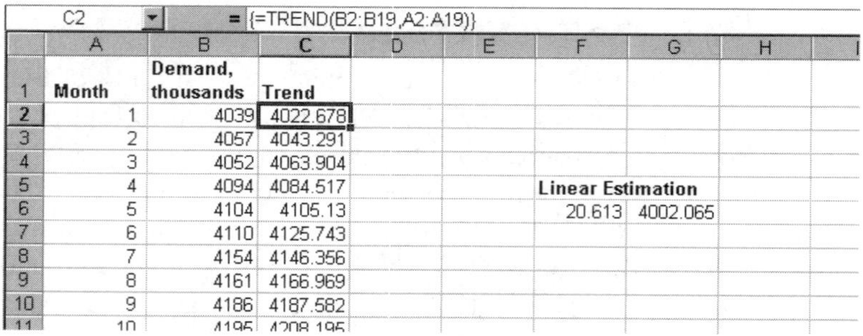

FIGURE 15-21.

The TREND function creates a data series that can be plotted as a line on a chart.

C2		= {=TREND(B2:B19,A2:A19)}						
	A	B	C	D	E	F	G	H
1	Month	Demand, thousands	Trend					
2	1	4039	4022.678					
3	2	4057	4043.291					
4	3	4052	4063.904					
5	4	4094	4084.517			Linear Estimation		
6	5	4104	4105.13			20.613	4002.065	
7	6	4110	4125.743					
8	7	4154	4146.356					
9	8	4161	4166.969					
10	9	4186	4187.582					
11	10	4195	4208.195					

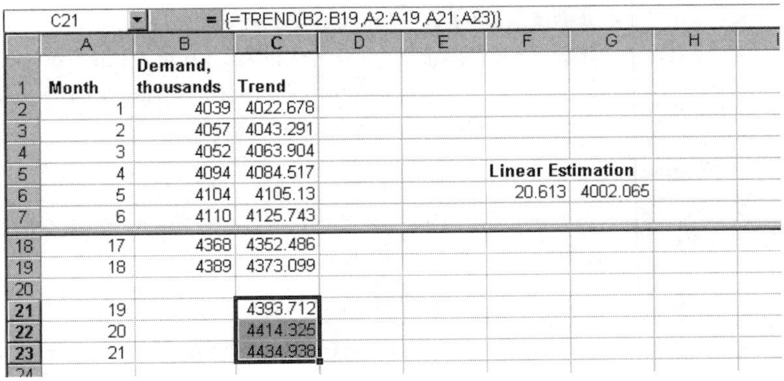

FIGURE 15-22.
TREND can predict the sales figures for months 19, 20, and 21.

The FORECAST Function

The FORECAST function is similar to TREND, except that it returns a single point along a line rather than returning an array that defines the line. This function takes the form

=FORECAST(x,known_y's,known_x's)

The x argument is the data point for which you want to extrapolate a value. For example, instead of using TREND, we can use the FORECAST function to extrapolate the value in cell C23 in Figure 15-22 by entering the formula

=FORECAST(21,B2:B19,A2:A19)

where the x argument refers to 21st data point on the regression line. You can use this function if you want to calculate any point in the future.

The SLOPE Function

The SLOPE function returns the slope of the linear regression line. The slope is defined as the vertical distance divided by the horizontal distance between any two points on the regression line. Its value is the same as the first number in the array returned by the LINEST function. In other words, SLOPE calculates the trajectory of the line used by the FORECAST and TREND functions to calculate the values of data points. The SLOPE function takes the form

=SLOPE(known_y's,known_x's)

To find the slope of the regression line that describes the data set from the example shown in Figure 15-20 on page 529, we can use the formula

=SLOPE(B2:B19,A2:A19)

which returns a value of 20.613.

The STEYX Function

The STEYX function calculates the standard error of a regression, a measure of the amount of error accrued in predicting a y for each given x. This function takes the form

=STEYX(known_y's,known_x's)

If we apply this function to the worksheet shown in Figure 15-20 on page 529, the formula

=STEYX(B2:B19,A2:A19)

returns a standard error value of 12.96562.

Calculating Exponential Regression Statistics

The equation that describes an exponential regression curve is

$$y = b*m_1^{x_1} * m_2^{x_2} * ... * m_n^{x_n}$$

If you have only one independent variable, the equation is

$$y = b * m^x$$

The LOGEST Function

 SEE ALSO

For more information about the LOGEST function's underlying equations and its arguments, see "The LINEST Function," page 527.

The LOGEST function works like the LINEST function, except that you use it to analyze data that is nonlinear. LOGEST returns coefficient values for each independent variable plus a value for the constant b. This function takes the form

= LOGEST(known_y's,known_x's,const,stats)

LOGEST accepts the same four arguments as the LINEST function and returns a result array in the same fashion. If you set the optional *stats* argument to TRUE, the function also returns validation statistics.

NOTE

> The LINEST and LOGEST functions return only the y-axis coordinates used for calculating lines and curves. The difference between them is that LINEST projects a straight line and LOGEST projects an exponential curve. You must be careful to match the appropriate function to the analysis at hand. The LINEST function might be more appropriate for sales projections, and the LOGEST function might be more suited to applications such as statistical analyses or population trends.

The GROWTH Function

For more information about the GROWTH function's arguments, see "The TREND Function," page 529.

Whereas the LOGEST function returns a mathematical description of the exponential regression curve that best fits a set of known data, the GROWTH function lets you find points that lie along that curve. The GROWTH function works exactly like its linear counterpart, TREND, and takes the form

=GROWTH(known_y's,known_x's,new_x's,const)

III

Analyzing Data

What-If Analysis

O ne of the most important benefits of spreadsheet software is that it lets you perform a what-if analysis quickly and easily. You can change key variables and instantly see the effect. For example, if you're using Microsoft Excel 2000 to decide whether to lease or purchase a car, you can test your financial model with different assumptions about interest rates and down payments, and you can see the effects of varying rates on "bottom-line" costs, such as the total interest you will pay.

Automatic recalculation provides you with instant feedback on your what-if experiments. When your model is set to recalculate automatically, you can change a value in a cell and watch as all cells whose values depend on the edited value are immediately recalculated.

Excel augments this basic capability with a number of advanced what-if features, which are also discussed in this chapter.

Data Tables

A data table, or *sensitivity table,* summarizes the impact of one or two variables on formulas that use those variables. You can use the Table command on the Data menu to create two kinds of data tables: a table based on a single input variable that tests the variable's impact on more than one formula, or a table based on two input variables that tests their impact on a single formula.

Data Tables Based on One Input Variable

Suppose you're considering buying a house that requires you to take on a 30-year, $200,000 mortgage, and you need to calculate monthly payments on the loan for several interest rates. A one-variable data table will give you the information you need.

To create this table, follow these steps:

1 Start by entering the inputs (that is, the interest rates) you want to test in a fresh worksheet. For this example, enter *6%, 6.5%, 7%, 7.5%, 8%,* and *8.5%* in cells B3:B8. We'll call this range the *input range,* because it contains the input values we want to test. If you want, you can also format the column for percentages.

2 Next enter the loan amount in a cell outside the data table area. We entered $200,000 in cell C1. This allows us to easily change the loan amount to test various scenarios.

3 Next enter the formula that uses the input variable. In this case, enter the formula

=PMT(A2/12,360,C1)

in cell C2. In this formula, A2/12 is the monthly interest rate, 360 is the term of the loan in months, and C1 refers to the cell containing the loan principal. Notice that this formula refers to cell A2, which is blank. (Excel assigns a value of 0 to a blank cell referenced in a numeric formula.) As shown in Figure 16-1, because A2 is blank, the function returns a spurious result: the payment required to amortize the loan at an interest rate of 0 percent. Cell A2 is a placeholder through which Excel will feed the values in the input range. Excel never actually changes the underlying value of this cell, so this placeholder can be any cell outside the table range. You'll see in a moment why this formula refers to cell A2.

 **ON THE WEB**

You can find Data Table.xls used in the following example on the Microsoft Press Web site at *http://mspress.microsoft.com/mspress/products/2050/.*

FIGURE 16-1.

Begin building the data table by entering the interest rates and the PMT function in the worksheet.

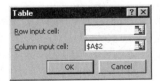

4   Select the data table range—the smallest rectangular block that includes the formula and all the values in the input range. In this case, select the range B2:C8.

5   Choose Table from the Data menu. (The Table command does not normally appear on shortened menus. Click the double arrow at the bottom of the Data menu to display the Table command.) In the Table dialog box, shown in Figure 16-2, specify the location of the input cell in the Row Input Cell or Column Input Cell edit box. The input cell is the placeholder cell referred to by the table formula—in this example, A2. If the input values are arranged in a row, enter the input cell reference in the Row Input Cell edit box. If the values in the input range are arranged in a column, use the Column Input Cell edit box. In this example, the input values are arranged in a column, so enter *$A$2* in the Column Input Cell edit box—or click in the edit box and then click cell A2.

FIGURE 16-2.

Use the Table dialog box to specify the input cell.

Table	? X
Row input cell:	
Column input cell:	$A$2
OK	Cancel

6   Click OK. Excel enters the results of the table formula (one result for each input value) in the available cells of the data table range. In this example, Excel enters six results in the range C3:C8, as shown in Figure 16-3 on the next page.

III

Analyzing Data

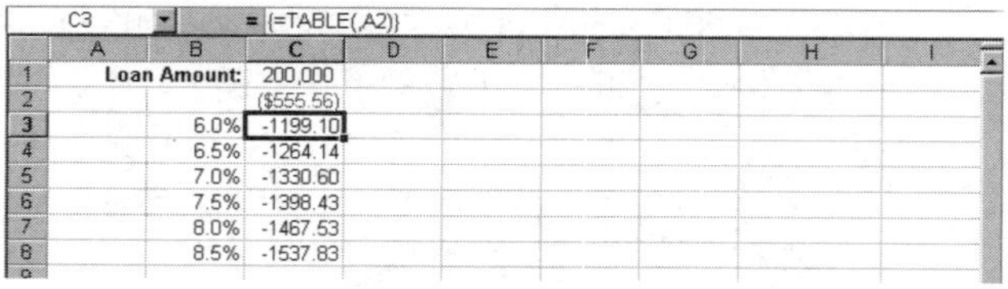

FIGURE 16-3.

The monthly loan payments for each interest rate now appear in the data table.

When you create this data table, Excel enters the array formula

{ =TABLE(,A2)}

in each cell in the range C3:C8 (what we'll call the *results range*). In the sample table, the TABLE formula computes the results of the PMT function using each of the interest rates in column B. For example, the formula in cell C5 computes the payment at a rate of 7 percent.

The TABLE function used in the formula takes the form

=TABLE(row input cell,column input cell)

Because the one-input table in the example is arranged in a columnar format, Excel uses the column input reference, A2, as the function's second argument and leaves the first argument blank, using a comma to indicate that an argument has been omitted.

After you've built the table, you can change the table formula or any of the values in the input range to create a different set of results. For example, suppose you decide to borrow only $185,000 to buy your house. If you change the amount in cell C1 to 185000, the values in the results range change, as shown in Figure 16-4.

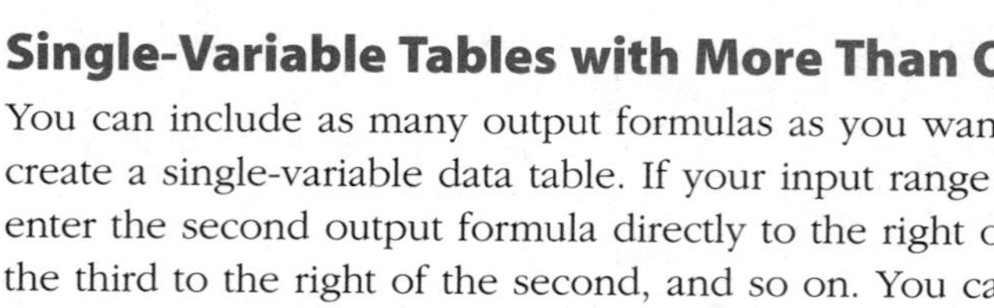

FIGURE 16-4.

When you change the loan amount, Excel recalculates the table.

Single-Variable Tables with More Than One Formula

You can include as many output formulas as you want when you create a single-variable data table. If your input range is in a column, enter the second output formula directly to the right of the first one, the third to the right of the second, and so on. You can use different formulas for different columns, but they must all use the same input cell.

Suppose you're also thinking about buying a house that would require you to take out a $180,000 mortgage. You want to know what your monthly payments would be on that mortgage at each of the interest rates in the input range, and you want to be able to compare these payments with those for the $200,000 mortgage calculated in Figure 16-3. You can expand the table in Figure 16-3 to include both formulas.

To add a new formula to the existing data table, follow these steps:

1 In the cell to the right of the existing formula—in this case, cell D2—enter the new formula. For this example, enter

=PMT(A2/12,360,D1)

Notice that this formula refers to cell A2, the same input cell as in the first formula.

2 Enter $180,000 in cell D1.

3 Select the table range—in this case, B2:D8.

4 Choose the Table command from the Data menu and then enter the input cell reference *$A$2* in the Column Input Cell edit box. Click OK. Figure 16-5 shows the result.

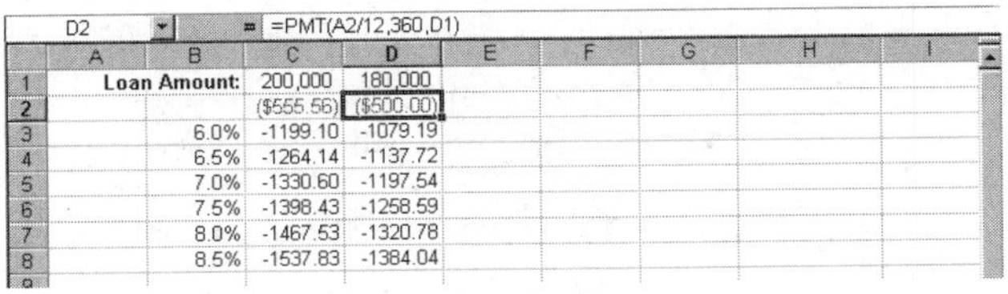

FIGURE 16-5.

This data table computes the monthly payments on two different loan amounts at various interest rates.

	A	B	C	D	E	F	G	H	I
	D2		= =PMT(A2/12,360,D1)						
1		Loan Amount:	200,000	180,000					
2			($555.56)	($500.00)					
3		6.0%	-1199.10	-1079.19					
4		6.5%	-1264.14	-1137.72					
5		7.0%	-1330.60	-1197.54					
6		7.5%	-1398.43	-1258.59					
7		8.0%	-1467.53	-1320.78					
8		8.5%	-1537.83	-1384.04					

As before, each cell in the range C3:D8 contains the formula

{ =TABLE(,A2)}

These formulas compute the results of the formulas in cells C2 and D2 at each interest rate in the input range. For example, the formula in cell D4 computes the result of the formula in cell D2 at the rate in cell B4, 6.5 percent.

Data Tables Based on Two Input Variables

The data tables considered so far compute the effect of a single variable on one or more formulas. You can also create tables that compute the effects of two variables on a single formula.

Suppose you want to build a data table that computes the monthly payment on a $200,000 mortgage, but this time you want to vary not only the interest rate but also the term of the loan. You want to know what effect changing the interest rate to 6, 6.5, 7, 7.5, 8, or 8.5 percent and changing the term to 15, 20, 25, or 30 years (180, 240, 300, or 360 months) will have on your monthly payment.

To create this table, follow these steps:

1 Enter the first set of input values you want to test in a column-oriented range. As before, enter the six interest rates in cells B3:B8.

2 Enter the second set of input values in a row-oriented range above and to the right of the first set. In this case, in cells C2:F2 enter the different terms for the loan: *180, 240, 300,* and *360*.

3 Enter the loan amount in a cell outside the table area; in this example, cell I2.

4 Now you can create the table formula. Because this is a two-variable table, the output formula must be entered in the cell at the intersection of the row and column that contain the two sets of input values—cell B2, in this example. Although you can include as many formulas as you want in a single-variable data table, you can include only one output formula in a two-variable table. The formula for the table in this example is

=PMT(A2/12,B1,I2)

In cell C1, enter the label *Months* and in cell A3 enter the label *Rate*. (We added some formatting to make the table easier to read.)

Figure 16-6 shows the result so far. The formula in cell B2 returns the *#DIV/0!* error value because the two blank cells A2 and B1, when used as arguments, produce a number either too large or too small for Excel to represent. As you'll see, this spurious result will not affect the performance of the table.

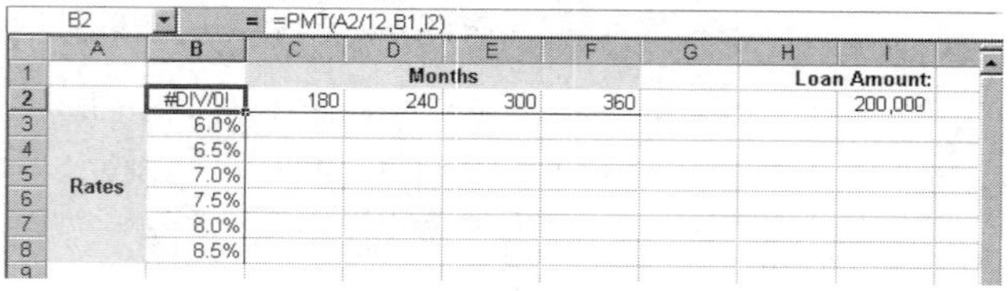

FIGURE 16-6.

Cell B2 contains the formula for this two-variable table.

B2		=	=PMT(A2/12,B1,I2)						
	A	B	C	D	E	F	G	H	I
1				Months					Loan Amount:
2		#DIV/0!	180	240	300	360			200,000
3		6.0%							
4		6.5%							
5	Rates	7.0%							
6		7.5%							
7		8.0%							
8		8.5%							
9									

5 Select the data table range—the smallest rectangular block that includes all the input values and the table formula. In this example, the table range is B2:F8.

6 Choose the Table command from the Data menu and specify the input cells. Because this is a two-variable table, you must define two input cells: one for the first set of input values and one for the second set. For this example, enter the reference for the first input cell, *$B$1*, in the Row Input Cell edit box and then enter the reference for the second input cell, *$A$2*, in the Column Input Cell edit box.

7 Press Enter or click OK to compute the table. Figure 16-7 shows the result. (We've formatted the payments in the table to two decimal places.)

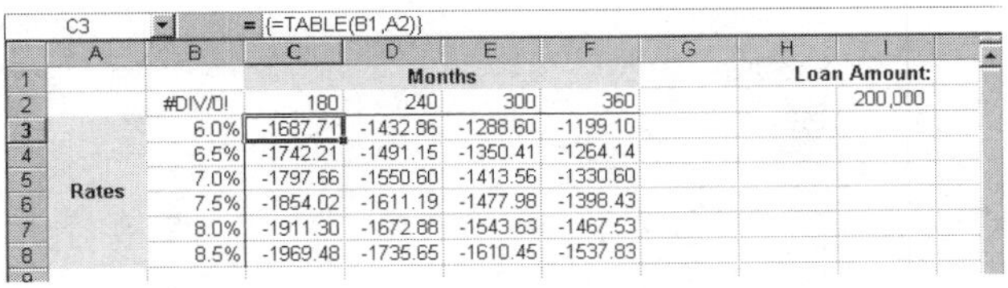

FIGURE 16-7.

This data table calculates the monthly payments using various interest rates and terms.

		A	B	C	D	E	F	G	H	I
C3				=(=TABLE(B1,A2))						
1					Months				Loan Amount:	
2			#DIV/0!	180	240	300	360			200,000
3			6.0%	-1687.71	-1432.86	-1288.60	-1199.10			
4			6.5%	-1742.21	-1491.15	-1350.41	-1264.14			
5		Rates	7.0%	-1797.66	-1550.60	-1413.56	-1330.60			
6			7.5%	-1854.02	-1611.19	-1477.98	-1398.43			
7			8.0%	-1911.30	-1672.88	-1543.63	-1467.53			
8			8.5%	-1969.48	-1735.65	-1610.45	-1537.83			

As in the previous examples, Excel enters TABLE array formulas in the results range C3:F8. Because this table has two sets of variables, the TABLE formula includes two references:

{ =TABLE(B1,A2)}

The values in the results range are the monthly payments required to amortize the mortgage at each combination of interest rates and terms. For example, the value in cell D6, -1611.19, is the payment required to amortize a $200,000 mortgage over 240 months at an interest rate of 7.5 percent.

Be careful not to reverse the input cells in a two-variable table. If you do, Excel uses the input values in the wrong place in the table formula, which creates a set of meaningless results. For example, if you reverse the input cells in the previous example, Excel uses the values in the input range C2:F2 as interest rates and the values in the input range B3:B8 as terms.

Editing Tables

Although you can edit the input values or formulas in the left column or top row of a table, you can't edit the contents of any individual cell in the results range because the data table is an array. For example, if you try to clear cell D7 in Figure 16-7, Excel displays an alert box with the message *Cannot change part of a table.* If you make a mistake when you set up a data table, you must select all the results, use the Clear command on the Edit menu, and then recompute the table.

SEE ALSO

For more information about copying and pasting ranges of cells, see "Moving and Copying with the Mouse," page 238.

You can copy the table results to a different part of the worksheet. You might want to do this to save the table's current results before you change the table formula or variables. To copy the results of the sample table in Figure 16-7 on the previous page from the range C3:F8 to the range C10:F15, select cells C3:F8, choose the Copy command from the Edit menu, select cell C10, and then choose the Paste command. As Figure 16-8 shows, the values in C10:F15 are constants, not array formulas. Excel changes the results of the table from a set of array formulas to their numeric values when you copy the results out of the table range.

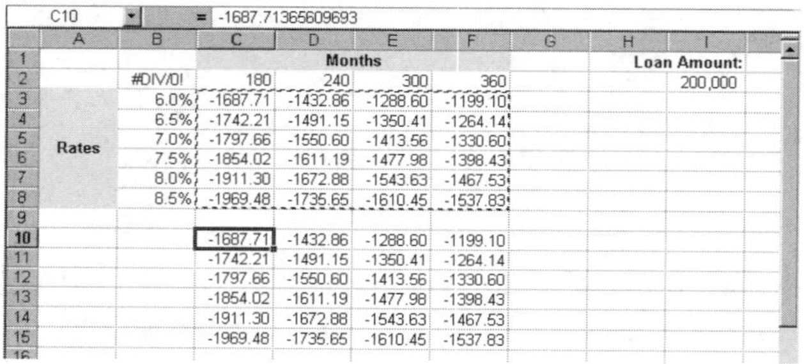

FIGURE 16-8.

Copying the results range to another part of the worksheet transfers the numeric values, not the formulas used to compute them.

The Scenario Manager

Data tables are fine for relatively simple situations that involve only one or two variables, but real-world decisions usually involve many more unknowns. To model more complicated problems that involve as many as 32 variables, you can call on the services of the Scenario Manager by choosing the Scenarios command from the Tools menu.

Before we get started, we'll define some terms so we're speaking the same language. A *scenario* is a named combination of values assigned to one or more variable cells in a what-if model. A *what-if model* is any worksheet, like the example in Figure 16-9, in which you can substitute different values for *variables,* such as Average Customer Visits, to see the effect on other values, such as Operating Profit, that are computed by formulas dependent on the variables. The Scenario Manager identifies cells that contain values you want to use as variables as *changing cells.*

You can find Grocery2000.xls used in the following example at *http://mspress.microsoft.com/mspress/products/2050/*.

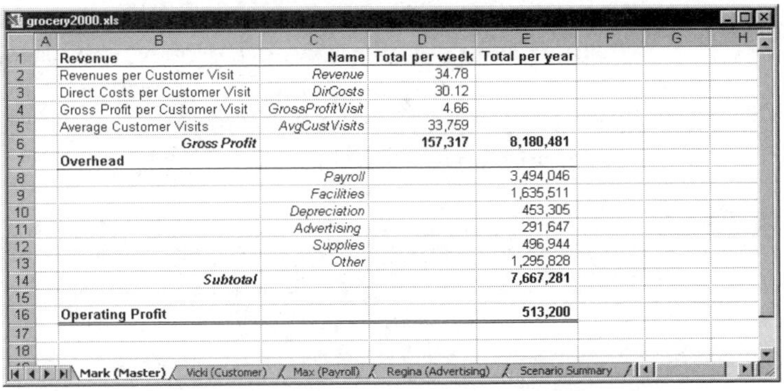

FIGURE 16-9.

We'll use the Scenario Manager to model the effects of changing values in D2:D3, D5, and E8:E13 of this worksheet.

	B	C	D	E
1	**Revenue**	Name	Total per week	Total per year
2	Revenues per Customer Visit	*Revenue*	34.78	
3	Direct Costs per Customer Visit	*DirCosts*	30.12	
4	Gross Profit per Customer Visit	*GrossProfitVisit*	4.66	
5	Average Customer Visits	*AvgCustVisits*	33,759	
6	*Gross Profit*		157,317	8,180,481
7	**Overhead**			
8		*Payroll*		3,494,046
9		*Facilities*		1,635,511
10		*Depreciation*		453,305
11		*Advertising*		291,647
12		*Supplies*		496,944
13		*Other*		1,295,828
14	*Subtotal*			7,667,281
15				
16	**Operating Profit**			513,200
17				
18				

Mark (Master) ╱ Vicki (Customer) ╱ Max (Payroll) ╱ Regina (Advertising) ╱ Scenario Summary

You can use the Scenario Manager to create as many scenarios as your what-if model requires, and you can then print reports detailing all the changing cells and result cells. The Scenario Manager includes the following features:

- You can create multiple scenarios for a single what-if model, each with its own sets of variables.

- You can distribute a what-if model to other members of your group so they can add their own scenarios. Then you can collect the multiple versions and merge all the scenarios into a single worksheet.

- You can track changes made to scenarios easily with the Scenario Manager's version-control features by recording the date and the user name each time a scenario is added or modified.

- You can password-protect scenarios from modification and even hide them from view.

SEE ALSO

For more information about PivotTables, see Chapter 27, "Using PivotTables."

- You can examine relationships between scenarios in which different sets of variables were created by multiple users by creating a Scenario Summary PivotTable using the PivotTable Report option. This adds another dimension to what-if analyses.

- You can define a scenario by simply selecting cells and typing a name with the Scenarios box on a custom toolbar that you can create.

III

Analyzing Data

To understand how the Scenario Manager works, imagine that you manage a grocery store whose profit picture is modeled by the worksheet in Figure 16-9. The numbers in D2:D5 and E8:E14 are recent historic averages; column C contains the names we've given to the relevant cells in columns D and E. You're interested in testing the impact of changes in these cells on the bottom line, which is shown in cell E15. Nine variables are far too many for the Table command, but the Scenario Manager can help.

> Before you begin using the Scenario Manager, it's a good idea to name the cells you plan to use for your variables, as well as any cells containing formulas whose values depend on your variable cells. This step is not required, but it makes the scenario reports, as well as some of the dialog boxes, more intelligible.

Defining Scenarios

To define a scenario, follow these steps:

1 Choose Scenarios from the Tools menu. (The Scenarios command does not normally appear on shortened menus. Click the double arrow at the bottom of the Tools menu to display the Scenarios command.)

2 In the Scenario Manager dialog box, shown in Figure 16-10, click the Add button.

FIGURE 16-10.

Choosing Scenarios from the Tools menu displays this Scenario Manager dialog box.

3 In the Add Scenario dialog box, shown in Figure 16-11, type a name for your scenario.

FIGURE 16-11.

Here we entered the references of the changing cells individually by selecting each one with the mouse and separating one reference from the next with a comma.

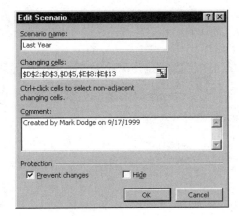

4 In the Changing Cells edit box, indicate which cells you plan to vary. By default, this edit box displays the reference of the cell or range that was selected when you chose the Scenarios command, but you can change it by typing new references or names or by selecting cells with the mouse. (If the Add Scenario dialog box is in your way, drag it to one side or click the Collapse Dialog button to the right of the Changing Cells edit box.) You can select nonadjacent cells and ranges by pressing the Ctrl key before selecting the cells or by separating their references or names with commas, as shown in Figure 16-11.

5 Click OK to create the first scenario.

6 The Scenario Values dialog box appears, displaying an edit box for each changing cell. If you have named the changing cells, the names are displayed adjacent to the edit boxes, as shown in Figure 16-12 on the next page; otherwise, the references of the changing cells are displayed. The edit boxes contain the corresponding values currently entered in the worksheet.

In each edit box, you can enter either a constant or a formula. For example, to increase the value of the first variable in Figure 16-12, click in front of the value in the first variable's edit box and type *=1.1** to create a formula that multiplies the current value by 1.1. (Note that although you can enter formulas in the Scenario Values dialog box, Excel alerts you that the formulas are converted to their resulting values when you click OK.) The Scenario Values dialog box displays only five variables at a time; use the scroll bar to display edit boxes for the other cells. To complete a scenario, you edit these values, but for this example, we'll leave the values as they are and just click OK.

FIGURE 16-12.

Enter a value for each changing cell. Because we previously named each changing cell, the names appear in the Scenario Values dialog box.

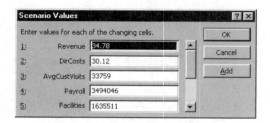

7 To create another scenario, click Add to return to the Add Scenario dialog box. (You can create as many scenarios as you want at this time.) When you have finished creating scenarios, click OK to return to the Scenario Manager dialog box. To return to the worksheet, click Close in the Scenario Manager dialog box. You can return to the Scenario Manager later to create or edit a scenario.

It's a good idea to define the values you start with as a scenario before changing any of them. You can name this scenario something like Starting Values or Last Year, as we did in the example. If you don't name the starting scenario, you'll lose your original what-if assumptions when you display the new changing cell values in your worksheet.

Using the Show Button to View Scenarios

After you've created a few scenarios, you'll probably want to start testing their effects on your worksheet. To do so, choose the Scenarios command, select a scenario name in the Scenario Manager dialog box, and then click Show. The Scenario Manager replaces the variable values currently in the worksheet with the values you specified when you created the selected scenario. Figure 16-13 shows how your worksheet might appear if you used the Show button with a scenario that increased average customer visits by 5 percent and decreased revenues per customer visit by the same percentage.

FIGURE 16-13.

Clicking the Show button replaces your current worksheet values with the values of a specified scenario.

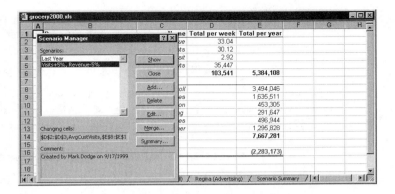

The Scenario Manager dialog box remains on screen when you use the Show button so that you can look at the results of other scenarios without returning to the worksheet. When you click Close or press Esc to close the Scenario Manager dialog box, the last scenario you looked at remains in the worksheet. As long as you have not made any other changes in the worksheet, you can reverse the effects of the last shown scenario by choosing the Edit menu's Undo Show command.

It's a good idea to save your worksheet before experimenting with the Scenario Manager's Show button, because the Show button replaces your worksheet's current values with the values from the selected scenario. After you've saved your worksheet, you can experiment to your heart's content, knowing that the original values are preserved. In any case, you can reverse the effects of the last few most recently displayed scenarios by repeated uses of the Edit menu's Undo command.

Adding, Editing, and Deleting Scenarios

Scenarios are saved with all other worksheet data when you use the File menu's Save command. Each worksheet in a workbook can contain its own set of scenarios, and each time you load a workbook, any scenarios associated with a particular worksheet are available. In the Scenario Manager dialog box, you add new scenarios by clicking Add, and you edit existing scenarios by clicking Edit.

Clicking the Edit button in the Scenario Manager dialog box displays the Edit Scenario dialog box, which is identical to the Add Scenario dialog box shown in Figure 16-11 on page 545. You can change the

III

Analyzing Data

name of the selected scenario, add changing cells, remove existing changing cells, or specify a completely different set of changing cells. When you click OK, the Scenario Values dialog box appears so you can edit the changing cell values.

As time goes by, you'll probably want to prune your scenario list. To erase a scenario, simply select the scenario's name in the Scenario Manager dialog box and click Delete.

How the Scenario Manager Tracks Changes

When someone edits a scenario, Excel adds a *Modified by* entry to the Comment box in the Scenario Manager dialog box, beneath the *Created by* entry that appears when a scenario is first added (see Figure 16-11 on page 545). Each time a scenario is modified, Excel adds the name of the user and the date of modification. This information is particularly helpful if you route your what-if models to others and then merge their scenarios into a single what-if model, as discussed below.

Merging Scenarios

If part of your job is to develop what-if models or projections for your company, you probably spend a lot of time gathering information about trends and market forces that might affect the company in the future. Often you need input from several people, each of whom knows about a particular aspect of the business, such as payroll costs or sales trends. In Excel, you can create scenarios with different sets of changing cells on the same worksheet. For example, you could create "best case" and "worst case" scenarios for payroll costs and sales trends. In addition, Excel includes two features to make this sort of information-gathering task easier: document routing and scenario merging.

? SEE ALSO

For more information about using routing slips, see Chapter 18, "Sharing Files with Others." For more information about Excel's file-sharing capabilities, see "Routing Workbooks to a Workgroup Using Electronic Mail," page 599.

If you are connected to a network that uses a compatible electronic mail system, you can use the Routing Recipient command on the Send To submenu of the File menu to attach the current workbook to an electronic mail message. Compatible electronic mail systems include Microsoft Outlook, Microsoft Mail, Lotus cc:Mail, and any other electronic mail application that complies with the MAPI (Messaging Application Programming Interface) or VIM (Vendor Independent Messaging) standards. Or, you can route workbooks using the Internet via Web documents and FTP sites. *For more information about using the Internet with Excel, see Chapter 19, "Hyperlinks and the Internet."*

If you are not connected to a network with a compatible electronic mail system, you can make copies of the worksheet containing your what-if model and distribute the copies to your coworkers the old-fashioned way—on floppy disks.

For example, suppose you want to distribute a what-if model to your coworkers: Vicki has expertise on customer trends, Max knows the payroll story, and Regina keeps track of advertising. You can consolidate their contributions in one of three ways: first, you can ask each person in turn to add his or her scenarios to the model in your original worksheet. Second, you can distribute a workbook with duplicates of the original model on four separate worksheets—one for you and one for each of them. To create this workbook, name each worksheet and select the worksheets as a group. Select the data to copy and choose Fill and then Across Worksheets from the Edit menu to copy all the data, formulas, and formats from the original model to the other three worksheets, as shown in Figure 16-14. You can then pass the workbook to each person in turn, with a request that they create their scenarios on their respective worksheets.

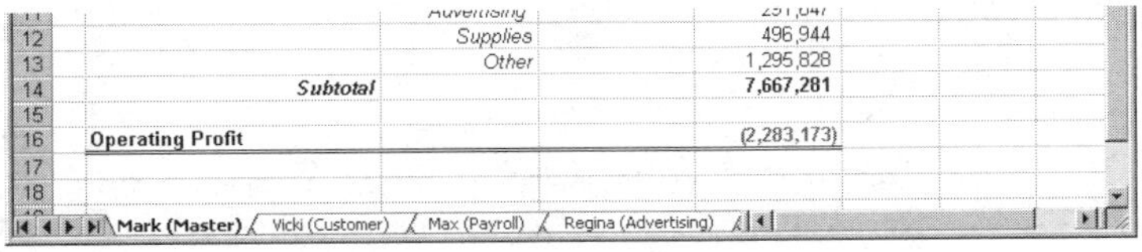

FIGURE 16-14.

This workbook is set up for distribution, with separate sheets for each coworker.

The third possibility is to make copies of the original workbook, each with a unique filename, so that each person can add his or her scenarios to a separate file.

With the second or third technique, after your coworkers add their what-if scenarios and return the workbook (or their copies of the workbook), you can merge the scenarios into a master worksheet. Simply open all of the workbooks containing the desired scenarios, activate the worksheet you wish to contain the merged scenarios, and use the Merge button in the Scenario Manager dialog box.

When you click the Merge button, a dialog box like the one in Figure 16-15 on the next page appears.

III

Analyzing Data

FIGURE 16-15.

Clicking Merge in the Scenario Manager dialog box displays the Merge Scenarios dialog box, with which you can import scenarios from any sheet in any open workbook.

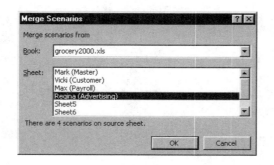

Merging scenarios works best if the basic structure of all the worksheets is identical. Although this uniformity is not a strict requirement, merging scenarios from worksheets that are laid out differently can cause changing cell values to appear in unexpected locations. For this reason, and because it's generally difficult to ascertain the skill level of everyone contributing data, you might try a fourth approach. Distribute a "questionnaire" requesting only the data you need, use external cell references to link the requested data with the appropriate locations in your master worksheet, and create the scenarios yourself or with a macro. *For more information about external cell references, see "Three-Dimensional Names," page 140, and "Defining Sheet-Level Names," page 136.*

In the Merge Scenarios dialog box, you select the workbook and worksheet from which you want to merge scenarios. As shown in Figure 16-15, when you select a worksheet from the Sheet list, a message at the bottom of the dialog box tells you how many scenarios exist on that worksheet. When you click OK, the scenarios on that worksheet are copied to the active worksheet. (The OK button appears dimmed if you try to merge a scenario from the active worksheet or from a worksheet on which there are no scenarios.)

After you've merged all the scenarios from your coworkers, the Scenario Manager dialog box for this example looks like the one shown in Figure 16-16 on page 552.

The Scenario Express

The quickest and easiest way to define and display scenarios is to add the Scenarios box to a standard or custom toolbar. To illustrate, let's create a custom Scenarios toolbar:

1 Choose Toolbars from the View menu and then choose Customize. Excel displays the Customize dialog box.

2 On the Toolbars tab, click the New button.

3 Excel presents the New Toolbar dialog box. Enter *Scenarios* and click OK. Excel displays a new, empty Scenarios toolbar.

4 In the Customize dialog box, click the Commands tab.

5 From the Categories list, select the Tools item.

6 In the Commands list, scroll down, find the Scenarios command and the Scenario box and drag them to your new Scenarios toolbar. After you've done this, the Scenarios toolbar should look like this:

To display your new Scenarios toolbar, from the View menu choose Toolbars and then Scenarios; the Scenarios box lists all the scenarios defined in the active workbook.

To use the Scenarios box, first enter new values in the changing cells, select them, click the Scenarios box, type a name for the new scenario, and then press Enter. Using this technique, you can define as many scenarios as you want, without ever using the Scenario Manager dialog box.

When you want to display a scenario, click the down arrow next to the Scenarios box and select the name of the scenario you want to show from the drop-down list.

You can also redefine scenarios using the Scenarios box. First, select the name of the scenario you want to redefine from the Scenarios drop-down list to display its changing cell values. Next, enter new values in the changing cells and again select the same scenario name from the Scenarios drop-down list. A dialog box appears, asking you to confirm that you want to redefine the scenario. (If you modify any of the current changing cell values, be careful not to inadvertently redefine the current scenario by selecting its name from the Scenarios drop-down list.)

III

Analyzing Data

FIGURE 16-16.

The merged scenarios now appear in the same worksheet. When identically named scenarios are merged, Excel assigns them unique names by appending creator names, dates, or numbers.

⑦ SEE ALSO

For more information about the Fill and Across Worksheets commands, see "The Across Worksheets Command," page 275. For more information about group editing, see "Editing Groups of Sheets Simultaneously," page 326.

Notice in Figure 16-16 that the Comment box displays the name of the creator and modifier of the selected scenario. Notice also that the Scenarios list includes similarly named scenarios. In this example, all the coworkers used the same three names—Expected, Best Case, and Worst Case—for their scenarios, and Excel avoided conflicts by appending the creation date when it encountered duplicate scenario names. Excel also used numbers to distinguish merged scenarios that were created on the same date, as shown by the last two scenarios listed in Figure 16-16. You can use the Edit button to rename the scenarios if you want, but you might find it useful to retain the creation dates.

Each group of scenarios provided by the coworkers uses different changing cells. Vicki's scenarios change the values in cells D2, D3, and D5, while Max's scenarios change only the value in E8, and Regina's scenarios change only the value in E11. You can display these different scenarios together and watch how the combinations affect the bottom line. For example, some of the values in the master scenarios have been changed in Vicki's, Max's, and Regina's scenarios. You could start out by displaying one of the master scenarios and then observe the effect of adding each of the other sets of changing cells to the model. The possibilities are virtually limitless.

Creating Scenario Reports

The Grocery2000 workbook, with its merged scenarios, has become quite a complex what-if model. However, you can create far more complex models that include as many scenarios as you want (or as many as your computer can handle) with up to 32 variables per scenario. The Scenario Manager's summary reports help you keep track of all the possibilities, and the PivotTable Report option gives you additional what-if functionality by allowing you to manipulate the elements of the report.

Clicking the Summary button in the Scenario Manager dialog box displays a dialog box with which you create a new worksheet containing a report that shows the values each scenario assigns to each changing cell. Optionally, this report can also show the impact of each scenario on one or more result cells. Figure 16-17 shows the dialog box that appears when you click the Summary button while working in the Grocery2000 workbook.

FIGURE 16-17.

Use the Scenario Summary dialog box to specify the type of report and the result cells you want to see.

In the top section of this dialog box, you select the type of report you want. At the bottom of the dialog box, you can identify any result cells you want to appear in the report, separated by commas (optional). For result cells, you want the cell that happens to be the final dependent of the changing cells—in this case, the Operating Profit value in cell E16 as well as cell E6, the yearly Gross Profit value.

The Scenario Summary Report

SEE ALSO

For information about moving worksheets in workbooks, see "Working with Sheets," page 311.

After you specify the result cells and then click OK, the Scenario Manager creates a report in a new worksheet. If you selected the Scenario Summary option in the Report Type section of the Scenario Summary dialog box, a fully formatted worksheet named Scenario Summary is inserted next to the active worksheet in your workbook, as shown in Figure 16-18. (We moved the Scenario Summary sheet to the end of the workbook. Also, in order to display more of the report on screen, we adjusted column widths and wrapped text in the row 3 headings.)

III

Analyzing Data

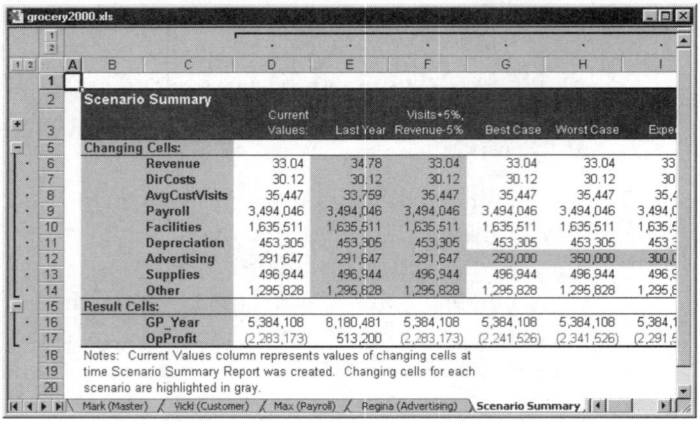

FIGURE 16-18.

The Scenario Summary option creates a report in a new worksheet named Scenario Summary.

SEE ALSO

For more information about adding notes to worksheets, see "Adding Comments to Cells," page 292.

Notice that the summary lists the changing cells and result cells by name if you have assigned names to them. The names of the scenarios appear as column headings, and the columns appear in the order in which the scenarios were defined. You might want to add a scenario description to each column by typing text in new rows inserted below the column headings, by creating text boxes, or by using the Comment command on the Insert menu. (The Comment command does not normally appear on shortened menus. Click the double arrow at the bottom of the Insert menu to display the Comment command.)

In Figure 16-18, notice that all the changing cell values in columns E and F are shaded in gray. The shading indicates the cells that were designated as changing cells in the Add Scenario dialog box when the scenario whose name appears at the top of the column was created.

SEE ALSO

For information about working with worksheet outlines, see "Outlining Your Worksheets," page 225.

Also notice that outlining symbols appear above and to the left of the summary report, allowing you to show and hide details. In Figure 16-18, the show detail symbol to the left of row 3 indicates that something is hidden here. As you can see in Figure 16-19, clicking this symbol displays the hidden data—the contents of the Comment box in the Scenario Manager dialog box, including the creation and modification date of each scenario.

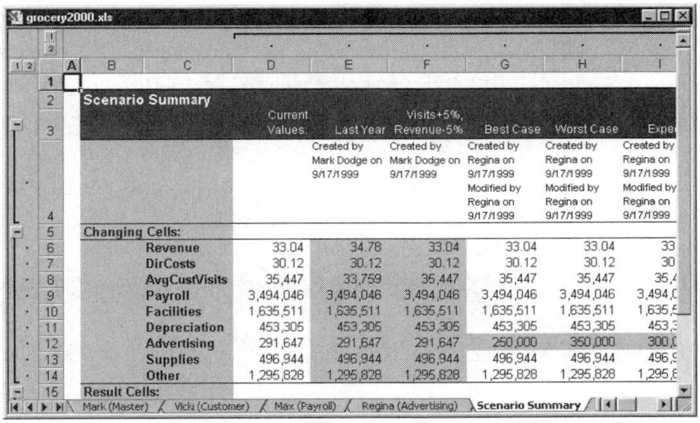

FIGURE 16-19.

The comments entered into the Scenario Manager dialog box are hidden in row 4 of the Scenario Summary report.

The PivotTable Report

? SEE ALSO

For more information about PivotTables and the PivotTable toolbar, see Chapter 27, "Using PivotTables."

The other report option in the Scenario Summary dialog box is Scenario PivotTable. Like the Scenario Summary option, the Scenario PivotTable option inserts a new worksheet in your workbook. However, pivot tables are what-if tools in their own right, allowing you to use direct mouse-manipulation techniques to mix and match different scenarios in the report and watch the effects on result cells.

Pivot tables are powerful analysis tools best suited to complex what-if models that include scenarios with different sets of changing cells created by different people. The more one-dimensional your what-if model, the less useful a PivotTable report becomes. Pivot tables take longer to create and consume more memory than summary reports. If you create all the scenarios yourself and use the same set of changing cells in each, you might find it easier to use the Scenario Summary option because you won't be able to make use of the advantages offered by the PivotTable report.

Figure 16-20 on the next page shows a PivotTable report created from a version of the merged-scenario Grocery2000 workbook. When you display a PivotTable report, the PivotTable toolbar appears.

The report cells containing numeric data represent the result cells as they would appear given the scenarios as they are currently displayed in the report. The row fields initially display the changing cells, whose

III

Analyzing Data

names appear in shaded boxes above the names of each scenario in which the changing cells are included. The result cells initially appear across the top of the table. To try a different arrangement, you simply drag any of the shaded boxes from one area to another. The boxes in the upper left corner of the report are drop-down lists with the names of the scenario creators. By default, the All option is selected, but you can select any individual name.

FIGURE 16-20.

The Scenario PivotTable report lets you manipulate the actual data in the report.

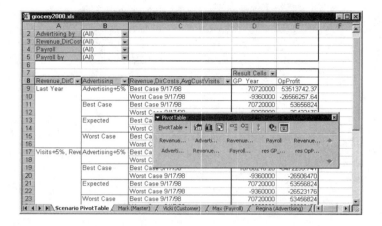

The Goal Seek Command

With the Tools menu's Goal Seek command, you can compute an unknown value that will produce a desired result. (The Goal Seek command does not normally appear on shortened menus. Click the double arrow at the bottom of the Tools menu to display the Goal Seek command.) For example, suppose you want to know the maximum 30-year mortgage you can afford if the interest rate is 6.5 percent and if you must limit your monthly payments to $2,000. To use the Goal Seek command to answer this question, follow these steps:

1   Set up the problem with trial values. For example, in the mortgage problem shown in Figure 16-21, a $500,000 mortgage would require monthly payments in excess of the $2,000 target. To define names for the cells B1:B4, select cells A1:B4 and choose Name from the Insert menu and then Create. Check the Left Column option and click OK.

 **ON THE WEB**

You can find Goal Seek.xls used in the following example on the Microsoft Press Web site at *http://mspress.microsoft.com/mspress/products/2050/*.

FIGURE 16-21.

Goal seeking helps find the maximum you can borrow with a given payment limit.

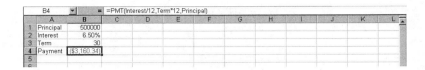

2 Make the formula cell—in this case, B4—the active cell. (This isn't absolutely necessary, but it simplifies the process.)

3 From the Tools menu, choose the Goal Seek command. (The Goal Seek command does not normally appear on shortened menus. Click the double arrow at the bottom of the Tools menu to display the Goal Seek command.)

4 In the Goal Seek dialog box, shown in Figure 16-22, accept the value in the Set Cell edit box (the absolute reference of the active cell).

FIGURE 16-22.

You might need Goal Seek to use more iterations for precision.

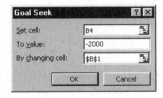

5 In the To Value edit box, type the maximum value you want as the result of the formula—in this case, *-2000*. (You enter a negative number because the payment represents cash spent rather than received.)

6 In the By Changing Cell edit box, type the reference or click the cell in the worksheet whose value is unknown—in this case, cell B1 (the Principal value). (Alternatively, if you have assigned a name such as *Principal* to cell B1, you can type that name in the By Changing Cell edit box.)

7 Click OK or press Enter. Excel displays the Goal Seek Status dialog box shown in Figure 16-23 on the next page. The answer you are looking for appears in the cell specified in the By Changing Cell edit box. In this example, the result 316,421.64 appears in cell B1.

8 To retain this value, click OK in the Goal Seek Status dialog box. To restore the value that was in B1 before you used the Goal Seek command, click Cancel.

III

Analyzing Data

FIGURE 16-23.

The Goal Seek Status dialog box informs you when a solution is found.

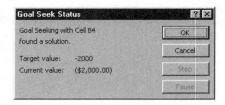

Excel uses an iterative technique to perform goal seeking. It tries one value after another for the variable cell specified in the By Changing Cell edit box until it arrives at the solution you requested. The mortgage problem we just looked at can be solved quickly. Other problems might take longer, and some might not be solvable at all.

While Excel is working on a complex goal-seeking problem, you can click Pause in the Goal Seek Status dialog box to interrupt the calculation and then click Step to display the results of each successive iteration. A Continue button appears in the dialog box when you are solving a problem in this stepwise fashion. To resume full-speed goal seeking, click Continue.

Precision and Multiple Solutions

For more information about worksheet calculation options, see "Calculating the Worksheet," page 149.

Suppose you enter the formula =$A2\textasciicircum2$ in cell A1 of a blank worksheet and then use the Goal Seek command to find the value of A2 that will make A1 equal to 4. (That is, in the Goal Seek dialog box enter $A$1 in the Set Cell edit box, 4 in the To Value edit box, and $A$2 in the By Changing Cell edit box.) The result, shown in Figure 16-24, might be a little surprising. Excel seems to be telling you that the closest value it can find to the square root of 4 is 2.000023.

FIGURE 16-24.

The Goal Seek command returns this result when asked to find the square root of 4.

	A	B	C	D	E	F	G	H	I	J	K	L
	A1		=	=A2^2								
1	4.000092											
2	2.000023											
3												
4												

By default, the Goal Seek command stops when it has either performed 100 iterations (trial solutions) or found an answer that comes to within 0.001 of your specified target value. If you need greater precision than this, you can change the default limits by choosing the Options command from the Tools menu, clicking the Calculation tab, and then changing the Maximum Iterations value to a number higher than 100, the Maximum Change value to a number less than 0.001, or both.

This example illustrates another factor you should be aware of when you use the Goal Seek command. The Goal Seek command finds only one solution, even though your problem might have several. In this case, the value 4 has two square roots: +2 and -2. In situations like this, the Goal Seek command gives you the solution with the same sign as the starting value. For instance, if you start with a value of -1 in cell A2, the Goal Seek command reports the solution as -1.999917, instead of +2.000023.

The Solver

The Goal Seek command is handy for problems that involve an exact target value that depends on a single unknown value. For more complex problems, you should use the Solver. The Solver can handle problems that involve many variable cells and can help you find combinations of variables that maximize or minimize a target cell. It also lets you specify one or more constraints—conditions that must be met for the solution to be valid.

The Solver is an add-in. If you performed a full installation of Excel, the Tools menu includes the Solver command. If you don't find that command on the Tools menu, choose the Add-Ins command instead and then select Solver Add-In in the Add-Ins Available list box. If the Solver isn't on the list, Excel asks whether you want to install it.

This section provides only an introduction to the Solver. A complete treatment of this powerful tool is beyond the scope of this book. For more details, including an explanation of the Solver's error messages, see Excel's online Help system. For background material on optimization, we recommend two textbooks: *Management Science,* by Andrew W. Shogan (Englewood Cliffs, New Jersey: Prentice-Hall, 1988) and *Operations Research, Applications and Algorithms,* by Wayne L. Winston (Boston: PWS-Kent Publishing Co., 1991).

As an example of the kind of problem that the Solver can tackle, imagine you are planning an advertising campaign for a new product. Your total budget for print advertising is $12,000,000; you want to expose your ads at least 800 million times to potential readers; and you've decided to place ads in six publications—we'll call them Pub1 through Pub6. Each publication reaches a different number of readers and charges a different rate per page. (To keep this analysis simpler, we'll ignore the issue of quantity discounts.) Your job is to reach the readership target at the lowest possible cost with the following additional constraints:

- At least six advertisements should run in each publication.

- No more than a third of your advertising dollars should be spent on any one publication.

- Your total cost for placing advertisements in Pub3 and Pub4 must not exceed $7,500,000.

Figure 16-25 shows one way to lay out the problem.

 **ON THE WEB**

You can find AdCampaign2000.xls used in the following example on the Microsoft Press Web site at *http://mspress.microsoft.com/mspress/ products/2050/.*

FIGURE 16-25.

You can use the Solver to determine how many advertisements to place in each publication in order to meet your objectives at the lowest possible cost.

	Publication	Cost per ad	Audience per ad (millions)	Number of ads placed	Total cost	Percent of total	Total audience (millions)
2	Pub1	$147,420	9.9	6.0	$884,520	26%	59
3	Pub2	$124,410	8.4	6.0	$746,460	22%	50
4	Pub3	$113,100	8.2	6.0	$678,600	20%	49
5	Pub4	$70,070	5.1	6.0	$420,420	13%	31
6	Pub5	$53,000	3.7	6.0	$318,000	9%	22
7	Pub6	$52,440	3.6	6.0	$314,640	9%	22
8	Total				$3,362,640		233
9	Total Pub3 + Pub4				$1,099,020		
10							
11		Constraints:			Total advertising budget		$12,000,000
12					Total budget for Pub3 + Pub4		$7,500,000
13					Minmum total audience (millions)		800
14					Maximum % of budget spent on any publication		33.30%
15					Maximum number of ads per publication		6

You might be able to work out this problem yourself by substituting many alternatives for the values currently in D2:D7, keeping your eye on the constraints, and noting the impact of your changes on the total expenditure figure in E8. In fact, that's what the Solver will do for you—but it will do it much more rapidly, and it will use some analytic techniques to home in on the optimal solution without having to try every conceivable alternative.

To use the Solver, choose the Solver command from the Tools menu. The dialog box shown in Figure 16-26 appears. To complete this dialog box, you must give the Solver three pieces of information: your objective, or *target* (to minimize total expenditure); your variables or *changing cells* (the number of advertisements you will place in each publication); and your *constraints* (the conditions summarized at the bottom of the worksheet in Figure 16-25).

FIGURE 16-26.

Use the Solver Parameters dialog box to set up your problem.

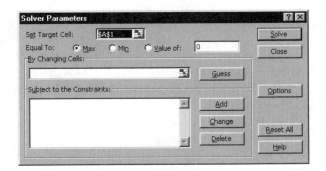

Stating the Objective

In the Set Target Cell edit box, you indicate the goal, or *target,* you want the Solver to achieve. In this example, you want to minimize your total cost—the value in cell E8—so you specify your objective by entering E8 in the Set Target Cell edit box and selecting Min as the Equal To option.

You can enter your objective in the Set Target Cell edit box by typing a cell's coordinates, typing a name that has been assigned to a cell, or clicking a cell in the worksheet. If you assign a name to the target cell, the Solver uses that name in its reports. If you don't name the cell, the Solver's reports construct a name based on the nearest column-heading and row-heading text, but these constructed names don't appear in the Solver dialog boxes. For clarity, it's a good idea to name all the important cells of your model before you put the Solver to work.

In this example, you want the Solver to set your target cell to its lowest possible value, so you select Min. In other problems, you might want to raise a target cell to its highest possible value by selecting the Max option—for example, if your target cell expresses profits. Or you might want the Solver to find a solution that makes your target cell equal to some particular value, in which case you would select the Value Of option and enter an amount (or a cell reference) in the adjacent edit box. (Note that by selecting the Value Of option, specifying only one variable cell, and specifying no constraints, you can use the Solver as a glorified Goal Seek command.)

SEE ALSO

For more information about the Show Iteration Results option, see "The Show Iteration Results Option," page 568.

You don't have to specify an objective. If you leave the Set Target Cell edit box blank, click the Options button, and select the Show Iteration Results option, you can use the Solver to step through some or all of the combinations of variable cells that meet your constraints. You will then get an answer that solves the constraints but is not necessarily the optimal solution.

Specifying Variable Cells

The next step is to tell the Solver which cells to change—that is, you need to specify your variable cells, or *changing cells*. In the advertisement campaign example, the cells whose values can be adjusted are those that specify the number of advertisements to be placed in each publication. These cells lie in the range D2:D7. As before, you can provide this information by typing cell coordinates, typing cell names, or selecting cells in the worksheet. If the variables are not in adjacent cells, you can separate variable cells (or ranges) with commas. (If you click nonadjacent cells to enter their references, hold down Ctrl while you select each cell or range.) Alternatively, you can click Guess, and the Solver will propose the appropriate changing cells based on the target cell you specified.

You must specify at least one variable cell; otherwise, the Solver will have nothing to do. If you specify a target cell (as you will in most cases), you must specify variable cells that are *precedents* of the target cell; that is, cells that the formula in the target cell depends on for its calculation. If the target cell's value does not depend on the variables, the Solver will not be able to solve anything.

Specifying Constraints

The last step, specifying constraints, is optional. To specify a constraint, click the Add button in the Solver Parameters dialog box and complete the Add Constraint dialog box. Figure 16-27 shows the constraint that total advertising expenditures (the value in cell E8 in the model) must be less than or equal to the total budget (the value in cell G11).

FIGURE 16-27.

Click the Add button in the Solver Parameters dialog box to add constraints.

As you can see, a constraint consists of three components: a cell reference, a comparison operator, and a constraint value. You specify the cell reference in the Cell Reference edit box, select a comparison operator from the drop-down list in the middle of the dialog box, and specify the constraint value in the edit box on the right. After specifying a constraint in this manner, you can either click OK to return to the Solver Parameters dialog box or click Add to specify another constraint.

Figure 16-28 shows how the Solver Parameters dialog box looks after all your constraints have been specified. Notice that the constraints are listed in alphabetical order, not necessarily in the order in which you defined them.

FIGURE 16-28.

The Solver lists the constraints in alphabetical order and uses defined cell and range names whenever possible.

Also notice that two of the constraints have range references on the left side of the comparison operator. The expression

$D$2:$D$7>=$G$15

stipulates that the value of each cell in D2:D7 must be 6 or greater, and the expression

$F$2:$F$7<=$G$14

stipulates that the value of each cell in F2:F9 must be no greater than 33.30 percent. Each of these expressions is a shortcut way of stating six separate constraints. If you use this kind of shortcut, the constraint value on the right side of the comparison operator must be a range of the same dimensions as the range on the left side, a single cell reference, or a constant value.

After completing the Solver Parameters dialog box, click Solve. As the Solver works, messages appear in the status bar. The Solver plugs trial values into your variable cells, recalculates the worksheet, and then tests the results. By comparing the outcome of each iteration with that of preceding iterations, the Solver homes in on a set of values that meets your objective and satisfies your constraints.

In the advertisement campaign example, the Solver succeeds in finding an optimal value for the objective cell while meeting all the constraints and displays the dialog box shown in Figure 16-29 on the next page. The values displayed in your worksheet at that time result in the optimal solution. You can leave these values in the worksheet by selecting the Keep Solver Solution option and clicking OK, or you can restore the values that your variables held before you activated the Solver by clicking Cancel or by selecting the Restore Original Values option and clicking OK. You also have the option of assigning the solution values to a named scenario.

III

Analyzing Data

FIGURE 16-29.

When the Solver succeeds, it presents the Solver Results dialog box.

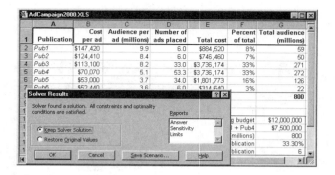

The solution values shown in Figure 16-29 indicate that you will expose your target audience to your advertisements 800 million times (assuming the publications' readership numbers are correct).

Specifying Integer Constraints

Notice that in Figure 16-29, the Solver arrived at 53.3 for the Number of Ads Placed in Pub4. Unfortunately, because it's not possible to run three-tenths of an advertisement, the solution is not practical. You can cope with the noninteger results by adding new constraints that force the results to be whole numbers.

To stipulate that your advertisement placement variables be restricted to whole numbers, you invoke the Solver as usual and then click the Add button in the Solver Parameters dialog box. In the Add Constraint dialog box, you select the range that holds your ad placement numbers—D2:D7. Next, display the drop-down list in the middle of the dialog box and then select *int*. The Solver inserts the word integer in the Constraint edit box, as shown in Figure 16-30. Click OK to return to the Solver Parameters dialog box.

FIGURE 16-30.

To specify an integer constraint, select the item labeled *int* in the drop-down list.

Note that when converting numbers to integers, Excel effectively rounds down; the decimal portion of the number is simply truncated. The integer solution shows that by placing 53 ads in Pub4, you can buy an additional ad in Pub5. For a very small increase in budget you can reach an additional 2 million readers.

> ### Do You Need Integer Constraints?
>
> Adding integer constraints to a Solver problem can geometrically increase the problem's complexity, resulting in possibly unacceptable delays. The example discussed in this chapter is relatively simple and does not take an inordinate amount of time to solve, but a more complex problem with integer constraints might pose more of a challenge for the Solver. Certain problems can only be solved using integer constraints. In particular, integer solutions are useful for problems in which variables can assume only two values, such as 1 or 0 (yes or no), but you can also use the bin (binary) option in the drop-down list in the middle of the Change Constraint dialog box.

Saving and Reusing the Solver Parameters

When you save a workbook after using the Solver, all the values you entered in the Solver's dialog boxes are saved along with your worksheet data. You do not need to respecify the problem if you want to continue working with it during a later Excel session.

Each worksheet in a workbook can store one set of Solver parameter values. To store more than one set of Solver parameters with a given worksheet, you must use the Solver's Save Model option. To use this option, follow these steps:

1   Choose Solver from the Tools menu.

2   Click the Options button, then in the Solver Options dialog box shown in Figure 16-31, click Save Model. Excel prompts you for a cell or range in which to store the Solver parameters on the worksheet.

FIGURE 16-31.

The Load Model and Save Model buttons in the Solver Options dialog box provide a way to store and retrieve your Solver parameters.

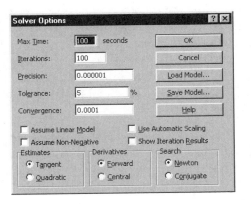

III

Analyzing Data

3   Specify a blank cell by clicking it or typing its reference and then click OK. If you specify a single cell, the Solver pastes in the model range, starting at the indicated cell and inserting formulas in as many of the cells below it as necessary. (Be sure the cells below the indicated cell do not contain data.) If you specify a range, the Solver fills only the specified cells with the model parameters. If the range is too small, some of your parameters will not be saved.

4   To reuse the saved parameters, click Options in the Solver Parameters dialog box, click Load Model, and then specify the range in which you stored the Solver parameters.

You'll find it easiest to save and reuse Solver parameters if you assign a name to each model range immediately after you use the Save Model option. You can then specify that name when you use the Load Model option.

Assigning the Solver Results to Named Scenarios

? SEE ALSO

For more information about what-if scenarios, see "The Scenario Manager," page 542.

An even better way to save your Solver parameters is to save them as named scenarios using the Scenario Manager. As you might have noticed, the Solver Results dialog box shown in Figure 16-29 on page 564 includes a Save Scenario button. Click this button to assign a scenario name to the current values of your variable cells. This option provides an excellent way to explore and perform further what-if analysis on a variety of possible outcomes.

Other Solver Options

The Solver Options dialog box shown in Figure 16-31 on the previous page contains several options that might need some explanation. With the Max Time and Iterations edit boxes, you tell the Solver, in effect, how hard to work on the solution. If the Solver reaches either the time limit or the number of iterations limit before finding a solution, calculation stops and Excel asks you whether you want to continue. The default settings are usually sufficient for solving most problems, but if you don't reach a solution with these settings, you can try adjusting them.

The Precision setting is used by the Solver to determine how closely you want values in the constraint cells to match your constraints. The closer this setting is to the value 1, the lower the precision. Specifying a setting that is less than the default 0.000001 results in a longer solution time.

The Tolerance setting applies only to problems that use integer constraints and represents a percentage of error allowed in the solution.

The Estimates, Derivatives, and Search options are best left at their default settings, unless you understand linear optimization techniques. If you want more information about these options, refer to Excel's online Help system.

The Assume Linear Model Option

A *linear* optimization problem is one in which the value of the target cell is a linear function of each variable cell; that is, if you plot XY charts of the target cell's value against all meaningful values of each variable cell, your charts are straight lines. If some of your plots produce curves instead of straight lines, the problem is nonlinear.

The Assume Linear Model option can be activated only for what-if models in which all the relationships are linear. Models that use simple addition and subtraction and worksheet functions such as SUM are linear in nature. However, most models are *nonlinear*. They are generated by multiplying changing cells by other changing cells, by using exponentiation or growth factors, or by using nonlinear worksheet functions such as PMT.

The Solver can handle both linear and nonlinear optimization problems. It can solve linear problems more quickly if you click the Options button in the Solver Parameters dialog box and then select the Assume Linear Model option. If you select this option for a nonlinear problem and then try to solve the problem, however, the Solver Results dialog box displays the message *The conditions for Assume Linear Model are not satisfied*. If you are not sure about the nature of your model, it's best not to use this option.

The Importance of Using Appropriate Starting Values

If your problem is nonlinear, you must be aware of one very important detail: your choice of starting values can affect the solution generated by the Solver. With nonlinear problems you should always do the following:

- Set your variable cells to reasonable approximations of their optimal values before running the problem.

- Test alternative starting values to see what impact, if any, they have on the Solver's solution.

III

Analyzing Data

For more information about the Sensitivity report, see "The Sensitivity Report," below.

If you select the Assume Linear Model option and then select the Sensitivity report option, the Solver produces a Sensitivity report in a slightly different form than for nonlinear problems.

The Show Iteration Results Option

If you're interested in exploring many combinations of your variable cells, rather than only the combination that produces the optimal result, you can take advantage of the Solver's Show Iteration Results option. Simply click the Options button in the Solver Parameters dialog box and then select the Show Iteration Results option in the Solver Options dialog box. After each iteration, the Show Trial Solution dialog box appears, which allows you to save the scenario and then either stop or continue with the next iteration.

You should be aware that when you use the Show Iteration Results option, the Solver pauses for solutions that do not meet all your constraints as well as for suboptimal solutions that do.

Generating Reports

In addition to inserting optimal values in your problem's variable cells, the Solver can summarize its results in three reports: Answer, Sensitivity, and Limits. To generate one or more reports, select the names of the reports in the Solver Results dialog box shown in Figure 16-29 on page 564. Select the reports you want and then click OK. (Hold down Ctrl to select more than one.) Each report is saved on a separate worksheet in the current workbook, with the tab identifying the name of the report.

The Sensitivity Report

The Sensitivity report provides information about how sensitive your target cell is to changes in your constraints. This report has two sections: one for your variable cells and one for your constraints. The right column in each section provides the sensitivity information.

Each changing cell and constraint cell is listed in a separate row. The Changing Cell section includes a Reduced Gradient value that indicates how the target cell would be affected by a one-unit increase in the corresponding changing cell. Similarly, the Lagrange Multiplier column in the Constraints section indicates how the target cell would be affected by a one-unit increase in the corresponding constraint value.

Note that if you place integer constraints on the results, Excel displays a message indicating *Sensitivity Report and Limits Report are not meaningful for problems with integer constraints.*

The Linear Model Sensitivity Report

If you select the Assume Linear Model option in the Solver Options dialog box, the Sensitivity report includes several additional columns of information.

For changing cells, the Reduced Cost column shows the increase in target cell value per unit of change in the changing cell value. The Objective Coefficient column shows the degree to which the changing cell and the target cell are related. The Allowable Increase and Allowable Decrease columns show the amount that the Objective Coefficient must change before the changing cells are affected.

For constraints, the Shadow Price column indicates the increase in the target value for each unit that the constraint increases. The Constraint RH Side column simply displays the constraint values used in the problem. And the Allowable Increase and Allowable Decrease columns show the amount that the constraint value (shown in the Constraint RH Side column) must change before the changing cells are affected.

The Answer Report

The Answer report lists the target cell, the variable cells, and the constraints. This report also includes information about the status of and slack value for each constraint. The status can be Binding, Not Binding, or Not Satisfied. The slack value is the difference between the solution value of the constraint cells and the number that appears on the right side of the constraint formula. A binding constraint is one for which the slack value is 0. A nonbinding constraint is a constraint that was satisfied with a nonzero slack value.

The Limits Report

The Limits report tells you how much the values of your variable cells can be increased or decreased without breaking the constraints of your problem. For each variable cell, this report lists the optimal value as well as the lowest and highest values that can be used without violating constraints.

III

Analyzing Data

When the Solver Is Unable to Solve

The Solver is powerful but not miraculous. It might not be able to solve every problem you give it. If the Solver can't find the optimal solution to your problem, it presents an unsuccessful completion message in the Solver Solution dialog box.

The most common unsuccessful completion messages are the following:

- **Solver could not find a feasible solution.** The Solver is unable to find a solution that satisfies all your constraints. This can happen if the constraints are logically conflicting (for example, if in separate constraints you ask that Pub1 be greater than 5 and less than 3) or if not all the constraints can be satisfied (for example, if you insist that your advertising campaign reach 800 million readers on a $1 million budget).

  In some cases, the Solver also returns this message if the starting values of your variable cells are too far from their optimal values. If you think your constraints are logically consistent and your problem is solvable, try changing your starting values and rerunning the Solver.

- **The maximum iteration limit was reached; continue anyway?** To avoid tying up your computer indefinitely with an unsolvable problem, the Solver is designed to pause and present this message when it has performed its default number of iterations without arriving at a solution. When you see this message, you can resume the search for a solution by clicking Continue, or you can quit by clicking Stop. (You can also assign the current values to a named scenario.)

  If you click Continue, the Solver begins solving again and does not stop until it finds a solution, gives up, or reaches its maximum time limit. If your problems frequently exceed the Solver's iteration limit, you can increase the default setting by choosing the Solver command from the Tools menu, clicking the Options button, and then entering a new value in the Iterations edit box.

- **The maximum time limit was reached; continue anyway?** This message is similar to the iteration-limit message. The Solver is designed to pause after a default time period has elapsed. You can increase this default by choosing the Solver command, clicking Options, and then modifying the Max Time value.

PART IV

Interfacing with the Rest of the World

Integrating Applications with OLE

Microsoft Excel 2000 fully supports Microsoft's OLE technology. With the help of OLE, your Excel worksheets can embed text, graphics, sound, or video created in other applications. Or you can link your worksheets to external data sources, so if the source numbers change, your worksheets can automatically stay in step. OLE also allows you to move data from one Excel worksheet to another, or from Excel to another OLE-supporting application, simply by dragging a cell range with your mouse.

Linking vs. Embedding

OLE has two components: *linking* and *embedding*. The difference between them is crucial. When you create a link to Excel data from another application, that application stores a set of pointers to the data's source in Excel; it does not store the data itself. If the source data changes, the document containing the link is updated, either automatically or on demand. In contrast, when you embed Excel data in another application, a copy of the embedded data is incorporated into the receiving document, and this embedded information is not updated if the source data changes. Typically, embedded data requires more disk space; linked data requires less disk space but also requires that the source document remain available.

The techniques you'll follow for linking and embedding depend on which application is your *source* and which is your *container*. This chapter provides both general instructions for where to look for linking and embedding commands in other applications and specific instructions on how to use Excel's linking and embedding commands.

OLE Terminology

Here's a list of terminology you may find useful when working with OLE:

- **Source** The application or document in which the embedded or linked object originates. For example, if you embed a Word paragraph in an Excel worksheet, Word is the source application. The source application is sometimes called the server application.

- **Container** The application or document that receives an embedded or linked object. For example, if you embed a Word paragraph in an Excel worksheet, Excel is the container application. The container application is sometimes called the client application.

- **Object** A linked or embedded data item.

- **Embed** To incorporate an object in a container document, so that the object becomes a permanent part of the container document.

- **Link** To store in a container document a pointer to an object. If the object changes in its source document, the container can be updated, automatically or on demand, to reflect the change.

- **In-place editing** An OLE service that allows you to edit an embedded object while remaining in the container application. During in-place editing, the menus and toolbars of the source application temporarily appear within the container application.

Why and How to Embed

You should embed rather than link when you want the source data in its current form to become a permanent part of the container document or when the source document will no longer be available to the container document. For example, suppose you plan to create a report in Microsoft Word that incorporates several Excel PivotTables and PivotCharts, and you need to take this report on the road. On your portable computer's hard disk, you have Excel and Word, but you keep your Excel data files on a file server at the office. In this case, it is appropriate to embed the Excel material in your Word document. While on the road, if you want to reformat or edit the Excel data, you can simply double-click it in your Word document to invoke Excel and then edit your Excel data.

Embedding is also useful when you want to be able to call on an OLE source for some simple ad hoc procedure. For example, Microsoft Office comes with an equation editor that can act as an OLE source application. While you work in Excel, you might want to use this equation editor to create a text box that shows an Excel formula in traditional mathematical notation. With embedding, you don't need to start the equation editor, create the equation, copy it to the Clipboard, and paste or link it into Excel. Instead, you can invoke the equation editor with Excel's Object command (which we will discuss in a moment), create your equation, and then use the editor's Update command to embed your work in the Excel document. You need not save the equation itself in its own file.

You can embed an object in two ways: by using the Copy and Paste (or Paste Special) commands and buttons or by using the Insert Object (or equivalent) command. To embed a data object with the Copy and Paste commands, follow these steps:

1. Copy the data from the source application to the Clipboard as usual.

2. Use the container application's Paste or Paste Special command. In many but not all situations, if the data on the Clipboard originated in an OLE source, the container application's Paste command automatically embeds the object.

   To be sure that you're embedding the data, use Paste Special instead of Paste. In the list of formats that appears, choose the one that includes the word "object."

Most OLE container applications offer an Insert Object command, typically on their Edit menus. In Excel, the Object command appears on the Insert menu. When you choose this command, a dialog box lists all the types of embeddable data objects known to your system. For example, you might see a listing similar to the one in Figure 17-1.

FIGURE 17-1.

You can use the Object command on the Insert menu to invoke an OLE source, create a data object, and embed that object in your Excel document.

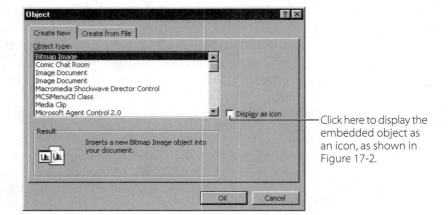

Click here to display the embedded object as an icon, as shown in Figure 17-2.

When you select the type of object you want to embed and then click OK, one of the following will happen (depending on the type of object): the object's source application will start, or a frame will appear in your container document and the menus and toolbars of your object's source application will be merged with those of the container application. If the source application itself starts, use it to create your object. When you've finished creating the object, use the application's Update command (typically on the File menu) to embed the data in your container document. If a frame appears and the source program's menus are merged with those of the container program, work within the frame exactly as you would in the source application. When you've finished, simply click outside the frame. For example, to use Microsoft Paint to create a visual adornment for an Excel worksheet, follow these steps:

1 In Excel, choose Object from the Insert menu. (The Object command does not normally appear on shortened menus. Click the double arrow at the bottom of the Insert menu to display the Object command.)

2 In the Object dialog box, select Paintbrush Picture and then click OK. The menus and toolbars change, and Paint provides a frame in the Excel window.

IV

3 Create the graphic. When you are finished, click outside the frame to return to Excel. Excel menus and toolbars reappear.

The Paint image is embedded as a picture at the current cell location in the Excel worksheet.

When you embed any form of data into Excel, Excel renders it as a graphic object and identifies it with a formula based on the EMBED function, as illustrated in Figure 17-2.

FIGURE 17-2.

This Excel worksheet has two embedded objects: a graphic from Paint and a block of text from Word, displayed as an icon.

The Name box identifies the selected object as Picture 2.

The formula bar displays the object's EMBED Formula.

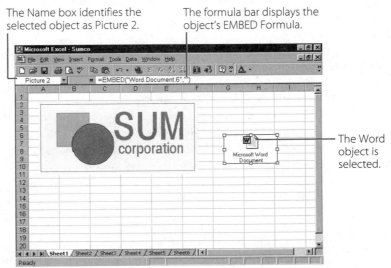

The Word object is selected.

NOTE

The designation Picture 2 means that the data is represented in the Excel worksheet by a graphic object (an icon). This object is in every way a normal Excel worksheet object. You can size it, move it, and manipulate it just as you would other worksheet objects.

SEE ALSO

For more information about embedding objects, see "Using Graphics from Other Programs," page 379.

If you're embedding information from Excel into a document created in a different OLE application, whether that data is represented as an icon depends entirely on the abilities and predilections of the container application.

To hear an embedded sound object or play an embedded video, double-click the icon representing that object. To edit an embedded sound or video object, right-click it, choose the Object command from the shortcut menu that appears, and then choose Edit from the next menu.

Why and How to Link

You should link rather than embed data in the following situations:

- When you want to use a data object in several container documents and you need to ensure that the data will be identical in each.

- When the data object is likely to change over time and you want to maintain it in its source application.

- When you simply want to avoid enlarging the container document.

For example, suppose you want an Excel worksheet to use sales information recorded in an OLE source document that's stored on a network file source. This data is frequently updated in the source document, and you want your Excel worksheet always to have access to the current values. In this case, you should create a link. As we'll see, you can designate the link as either automatic—in which case the changes to the data source are always reflected in the Excel worksheet—or manual—in which case the changes are read into the Excel document only when you ask for them.

You can create links either with source applications that support OLE or with older Microsoft Windows-based programs that support DDE but not OLE. The procedures for creating and maintaining the links are the same in both cases, and whether the application supports OLE or only DDE, the document that supplies the data is called the source, and the document into which the data is linked is called the container.

To create a link in Excel, follow these steps:

1 Save the document in the source application. Most source programs cannot copy a linkable format to the Clipboard from a document that has never been saved because such a document does not have a filename.

2 Copy the data to the Clipboard, just as you would if you were performing a static transfer.

3 Switch to your workbook and choose the Paste Special command from the Edit menu to display the dialog box. Excel creates automatic links by default. Depending on the source application, you might be able to select from several data formats as well as specify the automatic/manual status of the link. When you select

a format that can be linked, the Paste Link option becomes available. Choose this option and then click OK. When you click OK, the data is added in the selected cell. In the formula bar, the application name, file name, and the word OLE help you identify that the object is a link.

? SEE ALSO

For more information about link editing, see "Editing Links," page 582.

If you link data from Excel to another application, we recommend that you name the Excel range that contains your linked data before you create the link. If you do not name the range and you subsequently rearrange your worksheet, the odds are good that your container document will no longer be linked to the correct data. When a worksheet rearrangement causes the container document to be linked to an entirely new set of numbers, it's easy to overlook the fact that the link has, in effect, become corrupted.

When you name the Excel range before you create the link, the container application might not identify the source range by its name. Some applications insist on using the column and row coordinates even when the range has a name. Fortunately, you can use the container application's link-editing procedure to see how the link is identified and to change it if necessary.

Automatic vs. Manual Links

As we mentioned earlier, links are either automatic (updated whenever data changes) or manual (updated on demand). Some applications use other terms—such as *hot* and *cold*, *hot* and *warm*, or *active* and *inactive*—but the concepts are the same. No other forms of linkage exist.

To update a manual link in Excel, use the Links command on the Edit menu. As shown in Figure 17-3 on the next page, the Links dialog box lists all links to the current document and provides a set of command buttons. Clicking the button labeled Update Now produces the latest values for the link. To update a manual link in other applications, you typically choose a command with a name similar to Links from the File or Edit menu. Look for a command button labeled Update, Activate, or something similar to update the link.

In most applications, the same dialog box that lets you update a manual link also lets you change a link's status from manual to automatic or vice versa. In Excel, you change a link's status by choosing Links from the Edit menu, selecting the link to be changed, and clicking either the Automatic or Manual option.

FIGURE 17-3.

This dialog box lets you update, edit, or cancel a link, switch between automatic and manual linking, and open the source for the linked data.

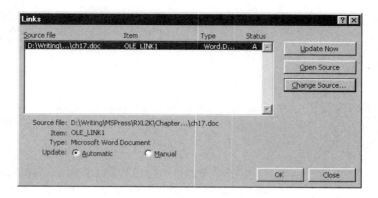

Opening a File that Contains Links

When you open a workbook that contains a remote reference to a document in another application, Excel asks whether you want to reestablish the link and update references to the source document. If you click Yes, Excel attempts to reestablish the link; if you click No, Excel freezes the linked references and displays the values shown when you last saved the workbook.

Suspending Links

To suspend a link temporarily, choose Options from the Tools menu, click the Calculation tab, and then clear the Update Remote References box. Excel then displays in the linked cells the last set of values received from the supporting document.

? SEE ALSO

For information about creating external references to Excel from another application, see documentation for that application.

In addition to initiating remote requests to other applications, Excel can also receive DDE requests. Excel automatically responds to any DDE request it receives. If you want to close Excel to DDE requests, choose the Options command from the Tools menu, click the General tab, and then select the Ignore Other Applications check box.

How Links Are Identified in Excel

Linked data is identified by three elements: the source application, the source document's filename, and the location of the data within the source document. In formal OLE parlance, these elements are referred to as the *application*, the *topic*, and the *item*.

When you link data to an Excel worksheet, Excel identifies the link with a remote reference by creating a formula that looks like this:

=Application|*Topic*'!'Item

For example, a link to a Word file named C:\WHATSUP.DOC might be identified in Excel's formula bar as follows:

=Word.Document.8|'C:\WHATSUP.DOC'!'OLE_LINK1'

You can create links manually by entering a remote reference formula in any worksheet cell. However, the only practical reason for creating a link manually is if you want to set up a link at a time when the source application or document isn't available. Otherwise, you'll probably find it simpler to use the Copy and Paste technique.

Linking Text vs. Linking Objects or Pictures

If the source application is a sophisticated word processor that handles both text and graphics, its Copy command probably supplies the Clipboard with data in both text and graphic formats. If you use Excel's Paste Special command with the Paste Link option selected, Excel links the default format, which is probably either an OLE object format or a picture (if the source does not support OLE).

If you don't need to see the linked text in your worksheet, the icon representation provided by the Display As Icon option in the Paste Special dialog box is a more compact way to annotate your worksheets sheets. Users who want to read the annotation can simply double-click the icon; those who don't are not distracted by the entire text.

To see the text, choose Paste Special from the Edit menu, select the Text format, select the Paste Link option, and then click OK. Each line of text in the source document appears in a separate row in Excel, and Excel turns the link formula into an array that spans the entire range occupied by the text. (Depending on the source, Excel might treat an entire paragraph as a single line of text and display it in one row.) If you select a single cell before creating the link, Excel uses as many rows as it needs to paste the source data.

Activating a Link

If the source application supports OLE, you can "activate" the link by double-clicking it. Windows then launches the source application (if it isn't already running). The source in turn loads the linked document and presents the linked item.

NOTE

> If the container application is Excel, double-clicking a cell containing a link formula might produce unexpected results. If the Edit Directly In Cell check box is selected, double-clicking activates the cell for editing. If you've attached a comment to the cell and the Edit Directly In Cell check box is clear, double-clicking the cell lets you edit the comment. Consequently, the most predictable way to display the Links dialog box is to choose the Links command from the Edit menu. *For more information about editing cells, see "Editing Directly in Cells," page 247, and "Adding Comments to Cells," page 292.*

An alternative to double-clicking—one that works with applications that don't support OLE as well as with OLE sources—is to choose Links (or its equivalent) from the File or Edit menu. (In some applications, this command is called Edit Links or something similar.) A dialog box lists all linked items and provides some command buttons. Select the item and then look for a command button called Open, Activate, or something similar. (In Excel, the button is called Open Source.)

Editing Links

The principal hazard with linking (as opposed to embedding) is that the source data might get moved or renamed, thereby "breaking" the link. Windows can sometimes keep track of a source file's location when you move it. But if a link does inadvertently get "broken," you'll need to repair the damage. Most container applications (Excel included) provide commands to help you in such cases. Typically, you choose the Links command from the File or Edit menu (again, this command might be called Edit Links or something similar), select the damaged link in the list box, and then click a Change or Edit command button. (In Excel, the button is called Change Source.) The application then provides a dialog box in which you can edit the link.

Sharing Files with Others

I t used to be that if you wanted to share your work sheets with other people, you copied everything onto floppy disks, carried them down the hall, and handed them to the person you wanted to share them with. This system (still a very effective one) is known affectionately as "sneakernet." The lucky few who worked in large companies might have been connected to a network. These days, even small companies have networks, and even if you are self-employed, you can also take advantage of the global network known as the Internet. Microsoft Excel 2000 makes it easier than ever to get connected and provides easy-to-use tools that can help foster the synergy that is the hallmark of effective collaboration.

Sharing Files Using a Network

For more information about Excel and the Internet, see Chapter 19, "Hyperlinks and the Internet."

If you're connected to a network or to the Internet, or if you're running Microsoft Outlook or Microsoft Exchange, using the features described in this section can make sharing information a lot easier.

Saving and Retrieving Files on Remote Computers

For more information about the Save As and Open commands, see Chapter 4, "Managing Files."

Using the Save In drop-down list on the Save As dialog box, you can save a workbook on any available network drive or at an FTP (File Transfer Protocol) site or Web folder on the Internet.

The dialog box that is displayed when you choose the Open command on the File menu contains a Look In drop-down list similar to the Save In list. You can use this list box to retrieve workbooks saved on the network or on the Internet.

Retrieving Busy Files Automatically

When you try to open a file that resides on a network drive while another user has the file open, Excel displays the File In Use dialog box, which allows you to open the file as read only. If the file was saved using the password-protection options available on the Save Options dialog box, you must also enter the appropriate password.

The File In Use dialog box that appears when you attempt to open a file that is in use is shown in Figure 18-1.

A Network on Your Desktop

Using the Direct Cable Connection command on the Accessories submenu of the Windows Start menu, you can connect two computers together using a null modem cable. Both computers act as if the other is an additional hard disk. This is a great file-sharing feature if you have both a laptop and a desktop system. Direct Cable Connection is an optional feature of Microsoft Windows 95/98, so you probably need to run the Windows Setup program to install it. *For more information about the Direct Cable Connection command, see the Windows Help index. For more information about network connections, see your Microsoft Windows or network software documentation.*

FIGURE 18-1.

The File In Use dialog box appears when you try to open a busy or protected file.

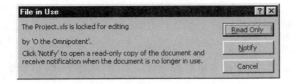

? SEE ALSO

For information about password-protection options, see "Protecting Files," page 71.

If you click the Notify button on the File In Use dialog box, you will automatically be alerted with the dialog box shown in Figure 18-2 when the file becomes available. The File Now Available dialog box contains a Read-Write button instead of a Notify button. If the file was saved with the Read-Only Recommended option selected, a Read-Only button also appears, with the suggestion that you open the file as read only.

If the file was saved with a password required for opening or modification, you are first prompted for the password in a separate dialog box before the File Now Available dialog box appears.

FIGURE 18-2.

The File Now Available dialog box alerts you when the file becomes available.

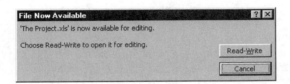

Sharing Workbooks on a Network

It has always been possible to share files on a network. You just had to make sure that you coordinated your efforts to avoid having more than one person open a file at the same time. But now, Excel allows two or more people to work on the same workbook simultaneously, using the Share Workbook command on the Tools menu.

When you check the Allow Changes By More Than One User At The Same Time box shown in Figure 18-3 on the next page, and click OK, the Save As dialog box appears to let you know that the workbook will be saved in order to consummate the command (you can change your mind and click Cancel before the deed is done). This is necessary because the workbook in the shared location must be saved as "sharable" before another user can open it. Once the workbook is saved, the bracketed word [Shared] appears in the title bar whenever anyone opens the workbook, and it persists unless the Allow Changes By

More Than One User At The Same Time option is turned off, which again causes the workbook to be saved.

To specify the name that other users see when the workbook is being shared, choose Options from the Tools menu, click the General tab, and type the name you want to use in the User Name box. You can see the names of all who have the workbook open at any given moment by choosing the Share Workbook command and looking at the Who Has This Workbook Open Now list, shown in Figure 18-3.

FIGURE 18-3.

The Editing tab of the Share Workbook dialog box displays the names of all who have the workbook open.

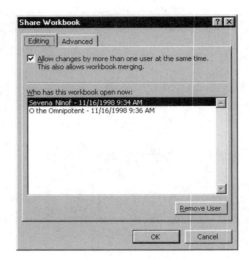

If you want to disconnect someone from the sharing session, click the Remove User button. You cannot remove yourself from the list in this manner. You must close the file instead. If the workbook is still in shared mode, however, that person can simply reopen the workbook and be right back in the sharing session again.

For more information about cell comments, see "Adding Comments to Cells," page 292.

Of course, there are inherent risks when several people work at the same time in the same place. Inevitable conflicts arise when several people are making changes that affect the same cells. When someone saves changes, Excel not only saves the workbook but also updates it if any changes have been saved by other users. If so, a dialog box informs you that changes have been incorporated. After you save, changes that have been made by other people are outlined with a colored border, and a special cell comment explains who made the change, as well as the date and time it was made. When you point to the cell, a comment box displays this information, as shown in Figure 18-4.

FIGURE 18-4.

Cells changed by others in a shared workbook are outlined and a comment is attached.

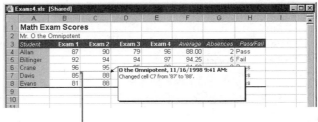

The triangular indicator for special cell comments appears in the upper left corner of the cell instead of in the upper right corner, as it does for regular cell comments.

 ON THE WEB

You can find Exams4.xls used to create the above figure on the Microsoft Press Web site at *http://mspress.microsoft.com/mspress/products/2050/*.

NOTE

Change tracking, which determines whether outlines and comment boxes appear in your worksheet, is turned on by default. You can control it by choosing Track Changes on the Tools Menu and then choosing the Highlight Changes command and selecting the Track Changes While Editing check box. (The Track Changes command is not normally visible on shortened menus. Click the double arrow at the bottom of the Tools menu to display this command.) Make sure this box is selected before the worksheet is first saved for sharing if you want to be able to track and review changes later.

What You Can't Do with a Shared Workbook

There are limitations to what you can do when a workbook is shared. Shared workbooks can be edited using Excel 97 and Excel 2000 only. Earlier versions of Excel, such as Microsoft Excel 7 for Windows 95, will not allow it.

When a workbook is activated for sharing, you can enter text and numbers, change cell formatting, edit formulas, as well as copy, paste, and move data by dragging with the mouse. You can insert columns and rows, but you can't insert blocks of cells. You can't merge cells, insert charts or other objects, create Hyperlinks, assign passwords, insert automatic subtotals, create outlines, create data tables or PivotTables, or insert worksheets. You can't do anything with macros except run them, although you can record macros if they are stored in a different, nonshared workbook. The Conditional Formatting, Scenarios, and Data Validation commands are disabled for a workbook in shared mode (although you can still see their effects), as are most of the buttons on the Drawing toolbar.

IV

Interfacing with the World

When a shared file is saved, Excel checks for conflicts and determines if any "mediation" is called for. Usually, a dialog box appears after saving that simply informs you that changes made by other users have been incorporated. However, if others' changes involve any of the same cells you changed, the "mediator" arrives in the form of the Resolve Conflicts dialog box shown in Figure 18-5.

When setting up a multiuser workbook, establish some working guidelines and design the workbook for maximum safety. For example, each person could have a separate named worksheet in the workbook, each worksheet reflecting their specific areas of responsibility. Then create a separate consolidation worksheet that pulls together all the relevant data from the personal sheets in order to present it in the necessary format. *For more information, see "Consolidating Worksheets," page 337.*

FIGURE 18-5.

If more than one person changes the same cells, the last person to save changes might get to decide which ones to keep.

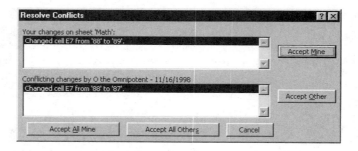

For each conflict identified, the Resolve Conflicts dialog box specifies the cells involved and allows you to decide whose changes to keep. You can resolve conflicts individually or use the buttons at the bottom of the dialog box to select all the changes entered by you or others.

Note that conflicts can exist only between the last saved version and the version you are trying to save. If more than two users have made changes to the same cells, each person who saves the workbook gets to decide who wins the conflict at the moment of saving. You can, however, revisit all the conflicts and accept or reject them individually later. *For more information, see "Reviewing Changes," page 592.*

Advanced Sharing Options

You can change some aspects of the default behavior of shared workbooks. To do so, choose Share Workbook from the Tools menu and click the Advanced tab of the Share Workbook dialog box, shown in Figure 18-6. Each shared workbook user can set these options separately.

FIGURE 18-6.

Use the Advanced tab to determine the way changes are handled.

Use the first section on the Advanced tab to specify the length of time you want to keep track of changes, or if, you want to track them at all.

> Turning off change tracking detracts from your ability to merge workbooks. *For more information, see "Merging Workbooks," page 594.*

In the Update Changes section, select when you want updates to occur. Normally, when anyone saves the file, their changes are saved, and their copy of the workbook is also updated with any changes made by others. The Automatically Every option is handy, allowing you to specify how often updates occur automatically. When you choose automatic updating, the normal procedure is as described above: your changes are saved, and changes made by others are incorporated into your copy. But you can also select the Just See Other Users' Changes option, which gives you the ability to hold your changes back until you decide to save them, while at the same time updating your file at regular intervals with any changes saved by others.

Normally, when conflicts arise, the Resolve Conflicts dialog box shown in Figure 18-5 appears. But if you select The Changes Being Saved Win in the Conflicting Changes Between Users section, all conflicts are essentially resolved by the last user to issue the Save command.

The Include In Personal View options allow you to change the print settings and any views set using the AutoFilter or Advanced Filter commands on the Filter submenu of the Data menu. With these options turned on, each person who has a shared workbook open can have different print and filter settings, which are recalled the next time that person opens the shared workbook.

> You can use the standard Excel password-protection options with shared workbooks, but you must apply the password before sharing. Choose Save As from the File menu, click the Tools button, and then choose the General Options command. In the File Sharing area, you can enter a password for opening the workbook and another password for making modifications to the workbook. Then you can disseminate the necessary passwords to members of your workgroup. *For more information, see "Protecting Files," page 71.*

Tracking Changes

Change tracking in Excel is closely linked with shared workbooks. If you choose Highlight Changes on the Track Changes submenu of the Tools menu and then select the Track Changes While Editing option, you automatically put your workbook into shared mode. The workbook is saved as a result, just as if you had chosen the Share Workbook command. Even if you select the Don't Keep Change History option on the Advanced tab of the Share Workbook dialog box, as shown in Figure 18-6 on page 589, you can still turn change tracking back on, using the Track Changes commands.

When you choose Highlight Changes from the Track Changes submenu of the Tools menu, the dialog box shown in Figure 18-7 appears.

> You don't have to share a workbook with another person to be able to track the changes you make yourself. Just turn on change tracking and save the resulting shared workbook on your own hard disk instead of on a shared network location.

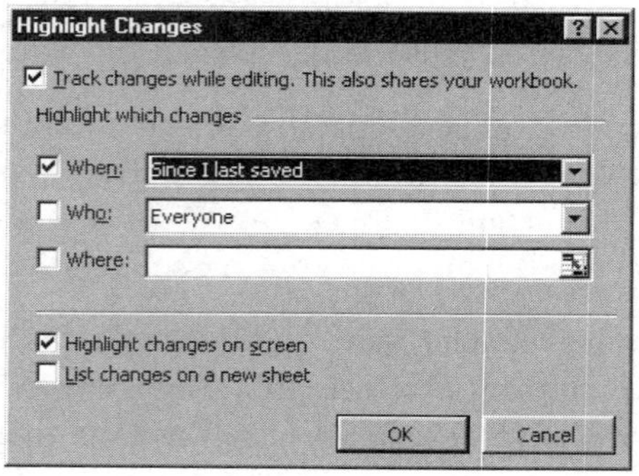

FIGURE 18-7.

Use the Highlight Changes command to show what's been done in a shared workbook.

You control which changes you want highlighted. Use the When drop-down list to select whether you want to see all the changes made since the workbook was first shared, only those changes that you haven't yet reviewed, those that have been made since the last time you saved, or those that have been made since a date you specify. The Who options include Everyone, Everyone But Me, and the name of every individual who has made changes to the shared workbook. If you want, you can enter a specific cell or range in the Where edit box. If you select a range before opening the Highlight Changes dialog box, its address is displayed in the Where edit box when you click the adjacent check box. If you click the check box next to the Where option, you can drag to select the cells directly on the worksheet while the dialog box is still open. Click the title bar to drag the dialog box out of the way or click the Collapse Dialog button, if need be.

Normally, the changes are highlighted on the screen with cell borders and attached cell comments. Click the check box to turn off the Highlight Changes On Screen option. You can also create a History worksheet detailing all the changes made. To do so, select the List Changes On A New Sheet option. The resulting worksheet is inserted after the last worksheet in the workbook, as shown in Figure 18-8.

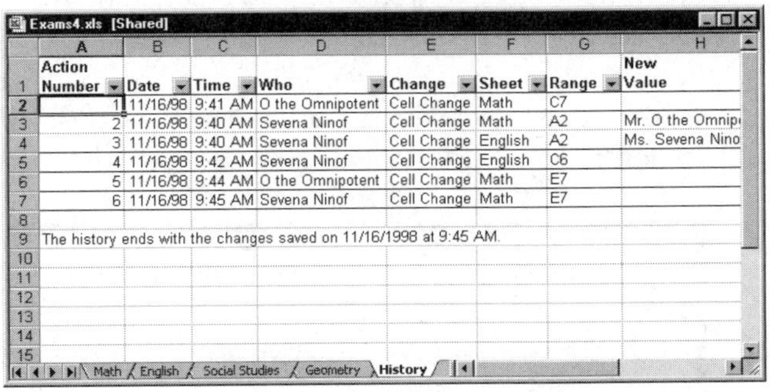
Exams4.xls [Shared]

Action Number	Date	Time	Who	Change	Sheet	Range	New Value
1	11/16/98	9:41 AM	O the Omnipotent	Cell Change	Math	C7	
2	11/16/98	9:40 AM	Sevena Ninof	Cell Change	Math	A2	Mr. O the Omnip
3	11/16/98	9:40 AM	Sevena Ninof	Cell Change	English	A2	Ms. Sevena Nino
4	11/16/98	9:42 AM	Sevena Ninof	Cell Change	English	C6	
5	11/16/98	9:44 AM	O the Omnipotent	Cell Change	Math	E7	
6	11/16/98	9:45 AM	Sevena Ninof	Cell Change	Math	E7	

The history ends with the changes saved on 11/16/1998 at 9:45 AM.

FIGURE 18-8.
You can choose to create a History worksheet detailing the changes made to a shared workbook.

The History worksheet is a special locked worksheet that can be displayed only when a worksheet is in shared mode—the worksheet disappears when you clear the Allow Changes By More Than One User option on the Editing tab of the Share Workbook dialog box. If you subsequently restart a shared workbook session, the history starts fresh, and any changes recorded in previous sharing sessions are lost.

TIP

To keep track of the change history after discontinuing the sharing session, copy the contents of the locked History worksheet and paste them into another worksheet.

Protecting the Change History

If you want to ensure that every change made during a sharing session is documented, choose Protection from the Tools menu, and then choose the Protect Shared Workbook command. When you do, the dialog box shown in Figure 18-9 appears.

FIGURE 18-9.

You can ensure that change tracking is protected in a shared workbook.

If you click Sharing With Track Changes and then click OK, change tracking for the shared workbook is protected so no one in your workgroup can turn it off directly. However, anyone can turn off the protection by choosing Protection from the Tools menu and then choosing Unprotect Shared Workbook. To eliminate this possibility, you can enter a password in the Protect Shared Workbook dialog box, but you must do so when the workbook is not in shared mode. Then anyone who tries to turn off protection must enter the identical, case-sensitive password.

> **⚠ WARNING**
>
> If you successfully enter a password to turn off Protect For Sharing mode, not only is protection turned off, but the workbook is also removed from sharing. Note that this is not the case unless there is a password. When you remove a workbook from sharing, you cut off anyone else who has the workbook open, and the change history is erased.

Reviewing Changes

You can decide at any time to go through each change that has been made to the shared workbook, provided the Track Changes While Editing check box was selected in the Highlight Changes dialog box when the worksheet was first saved for sharing. The Accept Or Reject Changes command on the Track Changes submenu of the Tools menu displays the dialog box shown in Figure 18-10. The drop-down lists are similar to those on the Highlight Changes dialog box, except that in the When list, the only options available are Not Yet Reviewed and Since Date.

FIGURE 18-10.

Use this dialog box to specify which changes you want to review.

When you click OK, the dialog box shown in Figure 18-11 appears, and the first change that meets the criteria you specified in the Select Changes To Accept Or Reject dialog box is highlighted on the worksheet. The dialog box describes the change, as well as who made it and the exact time it was made. At this point, you can accept or reject the change, or you can simply accept or reject all the changes. Once you've accepted or rejected all the changes, you cannot review them again. You can, however, still display the History worksheet.

FIGURE 18-11.

Each change is highlighted and described in order, allowing you to accept or reject it.

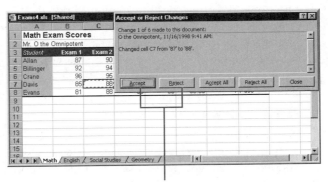

To review each change individually, click either the Accept or Reject button to move to the next change. Changes are displayed in chronological order from earliest to latest.

Canceling the Shared Workbook Session

You can discontinue the sharing session at any time by clearing the Allow Changes By More Than One User option on the Editing tab of the Share Workbook dialog box. Several things happen when you do this, however. First, the change history is lost. If you subsequently start a new sharing session, the history starts fresh. Also, any other users who still have the shared workbook open will not be able to save their changes to the same file. If they try to save, the Save As dialog box appears, and the best they can do is save a copy of the file under a different name. Even if you turn sharing off and then turn it back on again while another person still has the file open, a new session has been initiated, and the other person will not be able to save changes to the file. The other person will have to close the file left over from the old session and reopen it to rejoin the current sharing session.

You can click the Remove User button on the Editing tab of the Share Workbook dialog box if you want to disconnect someone from the sharing session manually. This way, the change history for the master workbook is maintained. You'll probably want to clear this with whomever you're disconnecting, of course.

Combining Changes Made to Multiple Workbooks

Another way to share workbooks is to make each person a separate copy of the workbook. This might be an option if not everyone in your workgroup has access to the same network server, or if there are no network or Internet file-sharing options available to you. In the scenario, after all the distributed copies have been updated with each person's changes, someone collects the copies and manually transfers all the changes to a master workbook. While this is a time-honored method, Excel now offers more efficient ways to handle this task.

Merging Workbooks

You can merge workbooks that were created equal—that is, a set of workbooks created from the same master. When you merge workbooks, all changes made to the merged workbooks are merged into the master workbook. Merging workbooks, like change tracking, is closely linked with the shared workbooks feature; you can only merge workbooks that have been saved with sharing turned on. Suppose we want to distribute the Exams4 workbook used in the previous shared workbook examples. The following procedure explains how to set up your workbooks for distribution and eventual merging:

1 Open the workbook you want to distribute.

2 Choose Share Workbook on the Tools menu. (You may need to expand the menu to see this option.)

3 On the Editing tab of the Share Workbook dialog box, select the Allow Editing By More Than One User check box.

4 Click the Advanced tab and make sure that there is a sufficient number of days specified in the Keep Change History For box for all the members of your workgroup to finish their edits and for you to collect and merge the workbooks. If you are unsure about how long to specify, just enter a large number, such as 500. If this time limit is exceeded, you will not be able to merge workbooks.

5 Click OK to save the workbook in shared mode.

6 Choose the Save As command on the File menu and save additional copies of the workbook under different names—one for each person on your distribution list. Because sharing is turned on, each copy you save is also in shared mode.

7 Distribute the copies to your workgroup.

SEE ALSO

For information about ways to distribute workbooks, see "Mailing Workbooks Using Electronic Mail," page 597.

Once you have prepared, distributed, and collected the edited workbooks, you are ready to merge. Open the workbook you want to use as the master workbook. All the changes made to the other workbooks you merge will be replicated in the master workbook. This workbook must have been saved from the same original shared workbook, just as the workbooks you distributed were. Open the master workbook, make sure none of the other workbooks you want to merge are open, and then choose Merge Workbooks from the Tools menu to display the dialog box shown in Figure 18-12. (The Merge Workbooks command is not normally visible on shortened menus. Click the double arrow at the bottom of the Tools menu to display this command.)

FIGURE 18-12.

We have Exams8 open already, so we select Exams5, Exams6, and Exams7 to merge.

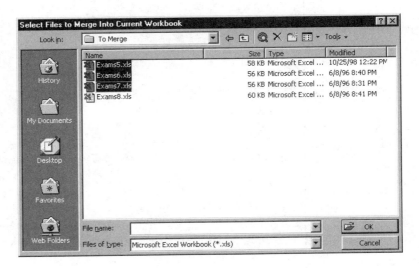

You can find the files Exams5.xls, Exams6.xls, Exams7.xls, and Exams8.xls that were used to create Figure 18-12 on the Microsoft Press Web site at *http://mspress.microsoft.com/mspress/products/2050/*.

Online Meetings and Discussions

The Online Collaboration menu, located on the Tools menu, contains commands that allow you to share information with others, *now*. The provocative Meet Now, Schedule Meeting, and Web Discussions commands all require additional connections and services before you can use them. Members of the Microsoft Office 2000 family, including Microsoft Excel 2000, have the capability to conduct online meetings using Microsoft NetMeeting, which has been integrated into all Microsoft Office 2000 programs. You can also take advantage of special Office Web server software to initiate Web discussions if you have access to a server running Office Server Extensions.

To begin an online meeting, click Online Collaboration on the Tools menu and then choose the Meet Now command to display the Microsoft NetMeeting dialog box. To use this feature, you need to be connected to a network or the Internet, and you also need to specify a directory server. The directory server provides the list of e-mail addresses you can connect to. Ask your network administrator for the name of your local directory server, or you can use any of the public Internet directory servers listed in the Server Name box at the bottom of the Microsoft NetMeeting dialog box. The Schedule Meeting command (on the Online Collaboration submenu of the Tools menu) allows you to set up a meeting in advance with multiple attendees using the scheduling features of Microsoft Outlook, which must also be installed on your system as well as on the systems of others in your workgroup.

Once you are set up and connected, you can conduct online meetings in real time. You can also use built-in NetMeeting tools, such as the Chat Window and the Whiteboard, which allows you to draw crude images that are transmitted to the whiteboards of all connected attendees. You can run a meeting from within Excel 2000 or from the Microsoft NetMeeting program. In the Programs folder of the Start menu, click the Internet Explorer folder and choose Microsoft NetMeeting. Web discussions are similar to online chat systems, except that each person's comments are visible within a special window in Excel, your browser, or another Microsoft Office 2000 program.

For more information about "Microsoft NetMeeting," consult the Help system in the Microsoft NetMeeting program or ask the Assistant in the Excel 2000 Help system about "online meetings." For more information about "scheduling online meetings in advance," see the Help system in Microsoft Outlook 2000.

The workbooks you select in this dialog box are merged one by one, in the order in which they appear in the dialog box. All changes made to the merged workbooks are, in turn, made to the master workbook. You can accept and reject changes and display the History worksheet just as you can with shared workbooks, as described in "Tracking Changes," page 590.

TIP

While merging workbooks combines all changes from a set of workbooks, consolidation combines only values from a set of worksheets (these worksheets can be in different workbooks). The Consolidate command on the Data menu can assemble information from as many as 255 supporting worksheets into a single master worksheet. *For more information, see "Consolidating Worksheets," page 337.*

Mailing Workbooks Using Electronic Mail

Excel provides built-in features to take advantage of electronic mail. If Microsoft Outlook, Microsoft Exchange, or another compatible mail program is present, the commands on the Send To submenu on Excel's File menu become available. When you choose the Mail Recipient command with Microsoft Outlook installed, Excel asks whether you want to send a message with a copy of the current workbook attached, or if you want to send the active sheet of the current workbook as the actual body of the message. A simple Outlook mail message is shown in Figure 18-13 with an Excel workbook attached.

FIGURE 18-13.

The Send To Mail Recipient command on the File menu activates the mail program and attaches a copy of the current workbook or worksheet.

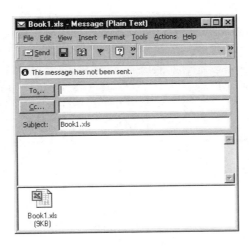

If You Have Microsoft Outlook

Microsoft Outlook is an information-management program that you already have if you purchased Excel as part of Microsoft Office 2000 (it is also available separately). Outlook combines features of several types of programs, including mail, scheduling, and contact management, and it even duplicates some file-management features of the Windows Explorer.

The Reviewing toolbar in Excel contains the Create Microsoft Outlook Task button, which you can use to create a task for yourself or anyone else who uses Outlook and to whom you are connected by electronic mail. The following figure shows a task created in Outlook after clicking the Create Microsoft Outlook Task button.

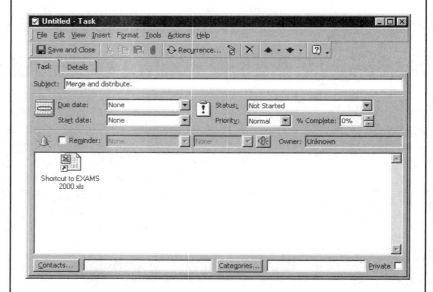

The Outlook task window appears with a shortcut to the currently active workbook. If you save this task, you will be reminded at the time you specify. Or you can use the Assign Task button in Outlook to send this task to someone else. For more information, see your Outlook documentation.

TIP

You can also send mail using the Send To Mail Recipient button on the Reviewing toolbar.

When you click the Send button, the message and attached copy of the workbook or worksheet are sent to the recipients listed in the To edit box. When the message is received, the recipients simply double-click the Excel icon in the mail message to open the workbook. Note that any changes you make to the workbook after sending the message are not reflected in the sent copy. If you choose to send the current worksheet as the message body, a representation of the worksheet is created in your e-mail program.

Routing Workbooks to a Workgroup Using Electronic Mail

If you are working on a project that involves a group of people whose input is crucial, you can route a workbook to the group using electronic mail. When you choose the Send To submenu on the File menu and then choose the Routing Recipient command, the Routing Slip dialog box shown in Figure 18-14 is displayed. (The Routing Recipient command is not normally visible on shortened menus. Click the double arrow at the bottom of the Send To submenu to display this command.)

FIGURE 18-14.

Route a workbook to a group using the Routing Recipient command.

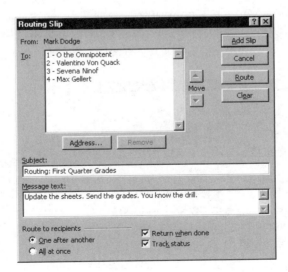

The Routing Recipient command offers several advantages over the Mail Recipient command. For example, the Routing Recipient command allows you to specify sequential routing. That is, if you construct a list of recipients using the Address button and select the One After Another option at the bottom of the dialog box, the workbook will be sent to the first person on the list. When that person has finished, the workbook will automatically be forwarded to the next person on the list. The To list box shows you the sequence, which you can modify by selecting a name in the list and clicking the Move buttons. Alternatively, you can choose to route the workbook to all recipients at the same time by selecting All At Once.

To send the message off on its appointed rounds, click the Route button on the Routing Slip dialog box. To simply attach the routing slip to the workbook, click the Add Slip button. Using the latter method allows you to continue working. Then, when you're ready to send the message, choose the Next Routing Recipient command (which replaces the Mail Recipient command when you have a routed workbook open) on the Send To submenu. (The Next Routing Recipient command is not normally visible on shortened menus. Click the double arrow at the bottom of the Send To submenu to display this command.) The dialog box shown in Figure 18-15 appears. If you click OK, the workbook is sent to the next person on your routing slip. You can also choose the second option, Send Copy Of Document Without Using The Routing Slip. If you do, a mail window appears as if you had chosen the Mail Recipient command, allowing you to send the workbook to anyone you choose. The original routing slip remains, and you can still send it to the next recipient on the list.

FIGURE 18-15.

This dialog box appears when you begin routing your workbook.

You can also reopen and edit the routing slip itself to include more or fewer people in the distribution by choosing the Edit Routing Slip command (which replaces the Add Routing Slip command when you have a routed workbook open).

If the Track Status option in the Routing Slip dialog box is selected, you will receive notification each time the workbook is forwarded so you can keep track of its progress. If the Return When Done option is selected, the workbook is automatically returned to you in the mail after it has made its rounds.

Workgroup Tools Mentioned Elsewhere in This Book

Excel has some other features that are very useful in workgroups and are covered elsewhere in this book. These include:

- **Get External Data** Some of the most powerful features of Excel involve the acquisition of data from remote sources. The three subcommands of the Get External Data command on the Data menu, Run Web Query, Run Database Query, and Create New Query, allow you to extract data from just about any type of database, even one located on the Internet. *For more information about queries, see Chapter 26, "Working with External Data."*

- **The Web** You can use your company's internal Web, or *intranet,* to publish your workgroup's reports or to search for and retrieve information to include in your workbooks. *For more information about Internet features, see Chapter 20, "Creating Web Pages with Excel," and Chapter 19, "Hyperlinks and the Internet."*

- **Scenarios** Spreadsheets have always been used for what-if analysis. The Scenarios command on the Tools menu starts the Scenario Manager, a powerful modeling tool that you can use to compare, contrast, combine, and recall the various possibilities that have been posed by different people in your workgroup. *For more information about scenarios, see "The Scenario Manager," page 542.*

- **Data Validation** You use the Validation command on the Data menu to apply a special kind of formatting to selected cells that allows you to determine precisely what kind of data may be entered. For example, you could first lock all the cells in the worksheet except for the ones you want others to fill in. Then use the Validation command to specify for each cell the specific type of value to enter there, such as date, time, whole number, and so forth. You can even specify minimum and maximum allowed values, a message that automatically appears when the cell is selected, and an error message that appears only if the entry does not meet the parameters you set. *For more information about specifying valid data, see "Validating Data Entry," page 785.*

- **Properties** Use the Properties command on the File menu to add summary information to your workbooks, as well as to other files you create using Microsoft Office applications. (The Properties command is not visible on shortened menus. Click the double-arrow at the bottom of the File menu to display the Properties command.) For example, properties make it easy to search for all the files related to a particular client or department. *For more information about properties, see "Adding Summary Information to Files," page 74.*

- **Auditing** The buttons on the Auditing toolbar make it easy to troubleshoot and verify worksheets that have been touched by many hands. You can use the Comments command to leave notes for others in your workgroup, or to explain why results might seem anomalous to your eventual audience. *For more information about auditing worksheets, see "Auditing and Documenting a Worksheet," page 288.*

Hyperlinks and the Internet

One of the nicest features offered in Microsoft Excel 2000 is an expression of Microsoft's intent to weave together all of the Microsoft Office applications with the explosive evolution of the Internet in the last few years. The intent is to provide seamless integration of the documents created by Excel, Microsoft Word, and other applications on your computer with those offered by others over the Internet.

Excel offers a rich array of features that make life on the Internet even more entertaining, engrossing, and *useful* than ever:

- Use Excel to navigate your hard disk, your intranet, the Internet, or the World Wide Web by inserting hyperlinks in workbooks. Create, format, and edit hyperlinks, and associate them with text, buttons, or drawing objects.

- View Excel documents that are linked to Web pages.

- View Web pages that are linked to Excel documents.

- Open and save documents at File Transfer Protocol (FTP) and Hypertext Transfer Protocol (HTTP) sites directly, almost as if they resided in a directory on your hard disk.

 SEE ALSO

For more information about saving worksheets in HTML format, see Chapter 20, "Creating Web Pages with Excel."

- Save worksheets and charts in the Hypertext Markup Language (HTML) format, so that fellow Web surfers can see the results of your work.

We will assume that you already have an account with an Internet service provider, that you've installed and are familiar with the procedure for connecting to your Internet account, and that you have a Web browser such as Microsoft Internet Explorer or Netscape Navigator. To keep from duplicating directions for both browsers in this chapter, we'll concentrate on Internet Explorer.

To download the most current version of whichever browser you like best, go to the application developer's Web site and follow the directions you find there. For example, to obtain the newest version of Microsoft Internet Explorer, go to *http://www.microsoft.com/ie*.

There's a listing of other useful Web sites at the end of this chapter.

Basic Internet Concepts

Originally, communication between people over the Internet consisted of e-mail, newsgroups, and FTP sites:

- **E-mail** is basically point-to-point transmission of a message in the form of text encoded in standard ASCII; you send a text message to an e-mail server, having specified a destination e-mail address in the form *name@server.orgtype*, where *.orgtype* is typically *.edu* for a university, *.com* for a commercial business, *.org* for a nonprofit organization, or *.gov* for a governmental site. To send and receive e-mail over the Internet, you need an

IV

e-mail browser (Eudora is probably the most well known, and Microsoft Outlook or Microsoft Outlook Express might be one you actually have right now, if you bought Microsoft Office) and an account on an Internet server.

- **A Newsgroup** is like a community bulletin board—you *post* a text message to the newsgroup, and everyone who reads the newsgroup (with an appropriate newsgroup browser) can read your message. The advantage of newsgroups is that you don't need to know the names or e-mail addresses of anyone in the group—all you need is the name of the group. There are thousands of newsgroups devoted to a huge range of topics, from Elvis sightings (*alt.elvis.sighting*) to research in nanotechnology (*sci.nanotech*).

- **FTP** (File Transfer Protocol) is another way for people to share information over the Internet; instead of sharing messages in a text format, you can share binary files, such as Excel workbooks. With FTP you can post files in their native binary format on an FTP site, and users who have the correct permissions can download the files directly to their machines.

As a system to support hypertext and linking was established on the Internet, the World Wide Web was born. The Web consists of a set of protocols and conventions that allow users to easily create and share documents despite their physical locations and regardless of computer platform and display requirements.

A fundamental convention of the Web is the document formatting standard called Hypertext Markup Language (HTML). HTML, a descendent of SGML (Standard Generalized Markup Language), is the foundation of an ever-evolving series of conventions for describing documents that appear on the World Wide Web. Any Web browser (or other program, such as Excel 2000) that conforms to the convention is theoretically able to read and display a Web document in the HTML format. Files in the HTML format are actually just plain text files containing relatively simple codes for formatting, document structuring, and hypertext.

Web browsers such as Netscape Navigator and Microsoft Internet Explorer have been evolving at an amazing rate. They now support not only "standard" Web browsing but also e-mail, newsgroups, FTP, and a variety of new data formats that can be viewed with a Web browser and in e-mail. These new formats include live audio "telephone" interaction, sound, video, and navigation inside three-dimensional graphic worlds, also called VRML, for Virtual Reality Markup Language.

A Brief History of the Internet

1940	The concept of the World Wide Web probably dates back to 1940, when Vanevar Bush discussed the idea of a *memex,* a huge machine that could store massive amounts of information, and *trails* that provided associative links through this information. In theory, you could store trails and make them available to other people—threading together areas of interest and ideas for research.
1965	Ted Nelson coins the term *hypertext.*
1969	The Internet is born as the ARPANET, for Advanced Research Projects Agency Network. This physical transmission system and communications protocol enhanced communication among Department of Defense researchers and military centers, and was said to be redundant and decentralized enough to survive an atomic attack.
1979	CompuServe goes live as the first *information service* (later joined by America Online, Genie, and Prodigy), offering a range of services without needing the technical background required of early adopters of Internet services.
1981	Ted Nelson uses the term *hypertext* in his book *Literary Machines* to describe the idea of creating a single global document, the parts of which are distributed among servers on a planetary scale. By activating a hypertext item called a *link*—a bibliographic reference in a research paper, for example—you could jump to the paper cited. The terms *link, hotlink,* and *hyperlink* have all developed from this concept and are roughly synonymous.
1983	Military networking is split off from ARPANET into an independent network called MILNET.
1989	Having read Ted Nelson's ideas, systems analyst Tim Berners-Lee, working at Conseil Européen pour la Recherche Nucléaire, in Geneva, Switzerland (a consortium of researchers in nuclear physics), publishes "Information Management: A Proposal," which lays the groundwork for the World Wide Web.
1990	Mosaic, the first Web browser, is developed. The browser reads documents in the HTML format and processes the links that let users easily jump from one document to another on the Web.
Now	Only ten years after the first one was first developed, the various flavors of browsers have become the most widespread and most often-used computer applications.

IV

Using Hyperlinks

A hyperlink is much like a link in any Web page: if you click a link in a document, the application viewing the document jumps to the document specified in the link. Other types of Excel links, such as those in an external cell reference, transfer an item of data back to the document containing the link. Hyperlinks are more a navigation tool than a method to transfer information.

A hyperlink in Excel can take the form of text, a drawing object, or a button. Whatever form the hyperlink takes, you activate the hyperlink by clicking it; when you do this, Excel jumps to the *destination document*. A destination document can be:

- A file in the HTML format (that is, a Web page) on a computer somewhere on the Internet

- A file in any format on your hard disk; in Excel, this is typically a workbook

- A file in any format somewhere on a computer attached to an internal network (an intranet) to which your computer is connected

- A file in any format at an FTP site somewhere on the Internet

Let's investigate each of these ways to use hyperlinks by creating a workbook in which you can experiment with the various types of hyperlinks in Excel.

Internet Addressing

All of the methods for accessing data on the Internet—whether you're accessing a file on a hard disk, e-mail, an FTP site, or a Web page—support a single convention for specifying the type and location of data. In this convention, files and locations are described by their URL, or Universal Resource Locator. A URL specifies the type of data, the name of the server that makes the data available, and (usually) a path name to the data.

A URL address can also specify another level of information—a location within the specified document. The name given to this location in a file depends on the file's format; it's called an *anchor* in a Web page, a *cell reference* or *named range* in an Excel document, or a *bookmark* in a Word document. Clicking a link takes you to the server and then activates the address or file specified in the link. (Depending on your privileges for the connection, however, a password might be requested.)

The following table lists the predominant types of services and presents examples of each.

You can find Hyperlinks.xls used to create the following table on the Microsoft Press Web site at *http://mspress.microsoft.com/mspress/products/2050/*.

Prefix	Type of Connection and a Sample Hyperlink
http://	Connects to a location on the World Wide Web. *http://www.microsoft.com*
ftp://	Connects to an FTP server to display a directory, transfers a file using FTP, or opens the file at the FTP site. *ftp://ftp.premier1.net/pub/users/quacky/hyperlinks.xls*
file://	Opens a file on your hard disk or network. *file://c:/My Documents/yourfile.xls*
gopher://	Connects to a Gopher server (this one at the University of Minnesota). *gopher://gopher2.tc.umn.edu/*
news://	Views new articles posted to a newsgroup. (This address opens the Nanotechnology newsgroup through your Internet service provider's news server, whose address you must supply, and to which newsgroup you must first subscribe.) *news://news.yourserver/sci.nanotech*
mailto://	Opens in your default e-mail program a mail message form ready to send to the specified address (in this case, Mark Dodge). *mailto://markrxl@quacky.net*

Creating a Hyperlink to a Web Page

Let's say you want to create a simple hit list of your favorite Web pages and other items you've found on the Web. To do this, you need to insert a URL address for each Web page in a cell on a worksheet. Let's assume you already know that the URL address for the destination document on the Web for which you want to create the link is

http://mspress.microsoft.com/

This URL gets you to the home page of Microsoft Press.

You can find LinkTest.xls used to create the following figures on the Microsoft Press Web site at *http://mspress.microsoft.com/mspress/products/2050/*.

To experiment with hyperlinks in a worksheet, do the following:

1   Choose New from the File menu to create a new, empty workbook. Enter headings and format them as shown in Figure 19-1. Finally, save the workbook as LinkTest.xls.

FIGURE 19-1.

A new workbook for experimenting with hyperlinks.

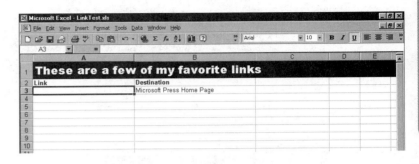

2   Select cell A3 and then choose Hyperlink from the Insert menu (or click the Insert Hyperlink button on the Standard toolbar). Excel may first present a dialog box requesting that you save the active workbook again. After you've saved the workbook, the dialog box in Figure 19-2 appears.

FIGURE 19-2.

The Insert Hyperlink dialog box.

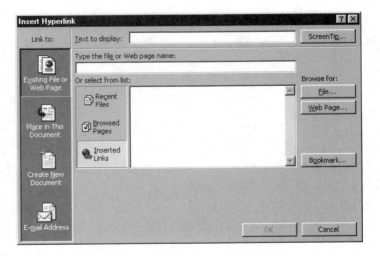

3   In the Type The File Or Web Page Name box, enter the Web address (URL)

http://mspress.microsoft.com

4   Ignore the rest of the options in the Insert Hyperlink dialog for now, and click OK.

Excel enters the address you entered as a hyperlink, much like a link you'd see in a Web browser such as Netscape Navigator or Microsoft Internet Explorer, as shown in Figure 19-3.

FIGURE 19-3.

The new hyperlink you've created.

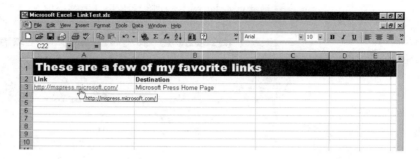

Editing a Hyperlink

Once a cell has been "formatted" as a hyperlink, you can't simply select the cell by clicking it with the mouse. Now when you click the hyperlinked cell, Excel launches you on a journey to the destination document, wherever it might be in cyberspace or your own hard disk.

You can select a cell that has a hyperlink by clicking with the *right* mouse button to display the shortcut menu and then choosing Select Hyperlink from the Hyperlink submenu. Or you can edit the hyperlink by choosing Edit Hyperlink from that same menu. You can also select a hyperlinked cell by clicking an adjacent cell and using the arrow keys to move the selection.

Follow these steps to edit the hyperlink we just created.

1 Click the *right* mouse button on the hyperlinked cell and choose Edit Hyperlink from the Hyperlink submenu.

2 In the Text To Display box, type

   Microsoft Press Home

3 Press Enter.

You'll see that the cell now displays the text you just typed, but it is still formatted as a hyperlink and still refers to the same URL. You can quickly check this by hovering the mouse over the hyperlink to display a yellow "tool tip" box that displays the underlying address for that hyperlink.

As with any cell, you can choose Copy or Cut from the Edit menu and paste a hyperlinked cell somewhere else without disturbing the link.

TIP

In Internet Explorer you can drag a link from a Web page to the desktop; when you do this, an icon appears for the link that contains the URL information you need to get to the page. You can double-click this icon to make your browser jump to the indicated site.

Once you have the shortcut, you can also drag the shortcut's icon into an Excel window; when you do this, Excel creates a new workbook containing the link. The title of the link becomes the name of the tab and the name of the document, and the link itself is inserted in cell A1 of the worksheet.

The Web Toolbar

You can view the Web toolbar by clicking Toolbars on the View menu and choosing Web. The Web toolbar contains many of the same controls as the toolbar visible in Microsoft Internet Explorer, as you can see in Figure 19-4. You can move backward and forward through a chain of hyperlinks you've used during the current session, open locations listed in your Favorites folder, open the page specified as Home in your browser, and more.

FIGURE 19-4.

The Web toolbar.

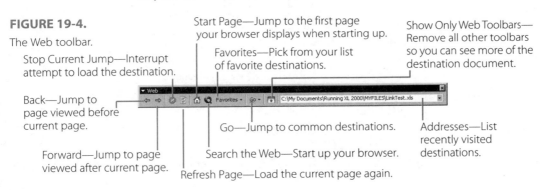

Start Page—Jump to the first page your browser displays when starting up.

Show Only Web Toolbars—Remove all other toolbars so you can see more of the destination document.

Stop Current Jump—Interrupt attempt to load the destination.

Favorites—Pick from your list of favorite destinations.

Back—Jump to page viewed before current page.

Go—Jump to common destinations.

Addresses—List recently visited destinations.

Forward—Jump to page viewed after current page.

Search the Web—Start up your browser.

Refresh Page—Load the current page again.

For pages that are jammed with information you need to see, click the Show Only Web Toolbar button to hide all other displayed toolbars and make room for more of the document you're viewing. To redisplay the hidden toolbars, click the Show Only Web Toolbar button again.

Cruising with a Web Hyperlink

Let's test the new hyperlink to the Microsoft Press home page. When you place the mouse pointer over the hyperlink, the pointer changes to a little hand with index finger extended, as shown in Figure 19-3. Click the hyperlink; if you haven't already logged on to your Internet service provider, you'll see a dialog box requesting you to log on. Next, Excel sends a message to Windows to launch your Web browser if it isn't already running. Your browser starts up and loads the page specified in the hyperlink, as shown in Figure 19-5.

> **NOTE**
>
> Unless you've been off-planet for the last couple of years, you're probably aware that the Web is changing much more quickly than any mortal could document accurately. Therefore, the Web pages you see when working through this chapter may differ from the ones we've printed in this book. In fact, we'd be shocked if they didn't.

FIGURE 19-5.

The Microsoft Press home page.

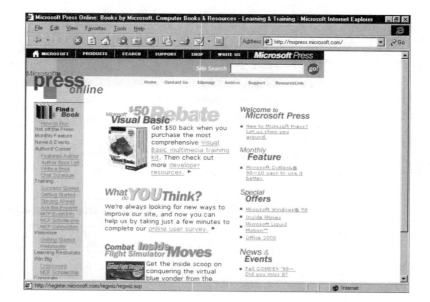

Changing Internet Settings

You can open the Internet control panel to customize certain aspects of the behavior of your browser and Windows applications that provide Internet access. To do this, choose Settings from the Start menu, then Control Panel, and in the window that appears double-click the Internet icon.

In the Internet Properties control panel, you can specify items such as the text color of links visited, characteristics related to connecting to your Internet provider, the addresses of your Start and Search pages, and programs used to access files across the Internet (such as sound, graphics, and multimedia files).

Copying a Link

Now let's take a link from the Microsoft Press Web page, move it to our list of favorite hyperlinks in Excel, and associate the address with text that we'll enter in the workbook.

1   On the Microsoft Press home page, find the Author's Corner link in the navigation column on the left side of the screen.

2   Place the mouse pointer over the words "Author's Corner," click the right mouse button, and then choose Copy Shortcut from the shortcut menu for the link.

3   Switch back to Excel, select cell A4, and then enter

   MS Press Author's Corner

4   Choose Hyperlink from the Insert menu, click in the Type The File Or Web Page Name box, and then press Ctrl+V to paste the Web address. You'll see the address

   http://mspress.microsoft.com/authors/

   appear in the box.

5   Click OK to dismiss the dialog box; you'll then see the workbook shown in Figure 19-6. You could also add the descriptive information shown in the figure in cells B3:B4.

FIGURE 19-6.

Cell B6 contains a hyperlink with display text.

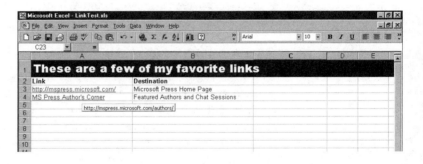

Let's test the new hyperlink to the Author's Corner page. If you place the mouse pointer over the link, you'll see the address to which the hyperlink points, as shown in Figure 19-6. If you click the hyperlink, Excel sends a message to Internet Explorer to display a window containing the document specified by the destination address, shown in Figure 19-7 on the next page.

FIGURE 19-7.

The Microsoft Press Author's Corner page.

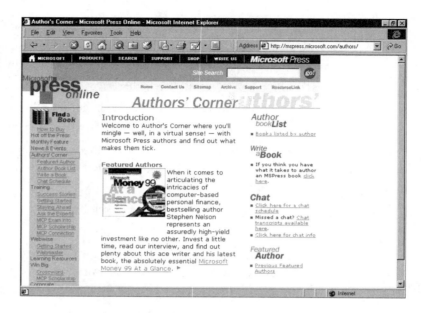

NOTE

If you click a hyperlink and Excel or your browser doesn't seem to respond, it might be that the server on which the document resides is experiencing too much traffic, or the connection to the remote server might be refused for some other reason—for example, the server might be off line. If this happens, simply click the Stop button on the Web toolbar and try again later.

More about Creating Hyperlinks

The Insert Hyperlink dialog box contains several convenient features to help you create hyperlinks. In addition to entering a URL that specifies a location on the Web, you can also enter the location of a document on your hard disk or on a network to which your computer is connected. You can also click one of the three buttons directly below the Type The File Or Web Page Name box—Recent Files, Browsed Pages, and Inserted Links (the default), as shown in Figure 19-2 on page 609—to choose from lists of files, pages, and hyperlinks previously used in your documents.

You can use the two Browse buttons on the Insert Hyperlink dialog box—File and Web Page—to locate a file or Web page whose address will then be used as the hyperlink. When you click the File button, Excel presents the Link To File dialog box (really a version of the Open dialog box) so you can find and select a file to which the new hyperlink points, as shown in Figure 19-8.

FIGURE 19-8.

The Link To File dialog box.

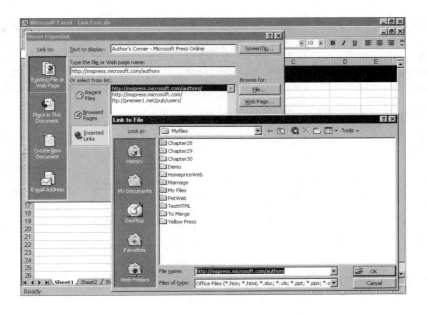

The other Browse button, Web Page, launches your browser, which you use to surf to the Web site you want. When you get there, switch back to Excel (press Alt+Tab) and you'll see that the URL of the page currently displayed in the browser appears in the Insert Hyperlink dialog box. This way, you know that you are using the correct address, without worrying about typing accuracy.

Linking to a Location in a Document

The Insert Hyperlink dialog box provides two ways to be more specific with your hyperlinks: the Place In This Document button, on the left side of the dialog box, and the Bookmark button, which is visible to the right of the main list box. When you click the Place In This Document button, an "outline" view of the active workbook appears in the main list box, as shown in Figure 19-9 on the next page.

⑦ SEE ALSO

For more information about defined names, see "Naming Cells and Ranges," page 133.

Two entries—Cell Reference and Defined Names—display the contents of the workbook. Click the plus or minus-sign bullets to the left of these two entries to expand or collapse the outline. (If there are no names defined in the current workbook, no plus sign appears next to Defined Names.) Cell Reference expands to display a list of sheets in the workbook. If you click a sheet name, you can enter a cell address in the Type The Cell Reference edit box. The Defined Names list expands to reveal any names you have defined in the current workbook. You can see the name *more_links* displayed in Figure 19-9 on the next page. When you specify a cell or a name, your hyperlink jumps to that specific location.

FIGURE 19-9.

Use the Place In This Document button to create a hyperlink to a named location in the current workbook.

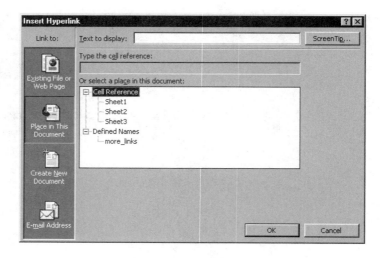

When you select any file or Web page and click the Bookmark button, the Select Place In Document dialog box appears, which displays a dialog box with essentially the same functionality as described above. The main difference is that you can select specific locations in any document Excel recognizes, including Web pages containing bookmarks (aka *anchors*), bookmarks in Microsoft Word, and other named locations in documents created by Microsoft Office programs. Notice in Figure 19-10 that the ScreenTip shows the path to the hyperlinked document as well as the named location within it.

FIGURE 19-10.

Creating a hyperlink to a named range in the current workbook.

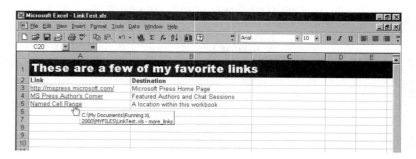

Making a Button or Drawing Object a Hyperlink

You can associate a hyperlink with a button or drawing object. Let's say you want to try and find a satellite photo of your hometown. You can create a hyperlink that you can use to access the Microsoft

Terraserver Web site by simply clicking a drawing of a star. To do this, perform the following steps with the LinkTest.xls workbook active:

1 From the View menu, choose Toolbars and then Drawing. The Drawing toolbar appears.

2 On the Drawing toolbar, choose Autoshapes, then Stars And Banners, and then 16-Point Star.

3 In the LinkTest workbook, drag to produce a star-shaped object.

4 With the star object selected, click Fill (the paint bucket icon) and then choose yellow to fill the star outline.

5 With the star still selected, from the Insert menu choose Hyperlink. In the Hyperlink dialog box, enter in the Type The File Or Web Page Name box

http://terraserver.microsoft.com

6 Click OK. You should see a worksheet similar to the one shown in Figure 19-11.

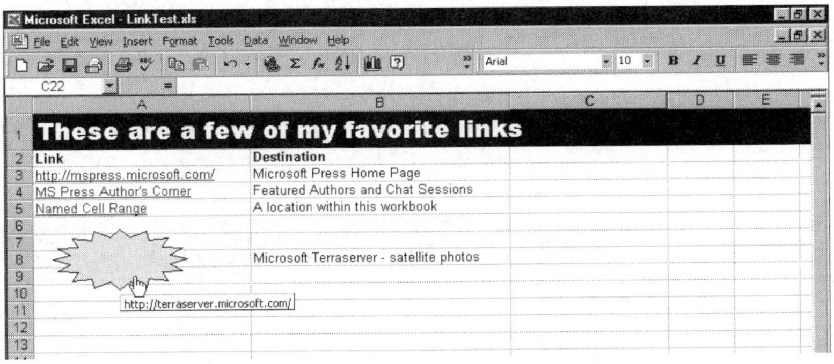

FIGURE 19-11.

After adding the star button hyperlinked to Terraserver.

If you find you've entered the URL for the hyperlink incorrectly, or if you want to edit the hyperlink, right-click the drawing object and from the shortcut menu for the object choose Hyperlink and then Edit Hyperlink. The Hyperlink dialog box appears, and you can change the information for the hyperlink.

Using the HYPERLINK Worksheet Function

There's a special worksheet function in Excel that you can use to manufacture a hyperlink as text, based on the evaluation of an expression in a formula that returns the URL of the intended hyperlink. To convert a URL in text format to an actual hyperlink, you use the HYPERLINK() function, which takes the form

HYPERLINK(link_location, friendly_name)

where *link_location* is the destination to which you want the hyperlink to point and *friendly_name* is the resulting text that appears in the cell. If you want to use the Paste Function dialog box (choose Function from the Insert menu), the HYPERLINK function is listed with the Lookup and Reference functions.

For example, let's say you're preparing a workbook for distribution that contains many hyperlinks. The workbook and the destination documents to which the hyperlinks point are on your computer, so you can prepare all the documents together. Before releasing the workbook into the world, however, you want to point all the hyperlinks to copies of the same documents on your Web server at a remote location.

To accomplish this, you might perform the following steps. Let's assume that the path to the directory on your computer containing the Web documents *is C:/My Documents/MyFiles/* and the base directory at your Web site is at *http://www.quacky.net/*.

1   From the Insert menu, choose Name and then Define. The Define Name dialog box appears; for each name, enter the name in the Names In Workbook field and the associated text in the Refers To box, and then click the Add button.

Names In Workbook	Refers To
LocalSite	="file://C:/My Documents/MyFiles/"
RemoteSite	="http://www.quacky.net/"
TheSite	=localSite

In the worksheet, wherever you want a hyperlink, use a variation on the following HYPERLINK function with the name of the destination document you want. For example, if the document you want to link to is sites.htm, for the links page at your Web site, you could use this formula:

=HYPERLINK(theSite&"sites.htm","My Links Page")

2   When you press Enter, Excel creates the hyperlink shown in Figure 19-12.

IV

Interfacing with the World

FIGURE 19-12.

Assembling a hyperlink with the HYPERLINK worksheet function.

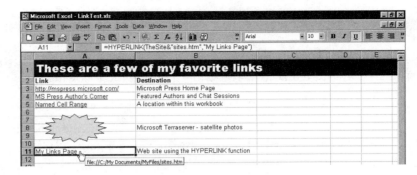

Now all you have to do to make all the hyperlinks in your workbook point to the remote Web server is use the Insert Name dialog box to redefine the name *theSite* as *remoteSite.*

Working with FTP Sites in Excel

Hyperlinks offer a wonderful way to bounce from one document to another on your hard disk or network, or over the Web, but what do you do if the priority is to make the data in an Excel workbook available to others? By saving an Excel document to an FTP site, you can let others access the workbook in several ways. With FTP access in Excel, you can:

- View a workbook as a read-only document at a public FTP site

- Download the workbook to your computer

- Use external references to the workbook to transfer data to cells in local worksheets on your computer

- Save a workbook to an FTP site, making it available to others

Let's take a look at each of these methods; first, though, you have to tell Excel the location of the FTP site you want.

> **NOTE**

You can also make data available to others by mailing workbooks for others to review and attaching routing slips to documents you've mailed. Or you can save worksheets and charts as Web pages in HTML format.

For more information about mailing and routing workbooks, see Chapter 18, "Sharing Files with Others." For more information about saving worksheets as Web pages, see Chapter 20, "Creating Web Pages with Excel."

Preparing for FTP Access

Before you can connect to an FTP site, you have to specify the location of the site and provide a password, if any, so you will be permitted access. To do this, perform the following steps:

1   Choose Open from the File menu to display the Open dialog box.

2   Pull down the Look In drop-down list and choose Add/Modify FTP Locations, as shown in Figure 19-13.

FIGURE 19-13.

The Open dialog box, showing the Add/ Modify FTP Locations option.

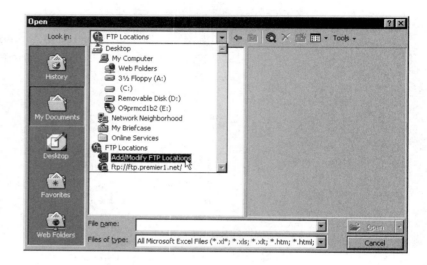

3   In the Add/Modify FTP Locations dialog box, shown in Figure 19-14, enter the location of the FTP site you want to access.

FIGURE 19-14.

Entering an FTP site in the Add/Modify FTP Locations dialog box.

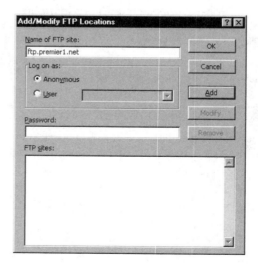

For this example, let's use

ftp.premier1.net/

4 In the Log On As area, make sure the Anonymous option is selected, giving you read-only, public access to the files stored there. Finally, click Add and then OK.

Opening a Workbook at an FTP Site

Now let's open a workbook at the public FTP site for Running Excel that we added in the last section. There are several ways to do this, each of which offers slightly different advantages.

First, you can use Open from the File menu to find the directory containing the file you want. Then follow these steps:

1 Open the Look In drop-down list and choose FTP Locations. Excel displays the URLs for all of your FTP locations in the dialog box.

2 Double-click the *ftp.premier1.net* icon to open it. If you're not connected to your Internet service provider, Excel brings up a Connect To dialog box, in which you enter your password to connect. When you click OK in the Connect To dialog box, Windows takes a moment to establish the connection and then displays in the Open dialog box a list of the directories at *ftp.premier1.net.*

3 Find and double-click the */pub* directory to open it. Next, find and open the */users* directory. Find and open the */quacky* directory. Your Open dialog box should look something like Figure 19-15.

FIGURE 19-15.

The public FTP site at *ftp://ftp.premier1.net/pub/users/quacky.*

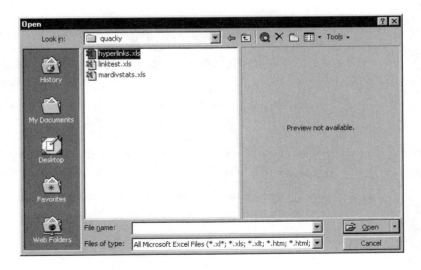

4 Double-click the MarDivStats.xls icon. After taking a moment for communication with the FTP site, Excel displays a Transferring File dialog box, then opens the workbook shown in Figure 19-16.

FIGURE 19-16.

The MarDivStats.xls workbook.

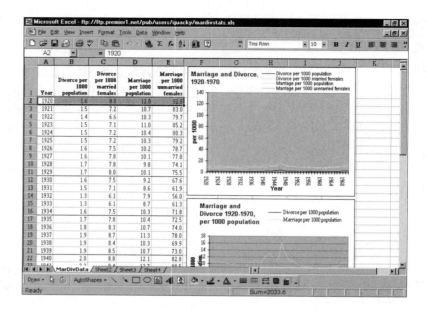

NOTE

If you happen to be in a Web browser, such as Microsoft Internet Explorer, rather than in Excel and you click a link to the workbook, the browser might use Excel as a viewer and display the document in an Excel window that appears within the browser.

Downloading a Workbook to Your Computer

Notice the path in the title bar at the top of the screen, showing that the location of the workbook is actually at the remote site. You can make alterations to the MarDivStats.xls workbook, but if you try to save the document, Excel displays a message stating that it can't save the document because you have read-only privileges for the folder at this public FTP site.

There are several ways to download a workbook from an FTP site to your computer:

- After you've opened the workbook and are viewing it in Excel, all you have to do is save the workbook on your hard disk.

■ You can also view an FTP directory through your browser and download the workbook without using Excel.

■ You can use FTP client software, such as CuteFTP, that allows you to view and work with files at an FTP site almost as if you were working with a directory on your hard disk.

Hyperlinks to an Excel Document at an FTP Site

Instead of using the Open dialog box to locate and open the desired workbook at an FTP site, you can create a hyperlink to the workbook and open the workbook by clicking the link.

You can try this out by opening the LinkTest workbook, selecting cell A12 (for example), and choosing the Insert Hyperlink command. In the Insert Hyperlink dialog box, type the address in the Type The File Or Web Page Name box:

ftp://ftp.premier1.net/pub/users/quacky/MarDivStats.xls

When you click OK in the Insert Hyperlink dialog box, Excel creates a hyperlink like that shown in Figure 19-17; if you click the hyperlink, Excel opens MarDivStats.xls from the remote location.

FIGURE 19-17.

Opening a workbook at an FTP site by clicking a hyperlink in a local workbook.

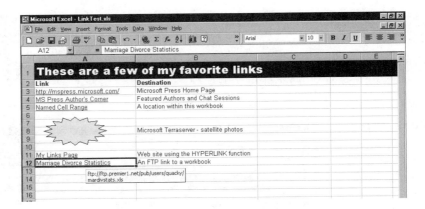

External References to Data in a Remote Workbook

As with any other workbook stored on your hard disk or network, you can look up information in a workbook at an FTP site by using an external reference, as long as you have an active connection to the remote FTP site and the workbook is open.

For example, let's look up a statistic in the MarDivStats.xls workbook at the FTP site by creating an external reference in the LinkTest.xls workbook. The MarDivStats workbook contains defined names for

 SEE ALSO

For information about using Query to return external data to a worksheet from a source on the Internet or the Web, see Chapter 26, "Working with External Data."

each column of data on the sheet MarDivData; the defined name of the data in the Year column is *year,* and the defined name of the data in the Divorce Per 1000 Population column is *divPop.* You can check this yourself, if you want, by opening the workbook and choosing Name and then Define from the Insert menu and looking at the list of defined names in the workbook.

Next, do the following:

1 In the LinkTest.xls workbook, set up a little table in cells B19:23, as shown in Figure 19-18.

For more information about the vector form of the LOOKUP function, see "Lookup and Reference Functions," page 443.

2 In cell C20 enter the scary formula

=LOOKUP(A15,'ftp://ftp.premier1.net/pub/users/quacky/ [MarDivStats.xls]MarDivData'!year,'ftp://ftp.premier1.net/ pub/users/quacky/[MarDivStats.xls]MarDivData'!divPop)

3 Press Enter. The formula looks up the divorce data for the year 1940 and returns the number 2 to the LinkTest.xls workbook.

Copy this formula into cells B16:B18 to complete the table. You can see our new formula in the formula bar in Figure 19-18.

You can make working with huge external references like this much less scary by assembling the reference with a couple of names you've defined in the Define Name dialog box, as described in "Using the HYPERLINK Worksheet Function," page 617.

FIGURE 19-18.

Setting up a table with external references to a workbook at an FTP site.

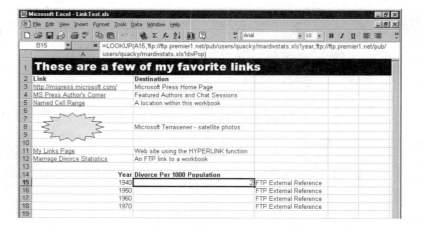

IV

Updating Links to a Remote FTP Site

SEE ALSO

For more information about accessing data on the Internet, see Chapter 26, "Working with External Data."

If and when you reopen a workbook containing external references to a workbook at an FTP site, Excel presents a dialog box saying that the workbook contains "automatic links to information in another workbook" and asks whether you want to update the information. If you click Yes, you'll see the Connect To dialog box so you can reestablish a channel between the remote FTP site and your computer.

SEE ALSO

For more information about linking workbooks together through external references, see "Working with Linked Workbooks," page 329.

Let's say, however, that you want to update the remote links in the workbook while the workbook is open. For example, you could be working with the LinkTest.xls workbook, doing the external linking example, and notice that there's an error in the statistics cited in the MarDivStats workbook. You pick up the phone on your other line (you're still connected to the Running Excel FTP site) and call me (don't try this at home), and I correct the error. The data in the remote MarDivStats workbook has changed, and you want to force Excel to update the linked data in the local workbook.

To do this, choose Links from the Edit menu; Excel presents the dialog box shown in Figure 19-19. In the Links dialog box, click the Update Now button to update information from MarDivStats.xls without opening the MarDivStats workbook.

FIGURE 19-19.

Updating external references in a linked workbook at a remote FTP site.

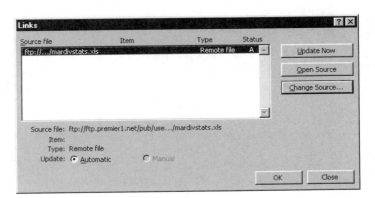

Uploading a Workbook to an FTP Site

There are two main methods for saving documents to an FTP or Web site on the Internet. The first, which we'll describe here, is simply to use the application that created the document—Excel, in this case—to save the workbook at the remote site. The second method is perhaps better for an HTML document you've created by converting a workbook into the HTML format: you can use an FTP-client application to open the remote FTP directory so you can upload your files directly.

Up until this point in the chapter, you have been using the Internet to access HTML documents and workbooks that have been saved by other people. These examples have required only that you have read-only, public access to the Web and FTP sites we've cited. To save a workbook to an FTP site yourself, you must have write privileges on the Internet account to which you want to save the workbook. Typically, you are allowed this type of access if you own the account.

> **NOTE**

> As an example of the first method of saving documents to an FTP or Web site, we'll describe the process you would use to upload the documents to our public FTP site. However, you won't be able to try this process exactly as described, because we won't give the password!

The first step in this process is to set up the connection to your FTP server so you can write to a directory at the site. This step is nearly identical to that described in "Preparing for FTP Access," page 620, except that you need to specify a password in order to gain access to the remote FTP server.

To set up the connection, do the following:

1 Choose Save As from the File menu; from the Save In drop-down list, choose Add/Modify FTP Locations. Enter the name of the server, the username for your account, and the password, and then click the Add button.

2 Pull down the Save In drop-down list again and choose the name of your FTP read-write service. Excel presents the FTP Log On dialog box requesting your password; enter the password and then click OK. Windows tries to connect to your Internet service provider.

3 When the connection is made, you'll see a collection of folders in the Save As dialog box; find and open the one that contains the account to which you've been granted access.

4 In the File Name box of the Save As dialog box, enter the name under which you want to save the workbook and then click Save.

Using Web Folders

The Web Folders feature lets you save and open documents located on a Web server. Web Folders works in a manner similar to the built-in FTP features, except that Web Folders allows you to open and save documents on a Web (HTTP) site rather than an FTP site, from within the Open and Save As dialog boxes in Excel. This is particularly handy when you are publishing your worksheets in HTML format for world-wide consumption on the Web because a Web folder effectively eliminates the need to use an FTP program when downloading or uploading your Excel documents.

> **NOTE**
>
> To use the Web Folders feature, your Web server must support the DAV Internet protocol, Microsoft Office Server Extensions, or Microsoft FrontPage Server Extensions.

To create a Web folder:

1 From the File menu, choose Save.

2 Click the Web Folders button on the left "navigation bar" in the dialog box.

3 Click the Create New Folder button. The Add Web Folder dialog box appears, as shown in Figure 19-20.

FIGURE 19-20.

Use the Add Web Folder dialog box to create shortcuts to frequently used folders on the Web.

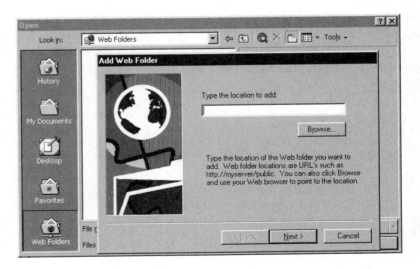

4 In the Add Web Folder dialog box, enter the address of the Web folder you want to add or click the Browse button to locate the Web folder using your browser. Click the Next button.

5 Enter your user name and password. Click OK.

6 Enter a display name for the Web folder. Click the Finish button.

If all goes well, you should now have a new Web folder icon that you can use to upload and download files on the Web.

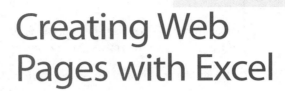

CHAPTER 20

Creating Web Pages with Excel

A s you probably know if you've done much surfing of the World Wide Web, you can use your browser to view a Web page, but what determines the actual content of the page is the underlying code. This is true of any document on your computer that consists of more than simple text, but the nice thing about documents coded with the Hyper Text Markup Language (HTML) is that HTML-coded text is just text and can still be read by human beings.

In the Dark Ages of Web design—a couple of years ago—Web designers had to write HTML code by hand, adding HTML codes one by one. Now there are dozens of applications such as Adobe PageMill and Microsoft FrontPage—and now Microsoft Excel—that you can use to edit Web pages and maintain your Web site without ever having to mess with the HTML code.

Converting an Entire Excel Workbook into HTML

To convert an Excel workbook into an HTML document that others can view on the Web, use the Save As Web Page command on the File menu.

For example, to convert the MarDivStats.xls workbook (shown in Figure 20-1) into an HTML file, do the following:

You can find MarDivStats.xls used to create the following figure on the Microsoft Press Web site at *http://mspress.microsoft.com/mspress/products/2050/*.

FIGURE 20-1.

We'll use the MarDivStats.xls workbook to test Excel's Save As Web Page command.

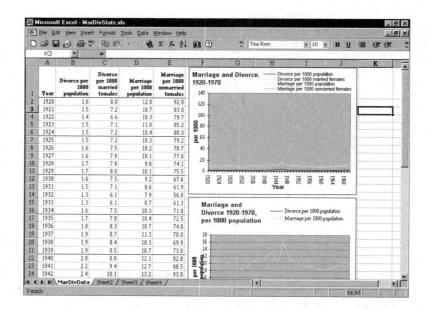

1   With the MarDivStats.xls workbook active, choose Save As Web Page from the File menu. (Save As Web Page does not appear on shortened menus. Click the double-arrow at the bottom of the File menu to diplay the Save As Web Page command.) Excel displays a special version of the Save As dialog box, as shown in Figure 20-2.

2   Click Save.

FIGURE 20-2.

The Save As dialog box provides special options when you choose the Save As Web Page command.

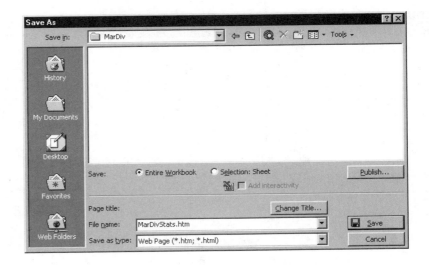

After you click the Save button, the dialog box disappears. The only evidence that anything actually happened is that the workbook name in the Excel title bar now has an .htm extension, rather than the familiar .xls. Our example file, MarDivStats.htm is now as fully editable as any other Excel workbook. If you do a lot of Web work, it may seem convenient to use HTML as your default file format for saving worksheets. However, you must avoid using features that cannot be translated into HTML. *A list of these features can be seen in the sidebar entitled "Lost in the Translation" on the next page.*

? SEE ALSO

For more information about files and file formats, see "Specifying a Default File Format," page 69, and "Working with Files," page 62.

Given the nature of the work most people do with spreadsheets, the best advice is to use the native .xls format as your default file format and use Save As Web Page only when needed. With this in mind, you should always close the workbook immediately after using the Save As Web Page command. If you want to continue working on the workbook, open the original by choosing the .xls version from the Recently Used Files list at the bottom of the File menu.

To get an idea of what happened when we saved our example workbook as an HTML file, choose Open from the File menu. The dialog box should open to the last location used, which in our example was the *MarDiv* folder. As you can see in Figure 20-3 on the next page, Excel created a "main" file, MarDivStats.htm, and a new folder, MarDivStats_files, which contains a number of supporting files.

FIGURE 20-3.

The Save As Web Page command created a new .htm file and a folder containing supporting files.

To see how well the HTML conversion went, select the MarDivStats.htm file in the Open dialog box, and then click the downward-pointing arrow to the right of the Open button and choose the Open In Browser

---

Lost in the Translation

When you convert a document into HTML, you nearly always lose some of the formatting options because the purpose of HTML is to describe the structure of a document, not merely the look of the resulting page. Consequently, HTML enables as many different computing environments as possible to access the information, regardless of the computing platform, operating system, or display characteristics of a given computer.

The following is only a *partial* list of features that either don't translate to the Web or may not behave as expected. If you want to use interactive data, the list is even longer. See "Adding Interactivity," page 637. For the complete list, see Help (for example, ask the Assistant "What is lost in HTML conversion?").

Custom views	Data consolidation	External cell references
Nested functions	Array formulas	Rotated or vertical text
Pattern fills	Dotted or dashed borders	Range names
Multiple fonts in a cell	Conditional formatting	Password protection
Cell comments	Data validation info.	1904 date system
Precision as displayed	Indented text	Scenarios

command, shown in Figure 20-3. When you do so, your browser starts up and displays the selected file. Figure 20-4 shows how MarDivStats.htm looks as a Web page displayed in Microsoft Internet Explorer. Notice that the HTML version of the file even displays a set of simulated "sheet tabs" at the bottom of the screen.

FIGURE 20-4.

The MarDivStats.xls workbook as a Web page displayed in Microsoft Internet Explorer, complete with "sheet tabs" along the bottom.

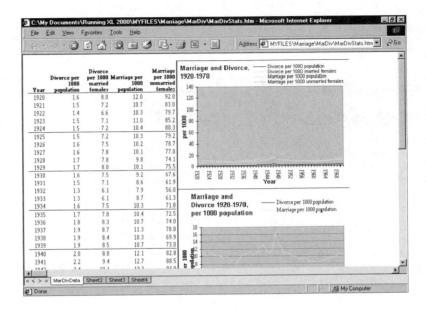

Where to Save?

When you choose Save As Web Page from the File menu, the Save As dialog box displays the standard locations in the navigation bar on the left side, including My Documents, Desktop, Favorites, and Web Folders. When you first create a Web page with Excel, it's recommended that you save your files in a location on your hard disk, so you can experiment and make changes. Once you get the results you're after, you can then publish your masterpiece to a public location.

Unless you specify otherwise, the My Documents folder is the default location offered. It probably doesn't make much sense to save your files on the Desktop, unless you have a thing for clutter. You can save files in the Favorites folder, but if you intend your files to be made available on the Internet or your company's intranet, you should try Web Folders. Web folders can be located anywhere in the world on any compatible Web server that you have permission to use. *For more information about Web folders, see "Using Web Folders," page 627.*

If you look in the MarDivStats_files folder, you'll find the rest of the essential files created by the Save As Web Page command. One .htm file is created for each sheet in the workbook. Also, there is one .gif image file for each chart or graphic object; a file called *tabstrip.htm,* which displays the simulated sheet tabs; and *stylesheet.css,* which controls formatting; along with several other data files. The folder and additional files are created only if you convert the entire workbook, and only then if more than one sheet contains data.

Converting Individual Excel Worksheets into HTML

You won't always want all the sheets in a workbook to be converted into Web pages, so Excel makes it easy for you to save specific sheets. For example, to convert only the first sheet in the MarDivStats.xls workbook into an HTML file, do the following:

1   In the MarDivStats.xls workbook, make sure that the MarDivData sheet is active and that only a single cell is selected.

2   Choose Save As Web Page from the File menu.

3   Click the Selection option (which currently displays *Selection: Sheet).*

⭐ **TIP**

> If you select a range of cells before choosing the Save As Web Page command, you can click the Selection option button in the Save As dialog box to publish only the selected cells rather than the whole sheet or the entire workbook. The label for the Selection option changes to identify the selected range. For example, if you select a range named SourceList and then choose the Save As Web Page command, the label for the Selection option reads *Selection: SourceList.*

4   Click the Publish button. The Publish As Web Page dialog box appears, as shown in Figure 20-5.

5   Click the Open Published Web Page In Browser option.

6   Click the Publish button.

The Publish As Web Page dialog box offers the convenient Open Published Web Page In Browser option, which eliminates an extra step

IV

when you are previewing your new Web page. When you look at this page in the browser, it looks identical to the one in the previous example, except that the simulated sheet tabs are absent this time.

FIGURE 20-5.

The Publish As Web Page dialog box affords some control over how elements on a sheet are converted to HTML.

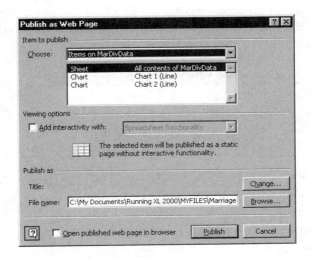

If you look at the location where you published the sheet, you'll notice that this time the default name of the file created is Page.htm. The new folder is named Page_files, and it contains fewer files this time—mainly, the .gif image files for the charts on the MarDivData sheet.

Other Web Publishing Options

The Save As dialog box that appears when you choose the Save As Web Page command on the File menu offers a few additional options you need to know about.

Changing the Title

You can click the Change Title button, shown in Figure 20-2 on page 631, to add or change the title of your Web page. The Set Page Title dialog box appears, allowing you to type in a title. After you do so and click OK, the title appears adjacent to the Change Title button in the Save As Web Page dialog box. This title will appear centered and at the top of the resulting Web page.

Choosing Other Items to Publish

When you click the Publish button in the Save As Web Page dialog box, the Publish As Web Page dialog box appears. While you can publish all the contents of a workbook or worksheet, you can also use the Item To Publish drop-down list to focus in on specific sheets or other publishable items on those sheets, as shown in Figure 20-6.

FIGURE 20-6.

The Item To Publish drop-down list identifies the publishable items in the current workbook.

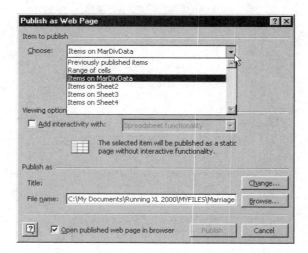

The Item To Publish list shows the publishable categories available for the active workbook. If you previously published all or any part of the workbook, selecting Previously Published Items allows you to republish the same items. If you published several different items from the current workbook, a list of these items is shown below the drop-down list box.

If you select Range Of Cells, you can enter a specific area on any sheet. You can either type the address of the cell range or select it by dragging the mouse. Click the Collapse button (on the right side of the edit box that appears below the drop-down list) to shrink the dialog box so you can select the range easily by dragging.

The rest of the items in the Items To Publish drop-down list correspond to sheets in the workbook. For example, you can see in Figure 20-5 the list of items that appears when *Items On MarDivData* is selected. Besides the item entitled All Contents Of MarDivData, the sheet also contains two charts. Figure 20-7 shows the Web page that resulted from publishing only Chart 2 from the MarDivData sheet.

FIGURE 20-7.

You can publish an individual chart from a worksheet.

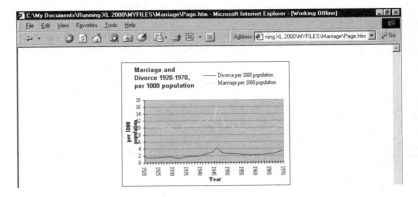

Adding Data to an Existing Web Page

If you want to do any serious editing of the Web pages you publish from Excel, the recommended approach is to use a dedicated HTML editing program, such as Microsoft FrontPage. If you simply want to append data to the bottom of an existing Web page, Excel can handle the job. Choose the Save As Web Page command, select the item you want to add, and publish it using the same filename as the file you want to amend.

For example, let's add Chart 1 from the MarDivData sheet to the bottom of the page we previously published, shown in Figure 20-4 on page 633. To do so, publish the new chart using the existing filename, Page.htm. Since the same filename is used, Excel displays the dialog box shown in Figure 20-8, asking how we want to proceed. Click the Add To File button instead of the Replace File button to add Chart 1 to the bottom of the Web page.

FIGURE 20-8.

If you publish an item using the same filename, you can replace it or add to it.

Adding Interactivity

Some of the coolest new features in Excel 2000 are interactive Web Components. These features allow you to publish worksheets, charts, and PivotTables as Web pages that actually allow others who view them to manipulate the data from within their browsers. Naturally, interactive data does not have the same degree of functionality on the Web as it does within Excel. Some features are not retained, and others are converted with some change in functionality. *For more information about application functionality on the Web, see the sidebar entitled "Lost in the Translation," on page 632.*

There are a few additional caveats about interactivity to keep in mind:

- Anyone who wants to create or use interactive data on the Web must have Microsoft Office 2000 Professional, Premium, or Standard Edition installed.

- You must use Internet Explorer 4.01 or later to view interactive data.

- Interactive charts and interactive worksheets must be created separately.

- Interactivity cannot be applied to an entire workbook, only to sheets and items on sheets.

Spreadsheet Functionality

Let's look at an example. If we want to add interactivity to the MarDivData sheet we published, first make it the active sheet, and then:

1 Choose Save As Web Page from the File menu.

2 Click the Publish button.

3 From the Item To Publish drop-down list, select All Contents Of MarDivData.

4 Click the Add Interactivity With check box, shown in Figure 20-9.

   When you select Add Interactivity With, the adjacent drop-down list becomes active. When a sheet or cell range is selected in the Item To Publish list, the drop-down list displays two options you can choose from, Spreadsheet Functionality and PivotTable Functionality.

5 From the Viewing Options drop-down list, choose Spreadsheet Functionality (if it is not already selected).

6 Click the Open Published Web Page In Browser option (if it is not already selected).

7 Click the Publish button.

The result is shown in Figure 20-10.

FIGURE 20-9.

Click the Add Interactivity With option to publish interactive Web pages.

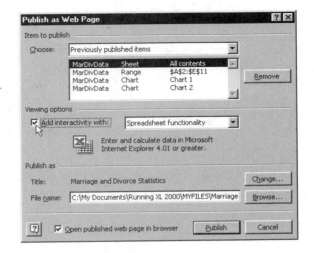

FIGURE 20-10.

An interactive spreadsheet displayed in Microsoft Internet Explorer.

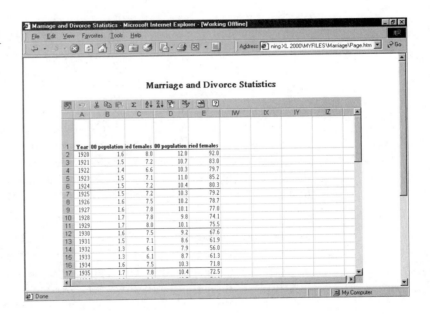

In Microsoft Internet Explorer 4.01 or later, you can view the published interactive Web page and actually click cells and change the values that appear there. Formulas respond to changes in cell values. You can even edit formulas, change formatting, and control the display of some visible features.

Notice that the two charts were not included in the conversion, even though we selected All Contents Of MarDivData as the item to publish. Because you can only specify one type of interactive data at a time—in this case, interactivity with spreadsheet functionality—only the spreadsheet was published. Also notice that the column headers appear truncated in the published spreadsheet. This is because when you choose to add interactivity, text wrapping in cells becomes disabled. This is just one of the little tradeoffs you'll have to take into account.

Take a closer look at the special toolbar shown in Figure 20-11 and you'll notice many familiar buttons and a few unfamiliar ones.

FIGURE 20-11.

The Web Spreadsheet Component toolbar.

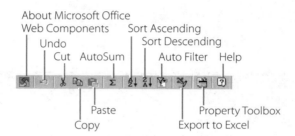

The first button, About Microsoft Office Web Components, displays what is commonly referred to in the software community as a "splash" dialog box—that is, a dialog box that displays the name and version number of the software, among other things. The most interesting thing about the "About" dialog box is that it contains live hyperlinks to a Technical Support Web site, as well as to the Microsoft Office Web site.

The next unfamiliar button is the Export To Excel button, which is somewhat self-explanatory. As suggested earlier, it would be better to return to the original .xls file rather than edit the converted Web page. But this button can be handy if you are looking at someone else's published worksheet and you want to massage the data in the comfort of your own copy of Excel 2000.

The other less-than-familiar button is the Property Toolbox button. Click this button to summon a floating box that behaves somewhat like a dialog box *and* a toolbar. The Spreadsheet Property Toolbox, shown in Figure 20-12, reveals the actual degree of control (or lack thereof) that you have over the Web Spreadsheet Component.

FIGURE 20-12.

The Spreadsheet Property Toolbox contains all the controls for the Web Spreadsheet Component.

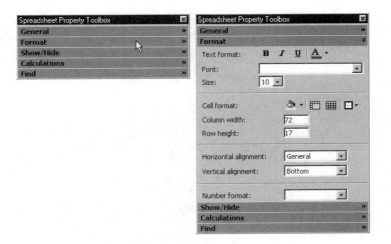

Each bar in the Spreadsheet Property Toolbox represents a category of controls you can apply to the published interactive worksheet. For example, Figure 20-12 shows the Spreadsheet Property Toolbox before and after clicking the Format bar. The format controls allow you to change various text, cell, and number formats. You use these controls the same way you would in Excel—select cells or ranges, then apply the formats. Click each bar to reveal a number of controls for that category. For example, the controls in the Show/Hide category allow you to hide gridlines, headers, the title bar, and the toolbar. If the toolbar is hidden on the Web page, you can click the right mouse button anywhere in the spreadsheet area and then choose the Property Toolbox command from the shortcut menu.

For complete information about the capabilities of the Spreadsheet Component, click the Help button on the toolbar to display a special Help file that contains topics specific to the Spreadsheet Component.

Chart Functionality

For more information about charting, see Chapter 21, "Basic Charting Techniques."

Now we'll look at another example, this time using the Web Charting Component. Even though the existing charts on the MarDivData sheet were easily converted to images in previous examples, they have been extensively formatted and so they make poor candidates for conversion to interactive Web charts. When you add interactivity, the charts are rendered in HTML, thereby limiting the formatting options. With this in mind, we created the new chart shown in Figure 20-13 to help illustrate both the strengths and the weaknesses of interactive charts.

FIGURE 20-13.

We'll use this chart to test the Web Charting Component.

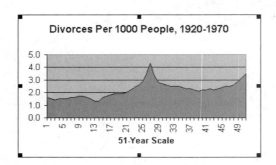

If we want to add interactivity to our new chart, first make sure MarDivData is the active sheet, then:

1   Choose Save As Web Page from the File menu.

2   Click the Publish button.

3   From the Item To Publish drop-down list, select Items On Mar-DivData and then select the new chart in the list box, shown in Figure 20-14. (Note that in our example the new chart is named Chart 5 because we previously created and discarded two charts.)

FIGURE 20-14.

You can publish individual charts as interactive Web pages.

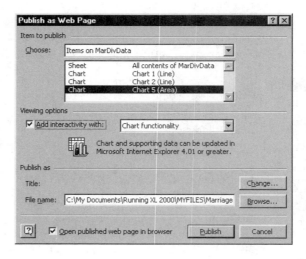

4   Click the Add Interactivity With check box.

When you select the Add Interactivity With option, the adjacent drop-down list becomes active. When a chart is selected in the Item To Publish list, the drop-down list displays only one option, Chart Functionality.

5 Click the Open Published Web Page In Browser option.

6 Click the Publish button.

The resulting Web page is shown in Figure 20-15.

FIGURE 20-15.

The published interactive chart, with its data table, as it appears in Microsoft Internet Explorer 4.01 or greater.

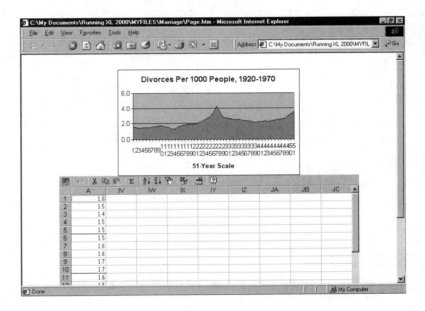

The first thing you'll notice about the published chart is what appears to be an interactive worksheet directly below it. This is the data table containing the values on which the chart is based, and this table is, in fact, what makes the chart interactive. That is, you can change values in the associated data table and the chart above immediately reflects your changes. For example, if we click cell A1 in the data table and change the existing value 1.6 to 10, the chart changes accordingly, as you can see in Figure 20-16 on the next page.

Another thing you might notice is that the numbers on the x-axis scale (at the bottom of the chart) seem to be displayed incorrectly. This error illustrates one of those little caveats we mentioned earlier—rotated text does not convert. Instead, the text is displayed in the only way possible in the current incarnation of HTML, which is "stacked" but not rotated. There may be other little problems like this, so we recommend experimentation, which should be no problem for you because it is so quick and easy to use the Web publishing feature to test each iteration. (Now you know why our example chart was Chart 5 instead of Chart 3!)

FIGURE 20-16.

Changes you make to values in the data table are immediately reflected in the interactive chart.

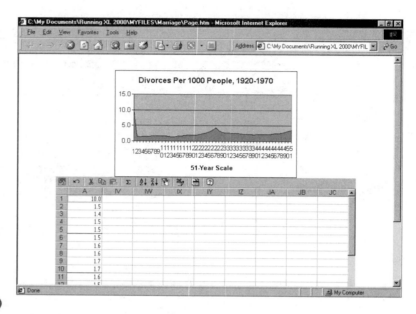

SEE ALSO

For more information about PivotTables, see Chapter 27, "Using PivotTables."

PivotTable Functionality

For the final example, we'll test the Web PivotTable Component with the BookSales.xls example workbook shown in Figure 20-17.

FIGURE 20-17.

We'll use this workbook to test the Web PivotTable Component.

	A	B	C	D	E	F	G	H
1	Year	Quarter	CatalogNo	Channel	Units	Sales		
2	1999	1	23524	International	149	349.11		
3	1999	1	23524	Mail Order	72	1,436.40		
4	1999	1	23524	Domestic	-468	(4,554.87)		
5	1999	1	26059	International	851	12,050.00		
6	1999	1	26059	Mail Order	55	1,361.25		
7	1999	1	26059	Domestic	10995	140,909.23		
8	1999	1	30782	International	896	12,678.40		
9	1999	1	30782	Mail Order	93	2,301.75		
10	1999	1	30782	Mail Order	29	703.25		
11	1999	1	30782	Domestic	5872	80,188.00		
12	1999	1	41210	Domestic	6208	77,600.00		
13	1999	1	41210	International	741	10,485.15		
14	1999	1	41210	Mail Order	100	2,475.00		
15	1999	1	50724	Domestic	6453	80,662.50		
16	1999	1	50724	International	620	15,345.00		
17	1999	1	50724	Mail Order	15	212.25		

ON THE WEB

You can find BookSales.xls used to create Figure 20-17 on the Microsoft Press Web site at *http://mspress.microsoft.com/mspress/products/2050/*.

First, make sure Sheet1 is the active sheet, and then:

1 Choose Save As Web Page from the File menu.

It's a good idea to create a new folder for each test. Just click the New Folder button at the top of the Save As Web Page dialog box and then give the new folder a name.

2 Click the Publish button.

In the Item To Publish box, Items On Sheet1 and All Contents Of Sheet1 should already be selected.

3 Click the Add Interactivity With check box.

When you select the Add Interactivity With option, the adjacent drop-down list becomes active.

4 Click the arrow to the right of the Add Interactivity With drop-down list and select PivotTable Functionality (if it isn't already selected).

5 Click the Open Published Web Page In Browser option.

6 Click the Publish button.

The resulting Web page is shown in Figure 20-18.

FIGURE 20-18.

You can publish an interactive worksheet with PivotTable functionality without even creating a PivotTable.

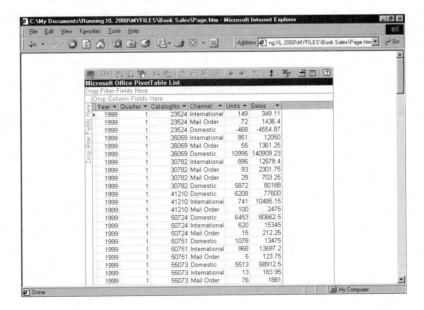

We actually published a PivotTable before we even created one—call it a *potential* PivotTable—but you might want to first create your PivotTable in Excel and then publish it. For this example, our potential PivotTable highlights the capabilities of the Web PivotTable Component within your browser.

NOTE

When you publish a workbook that already contains a PivotTable, the PivotTable appears in the Item To Publish list as a separate item you can select for publication.

The toolbar that appears in your browser for the Web PivotTable Component, shown in Figure 20-19, has a few tools in common with the Web Spreadsheet Component toolbar shown in Figure 20-11 on page 640, as well as a few buttons you'll also find elsewhere in Excel. But there are a few tools specific to PivotTables that you won't find anywhere else. Note that some of these tools will remain shaded until you either select a cell or a column in the PivotTable. The AutoCalc button—which looks like the AutoSum button with a little arrow next to it—is a drop-down menu that allows you to insert not only Sum formulas, but also Count, Min, and Max formulas as well. The Subtotal button shows or hides subtotals. The four Move To buttons provide the toolbar equivalents of dragging fields to the locations you want. For example, if you are unsure where the "filter area" actually is, clicking the Move To Filter Area button lets you know. If you have more than one row or column field, the Promote and Demote buttons allow you to move selected rows or columns closer or further away from the data in the table.

FIGURE 20-19.

The toolbar for the Web PivotTable Component.

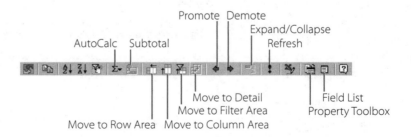

The Property Toolbox button displays a floating box similar to the one for the Spreadsheet Component but with a number of different controls, as shown in Figure 20-20. For example, the Show/Hide category allows you to control the display of the plus and minus sign expand indicators, among other things. The contents of the Property Toolbox change, depending on what's currently selected in the PivotTable. The Field List button displays the PivotTable Field List, also shown in Figure 20-20, which allows you to add any additional fields available in the data source to the PivotTable. To do so, select the field you want to add, select the location you want from the drop-down list at the bottom of the box, and then click the Add To button.

FIGURE 20-20.

The PivotTable Property Toolbox and the PivotTable Field List.

Manipulating the PivotTable fields in your browser is as easy as dragging field buttons to the desired locations or clicking field headers and using the Move To buttons on the toolbar. Use our example to try the following:

1 Click the Units field header with the right mouse button and choose Remove Field from the shortcut menu. (You can always restore it later by dragging it from the Field List box.)

2 Click the Year field header and then click the Move To Filter Area button.

3 Click the CatalogNo field header and then click the Move To Row Area button.

4 Click the Channel field header and then click the Move To Row Area button.

5 Click the Quarter field header and then click the Move To Column Area button.

Figure 20-21 shows the result.

FIGURE 20-21.

You can create different views of your data easily by dragging fields or using buttons on the toolbar.

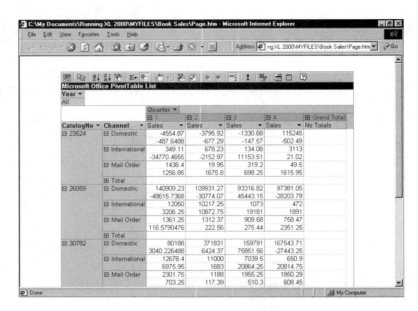

As with the other interactive Web components, there are many things you can do with PivotTables within Excel that you can't do once you save them as Web pages. For the complete, up-to-date list, consult the online Help system.

Charts

Basic Charting Techniques

With Microsoft Excel 2000, you can create sophisticated charts from your worksheet data. You can choose from a wide range of standard business and technical chart types, each of which is available in several subtypes. For example, if you're creating a column chart, you can choose overlapped, clustered, stacked, or 100 percent-stacked columns. You can also combine the basic chart types. For example, you can lay a line chart over a column chart to plot a stock's price together with its volume. You can even create picture charts that represent values with graphic images instead of ordinary columns or lines. All these chart types, combined with Excel's custom formatting options, provide you with a virtually endless variety of charting possibilities.

This chapter covers the basics of chart creation and includes a tour of Excel's standard chart types. Chapter 22, "Changing the Appearance of Your Charts," shows you how to tailor the appearance of a chart as well as how to add your own customized chart types to Excel's standard offerings. In Chapter 23, "Working with Chart Data," we look at the procedures for modifying the content of your charts—adding and removing data, adding trendlines and error bars, and so on. Excel also includes a facility for turning geographic data into attractive maps, which we survey in Chapter 24, "Mapping Geographic Data."

Creating a New Chart

To create a new chart, start by selecting any cell within the data you want to plot. Then do either of the following:

- Choose Chart from the Insert menu.

- Click the Chart Wizard button. (See Figure 21-1.)

Either way, Excel responds by displaying the first Chart Wizard dialog box. Using a four-step sequence of dialog boxes, the Chart Wizard gathers all the information Excel needs to build your chart.

FIGURE 21-1.

To create a new chart, select a cell in the data to be plotted and then click the Chart Wizard button.

The Chart Wizard button

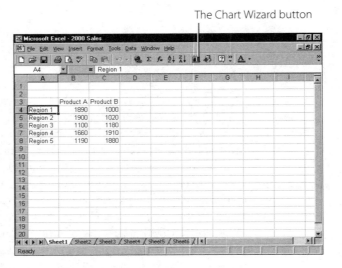

<table>
<tr><td>Product A</td><td>Product B</td></tr>
<tr><td>Region 1</td><td>1890</td><td>1000</td></tr>
<tr><td>Region 2</td><td>1900</td><td>1020</td></tr>
<tr><td>Region 3</td><td>1100</td><td>1180</td></tr>
<tr><td>Region 4</td><td>1660</td><td>1910</td></tr>
<tr><td>Region 5</td><td>1190</td><td>1880</td></tr>
</table>

⭐ TIP

The Fastest Way to Plot

To create a chart directly, without using the Chart Wizard, select a cell within the data you want to plot and then press F11. Excel uses the default chart type and creates your chart on a new chart sheet.

Step 1: Choosing a Chart Type

The Chart Wizard's Step 1 dialog box, shown in Figure 21-2 asks you to choose a chart type. You can see a sample of each chart type, applied to your own data, by clicking and holding the button near the lower right corner of this dialog box.

V

Charts

FIGURE 21-2.

The Step 1 dialog box lets you select and see samples of chart types.

1 Select a chart type from this list.

2 Select a subtype from this gallery.

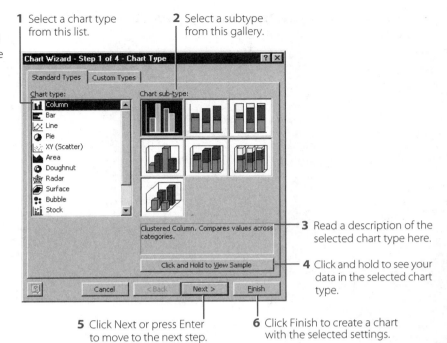

3 Read a description of the selected chart type here.

4 Click and hold to see your data in the selected chart type.

5 Click Next or press Enter to move to the next step.

6 Click Finish to create a chart with the selected settings.

The Step 1 dialog box has two tabs, one for built-in chart types and one for "custom" chart types. The latter include chart types that you create yourself (by customizing the built-in types) as well as certain combination charts defined by Excel. These combinations include line-over-column charts, column-over-area charts, and line charts with two value axes.

Step 2: Specifying the Data to Plot

In the Chart Wizard Step 2 dialog box, shown in Figure 21-3 on the next page, you tell Excel what data to plot.

If you selected a single cell within your chart's data range before starting the Chart Wizard, the Data Range entry box in this dialog box contains the range address of the entire data range. This entry box will also be correct if you selected the entire data range before starting the Chart Wizard. To help you see what data it will plot, Excel also draws a marquee around the range. If for any reason the data range isn't correct, you can fix it by pointing to the range you want to plot.

FIGURE 21-3.

The Step 2 dialog box lets you confirm or specify the data you want to plot.

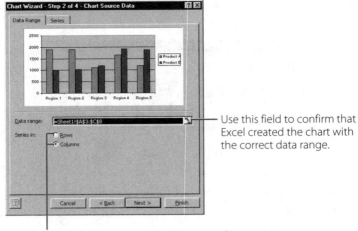

Use this field to confirm that Excel created the chart with the correct data range.

Use these buttons to switch between plotting by rows and plotting by columns.

In Figure 21-3, the sample chart shows that Excel will plot two data series, each of which has five points. The series are called Product A and Product B, and the points are Region 1, Region 2, Region 3, Region 4, and Region 5. If instead we wanted five data series, each with two points, we would click the Rows option button, causing Excel to switch from plotting by columns to plotting by rows. Excel would then redraw the sample chart in the Chart Wizard dialog box, to allow us to confirm the new orientation.

You'll find that Excel usually makes the right judgment about whether to plot by rows or by columns. It does so by assuming that your chart will include more points and fewer series. But you'll want to check the sample, just to make sure the chart represents your data effectively.

Like the Step 1 dialog box, the Step 2 dialog box includes two tabs. To make sure Excel has the correct name and range for each series in your chart, click the Series tab. You'll see the dialog box shown in Figure 21-4.

⭐ **TIP**

Plotting Noncontiguous Data
The data in your chart does not have to reside in a single contiguous block. In Figure 21-1 on page 652, for example, you could plot only Regions 1, 3, and 5, omitting Region 2 and Region 4. To plot noncontiguous data, hold down the Ctrl key while selecting each block that you want to plot, and then start the Chart Wizard.

FIGURE 21-4.

Use the Series tab to check the names and values of series in your chart.

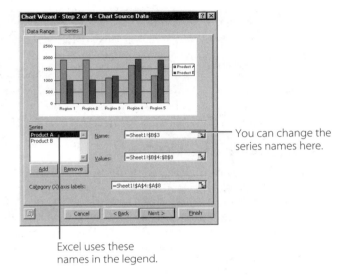

You can change the series names here.

Excel uses these names in the legend.

On this tab of the Step 2 dialog box, each series in the chart has a name in the list box at the left. To see what values Excel plans to use for a series, as well as the name that will appear in the legend, select the series name in the list box.

If the data does not include column or row headings that identify the names of the data series, Excel uses the default names Series 1, Series 2, and so on. You can replace the defaults with something more meaningful either by typing text directly into the Name edit box or by selecting the Name edit box and then pointing to a worksheet cell that contains the appropriate text.

If the chart data does include headings that identify the data series names, a cell reference for each series appears in the Name field. The data series is linked to the referenced cell: if the text there changes, the series name changes automatically.

If the chart data does not include column or row headings that identify points in the data series (the text that typically appears along the x axis), Excel uses the default identifiers 1, 2, 3, and so on. You can replace the defaults either by pointing to a worksheet range that contains the appropriate text or by typing names directly into the category-axis label field. If you type text in directly, use commas to separate the names. Click Next to move to Step 3 when you are finished identifying the data to chart.

Step 3: Choosing Chart Options

The Chart Wizard Step 3 dialog box includes six tabs. This dialog box is where you specify details about the chart's axes, the titles to be associated with the chart and its axes, the legend, labels for data points, and so on. You can take care of all these matters now, while you're building the chart, or you can return to this dialog box to make changes after you've already created a chart.

Specifying Chart Titles

The Titles tab of the Step 3 dialog box, shown in Figure 21-5, lets you assign a title for the chart and descriptive text for each axis.

Excel displays the text using default fonts, alignments, and positions. The titles are ordinary text-box objects, which you may reposition, realign, reformat, and edit after the chart has been created.

FIGURE 21-5.

This dialog box has at least three edit boxes—and may make available as many as five for certain kinds of charts—where you type title text.

Enter title text for the chart and axes here.

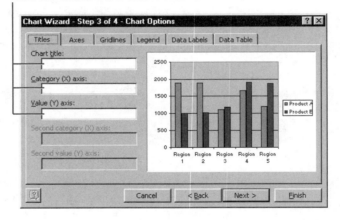

Displaying or Hiding Axes

? **SEE ALSO**

For more information about modifying your chart, see Chapter 22, "Changing the Appearance of Your Charts."

Occasionally, you may find that a chart looks best if it's drawn without one or more of its customary axes. You can prevent the display of any axis on the Axes tab of the Step 3 dialog box, as shown in Figure 21-6.

To hide an axis, clear the check box. The Chart Wizard redraws the sample to show what your chart will look like without that axis.

FIGURE 21-6.

Use the Axes tab to control the display of axes.

To remove the Category (x) axis, clear this check box.

Value axis

Series axis

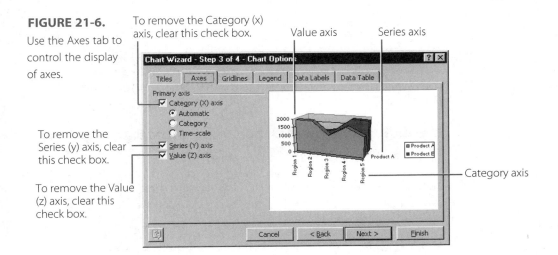

To remove the Series (y) axis, clear this check box.

To remove the Value (z) axis, clear this check box.

Category axis

> **NOTE**
>
> Pie and doughnut charts do not use axes, so the Axes tab does not appear if you selected one of these chart types.

Category vs. Time Scaling

If the data for the category axis consists of dates, Excel recognizes that fact and automatically applies time scaling to the axis. Time scaling differs from ordinary ("category") scaling in the following ways:

- Excel positions all data points in accordance with their chronological locations. For example, if a time-scaled axis includes points for January 1, January 2, and January 6, the January 2 point appears closer to the January 1 point than to the January 6 point.

- Excel automatically plots time-series points in ascending chronological order, even if your data is not sorted chronologically.

- Excel uses the smallest time difference between your data points as its base unit, but you can switch to a larger base unit to get a different perspective on your data. For example, if you plot daily stock prices, Excel uses 1 day as its base unit. But you can switch to a weekly or monthly view by changing the base unit. *For information about changing the base unit, see "Changing the Base Unit," page 685.*

Time scaling is available in both two-dimensional and three-dimensional line, column, bar, and area charts. For these chart types, you can specify either category or time scaling by selecting the Category or Time-scale option button on the Axes tab of the Step 3 dialog box in the Chart Wizard. If instead you leave the setting at Automatic, Excel will make the decision for you—which usually works out fine.

Manual Scaling and Other Axis Formatting Options

To scale an axis manually—that is, to specify an axis's maximum value, minimum value, or tick-mark interval—first create the chart with automatic scaling. Then adjust the axis as described in *"Formatting and Scaling Axes," page 677*. The Chart Wizard does not include manual scaling options.

You can also use procedures described in Chapter 22 to change the font and alignment of axis labels, change the numeric formatting used for values and dates, and change the line style or color of the axes themselves.

Displaying Gridlines

Gridlines are horizontal or vertical lines that help clarify the position of data markers relative to axis scales. Most of Excel's chart types use some form of gridlines by default. You can add gridlines or remove them by clicking the Gridlines tab of the Chart Wizard Step 3 dialog box, shown in Figure 21-7.

FIGURE 21-7.

Use the Gridlines tab to change Excel's default gridline settings.

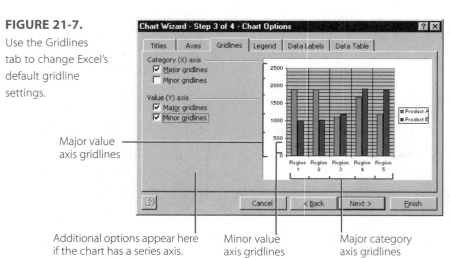

Major value axis gridlines

Additional options appear here if the chart has a series axis.

Minor value axis gridlines

Major category axis gridlines

SEE ALSO

For more information about gridlines, see "Displaying and Formatting Gridlines," page 688.

Major gridlines emanate from axis subdivisions called major tick marks. Minor gridlines are drawn from further subdivisions known as minor tick marks. Excel determines the position of these tick marks automatically, but you can use formatting commands to change their positions. You can also alter the colors and styles of the gridlines themselves.

NOTE

Pie and doughnut charts do not use gridlines, so the Gridlines tab does not appear if you have chosen one of these chart types.

Displaying or Hiding a Legend

Excel normally displays a legend at the right side of the chart. You can choose a different location for the legend or dispense with it altogether by clicking the Legend tab, shown in Figure 21-8, in the Chart Wizard Step 3 dialog box.

FIGURE 21-8.

Use the Legend tab to move or remove a legend.

Clear this check box to remove the legend.

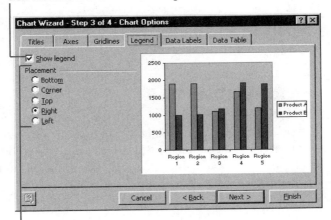

Select an option to specify the legend's position.

SEE ALSO

For more information about formatting text in your chart, see "Formatting Text Elements," page 672.

Once the chart is created, you can reposition the legend by dragging it with the mouse. You can also use formatting commands to change the text font.

Displaying Data Labels

The Chart Wizard can attach various kinds of labels to data markers. Pie and doughnut slices, for example, can be identified with percentages, absolute values, or both. Columns in a column graph and markers in a line graph can have labels indicating the value of each point or the category-axis text associated with each point, and so on. To add data labels, click the Data Labels tab in the Chart Wizard Step 3 dialog box, shown in Figure 21-9. *For more information on how to label data, see Chapter 22, "Changing the Appearance of Your Charts."*

FIGURE 21-9.

The Data Labels tab labeling options apply to all data points in the chart.

Select a label option.

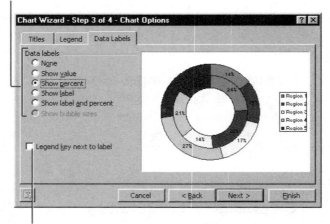

Select this check box to add legend symbols next to labels.

Adding a Data Table

Depending on the type of chart you're creating, Excel might give you the option of including a data table along with the chart. A data table is simply a table of the values from which the chart is derived. To include a data table, click the Data Table tab in the Chart Wizard Step 3 dialog box, shown in Figure 21-10.

FIGURE 21-10.

Use the Data Table tab to include a table that shows the values used to create the chart.

To add a data table to a chart, select this check box.

Select this check box to include legend symbols in the table.

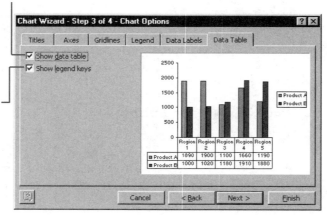

Once you create the chart, you can use formatting commands to modify the line styles and font used in the data table, *as described in "Formatting Text Elements," page 672.*

Step 4: Deciding Where to Put the Chart

Excel can place the chart either as an object on a worksheet or on a separate chart sheet. You express your preference in the Chart Wizard Step 4 dialog box, shown in Figure 21-11.

FIGURE 21-11.

The Step 4 dialog box lets you decide where to locate the chart.

To place the chart on a separate chart sheet, select this button.

Type a name for the chart sheet here.

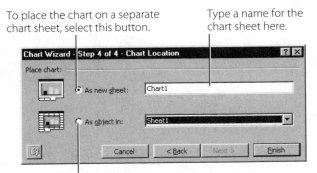

To place the chart in an existing worksheet, select this button and choose a worksheet from the drop-down list.

Changing a Chart's Size and Position

If you place the chart as an object on an existing worksheet, Excel creates the chart in a default size and position, as shown in Figure 21-12 on the next page. Drag the mouse to adjust the position and size of the chart. Hold down Ctrl or the Shift key to maintain the chart's center point or aspect ratio (the ratio of its length to its height).

When you resize a chart, Excel adjusts the size of all chart text. If you're not happy with the adjustment, you can use formatting commands to increase or decrease the text size, as *described in "Formatting Text Elements," page 672.*

If you place the new chart on a separate chart sheet, Excel creates it at a standard size, and the chart maintains that size even if you make the window larger or smaller. For example, if your workbook window is maximized, the chart will be fully visible on its new chart sheet. But if you subsequently reduce the size of the workbook window, only some of the chart will be visible.

FIGURE 21-12.

You can use the mouse to adjust the chart's size and position.

To move a chart object, click within the chart and drag.

To resize a chart, drag one of the handles.

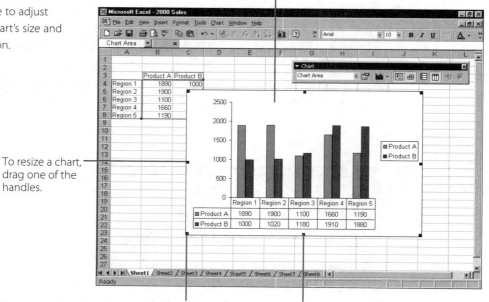

To resize and maintain aspect ratio, hold down Shift while dragging a corner handle.

To resize and maintain center point, hold down Ctrl while dragging a handle.

You can switch to an alternative display mode, in which the chart's size automatically changes if you change the size of the window. To do this, activate the chart sheet, choose Options from the Tools menu, click the Chart tab, and select the Chart Sizes With Window Frame check box.

Plotting Hidden Cells

Excel normally ignores any hidden rows or columns in a chart's data range. If you want hidden cells to be plotted, create the chart in the normal way. Select the chart, choose Options from the Tools menu, click the Chart tab, and then clear the Plot Visible Cells Only check box.

How Excel Handles Missing Values

In line, radar, xy, and surface charts, Excel normally skips over any blank cells. Missing data points thus appear as discontinuities in the chart. You have two other options:

- Plot the missing data points as zeros.

- Interpolate the missing points.

If you interpolate, Excel uses a straight line to bridge the gap created by a missing value. It does not actually create a new, interpolated, data point.

To select a missing values option, first create a chart and select it. Choose Options from the Tools menu and then click the Chart tab. You'll see the dialog box shown in Figure 21-13.

FIGURE 21-13.

Select an option to determine how Excel handles missing values in line, radar, area, xy, and surface charts.

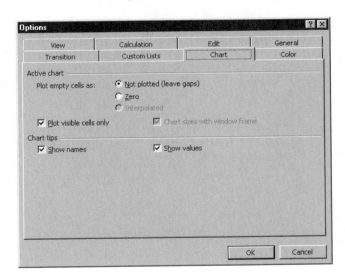

Note that these options have no effect in charts with discontinuous data markers, such as bar charts and column charts. Also, in area charts and surface charts, missing points are plotted as zeros, regardless of how you set the interpolation option.

Changing the Default Chart Type

Excel's "factory" default chart type is a two-dimensional clustered-column chart—that is, a vertical bar chart in which series are plotted side by side along a single category axis. This is the style of chart you will get if you simply select your chart data and then press the F11 key. To make a different chart type the default, create a chart, then select the chart and choose the Chart Type command from the Chart menu (this menu is usable only when a chart is selected). You will see the dialog box shown in Figure 21-14, which looks almost identical to the Step 1 dialog box of the Chart Wizard. To change the default chart type, do the following:

FIGURE 21-14.

Use the Chart Type Selection dialog box to change the default chart type.

1 First, select a type category.

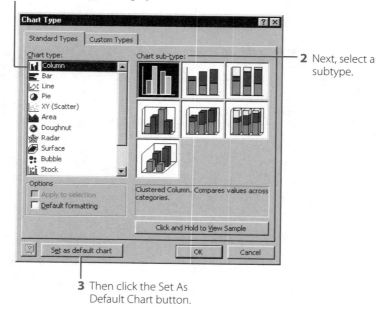

2 Next, select a subtype.

3 Then click the Set As Default Chart button.

The only difference between this dialog box and the one you saw in Step 1 of the Chart Wizard is that this dialog box includes the Set As Default Chart command button. Click here, answer the confirmation prompt, click OK, and you have a new default chart type.

You must select an existing chart to open this dialog box. Changing the default chart type changes this existing chart to the selected type. Once you arrive at this dialog box, you can select any of Excel's built-in chart types and subtypes and make a new default.

You can also use the Chart Type command to make a customized chart the default. Chapter 22 explains how to do this. *For more information on Custom Charts, see "Adding a Customized Chart to the Chart Wizard Gallery," page 671.*

Printing Charts

To print a chart that appears on a separate chart sheet, simply activate the sheet and follow the printing procedures described in Chapter 11, "Printing and Presenting." To print a chart that appears as an object on a worksheet page, you can do either of the following:

- To print the chart by itself, select it and then choose the Print command from the File menu.

- To print the chart with surrounding worksheet data, select any part of the worksheet (but not the chart). Then choose the Print command from the File menu.

If you print the chart with surrounding data, the printout will resemble what you see on the screen. That is, cells covered by the chart on-screen will also be covered on the printout.

Saving, Opening, and Protecting Charts

Charts are saved with the workbook in which they reside. To save a chart, simply save the workbook file by choosing either Save or Save As from the File menu. The chart is available whenever the workbook is open, so to open a chart, simply open its workbook.

After you create a chart, you can use the Protection command on the Tools menu to lock the worksheet or chart sheet containing the chart. Then other people can't change the sheet and, therefore, the chart. The Protection command works the same way for both worksheets and chart sheets.

V

Charts

CHAPTER 22

Changing the Appearance of Your Charts

A fter you've created a chart, either by pressing F11 or stepping through the Chart Wizard's dialog boxes, you can do many things to modify its appearance. Microsoft Excel 2000 offers a wide assortment of commands for tailoring your charts to suit your tastes, your presentation needs, and your company's visual standards. Those commands are the subject of this chapter.

This chapter describes only the formatting features that are provided on the Chart and Format menus. You can also do a lot to enhance the appearance of your charts by using drawing tools. For example, you can add arrows, ellipses, or text objects to highlight or explain significant data shown in your chart. *For details about the use of drawing tools, see Chapter 10, "Graphics."*

Working with the Chart Menu and Chart Toolbar

The first step in customizing any chart is to select it. If the chart is on a separate chart sheet, activate that sheet. If it's an object on a worksheet, select it there. When you activate a chart sheet or select a chart object, Excel replaces the Data menu with the Chart menu. As Figure 22-1 shows, it also displays a handy Chart toolbar.

FIGURE 22-1.

When a chart is selected, Excel displays a Chart menu and a Chart toolbar.

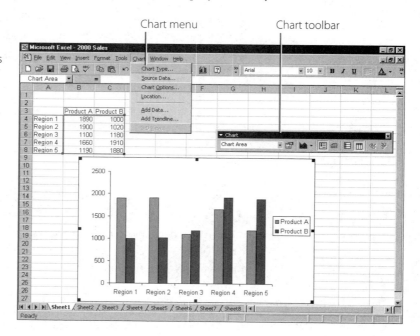

Chart menu

Chart toolbar

Click the down arrow at the bottom of the Chart menu and the first four commands display dialog boxes that are almost identical to those of the Chart Wizard. Thus, you can use the Chart menu to revise any decision you made while creating your chart. If you created a column chart, for example, and you decide you'd rather have a bar chart, simply select the Chart Type command from the Chart menu. This will take you to a dialog box almost identical to the one you saw in the first step of the Chart Wizard. If you want to add titles to your axes, choose Chart Options from the Chart menu, and then click the Titles tab. Any chart-building choice you can make using the Chart Wizard you can also make after the fact using the Chart menu.

The Chart toolbar's features are labeled in Figure 22-2. This toolbar normally appears whenever you select a chart and disappears when you select anything else. Most users find it both helpful and unobtrusive. If it gets in your way, though, you can click the Close box to send it packing. To make the toolbar visible again, click the menu bar or any part of any visible toolbar with the right mouse button, or choose Toolbars from the View menu. Then select Chart from the Toolbar menu.

NOTE

If you close the Chart toolbar while a chart is selected, the toolbar will not appear automatically the next time you select a chart. You need to click Toolbars from the View menu and select Charts to view this toolbar again.

FIGURE 22-2.

The Chart toolbar provides the tools you need to improve the chart's appearance.

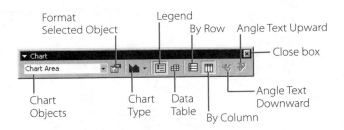

Selecting Chart Elements

To change the appearance of any particular chart element, such as the legend or the category axis, first select that element. You can do this by choosing the appropriate item from the Chart Objects drop-down list, the first item on the Chart toolbar. Or you can simply click the chart element you want to modify. Excel makes it easy to verify that you've selected the right element. As you move the pointer around a chart, Excel displays chart tips that identify the chart element you're currently pointing to. When you click to select an element, Excel also changes the current item in the Chart Objects drop-down list, so a quick glance will confirm that you're in the right spot. Finally, just in case you're not using the Chart toolbar, Excel also shows what you've selected in the Name box, to the left of the formula bar. Figure 22-3 on the next page illustrates all three navigational aids.

V

Charts

TIP

A chart tip should appear automatically when you point to a chart element. If you're not seeing chart tips, choose the Options command from the Tools menu and then click the Chart tab. Select the Show Names check box, in the Chart Tips group near the bottom of the dialog box. If you want your tips to include data-point values, also select the Show Values check box.

FIGURE 22-3.

Chart tips, the Chart Objects drop-down list, and the Name box all help you select the right element for formatting.

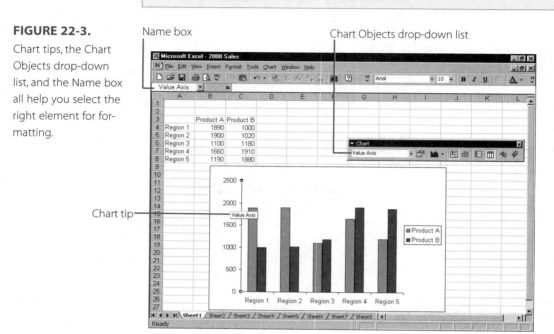

Copying Formats from One Chart to Another

SEE ALSO

For more information about adjusting the scaling of a chart, see "Scaling Axes Manually," page 679.

Most of this chapter is devoted to procedures for changing the appearance of particular chart elements. But if you've already got one chart set up just the way you want it, you can use that chart as a model for others. To use the formats of one chart in another, first select the chart area of the chart whose formats you want to copy. Choose Copy from the Edit menu, select the other chart, and then choose Paste Special from the Edit menu. In the Paste Special dialog box, choose the Formats option. Note that when you do this, *all* formats are copied from the first chart to the second, including any scaling changes you have applied to any axis. If you want your second chart to look like your first, but the range of data values that it plots are different, you'll need to adjust the scaling on the second chart after you use the Paste Special command.

Adding a Customized Chart to the Chart Wizard Gallery

If you want to use a particular combination of charting formats again and again, it's best to add that combination to the gallery of chart types presented by the Chart Wizard. You can do that following these steps:

1 Format your chart to look exactly as you want, using procedures described in the remainder of this chapter.

2 Select the chart and choose Chart Type from the Chart menu.

3 Click the Custom Types tab.

4 Click the User-Defined option button in the Select From group.

5 Click Add.

6 In the Add Custom Chart Type dialog box, type a name for the custom chart and (if you like) a description of it.

7 Click OK twice to return to the chart.

To delete a customized chart from the Chart Wizard Gallery, select any chart, choose Chart Type from the Chart menu, and then click the Custom Types tab. Choose the User-Defined option button, select the name of the customized chart type you want to delete, click the Delete button, and then answer the confirmation prompt.

Repositioning Chart Elements with the Mouse

You can move the chart title, axis titles, data labels, and legend simply by dragging with the mouse. You can also "explode" a pie or doughnut chart by dragging slices with the mouse. Note, in particular, that you can adjust the positions of individual data labels without moving an entire series of labels and that, although the Chart Wizard lets you create a legend only in certain fixed positions, you're free to drag the legend anywhere, including into the middle of the chart itself.

To restore the default position for an object, you can drag it back to where you first found it. To recreate the default position more precisely, first delete the object, and then recreate it. For example, if you drag the legend onto the middle of the chart, and then decide it really looked better back in its original location, simply click the Legend tool on the Chart toolbar twice. The first click eliminates your customized legend, and the second recreates a standard legend.

TIP

> You don't have to use a dialog box to delete a legend, an axis, a data table, or a set of gridlines or data labels. Simply select the element you want to get rid of and then press Delete. If you change your mind immediately, choose Undo from the Edit menu.

Moving and Resizing the Plot Area

The *plot area* is the part of your chart that displays data, as distinguished from the *chart area,* which surrounds the plot area. You can use the mouse to change the size and position of the plot area within the chart area. Start by selecting the plot area. Excel displays a border around the plot area and handles in the corners. To change the size of the plot area, drag one of the handles. To change the position of the plot area, drag one of the borders.

Formatting Text Elements

The text-formatting options described in the following paragraphs apply to these chart elements:

- Chart title
- Axis titles
- Legend text
- Axis tick-mark labels
- Data labels

Some of the text-formatting options can also be used with the text that appears in a data table. Additional formatting options are available with text objects that you create with drawing tools.

⭐ **TIP**

To quickly format any chart element, you can begin by simply double-clicking it. Excel displays the appropriate formatting dialog box when you do this. Alternatively, you can select an element and press Ctrl+1, or select an element and click the Format [Selected Object] button on the Chart toolbar. Note that the name of [Selected Object] will change according to what you have selected. And if these are not shortcuts enough, the command described in this chapter as "the first command on the Format menu" is also always the first command on the shortcut menu that appears when you click a chart object with the right mouse button. To format an axis, for example, you can simply click the axis with the right mouse button and then choose the first command from the shortcut menu.

Changing the Font and Color

To change the typeface, point size, type style (for example, bold or italic), or color of a text element, select the element and choose the first command on the Format menu. (This command changes according to what you have selected. If you select an axis title, for example, it says Format Selected Axis Title.) Then click the Font tab of the Format dialog box, as shown in Figure 22-4.

V

Charts

FIGURE 22-4.

The Font tab looks and works just like the one you use to format text in worksheet cells, except that it has two additional controls.

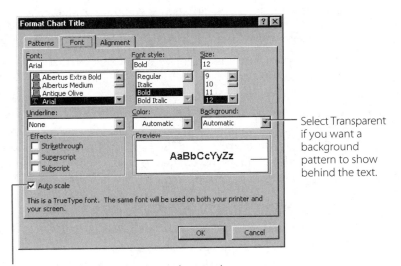

Select Transparent if you want a background pattern to show behind the text.

If you don't want the point size to change when you resize your chart, clear this check box.

Excel normally resizes all chart text whenever you change the size of the chart. If you'd rather Excel did not do this, clear the Auto Scale check box. Excel also normally makes the background area of your text opaque. Any pattern underlying the text block is thus invisible. If you'd rather see the underlying pattern, choose Transparent from the Background drop-down menu. Otherwise, leave this setting on Automatic or set it to Opaque.

> Many of the dialog boxes you see while formatting charts include options identified as Automatic. Choosing Automatic tells Excel to exercise its own judgment. If you're in doubt about a formatting choice, it's best to leave the setting on Automatic.

Formatting All Chart Text at Once

To change the font and color of all text in a chart—titles, tick-mark labels, data labels, and legend—select Chart Area, choose Selected Chart Area from the Format menu, and then click the Font tab. This changes all the default text elements—the legend and axis labels, for example—but has no effect on custom text elements. For example, if you have added a label to an arrow that points to part of a pie chart, changing the default text elements does not affect this label.

Formatting Individual Words and Letters

If you click a text block once—your chart title, for example—Excel draws a border around the block and displays handles along the border. Any formatting command you issue applies to the entire block. To format a portion of the block, such as a particular word, first click the text block as you normally would. Second, drag over the part you want to format to highlight it. Excel removes the border and handles and highlights the characters you selected. Finally, choose the first command from the Format menu.

Formatting Individual Data Labels

To change the formatting for a particular data label, click the label twice. The first click selects all labels for the data series. The second click refines the selection to the current point. Then choose the first command from the Format menu. (Don't be too quick about selecting twice! If Excel thinks you've given it a double click instead of two successive single clicks, it displays a formatting dialog box for the entire series of labels.)

To make the same formatting change to several, but not all, labels in a data series, first make the change to one label, as described in the previous paragraph. Then select the next label you want to change and press the F4 key. (The F4 key repeats your most recent command.)

Creating a Multiline Title

You cannot create a title that extends over two or more lines in the Chart Wizard. But after you have created your chart, you can split an existing title across multiple lines. Click the title twice—once to select the entire title and a second time to place an insertion point in the title text. Move the insertion point to the place where you want the line break and press the Shift key and Enter simultaneously.

Changing Text Rotation

Excel normally displays the chart title and category axis title text horizontally, value axis title text vertically, and category axis labels with an upward slant (if necessary to make the labels fit). To change one of these default orientations, start by selecting the element you want to change. Choose the first command from the Format menu to reveal the Format Chart Title dialog box. Click the Alignment tab as shown in Figure 22-5.

FIGURE 22-5.

Use the Alignment tab to change Excel's default orientations.

These drop-down lists adjust the alignment of multiline titles.

Click here to stack letters vertically.

To give text a new slant, click this semicircle . . .

. . . or enter a number between -90 and 90 here.

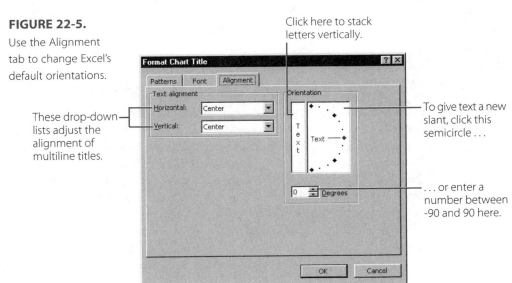

Changing the Orientation of Particular Data Labels

You can change the orientation of an entire series of data labels or of individual labels. To change an individual label, click it twice (slowly). Then choose the Format menu's first command.

Repositioning Data Labels

In many chart types, you can change the position of data labels relative to their markers. When you select a data label on one of these chart types, the Alignment tab of the Format dialog box for data labels includes a Label Position area in addition to the controls shown in Figure 22-5 on the previous page. Use the drop-down list in this area to select a different position for your data labels. The options that appear in the list depend on the kind of chart you're working with. With column charts, for example, you can put your labels above the columns, at the base of the columns, or to the left or right of the columns' tops.

Changing the Alignment of Multiline Titles

The Text Alignment drop-down lists, on the left side of the dialog box shown in Figure 22-5 on the previous page, are meaningful only when the selection is a multiline text block—a two-line chart title, for example. Excel normally centers multiline text, but you can choose a different form of alignment.

Changing the Numeric Format Used by Tick-Mark and Data Labels

Excel normally uses the same format for axis tick-mark labels and data labels as the associated worksheet data uses. If you plot a column of cells formatted as currency, for example, data labels for that series will have the same currency format. (If not all cells in a series have the same format, Excel uses the format assigned to the first cell in the series.) You can change either the tick-mark label or data label display to any other built-in or custom numeric format. Select the axis or data labels you want to change. Then choose the Format menu's first command to reveal the Format Axis dialog box. Click the Number tab as shown in Figure 22-6.

When you choose a format from the Category box, Excel automatically clears the Linked To Source check box. To restore the use of the formats assigned to the associated worksheet cells, simply reselect this check box.

FIGURE 22-6.

Select a numeric format from the Category box or select the Linked To Source check box to use the associated worksheet cells' format.

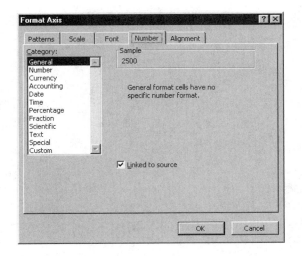

You can create a custom format that applies a scaling format to a set of numbers—making 1000000 appear as 1000, for example. *See "Formatting Numbers and Text," page 163, for more details.*

Formatting the Borders and Backgrounds of Text Areas

The procedures for formatting the borders and backgrounds of text blocks are the same as those for formatting the larger background areas of your chart. *For information about formatting background areas, see "Formatting Background Areas," page 701.*

Formatting and Scaling Axes

Excel gives you a great deal of control over the format, position, and scale of your charts' axes. You can specify the line style, color, and weight of the axes, as well as the presence or absence of tick marks and tick labels. You can also override Excel's default scaling and set the positions at which vertical and horizontal axes intersect.

Specifying Line Style, Color, and Weight

To change the line style, color, or weight of an axis, select it and then choose the first command from the Format menu. Then click the Patterns tab of the Format Axis dialog box, shown in Figure 22-7 on the next page.

Charts

FIGURE 22-7.

Change the properties of an axis by clicking the Patterns tab of the Format Axis dialog box.

Select line style, color, and weight.

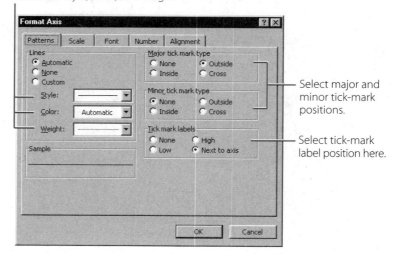

Select major and minor tick-mark positions.

Select tick-mark label position here.

The default axis is a thin solid black line, but Excel gives you eight line styles and four weights to choose from. Note that your tick marks are drawn in the same style as your axis, so if you choose a heavy red line for the axis, you'll get heavy red tick marks as well—unless, of course, you opt for no tick marks.

Specifying the Position of Tick Marks and Tick-Mark Labels

Tick marks are short lines that either cross or abut an axis at regular intervals. Like the lines that mark inches and fractions of an inch along a ruler, tick marks help define the axis scale. Tick marks come in two degrees, major and minor. Minor tick marks delineate subdivisions between major tick marks.

Tick-mark labels are the labels that identify positions along the axis. In Figure 22-8, for example, the value-axis tick-mark labels are the currency figures at the left edge of the chart. The category-axis tick-mark labels are Quarter 1, Quarter 2, and so on.

By default, Excel displays major tick marks on the outside of axes and does not display minor tick marks. A tick-mark label is displayed for each major tick mark, adjacent to the axis.

FIGURE 22-8.

We selected Low
for the category-axis
tick-mark labels, to
keep them out of the
plot area.

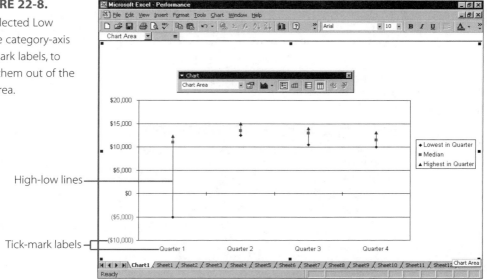

High-low lines —

Tick-mark labels —

To reposition tick marks or tick-mark labels, select the appropriate axis, choose the first command from the Format menu, and click the Patterns tab of the Format Axis dialog box, shown in Figure 22-7.

You will probably want to reposition your tick-mark labels in charts where the category and value axes intersect somewhere other than the lower left corner of the chart. In Figure 22-8, for example, the inclusion of negative values causes the category axis to cross the value axis above the bottom of the chart. If the category-axis tick-mark labels remained in their default stations, adjacent to the axis, they'd be in the middle of the plot area. Therefore, we selected Low in the Tick-Mark Labels section of the Patterns tab of the Format Axis dialog box.

Scaling Axes Manually

Excel usually creates satisfactory scales for your axes, but you're not required to use them. You can specify your own maxima and minima, change the positions of major and minor tick marks (as well as the gridlines that may extend from those tick marks), and switch between normal and logarithmic scaling.

Scaling a Value Axis Manually

To scale a value axis manually, select it, choose the first command from the Format menu, and then click the Scale tab of the Format Axis dialog box, as shown in Figure 22-9.

FIGURE 22-9.

Click the Scale tab to scale a value axis manually.

Select Auto check boxes to restore scaling defaults.

Enter values in the edit boxes to override scaling defaults.

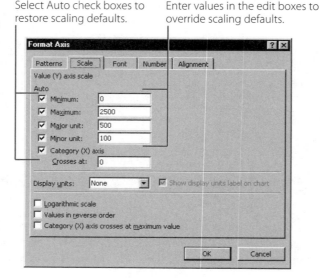

Setting Minimum and Maximum Values

When all the values in your chart data are positive, Excel's default value axis usually begins at 0 and ends at (or just above) the highest value in the chart. If all the chart values are negative, the scale normally begins at (or just below) the lowest value and ends at 0. If the chart includes both negative and positive values, the default scale starts at (or just below) the lowest value and ends at (or just above) the highest value.

In a chart with only positive values, you can zoom in on the plot area by changing the minimum scale value from 0 to a number that approximates the lowest value in the chart. In a chart with only negative values, you can zoom in on the plot area by making a similar change to the maximum value. To change either end point of the scale, simply enter the value of your choice in the Minimum or Maximum edit box on the Scale tab of the Format Axis dialog box.

When you change the Minimum or Maximum value, Excel clears the Auto check box to the left of the option. To restore the automatic Minimum or Maximum value, reselect the appropriate Auto check box.

Changing the Position of Tick Marks and Gridlines

The Major Unit and Minor Unit values on the Scale tab of the Format Axis dialog box determine the position of major and minor tick marks. The Major Unit and Minor Unit values determine the position of major and minor gridlines, if you choose to display them. For example, to increase the space between gridlines, increase the Major Unit value, the Minor Unit value, or both, by typing new values in the Major Unit and Minor Unit edit boxes.

Changing the Intersection of the Category Axis

Normally, the category axis crosses the value axis at 0. To position it elsewhere, enter a value other than 0 in the Category (X) Axis Crosses At edit box on the Scale tab of the Format Axis dialog box. Excel then clears the associated Auto check box. To restore the normal position of the category axis, reselect the Auto check box.

You can also modify the position of the category axis by selecting the Category (X) Axis Crosses At Maximum Value option at the bottom of this dialog box. Excel then displays the category axis at the top of the chart (unless you also select the Values In Reverse Order option).

Using Logarithmic Scaling

In a logarithmic scale, each power of 10 is separated by the same distance. For example, in a logarithmic scale that runs from 1 to 10,000, the numbers 1, 10, 100, 1,000, and 10,000 are equally spaced. Scientific and other types of technical charts often use logarithmic scaling.

To use logarithmic scaling, select the Logarithmic Scale option on the Scale tab of the Format Axis dialog box. To restore linear (normal) scaling, clear this option.

In a logarithmic scale, the lowest value is typically 1. Negative and 0 values cannot be plotted. If you apply logarithmic scaling to a chart that contains negative or 0 values, Excel displays an error message and removes those values from the chart. To restore them, simply restore linear scaling.

Reversing the Value-Axis Scale

You can turn the value-axis scale upside down so that the highest values appear near the bottom of the chart and the lowest values appear near the top. This option is convenient if all your chart values are negative and you're interested primarily in the absolute values of each point. You may also find it handy if lower values are considered better—for example, in a chart that plots interest rates. To reverse the scale, select the Values In Reverse Order option on the Scale tab of the Format Axis dialog box.

Scaling Manually a Non-Time-Scaled Category Axis

To scale manually a non-time-scaled category axis, select it, choose the command from the Format menu, and then click the Scale tab of the Format Axis dialog box, as shown in Figure 22-10.

FIGURE 22-10.

The Scale tab also allows you to scale manually a non-time-scaled category axis .

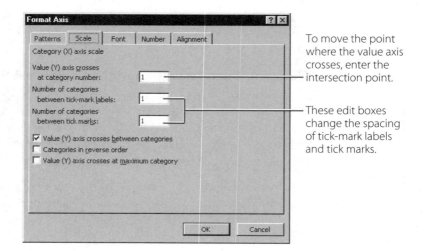

To move the point where the value axis crosses, enter the intersection point.

These edit boxes change the spacing of tick-mark labels and tick marks.

Changing the Intersection of the Value Axis

Normally, the value axis crosses the category axis to the left of the first category's data markers. You can position its crossing point elsewhere, however. Simply enter a value other than 1 in the Value (Y) Axis Crosses At Category Number edit box on the Scale tab of the Format Axis dialog box. To restore the normal position of the value axis, change the value back to 1.

You can also modify the position of the value axis by selecting the Value (Y) Axis Crosses At Maximum Category option. Excel then displays the value axis at the right side of the chart (unless you also select the Categories In Reverse Order option).

Changing the Intervals Between Category Labels

Excel normally displays one category label for each data cluster (or for each data point in a single-series chart). If the chart has a lot of data points, the program draws the labels at an angle so they won't overlap. If you specify horizontal alignment *(see "Changing Text Rotation," page 675)*, Excel automatically skips a certain number of labels to avoid overlap. If, despite these measures, you still find your horizontally aligned labels overlapping, or if you just want to see fewer labels, enter a number other than 1 in the Number Of Categories Between Tick-Mark Labels edit box on the Scale tab of the Format Axis dialog box. If you enter 2, for example, Excel displays a label for every other category. If you enter 3, Excel displays a label for every third category, and so on.

Changing the Intervals Between Tick Marks and Gridlines

The values in the Number Of Categories Between Tick Marks box on the Scale tab of the Format Axis dialog box determine the position of major tick marks along the category axis. By default, Excel creates a major tick mark for every category name. You can make them appear less frequently if you enter a value greater than 1 in this box.

The presence or absence of tick marks along the category axis doesn't have much of an impact on the appearance of your chart. But major gridlines emanate from major tick marks, so if you display major category-axis gridlines, you can control the frequency at which they appear by altering the interval between tick marks.

Excel draws minor category-axis gridlines halfway between each pair of major gridlines. You cannot customize this interval independently.

Changing Where the First Point Appears

The Value (Y) Axis Crosses Between Categories option on the Scale tab of the Format Axis dialog box determines where the first point in each series appears, relative to the value axis. This option is selected by default for bar and column charts and cleared for area and line charts. As a result, Excel draws bar and column charts with a little space between the axis and the first marker, and area and line charts with their first markers flush against the value axis.

Reversing the Category-Axis Scale

You can invert the category-axis scale so the first category appears on the right side of the chart and the last category appears on the left. This option is convenient if you want to emphasize the last category. To reverse the scale, select the Categories In Reverse Order option on the Scale tab of the Format Axis dialog box.

Scaling a Time-Scaled Category Axis Manually

As mentioned in Chapter 21, "Basic Charting Techniques," Excel treats time-scaled category axes differently from ordinary category axes. On a time-scaled axis, Excel spaces points at equal temporal intervals, resulting in discontinuities or interpolations if there is no data associated with particular dates. On a time-scaled axis plotting daily stock prices, for example, weekends and holidays will show up as gaps in the plot.

Scaling options for time-scaled category axes are different from the ones for ordinary category axes. To see these options, select a time-scaled category axis, choose the first command on the Format menu, and then click the Scale tab of the Format Axis dialog box, as shown in Figure 22-11.

FIGURE 22-11.

Select Scaling Options for time-scaled category axes by clicking the Scale tab.

Change these values to zoom in on a segment of your data.

Increase the Base Unit to consolidate chart data.

Change these values to alter the spacing between tick-mark labels and gridlines.

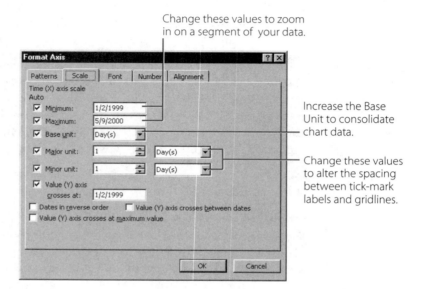

Changing the Maximum and Minimum

Excel ordinarily makes your earliest time value the minimum point on the scale and the latest time value the maximum. By specifying different values for these parameters, you can focus on a subset of your data.

For example, if your chart plots monthly information from January through December 1999, you can zoom in on the third quarter by changing the minimum to 7/1/99 and the maximum to 9/1/99. Or, if you want to show graphically that the year 2000's outcomes are unknown, you can change the maximum to 12/1/2000. Excel will then compress the plot into the left side of the chart, leaving white space on the right.

Changing the Major and Minor Units

The Major Unit setting determines the spacing of major tick marks, tick-mark labels, and major gridlines. To move labels and gridlines farther apart, increase the value of the Major Unit by choosing a number in the left edit box and a time unit in the right. Note, however, that the Major Unit value may not be smaller than the Base Unit value.

The Minor Unit setting determines the spacing of minor tick marks and minor gridlines. You can increase or decrease the interval between these items by specifying different values in the two Minor Unit edit boxes. Note that the Minor Unit value must be a smaller time interval than the Major Unit value.

Changing the Base Unit

The Base Unit setting determines the "granularity" of your time-scaled chart. If your chart plots monthly figures, for example, and you change the Base Unit to Day(s), you will get nearly a month's worth of blank space between each pair of data points. Going in the other direction, by increasing the Base Unit value, you can achieve a crudely consolidated chart (see Figure 22-12 below, and Figure 22-13 on the next page).

FIGURE 22-12.

In this time-scaled open-high-low-close chart, the Base Unit is Day(s), and the Major Unit is 14 days. We've added gray dotted gridlines to delineate two-week intervals.

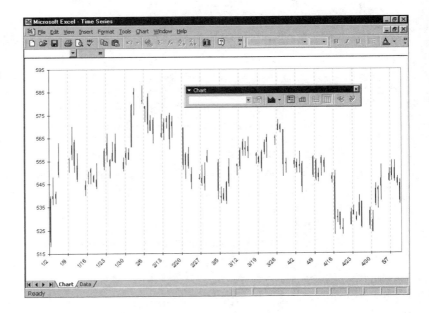

The consolidation is crude because Excel performs no analysis of the rolled-up data. It simply plots all points for each month in one place—

on top of one another. Thus, in Figure 22-13, we can see the high and low points for each month, but the superimposition of daily points makes it impossible to tell where prices opened and closed.

FIGURE 22-13.

We've changed the Base Unit in Figure 22-12's chart from Day(s) to Month(s). Now we can see at a glance the high and low prices for each month, but we can't tell where prices opened and closed.

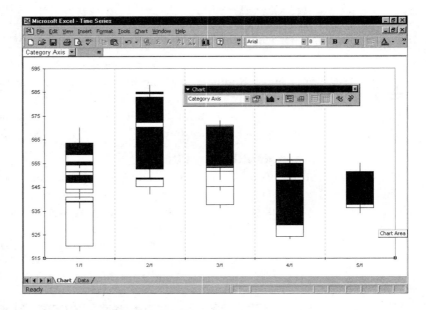

Setting the Value-Axis Cross Point and Reversing the Scale

The remaining options in the Scale dialog box for a time-scaled category axis are comparable to those for a value axis, as discussed in "Scaling a Value Axis Manually," page 680. You can use these options to reverse the plotting order of your data and to specify the point at which the category axis and value axis cross.

Scaling the Series Axis Manually

The series axis appears only in certain three-dimensional charts, such as that shown in Figure 22-14. When each series appears on a separate plane, Excel displays two axes along the floor of the chart and a third axis that rises straight up from the floor. One of the axes along the floor of the chart becomes the category (x) axis, and the other becomes the series (y) axis.

You can change the scale of a series axis by selecting it, choosing the first command from the Format menu, and then clicking the Scale tab of the Format Axis dialog box. As Figure 22-15 shows, your options are few.

FIGURE 22-14.
This three-dimensional area chart has a series as well as value and category axes.

Value (z) axis

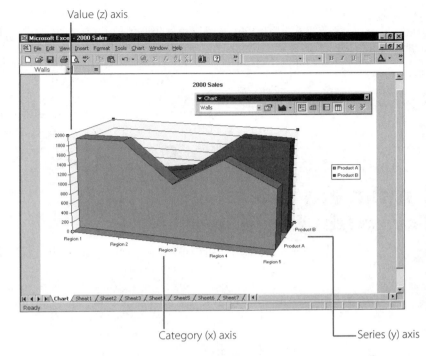

Category (x) axis

Series (y) axis

FIGURE 22-15.
The Scale tab also lets you change the scale of a series axis.

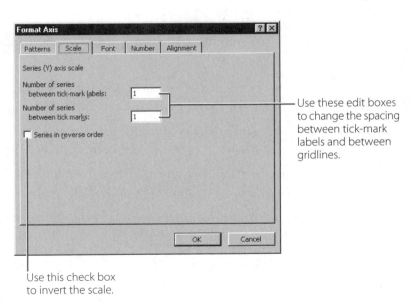

Use these edit boxes to change the spacing between tick-mark labels and between gridlines.

Use this check box to invert the scale.

For information about rotating a chart, see "Changing the Rotation," page 708.

To increase the space between series labels, enter a number greater than 1 in the Number Of Series Between Tick-Mark Labels edit box. To increase the space between tick marks (and gridlines, if you choose to display them), enter a value greater than 1 in the Number Of Series Between Tick Marks edit box. To reverse the order in which Excel plots the series, select the Series In Reverse Order option. This last option might be useful if the points in your first series obscure those in subsequent series. You can also deal with that problem by rotating the chart.

Displaying and Formatting Gridlines

Gridlines are horizontal or vertical lines that help clarify the position of data markers relative to axis scales. Figures 22-3 on page 670 and 22-8 on page 679 include value-axis (horizontal) gridlines. Figures 22-12 on page 685 and 22-13 on page 686 have category-axis (vertical) gridlines. To add gridlines to a chart, choose Chart Options from the Chart menu, and then click the Gridlines tab of the Chart Options dialog box. Major gridlines emanate from major tick marks, and minor gridlines emanate from minor tick marks. You can change the position of both kinds of tick marks (and thus the number of gridlines that appear) in either of two ways:

- Select the axis whose gridlines you want to change and then choose the first command from the Format menu.

- Select a gridline from the set of gridlines you want to change and then choose the first command from the Format menu.

After choosing the Format command, click the Scale tab and then change the values in the Major Unit and Minor Unit boxes.

To change the line style, weight, or color of a set of gridlines, select one of the gridlines you want to format, choose the first command from the Format menu, and then click the Patterns tab of the Format Gridlines dialog box as shown in Figure 22-16.

FIGURE 22-16.

Select your gridlines' style, color, and weight from the drop-down lists in the Patterns tab.

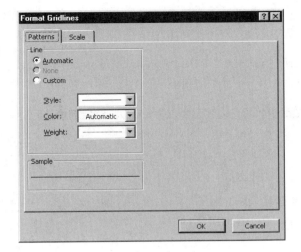

Formatting Data Series and Markers

Excel provides plenty of options for formatting the appearance and arrangement of both entire data series as well as individual markers within a series. Many of these options apply to all charts, while others are for specific chart types. We'll look at the generally applicable options first, followed by options for specific chart types.

 **TIP**

Many formatting options can be applied to data markers singly as well as to a whole series of markers. To select a single marker, first select its series. Then click a second time on the particular marker you want to format. If Excel cannot apply your formatting command to individual markers, it applies it to the entire series of which the selected marker is a part. In that case you might want to make use of the Edit menu's Undo command.

Assigning a Series to a Secondary Value Axis

A secondary value axis makes it possible to plot series that fall within widely divergent value ranges. The secondary axis, usually positioned on the right side of the chart, can have a completely different scale from the primary axis. You can assign as many series as you like to the secondary axis.

To switch a series from the primary axis to a secondary axis (creating the secondary axis in the process, if you don't already have one), or to move a secondary-axis series back to the primary axis, select the series, choose the first command from the Format menu, and click the Axis tab of the Format Data Series dialog box as shown in Figure 22-17.

FIGURE 22-17.

Select an option on the Axis tab to change the axis assignment for a series.

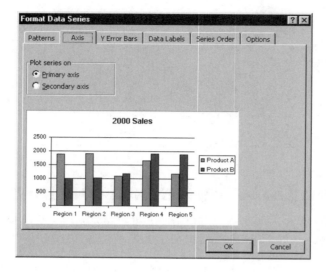

After you select an option, Microsoft Excel displays a sample of the rearranged chart.

Using Two or More Chart Types in the Same Chart

Some charts look best if one data series is plotted as columns, while another is plotted as a line or area. Excel lets you create many such "composite" charts. Simply select the series that you want to move to a different chart type. Then choose Chart Type from the Chart menu and select the kind of chart you want from the chart gallery.

Certain combinations are not possible. For example, you cannot mix a two-dimensional chart with a three-dimensional chart. If you try to create a composite chart that isn't allowed, Excel displays an error message.

If you mix a bar chart with any kind of vertically oriented chart, Excel creates a new category axis at the top of the chart. At that point you have a value axis and a category axis for your bars and another value axis and category axis for your vertical markers. You can format the second category axis just as you would the first.

Changing the Series Order

Excel normally plots series following the column or row order of the data on your worksheet, but you're not obliged to stick with the default order. To change the series order for your chart, select any of its data series, choose the first command from the Format menu, and then click the Series Order tab of the Format Data Series dialog box as shown in Figure 22-18.

FIGURE 22-18.

To change the series order, use the Series Order tab to select the series you want to move, then click Move Up or Move Down.

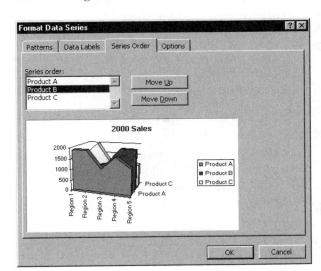

Changing the series order is one way to make a partly obscured series visible in a three-dimensional chart. In the chart depicted above, for example, we could make the first data point in the second series easier to read by selecting Product B and clicking Move Up. You can also improve the readability of three-dimensional charts by changing their viewing angles. *For information on how to do this, see "Changing Three-Dimensional Viewing Angles," page 706.*

Toggling the Column/Row Orientation

As mentioned in Chapter 21, Excel usually makes the appropriate decision about whether to plot your series by row or by column. You can overrule it easily, however, by simply clicking the By Row or By Column button on the Chart toolbar. You can use these buttons to switch instantly between the two orientations. If you'd rather not use the toolbar, choose Source Data from the Chart menu, click the Data Range tab, and then select either the Series In Rows or Series In Columns option.

Changing Colors, Patterns, Fills, and Borders for Markers

To change the color, pattern, fill, or border for a marker or set of markers, select the series or marker, choose the first command from the Format menu, and then click the Patterns tab of the Format dialog box. Your options here are essentially the same as your options for formatting the background areas of your chart. *For details, see "Formatting Background Areas," page 701.*

TIP

You can create column and area charts in which your markers are replaced by pictures. *For details, see "Formatting Background Areas," page 701.*

The Invert If Negative Option

In the Patterns dialog box for many types of data series, you'll find a check box labeled Invert If Negative. If you select this option for a series, Excel displays any negative markers in that series in a contrasting color. Figure 22-19 shows a two-series column chart in which the Invert If Negative option is selected for both series. Unfortunately, while the negative-value colors contrast well with the positive-value colors, both series use the same negative-value color, potentially eliminating the contrast between the two series.

FIGURE 22-19.

We used the Invert If Negative option to make the negative markers appear in a contrasting color. Unfortunately, both series employ the same contrasting color (white).

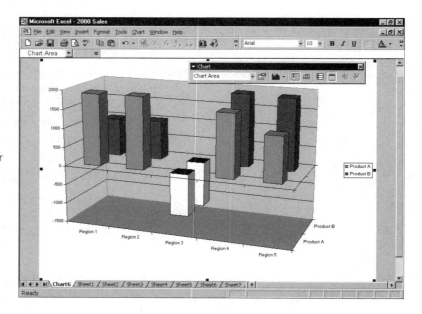

The Vary Colors By Point (Slice) Option

Charts that plot a single series might or might not use distinct colors for each point in the series. By default, Excel varies colors by point (or, rather, by "slice") in pie charts, but not in column or bar charts. In any case, you can override the default by means of the Vary Colors By Point check box. To change this option, select the data series, choose the first command from the Format menu, and then click the Options tab of the Format Data Series dialog box.

Adjusting Marker Spacing in Two-Dimensional Column and Bar Charts

To adjust the spacing of markers in a two-dimensional column or bar, select a series (any series in the chart will do), choose the first command from the Format menu, and then click the Options tab of the Format Data Series dialog box as shown in Figure 22-20. The Overlap option controls the distribution of markers within a cluster, and the Gap Width option determines the space between clusters. The default settings for the kind of chart shown in Figure 22-20 are 0 percent overlap and 150 percent gap width. As a result, Excel displays markers within a cluster side by side with no overlap and no space between them, and the space between clusters equals one-and-one-half times the width of an individual marker.

FIGURE 22-20.

Use the Options tab to adjust marker spacing.

Enter an Overlap value between -100 and 100 to change the space between series.

Enter a Gap Width value between 0 and 500 to change the space between clusters.

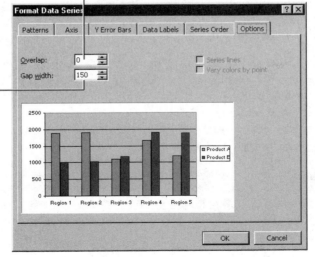

Note that if you specify a 100 percent overlap, Excel displays all the markers in a given cluster on top of one another, but it doesn't stack them. When you select a stacked bar or column chart, however, the default Overlap value is 100 percent. By entering a number less than 100, you can create a column or bar chart that is both stacked and staggered.

To change the amount of space between clusters, enter a value from 0 through 100 in the Gap Width edit box. The smaller the gap width, the wider your bars or columns. By specifying a 0 percent gap width, you can create a step chart—a bar or column chart in which all markers are lined up next to each other, with no intervening spaces.

Adjusting Marker Spacing in Three-Dimensional Charts

? SEE ALSO

For more information about changing the appearance of a three-dimensional chart by rotating or tilting it, see "Changing Three-Dimensional Viewing Angles," page 706.

In three-dimensional charts that use a series axis, the spacing of markers is controlled by three parameters. Gap depth and gap width specify the relative intermarker space along the series axis and category axis, respectively, while chart depth determines the relative length of the series axis. Reducing gap depth or gap width brings markers closer together; increasing these values moves the markers farther apart. Increasing chart depth, meanwhile, generates a chart that appears to recede further into the page, while decreasing chart depth flattens the chart.

To change any of these parameters, select any series from a three-dimensional chart, choose the first command from the Format menu, and then click the Options tab of the Format Data Series dialog box as shown in Figure 22-21.

You'll find that getting the right look in a three-dimensional chart is a matter of balance. Increasing the chart depth, for example, can produce a more dramatic three-dimensional look, but tends to scrunch the chart along its value axis. If experimentation leads you astray, you can restore the original look by setting the gap width and gap depth to 150 and the chart depth to 100.

★ TIP

By default, Excel creates a legend even for charts with a series axis. The legend significantly reduces the amount of space available to the chart. If you don't need it, you can get a better-looking chart by deleting it.

FIGURE 22-21.

Excel provides an immediate sample of any parameter changes you make.

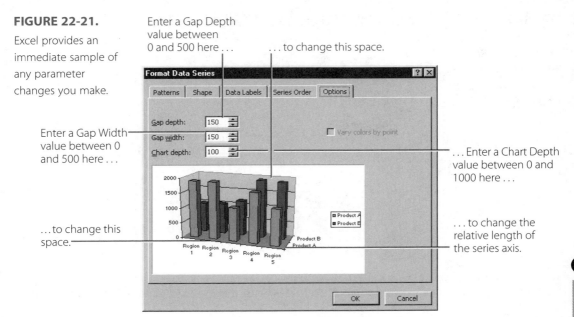

Enter a Gap Depth value between 0 and 500 here . . .   . . . to change this space.

Enter a Gap Width value between 0 and 500 here . . .

. . . to change this space.

. . . Enter a Chart Depth value between 0 and 1000 here . . .

. . . to change the relative length of the series axis.

Adding Series Lines in Stacked Column and Bar Charts

Series lines connect markers in stacked column or bar charts. They can help you follow the changes in magnitude of markers that don't originate on the category axis. To add series lines, click any series in a stacked column or bar chart, choose the first command from the Format menu, click the Options tab of the Format Data Series dialog box, and then select the Series Lines check box. Note that Excel draws series lines for each series in the chart, not just the one you select.

Changing Marker Shapes in Three-Dimensional Column and Bar Charts

In certain three-dimensional column or bar charts, you can switch the marker shape of individual series between rectangles, cylinders, cones, and pyramids. To do this, select the series or individual marker you want to change, choose the first command from the Format menu, and then click the Shape tab of the Format Data Series dialog box as shown in Figure 22-22 on the next page.

V

Charts

FIGURE 22-22.

Select one of the shapes on the Shape tab to change an individual marker or series of markers.

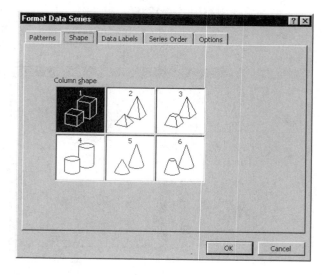

This option is not available with three-dimensional charts that use a series axis.

Options 2 and 3 are very similar to one another, as are options 5 and 6. The difference is only that with options 3 and 6, the shorter of the corresponding marker(s) in each set of data (representing lower value(s)) are drawn with "flat" tops. A shorter data marker in option 3, for example, would appear as a pyramid without the point on top.

Smoothing the Lines in Line and XY (Scatter) Charts

Excel can apply smoothing to line and xy (scatter) chart series. To use this capability, select the series you want to smooth. Choose the first command from the Format menu, click the Patterns tab of the Format Data Series dialog box, and then select the check box labeled Smoothed Line.

> **NOTE**
>
> This smoothing option should not be confused with the exponential smoothing feature provided in the Analysis ToolPak. *For details about the Analysis ToolPak, see Chapter 15, "Statistical Analysis."*

Changing Line and Marker Styles in Line, XY (Scatter), and Radar Charts

To change the line style, weight, or color in a line, xy (scatter), or radar chart series, select the series, choose the first command from the Format menu, and then click the Patterns tab of the Format Data Series dialog box as shown in Figure 22-23. You can also change the style, color, and size of your markers—or eliminate the markers from your series.

FIGURE 22-23.

Use the options in the Patterns dialog box to format lines and markers.

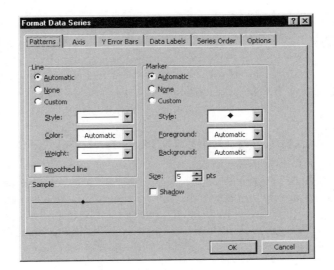

Adding High-Low Lines and Up-Down Bars in Line Charts

High-low lines are straight lines that extend between the highest and lowest points in a cluster. You can use them to indicate the range over which a value varies. Figure 22-8, shown on page 679, illustrates the use of high-low lines. High-low lines are available only in two-dimensional line charts.

Up-down bars are rectangles drawn between corresponding points of two or more line series. Excel fills the bars with one color or pattern if the first series is higher than the last and with a contrasting color or pattern when the opposite is true. Up-down bars are used chiefly in charts that track opening and closing prices (so-called "candlestick" charts), but you can add them to any two-dimensional line chart that includes at least two data series.

To add high-low lines or up-down bars to a chart, select any series, choose the first command from the Format menu, click the Options tab of the Format Data Series dialog box, and then select either the High-low lines check box or the Drop lines check box—or both.

When you use the Up-Down Bars option, Excel also lets you modify your chart's gap width. This option is normally available only with bar and column charts, but Excel treats a line chart with up-down bars as a kind of column chart. Increasing the Gap Width number in the edit box makes the up and down bar rectangles narrower, and decreasing the number makes the bars wider.

? SEE ALSO

For more information about adding a texture or picture to up-down bars, see "Formatting Background Areas," page 701.

To change the appearance of your high-low lines or up-down bars, simply select one of them and choose the first command from the Format menu. You can change the color, weight, and style of your high-low lines, and the color, pattern, and border of your up-down bars. You can even supply the up-down bars with a texture or picture.

Adding Drop Lines in Area and Line Charts

Drop lines are straight lines that extend from a data point to the category axis. Drop lines are particularly useful in multiple-series area charts, but you can add them to any two-dimensional or three-dimensional line or area chart. Select a series, choose the first command from the Format menu, click the Options tab of the Format Data Series dialog box, and then select the Drop Lines check box.

Once you've added your drop lines, you can change their appearance by selecting a line and choosing the first command from the Format menu.

Exploding Pie Slices and Doughnut Bites

Your mouse can detonate pies and doughnuts. Simply click a marker and drag it away from the chart's center. (You can explode only the outermost ring of a doughnut chart, however. The inner rings are immovable.) To reverse the explosion, simply drag a marker back toward the center of the chart.

To explode a particular pie slice or doughnut marker, without affecting the rest of the series, click the marker twice. The first click selects the series, and the second click selects the individual marker. Then drag the individual marker.

Split and Formatting Options in Pie-Column and Pie-Pie Charts

Pie-column and pie-pie charts are pie charts in which one or more series are "split out" into a second chart, a column chart, or a second pie chart, as the case may be. The second chart provides a more detailed look at a portion of the first chart.

To convert an ordinary pie chart into a pie-pie or pie-column chart, select any part of the chart and choose Chart Type from the Chart menu. You'll find the pie-pie and pie-column subtypes on the right side of the Pie gallery.

By default, Excel derives the "detail" portion of your pie-pie or pie-column chart from the last two series of the main chart. You have many other options about how to split the chart, however. To see these options, select a series from an existing pie-pie or pie-column chart, choose the first command from the Format menu, and then click the Options tab of the Format Data Series dialog box. Figure 22-24 shows some of your choices.

FIGURE 22-24.

Use the Options tab to split pie charts.

Use this drop-down list to split by position, value, percent value, or to create a custom split.

Use this option to control the relative size of the two charts.

Use this option to control the space between the charts.

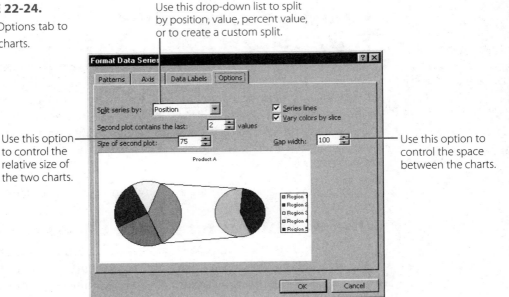

You can split your chart by position (the last n points in a series go to the detail chart), by absolute value (all points less than n go to the detail chart), or by percent value (all slices less than n percent of the total go to the detail chart). Alternatively, you can select Custom from the Split Series By drop-down list, and then simply drag slices from the main chart to the detail chart. However you choose to split, your options are the same for pie-pie and pie-bar charts. The only difference between the two kinds of chart lies in the shape of the detail component. Also, however you choose to split, Excel redraws the main chart to show a single slice representing all slices shown in the detail chart. Series lines are drawn by default from the edges of this single main-series chart to the entire detail chart. You can remove the series lines by clearing the Series Lines check box.

By default, Excel makes the diameter of the detail pie or the height of the detail bar 75 percent of the corresponding dimension in the main chart. To change these relative sizes, enter a different value in the Size Of Second Plot edit box. You can also move the detail plot closer to or farther away from the main plot by entering larger or smaller values in the Gap Width edit box.

Changing the Angle of the First Pie Slice or Doughnut Bite

By default, Excel draws the beginning radius for the first marker in a doughnut or pie series at a 45-degree angle from the vertical. In other words, if the pie or doughnut were a clock face, that first radius would point toward a spot midway between one o'clock and two o'clock. You can change the angle by selecting a series, choosing the first command from the Format menu, and then clicking the Options tab of the Format Data Series dialog box.

Pie and doughnut slices are always drawn in clockwise order.

Display Options for Bubble Charts

A *bubble chart* is a special type of xy chart, in which the size of the data markers (the bubbles) is determined by a third column or row of data. By default the third column or row determines the area of the bubbles. If you prefer, you can have the third column or row determine the width of the bubbles instead. To make this change, select the data series in question, choose the first command from the Format menu, click the Options tab, and then select the Width Of Bubbles option button.

In the same dialog box, you'll find a spinner labeled Scale Bubble Size To. You can increase or decrease the size of your bubbles by manipulating this spinner. Values between 0 and 300 are permitted. Choosing 0 makes the bubbles disappear. Choosing 300 makes each selected bubble three times as large as Excel would normally draw it.

Formatting Background Areas

Excel provides a rich set of options for formatting the background areas of your charts—including the plot area, the chart area, and the walls and floors of three-dimensional charts. You can also apply these formatting options to legends, to the background areas of text objects (chart titles and data labels), and to certain kinds of chart markers—including columns, bars, pyramids, cones, cylinders, areas, bubbles, pie slices, and doughnut bites.

All of the formatting options described in this section are on the Patterns tab of the Format dialog box. To get there, select the element you want to format, choose the first command from the Format menu, and then click Patterns. Figure 22-25 shows how the Patterns tab typically looks (but the options depend on your chart type).

FIGURE 22-25.

Access background formatting options with the Patterns tab.

To add a border, select a style, color, and weight. To remove a border, select None. The Shadow option is available only for certain objects.

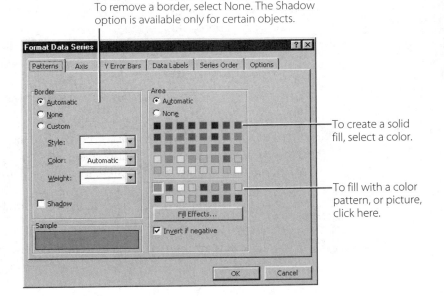

To create a solid fill, select a color.

To fill with a color pattern, or picture, click here.

Formatting the Border

To change the appearance of an area's border, use the controls on the left side of the Patterns dialog box. As with axes, you can specify the color, weight, and style of the line used to form the border. Or you can click None to get rid of the border. With some kinds of areas, you can add a shadow to the border. The shadow appears along the lower and right edges of the area.

Filling an Area with a Solid Color

To fill an area with a solid color, simply click the color you want in the right side of the Patterns dialog box. Note that if you're using a 16-color display, many of the 48 color choices shown in the dialog box will be *dithered*; that is, they will simulate unavailable colors by densely interweaving two or more available colors.

Filling an Area with a Color Gradient

A color gradient is a smooth progression of color tones from one part of an area to another—such as from the top of a column marker to the bottom. Color gradients can give your chart areas a classy, professional appearance.

Excel offers two basic kinds of color gradients—one-color gradients and two-color gradients. In a one-color gradient, the chosen color is varied by adding or subtracting luminosity, so you typically get a progression from white at one end to black at the other, with varying shades of the chosen color in between. In a two-color gradient, the balance of the chosen colors is varied so the first color predominates at one end of the gradient and the second color predominates at the other end.

If you opt for a two-color gradient, you can either specify the two colors yourself or choose from a palette provided by Excel. The preset palette includes "atmospheric" choices, such as "Early Sunset" and "Fog"; choices that mimic familiar materials, such as "Mahogany" and "Parchment"; and a variety of other interesting color combinations.

In any case, to specify a color gradient, click the Fill Effects button on the right side of the Patterns dialog box, and then click the Gradient tab of the Fill Effects dialog box as shown in Figure 22-26.

FIGURE 22-26.

Specify a color gradient in the Gradient tab.

For a one-color gradient, click here and select a color.

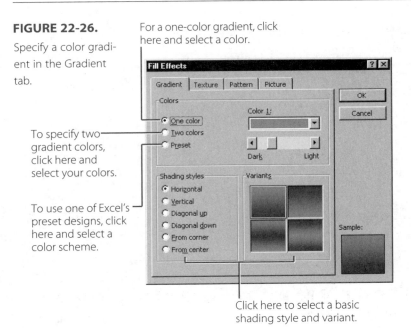

To specify two gradient colors, click here and select your colors.

To use one of Excel's preset designs, click here and select a color scheme.

Click here to select a basic shading style and variant.

Select the kind of gradient you want by clicking one of the option buttons in the Colors section of this dialog box. When you make your selection, Excel displays the appropriate number of color drop-downs. (If you select Preset, Excel displays a drop-down list of its "designer" gradient offerings.)

In the bottom portion of the dialog box, choose a basic shading style—such as horizontal or vertical—and a variant of that style. The Variants boxes show samples, in your chosen colors, of the basic shading style you select.

Filling an Area with a Pattern

Like a two-color gradient, a pattern provides a mix of two colors—called, in this case, the foreground color and the background color. But in a pattern, the two colors are varied in accordance with a repeating geometrical design. To specify a pattern, click the Fill Effects button on the right side of the Patterns dialog box and then click the Pattern tab of the Fill Effects dialog box. Figure 22-27 on the next page shows you a sample of what you'll see.

V

Charts

FIGURE 22-27.

Use the Pattern tab to apply a pattern to an area.

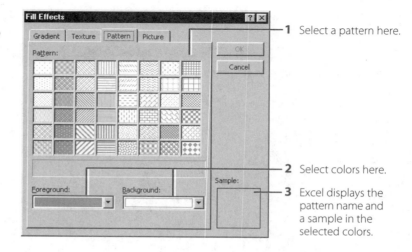

1 Select a pattern here.

2 Select colors here.

3 Excel displays the pattern name and a sample in the selected colors.

Filling an Area with a Texture or Picture

If you don't care for solids, gradients, or patterns, how about filling your background areas or markers with pictures? You can use images in a wide variety of supported graphic formats, or you can use one of twenty-four "texture" images supplied by Excel. The latter evoke familiar materials, such as oak, marble, and cloth. Figure 22-28 shows a "fish fossil" texture applied to a chart's plot area.

FIGURE 22-28.

We've applied a "fish fossil" texture to the plot area of this chart.

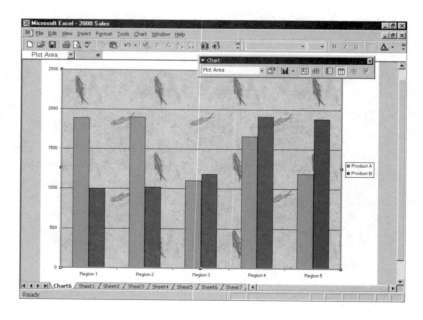

To apply a texture to an area, click the Fill Effects button on the right side of the Patterns dialog box and then click the Texture tab of the Fill Effects dialog box as shown in Figure 22-29.

FIGURE 22-29.

Use the Texture tab to apply texture to an area.

Select a texture here.

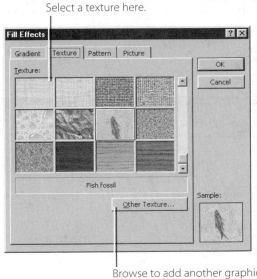

Browse to add another graphic file to the texture gallery.

To apply a picture to an area, click Fill Effects and then click the Picture tab of the Fill Effects dialog box shown in Figure 22-30.

FIGURE 22-30.

Use the Picture tab to select the image used to fill a chart area.

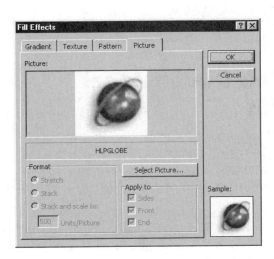

If you apply a picture to a chart marker (as opposed to a background area), you can choose from three formatting options for pictures applied to markers. Stretch, the default option, displays one copy of your picture per marker and simply stretches the picture to fit. Stack displays as many copies of the picture as needed to fill the marker, leaving each copy at its original size. Stack And Scale lets you make each copy of the picture represent some number of units along the value axis.

Figure 22-31 shows a chart with stacked pictures applied to column markers.

FIGURE 22-31.

Pictures applied to column or area markers can make your point graphically.

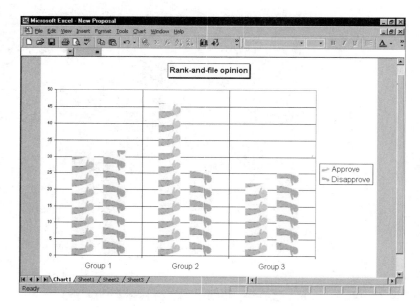

Changing Three-Dimensional Viewing Angles

The simplest way to change the viewing angle of a three-dimensional chart is to select one of the chart's corners and drag it with the mouse. While you're dragging, Microsoft Excel 2000 displays an outline of the chart. (If you want to see the chart, hold down the Ctrl key.)

This direct-manipulation approach is simple, but it also lets you easily turn an intelligible chart into something quite the opposite. A mere flick of the wrist, for example, is all it takes to transform Figure 22-32 into Figure 22-33.

FIGURE 22-32.

You can change the appearance of a three-dimensional chart dramatically by dragging one of its corner handles.

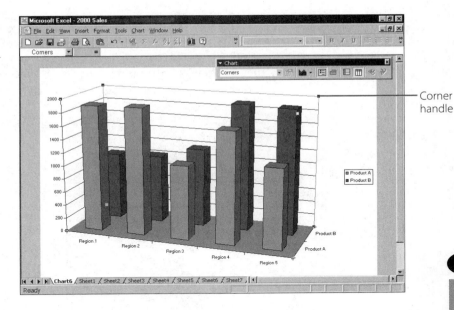

Corner handle

FIGURE 22-33.

If you change the chart too dramatically, you can click the Default button in the 3-D View dialog box to restore the original view.

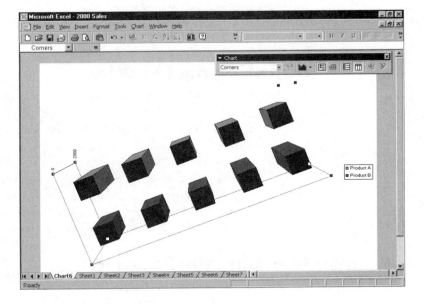

Fortunately, the 3-D View dialog box, shown in Figure 22-34, includes a Default button, which you can click to return a chart to its original viewing angle. The 3-D View dialog box also lets you fine-tune the appearance of your chart by modifying its elevation, rotation, perspective, and height. To use this dialog box, select your chart and choose 3-D View from the Chart menu.

FIGURE 22-34.

Use the 3-D View dialog box to adjust chart appearance.

As you change the view of your chart, Excel shows a preview of the chart.

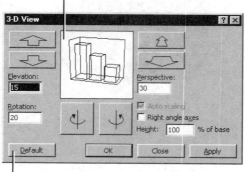

Click the Default button to restore your chart's original appearance.

Adjusting the Elevation

The Elevation setting changes your viewing angle relative to the floor of the chart. The default setting is 15, and you can specify any value from -90 through 90. (With three-dimensional pie charts, you're limited to a value from 10 through 80.) A setting of 90 places you directly above the chart, as if you were looking down on the tops of markers. With a -90 setting, you look up through the chart's floor (which, incidentally, is always transparent regardless of how you format it). To change the elevation, type a number in the Elevation edit box or click the large Up or Down arrow in the upper left corner of the dialog box.

Changing the Rotation

Imagine that your chart is anchored to a turntable. The Rotation setting allows you to spin the turntable. Technically, the rotation setting specifies the angle formed by the category axis and a line drawn horizontally across your screen. The default angle is 20 degrees (except for pie charts, where it's 0). You can specify any angle from 0 through 360 by entering it in the Rotation edit box or by clicking the clockwise and counter-clockwise buttons to the right of the edit box.

Changing the Height

The Height setting changes a chart's value-axis-to-category-axis ratio. The default is 100 percent; you can select any value from 5 through 500. The higher the value, the taller your chart. This option is unavailable for three-dimensional bar charts.

Changing the Perspective

The Perspective setting determines the apparent depth of three-dimensional area, column, line, and surface charts (as long as the Right Angle Axes option is not selected). The default setting is 30, and you can specify any value from 0 through 100. Low values make the chart look flatter, as though you were looking at the chart through a telescope or telephoto lens. High values have the opposite effect, making it appear as though you were looking through the wrong end of a pair of binoculars or a wide-angle lens.

The default setting, 30, specifies that the far side of the chart is 30 percent smaller than the near side. This means that with a rotation of 0, the back of the floor is 30 percent narrower than the front of the floor. Similarly, if the elevation is 90, the bottom of the tallest column in a three-dimensional column chart is about 30 percent smaller than the top of the column.

To change the Perspective setting, enter a new number in the Perspective edit box or click the Up or Down arrow above the Perspective option. You can also eliminate all perspective from a chart by selecting the Right Angle Axes option.

Changing the Axis Angle and Scale

The Right Angle Axes option sets the axes at right angles independent of chart rotation or elevation. To see axes in perspective, turn off this option. For three-dimensional bar charts, this option is always turned on.

Auto Scaling is available only if the Right Angle Axes option is selected. When you change a two-dimensional chart into a three-dimensional chart, it is sometimes drawn smaller. For charts with right-angle axes and a rotation of less than 45 degrees, the Auto Scaling option scales the three-dimensional chart so it is closer in size to the two-dimensional version.

CHAPTER 23

Working with Chart Data

Charts have a way of changing over time. New data arrives, old data becomes irrelevant, and new visual comparisons become meaningful. In this chapter you'll look at Microsoft Excel 2000's procedures for working with the data that drives your charts. You'll see how to add new points and series to a chart, how to change the order in which series are plotted, and how to plot multilevel categories of information. You'll also look at Excel's features for adding trendlines and error bars.

Note: Excel 2000 can also create charts from PivotTable data that pivot to stay in step with the source data. *For information about these PivotCharts, see Chapter 27, "Using PivotTables."*

Adding Data

Excel provides several ways to add new data to a chart. We'll look at the simplest method first.

Figure 23-1 plots data through May 2. The figure shows a week's worth of data that hasn't yet been added to the chart. Notice that, because Chart Area is selected, Excel draws two rectangles around the chart's worksheet data. The first rectangle, in column A, outlines the worksheet range that the chart is using for its category-axis labels. The second rectangle, in columns B through E, outlines the four data series.

To extend the chart so it includes the new data in rows 750 through 755, drag the fill handle in the lower right corner of either rectangle.

Alternatively, you can use drag-and-drop copying procedures:

1 Select the new data, including the category-axis labels (the dates in column A of Figure 23-1).

2 Position your mouse on the border of the selection, so that the mouse pointer changes to an arrow.

3 Drag the selection and drop it anywhere on the chart.

FIGURE 23-1.

When you select a chart's chart area, Excel outlines the data area on your worksheet.

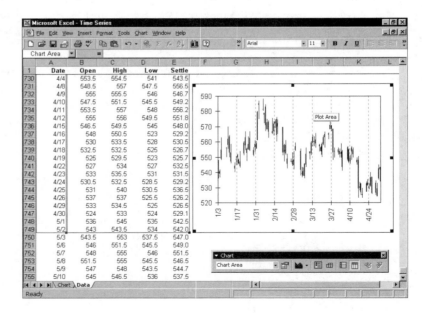

Note that while the chart area is selected Excel draws lines on the worksheet to show the cell range that's currently plotted. You can use these lines as a confirmation that your new data points have been added.

The methods just described work fine if your chart and its data are close together on the same worksheet. If they're not, you can use standard copy and paste procedures. Select the new data, choose Copy from the Edit menu, select the chart, and then use Paste from the Edit menu. Alternatively, you can use the Add Data command from the Chart menu. (The Add Data command does not normally appear on shortened menus. Click the double arrow at the bottom of the Chart menu to display the Add Data command.) The Add Data dialog box appears, as shown in Figure 23-2.

FIGURE 23-2.

Type the data range here or point to it on your worksheet.

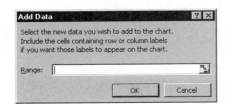

Enter a reference of the range you want to add in the Range edit box by typing cell coordinates, typing a range name, or selecting the range with the mouse. If you use the mouse, you might first want to click the Collapse Dialog button at the right side of the edit box, but this step isn't required.

Adding a new data series is just like adding new points to existing series: simply select the data series you want to add, copy it, and then paste it onto the chart (or drag the selection to the chart). Assuming the new data series is adjacent to the existing data, Excel has no difficulty in determining that you want to add a whole new series, as opposed to a set of new points. If the new data is not adjacent to the old, Excel may still be able to add the data correctly. For example, in Figure 23-3 on the next page, Excel can correctly paste the selected data as a new series, because the selection is a column and has the same row positions as the existing three series. If the selection were in H3:H7 instead of H2:H6, however, as shown in Figure 23-4 on the next page, Excel would no longer know what to do. Pasting *that* data block creates the meaningless chart shown in Figure 23-4.

FIGURE 23-3.

If you paste this block onto the chart, Excel knows you want to add a series.

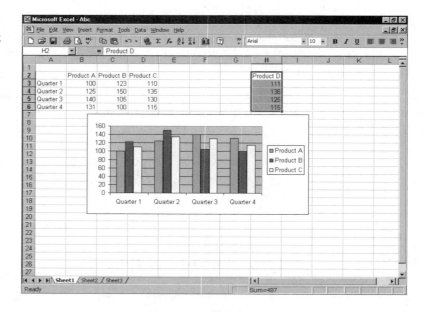

FIGURE 23-4.

When Paste doesn't give you what you want, use Undo, and then try again with Paste Special.

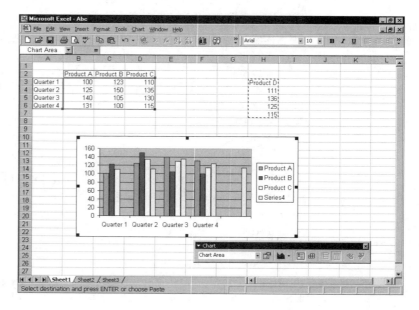

To help Excel out when it can't discern exactly how you want to paste new data, use Paste Special instead of Paste. Select the data you want to add, select the chart, and then choose Paste Special from the Edit menu. (Select the chart before you choose Paste Special or you'll see an entirely different set of options.) With a chart selected, the Paste Special dialog box appears, as shown in Figure 23-5.

FIGURE 23-5.

Use the Paste Special dialog box to tell Excel exactly how to display the new data.

Removing Data

Removing a data series from a chart is simple, provided you remember to delete from the chart, not from the underlying worksheet. For example, suppose you want to remove Product C from the chart shown in Figure 23-3. If you simply clear the data from cells D2:D6 (by selecting that range and pressing the Delete key), Excel adjusts the chart, as shown in Figure 23-6.

FIGURE 23-6.

Clearing the worksheet data generates a blank series. Instead, select the series on the chart and then press Delete.

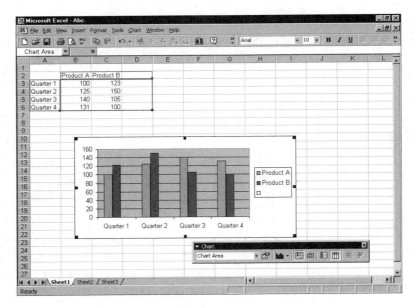

If you delete the range D2:D6 instead of clearing it (that is, if you actually remove the cells from the worksheet by selecting them and choosing the Delete command from the Edit menu), the chart's third series generates a #REF! error, and Excel displays an alert message. To avoid these errors, activate the chart, select the series you want to delete, and then press Delete. To remove particular data points rather than entire series, select your chart. Then drag the blue rectangle at the lower right corner of the bounding box that appears around your data. Drag it upward to remove the unwanted data.

Alternatively, choose Source Data from the Chart menu and click the Data Range tab. The dialog box shown in Figure 23-7 appears. Select the range you want to change and, as usual, you can modify the specification by typing the range or selecting it in the worksheet.

FIGURE 23-7.

To remove data points, change the range in the Data Range box.

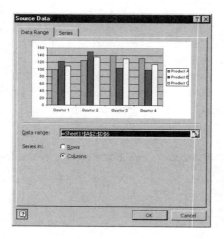

Replacing Data

To make your chart plot a different set of data, select the chart area and drag the rectangle on your worksheet, just as you would if you were simply adding new data. In this case, however, don't drag the fill handle. Instead, drag the upper or lower boundary of the rectangle.

Alternatively, you can use the Series tab of the Source Data dialog box, shown in Figure 23-8, to change the data the chart illustrates. Select the chart, choose Source Data from the Chart menu, click the Series tab, and then change the contents of edit boxes on the Series tab of the Source Data dialog box.

Note that you can also use this dialog box to add and remove entire series. In most cases, however, you'll find it easier to use the cut-and-paste method for adding and the Delete key for deleting.

FIGURE 23-8.

The Series tab of the Source Data dialog box specifies the data series that make up a chart.

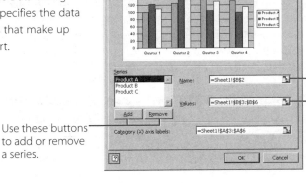

Change the entry in this box to make a different name appear in the legend.

Change the entry in this box to change the labels on the x-axis.

Use these buttons to add or remove a series.

Changing the Plot Order

To change the order in which series are plotted, select any series, choose Selected Data Series from the Format menu, and then click the Series Order tab. The dialog box shown in Figure 23-9 appears.

Note that scrambling the series order may be an effective way to make all series visible in a three-dimensional chart type.

FIGURE 23-9.

Use the Series Order tab of the Format Data Series dialog box to change the plot order.

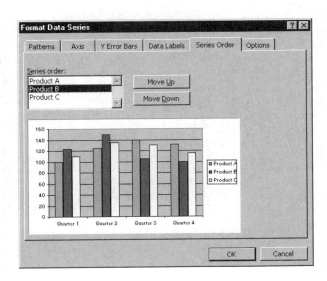

Using Multilevel Categories

Excel lets you categorize your categories. This sounds redundant, but a quick example will illustrate the technique. Suppose you want to plot the data shown in Figure 23-10 (the result is shown in Figure 23-11). Here, the series are months and the categories are the sales offices located in different cities. The categories—the city sales offices—are further classified by state, however.

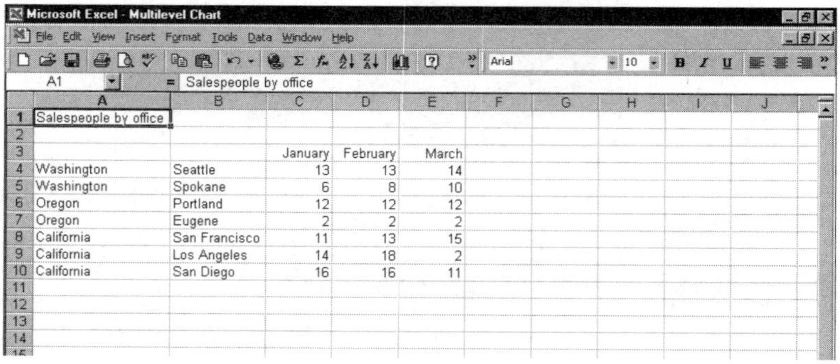

FIGURE 23-10.

This worksheet uses multilevel categories: city sales offices are grouped by the states in which the cities are located.

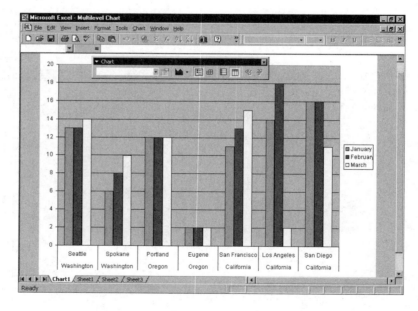

FIGURE 23-11.

A multilevel category chart uses two or more sets of category names to label the category axis.

To plot the data in Figure 23-10 in a chart with multilevel categories, select the range A3:E10 and use the Chart Wizard or the Chart Command on the Insert menu to plot the data in a simple column chart. Excel displays both the city names and the state names below the category axis, as shown in Figure 23-11.

Adding Trendlines

A *trendline* is either a regression line that best fits the plotted data of a series or a line that plots a moving average of the values in a series. To add a trendline to a series in an area, bar, column, line, or xy chart, select the series and then choose Add Trendline from the Chart menu. (The Add Trendline command does not normally appear on shortened menus. Click the double arrow at the bottom of the Chart menu to display the Add Trendline command.) Excel displays the Add Trendline dialog box shown in Figure 23-12.

FIGURE 23-12.

A trendline illustrates the trends your data series predicts.

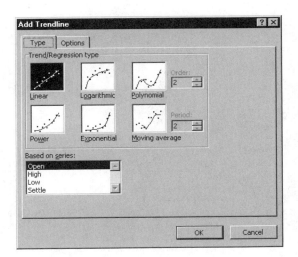

To specify how Excel should draw the trendline, select one of the Trend/Regression Type options. If you select Polynomial, indicate the highest power (from 2 through 6) for the independent variable in the adjacent Order box. If you select Moving Average, indicate how many periods Excel should use in its calculations in the adjacent Period box.

After you've indicated the type of trend/regression line Excel should draw, select the Options tab if you want to name this trendline specification. As long as you're not working with a moving average trendline, you can also use the Forward and Backward spinners to extrapolate the trendline. For linear, polynomial, and exponential trendlines, you can set the y-intercept in the Set Intercept edit box. And, if you want, you can display the regression equation and the R-squared value alongside the trendline plot.

Adding Error Bars

When you are charting statistical or experimental data, it is often helpful to show the confidence level of your data. Excel's error-bar feature makes this easy. To add error bars to a data series in an area, bar, column, line, or xy chart, select the data series, choose Selected Data Series from the Format menu, and then click the Y Error Bars tab. Excel then displays the Error Bars dialog box shown in Figure 23-13.

FIGURE 23-13.

Use error bars to illustrate the potential error for each data point in a series.

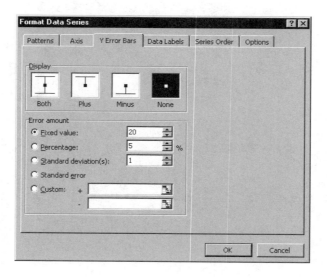

Error bars can be shown as the actual data point value plus some amount, minus some amount, or both plus and minus some amount. Use the options in the Display section to indicate which of these error bar styles you want. Use the Error Amount options—Fixed Value, Percentage (of the data point value), Standard Deviation(s), Standard Error, and Custom (an amount specified manually)—to calculate the amount depicted by the error bar.

Dragging Chart Markers to Change Data

Because charts are linked to worksheet cells, you can use them to construct visual "what-if" scenarios with your data. For example, if you set up a break-even analysis in a worksheet and then plot fixed costs, variable costs, total costs, and gross margin in a chart, you can change fixed-cost assumptions in the worksheet and immediately see the effect on the gross-margin line in the chart.

You can also reverse this process in two-dimensional bar, column, line, and xy charts. You can drag chart data markers—including picture markers—upward or downward and have Excel adjust the underlying worksheet. In the break-even analysis, for example, you can drag the chart's gross-margin line upward so it crosses 0 at a different point and then find out on the worksheet exactly how much you would need to reduce your fixed costs to achieve the increase in profit. This process is called graphical goal-seeking.

Let's look at a simple example. Suppose that, after examining the chart in Figure 23-14, you decide that the fourth-quarter data doesn't look quite right. Product B appears to lag behind Products A and C in that quarter, when in fact you expected B to do better than C—if not quite as well as A. Instead of going back to the worksheet and entering new values, you can change the chart directly.

FIGURE 23-14.

This simple chart demonstrates Excel's graphical goal-seeking capabilities.

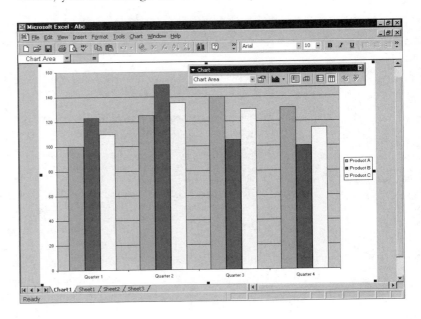

To adjust the worksheet's values from the chart, follow these steps:

1 Select the data marker you want to adjust. (You may have to click twice.) Black handles appear on the marker. In our example, you would select the fourth-quarter marker for Product B.

2 Point to the top center black handle. The pointer becomes a double-headed arrow. Drag the marker upward until the marker's height is somewhere between that of Product A and Product C. As you drag Product B's marker, your screen looks like Figure 23-15.

FIGURE 23-15.

As you drag a marker, Excel displays the marker's current value. Here we've dragged the marker from its original value to 126.9. If we release the mouse button, Excel changes the associated worksheet cell to 126.9.

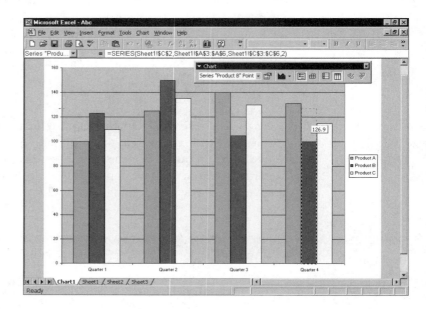

3 Release the mouse button when the data marker reflects the value you want. Excel redraws the chart and updates the underlying worksheet cell.

? SEE ALSO

For more information about the Goal Seek command, see "The Goal Seek Command," page 556.

In this example, all Excel must do to make the chart display the new value is modify one cell in the underlying worksheet. If that cell contains a formula instead of a constant, however, the situation is different. Excel understands then that you want the result of the formula producing the data point value to change, but you don't want to replace the formula with a constant. To clarify your intentions, Excel presents the Goal Seek dialog box—the same dialog box you see when you use the Goal Seek command on the Tools menu. In the Goal Seek dialog box, specify what value the formula should return and which formula input the Goal Seek command should adjust.

CHAPTER 24

Mapping Geographic Data

In the past, applications that allowed you to display data in a geographic context were highly specialized, expensive, and relatively complex to operate. Excel brings this capability down to earth with Microsoft Map—an optional component that you can use to make geographic information highly presentable.

Like all Excel charts, data maps allow you to present rows and columns of information in a more immediately understandable format. You can use data maps in many ways. Perhaps the most obvious application is the display of inherently geographic statistics such as census or environmental data. You can display certain specific features, depending on the map, including highways, cities, airports, and rivers. And you can display data by country, state, province, or even by postal code.

> **NOTE**
>
> Microsoft Map is an installation option. It is not installed if you performed a "typical" installation. You might have to rerun Setup to install it.

Preparing Your Data

The first step in creating a data map is to make sure your worksheet data is organized in a way that makes sense for mapping. A geographic data table doesn't need to be complex, but you do need to apply labels to your data that Microsoft Map can understand. Therefore, your worksheet should include a column listing state names, country names, or postal codes. You can use the standard spellings of state or country names, or you can use standard abbreviations. Note that Microsoft Map requires that these map "feature names" be in a column. You cannot use a transposed table layout in which the feature names appear across the top in a single row.

To begin constructing a data map, first select the worksheet data you want to use. Figure 24-1 shows a sample worksheet that is organized for data mapping. Your selection should include the row and column headers and, of course, the data itself. Microsoft Map scans the column containing the geographic locations and automatically determines the necessary map to use.

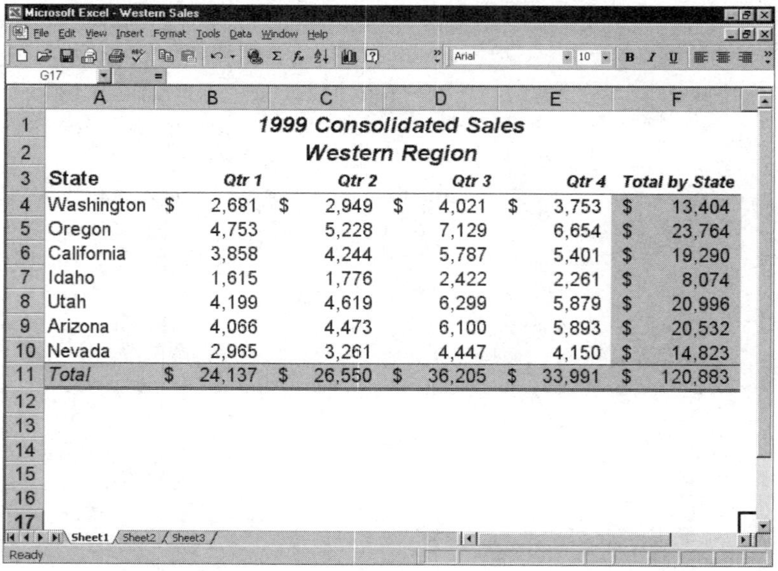

	A	B	C	D	E	F
1			*1999 Consolidated Sales*			
2			*Western Region*			
3	**State**	***Qtr 1***	***Qtr 2***	***Qtr 3***	***Qtr 4***	***Total by State***
4	Washington	$ 2,681	$ 2,949	$ 4,021	$ 3,753	$ 13,404
5	Oregon	4,753	5,228	7,129	6,654	$ 23,764
6	California	3,858	4,244	5,787	5,401	$ 19,290
7	Idaho	1,615	1,776	2,422	2,261	$ 8,074
8	Utah	4,199	4,619	6,299	5,879	$ 20,996
9	Arizona	4,066	4,473	6,100	5,893	$ 20,532
10	Nevada	2,965	3,261	4,447	4,150	$ 14,823
11	*Total*	$ 24,137	$ 26,550	$ 36,205	$ 33,991	$ 120,883

FIGURE 24-1.

A geographic data table includes a column containing location names or postal codes.

⭐ **TIP**

Displaying Postal Codes

Excel normally doesn't display the leading zeros that many postal codes use. To create a data map using postal codes, therefore, you can either enter the postal codes as text (precede the postal code number with an apostrophe, which tells Excel to treat the entire cell entry as text) or select the entire column, press Ctrl+1, click the Number tab, click the Special category, and then select one of the zip code formats.

Creating a Data Map

After you select all of the worksheet data, choose Object from the Insert menu. In the Object dialog box, click the Create New tab and then select Microsoft Map from the list of available object types. Microsoft Map responds by creating a new map object on your worksheet. You can drag the handles of the object to change its size or drag the body of the map to reposition it. Before the map actually appears, you might have to answer a few questions. Figure 24-2 shows a dialog box that appears if more than one map makes sense for your data.

FIGURE 24-2.

If more than one map is available for your data, select the one you want.

Figure 24-3 on the next page shows a dialog box that appears if Microsoft Map can't figure out the geographic locations listed in your table. This can happen because of misspelling or if you simply forget to select the column containing the locations before choosing the Map command. In any case, it's easier at this point to cancel and correct the spelling error or select the necessary cell range. (Note that Microsoft Map goes ahead and creates a dummy map on your worksheet when you cancel out of the Unable To Create Map dialog box. Simply press the Delete key while the dummy map is selected to get rid of it.)

FIGURE 24-3.

If Microsoft Map has a problem interpreting the geographic locations in your data table, this dialog box appears.

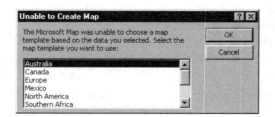

You can adjust the amount of time allotted to the matching of your geographic data using the Options command on Microsoft Map's Tools menu. As you can see in the dialog box shown in Figure 24-4, the Time Limit associated with the Thorough matching option is normally 5 seconds. You can increase this number to as much as 120 seconds if you are having trouble getting the results you need. If you're using a large worksheet or database to create a map, and if you are certain that your geographic location names are valid, increasing the time limit could solve the problem. Use the Quick matching option if you have a small amount of data or are using either postal codes or abbreviations as your geographic names.

FIGURE 24-4.

The Map Matching options control the amount of time Microsoft Map spends matching maps to geographic names.

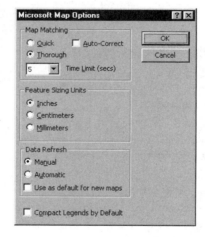

Once Microsoft Map has the necessary information, the map appears on the worksheet and the Microsoft Map Control dialog box appears, as shown in Figure 24-5.

★ TIP

If column names are not fully displayed in the Microsoft Map Control dialog box, simply drag the borders of the box to enlarge it.

FIGURE 24-5.

As soon as the map is drawn, you can modify it to suit your needs.

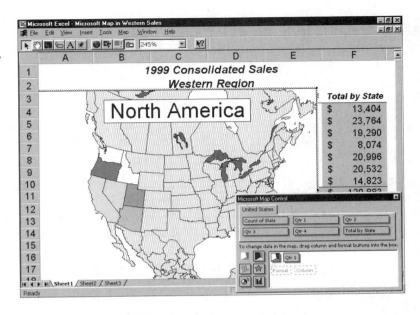

SEE ALSO

For more information on map formats, see "Single-Series Map Formats" on page 728.

In Figure 24-5, you can see three distinct areas in the Microsoft Map Control dialog box. At the top of the United States tab are *column buttons*—boxes with names like "Qtr 1" and "Total By State" that correspond to names of columns in the data table that you can display in the map. On the lower left of the dialog box are six *format buttons* you use to determine the way the data is to be displayed in the map. To see what the buttons mean, move the pointer over a button. A ScreenTip appears showing you its name. The white area at the bottom of the dialog box is where you specify the format and column you want to use. The two dotted boxes, labeled "Format" and "Column," indicate what the icons above them signify. In Figure 24-5, the icon above the Format box is the Value Shading format button. The icon above the Column box indicates that Qtr 1 is the column of data currently displayed in the map. If you want to change the map to display Total By State rather than Qtr 1, click the Total By State box and drag it over the Qtr 1 box in the white area of the dialog box.

TIP

Displaying Column Ranges

If it's not clear exactly what a column button at the top of the Microsoft Map Control dialog box refers to on the worksheet, double-click it to display a dialog box with the corresponding sheet and range reference. (Notice that when you double-click column buttons in the white active section at the bottom of the dialog box, the add-in displays the Value Shading Options tab of the Format Properties dialog box rather than the reference.)

Single-Series Map Formats

The Value Shading, Category Shading, Dot Density, and Graduated Symbol formats can describe only one data series, while the Pie Chart and Column Chart formats can display multiple related data series. The default map format is Value Shading, which divides the values in the specified column into ranges and then color-codes each map region according to where its value falls. In Value Shading maps, the legend indicates the values of each range.

You can adjust the number of value ranges and how they are determined by double-clicking the Value Shading button while it is in the white active section of the Microsoft Map Control dialog box. When you do so, the Value Shading Options tab of the Format Properties dialog box appears, as shown in Figure 24-6. (Alternatively, you can display this dialog box by choosing the Value Shading Options command from the Map menu.)

FIGURE 24-6.

When a Value Shading map is active, choose the Value Shading Options command on the Map menu to display this dialog box.

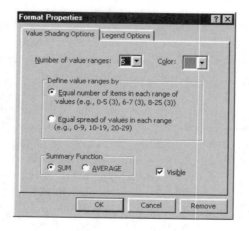

The Number Of Value Ranges control allows you to choose the number of ranges you want. Using the Color drop-down list, select the base color to be used to indicate the different value ranges on the map. Only one color is used, and the value ranges are distinguished by using different shadings of this base color. Use the Define Value Ranges By options to choose between two approaches: dividing the ranges into equal numbers of geographic locations or dividing them into equal ranges of values.

You change the format of a map the same way you change a data series. Drag one of the format buttons on the lower left of the

Microsoft Map Control dialog box over an existing button in the white active section. For a single data series like the one in our example, you can use the Value Shading, Dot Density, and Graduated Symbols formats. Figure 24-7 shows examples of the Dot Density and Graduated Symbol formats.

Both the Dot Density and the Graduated Symbol formats are useful when you are creating maps showing geographic concentrations. Each dot in a Dot Density map represents a fixed amount. More dots are added to represent a higher value in a geographic region. Each geographic region in a Graduated Symbol map is represented by a single symbol. Each region's symbol size is proportionate to the region's value.

FIGURE 24-7.

The Dot Density format on the left shows relative concentration by geographic region. The Graduated Symbol format on the right shows relative size.

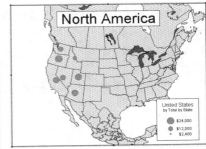

Microsoft Map and OLE

Microsoft Map is an Object Linking and Embedding (OLE) source application. While you're working in Map, the menu for Map merges with Excel's, and Map's toolbar appears in place of the standard Excel toolbar. The Microsoft Map Control dialog box also appears. (You can hide and redisplay this dialog box by means of Map's View menu.)

To return from Map to Excel, simply click anywhere outside the map. Map responds by creating your map as an embedded object on your Excel worksheet. To edit the map, double-click it.

To change the size of a map after it appears on your worksheet, first click outside the map to return control to Excel. Then click once on the map. Now drag the white handles (to change the map's size) or the map itself (to reposition).

To delete a map, click outside the map, then click the map once. While the map is thus selected, press the Delete key.

The Category Shading format is a bit different in that it groups geographic regions into subgroups that share a common characteristic. You could try using the Category Shading format button on our example map, but in this case it wouldn't make much sense. Because each state in our data table has a unique sales total associated with it, each state becomes a different category. But when your sample data includes a column listing each sales representative for that state, you can create a map showing each representative's sales region, as shown in Figure 24-8.

FIGURE 24-8.

We added a Rep column and used the Category Shading format to show sales representatives' regions. (By default, Map draws Jones's territory in red and Smith's in green.) Use the Map Control dialog box to update the map itself.

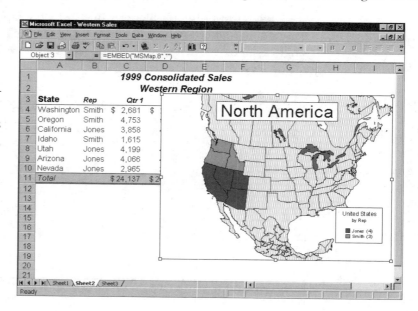

> **NOTE**
>
> If your source data includes a column of five-digit postal codes, Microsoft Map automatically scans this column and positions the dots or symbols accordingly.

Changing the Look of a Map

So far, our sample looks a little silly with only seven states active on a big North American map. But we can customize the map to feature the Western region a little more prominently. The Microsoft Map toolbar shown in Figure 24-9 includes several buttons we can use.

FIGURE 24-9.

You can use the Microsoft Map toolbar to change the appearance of your map.

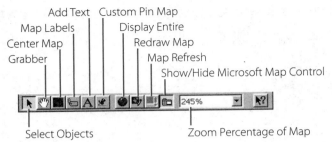

The Select Objects button is active when you start Microsoft Map. Use it to reposition titles and legends. Use the Grabber to drag the map around inside the object box as if you were sliding a picture around inside a frame to position it for cropping.

The Center Map tool actually does not center the map based on its boundaries. Instead, it lets you select a point on the map to be drawn in the center of the frame. In Figure 24-8, for example, you could make Oregon appear in the center of the frame by clicking first on the Center Map tool and then on the state of Oregon.

The Map Labels tool, in conjunction with the Map menu's Features command, lets you add symbols and text to selected points of interest on your map. *These components of Microsoft Map are discussed in "Adding Map Features," page 735.*

The Zoom Percentage Of Map drop-down list lets you control the size of the map relative to its frame. If you want to focus on a particular area of a map (the western states in a map of North America, for example), you can increase the zoom percentage, and then use the Grabber tool to move the area of interest into the center of the frame.

Using the toolbar buttons, you can reorient the map to emphasize the area you want to focus on, as shown in Figure 24-10 on the next page.

It's easy to edit the text in the title—just double-click the title object to activate and then edit it. You can control the display of the title using the Title command on the View menu. This command is a toggle, so you can turn it on and off to try different effects. The View menu also includes the Subtitle command, which, as you might expect, adds a smaller title box beneath the title that you can also edit and display until you get the effect you want.

FIGURE 24-10.
Change your map's point of view using the Zoom drop-down list and the Grabber button.

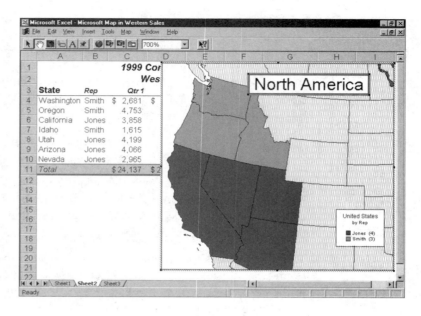

Double-click the legend to display the Legend Options tab of the Format Properties dialog box, shown in Figure 24-11. Here you can modify more than just the text content.

FIGURE 24-11.
The Legend Options tab of the Format Properties dialog box offers total control over the way legends appear.

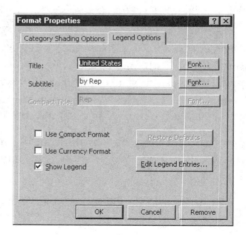

You can change the fonts used for each element in the legend, specify whether currency format should be used for numeric values, and even specify a different title for the legend when it is displayed in "compact" format. Figure 24-12 shows our sample map with more meaningful titles and legend text.

FIGURE 24-12.

You can add a subtitle, edit the title, and position the titles and legend to help your map communicate more clearly.

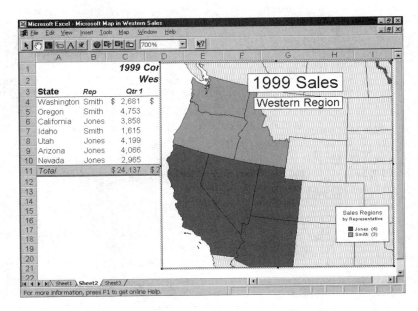

Adding New Layers to a Map

Each row of icons in the active white section of the Microsoft Map Control dialog box represents one map layer. You can usually add more than one layer to a data map by dragging format and column icons to a new row below the existing ones in the white area. Certain types of data can peacefully coexist in layers on a map, and others cannot. The Microsoft Map Control dialog box is smart about this—most of the time it doesn't let you do things that don't make sense. Pairs of format symbols in the dialog box (ones adjacent to each other) cannot coexist in the same layer. Other behavior is not permitted, such as adding more than one column to the same layer in a Value Shading map. (You *can* do this, however, when you have a Pie or Column Chart format map displayed, which we'll discuss a bit later.)

TIP

To remove a layer from the map, open the Map Control dialog box and drag the corresponding buttons in the white active section outside the dialog box.

We can get more information into our map in Figure 24-12 on the previous page by adding a layer. Now this map uses the Category Shading format to show sales regions. We can add a new layer using the Graduated Symbol format. To do this, click the Graduated Symbol button and drag it to the white section of the dialog box, below the row containing the Category Format and Rep column buttons. Next drag the Total By State column button to the same row. After a little recalculating time, the symbols appear on the map. If they don't look like what you had in mind, you can edit them by double-clicking the Graduated Symbols button. This action displays the dialog box shown in Figure 24-13.

FIGURE 24-13.

Display this dialog box by double-clicking the Graduated Symbol button in the Microsoft Map Control dialog box.

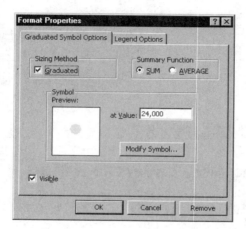

⭐ **TIP**

Formatting Options

Each format button in the Microsoft Map Control dialog box has an associated options dialog box that you display by double-clicking the button. Note, however, that you can display these dialog boxes only when the format button, along with an associated column button, is in the active white section of the Microsoft Map Control dialog box. Besides double-clicking the button, you can also display these dialog boxes by choosing commands from the map menu. Each format currently active in the map has a corresponding command appearing at the bottom of the Map menu.

From the Graduated Symbol Options tab, you can select a different symbol (click the Modify Symbol button), change from summary calculation (the default) to averaging, switch from graduated symbols to fixed-size symbols, or remove the symbols altogether. The number in the At Value edit box is a rounded-up approximation of the highest value in the column used for the calculation. The size of symbols is determined by this number—symbols whose values match this number are the same size as the symbol you have selected in the dialog box. Symbols are scaled according to the relative value associated with a geographic location.

When you add another layer to your map, Microsoft Map adds another legend to the map.

⭐ **TIP**

Sizing Symbols

Use the font size, not the At Value number, to determine symbol sizing. It's true that you can type a smaller number in the At Value box, which causes larger values to scale the associated symbol proportionately larger than the selected point size. However, each time the map is opened or recalculated, this number is reset to encompass the largest value.

⭐ **TIP**

Hiding Symbols

To hide graduated symbols, clear the Visible check box on the Graduated Symbols Options tab of the Format Properties dialog box. When you do so, the symbols and the legend both disappear from the map, but you can restore them easily by reselecting the option.

Adding Map Features

If states, provinces, or countries aren't enough, you can add some other map details, such as airports, highways, and cities. Choose the Features command on the Map menu to display the Map Features dialog box, shown in Figure 24-14 on the next page. This dialog box lists most of the features available for the current map. For each item, you can use a small check box to control its display. To see all the features available for all maps, click the Add button. When you choose to add a feature from the Add Map Feature dialog box, it becomes a resident of the Map Features dialog box, and its check box is automatically selected. For example, to add U.S. cities to a map, click the Add button and double-click the "US Cities (AK&HI Inset)" feature.

The middle area of the dialog box shows the properties of the map feature. You can modify the feature's appearance by clicking the Custom option and then clicking the button below.

V

Charts

FIGURE 24-14.

Use the Map Features dialog box to add more detail to a map.

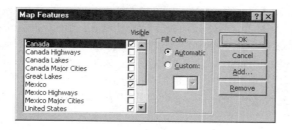

When you finish, symbols appear on your map, although no city names are displayed. Don't worry—this is for your own good, as you'll see. In a small map like our example, city names would be stacked up so thickly in places like Southern California that you wouldn't be able to read them at all. For this reason, the Labeler feature was created so you can choose exactly which feature names to show in your map. Click the Map Labels button on the toolbar to display the dialog box shown in Figure 24-15. (The Tools menu includes the Labeler command, which also displays this dialog box.)

FIGURE 24-15.

Use the Map Labels dialog box to add selected labels to a map.

TIP

Cities and Major Cities

Contrary to what you might expect, the various "Cities" features include many fine cities, but they do not include the major cities. To display symbols for all the cities available for a geographic region, select both the "Cities" and the "Major Cities" features.

Features displayed on the current map are listed in the Map Feature To Label drop-down list. You can also add labels based on the entries in the worksheet columns, which are listed in the Values From drop-down list. Once you select a feature to label and then click OK, it seems as if nothing happens to the map. But when you move the mouse pointer over a feature symbol on the map, the name of the feature—in this case, the name of the city—appears as long as the pointer stays over the symbol. If you want to affix a label to the map, click the mouse button when the label is visible. A small text box appears containing the city name. This way you can choose only the labels you want to add. You can drag the text box to a better viewing position on the map, if necessary. Figure 24-16 shows what the map looks like with city symbols added, then with selected labels added and symbols removed.

FIGURE 24-16.

You can add or remove labels selectively, as shown on this map.

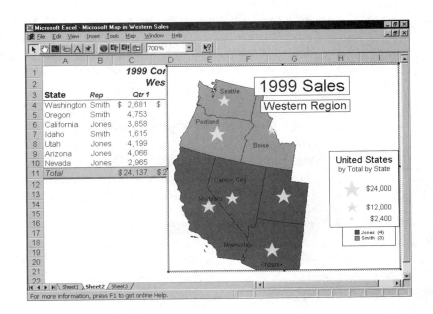

TIP

If you want to add labels for more than one feature (for instance, "Cities" and "Major Cities"), you'll need to use the Labeler separately for each one.

You can copy, paste, edit, and delete labels. If labels are too long, break them into two labels. To change the font, click the right mouse button on a selected label and then choose the Format Font command from the shortcut menu. If the Labeler doesn't provide exactly what you need, you can use the Add Text toolbar button to create your own labels.

TIP

Don't Overdo It
Be careful about adding too much to your maps. There is a fine line between good communication and "chart junk." It's better to create several separate maps that are clear and easy to understand than to cram everything into one.

V

Charts

Refreshing the Map

A map recalculates each time you open the worksheet, unless you turn off automatic calculation in Excel's Options dialog box (not Microsoft Map's). Subsequent worksheet recalculations do not refresh the map automatically, however. To ensure that your map reflects the latest changes on your worksheet, double-click the map and choose Refresh from the Map menu. If the Refresh command is gray, the map is current. Even though this recalculation occurs, the map drawing itself does not change. Instead, a small icon appears in the upper left corner of the map object, letting you know that you need to activate and refresh the map.

Saving the Map Template

When you've worked hard to get the map just the way you want it, you can save yourself the trouble of recreating it next time by using the Save Map Template command on the Map menu. When you choose this option, the dialog box in Figure 24-17 appears.

FIGURE 24-17.

Save your map as a template so you can use it again as the basis for other maps.

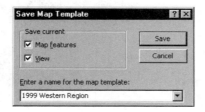

When you save a map template, you can give it a new name that is then added to the list of available maps. For example, suppose you create and name a template similar to the United States map used in our examples. The new template name appears in the Multiple Maps Available dialog box (shown in Figure 24-2 on page 725) the next time you create a map containing geographic location names that apply to this area.

Note that the overall format of the map is not saved since the type of data you select when creating the map determines the format. For example, if you save a template while a multiple-series map is displayed, the charts are not part of the template and will need to be reapplied. Only the map features you add and the current view are saved with the template.

Use the Delete Map Template command on the Map menu to remove unwanted templates.

Multiple-Series Map Formats

The Pie Chart and Column Chart formats can display multiple data series that are related in the sense of parts-to-the-whole. Using our sample data, we can add column charts that show the relative quarterly sales for each state in the map. To start with, we removed the graduated symbols from the map by dragging the Graduated Symbol button outside the white section in the Microsoft Map Control dialog box. (When you do this, the associated column button is also removed.) Next we dragged the Column Chart button and the four quarterly sales column buttons to the same row in the active white section of the Microsoft Map Control dialog box. The result is shown in Figure 24-18, where we also edited the legend's title.

TIP

> **Showing the Control Dialog**
>
> If the Microsoft Map Control dialog box is not currently visible, click the Show/Hide Microsoft Map Control button on the toolbar. Click the toolbar button again to hide the dialog box.

FIGURE 24-18.

The Column Chart format illustrates the relative values of several columns of data in each geographic region.

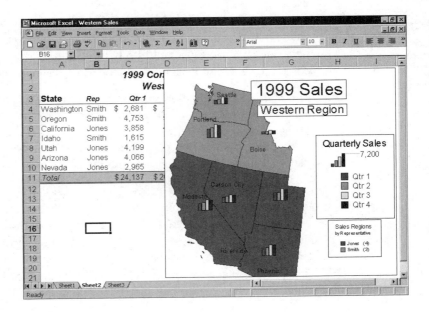

As with all formats added to a map, a command appears at the bottom of the Map menu that allows you to choose options associated with the format. Choose the Column Chart Options command to display the dialog box shown in Figure 24-19. (You can also double-click the Column Chart button in the active white section to display this dialog box.)

FIGURE 24-19.

Double-click the Column Chart button to display the Column Chart Options tab.

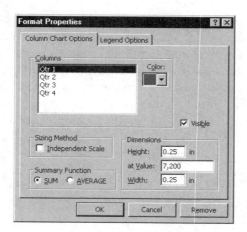

The Independent Scale option is useful if each column button you drag into the active white section represents a different type of data. For example, you could show the number of customers per state, total sales per state, and average sale amount per customer in the same column chart. Because these are each very different units of measure, the Independent Scale option would be helpful. In our example, however, the column data are all related, so independent scaling is not recommended.

The Summary Function options give you the choice of summing or averaging the data, and the Dimensions options allow you to control the size of the column charts on the map. Clicking the Remove button is the same as dragging the Column Chart button outside the Microsoft Map Control dialog box, completely removing the column chart layer from the map.

Instead of using column charts, you can use the Pie Chart format button to better express your data. For example, you could show how each quarter contributed to the total "pie" for each state. The Pie Chart Options dialog box is identical to the Column Chart Options dialog box, except that the Height and Width edit boxes in the Dimensions group are replaced with a single Diameter edit box and the Independent Scale check box is replaced by a Graduated check box.

You use the Graduated check box to specify that the pie charts are scaled like graduated symbols—the larger the total for each geographic region, the larger the pie itself. If your data is based on percentages, such as demographic data showing the ethnic breakdown within a population, the Graduated option might not be desirable.

A Demographic Database

If you work with data that involves people, there are times you might like some perspective. For instance, if you want to gauge the potential market for a product, it might be helpful to know some details about the population in a particular area. While this sort of information is sliced and diced every way imaginable by the advertising industry, it isn't always readily available to most of us.

Microsoft Map comes with a workbook entitled Mapstats (you can use the Windows Find command to locate it), which contains a wealth of helpful demographic information. For example, Mapstats contains such detailed information as the total population of females between the ages of 15 and 64 in Angola and the median household income in Wyoming. It also has worksheets containing data for the United States, Mexico, and Australia by state; Europe and the world by country; the United Kingdom by standard regions; and Canada by province. One helpful aspect of the Mapstats workbook is that it is a spelling reference for all the state, province, region, and country names recognized by Microsoft Map, along with their valid abbreviations.

As you can see in the illustration, you move the pointer over column titles in Mapstats to see ScreenTips describing the data.

Even if you can't apply this information to your work, it's fun and interesting to create data maps using the Mapstats data itself, plus it's a great tool for school projects.

 **TIP**

> **Changing Measures**
>
> If you want to use units of measure other than inches for the dimensions options, choose the Options command from the Tools menu and select Centimeters or Millimeters. (See Figure 24-4 on page 726.)

Inserting Data into a Map

Microsoft Map's Insert menu includes two commands, Data and External Data, that allow you to import data into your map that you didn't originally select when you created the map.

When you choose the Data command from the Insert menu, the dialog box in Figure 24-20 appears. You can add data from any open workbook using this command. Simply type the worksheet name and cell reference into the edit box. A more foolproof method of entering the reference is to either click the sheet tab (if the data is in the active workbook) or use the Window menu to activate another open workbook and then select the range you want to include. You can do all this while the Microsoft Map dialog box is open. This way, the reference is automatically entered in the correct syntax. You can also use a named range instead of a cell reference.

FIGURE 24-20.

Use the Data command to display this dialog box, in which you enter the range you want to use.

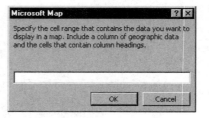

After you indicate the new data range and then click OK, a new column button is added to the Microsoft Map Control dialog box for each column in the new range.

The External Data command on the Insert menu performs similarly, except that instead of using open workbooks, it first presents you with the "file open" type of dialog box you use to open files created by database programs such as Microsoft Access. Note that you'll need to include a column of geographic information from your database so that Microsoft Map knows where to put the data.

Creating Custom Pin Maps

A custom pin map is like an overlay. You create a pin map using the Custom Pin Map button on the toolbar. The first time you click the button, the Custom Pin Map dialog box appears and asks you to provide a name for the pin map you are about to create, as shown in Figure 24-21.

FIGURE 24-21.

The Custom Pin Map dialog box is used for both creating and opening custom pin maps.

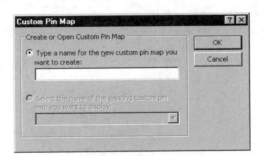

After you name the pin map and then click OK, the pointer changes to the "push-pin" cursor you use to add pins or other symbols to the map. Each time you click the mouse, another pin is added to the map wherever your cursor is positioned.

As soon as you add a pin to the map, a dialog box appears in which you can type a label for the new pin. (If you don't want a label associated with the pin, click OK without entering any text.) Note that the pin symbol and the label are linked, so when you drag the pin symbol, the label moves along with it. If you want to reposition the label with respect to the pin symbol, first click the Select Objects tool, then drag the label's text box.

You format pins by clicking the right mouse button on the pin and choosing Format from the shortcut menu. In the dialog box that appears, you can change the size and color of the pin symbol, as well as the symbol itself. (You might need to change the color to make the pin contrast with the color of the underlying map.) In the pin map shown in Figure 24-22 on the next page, we've enlarged the pins to 24 points to make them stand out.

⭐ **TIP**

Formatting the Pins

The pin images that appear when you first use the Custom Pin Map button might not look quite the way you'd like them to. To avoid unnecessary work, add one pin to your map, then format it immediately. Subsequent pins you add will be displayed in the same format, so you won't need to format each one.

The Map menu has three commands—Open Custom Pin Map, Close Custom Pin Map, and Delete Custom Pin Map—that you use to manage your pin map collection. You can create different pin maps for different purposes, and you can save them and apply them to any other maps you create.

FIGURE 24-22.

Create a custom pin map to indicate special locations or points of interest.

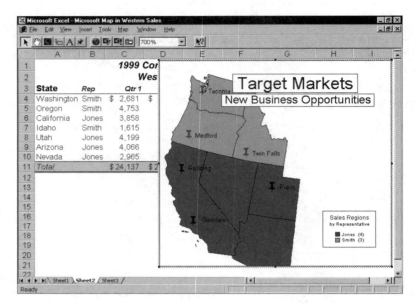

TIP

Mixing Symbols

Note that you cannot open more than one pin map at a time. But if you want to, you can include several different types of symbols in the same pin map. For example, you can use different symbols to indicate sales offices, distribution warehouses, and subsidiaries in the same pin map. You can format each data series with a different symbol, color, and label font.

PART VI

Database and List Management

Managing Information in Lists

O ne of the tasks most commonly performed with spreadsheets is the management of lists—phone lists, client lists, task lists, lists of transactions, lists of assets and liabilities—you name it. Accordingly, Microsoft Excel 2000, with a richer set of list-management features than any other spreadsheet on the market, makes it easy to organize and analyze this kind of information. We'll look at Excel's list-management features in this chapter and the two following chapters.

Building and Maintaining a List

To function effectively, a list should have the following characteristics:

- Each column should contain the same kind of information. In a personnel list, for example, you might devote one column to employees' ID numbers, another to their last names, a third to first names, a fourth to date of hire, and so on.

- The top one or two rows of the list should consist of labels, with each label describing the contents of the column beneath it.

- The list should not contain any blank rows or blank columns.

- Ideally, the list should occupy a worksheet by itself. If that's not possible, the list should be separated from any information on the same worksheet by at least one blank row and one blank column.

- A list you plan to filter should not contain any other information in the rows occupied by the list. *For more information about filtering, see "Using Filters to Analyze a List," page 760.*

> **NOTE**
>
> Excel's Share Workbook command lets two or more users work with the same list at the same time.

SEE ALSO

For more information about the Freeze Panes command, see "Freezing Panes," page 320. For more information about the Format Cells dialog box, see Chapter 7, "Formatting a Worksheet."

Figure 25-1 shows an example of a seven-column list. Notice that the column headings in the first row appear to be underscored. Actually, we used Excel's Freeze Panes command to lock the top row so it would remain visible as we scrolled through the list, and Excel marked the pane boundary with a rule.

If you want to underscore your headings, use the Font or Border tab of the Format Cells dialog box. (You can open this dialog box by choosing Cells from the Format menu.) Don't create a separate row and fill it with hyphens or equal signs because Excel might treat your "underscores" as data.

> **TIP**
>
> Excel has a Text To Columns command on the Data menu that makes it easy to build lists from data stored in text files.

FIGURE 25-1.

Each column in a list should contain a particular kind of information, and the first row should consist of labels describing the columns' contents.

	A	B	C	D	E	F	G	H
1	**Last Name**	**First Name**	**Date of Hire**	**Date of Birth**	**Sex**	**Salary**	**Age**	
2	White	Connie	5/16/74	3/15/49	F	32000	50	
3	Jacks	Kris	1/16/93	10/19/66	M	57300	33	
4	Falconer	Charles	10/23/81	4/24/51	M	49400	48	
5	Miller	Zachary	5/2/84	10/7/56	M	42000	43	
6	Pall	Dick	11/3/88	7/19/41	M	33290	58	
7	Davidson	Paul	8/27/85	8/17/60	M	59950	39	
8	Halvorson	Monica	4/20/93	6/26/61	F	36700	38	
9	Ford	Hunter	3/18/87	4/5/58	M	32700	41	
10	Gay	Michael	8/9/65	9/15/52	M	45200	47	
11	Neal	Steve	12/6/91	10/8/47	M	55300	52	
12	Edelhart	Catherine	12/28/83	3/22/58	F	33600	41	
13	Andrews	Frances	12/14/82	12/22/44	F	49200	55	
14	Lake	Lisa	5/24/87	1/22/43	F	31350	56	
15	Bach	Shirley	11/12/81	9/15/51	F	39250	48	
16	Gandet	Debbie	5/27/85	3/31/64	F	54200	35	
17	Valdiviezo	Julia	4/1/92	11/26/50	F	51825	49	
18	Kahn	Bob	8/6/94	9/24/50	M	44150	49	

Using a Form to Add, Change, or Delete Rows

SEE ALSO

For information on how to use a form instead of filters to access information, see the sidebar "Using a Form to Find List Information" on page 765.

You can add new information to a list by moving to the first blank row below the list and typing. But you may find it easier to use Excel's Form command, which displays your list one row at a time. To do this, select any single cell in your list and then choose Form from the Data menu. (The Form command does not normally appear on shortened menus. Click the double arrow at the bottom of the Data menu to display the Form command.) Figure 25-2 shows the form display for the list in Figure 25-1.

FIGURE 25-2.

The Form command displays lists one row at a time.

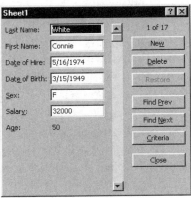

Database and List Management

Converting an Excel List to an Access Database

Excel is a superb tool for managing lists of moderate size and complexity, but it doesn't offer all the power and convenience of a full-fledged relational database management system. If you have Microsoft Access version 7 or later, you might want to convert some of your larger lists to Access files. The Convert To MS Access command appears on Excel's Data menu if you have installed Microsoft Access. When you choose Convert To Access, the Import Spreadsheet Wizard takes you through the process of converting your file to an Access database. Once you've made this conversion, you do all further work with the database in Access instead of in Excel.

After the Import Spreadsheet Wizard finishes, another Wizard, the Table Analyzer Wizard, helps you find inconsistencies in your data. For example, if you've used two or more different spellings for the same data item, the Table Analyzer Wizard notices the problem and helps you correct it. If appropriate, the Table Analyzer Wizard will also break a large table into smaller but related tables. For example, it might separate a transaction database into separate tables containing customer information, product information, and purchase records. Breaking up the data in this manner makes it easier for you to maintain the database and allows your software to perform more efficiently.

If you transfer your database from Excel to Access, you can still use Excel to analyze the data. Microsoft Query, described in Chapter 26, makes it easy to import data from an Access (or other) database into an Excel worksheet.

At the top of the form, Excel displays the name of the worksheet (not the workbook) that contains the list on which the form is based. Immediately below this title bar are all the list's column headings. If you've already entered some rows in your list, you'll see the entries for your first row of data alongside the column headings.

In the upper right corner of the form is a notation that tells you which row is currently displayed and how many rows the list contains. Notice that the headings row is excluded from this accounting. At the right side of the form are several command buttons that let you work with your list. (If it does not appear, you need to install the Accesslinks add-in program. *For more information, search for "install features" in Microsoft Excel Help.*)

Naming a List

If you assign the name Database to your entire list (including the column headings) and use the Form command's New button to add rows to the list, Excel automatically adjusts the definition of the name Database to include the new rows. Excel does not automatically adjust the definitions of any names other than Database, however.

Assigning a name to a list and updating the definition of that name as the list grows can be very useful. Among other things, you can then use worksheet formulas based on the INDEX function to reference particular values in the list. For example, the formula

=INDEX(Database,ROWS(Database),2)

would give you the last value in column 2 of a list named Database. The formula

=MAX(INDEX(Database,2,5):INDEX(Database, ROWS(Database),5))

would report the highest value in column 5, and so on.

For more information about the INDEX function, see Chapter 12, "Common Worksheet Functions."

The form provides an edit box next to each column heading, unless the column contains values calculated by formulas. In our example, the values in the Age column are calculated by formulas, so the Age heading does not have an edit box.

To add a new row to your list, click the New button. Excel displays a blank form, in which you can enter the values for your new row. To add another new row, click New again; to return to the worksheet, click Close.

When you add new rows to your list with the Form command, Excel expands the list downward without affecting any cells outside the list. If expanding the list will overwrite existing data, Excel alerts you that the list cannot be expanded.

To change a value in the list (other than a value that results from a formula), use the scroll bar in the Form dialog box to move to the row that contains the value you want to change and then make your changes in the appropriate edit box. To delete a row in the list, use the scroll bar to move to that row and then click Delete. You cannot undo deletions made in the Form dialog box, so Excel displays a confirmation prompt when you click the Delete button.

V

List Autofill

A new feature in Excel 2000, List Autofill eliminates the need to copy formulas and formatting when you add new rows to a list. If Excel sees a consistent pattern of formulas or formatting, it replicates that pattern automatically as you build your list.

For example, suppose your list includes columns for date, item, quantity, list price, discount, extended price, sales tax, and total. And suppose the entries in your extended price, sales tax, and total columns contain formulas that reference the entries in your quantity, list price, and discount columns. As you add new transactions to the list, Excel will automatically perform the appropriate calculations for you—without your having to copy formulas. It will also copy a consistent pattern of formatting (not including borders, however).

For List Autofill to copy a formula or formatting pattern into a new row, Excel must see at least five rows that follow the pattern above the new row. Thus, you won't see the feature take effect before you get to the sixth row of your list. And if you change something in a row near the bottom of your list, you may need to reestablish the pattern with a few new rows before the feature takes effect again.

Sorting Lists and Other Ranges

Excel provides numerous ways to sort worksheet ranges regardless of whether Excel considers those ranges to be lists. You can sort by columns or rows, in ascending or descending order, and with capitalization considered or ignored. (When you sort by rows, the rows of your list are rearranged, while the columns remain in the same order. When you sort by columns, the opposite kind of rearrangement occurs.) You can even define custom sorting sequences so that, for example, your company's division names always appear in the order North, South, East, and West, rather than in alphabetical order. And issuing a sort command is easy in Excel.

A Simple Example

To sort a list, select one cell from the list. Then choose the Sort command from the Data menu. Excel examines your data to determine the extent of the list, determines whether the list includes a heading row that should not be sorted, and then displays the Sort dialog box.

To demonstrate how the Sort command works, we'll use the unsorted list shown in Figure 25-3. To sort this list by recipient, select any single cell (not a range of cells) in the list, and then choose Sort from the Data menu. Excel displays the dialog box shown in Figure 25-4.

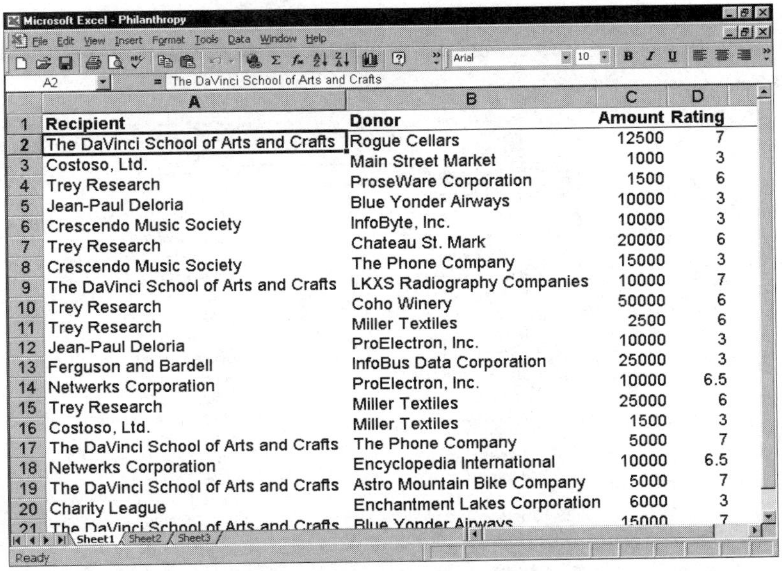

FIGURE 25-3.

This list is now unsorted. We'll use the Sort command to sort it by recipient.

FIGURE 25-4.

You can use the options in the Sort dialog box to tell Excel how you want your list sorted.

In the Sort By drop-down list box, make sure Recipient, the heading for the column on which you want to sort the list, is selected. To sort in ascending order (that is, A before Z and 1 before 2), leave the Ascending option selected. To sort in the opposite order, select the Descending option. Be sure the Header Row option at the bottom of

V

Database and List Management

the Sort dialog box is selected and then click OK. Excel reorders the list, as shown in Figure 25-5. Notice that because the Header Row option was selected, the column headings were not included in the sort. Instead, the headings remain at the top of the list after the sort is performed.

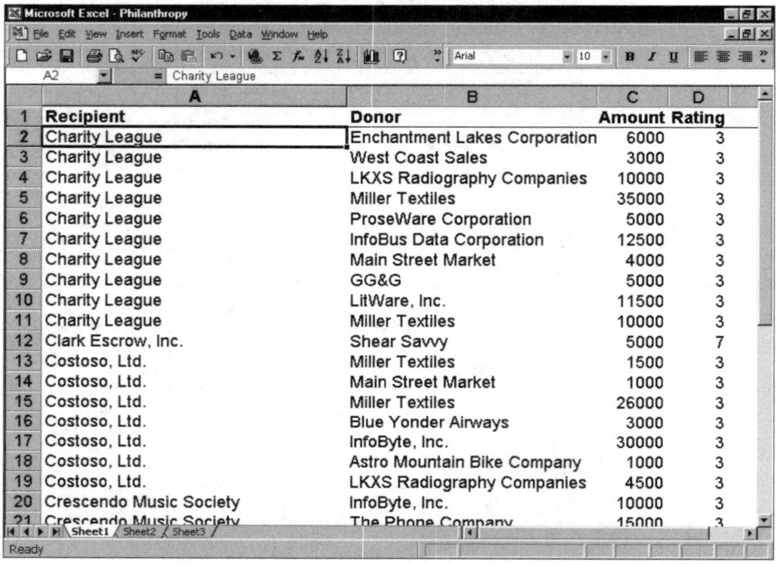

FIGURE 25-5.

After an ascending sort on the Recipient column, the list shown in Figure 25-3 looks like this.

	A	B	C	D
1	**Recipient**	**Donor**	**Amount**	**Rating**
2	Charity League	Enchantment Lakes Corporation	6000	3
3	Charity League	West Coast Sales	3000	3
4	Charity League	LKXS Radiography Companies	10000	3
5	Charity League	Miller Textiles	35000	3
6	Charity League	ProseWare Corporation	5000	3
7	Charity League	InfoBus Data Corporation	12500	3
8	Charity League	Main Street Market	4000	3
9	Charity League	GG&G	5000	3
10	Charity League	LitWare, Inc.	11500	3
11	Charity League	Miller Textiles	10000	3
12	Clark Escrow, Inc.	Shear Savvy	5000	7
13	Costoso, Ltd.	Miller Textiles	1500	3
14	Costoso, Ltd.	Main Street Market	1000	3
15	Costoso, Ltd.	Miller Textiles	26000	3
16	Costoso, Ltd.	Blue Yonder Airways	3000	3
17	Costoso, Ltd.	InfoByte, Inc.	30000	3
18	Costoso, Ltd.	Astro Mountain Bike Company	1000	3
19	Costoso, Ltd.	LKXS Radiography Companies	4500	3
20	Crescendo Music Society	InfoByte, Inc.	10000	3
21	Crescendo Music Society	The Phone Company	15000	3

TIP

Check the result of a sort immediately. If you don't like what you see, use the Undo command on the Edit menu to restore the previous order.

If you want to be able to restore the previous order of a list after several sort operations, create a row-number column before you perform the first sort. Simply add a new column to the list and fill that column with a numeric sequence. Then, to restore the previous order after sorting, sort again on the row-number column.

Sorting on More Than One Column

In our simple example, we sorted the list shown in Figure 25-3 on page 753 on just one column, the Recipient column. We now have rows grouped by recipient, and the recipients are in alphabetical order. But within each group of recipients, the rows are in no meaningful sequence.

Suppose we had wanted the recipients in ascending alphabetical order, and within each recipient group, the amount values in descending order. To produce this arrangement, we would have to sort on two separate columns: the Recipient column and the Amount column. Figure 25-6 shows the Sort dialog box that would produce such a sort, and Figure 25-7 shows the list after the two-column sort was performed.

FIGURE 25-6.

To sort on two columns, we supplied the names of the column headings in the Sort By and Then By drop-down list boxes.

We could even specify a third sort column in the Sort dialog box. For example, by entering the Donor heading in the second Then By list box, we could ensure that any rows with duplicate recipient and amount values will appear in ascending (or descending) alphabetical order.

FIGURE 25-7.

A sort on two columns produced this list. The recipients are in ascending alphabetical order. Within each group of identical recipients, the rows are sorted by Amount in descending numeric order.

	A	B	C	D
1	**Recipient**	**Donor**	**Amount**	**Rating**
2	Charity League	Miller Textiles	35000	3
3	Charity League	InfoBus Data Corporation	12500	3
4	Charity League	LitWare, Inc.	11500	3
5	Charity League	LKXS Radiography Companies	10000	3
6	Charity League	Miller Textiles	10000	3
7	Charity League	Enchantment Lakes Corporation	6000	3
8	Charity League	ProseWare Corporation	5000	3
9	Charity League	GG&G	5000	3
10	Charity League	Main Street Market	4000	3
11	Charity League	West Coast Sales	3000	3
12	Clark Escrow, Inc.	Shear Savvy	5000	7
13	Costoso, Ltd.	InfoByte, Inc.	30000	3
14	Costoso, Ltd.	Miller Textiles	26000	3
15	Costoso, Ltd.	LKXS Radiography Companies	4500	3
16	Costoso, Ltd.	Blue Yonder Airways	3000	3
17	Costoso, Ltd.	Miller Textiles	1500	3
18	Costoso, Ltd.	Main Street Market	1000	3
19	Costoso, Ltd.	Astro Mountain Bike Company	1000	3
20	Crescendo Music Society	The Phone Company	15000	3
21	Crescendo Music Society	InfoByte, Inc.	10000	3

> To find out the sum, average, count, maximum, or minimum of any group of entries in a list, simply select those entries. Excel displays in the status bar the number you're interested in. For example, if you select cells C2:C11 in Figure 25-5 on page 754, the status bar reports "SUM=102000." To see the average or count instead, right-click the status bar and make a selection from the shortcut menu.

Sorting on More Than Three Columns

Excel allows you to sort a worksheet on up to three columns at once, and in most applications that's plenty. Should ever need to sort on more than three columns, you can do so by doing successive single-column or multiple-column sorts. Simply sort the least important column first, repeat the sort on the next-least important column, and so on.

Sorting Only Part of a List

CAUTION

Be sure to select all columns when you're sorting part of a list by rows. In Figure 25-3 on page 753, if you selected A10–B17 instead of A10–D17, Excel would rearrange the rows in the first two columns and leave the rows in the third and fourth columns alone, resulting in a scrambled list.

If you select a single cell before choosing the Sort command, Excel scans the area surrounding the selected cell, highlights the entire contiguous range of cells, and assumes you want to sort that entire range. If you want to sort only part of a list (a subset of a contiguous range), select only those rows and columns you want to sort. Then choose the Sort command from the Data menu. To sort rows 10 through 20 in Figure 25-3 on page 753, for example, you would start by selecting A10 through D20.

Note that you can't specify a sort range in the Sort dialog box; you must select the range before you open the dialog box. Also note that the dialog box itself doesn't indicate what Excel is about to sort. Check your worksheet immediately after a sort and use the Undo command if you don't like what you get.

The Header Row Option

Whether you ask Excel to sort a complete list or only part of a list, the program always looks for a row of column-heading labels at the top of the sort area. If Excel finds such a row, the Header Row option in the My List Has section of the Sort dialog box is selected by default. If you accept this default, Excel sorts the body of your list without moving the column headings.

To determine whether your list includes column headings, Excel examines the top two rows of the list. If the first row differs from the second in terms of data type, font, underscoring, alignment, or capitalization, Excel assumes the first row is a header. If the first and second rows are alike in these respects, Excel compares the second row with the third. If those rows differ, the first two rows are assumed to be headers and both are excluded from the sort.

The upshot of this is that in nearly all cases, Excel will correctly determine whether it should include the top one or two rows in the sort. Just to be sure the program doesn't make an error, it's a good idea to verify the options at the bottom of the Sort dialog box.

Sorting by Columns

All the examples presented so far have been sorted by row, or top to bottom. That is, we've rearranged the rows of a list, while leaving the order of the columns alone. Excel also allows you to sort by columns, while leaving the order of the rows alone. To sort by columns, click the Options button in the Sort dialog box and select the Sort Left To Right option. Figure 25-8 below and Figure 25-9 on page 759 show a worksheet before and after a left-to-right sort.

FIGURE 25-8.

A simple financial worksheet.

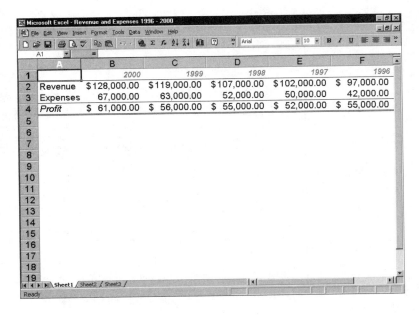

Watch Out for Formulas!

When you sort lists and ranges, watch out for cells that contain formulas. If you sort by row (top to bottom), references to other cells in the same row will be correct after the sort, but references to cells in other rows of the list will no longer be correct after the sort.

Similarly, if you sort by column (left to right), references to other cells in the same columns will be correct after the sort, but references to cells in other columns will no longer be correct after the sort.

The following before-and-after illustrations demonstrate the hazards of sorting lists and ranges that contain formulas. Row 5 of the worksheet calculates the year-to-year change in profit, using relative-reference formulas. Cell C5, for example, uses the formula =C4-B4 to calculate the difference between 1997's profit and 1996's.

	A	B	C	D	E	F
1		1996	1997	1998	1999	2000
2	Revenue	$ 97,000.00	$ 102,000.00	$ 107,000.00	$ 119,000.00	$ 128,000.00
3	Expenses	42,000.00	50,000.00	52,000.00	63,000.00	67,000.00
4	Profit	$ 55,000.00	$ 52,000.00	$ 55,000.00	$ 56,000.00	$ 61,000.00
5	Y/Y Change		$ (3,000.00)	$ 3,000.00	$ 1,000.00	$ 5,000.00
6						

After sorting by column, the formula in C5 is still =C4-B4, but it now reports the wrong year-to-year change! To continue reporting year-to-year changes correctly, C5 would have to contain the formula =C4-D4. The other formulas in row 5 are also incorrect.

	A	B	C	D	E	F
1		2000	1999	1998	1997	1996
2	Revenue	$ 128,000.00	$ 119,000.00	$ 107,000.00	$ 102,000.00	$ 97,000.00
3	Expenses	67,000.00	63,000.00	52,000.00	50,000.00	42,000.00
4	Profit	$ 61,000.00	$ 56,000.00	$ 55,000.00	$ 52,000.00	$ 55,000.00
5	Y/Y Change	#VALUE!	$ (5,000.00)	$ (1,000.00)	$ (3,000.00)	
6						

To avoid the problems associated with sorting lists and ranges that contain formulas, observe the following rules:

- In formulas that depend on cells outside the list, use only absolute references.

- When sorting by row, avoid formulas that reference cells in other rows.

- When sorting by column, avoid formulas that reference cells in other columns.

FIGURE 25-9.

We used the Sort Left To Right option to reorder the years on the financial worksheet.

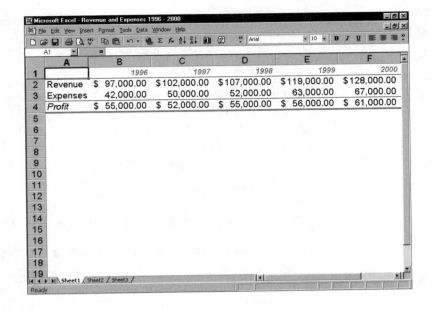

To perform this sort, select B1:F4, choose Sort from the Data menu, and then click the Options button. Make sure that Sort left to right is selected, and then click OK to return to the worksheet.

Note that it's best to select all the data you want to sort, rather than just a single cell, when you're sorting laterally. If you select only one cell, Excel will propose to sort everything in the worksheet, including the labels in your first column. (In other words, Excel doesn't recognize row headings in column-oriented sorts.)

Creating and Using Custom Sort Orders

Excel doesn't limit you to the standard sorting sequence. If you want a set of labels to be sorted in a particular nonalphabetical order, you can define a custom sorting series. Excel has already defined the days of the week and the months of the year as custom sort orders, as you can see by choosing the Sort command, clicking the Options button, and opening the First Key Sort Order drop-down list box. To create a new custom sort order, follow these steps:

1   Choose the Options command from the Tools menu and click the Custom Lists tab.

2   Select NEW LIST from the Custom Lists list box.

3 In the List Entries section of the dialog box, type the items of your list in the order in which you want them sorted, placing each item on a new line or using commas to separate the items. Then click OK.

The items in your custom list can include spaces. For example, you could create the following list: Pitcher, Catcher, First Base, Second Base, Third Base, and so on. Remember to separate the items with commas or place each item on a separate line. To delete a custom list, select the list on the Custom Lists tab and click the Delete button.

To use a custom list, choose the Sort command from the Data menu and click the Options button in the Sort dialog box. Then open the First Key Sort Order list box and select your custom list.

Importing a Custom List from the Worksheet

If the items in your custom list already appear in the desired order as text in your worksheet, you don't have to type them on the Custom Lists tab of the Options dialog box. Select the list before choosing the Options command from the Tools menu. Your selection will appear in the edit box at the bottom of the dialog box, and you can click the Import button to add the new sequence to Excel's repertoire of custom lists.

Using Filters to Analyze a List

To *filter* a list means to hide all the rows except those that meet specified criteria. Excel provides two filtering commands—AutoFilter, for simple criteria, and Advanced Filter, for more complex criteria.

The AutoFilter Command

To use the AutoFilter command, first select any cell in your list. Then choose AutoFilter from the Filter submenu of the Data menu; Excel displays drop-down arrows next to each of the column headings in your list. Clicking the arrow next to any heading reveals a list of that heading's unique values, which you can use to specify filtering criteria.

If you plan to use only one column for your filtering criteria, you can eliminate the drop-down arrows for the other columns. Select the heading cell for the column you want to use and hold down the Shift key while pressing Ctrl and the Down arrow key. Then choose the AutoFilter command.

Let's look at an example. Suppose that from the list shown in Figure 25-7 on page 755, we'd like to see only those rows in which the donor is Miller Textiles. To generate this subset, we would choose the AutoFilter command and then select Miller Textiles from the drop-down list next to the Donor heading. The result would look like Figure 25-10.

FIGURE 25-10.

We used the AutoFilter command to display only those rows for which the donor is Miller Textiles.

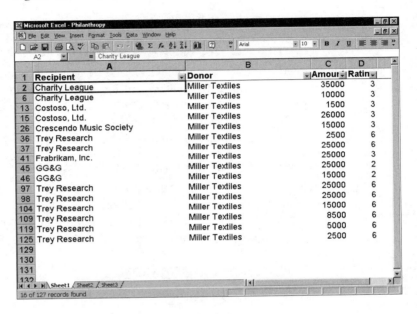

Notice the row-number gaps in Figure 25-10. When you use the AutoFilter command or the Advanced Filter command to display a subset of your list, Excel simply hides all the rows that don't meet your criteria. To remind you that you have filtered your list, Excel also displays the filtered row numbers in a contrasting color.

 **TIP**

> You can use Excel's Subtotals command to analyze the rows that pass your filter. *For more information, see "Using Subtotals to Analyze a List," page 777.*

When you first filter a list, Excel lets you see at a glance how many rows have met your filtering criteria. Excel displays the number of records found out of the total in the status bar.

Because Excel creates filters by hiding rows, any data stored alongside a list might be hidden by the filtering process. Of course, you can restore this data to view by removing the filter, but it's simpler to avoid the problem altogether by placing your lists on worksheets by themselves. If you want to include other information in the same worksheet as the list, place the information above or below the list.

Using AutoFilter Criteria in More Than One Column

You can specify AutoFilter criteria for your list in as many columns as you want. Simply filter your list on one column, then filter the resulting list on another column, and so on. For example, to show only the $25,000 donations made by Miller Textiles, open the Amount drop-down list in Figure 25-10 and select 25000.

Using AutoFilter to Find the Top Ten

Use AutoFilter to find the top or bottom *n* items in a list, or those items that make up the top or bottom *n* percent of a column's total. Click the drop-down arrow for the column and then select Top 10 from the list. Excel displays the dialog box shown in Figure 25-11.

FIGURE 25-11.

Excel's Top 10 option lets you zero in on the top or bottom *n* list items.

The Top 10 AutoFilter dialog box has three boxes. In the first, you can select either Top or Bottom. In the second, you can specify any number between 1 and 500. In the third, you can select either Items or Percent.

Using AutoFilter to Find Blank Cells

If a column contains blank cells, you'll find the entries Blanks and NonBlanks at the bottom of its AutoFilter drop-down list. If you want to locate those rows in which a particular column has no entry, specify Blanks as your AutoFilter criterion. If you want to eliminate rows with blank entries from the filtrate, specify NonBlanks.

Using the Custom Option to Specify More Complex Criteria

The example in Figure 25-10 on page 761 used a single equality comparison for its criterion. That is, we asked Excel to display only those rows in which the Donor column was equal to a particular value. With the help of the Custom option, you can filter on the basis of an inequality or find rows that fall within a range of values. To use the Custom option, open the drop-down list for the column you're interested in and select Custom. You'll see the dialog box shown in Figure 25-12.

FIGURE 25-12.

The Custom option lets you specify more complex AutoFilter criteria.

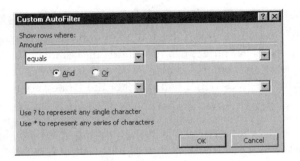

You can enter one or two criteria in the Custom AutoFilter dialog box, and you can select from a full range of Excel's relational operators. The drop-down list boxes on the left side of the dialog box provide a selection of relationships (equals, does not equal, is greater than, and so on), and the drop-down list boxes on the right allow you to select the values that appear in your list.

Suppose, for example, that you want to see all the donations shown in Figure 25-7 on page 755 in which the Amount value is between $50,000 and $100,000. First, open the upper left drop-down list box in the Custom AutoFilter dialog box and select *is greater than or equal to*. Then open the top right drop-down list box and select 50000. (You could also type *50000* directly in the edit box.) Then select *is less than or equal to* from the lower left drop-down list box, and 10000 from the lower right list box, as shown in Figure 25-13 on the next page.

Notice that we selected the And option in Figure 25-13, not the Or option. If we selected Or, our filtered list would no longer be a subset of the original list, but rather the entire list—all donations in that list are either less than $100,000 or greater than $50,000.

V

Database and List Management

FIGURE 25-13.

Filling out the Custom AutoFilter dialog box this way would produce a list of donations between $50,000 and $100,000, inclusive.

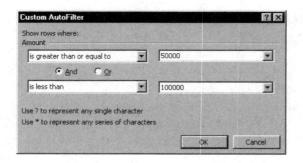

Finding All Text Values within a Particular Alphabetical Range

To find all the text values in a column that fall within a particular alphabetical range, use the AutoFilter command's Custom option and specify two criteria joined by And. For example, to find all the donors whose names begin with B, filter the Donor column and specify

>B And <C

in the Custom AutoFilter dialog box. In this case, the values B and C would probably not be found in the drop-down list boxes, so you would simply type them in the edit boxes.

Using Wildcards in Custom Criteria

As you can see in Figure 25-12 on page 763, and Figure 25-13 above, the Custom AutoFilter dialog box accepts two kinds of wildcard criteria:

- Use the asterisk character (*) as a proxy for any sequence of characters.

- Use the question-mark character (?) as a proxy for any single character.

The following table shows examples of wildcard specifications and the values that would pass through the resulting filters:

The Entry	Allows These Names to Pass
=Sm?th	Smith, Smyth
=H??t	Hart, Heit, Hurt
=S*n	Stevenson, Svenson, Smithson

Note that you can combine these wildcards in just about any way. You can even use multiple asterisks in the same criterion. For example, filtering the Recipient column of Figure 25-5, on page 754, with the specification =*Music* would result in all rows whose recipient values include the word Music, such as Crescendo Music Society.

TIP

If you want to include a literal question mark (?) or asterisk (*) in a filter, precede the ? or * with a tilde (~).

Using a Form to Find List Information

Filters are an effective way to find list information, but they're not the only way. You can also use the Form command to locate rows that meet stated criteria. Here's how:

1 Select any cell in your list.

2 Choose the Form command from the Data menu, and when the dialog box appears, click the Criteria button.

3 Complete the edit boxes in the form as though you were creating a criteria range:

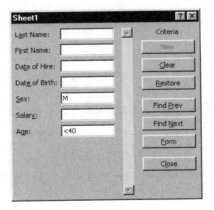

The accompanying figure shows how you might complete the form if you wanted to see the names and other particulars for all male employees under the age of 40.

4 Click the Find Next button to display the first row in the list that meets your criteria.

5 Continue clicking Find Next to see subsequent rows or click Find Prev to return to previous rows.

Removing AutoFilters

To remove an AutoFilter for a particular column, open the column's drop-down list and select (All). To remove all AutoFilters currently in effect from the Data menu, choose Filter and then Show All. To remove all AutoFilters and the drop-down arrows, choose the AutoFilter command again—thereby removing the check mark next to its name on the Filter submenu of the Data menu.

Copying AutoFiltered Data to Another Location

At times you might want to copy, or extract, the rows that meet AutoFilter criteria to some other part of your worksheet or to another worksheet altogether. Like any other type of worksheet data, AutoFiltered rows can be copied with the Copy and Paste commands on the Edit menu.

If you want to extract selected rows in a single step, without having to use the Copy and Paste commands, use the Advanced Filter command, described in the next section. Note, however, that the Advanced Filter command will not automatically copy selected rows to a new file or to a new worksheet within the current workbook. To do these tasks, you must still use the Copy and Paste commands.

The Advanced Filter Command

In contrast to the AutoFilter command, the Advanced Filter command allows you to do the following:

- Specify criteria involving two or more columns and the conjunction OR. For example, you could restrict your personnel list to all employees who are either older than 50 or earning more than $50,000. (You could also use Advanced Filter if you wanted to see rows that met both criteria, >50 and >$50,000, but it would be simpler to use the AutoFilter command twice in succession.)

- Specify three or more criteria for a particular column, where at least one OR conjunction is involved. For example, you could list the names of all employees in Division A, Division C, or Division D.

- Specify computed criteria. For example, you could list only those employees whose salaries are more than 25 percent greater than the median salary.

In addition, the Advanced Filter command can be used to extract rows from the list, placing copies of those rows in another part of the current worksheet. You can create extracts with the AutoFilter command as well, but you have to do the copying and pasting yourself. The Advanced Filter command will offer to do it for you.

Specifying a Criteria Range

The Advanced Filter command, unlike AutoFilter, requires that you specify filtering criteria in a worksheet range separate from your list. Because entire rows are hidden when the filter is executed, it's inadvisable to put the criteria range *alongside* the list. Instead, put it above or below the list. If you think your list may get longer over time, you'll probably find it more convenient to store the criteria range above the list.

For more information about computed criteria, see "Using Computed Criteria," page 772.

A criteria range must consist of at least two rows. You enter one or more column headings in the top row and your filtering criteria in the second and subsequent rows. With the exception of computed criteria, the headings in your criteria range must exactly match those in your list. To ensure accuracy, the best way to create these headings is by selecting the column headings in your list and then using the Copy and Paste commands on the Edit menu to paste copies of the headings into the top row of the criteria range.

Keep in mind that a criteria range does not have to include headings for every column in the list. Columns that are not involved in the selection process can be eliminated.

If you use two or more sets of criteria regularly to filter the same list, it's a good idea to set them up in separate criteria ranges. Assigning names to these criteria ranges and then specifying the names, instead of the range addresses, in the Advanced Filter dialog box will make it easy to switch between filters.

An Example Using Two Columns Joined by OR

Suppose that from the personnel list shown in Figure 25-1, page 749, you want to see the names of employees who are either earning salaries of more than $50,000 or over 50 years of age. To create this filter, follow these steps:

1 Insert some new rows at the top of the worksheet to make room for the criteria range.

2 Create the criteria range shown in Figure 25-14 on the next page.

Database and List Management

FIGURE 25-14.

The criteria range in cells A1:B3 will filter the list to show only those employees who earn $50,000 or more or who are at least 50 years of age.

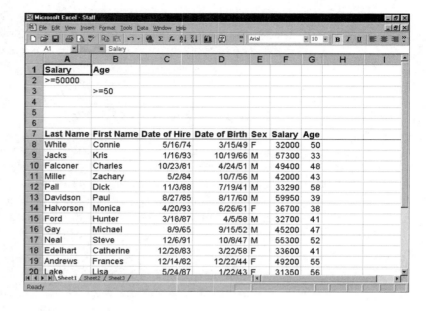

3 Choose the Advanced Filter command from the Filter submenu of the Data menu and enter the information in the Advanced Filter dialog box as shown in Figure 25-15.

FIGURE 25-15.

Enter the locations of your list and criteria range in the Advanced Filter dialog box.

4 Be sure the Filter The List, In-Place option is selected and then click OK. Figure 25-16 shows the results.

Like AutoFilter, the Advanced Filter command will hide all rows that don't pass the filter. It also displays the qualifying row numbers in a contrasting color and the number of records found in the status bar.

FIGURE 25-16.

After we created the criteria range shown in Figure 25-14, on page 768, and completed the Advanced Filter dialog box shown in Figure 25-15, on page 768, Excel displayed this list.

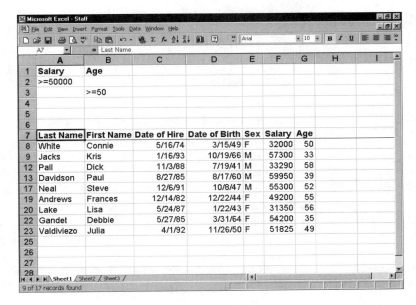

In Figure 25-14, notice that the criteria in cells A1:B3 are entered as ordinary labels. You simply type *>=50000* under the Salary heading and *>=50* under the Age heading.

Notice also that the two criteria must be specified on separate lines. If you put both criteria on the same line, you'd be asking Excel to display only those rows where both criteria are met—that is, the rows for employees who earn more than $50,000 a year and are over 50 years of age.

You can enter as many criteria as you like in a criteria range. Excel interprets the range according to these rules:

- Criteria on the same line are considered to be joined by AND.

- Criteria on separate lines are considered to be joined by OR.

WARNING

A blank cell in a criteria range means "accept any value for this column." If you include a blank row in the criteria range, you will get an unfiltered list. To avoid this, be careful when removing criteria rows from a range. If you no longer need a row, it's not enough simply to delete the row's contents. You must also change the criteria range in the Advanced Filter dialog box to show the reduced range.

Database and List Management

TIP

When you specify a criteria range in the Advanced Filter dialog box, Excel assigns the name Criteria to that range. You can use this name as a navigation aid. For example, if you need to return to the range to change the criteria, press F5 and then select Criteria from the Go To dialog box.

An Example Using Three ORs on a Column

Now let's suppose you want the list in Figure 25-1, on page 749, to display only those employees whose names begin with A, F, or M. You would include the Last Name heading in your criteria range, and you would enter the letters A, F, and M in the three rows immediately below that heading. After you choose the Advanced Filter command and enter the locations of the list and criteria range in the Advanced Filter dialog box, Excel displays the list shown in Figure 25-17.

FIGURE 25-17.

Using the criteria range in cells A1:A4, we reduced the list to those employees whose last names start with A, F, or M.

	A	B	C	D	E	F	G	H	I
1	**Last Name**								
2	A								
3	F								
4	M								
5									
6									
7	**Last Name**	**First Name**	**Date of Hire**	**Date of Birth**	**Sex**	**Salary**	**Age**		
10	Falconer	Charles	10/23/81	4/24/51	M	49400	48		
11	Miller	Zachary	5/2/84	10/7/56	M	42000	43		
15	Ford	Hunter	3/18/87	4/5/58	M	32700	41		
19	Andrews	Frances	12/14/82	12/22/44	F	49200	55		
25									
26									
27									
28									
29									
30									
31									
32									
33									

4 of 17 records found

An Example Using Both OR and AND

What if we need the employees whose last names begin with A, F, or M and who are also at least 40 years of age? In this case, we would set up the criteria range as shown in Figure 25-18. Notice that the criterion >=40 must be repeated in each row because for each alphabetical category (A, F, and M) we want only those employees who meet two criteria—the alphabetical criterion *and* the age criterion.

FIGURE 25-18.

To display a list of employees whose names start with A, F, or M and who also belong to the over-40 set, we need to repeat the >=40 criterion in each line of the criteria range.

	A	B	C	D	E	F	G	H	I
1	Last Name	Age							
2	A	>=40							
3	F	>=40							
4	M	>=40							
5									
6									
7	Last Name	First Name	Date of Hire	Date of Birth	Sex	Salary	Age		
10	Falconer	Charles	10/23/81	4/24/51	M	49400	48		
11	Miller	Zachary	5/2/84	10/7/56	M	42000	43		
15	Ford	Hunter	3/18/87	4/5/58	M	32700	41		
19	Andrews	Frances	12/14/82	12/22/44	F	49200	55		
25									
26									
27									
28									
29									
30									
31									
32									
33									

4 of 17 records found

 TIP

> Each time you use the Advanced Filter command, Excel reexamines the entire list rather than only the current filtrate. Therefore, you don't have to use the Show All command before changing the filter.

So far, our examples have involved only what are called *comparison* criteria. No computations were required. We'll give some examples of *computed* criteria in a moment. But first, we need to look more closely at the way Excel handles text criteria.

Specifying Text Criteria

The rules for specifying text criteria are not as obvious as you might like. The following paradigms should help you think the way Excel does:

- A single letter means "Accept any value that starts with this letter." Example: Entering *M* returns Mary, Martha, and Mr. Rogers.

- Greater-than and less-than symbols mean "Accept any value that falls after or before this point in the alphabet." Example: Entering *>M* under a Last Name heading returns all last names that begin with M through Z. Conversely, entering *<M* returns all last names that begin with A through L.

VI

Database and List Management

- The formula ="=text" means "Accept only those rows that contain the value *text*." Example: Specify *="=Smith"* to return the exact match Smith. If you specify Smith without the formula, Excel returns Smith, Smithsonian, Smithy, and so on.

Wildcards are permitted. Wildcards work the same way in an Advanced Filter as they do in an AutoFilter. *For more information about using wildcards, see "Using Wildcards in Custom Criteria," page 764.*

Using Computed Criteria

Computed criteria are criteria that involve any test other than a simple comparison of a column's value to a constant. Asking Excel to find employees with salaries above $50,000 does not require a computed criterion. Asking for employees with salaries greater than the median salary does.

Even experienced Excel users can get tripped up when using computed criteria. Here are three rules to help you stay on your feet:

- The column heading above a computed criterion must *not* be a copy of a column heading in the list. The criteria-range heading can be blank, or it can contain anything else you like. (Note that this requirement is the opposite of what noncomputed criteria require.)

- References to cells outside the list should be absolute.

- References to cells within the list should be relative.

This last rule has one exception, as you'll see. Now for some examples.

Referencing a Cell Outside the List

Figure 25-19 on the next page shows an Advanced Filter that finds all employees with salaries greater than the median salary. In setting up this filter, we first stored the formula

    =MEDIAN(F8:F26)

outside the list, in cell H2. Then, in cell A2, we entered a computed criterion that references this "outside" cell. The criteria range is A1:A2, and the computed criterion formula in cell A2 reads =F8>$H$2.

As the status bar in Figure 25-19 indicates, this filter admits 8 of the original 17 rows. In other words, just under half the employees have salaries above the median—which is exactly what you would expect.

FIGURE 25-19.

We use an Advanced Filter in this list to find all employees with salaries greater than the median salary. The computed criterion at A2 makes absolute reference to a cell outside the list.

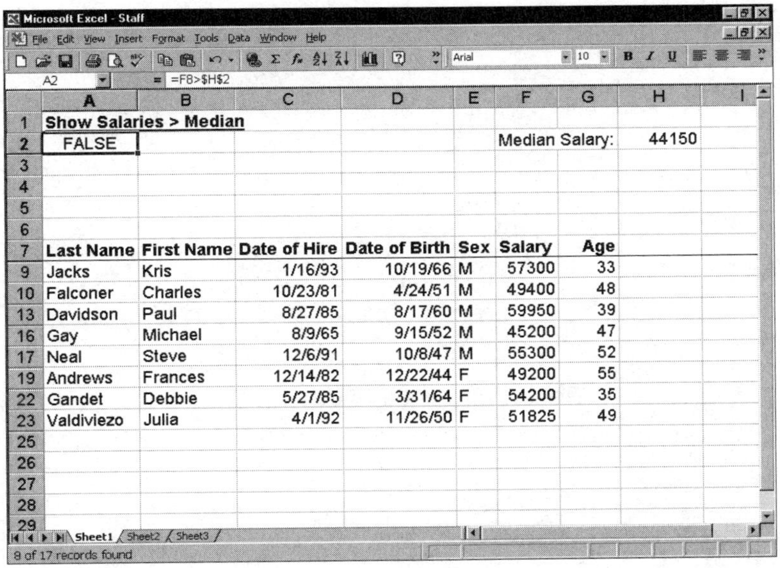

In the previous example, note the following:

- The heading for the criteria range does not duplicate any of the headings in the list. (If it did, the Advanced Filter would not work correctly.)

TIP

As mentioned, the column heading in a computed criterion can be blank, or it can contain text, as long as the text is not a duplicate of any other heading in the list. If the column heading is blank, you must still include it in the criteria range when you specify the range in the Advanced Filter dialog box.

- The criterion formula compares cell F8 with cell H2. Cell F8 is the first cell in the Salary column of the unfiltered list, and the computed criterion formula instructs Excel to evaluate this first cell in the column. As Excel processes the filter, it substitutes each member of the list, in turn, for this first value; that is, Excel evaluates F8, followed by F9, followed by F10, and so on until it reaches the end of the list.

- The reference to cell H2 is absolute. In cell A2 of the criteria range, if we entered the formula *=F8>H2* (that is, if we used a relative reference to H2), Excel would compare F8 with H2. Then it would compare F9 with H3, and so on. All tests except the first would be invalid.

V

Database and List Management

TIP

> If you want to see the formula in the criteria range, open a new window and turn on the Formulas display option. (First choose New Window from the Window menu. Then, in the new window, choose Options from the Tools menu, click the View tab, and select the Formulas option.) You can size and position the two windows so the formula remains visible while you work with the list.

- The value returned by the criterion formula itself is irrelevant. In our example, the formula returns FALSE—but only because the first employee in our unfiltered list happens to make less than the median salary.

Referencing Cells Within the List

The Advanced Filter in Figure 25-20 subtracts the date of birth from the date of hire and compares the result against the product of 18 and 365 to determine whether any employee joined the firm before turning 18. The filter results reveal a flagrant violation of the child labor laws!

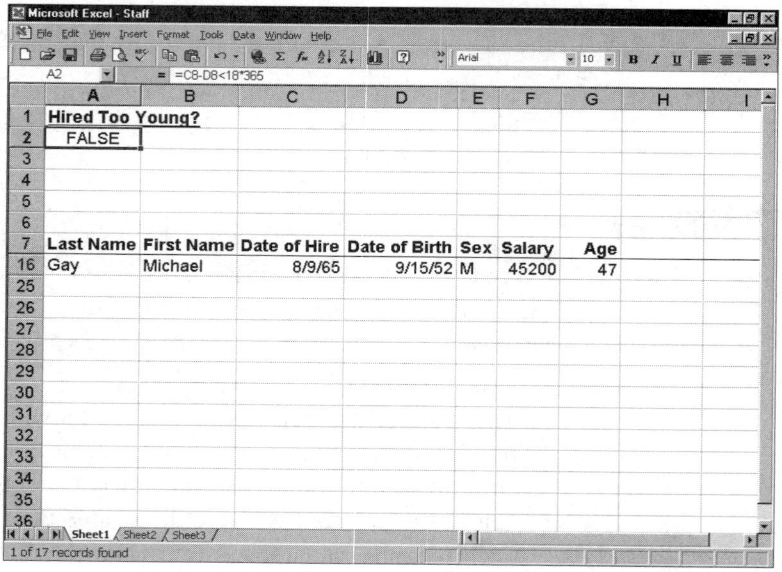

FIGURE 25-20.

The computed criterion in this example uses only relative references.

	A	B	C	D	E	F	G	H	I
1	Hired Too Young?								
2	FALSE								
3									
4									
5									
6									
7	Last Name	First Name	Date of Hire	Date of Birth	Sex	Salary	Age		
16	Gay	Michael	8/9/65	9/15/52	M	45200	47		

A2 = =C8-D8<18*365

Microsoft Excel - Staff

1 of 17 records found

The criterion formula

=C8-D8<18*365

uses only relative references because we want Excel to first subtract D8 from C8, then D9 from C9, and so on.

An Exception to the Rule

Like the worksheet shown in Figure 25-19 on page 773, the worksheet in Figure 25-21 contains a filtered list displaying records of employees with salaries above the median. But the formula in this case,

=F8>MEDIAN($F$8:$F$24)

makes direct reference to the Salary column, rather than referencing an outside cell. According to the rules listed on page 772, references to cells within the list should be relative; however, the references to cells F8 through F24 are absolute. We used absolute references because we want Excel to evaluate the same range of cells at each step of the filtering process. That is, we want Excel to compare F8 with the median of F8:F24, then F9 with the median of F8:F24, and so on. If we used a relative reference to F8:F24, only the first comparison would be valid.

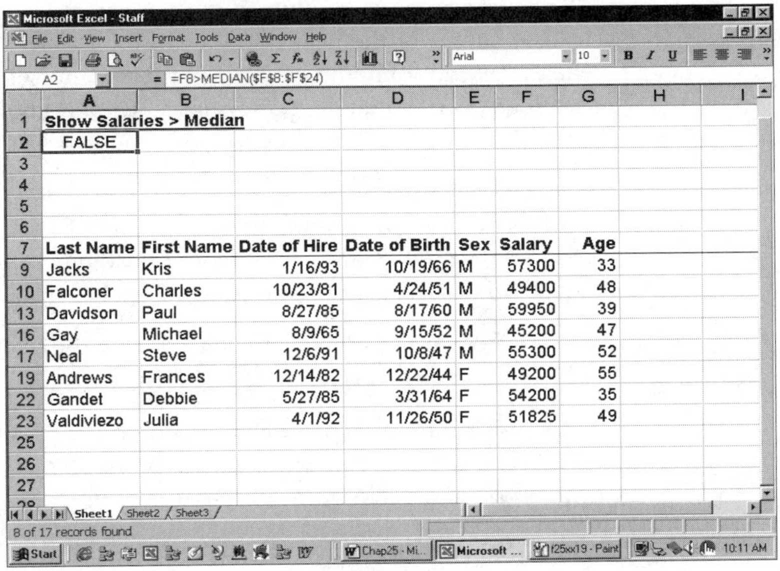

FIGURE 25-21.

References to cells within the list are usually relative. In this case, however, the reference to F8:F24 must be absolute.

Copying Filtered Rows to Another Worksheet Location

The Advanced Filter dialog box, shown in Figure 25-15 on page 768, includes an option for copying the selected rows to another worksheet location, instead of displaying a filtered list. To copy rows rather than display them, select the Copy To Another Location option in the Advanced Filter dialog box and supply the name or address of the range where you want the information to appear in the Copy To edit box.

The easiest way to specify the Copy To range is to click a blank cell in your worksheet where you want the range to start. Be sure the cell has plenty of blank space below and to the right of it. Excel will then copy your list's column headings and all the rows that meet the Advanced Filter criteria to the range that begins with the cell you specified. Be careful, though: any data already stored in the selected range will be overwritten. Alternatively, if you specify a range of cells, Excel will copy the rows that pass the filter but will stop when the range is full.

> **TIP**
>
> When you specify a Copy To range in the Advanced Filter dialog box, Excel assigns the name Extract to the range. You can use this name as a navigation aid. For example, when you need to return to the range to change column headings, press F5 and then select Extract from the Go To dialog box.

To copy only certain columns of your list to a new worksheet range, create copies of the headings for those columns. Then specify the headings (not only the first cell but the entire set of copied headings) as your Copy To range. For example, to filter the personnel list in Figure 25-1 on page 749 and copy only the Last Name, First Name, and Salary columns to the range beginning at cell A100, follow these steps:

1 Copy the Last Name, First Name, and Salary headings to A100:C100. (You can copy the headings in any order, depending on how you want your filtered data to appear.)

2 Choose the Advanced Filter command from the Filter submenu of the Data menu.

3 When the Advanced Filter dialog box appears, specify your list and criteria ranges and then type *A100:C100* in the Copy To edit box and click OK.

The Unique Records Only Option

The Unique Records Only option in the Advanced Filter dialog box adds an additional filter to whatever you specify in your criteria range. It eliminates rows that are exact duplicates. (Note that Unique Records Only works only in conjunction with the Copy To Another Location option.) For example, suppose that from the list shown in Figure 25-7, on page 755, you want to see all recipients who have a rating of 3. You don't need to see every row in which the rating-3 recipients appear. You just want a simple list:

1 Above or below the list, set up a criteria range consisting of the number 3 in the cell below the Rating heading.

2 In another, blank region of the worksheet, enter the heading *Recipient*. The cell you use is your Copy To range.

3 Choose the Advanced Filter command from the Filter submenu of the Data menu.

4 Select any cell in the database.

5 Enter the criteria ranges as well as the Copy To range in the Advanced Filter dialog box. Select the Copy To Another Location option and the Unique Records Only option and then click OK. Figure 25-22 shows the results.

FIGURE 25-22.

This list was filtered using the Unique Records Only option.

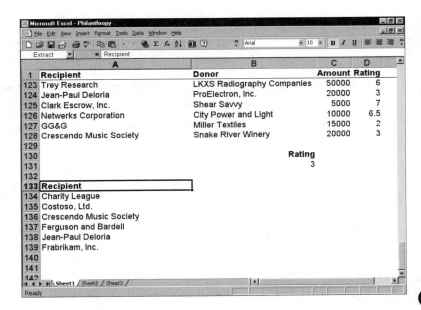

Using Subtotals to Analyze a List

After you've sorted your list properly and filtered out any information you don't (for the moment) need, you can use the Subtotals command on the Data menu to provide many kinds of summary details. The Subtotals command can do as its name suggests—add subtotal lines for each group of entries in your list. It can also supply other aggregate calculations at a group level. For example, you can use the Subtotals command to calculate the average of the values in a particular column for each group of rows, the number of rows in each group, the number of blank items in each group, the standard deviation for each group, and so on.

V

Database and List Management

The Subtotals command also creates grand totals. That is, it applies the aggregation function you use, such as SUM or AVERAGE, to the entire body of your list, as well as to subgroups within the list. You can even choose whether you want the grand totals to appear above or below the list. With long lists, you may find it more convenient to place this "bottom-line" calculation on top so you won't have to scroll to the end of the list. You shouldn't have to do much scrolling in any case, though, because Excel builds an outline of your list when it creates subtotals. You can then click the outline symbols to see whatever level of detail you need.

To show you how the Subtotals command works, we'll use the list in Figure 25-23, which displays financial transactions imported from Microsoft Money. The list has columns for date, payee, budget category, and amount, and it is currently sorted by date.

FIGURE 25-23.

We'll use the Subtotals command to analyze this list of transactions.

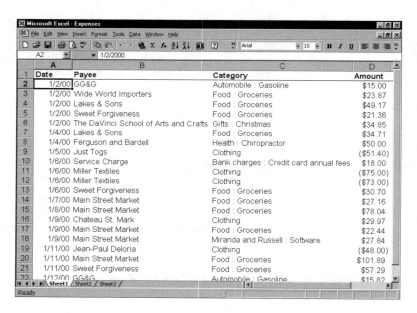

Now suppose you want to know how much money was spent in each budget category. The following steps will elicit this information:

1 Select a cell in the Category column and choose the Sort command from the Data menu. Leave the default information in the Sort dialog box, and then click OK to sort the list by category.

2 Choose the Subtotals command from the Data menu.

3 Complete the Subtotal dialog box as shown in Figure 25-24.

FIGURE 25-24.

Filling out the Subtotal dialog box as shown here produces subtotals for each budget category.

4   Be sure the Replace Current Subtotals and Summary Below Data options are selected and then click OK. Figure 25-25 shows the results.

FIGURE 25-25.

The transactions list now contains subtotals for each budget category. Notice the row level symbols on the left.

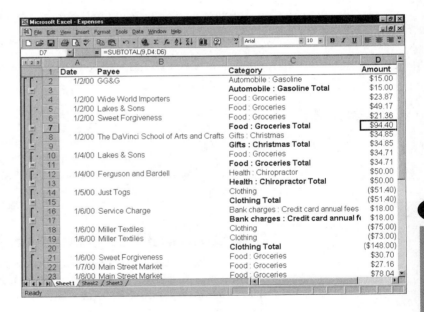

By completing the Subtotal dialog box as shown in Figure 25-24, we asked Excel to do the following three things:

■ Create a new aggregation formula for each change in the Category column.

■ Build the formula with the SUM function and apply it to the Amount column (that is, add up the amounts in each group).

Database and List Management

■ Place the subtotals below each group and the grand total at the bottom of the list.

In Figure 25-25 on the previous page, notice that Excel has also outlined the list. You can use this outline as follows:

■ To see only the grand total, click the row 1 level symbol.

■ To see only the subtotals and grand total, click the row 2 level symbol.

■ To see the list in full detail, click the row 3 level symbol.

SEE ALSO
For more information about using outlines, see "Outlining Your Worksheets," page 225.

You can also use the outline to sort the list by the values of the subtotals. For example, if you wanted to rearrange the list so the budget categories that put the biggest dent in your wallet appeared at the top, do the following:

1 Click the row 2 level symbol to "collapse" the list and make the outline display the subtotals and grand total only.

2 Sort the Amount column in descending order.

All the detail rows would still be associated with the appropriate summary rows after the sort.

TIP

> Outline level symbols can eat valuable screen real estate, pushing columns out of view. You can restore the columns to view by using the Zoom command on the View menu. Alternatively, you can hide the outline symbols. To do this, from the Tools menu, choose Options. Then click the View tab and clear the Outline Symbols check box.

How Subtotal Formulas Are Built

The formula in cell D7 in Figure 25-25 on the previous page provides an example of how Excel calculates subtotals. It uses the SUBTOTAL function, rather than the SUM function, and its first argument, 9, indicates the kind of calculation that is being performed.

The important things to know about the SUBTOTAL function are:

■ You don't have to worry about how it works because the Subtotals command automatically creates it for you.

■ You do have to be careful not to apply your own aggregation formulas "by hand" to a range that includes SUBTOTAL formulas. For example, if you moved to a cell below the subtotaled list and created your own SUM formula to calculate a grand total, the SUM formula would add up everything in the range— details, subtotals, and the existing grand total. It would not "skip over" the SUBTOTAL formulas.

 TIP

Using AutoFormat

If you apply the AutoFormat command to a subtotaled list, Excel will give each subtotal formula a contrasting format, making it easy for you to see both details and summary data at a glance.

Using Automatic Page Breaks

The Page Break Between Groups option in the Subtotal dialog box is handy if you plan to print your subtotaled list. When you select this option, Excel prints each group on a separate page.

Applying More Than One Aggregation Formula to a Column

After looking at the list shown in Figure 25-25 on page 779, you might be curious to know what the average expenditure in each category was. You can find that by choosing the Subtotals command again, selecting Average as the aggregation function, and clearing the Replace Current Subtotals option. Figure 25-26 shows the results.

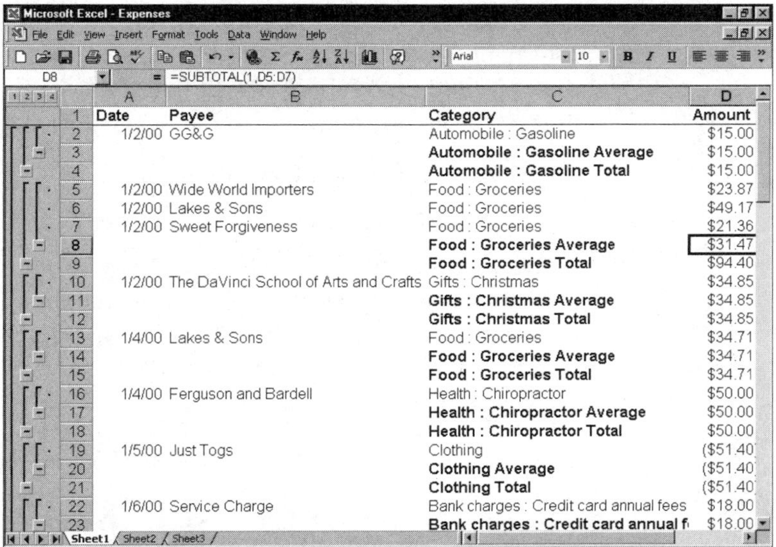

FIGURE 25-26.

In addition to the SUM function, we applied the AVERAGE function to the Category column.

Database and List Management

Removing or Replacing Subtotals

To remove the subtotals and outline, open the Subtotal dialog box and select Remove All. To replace the current subtotals, open the Subtotal dialog box and be sure the Replace Current Subtotals option is selected.

Using Functions to Analyze a List

Microsoft Excel 2000 offers 14 functions—COUNTIF, SUMIF, DAVERAGE, DCOUNT, DCOUNTA, DGET, DMAX, DMIN, DPRODUCT, DSTDEV, DSTDEVP, DSUM, DVAR, and DVARP—that are tailored for working with lists. Each of these functions returns information about the elements in a range that meet some criterion or criteria.

 TIP

COUNTBLANK is another important function to know about. The formula =COUNTBLANK(range) returns the number of cells in a range that are either empty or contain formulas that return null strings. If your application would be invalidated by the presence of blank elements in particular columns of a list, you might want to create some COUNTBLANK formulas as "flags." Format the COUNTBLANK cells to display a contrasting color if the formulas return any value other than 0.

Using the COUNTIF and SUMIF Functions

The COUNTIF and SUMIF functions are easier to use than the other list-oriented functions because they let you specify your criteria directly within the formula. With both functions, however, you're limited to simple comparison criteria.

The COUNTIF function takes the form

    =COUNTIF(range,criteria)

where *range* is the range whose values you want to count and *criteria* is a text value expressing the required criterion. To count the number of women employees in the list shown in Figure 25-1 on page 749, for example, you could use the formula

    =COUNTIF(E2:E24,"F")

To count the number of employees who are 45 or older, you could use

    =COUNTIF(G2:G24,">=45")

Note that the criteria argument can be applied only to the range that you are counting.

The SUMIF function takes the form

=SUMIF(range, criteria, sum_range)

Here the *criteria* argument is applied to *range*, while *sum_range* is the range whose values you want to add. For example, in Figure 25-1 on page 749, to calculate the total spent on salaries for workers below the age of 30, you could use the formula

=SUMIF(G2:G24,"<30",F2:F24)

Because an average is a sum divided by a count, you can use the SUMIF and COUNTIF functions together to calculate averages. For example, the formula

=SUMIF(G2:G24,"<30",F2:F24)/COUNTIF(G2:G24,"<30")

returns the average salary paid to employees under 30 years of age.

Using the D Functions

The remaining list-oriented functions belong to a group known as the D functions, which include DAVERAGE, DCOUNT, DCOUNTA, DGET, DMAX, DMIN, DPRODUCT, DSTDEV, DSTDEVP, DSUM, DVAR, and DVARP.

? SEE ALSO

For more information about statistical functions, see Chapter 15, "Statistical Analysis."

Each of these functions, with the exception of DGET, is the counterpart of a "normal" statistical function. The DSUM function, for example, is the counterpart of the SUM function, the DSTDEV function is the counterpart of the STDEV function, and so on.

The difference between the D functions and their counterparts is that the D functions operate only on those members of a range that meet stated criteria. In Figure 25-27 on the next page, for example, we used the formula

=DAVERAGE(A7:G26,"Salary",A1:A2)

to calculate the average salary of employees 40 and over.

Note the following points about the form of the D functions:

- The first argument specifies the entire list, not just a particular column.

- The second argument identifies the column you want to sum, average, count, or otherwise calculate.

■ For the second argument, you can use the column heading, expressed as a text value. Or you can use a number representing the column's position in the list. For example, in the formula in Figure 25-27, the second argument could have been 6 (the quotation marks aren't necessary when you are using a number rather than text) because Salary is the sixth column in the list.

FIGURE 25-27.

The database statistical functions are useful for analyzing list information that meets particular criteria. Here we used DAVERAGE to find the average salary of workers 40 and over.

Microsoft Excel - Staff

E4 =DAVERAGE(A7:G24,"Salary",A1:A2)

	A	B	C	D	E	F	G	H
1	Age							
2	>=40							
3								
4			Average salary for Employees over 40:		41482			
5								
6								
7	Last Name	First Name	Date of Hire	Date of Birth	Sex	Salary	Age	
8	White	Connie	5/16/74	3/15/49	F	32000	50	
9	Jacks	Kris	1/16/93	10/19/66	M	57300	33	
10	Falconer	Charles	10/23/81	4/24/51	M	49400	48	
11	Miller	Zachary	5/2/84	10/7/56	M	42000	43	
12	Pall	Dick	11/3/88	7/19/41	M	33290	58	
13	Davidson	Paul	8/27/85	8/17/60	M	59950	39	
14	Halvorson	Monica	4/20/93	6/26/61	F	36700	38	
15	Ford	Hunter	3/18/87	4/5/58	M	32700	41	
16	Gay	Michael	8/9/65	9/15/52	M	45200	47	
17	Neal	Steve	12/6/91	10/8/47	M	55300	52	
18	Edelhart	Catherine	12/28/83	3/22/58	F	33600	41	
19	Andrews	Frances	12/14/82	12/22/44	F	49200	55	
20	Lake	Lisa	5/24/87	1/22/43	F	31350	56	

■ The third argument specifies a criteria range.

SEE ALSO

For more information about criteria ranges, see "The Advanced Filter Command," page 766.

Because the D functions require a criteria range, they're a bit more difficult to use than the SUMIF and COUNTIF functions. However, they allow you to perform more complex calculations. While SUMIF and COUNTIF are limited to simple comparison criteria, the D functions can use any criteria that can be expressed in a criteria range.

The DGET Function

The DGET function returns the value of any cell in a column that meets the criteria expressed in a criteria range. If no cell meets the criteria, the function returns the #VALUE! error value. If more than one cell meets the criteria, the function returns the #NUM! error value.

Validating Data Entry

You can use Microsoft Excel's Data Validation command to ensure that new entries to a list or database meet certain criteria. You can specify the type of data you'll allow (whole numbers, dates, times, or text, for example), as well as the range of acceptable values (for example, whole numbers between 1 and 100). You can even set up a list of acceptable values (the names of your operating divisions, for example) and have Excel create a drop-down list of those values. None of this requires any programming on your part.

CAUTION

Data validation criteria can restrict the value a user enters directly into a cell. The user can still use Copy and Paste to transfer invalid information into a restricted cell, however.

To set up data validation criteria, select the range of cells where you want the criteria to apply, and then choose Validation from the Data menu. Excel presents the Data Validation dialog box. In the Settings tab of this dialog box, indicate what kind of data and what range of values you want to allow. The Input Message tab lets you create a prompt that tells the user (or you, if you're setting up the criteria for yourself) what kind of data is allowed. The Error Alert tab lets you specify the message that appears if an entry is invalid.

Specifying Data Type and Acceptable Values

To specify the kind of data you'll allow, open the Allow drop-down list in the Data Validation dialog box. You can choose from the following types: any value, Whole number, Decimal, List, Date, Time, Text length, and Custom. After you choose a data type, Excel modifies the dialog box so you can enter additional information about the chosen type. If you choose Whole number, for example, you'll be asked to specify a minimum and a maximum value.

Supplying a List of Acceptable Values

To set up a list of acceptable values, choose List from the Allow drop-down list, then specify the worksheet range where your list appears. For example, if you want the user to enter only North, South, East, or West in cell A1, you could type those four values in some other part of your workbook—say, the range Z1:Z4. Then you would select A1, choose the Validation command, choose List from the Allow drop-down list, and specify Z1:Z4 as your list range.

VI

Database and List Management

Using a Formula to Validate Input

To use a formula for validation, choose Custom from the Allow drop-down list, and specify a formula in the Formula box that appears. For example, to ensure that cell A1's value is greater than cell B1's, you would select A1, choose the Validation command, choose Custom from the Allow drop-down list, and then specify =A1>B1 in the Formula box.

If you select a range of cells before choosing the Validation command, your formula must make appropriate use of relative and absolute references. Here's how this works. Suppose you validate A1:A10 and your formula reads =A1>B1. Excel will then ensure that A1 is greater than B1, A2 is greater than B2, and so on. If instead your formula reads =A1>$B$1, Excel will make sure A1>B1, A2>B1, A3>B1—and so on.

Specifying an Input Message

To supply an input prompt to guide your user, click the Input Message tab in the Data Validation dialog box. You'll have the opportunity to specify both the title and the content of your message. The message will be displayed as a comment beside the validated cell whenever the user selects that cell.

Specifying Error Alert Style and Message

If you do no more than supply validation criteria for a cell or range, Excel displays a standard error message when the user enters invalid data and forces the user to retry or cancel (canceling leaves the cell's contents unchanged). To supply your own error message, click the Error Alert tab in the Data Validation dialog box. In the dialog box that appears, you can supply title and text for your message.

You can also use the Error Alert tab to specify the style of message that appears. Your choices in the Style drop-down list are Stop, Warning, and Information. These three message styles display different icons beside your message text, and they have differing consequences for the user. If your message style is Stop (the default), the user is forced to retry or cancel. If you choose Warning, the user will be told that his or her data is invalid but will be given the option to leave it in the cell anyway. If you choose Information, the user will be told about the error but will not be given a retry option.

CHAPTER 26

Working with External Data

I n Chapter 25, "Managing Information in Lists," we looked at Microsoft Excel's tools for analyzing lists and databases that reside on Excel worksheets. Now we'll turn our attention to the program's facilities for tapping external data sources—text files, Internet Web sites, and files created in traditional database management systems.

Like earlier versions of Excel, Excel 2000 includes a tool called Microsoft Query that you can use to import selected records from database files. You specify your search criteria using Query's friendly interface, and Query forwards your request as an SQL (Structured Query Language) command to your external data source. The heavy lifting required to locate the records you need takes place outside Excel (on your database server, for example), saving time and memory on your own computer. Once you've created a query in Query, you can refresh the imported data at regular intervals or whenever you'd like. You can also save the query as a data query file (.dqy file), thereby making it available to other users or from other worksheets.

We'll take a close look at Query in this chapter. We'll also look at Excel's features for importing data from text files and for querying sites on the World Wide Web.

Getting Data from Text Files

Excel offers three distinct ways to fetch data from text files:

- You can simply import a text file, using the Open command from the File menu.

- You can choose Get External Data from the Data menu, and then choose Import Text File from the ensuing submenu.

- Or you can use Microsoft Query.

If you use the Open command to import a text file, the text file arrives as a new single-worksheet workbook. Once the data arrives in Excel, you can't refresh it from the text-file source. If you think the text file might have changed since you opened it, you'll need to import it again.

If you use the Import Text File command that appears on the Get External Data submenu of the Data menu, Excel displays the imported data at a selected location on the current worksheet. It also treats the imported data as an external data range, allowing you to refresh the data as needed or at specified intervals. (An external data range is like any other worksheet range, except that its contents are derived from external data. Excel remembers where the external data came from and can reconnect to the source whenever you perform a refresh.) At the time you refresh your query, you can specify a different text file or the same file. Thus, for example, you can use this facility for creating periodic reports from mainframe data. All you need to do is refresh your query and point Excel to the text file on which your current report is to be based.

If you use either the Open or Import Text File command, Excel gives you the option of excluding one or more rows at the top of the file, but otherwise your data arrives unfiltered. If your text file is large, and you need only particular records from it, you'll want to use Microsoft Query. With Query you can specify criteria that limit the import to those records you actually need.

We'll save the discussion of Query for later in this chapter and focus now on the File Open and Import Text File methods. Both of these approaches to text-file import lead you first to the Text Import Wizard, shown in Figure 26-1.

FIGURE 26-1.

The Import Text File Wizard gives you some control over the manner in which Excel parses your text data.

Use this to exclude header rows at the top of your file.

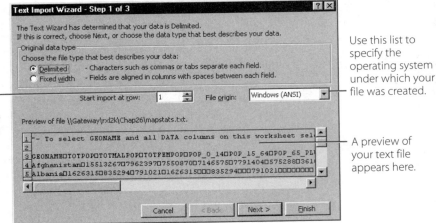

Use this list to specify the operating system under which your file was created.

A preview of your text file appears here.

The Import Text File Wizard

Although the Import Text File Wizard doesn't let you specify particular records to import, it does give you other forms of control over the import process. Among other things, it lets you exclude particular columns (fields) from the import and tell Excel whether each imported column should be treated as text, numbers, or dates.

The wizard's first screen, shown in Figure 26-1, presents a preview of the data that Excel is about to import. It also indicates whether Excel regards your file as *delimited* or *fixed width*. A delimited file is one in which one or more particular characters mark the divisions between columns. Common delimiting characters are the comma and the tab (a comma-delimited file is sometimes called a comma-separated-values, or CSV, file), but, as we'll see, Excel can recognize other delimiters as well. A fixed-width file, sometimes called a formatted-text file, is one in which space characters have been inserted into the file to achieve columnar alignment. Print (.prn) files saved from Lotus 1-2-3, for example, are fixed width.

It's unlikely that the Import Text File Wizard will misread a delimited file as fixed width, or vice versa, but should that ever happen, you can use the option buttons on the wizard's first screen to fix the problem.

The file previewed in Figure 26-1 is delimited, but it has a header row (row 1) that is structured completely differently from the rest of the file. It also has a blank row below the header. When your text file has rows at the top either that you don't need or that Excel might not know how to parse into columns, you might want simply to eliminate them from the import. You can do that with the Start Import At Row box in the center of the dialog box. In our example case, we would click twice on the up arrow to start the import at row 3.

Different operating systems have different ways of encoding special characters such as accented letters and commercial symbols. Excel can correctly import files created in Microsoft Windows, MS-DOS, or Macintosh. Use the File Origin list to tell the Import Text File Wizard the system under which your file was created. (For a mainframe file, specify MS-DOS.)

When you click the Next button to move to the wizard's second screen, you see something resembling either Figure 26-2 or Figure 26-3, depending on whether your text file is delimited or fixed width. In both cases, the vertical lines in the Data Preview window show how Excel proposes to parse (split) your file into columns. The Data Preview window initially shows only the top few rows, but you can see other parts of the file by using the vertical scroll bar.

FIGURE 26-2.

If your file is delimited, the wizard's second screen indicates what character Excel has recognized as the delimiter, and the Data Preview window shows how Excel will parse your file into columns.

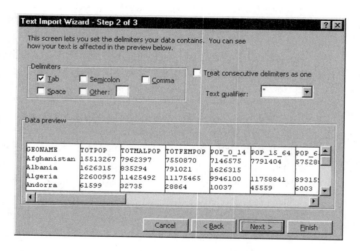

If your file is delimited, the wizard's second screen indicates what character Excel regards as the delimiter. You can override its choice and see the effect immediately in the Data Preview window. Because the delimiter controls are check boxes, not option buttons, you can specify more than one delimiting character. If you specify two or more, Excel breaks to a new column whenever it sees any of your choices. A separate check box lets you specify that consecutive delimiting characters in your text file should be regarded as a single delimiter.

Because both numeric and text fields in a comma-delimited file might themselves contain significant commas (thousands separators in numbers, for example), such files commonly surround field contents with double-quote marks, in addition to using the delimiting character. For this reason, you should generally leave the double-quote mark in the Text Qualifier list. If your file uses single-quote marks instead, choose the single-quote symbol from the drop-down list.

If your file is fixed width, it's possible that Excel's initial attempt to parse it might give you less-than-optimal results (see, for example, the Data Preview window in Figure 26-3). You can set Excel straight by dragging the vertical lines to reposition them. Click the ruler above the Data Preview window to create a new line, or double-click a line to get rid of it.

FIGURE 26-3.

If your file is fixed width, be sure to check the Data Preview window to see how Excel proposes to parse your data into columns. If Excel doesn't get it right (not an unlikely occurrence), you can correct it by manipulating the vertical lines.

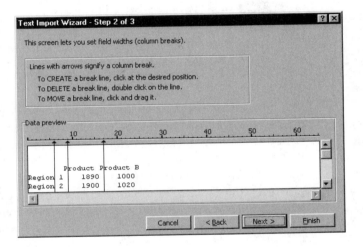

Click the Next button to arrive at the wizard's third dialog box (see Figure 26-4 on the next page), which lets you specify the formatting for each column of your imported text file. Your choices here are the same in delimited and fixed-width files. Click a column to see the format that Excel plans to apply and use the option buttons if necessary, to override its decisions.

In columns marked General, Excel applies either text or numeric formatting as the data warrants. In column 2 of the data shown in Figure 26-4 on the next page, for example, the top row (containing the heading TOTPOP) would be given text treatment, while the ensuing rows would be formatted as numbers.

If you assign Date format to a column, you can also use the drop-down list to specify your preference of six available date formats.

And if you find a column you don't need, you can choose the fourth option button to tell Excel not to import it.

FIGURE 26-4.

You can use the wizard's third dialog box to control the formatting of individual columns. You can also tell Excel not to import particular columns.

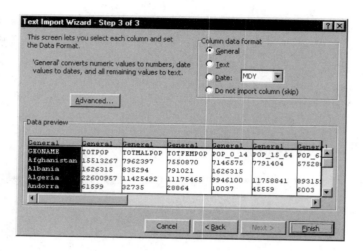

The third dialog box also includes an Advanced button. By clicking this button, you can change the way the wizard handles commas and periods in numeric data. By default, the wizard uses the settings specified in the Regional Settings section of the Control Panel. This default should be fine if the external text file was created in the same country in which you work. If, however, you work in the United States and your text file was created in a country that uses commas for decimal points and periods for thousands separators, you will want the import wizard to interpret your text file using the other country's conventions. You can accomplish this by clicking the Advanced button and making the appropriate selections in the Advanced Text Import Settings dialog box.

Parsing Long Labels into Separate Columns

Occasionally when working with external text data, you may find long text strings that need to be broken into separate columns. This can happen, for example, if you paste text into Excel from the Clipboard (although Excel often parses Clipboard text correctly, under some conditions it does not). To parse such data, simply select it and then choose Text To Columns from the Data menu. You'll find yourself in the hands of the Import Text File Wizard again—although in this case the wizard will be identified as a Convert Text To Columns Wizard. Despite the name change, the wizard works exactly like the one used for importing text files.

★ **TIP**

> **Postal Codes and Credit Card Numbers**
> Some data that looks numeric to Excel is better treated as text. Postal codes with trailing zeroes are one example. Sixteen-digit credit card numbers are another. If you import a sixteen-digit number as a number, Excel will turn the last digit into a zero because it can handle only fifteen digits of precision. To avoid havoc, be sure to import credit card or other long account numbers as text.

After you click the Finish button in the wizard's third dialog box, Excel either opens the parsed text file (if you used the Open command from the File menu) or presents one more dialog box asking where the data should go (if you used the Import Text File command). In this last dialog box, in addition to specifying a worksheet destination, you can click a Properties button to examine or modify the properties of your query. In the property sheet you can, among other things, specify an automatic refresh interval for your query. We'll look at the property sheet for text queries in a moment.

Working with the External Data Toolbar

When you import text data, Excel customarily displays the External Data toolbar. If this toolbar does not appear and you wish it did, right-click any visible toolbar and choose External Data from the list that appears. To banish the toolbar, click its close button.

When you select a cell within a text query, four buttons on the External Data toolbar become active (available): Edit Text Import, Data Range Properties, Refresh Data, and Refresh All. The remaining buttons appear dimmed because they are not applicable to text queries.

Revisiting the Import Text File Wizard

If the wizard didn't do its job to your satisfaction, you don't need to delete the imported data and start over. Instead you can leave the data in place and click the Edit Text Import button on the External Data toolbar. (Alternatively, you can choose Get External Data from the Data menu, then Edit Text Import from the submenu.) After you specify the text file you want to import, the wizard will reappear, allowing you to make appropriate changes. When you click Finish, the incoming data will replace the existing data.

Refreshing a Text Query

To refresh (update) a text query, click the Refresh Data tool on the External Data toolbar, or choose Refresh Data from the Data menu. Either way, Excel first presents a file-selection dialog box, allowing you to specify the file you want to refresh your data from. This step may seem unnecessary if you're simply updating your query with the latest version of the same file you imported in the first place. But it gives you the opportunity to refresh your data with a different file—something that may prove useful if you produce periodic reports from external data, using on each occasion the same format but a different data file.

> If you don't want to be prompted for a filename each time you refresh a text query, clear the Prompt For File Name On Refresh check box on the query's property sheet.

When you refresh a text query, the new data arrives in accordance with settings specified in the query's property sheet. By default, Excel inserts new rows or columns as needed to accommodate new data and deletes rows or columns if they have been removed from the source file. Column widths are adjusted to accommodate the longest entries in each column, and if you have applied your own formatting to any part of your external data range, that formatting is preserved after the refresh.

You can change any of these options by visiting the query's property sheet.

Refreshing All Queries at Once

If you have more than one query on your worksheet, you can refresh them all with a single command. Click the Refresh All tool on the External Data toolbar. Note that this tool does not have a menu equivalent.

> To check the status of a refresh that's taking a long time, click the Refresh Status tool on the External Data toolbar.

Working with the Text Query's Property Sheet

To change refresh properties and other matters pertaining to a text query, open the query's property sheet. As mentioned, you can display the property sheet at the time you create the query (by clicking the Properties button in the last dialog box that appears before your data is imported). Alternatively, you can click the Data Range Properties button on the External Data toolbar or choose Get External Data from the Data menu and then choose Data Range Properties from the submenu. The property sheet for a text query, with default settings in place, is shown in Figure 26-5.

FIGURE 26-5.

The External Data Range Properties dialog box, or property sheet, lets you adjust the way your query is formatted and refreshed. Shown here are the default settings and available options for a text query.

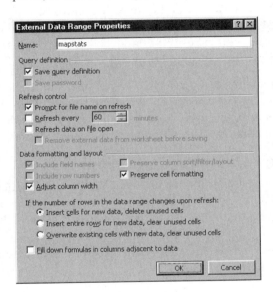

You'll notice that the property sheet shown in Figure 26-5 includes a number of shaded options. That's because Excel uses the same property sheet for text queries, Web queries, and data queries (queries that you create with Microsoft Query). Options unavailable in the text-query context are shaded in Figure 26-5.

Name

The edit box at the top of the property sheet supplies the name by which your external range is known on your Excel worksheet. You can use this name exactly as you would any other range name. For example, you can navigate to an external data range by pressing F5 and choosing the name of the range you want to go to.

By default, this name is the name of the first external file imported via the query. You can choose whatever name pleases you, however, and changing the name does not change Excel's behavior when you refresh the query.

Query Definition

Below the Name edit box is a check box labeled Save Query Definition. If you clear this check box, your imported text data is no longer an external data range. Excel issues a warning to this effect if you clear the check box.

Refresh Control

The first check box in the Refresh Control section of the property sheet is checked by default, causing Excel to prompt for a filename each time you refresh. If you always use this query with the same file, you'll probably want to clear this check box.

The remaining two available check boxes in the Refresh Control section let you specify an automatic refresh interval (every 60 minutes, by default), tell Excel to update the query every time you open the file, or do both. These options are cleared by default.

Data Formatting and Layout

Two formatting options are available for text queries. You can have Excel automatically adjust column widths when you refresh your query, so that columns are always just wide enough to accommodate the longest entry. And you can have Excel preserve any formatting that you apply yourself to cells within an external data range. These options are both on by default.

If the Number of Rows Changes on Refresh

The three options near the bottom of the property sheet determine what Excel does if the size of your external data range changes on refresh. If you choose the first option, (Insert Cells For New Data, Delete Unused Cells), Excel adjusts the size of the external data range without moving cells in the rest of your worksheet. This option is the default.

If you choose the second option (Insert Entire Rows For New Data, Clear Unused Cells), Excel inserts whole new rows into the external data range when necessary, moving cells to the left or right of the external data range downward in the process. If a refresh produces a smaller block of query data, Excel erases the contents of unused cells, without deleting them.

If you choose the third option (Overwrite Existing Cells With New Data, Clear Unused Cells), Excel never inserts new rows. If a refresh produces more data, Excel simply expands the external data range without worrying about whether such expansion may overwrite data below the external data range. If a refresh produces less data, Excel erases the contents of unused cells without deleting them. The advantage of this option is that cells lying outside the external data range are never moved. The disadvantage is that, under some circumstances, an expanding external data range may overwrite existing information.

Extending Formulas Downward in Adjacent Columns

You can perform calculations based on imported text data and have Excel automatically update those calculations when you refresh the query. All you need to do is place your calculations in one or more columns directly adjacent to the external data range and, in the query's property sheet, select the check box labeled Fill Down Formulas In Columns Adjacent To Data.

Be aware when you do this that Excel will assume that all rows of an adjacent column are to be calculations. If you place a constant (a label, for example, or a number that doesn't result from a formula) in one of the rows of a calculation column, that constant will be overwritten by a formula when you refresh.

Note also that Excel assumes that all formulas in an adjacent calculation column should be replications of the first formula that it encounters. For example, suppose your external data range extends from A1 to N100, and at O1 you write the formula =SUM(A1:N1). On refresh, Excel will enter =SUM(A2:N2) at O2, =SUM(A3:N3) at O3, and so on down to O100. If instead you put =SUM(A1:N1) in O1 and =AVERAGE(A2:N2) at O2, Excel will still create a column of sum formulas on refresh, overwriting your average formula in the process.

Using Web Queries to Get Information from the Internet

Web queries let you grab specific information, such as stock quotes, sports scores, or your company's current sales data from the Internet or an intranet. Queries can be set up either to prompt you for the data you want (for a set of stock ticker symbols, for example) or to get the same information every time they're executed. You can try out the Web query facility using a set of sample queries that come with Excel 2000.

When you execute a Web query, the data that lands on your worksheet becomes an external data range. You can have Excel refresh the query automatically at specified time intervals, or you can refresh it manually by simply clicking a toolbar button. Because the information that Excel needs to perform the query is stored invisibly with the external data range, you can refresh a Web query even if you lose the query (*.iqy) file on which it was originally based.

Executing an Existing Web Query

To run an existing Web query—one of the samples supplied with Excel or one that you or someone else has already set up—choose Get External Data from the Data menu and Run Saved Query from the submenu. The Run Query dialog box that appears will initially list all query files saved in the default query-file folder. That is, you may see database and OLAP queries (*.dqy and *.oqy files created with Microsoft Query) as well as Web queries listed there. You can use the Files Of Type drop-down list to limit the display to Web queries, and you can use standard folder navigation tools to find query files stored in other folders.

After you select the query file you want to run and click the Get Data button, Excel presents a dialog box similar to the one shown in Figure 26-6. The only thing you have to do here is tell Excel where you want the incoming Web data to go—by specifying a location on the current worksheet or telling Excel to put the data on a new worksheet. By clicking the Properties button, you can do such additional things as specifying an automatic refresh interval. But you can do that later as well, by opening the query's property sheet. We'll examine the property sheet for Web queries momentarily.

FIGURE 26-6.

Before your Web query runs, you'll need to tell Excel where you want the data displayed.

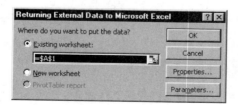

If the query you're running requires information from you at runtime, the Parameters button will be available in the dialog box shown in Figure 26-6. An example might be a stock query that requires you to supply one or more ticker symbols when you run the query. You don't have to click the Parameters button to run the query, but you can. If you do not click Parameters, the query will prompt you for the information it needs. If you do click Parameters, you will see a dialog box similar to the one shown in Figure 26-7.

FIGURE 26-7.

You can supply parameters to a Web query by filling out this dialog box, or you can let the query prompt you when it runs.

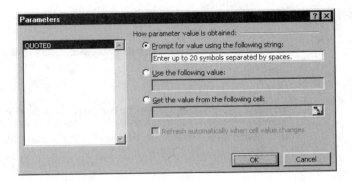

To supply parameters via the Parameters dialog box, either select the second option and type one or more parameters, or select the third option and specify a worksheet range containing your parameters. If you specify a multicell range, Excel parses the range moving across, then down. For example, specifying H2:I4 would be equivalent to typing the value of H2, and then the value of I2, and then the value of H3, and so on.

If you use a worksheet range to feed parameters to your Web query, you can also stipulate that the query be refreshed automatically any time the worksheet range changes. To do this, check the Refresh Automatically When Cell Value Changes check box at the bottom of the Parameters dialog box.

Some queries might include more than one item in the list on the left side of the dialog box. A query designed to get financial planning information, for example, might ask you to supply parameter values for several different variables. In such a case, you would select a variable in the list on the left, read the prompt that appears beside the first option, supply a value or a worksheet range, and then move on to the next item in the list, and so on.

Figure 26-8 on the next page shows an example of data returned by one of the Web queries supplied with Excel 2000. Note that this particular query is set up to return the names of companies as hyperlinks and to provide AutoFiltering capability for the columns. (The AutoFiltering capability is enabled by means of Excel-specific HTML tags at the Web site, not by information stored in the query file.) You can click the hyperlinks to get more information about a company, and you can use the AutoFilter lists to limit your display to particular records. Notice also that Excel displays the External Data toolbar next to the external data range. You can use the toolbar to examine the query's definition, parameter dialog box, or property sheet, or to refresh the query.

FIGURE 26-8.

Data returned by this Web query includes hyperlinks and AutoFilters.

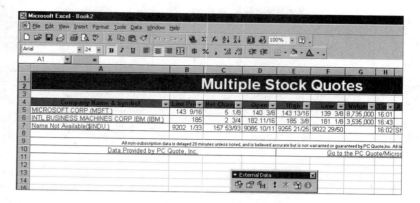

Refreshing a Web Query

Once a Web query has returned data to a worksheet, you can refresh it as often as you like, whether or not you still have the query file (the *.iqy file that told Excel how to execute the query the first time). As we've seen, if you've supplied parameters to the query via a worksheet range, you can set things up so that any change to that worksheet range triggers an update. You can also refresh the query at any time by clicking the Refresh button on the External Data toolbar or choosing Refresh Data from the Data menu. Finally, you can set up the query's property sheet so that the query is updated at regular time intervals, whenever you open the workbook containing the external data range, or in both instances.

Working with the Web Query's Property Sheet

To display the property sheet for your Web query, click the Data Range Properties tool on the External Data toolbar or choose Get External Data from the Data menu and then Data Range Properties from the submenu. (If the Data Range Properties command is not available, you need to select a cell within the external data range.) The property sheet for a Web query looks exactly like the one for a text query (see Figure 26-5 on page 795), except for one change: in place of the text query's Prompt For File Name On Refresh check box, the Web query has a check box labeled Enable Background

Refresh. With this check box selected (its default state), you can continue working in Excel while your query is updated. Normally, you'll want to enable background refresh.

Creating Your Own Web Queries

To create your own Web query, choose Get External Data from the Data menu and then New Web Query from the submenu that appears. (If you've already run a Web query, you first may need to select an empty section of your worksheet.) You'll see the dialog box shown in Figure 26-9.

FIGURE 26-9.

A new dialog box in Excel 2000 simplifies the task of creating and editing Web queries.

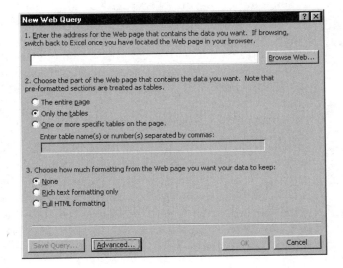

Creating a Web query entails three steps, marked by the numbers 1, 2, and 3 in the dialog box. First you supply the URL of the Web page from which you want to extract data. Second, you indicate whether you want to download all text from that Web page or only particular items. Third, you specify how much of the Web page's own formatting you want to preserve. Once you have done these things, you have the option of saving your query in an *.iqy file.

Specifying the URL

The simplest way to specify the URL is to click the Browse Web button and move to the Web page in your browser. When you have arrived at the page you want to download, return to Excel. The edit field at the top of the dialog box will be filled in for you.

Database and List Management

Indicating What Data You Want to Retrieve

You have three options regarding the data you want to retrieve. You can download all textual elements (choose the first option), all tables and preformatted sections (the second option), or only particular tables or preformatted sections (the third option). A preformatted section is a section of a Web page that has been formatted with tabs and spaces, instead of HTML tags, making it suitable for display in another program, such as Excel.

To retrieve only specific tables or preformatted sections, you must identify them by their names or numbers. To do this, you might find it helpful to display the Web page's HTML code. In Microsoft Internet Explorer, right-click the page and choose View Source from the context menu that appears. The source HTML code appears in Notepad or another text editor. You can then use the editor's search commands to find tables and preformatted sections. Tables are enclosed between the HTML tags <TABLE> and </TABLE>. Preformatted sections are enclosed between the tags <PRE> and </PRE>. If you're having difficulty identifying the sections you need by name or number, you might need to contact the owner or author of the Web page.

By default, Excel breaks preformatted text into separate columns on your worksheet, using delimiting characters embedded in the text. Also by default, Excel treats two or more consecutive delimiters as single delimiters. You can override these defaults by clicking the Advanced button on the New Web Query dialog box and entering information in the ensuing dialog box.

In the Advanced dialog box, you can also disable date recognition so that numbers within preformatted text are imported strictly as numbers, even if Excel would otherwise parse them into dates. You might need to exercise this option if you are downloading part numbers or other items from the Web that Excel is incorrectly handling as dates.

Formatting Options

You can format incoming Web query data in three ways: minimally, with rich text formatting (RTF), or with full HTML formatting. If you choose the first option, None, Excel breaks tabular data into worksheet columns but ignores fonts, colors, and other details. If you choose Rich Text Formatting Only, you get colors and fonts, but other elements (such as hyperlinks) are not imported. For the most complete replication of your Web page's formatting, choose Full HTML Formatting. (Without full HTML formatting, for example, the hyperlinks in figure 26-8 on page 800 would have been imported as plain text and AutoFiltering would not have been enabled.)

Creating Parameter-Based Queries

To create a query that prompts the user for one or more parameters, you need some knowledge of HTML, which is beyond the scope of this book.

To get more information, run the query Get More Web Queries, which is included with Excel. On the Web page that is retrieved by this query, look for a hyperlink marked Click Here To Get The Microsoft Excel Web Connectivity Kit. Clicking this link takes you to a site from which you can download details about encoding Web queries.

Saving Your Query

To save your query as an *.iqy file, click Save Query and enter information in the ensuing dialog box. By default, your query is stored in the folder C:\Windows\Application Data\Microsoft\Queries.

Saving your query file enables you and others to reuse it. If you omit this step, you will still get your query data on the current worksheet, and you will be able to refresh the query from that worksheet. But it will not be available in other contexts.

Editing a Query File

Query files are stored as plain text, as shown in Figure 26-10, which means that you can edit them in Notepad, WordPad, or any other plain-text editor. You can open a query file easily in Notepad by right-clicking its name in a Windows Explorer window and choosing Edit With Notepad from the context menu that appears.

FIGURE 26-10.

A Web query file is stored as plain text, suitable for editing in Notepad.

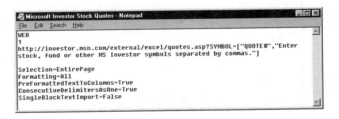

If your query does not include parameter statements, you can edit it more easily by selecting any cell within the range of data downloaded by the query and then clicking the Edit Query tool on the External Data toolbar. (Alternatively, choose Get External Data from the Data menu and then Edit Query from the submenu.) This action takes you back to the dialog box in which you created the query, allowing you to make the necessary changes.

VI

Database and List Management

Using Microsoft Query to Create Database Queries

Microsoft Query lets you import selected records from external data sources and create reusable query files. By default, Query is installed the first time you use Query. If it was not included when Excel or Microsoft Office was installed on your system, you'll need to rerun the Office or Excel setup program. Click the plus sign icon next to the heading Office Tools, and then click the icon next to Microsoft Query to select the type of installation you want.

Microsoft Query Terminology	
Data source	A stored set of information that allows Excel to connect to an external database.
Field/column	Equivalent to a column in an Excel list. (Query uses the terms *field* and *column* interchangeably.)
Field name	Equivalent to a column heading in an Excel list.
Inner join	A connection between fields in two tables that selects only the records that have the same value in the joined fields.
OLAP	Online analytical processing, a technology that has been optimized for querying and reporting, instead of processing transactions. OLAP data is structured hierarchically and stored in "cubes" instead of tables. Query can supply selected OLAP data to an Excel PivotTable.
Outer join	A connection between fields in two tables that selects all the records in one table, whether or not there are matching records in the other table.
Query	A stored, reusable specification for getting data.
Record	Equivalent to a row in an Excel list.
Result set	The records that meet your current criteria. Query displays the result set in the data pane.
SQL	Structured Query Language, the language used by Query to get information from an external database.
Table	A collection of information on a single topic, organized into fields and records. Equivalent to a list in Excel.

You can use Query with any data source for which a suitable ODBC, OLE-DB, or OLAP driver is installed. Excel provides drivers for the following data sources:

- Microsoft Access 2000

- Microsoft SQL Server

- Microsoft FoxPro

- dBASE

- Excel

- Oracle

- Paradox

- Text files

- Microsoft SQL Server OLAP Services

For additional drivers that might be available from Microsoft (but not shipped with Excel), see the Excel and Office readme files. Other drivers not provided by Microsoft might be available from database or OLAP vendors.

With the exception of data from OLAP sources, data returned by Query can arrive on your worksheet in either of two formats: as an Excel table or as a PivotTable report. (Data from an OLAP source can arrive only as a PivotTable.) *We'll look at the use of Query in conjunction with PivotTables in Chapter 27, "Using PivotTables."* For now we'll focus on using Query to supply data to an Excel table.

When to Use Query, When to Use the Query Wizard

For simple queries, you can take advantage of the Query Wizard, an interface to Query itself. The wizard makes it easy for you to specify selection criteria and sort preferences and not have to learn a new program. Using the wizard is an ideal way to perform simple queries, but it doesn't provide access to all of Query's power. You'll need to work directly with Query if your query uses criteria involving calculations (other than simple comparisons) or if you want to create a query that prompts the user for one or more parameters when run. Query, but not the Query Wizard, also lets you do the following: rename columns, filter out fields that are not included in the result set, limit the result set to unique entries, and perform aggregate calculations.

Specifying a Data Source

Whether you use the Query Wizard or interact directly with Microsoft Query, the first step in creating a new query is to specify a data source. A data source is a set of information, stored in a file with the extension .dsn, that tells Query how to connect to an external database. The .dsn file can include the name and location of the database server, the name of the driver used to connect to the database, logon information, and various other details. Like Web query (.iqy) and data query (.dqy) files, a .dsn file (see Figure 26-11) is plain text, suitable for viewing and editing in Notepad or WordPad.

FIGURE 26-11.

A data source (.dsn) file consists of several lines of plain text that specify information Query needs in order to connect to the external data source.

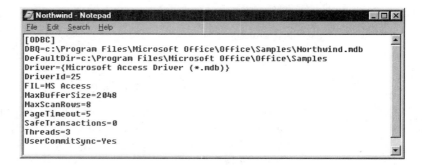

To specify a data source, choose Get External Data from the Data menu, and then New Database Query from the submenu that appears. You'll see the Choose Data Source dialog box, shown in Figure 26-12.

FIGURE 26-12.

To specify a data source, choose one of the entries that appear in this dialog box or double-click <New Data Source>.

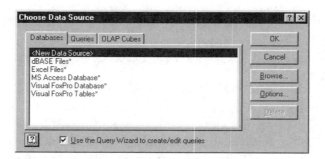

The dialog box initially displays all existing data sources whose .dsn files are stored in default folders, plus (optionally) any available registry DSNs. A registry DSN is a data source created with a version of Query prior to Query 97. Registry DSNs are recorded in your Windows registry, not in a disk file, and can be used only on your own system. In the Choose Data Source dialog box, Query displays an asterisk after the name of each registry DSN. If you don't want to see the names of registry DSNs, click the Options button and then clear the check box at the bottom of the Data Source Options dialog box.

In the Data Source Options dialog box, you can also indicate in which default folders you want Query to search for .dsn files. If you regularly use data sources whose .dsn files reside on a server, you can add that server to the default list by clicking the Options button in the Choose Data Source dialog box, and then browsing to the server in the Data Source Options dialog box. When you've found the server, click the Add button. To specify a .dsn location without adding it to the default list, click the Browse button in the Choose Data Source dialog box.

To connect to an existing data source, select it in the list of available .dsn files. Then either select or clear the check box at the bottom of the Choose Data Source dialog box (see Figure 26-12 on the previous page), depending on whether or not you want to use the Query Wizard.

Defining a New Data Source

To define a new data source, follow these steps:

1 Double-click the <New Data Source> entry at the top of the Choose Data Source dialog box. The dialog box shown in Figure 26-13 appears.

FIGURE 26-13.

Define a new data source in the Create New Data Source dialog box.

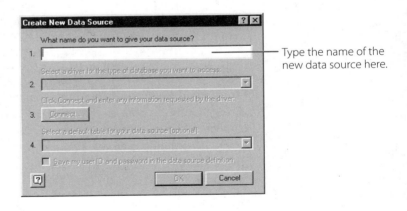

Type the name of the new data source here.

As the numbers along the left side of this dialog box suggest, creating the new data source entails a sequence of steps. Each numbered step becomes available only when the preceding step has been completed. The fourth step is optional.

2   Begin by supplying a name for your new data source. The name can be short or long. It does not have to be the name of the database file or table you plan to work with.

3   After naming your new data source, click the arrow at the right side of step 2 to display a drop-down list of installed drivers, as shown in Figure 26-14.

FIGURE 26-14.

Select the driver for the type of database you want to query.

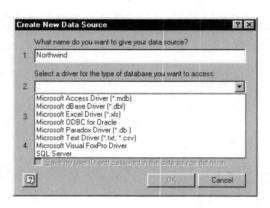

4   After selecting the appropriate driver, click the Connect button. A new dialog box appears, in which you will be asked to supply information appropriate for the selected driver. Depending on what driver you selected, you might be asked to enter a logon name and password, the version of the driver you need (for example, dBASE II, III, or IV), and the location of the database files. If you're not sure what is required, click the Help button.

5   After entering information in the Connect dialog box, click OK. Query returns you to the Create New Data Source dialog box shown in Figure 26-13 on the previous page. If your data source consists of multiple tables, you can then select a default table from the drop-down list in step 4 of this dialog box. This step is optional.

6   After entering all of the required information, click OK one more time. Query returns you to the Choose Data Source dialog box shown in Figure 26-12 on page 806, and the new data source appears in the list box.

7 Select the data source you want, select or clear the check box about using the Query Wizard, and then click OK to proceed.

Using the Query Wizard

The Query Wizard makes selecting and sorting database records a simple four-step process. The steps are as follows:

1 Select tables and fields (columns).

2 Supply filter criteria.

3 Sort records.

4 Name and save the query.

All steps except the first are optional, and after you complete this sequence, you can either return your external data directly to Excel or send it first to Query for additional processing.

Choosing Tables and Fields

In step 1, you'll see a dialog box similar to the one shown in Figure 26-15.

FIGURE 26-15.

Use the first Query Wizard dialog box to select tables and fields.

Table names

Field names

Click a field name and then click here to see a sample of the selected field.

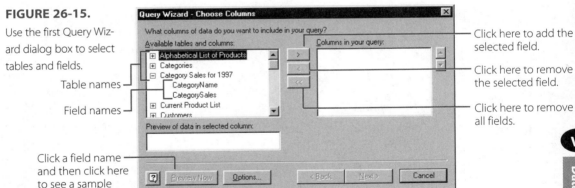

Click here to add the selected field.

Click here to remove the selected field.

Click here to remove all fields.

The list on the left side of the first Query Wizard dialog box shows available tables and the fields those tables contain. The list on the right side, initially empty, shows the fields that will be included in your query. Use the arrows in the middle of the dialog box to copy selected tables and fields from the left list to the right list.

A plus sign in the left list box indicates a table name that can be expanded to reveal fields within the table. A minus sign indicates a table that can be collapsed so the table's fields are not visible.

To include all fields from a table in your query, simply select the table name
and then click the right arrow.

Filtering Records

After filling out the Wizard's first dialog box, click Next to arrive at
step 2, the dialog box shown in Figure 26-16.

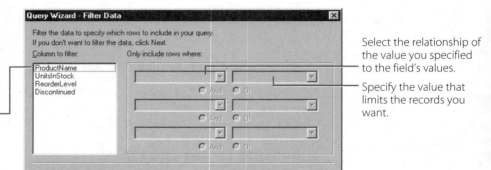

FIGURE 26-16.

Filters select the
records that meet
criteria you specify.

Select the field
to filter here.

Select the relationship of
the value you specified
to the field's values.

Specify the value that
limits the records you
want.

Here you can specify one or more filter criteria. This is an optional
step; if you skip it, Query returns all records from the selected tables
to your Excel worksheet.

A filter criterion has three components: a field name, a relationship,
and a value. For example, if you want to see only those records in
which the Discontinued field is 0, your field name would be Discontinued, the relationship would be "equals," and the value would be 0.

The list at the left side of the dialog box shown in Figure 26-16 contains the names of all the fields on which you can filter. The name of
the field you selected appears above the list in the center of the dialog
box. Opening the list reveals all the available relationships. After
you select a relationship, the list on the right side of the dialog box
becomes available. Opening that list reveals the values for the
selected field of all records in your database. You can select a value
from this list or type directly in the edit field.

To remove a filter criterion, open the relationship list and then choose the
blank entry at the top of the list.

As you can see in the following list, Query offers a rich set of relationships that you can use in your filter criteria:

- Equals
- Does not equal
- Is greater than
- Is greater than or equal to
- Is less than
- Is less than or equal to
- Begins with
- Does not begin with

- Ends with
- Does not end with
- Contains
- Does not contain
- Like
- Not like
- Is null
- Is not null

When you work directly with Query (that is, without using the Wizard), the following additional relationships are available:

- Is one of
- Is not one of

- Is between
- Is not between

These additional relationships are designed to work with two or more values. For example, *Is between* and *Is not between* both require two values. *Is one of* and *Is not one of* can use a list of values.

Specifying More Than One Filter Criterion

To enter a second filter criterion, begin by clicking the And or the Or button below your first criterion. If you click And, your filter admits only those records that satisfy both your first and second criteria. If you click Or, the filter admits all records that satisfy either criterion. You may specify as many criteria as you want.

Note that when you specify a first criterion and click And, the Query Wizard retains your first criterion but removes it from view. Your second criterion then appears on the top line of the dialog box, where you just finished entering your first criterion. You might be disconcerted not to see both criteria at once in the dialog box, but the Query Wizard will give you the option of inspecting your entire filter specification before returning any data to Excel. To do this, simply choose View Data In Microsoft Query in the Query Wizard's fourth dialog box, described in the section after next.

Sorting Records

After entering all of your filter criteria, click Next to move to the wizard's third step, the dialog box shown in Figure 26-17.

FIGURE 26-17.

Use the Sort Order step to arrange the records that are returned to Excel.

Select the field(s) to sort on.

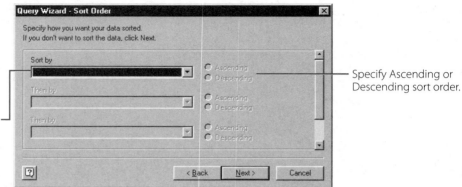

Specify Ascending or Descending sort order.

Like the filter step, the sort step is optional. If you omit it, Query returns records in the order in which they're stored in your external database file.

To sort, begin by clicking the Sort By list. There you'll find the name of each field in the table you're querying. Select a field, then click the Ascending or Descending option to the right of the list. To sort on a second field, repeat this process on the next line of the dialog box. You can sort on as many fields as you want.

Naming and Saving the Query

After sorting, click Next to get to the Query Wizard's fourth and final dialog box, shown in Figure 26-18.

FIGURE 26-18.

Indicate whether you want to return the data to Excel or continue by working directly in Query.

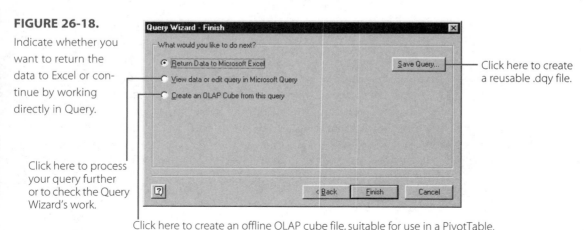

Click here to create a reusable .dqy file.

Click here to process your query further or to check the Query Wizard's work.

Click here to create an offline OLAP cube file, suitable for use in a PivotTable.

To store your query specification in a reusable .dqy file, click the Save Query button and supply a filename. This step is optional. If you do not save the query, you will still be able to refresh it from the external data range that it creates on your Excel worksheet. You will not be able to use it again on another worksheet, however.

Returning Your Data to Excel or to Query

If you're satisfied that the Query Wizard has fetched exactly the data you're looking for, choose the Return Data To Microsoft Excel option in the dialog box shown in Figure 26-18 and then click the Finish button. Alternatively, if you'd like to inspect the query definition or manipulate it further, choose the View Data In Microsoft Query option before clicking Finish. *For more information about what you can do with the query definition in Query, see "Working Directly with Microsoft Query" below.*

To create an offline OLAP cube file from your query, suitable for use in a PivotTable report, choose the Create An OLAP Cube From This Query option. You will then be taken to the OLAP Cube Wizard.

When you return your data to Excel, Excel displays a dialog box similar to the one shown in Figure 26-6, on page 798. As with text queries and Web queries, you can inspect the new data query's property sheet before creating an external data range on your worksheet. But you can always return to the property sheet later by clicking Data Range Properties on the External Data toolbar.

Working Directly with Microsoft Query

To create your query directly in Microsoft Query, without the help of the wizard, follow these steps:

1   Choose Get External Data from the Data menu.

2   Choose New Database Query from the submenu.

3   Specify the data source you want to use.

4   Make sure the Use The Query Wizard check box is cleared.

5   Click OK.

 SEE ALSO

For more information about working with multiple tables, see "Joining Tables," page 831.

These steps launch Query, and Query displays the Add Tables dialog box. To make a table available to your query, select the table and then click Add. You can select as many tables from the list as you want.

When you have finished selecting tables, click the Close button. You can now work with your query window, which looks similar to Figure 26-19.

FIGURE 26-19.

A new query window includes a table pane and a data pane. When you specify filter criteria, the window includes a criteria pane as well.

Field list

Field box

Data pane

Scrolling buttons

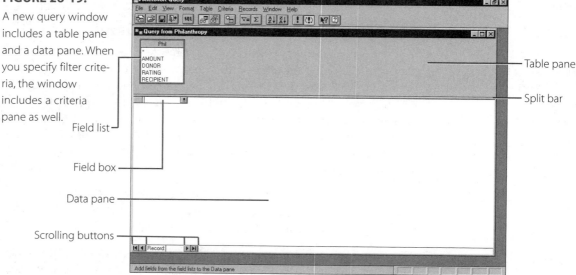

Table pane

Split bar

Initially, the query window is divided into two sections. A table pane occupies the top section, and a data pane occupies the bottom section. As you'll see, your query window can include a criteria pane as well. Notice that you can have more than one query window open at a time.

TIP

While you are working in Query, you can add tables by clicking the Add Tables button on Query's toolbar.

In the table pane, you'll see one or more field lists labeled with the name of the table you're working with and the fields each table contains. In our example, we have just one table: a dBASE file called Phil.dbf. As Figure 26-19 shows, the Phil.dbf table contains four fields: AMOUNT, DONOR, RATING, and RECIPIENT.

The data pane is where Query displays the records that meet the specified criteria. These records are known as the result set. Initially, the data pane displays one empty field list box with a drop-down arrow beside it. As you add fields to your data pane, Query continues to display an empty list box so you can add more fields to the query window.

⭐ **TIP**

Resizing the Panes

You can change the size of the panes in a query window by dragging the split bar that divides the table pane from the data pane. If your table has relatively few fields, for example, you can increase the default size of the data pane without covering up information in the table pane. You can then see more records in the data pane.

As shown in Figure 26-20, Microsoft Query has its own toolbar, which you can use to perform queries and return data to your Excel worksheet.

FIGURE 26-20.

Use the Microsoft Query toolbar as you query and retrieve data.

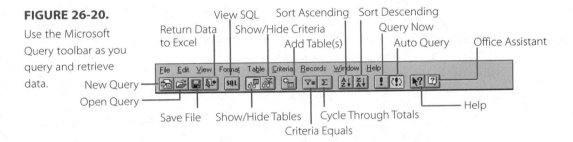

Automatic Query vs. Manual Query

By default, Microsoft Query updates the result set every time you add a new field to the data pane, rearrange the order of the existing fields in the data pane, change a sort specification, or change a filter criterion. In response to these actions, Query creates a new SQL statement and executes that statement against your data source. (You can see the SQL code by clicking the View SQL button on the toolbar.) If your data source is particularly large or network traffic is high, Automatic Query can cause annoying delays. You can turn off the Automatic Query feature so that Query executes the current SQL statement only when you ask it to.

You can determine whether Automatic Query is on by checking whether the Auto Query button on the toolbar is selected or not. You can turn the feature off by clicking the Auto Query button or by choosing the Automatic Query command from the Records menu.

To execute the current query while you're in manual query mode, click the Query Now button or choose the Query Now command from the Records menu.

V

Database and List Management

Choosing and Arranging Fields

You can ask Microsoft Query to display records from your table using some or all of the fields in the table, and you can arrange the fields in any order you want. You bring a field into view in one of four ways:

- In the table pane, double-click the name of the field you want.

- Drag the name of the field you want from the table pane to the empty list box at the top of the data pane.

- Click the arrow beside the data pane's empty list box and select the field you want.

- Choose the Add Column command from the Records menu and select the name of the field you want. You can add as many columns as you want from this dialog box. When you are finished, click close.

Adding All Fields to the Data Pane

To add all of your table's fields to the data pane, drag the asterisk in the table pane's Field list box to the data pane's empty field list box. (You can also double-click the asterisk, or choose the Add Column command and then select the asterisk.) Query displays the fields in the order they appear in your database field, which might or might not reflect their alphabetical order in the field list. You can rearrange the fields after they appear in the data pane.

> **Hiding the Table Pane**
>
> After you have finished adding fields to the data pane, you might not need to see the table pane anymore. You can hide the table pane by clicking the Show/Hide Tables button on the Query toolbar. When you want to redisplay the table pane, simply click the Show/Hide Tables button again.

Rearranging Fields

You can move fields in the data pane by dragging them with the mouse. Click a field heading to select the field, and then drag the field to its new position.

Removing Fields

If you decide you no longer need a particular field, you can remove it from the data pane. Simply select the field heading and then press the Delete key.

Resizing and Hiding Columns

You can change the width of the column in which a field is displayed by employing the same techniques you use to resize a column in Excel. Simply drag the column border to the right of the field heading. For more precise positioning, you can choose the Column Width command on the Format menu.

To make a column just wide enough to accommodate its longest entry, double-click the border to the right of the column heading. Alternatively, select the column, choose the Column Width command from the Format menu, and then click the Best Fit button. Note that in adjusting column widths, the Best Fit command takes into account only those records currently displayed in the result set, not all the records in your database. When the result set changes, you might need to reuse Best Fit.

To hide a column, drag it to zero width or select the column and choose the Hide Columns command from the Format menu. To restore a hidden column to view, choose the Show Columns command from the Format menu.

Renaming Columns

By default, Microsoft Query uses the names of your fields as field headings. If these field names are short and cryptic, you might want to supply different headings.

First, select the column you want to change and choose the Edit Column command from the Records menu (or double-click the field heading). Then type a new name in the Column Heading edit box and then click OK. (Note that this action has no effect on the underlying database; it simply supplies a different heading for display purposes.)

Navigating the Data Pane

Figure 26-21 on the next page shows all four fields of the first 25 records in the Phil.dbf table. You can use the vertical and horizontal scroll bars to make additional records and fields visible. Note, however, that scrolling with the scroll bar does not change the selection; it only moves different records into view.

Some of Excel's navigation keystrokes also work in Query. For example, you can move directly to the last record in your database by pressing Ctrl+End or to the first record by pressing Ctrl+Home. The End key used in combination with the Up or Down arrow key does not work in Query, however.

FIGURE 26-21.

You can use the data pane's vertical scroll bar to move between records.

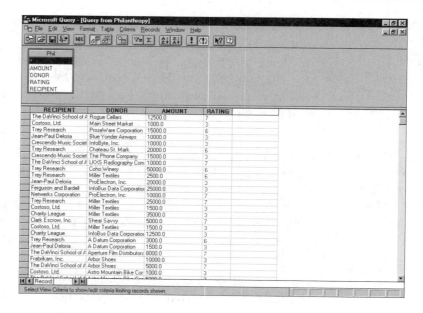

Sorting the Result Set

Microsoft Query initially displays records in the order in which they're stored in the underlying database. You can use sorting commands to change their order in the result set without affecting the order of the underlying database. You can sort by using the Sort command or by clicking buttons on the Query toolbar.

Using the Sort Command

Suppose you want to see the result set shown in Figure 26-21 in ascending order by donor. Start by choosing the Sort command from the Records menu to display the Sort dialog box shown in Figure 26-22.

FIGURE 26-22.

The Sort dialog box displays the current sort order and lets you add fields from a drop-down list.

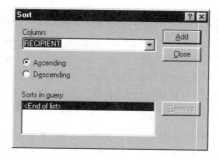

The Sorts In Query list in the Sort dialog box indicates what sort specification, if any, is currently in effect. In Figure 26-22, the Sorts In Query list is empty except for the [End Of List] entry, indicating that the result set is currently unsorted. The Column drop-down list at the top of the Sort dialog box lists all the table fields available for sorting.

To sort the result set by donor, select DONOR from the Column list and then click the Add button. Query adds the DONOR heading to the Sorts In Query list, preceding it with (Asc) to indicate that you've sorted on the DONOR column in ascending order. If Automatic Query has been selected, Query sorts the result set by donor but leaves the Sort dialog box open in case you want to specify another sort field. Figure 26-23 shows the dialog box and the result set after this initial sort.

FIGURE 26-23.

After you add a field to the sort specification, Query resorts the result set and updates the Sort dialog box, leaving the dialog box open in case you want to do additional sorting.

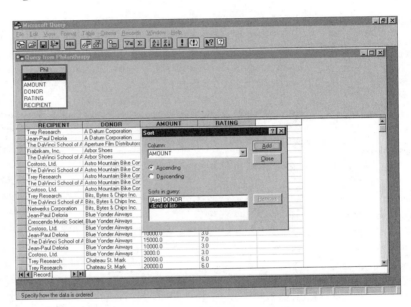

Now suppose you want to sort the records with identical DONOR fields by the values in their AMOUNT fields, with the highest amounts at the top of each group. To sort the records in this order, specify two sort fields: DONOR and AMOUNT. DONOR will be the primary sort field because you want Query to sort the entire table by the DONOR field. AMOUNT will be the secondary field because you want Query to sort AMOUNT values only within groups of matching DONOR fields. If you wanted to sort matching AMOUNT values by another field, that additional field would be a tertiary, or third sort field.

You can sort on as many fields as you like in Query. Simply add fields to the Sorts In Query list in descending order of precedence. That is, add your primary sort field first, then your secondary sort field, and so on.

In our example, we have already sorted on the DONOR field. To sort on the AMOUNT field, add this field to the Sorts In Query list after the DONOR field. To add the AMOUNT field after the DONOR field, do the following:

1 With the Sort dialog box shown in Figure 26-23 on the previous page still open, select <End Of List> in the Sorts In Query list.

2 Select AMOUNT from the Column drop-down list and then select the Descending option.

3 Click the Add button.

Query adds (Desc) next to the AMOUNT field in the Sorts In Query list to indicate that you've sorted on the column in descending order, and then resorts the result set. Figure 26-24 shows how the Sort dialog box and result set look after this secondary sort.

FIGURE 26-24.

This list was first sorted by DONOR and then by AMOUNT. Notice that the primary sort field appears first in the Sorts In Query list box, followed by the secondary field, and so on.

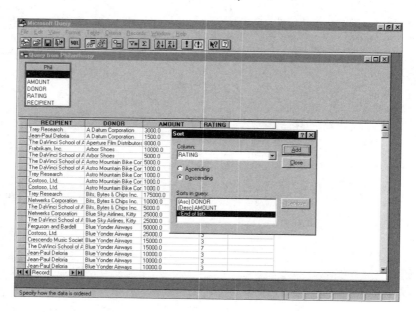

Rearranging Sort Fields

When you click the Add button in the Sort dialog box, Query adds your new sort field above the currently selected field in the Sorts In Query list. If you accidentally add a sort field in the wrong order, select the field and click the Remove button. Then add the field in the correct position.

Sorting with the Toolbar

Sorting with the buttons on the toolbar is a little simpler than using the Sort command, although you don't get the benefit of seeing the names of any fields on which the result set is already sorted. To sort our example table first on DONOR (in ascending order) and then on AMOUNT (in descending order), do the following:

1   Select any cell in the DONOR field.

2   Click the Sort Ascending button. (See Figure 26-20 on page 815.)

3   Select any cell in the AMOUNT field.

4   Hold down Ctrl and click the Sort Descending button.

When you click a sort button without holding down Ctrl, Query replaces any current sort specification with your new sort. In order words, it applies your new sort to the records as they are ordered in the underlying database. When you hold down Ctrl and click a sort button, Query sorts the records on the new sort field after it sorts them on the previous sort fields.

Filtering the Result Set

Microsoft Query provides a variety of methods by which you can filter the result set so that it lists only the records you're actually interested in. As with the Query Wizard, you create a filter by specifying one or more criteria—conditions that particular fields must meet.

Exact-Match Criteria

The simplest kind of criterion is one in which you stipulate that a field exactly equal some value. Query makes it extremely easy to create such criteria:

1   Select a field value that meets your exact-match criterion.

2   Click the Criteria Equals button on the toolbar (see Figure 26-20 on page 815).

For example, suppose you want to filter the result set shown in Figure 26-21 on page 818 so that it displays only those records in which the RATING field equals 7. To do this, select any record in the RATING field that already equals 7 (such as the first record in Figure 26-21 on page 818) and click the Criteria Equals button. Query responds by displaying the criteria pane (if it's not already displayed) and applying the new filter to the table, as shown in Figure 26-25 on the next page.

FIGURE 26-25.

When we clicked the Criteria Equals button, Query displayed the criteria pane and applied the filter to the result set.

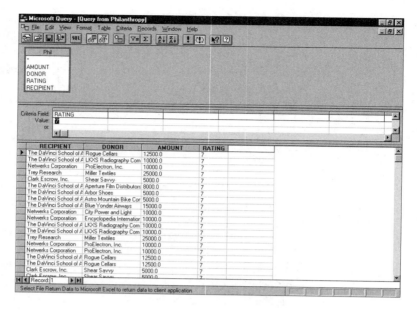

TIP

Switching Matches

After you use the Criteria Equals button to specify an exact-match criterion, you can quickly switch to a different match. Simply type a new value in the criteria pane to replace the current one. For example, to change the result set shown in Figure 26-25 to show records with RATING values of 6, simply type 6 in the criteria pane where 7 now appears. Then press Enter.

SEE ALSO

For more information on Excel's Advanced Filter command, see "The Advanced Filter Command," page 766.

If you've ever used Excel's Advanced Filter command, you'll notice that the criteria pane in the query window looks a lot like a criteria range in an Excel worksheet. Field headings appear in the top row, and criteria are stated in subsequent rows. Although you can enter new criteria or edit existing criteria directly in the criteria pane, it's not necessary, because Query's menu commands take care of entering information in the criteria pane for you. In fact, you don't need to have the criteria pane on your screen at all.

TIP

Hiding Panes

To make more room for the result set, you can remove the criteria pane by clicking the Show/Hide Criteria button on the Query toolbar or by choosing the Criteria command from the View menu.

Using Multiple Exact-Match Criteria

Suppose you want to see records in which the DONOR field is Shear Savvy and the RATING field is 7. You can do this by simply adding another exact-match criterion, as follows:

1 Select a cell in which the DONOR field is Shear Savvy. (The fifth record in Figure 26-25 on the previous page will do.)

2 Click the Criteria Equals button on the toolbar.

As Figure 26-26 shows, Query adds the new criterion to the criteria pane, placing it in the same row as the first criterion. As in an Advanced Filter criteria range in Excel, criteria that appear in the same row of the criteria pane are joined by AND; the filter admits only those records that meet both criteria.

FIGURE 26-26.

When you use the Criteria Equals button in two separate fields, Query's filter admits only those records that meet both criteria.

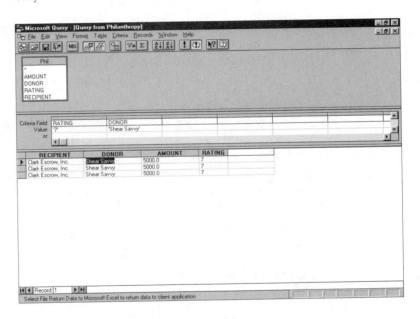

To see records in which the RATING field equals *either* 7 or 6, we can do the following, starting with the result set shown in Figure 26-26:

1 Turn off the Automatic Query feature (if it's on) by clicking the Auto Query button or by choosing the Automatic Query command from the Records menu.

2 In the RATING field, select a cell that equals 7 and then click the Criteria Equals button.

3 In the RATING field, select a record that equals 6 and then click the Criteria Equals button.

4 Turn on Automatic Query by clicking the Auto Query button or by choosing Automatic Query from the Records menu.

When you use the Criteria Equals button to add two or more values from the same field to the criteria pane, Query creates a filter in which the criteria are joined by OR; the filter admits records that meet either criterion.

Using Menu Commands to Specify Exact-Match Criteria

If you prefer to use menu commands rather than toolbar buttons, you can specify an exact-match criterion as follows:

1 Select a field value that meets your specification.

2 Choose the Add Criteria command from the Criteria menu and when the Add Criteria dialog box appears, click the Add button. (The Add Criteria dialog box should already contain the correct settings when you choose the Add Criteria command.)

Removing Criteria

The simplest way to remove a filter criterion is to select the criterion's heading in the criteria pane and press the Delete key. Then assuming that the Automatic Query feature is turned on, select something else— another cell in the criteria pane or a cell in the result set, for example. As soon as you move the selection away from the deleted criterion's location, Query updates the result set.

To remove all criteria and restore the unfiltered result set, choose the Remove All Criteria command from the Criteria menu.

Comparison Criteria

To specify a comparison criterion, follow these steps:

1 Choose the Add Criteria command from the Criteria menu. You'll see a dialog box similar to the one shown in Figure 26-27.

FIGURE 26-27.

The Add Criteria dialog box lets you select fields, comparison operators, and values.

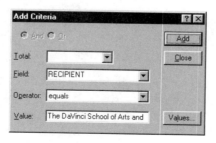

In the Add Criteria dialog box, you can construct your criteria by selecting options from various drop-down lists. For example, you can select a field from the Field list and then select an operator, such as *Is Greater Than*, from the Operator list. You can also enter a value in the Value text box by typing it or by clicking the Values button and selecting the value you want.

When you click the Values button, a list containing all the entries for the selected field is displayed. In many cases, however, it's easier to type the value rather than select it. For example, to filter out amounts greater than 100,000 simply select *Is Greater Than* from the Operator list and then type *100000* in the Value text box.

 NOTE

For comparison criteria that don't involve computed fields, be sure the Total drop-down list in the Add Criteria dialog box is blank, as it is in Figure 26-27. *(We'll discuss the Total list later in the chapter, in "Filtering on Calculated Fields," page 830.)*

2 After you complete the Add Criteria dialog box, click the Add button.

Query responds by creating the appropriate entry in the criteria pane and if the Automatic Query feature is on, executing the new query. The Add Criteria dialog box remains open so you can specify more criteria.

3 To add another criterion, select the And option or the Or option at the top of the dialog box and then enter the information as before.

4 When you've finished entering criteria, click the Close button.

The And and Or Options

A criterion added with the And option selected appears in the criteria pane on the same row as the previously added criterion. When you add a criterion using the Or option, the value of the new criterion appears on a new row.

As mentioned earlier, when Query evaluates the criteria pane, it treats all entries sharing a common row as a single criterion. As a result, the filter admits only those records that satisfy every entry on the row. When criteria appear on separate rows, the filter admits all records that satisfy the entries on any row. Note that Query interprets the information in a criteria pane in exactly the same way that Excel's Advanced Filter command interprets the information in a criteria range.

V

Database and List Management

If an entry in the criteria pane is not arranged the way you want it, you can delete the entry and use the Add Criteria dialog box to reenter it, or you can use the Cut and Paste commands on the Edit menu to position the entry on the row where it belongs.

Filtering on Fields That Are Not in the Result Set

Your filter criteria can be based on fields that are not currently displayed in the result set. For example, if you want a list of all the recipients from the Phil table who were given donations greater than $50,000, you can do the following:

1 Show only the RECIPIENT field in the data pane.

2 Choose the Add Criteria command from the Criteria menu.

3 When the Add Criteria dialog box appears, select AMOUNT from the Field drop-down list, select Is Greater Than from the Operator list, and type *50000* in the Value text box.

When you click the Add button, Query lists the recipient of each donation greater than $50,000, displaying one record for each donation.

Limiting the Result Set to Unique Entries

In a case like the preceding example, you would probably rather see each recipient's name listed only once, no matter how many donations greater than $50,000 that recipient received. To limit the result set, choose Query Properties from the View menu. In the dialog box shown in Figure 26-28, select Unique Values Only. You can make this selection before or after you create your filter.

FIGURE 26-28.

You can restrict your result set to unique entries.

Performing Aggregate Calculations

You can analyze your result thoroughly after you get into your Excel worksheet. If you prefer, however, you can have Microsoft Query do some of the calculating for you. With Query, you can make *aggregate calculations* the basis of filtering criteria—as you'll see in a moment. First we'll consider some details about how to perform the calculations.

Query refers to all calculations as *totals*, although summing values is only one of the functions Query has to offer. The aggregate functions that are common to all database drivers (for example, dBase or MS Access Database File) are AVG (Average), COUNT, MIN (Minimum), and MAX (Maximum). Your driver may support additional functions as well.

Using the Totals Button

One way to perform aggregate calculations is by clicking the Cycle Through Totals button on the Query toolbar. (See Figure 26-20 on page 815.) For example, to find the total amount of all donations recorded in the Phil table, do this:

1   Display only the AMOUNT field in the data pane and remove all filtering criteria from the criteria pane.

2   Select the AMOUNT column and then click the Cycle Through Totals button.

As shown in Figure 26-29, Query then displays the donation total in the data pane.

FIGURE 26-29.

We used the Cycle Through Totals button on the Query toolbar to calculate the sum of all donations recorded in the table.

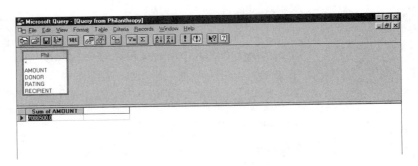

Cycling Through the Functions

In the previous example, clicking the Cycle Through Totals button a second time changes the aggregate function from SUM to AVG, and the amount shown in the data pane then changes to reflect the average of all the donations recorded in the Phil table. Successive clicks on the Cycle Through Totals button result in the count of all donations, the minimum donation, and the maximum donation, as the button cycles through the other aggregate functions. One more click returns the result set to its original, unaggregated state.

 NOTE

Not all of the aggregate functions are available for every field type.

V

Database and List Management

Using Menu Commands

If you prefer to use menu commands rather than toolbar buttons, you can use the Edit Column command:

1 Choose Edit Column from the Records menu.

2 When the Edit Column dialog box appears, select the function you want from the Total drop-down list, as shown in Figure 26-30.

FIGURE 26-30.

Instead of clicking the Cycle Through Totals button, you can use the Edit Column command to perform calculations on your result set.

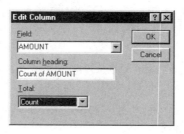

To access the Edit Column dialog box quickly, double-click the field heading in the data pane.

Changing the Displayed Field Heading

As mentioned, you can also use the Edit Column dialog box to change field headings. For example, to use Grand Total rather than Sum Of AMOUNT for your field heading, type Grand Total in the Column Heading edit box.

Aggregating Groups of Records

In addition to grand totals, you can also calculate totals for groups of records. For example, suppose you want to calculate the total amount of donations made for each value of the RATING field in the Phil table:

1 In the data pane, display the RATING column first, followed by the AMOUNT column.

2 Select the AMOUNT column and then click the Cycle Through Totals button on the toolbar.

As Figure 26-31 shows, Query displays one record for each rating value and shows the sum of all donations made to organizations in each rating category.

FIGURE 26-31.

You can apply aggregate calculations to groups of records. Here we calculated the total amount of donations made to recipients in each rating category.

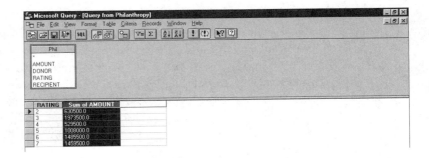

Aggregating Subgroups

By adding the RECIPIENT field to the data pane between the RATING field and the Sum Of AMOUNT field, you can make Query tally the total amount donated to each recipient within each rating category. The result of that calculation is shown in Figure 26-32.

FIGURE 26-32.

When an aggregate field appears to the right of two other fields, Query aggregates groups within groups. The result set shows the total donated to each recipient in each rating group.

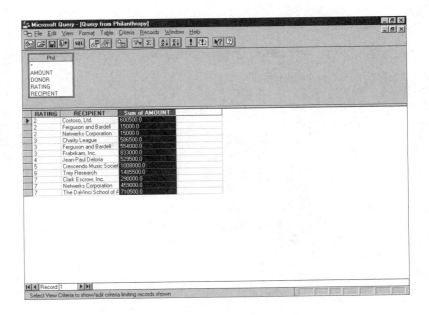

Using More Than One Aggregate Field

You can add as many aggregate fields to your result as you need. For example, to display average donations as well as total donations in Figure 26-32, you can drag the AMOUNT heading from the Field list in the Table pane to the empty Field list box in the Data pane. Click the Cycle Through Totals button until you display the Avg Of Amount heading.

V

Database and List Management

Sorting on an Aggregate Field

Notice that the records in Figure 26-31 and Figure 26-32 on the previous page are sorted in ascending order, first on the leftmost column and then on the next column. Query performs these sorts automatically. Depending on the capabilities of your driver, you might also be able to sort the records yourself, using the aggregate field. For example, you might want to sort the result set in Figure 26-32 on the Sum Of AMOUNT column rather than the RATING field.

If your driver does not allow this kind of sort, you can always sort the data after you return it to your worksheet.

Filtering on Calculated Fields

A field that performs an aggregate calculation is also known as a *calculated* field. You can use calculated fields as the basis for filtering criteria. For example, in Figure 26-33, the result set shows the names of all recipients in the Phil table who have received at least 10 donations totaling at least $50,000.

FIGURE 26-33.

We used calculated fields as the basis for filters, restricting the result set to recipients who have received 10 or more donations totaling at least $50,000.

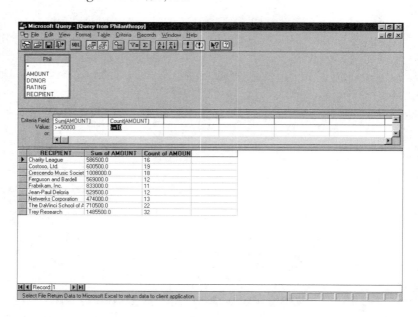

To create the filter shown in Figure 26-33, follow these steps:

1   In the Data pane, add the RECIPIENT field to the empty Field box. Then add the AMOUNT field twice.

2   Select the first AMOUNT field and click the Cycle Through Totals button to display the SUM OF AMOUNT function.

3 Select the second AMOUNT field and click the Cycle Through Totals button until you arrive at the COUNT OF AMOUNT function.

4 Select Add Criteria from the Criteria menu, and then complete the Add Criteria dialog box shown in Figure 26-34. Be sure to select the SUM function in the Total drop-down list, and then click the Add button.

FIGURE 26-34.

To filter on a calculated field, select the calculation function in the Total list and the name of the uncalculated field in the Field list.

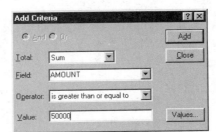

5 With the Add Criteria dialog box still open, select COUNT in the Total list, type *10* in the Value text box, and then click Add again.

6 Click Close to return to the Query window.

Joining Tables

In the examples thus far, we've queried a single external table. We've kept things simple in order to focus on the mechanics of sorting, specifying criteria, and performing calculations. In your own work, you might often need to query two or more related tables. Figure 26-35 on the next page shows a query against two related tables.

In this query, the ProductName and UnitsInStock fields come from the Products table, while the CompanyName and Address fields come from the Suppliers table. We've asked Query to return only those records in which the UnitsInStock field is less than 50.

Query automatically joins related tables when it recognizes a primary key field in one table and a field with the same name in another table. In the table pane, Query draws a line between the two tables to indicate they are joined. You can double-click the join line or choose Joins from the Table menu to get more information about how the tables are joined. Figure 26-36 on the next page shows what you would see if you double-clicked the join line in Figure 26-35.

Database and List Management

FIGURE 26-35.

We joined two tables that share a common field, SupplierID. In the result set, the ProductName and UnitsInStock fields come from the Products table, while the other two fields come from the Suppliers table.

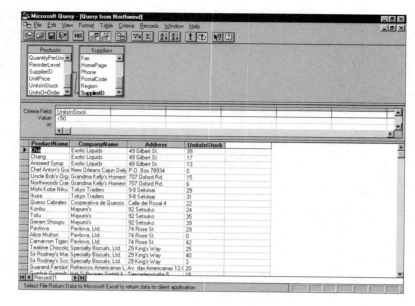

As Figure 26-36 shows, Query has in this case performed an *inner join,* a type of join in which only those records that have common values in the joined fields appear. Using the Joins dialog box, you can change the type of join that Query has performed, as well as create new joins or remove existing ones. (You can also create new joins by simply dragging a field in one table to a field in another.) Options 2 and 3 in the Joins dialog box create *outer joins*—joins that admit all records from one table but only those records in the second table whose values match in the joined field.

FIGURE 26-36.

The Joins dialog box provides information about all joins in the current query. It also enables you to add or remove existing joins and to change the type of join that Query has performed.

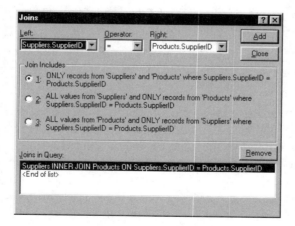

Figure 26-37 shows an example of a *self join*—a join that relates fields within a single table. Here we've asked Query to return all records in which the value of the UnitsInStock field from the Products table is less than the ReorderLevel field from the Products table. To get the supplier address for each product, we've also maintained the inner join between the Products and Suppliers tables.

FIGURE 26-37.

We've added a self join between two instances of the Products table in order to get those records in which the UnitsInStock field is less than the ReorderLevel field.

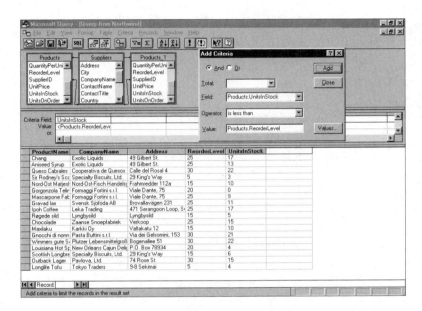

To create a self join, you need to add a second instance of the joined table. To do this, choose Add Tables from the Table menu and answer the confirmation prompt that appears. To create the filter criterion, choose Add Criteria from the Criteria menu.

Creating a Parameter-based Query

A parameter-based query is one in which a filter criterion is based upon a value supplied by the user when the query is executed. To do this, first turn the Auto Query feature off by clicking the Auto Query button on the Query toolbar. Then specify a criterion in the normal way—either with the Add Criteria dialog box or by entering values directly in the criteria pane. Instead of entering a value, though, type a left bracket character, then a prompt of your choosing, and then a right bracket character. (The prompt must not be identical to the field name, although it can include the field name.) When you execute the query, either from within Query or from Excel, a dialog box containing your prompt text appears. Figure 26-38 on the next page shows a parameter-based query.

Database and List Management

FIGURE 26-38.

Because the Value line of the criteria pane includes a prompt enclosed between brackets, this query, when executed, will prompt the user for a product name.

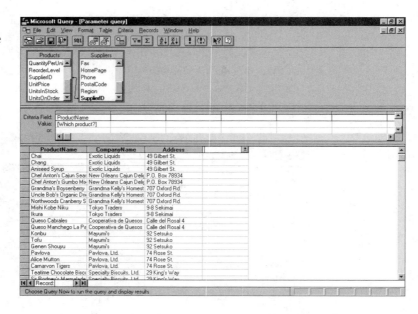

You can use as many parameters as you want in a query.

Saving a Query

To store your query specification in a reusable .dqy file, choose Save from the File menu and supply a filename. This step is optional. If you do not save the query, you will still be able to refresh it from the external data range that it creates on your Excel worksheet. You will not be able to use it again on another worksheet, however.

Returning the Result Set to Excel

To return your data to your Excel worksheet, choose Return Data To Microsoft Excel from the File menu. A dialog box will appear, asking you to specify a worksheet address where you want to create your external data range: an existing worksheet, a new worksheet, or a PivotTable report. As with the other types of queries we've looked at in this chapter, you can visit the query's property sheet by clicking Properties on this dialog box. But you can display the property sheet later as well, by clicking the Data Range Properties button on the External Data toolbar.

CHAPTER 27

Using PivotTables

A PivotTable is an analytical tool that summarizes information from particular fields of an Excel list, a relational database file, or an OLAP cube. (An OLAP cube is a file containing OLAP data. For a definition of OLAP, see page 804. When you create a PivotTable, you specify which fields you're interested in, how you want the table organized, and what kinds of calculations you want the table to perform. After you have built the table, you can rearrange it to view your data from alternative perspectives. This ability to "pivot" the dimensions of your table—for example, to transpose column headings to row positions—gives the PivotTable its name and makes it a very powerful tool.

PivotTables are linked to the data from which they're derived. You can choose to have your table automatically recalculated, or *refreshed* at regular time intervals, or you can refresh it manually by clicking a button on the PivotTable toolbar, which appears by default whenever you create or select a PivotTable.

A Simple Example

Figure 27-1 shows a list of sales figures for a small publishing firm. The list is organized by year, quarter, catalog number, distribution channel, units sold, and sales receipts. The data spans a period of eight quarters (1998 and 1999), and the firm uses three distribution channels—domestic, international, and mail order. With just a few keystrokes you can turn this "flat" list into a table that provides useful information at a glance. One of the many possible arrangements for this PivotTable is shown in Figure 27-2.

In Figure 27-2, the Year and Quarter fields have been positioned along the table's *column axis*, and the CatalogNo and Channel fields have taken up positions along the *row axis*. The body of the table displays the total sales numbers for each column-and-row intersection. Cell H6, for example, shows that the total domestic sales in the first quarter of 1999 for the book whose catalog number is 23524 were negative $488—meaning that returns outnumbered sales for that title, in that time period, in that distribution channel.

What's New in Excel 2000

Three things are new in Excel 2000's PivotTables:

- The user interface has been simplified. Instead of making you build your table completely within the PivotTable Wizard, Excel now gives you a blank table layout, displays your field buttons in the PivotTable toolbar, and lets you build the table by dragging buttons to the layout. It's simpler, cleaner, and easier to learn and use. (If you prefer to continue building PivotTables the way you did in Excel 97, you can do that as well.)

- You can now create PivotCharts as well as PivotTables. You can drag fields from axis to axis on a PivotChart, exactly as you would on a PivotTable.

- Excel now lets you construct PivotTables from OLAP data sources. OLAP is a faster way to analyze large amounts of corporate data. OLAP queries execute more quickly than traditional relational database queries, and when you build a PivotTable from an OLAP source, Excel downloads only the data you need, saving memory as well as time. With this new capability, you can build a PivotTable to analyze a gigabyte-sized or terabyte-sized data warehouse, without exceeding the memory limitations of your client machine.

FIGURE 27-1.

It's difficult to see the bottom line in a flat list like this. The PivotTable And PivotChart Report command can help.

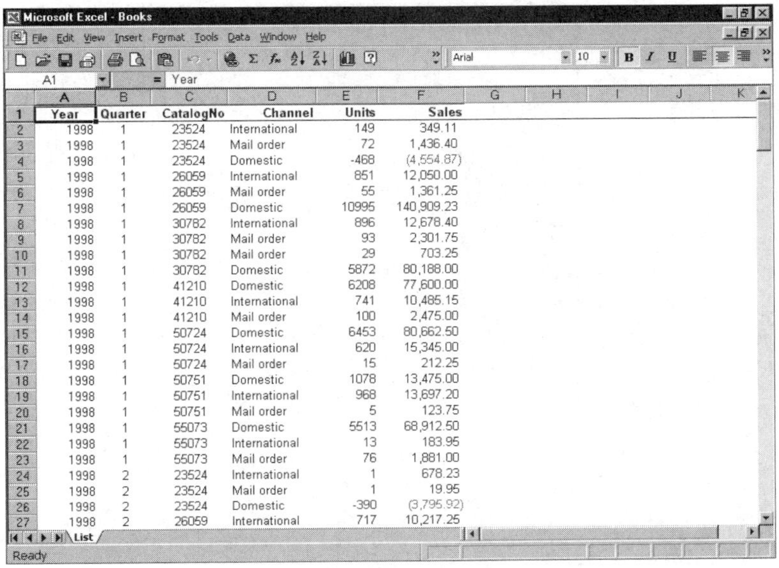

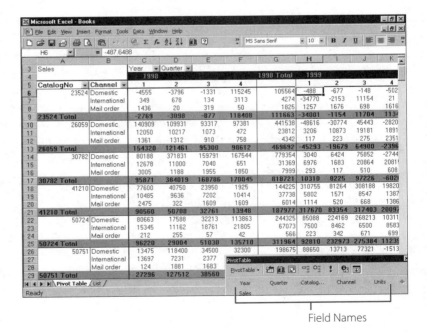

FIGURE 27-2.

This PivotTable provides a summary view of the information in Figure 27-1.

Field Names

Excel displays field buttons at the bottom of the PivotTable toolbar for the four category fields used in this table—Year, Quarter, CatalogNo, and Channel. Rearranging the table is as simple as dragging these field buttons into new positions.

Database and List Management

PivotTable Terminology	
Axis	A dimension in a PivotTable, such as a column, row, or page.
Data source	The list, table, or cube from which the PivotTable is derived.
Field	A category of information, equivalent to a column in a list.
Field heading	A label describing the contents of a field. You can pivot a PivotTable by dragging its field headings.
Item	A member of a field. In Figure 27-2, 1998 and 1999 are items in the Year field.
Pivot	To rearrange a PivotTable by repositioning one or more fields.
Summary function	The worksheet function used by Excel to calculate values in the body of the table. The default summary function is SUM for numeric values and COUNT for text.
Refresh	To recalculate the PivotTable so that its values reflect the current state of the data source.

Rows 9, 13, 17, 21, 25, and 29 in Figure 27-2 on the previous page display subtotals for the various items in the catalog number field. Column G displays subtotals for the four quarters of 1998. Beyond the boundaries of the figure lie additional subtotals, and at the outer edges the PivotTable includes a grand total column and a grand total row. If you scrolled the table in Figure 27-2 to the bottom cell in column C, for example, you would find the total first quarter 1998 sales for all titles across all distribution channels. The PivotTable And PivotChart Report command creates these subtotals and grand totals automatically, unless you tell it not to.

The PivotTable shown in Figure 27-2 makes it easy to find almost all the information recorded in the list in Figure 27-1. The only details that do not appear are the unit sales. If you had wanted to make the table a bit more complex, you could have shown those also. Suppose, however, that instead of more detail, you want less. The PivotTable can accommodate that need as well. Figure 27-3 on the next page shows one of the many ways in which the table in Figure 27-2 can be modified to focus on a particular section of the data. Here we have transposed the Channel field from the row axis to the column axis and moved both the Year and Quarter fields to the *page axis*. Moving these fields to the page axis allows you to "zoom in" on the numbers for a particular year and quarter. When you want to see a different time period, you can simply select a different year or quarter from the drop-down lists next to the Year and Quarter field headings.

FIGURE 27-3.

Using a PivotTable, you can also focus on a particular section of the data in a table.

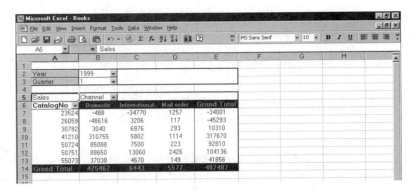

Creating a PivotTable

You can create PivotTables from four kinds of data:

- An Excel list

- An external data source

- Multiple "consolidation" ranges (separate Excel lists that the PivotTable And PivotChart Report command will consolidate as it builds your PivotTable)

- Another PivotTable

In the example that follows, we'll create a PivotTable from an Excel list—the list shown in Figure 27-1 on page 837.

   You can find the Books.xls used in Figures 27-1 and 27-2 on the Microsoft Press Web site at *http://mspress.microsoft.com/mspress/products/2050/*.

Starting the PivotTable and PivotChart Wizard

To create a PivotTable, begin by selecting any cell within the list from which you want to create your table. This step is optional, but it saves time. Then choose the PivotTable And PivotChart Report command from Excel's Data menu. (The PivotTable and PivotChart Report command is not visible on shortened menus. Click the double arrow at the bottom of the Data Menu to display this command.) This action

Database and List Management

summons the PivotTable and PivotChart Wizard, which initiates the table creation process. The wizard will prompt you to follow these steps:

1 Specify the type of data source on which the table will be based and whether you want to create a PivotTable or a PivotChart.

2 Indicate the location of your source data.

3 Indicate where you want the table to appear.

After you complete these steps, you work with the PivotTable toolbar to specify which fields you want in your table, how you want the table organized, and what calculations you want the table to perform.

Step 1: Specifying the Type of Data Source

The wizard's initial dialog box is shown in Figure 27-4.

FIGURE 27-4.

The PivotTable and PivotChart Wizard walks you through the table creation process.

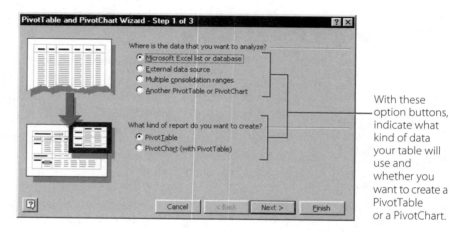

With these option buttons, indicate what kind of data your table will use and whether you want to create a PivotTable or a PivotChart.

Notice that Excel uses graphics on the left side of this dialog box to confirm your selection. If you select External Data Source, for example, the picture on the left changes to show a mainframe computer transferring data to a desktop terminal. If you choose PivotChart, the image in the lower left corner of the dialog box changes from a table to a chart.

Step 2: Indicating the Location of Your Source Data

After you indicate your data source type and then click Next, the wizard displays its second dialog box, which asks you for the location of your data. If you're basing your PivotTable on an Excel list, and you selected a cell in that list before invoking the PivotTable and PivotChart

Wizard, the wizard already knows the location of your data and merely asks you to confirm it. The wizard's second dialog box, in that case, looks something like the one shown in Figure 27-5.

FIGURE 27-5.

If you're building your table from an Excel list, choose or confirm the location of your list in this dialog box.

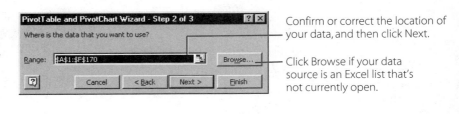

Confirm or correct the location of your data, and then click Next.

Click Browse if your data source is an Excel list that's not currently open.

> If your source data is an Excel list, the list must include a field name at the top of each column.

If your data source is an Excel list that isn't currently open, you can click the Browse button in the dialog box shown above and find it. Once you've specified the file, you will still need to type a range name or reference so that the wizard will know which part of the file you want to use.

SEE ALSO

For more information on Microsoft Query, see "Using Microsoft Query to Create Database Queries," page 804.

If you're building a PivotTable from an external data source, you'll see the dialog box shown in Figure 27-6. Click the Get Data button in this dialog box. Excel will then transfer control to Microsoft Query, which will display the Choose Data Source dialog box (see Figure 26-12, on page 806). Here you can either select an existing relational database source (select an item listed on the Databases tab), execute a saved query (click the Queries tab), or specify an OLAP source (click the OLAP Cubes tab).

FIGURE 27-6.

If you're building your table from an external data source, click the Get Data button on this dialog box.

If your data source is "multiple consolidation ranges," the wizard will take you down quite a different path. *For information about using PivotTables to consolidate ranges, see "Using a PivotTable to Consolidate Ranges," on page 871.*

If your data source is another PivotTable or PivotChart, the wizard will display a list of existing PivotTables and PivotCharts, allowing you to pick the one you want to use.

Basing one PivotTable on another is the most memory-efficient way to create two tables derived from the same data source. When you create a PivotTable from a new data source, Excel copies that source into an area of memory called a *cache*. If you base one table on another, the two tables share the cache. If you create a new table from scratch and that table uses the same data source as an existing table, Excel simply duplicates the cache, wasting memory in the process.

If you happen to specify an Excel list in step 1, and that list is already being used by an existing PivotTable or PivotChart, Excel will advise you to base your new PivotTable on the existing one. You can ignore this advice if you really want two independent tables based on a common data source.

Step 3: Telling the Wizard Where to Put Your PivotTable

In the wizard's last dialog box, shown in Figure 27-7, you indicate where you want your PivotTable.

FIGURE 27-7.

To create your table on an existing worksheet, type a range name or reference in the text box.

To put the table on a new worksheet (always a safe choice), select the New Worksheet option. Otherwise, select Existing Worksheet and supply a range reference or name in the edit box. (Do not put a sheet name in the text box; Excel will try to interpret it as a range name.)

Before clicking Finish, you can click Options and specify such things as an automatic refresh-time interval for your table. But you can always return to the Options dialog box later.

⭐ **TIP**

If you prefer to create PivotTables the way you did in Microsoft Excel 97 and earlier versions, click the Layout button on the dialog box shown in Figure 27-7.

TIP

Moving a PivotTable

After you create a PivotTable, you can easily move it. Select any cell within the table, then choose the Data menu's PivotTable And PivotChart Report command (or click the PivotTable Wizard tool on the PivotTable toolbar). Click Next to get to the wizard's Step 3 dialog box. Then select New Worksheet or select Existing Worksheet and specify a range name or address in the text box.

Laying Out the PivotTable

After you've told the wizard where your source data resides and clicked Finish, Excel displays a blank table layout similar to the one shown in Figure 27-8. It also displays the PivotTable toolbar, which includes buttons for each field in your data source. You create the initial organization for your table by dragging field buttons from the toolbar to the table layout.

FIGURE 27-8.

You specify the initial organization for your table by dragging field buttons from the toolbar to the layout.

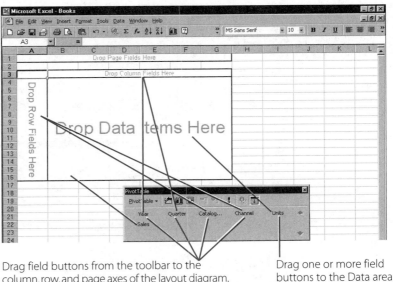

Drag field buttons from the toolbar to the column, row, and page axes of the layout diagram.

Drag one or more field buttons to the Data area.

To create the PivotTable shown in Figure 27-2 on page 837, drag the Channel and CatalogNo buttons to the row axis (the area marked Drop Row Fields Here), the Quarter and Year buttons to the column axis (the area marked Drop Column Fields Here), and the Sales button to the data area (the area marked Drop Data Items Here). The table shown here does not use the page axis (the area marked Drop Page Fields Here).

You can put as many fields as you like in any of the areas of the layout. To remove a field, drag its button off the layout.

Changing the Layout of a PivotTable

To pivot, or rearrange, your finished PivotTable, drag one or more field buttons. To move a field from the column axis to the row axis, for example, all you have to do is drag its button from the column area to the row area.

In addition to transposing columns and rows, you can change the order in which fields are displayed on the column or row axis. For example, using Figure 27-2 on page 837 as an example, drag the Channel heading to the left of the CatalogNo heading. As shown in Figure 27-9, the catalog number items now appear within channel groups, and subtotals summarize revenue by channel.

FIGURE 27-9.

By dragging the Channel heading to the left of the CatalogNo heading, you can change the organization of the PivotTable shown in Figure 27-2 on page 837.

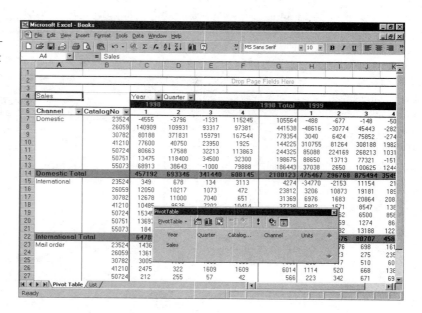

Using the Page Axis

When you display a field on either the row axis or column axis, you can see all of that field's items just by scrolling through the table. On the page axis, however, each field can show only one item at a time. In Figure 27-3, on page 839, you see only the 1998 item for the Year field and the 1 item for the Quarter field. To see other items in a field, select from that field's drop-down list. By selecting each entry in the list in turn, you can see a two-dimensional slice corresponding to each value in the field in the Page area.

Displaying Totals for a Field in the Page Area

At the top of each field's drop-down list, you'll find the (All) option. You can select this option to display total values for each field on the page axis. Figure 27-10 shows the result of selecting the (All) option for the Year and Quarter fields shown in Figure 27-3 on page 839.

FIGURE 27-10.

Select (All) in a field's drop-down list to insert total values for that field. Here you'll see the sales figures for all quarters of all years, broken out by channel and catalog number.

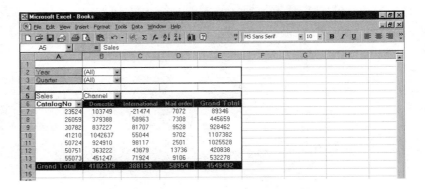

Moving Page Fields to Separate Workbook Pages

Even though a PivotTable might include a page axis, the table is stored on only one workbook page. By choosing the Show Pages command, however, you can create a series of linked PivotTables, each of which can show one item in a page field. (To get to the Show Pages command, click PivotTable on the PivotTable toolbar. You'll find the command on the menu that opens.) For example, as shown in Figure 27-11, you can use Show Pages to create a separate copy of your PivotTable for each item in the Year field. Notice that Excel creates a new worksheet for each item in the Year field, positions the new worksheets in front of the original PivotTable worksheet, and assigns names to the sheets based on the items in the Year field.

 TIP

Copying a PivotTable

If you copy a PivotTable and paste it somewhere else using the Copy and Paste commands on the Edit menu, Excel creates a second PivotTable. If you want to replace a formula or range of formulas with their resulting values, first copy the table as usual. Then use the Paste Special command and select the Values option.

FIGURE 27-11.

Use the Show Pages command to create separate copies of the PivotTable for each item in the Year field.

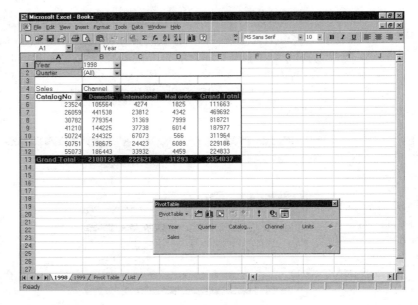

Selecting Items to Display on the Row and Column Axes

Initially, when you drag a field button to either the row axis or column axis, your PivotTable displays all items for that field. In Figure 27-11, for example, all three distribution channels appear along the column axis and all seven catalog numbers appear along the row axis. To limit the display to particular items, click the drop-down arrow at the right side of the field button, make your selections from the set of check boxes that appear, and then click OK.

You can also use an AutoShow feature to limit the display to particular items, based on their data values. *For information about modifying the items you display in your PivotTable, see "Showing the Top or Bottom Items in a Field," page 858.*

Creating a PivotChart

You can create a PivotChart from the PivotTable and PivotChart Wizard (see Figure 27-4 on page 840). Or you can first create a PivotTable, and then, while any cell within the table is selected, click the Chart

Wizard button on the PivotTable toolbar. If you take the first approach, Excel creates both a new PivotTable and a new PivotChart. If you take the second approach, Excel creates a PivotChart based on the current PivotTable.

Either way, the chart and table are linked. Changes to one are reflected immediately in the other. Figure 27-12 shows a PivotChart that's linked to the PivotTable shown in Figure 27-11. Notice that the page fields of the PivotTable shown in Figure 27-11 appear at the upper left corner of the PivotChart, while the table's row and column fields appear as the category and value axes of the chart, respectively.

FIGURE 27-12.

You can create a PivotChart linked to the PivotTable shown in Figure 27-11.

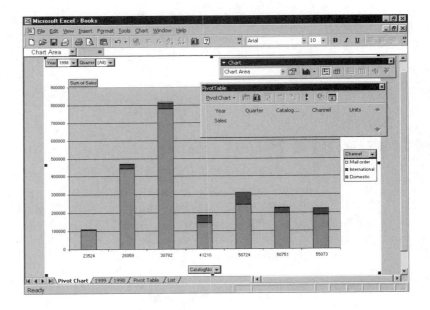

You can rearrange a PivotChart exactly as you would a PivotTable—by dragging field buttons from one axis to another. To add fields, drag them from the PivotTable toolbar. To remove fields, drag them off the chart. (Because chart and table are always in lockstep with one another, you can also rearrange a chart by rearranging the table to which it's linked.) Figure 27-13 shows the PivotChart from Figure 27-12 rearranged to reflect the structure of the PivotTable shown in Figure 27-2 on page 837.

Database and List Management

FIGURE 27-13.
You can rearrange the
PivotChart from Figure
27-12 by dragging
field buttons.

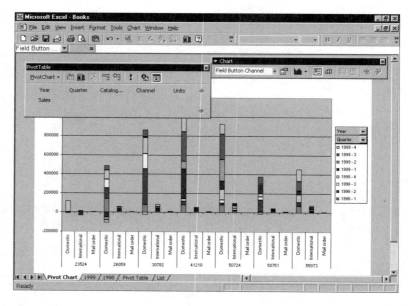

Refreshing a PivotTable

PivotTables are not automatically updated each time a change occurs
in their source data. To update a table, select any cell within it. Then
choose Refresh Data from the Data menu or select Refresh Data from
the PivotTable toolbar.

Refreshing on File Open

If you want Excel to refresh your PivotTable every time you open the
worksheet on which it resides, choose Table Options from the PivotTable
menu on the PivotTable toolbar. (Table Options is not visible on shortened menus. Click the double arrow at the bottom of the PivotTable to
display this option.) Then select the Refresh On Open check box in
the PivotTable dialog box that appears. If you want to prevent Excel
from updating the table automatically each time you open the table
(for example, if the table is based on a time-consuming query of external data), be sure this check box is cleared.

Refreshing Linked PivotTables

When one PivotTable serves as the data source for another PivotTable,
refreshing either table refreshes both.

Refreshing a PivotTable Based on External Data

If your PivotTable is based on a query of external data, you might want to let Excel execute the query in the background so that you can continue working while your PivotTable is refreshed. To do this, select any cell in the table, choose Table Options from the PivotTable menu on the PivotTable toolbar, and then select the Background Query check box in the PivotTable Options dialog box. This option is available only for tables created from external data.

If your PivotTable uses page fields, you can choose a querying mode in which Excel fetches only the data needed for the page you're currently looking at. This option uses less memory and may serve you best if you're working with a large external database and your computer's memory is limited. You might also prefer to use this option if you switch pages infrequently.

To query your external data source a page at a time, double-click the field button for any page field in your table. In the PivotTable Field dialog box that appears, click Advanced. In the PivotTable Field Advanced Options dialog box, click the option labeled Query External Data Source As You Select Each Page Field item.

Refreshing at Regular Time Intervals

To have your table automatically refreshed at periodic intervals, choose Table Options from the PivotTable menu on the PivotTable toolbar. Select the Refresh Every check box and then specify a time interval in minutes. This option is available only for tables created from external data.

Selecting Elements of a PivotTable

Normally, when you click an element in a PivotTable, you select only that cell where you have clicked. With a command on the PivotTable menu, you can extend the selection to all other instances of the same element. For example, if you select the Domestic label in cell B6 of the table shown in Figure 27-2 on page 837, you can extend the selection to include *all* the Domestic labels, as well as all the data falling under those headings. Figure 27-14 shows an example of this *structured selection*.

Structured selection makes it easier for you to compare related items in a PivotTable. Equally important, with structured selection turned on, formatting changes that you make to selected cells are retained even if you refresh or reorganize (pivot) your table. With structured selection off, those formatting changes are not retained.

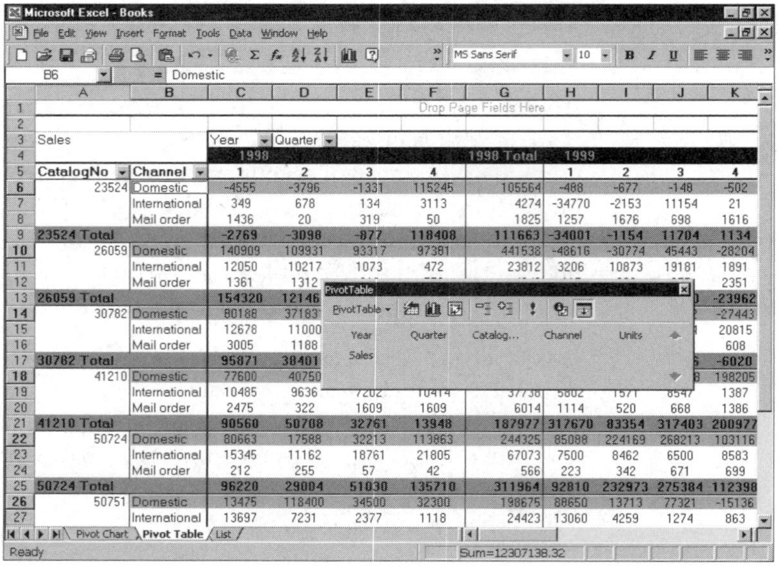

FIGURE 27-14.

With structured selection on, Excel can select all instances of a field label as well as all the data falling under that label.

Turning Structured Selection On or Off

The structured selection feature is off by default. To extend the selection to all common elements using structured selection, first select one element. Then choose the PivotTable menu on the PivotTable toolbar and choose Select from the PivotTable menu. You'll see the cascading submenu shown in Figure 27-15.

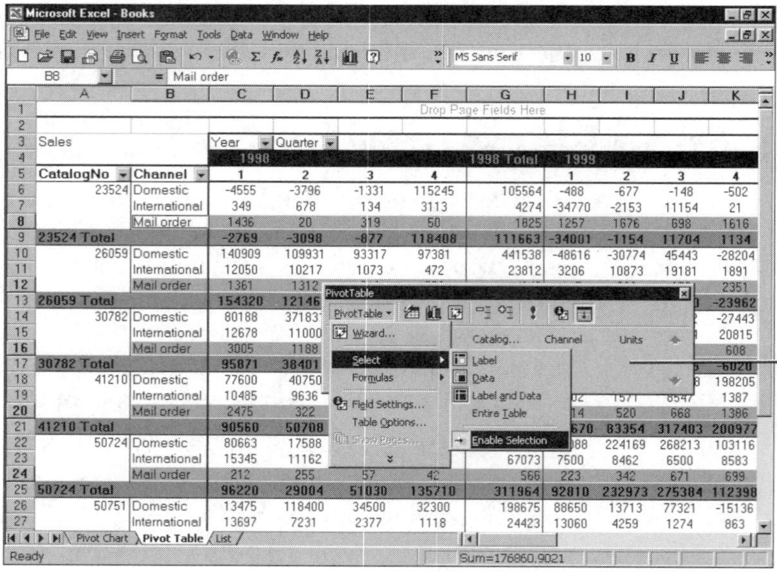

FIGURE 27-15.

With structured selection on, a single click can select all instances of a field label as well as all the data falling under that label.

If these commands are available, structured selection is on

When the Enable Selection feature is on, the button to the left of the Enable Selection command is selected and the three commands at the top of the Select submenu are available. When the feature is off, the button is cleared and the three commands are unavailable.

Selecting Labels Only or Data Only

You can use commands on the Select submenu (see Figure 27-15) to select labels only or data only. For example, if you had wanted to select only the Domestic data shown in Figure 27-2 on page 837, omitting the Domestic field labels, you could have clicked on one of the Domestic labels, turned structured selection on, and then chosen the Select Data command. Had you wanted to select the Domestic labels *without* their associated data, you could have chosen instead the Select Label command. To restore the normal labels-plus-data selection mode, you would choose Select Label And Data.

Selecting an Entire PivotTable

To select all of a PivotTable, click the PivotTable menu on the PivotTable toolbar, choose Select, and then choose Entire Table from the cascading submenu (see Figure 27-15 on the previous page).

Formatting a PivotTable

You can use standard formatting techniques to modify the appearance of cells in a PivotTable. Excel will retain your formatting preferences when you refresh or pivot your table, provided you have not cleared the Preserve Formatting check box in the PivotTable Options dialog box. If you're losing formats when you pivot or refresh, you can fix the problem as follows:

1   Select any cell in the PivotTable.

2   Choose Table Options from the PivotTable menu on the PivotTable toolbar. The PivotTable Options dialog box opens.

3   Select the check box labeled Preserve Formatting.

 NOTE

You cannot apply conditional formatting to PivotTable cells. Border formatting will not be preserved, even if you select Preserve Formatting in the PivotTable Options dialog box.

Using AutoFormat with PivotTables

? SEE ALSO

For more information about formatting, see Chapter 7, "Formatting a Worksheet."

Excel provides more than twenty autoformatting options for PivotTables. You can apply these by selecting any cell within the table and then clicking the Format Report button on the PivotTable toolbar. Alternatively, choose AutoFormat from the Format menu.

To remove autoformatting from an existing table, select any cell within the table, choose Table Options from the PivotTable menu on the PivotTable toolbar, clear the AutoFormat Table check box, and then click OK. Then choose Select from the PivotTable menu and choose Entire Table from the Select submenu. Finally, choose Style from the Format menu and apply the Normal style.

Any formatting that you apply with other formatting techniques, either before or after you choose an AutoFormat, takes precedence over the AutoFormat setting. Thus, for example, you can have the majority of your table use an AutoFormat but override that AutoFormat for particular cells.

Changing the Number Format for All Cells in a PivotTable

You can change the numeric format for particular cells in a PivotTable simply by selecting those cells and using standard formatting techniques. To apply a numeric format to all PivotTable cells at once, follow this procedure:

1 Select any cell in the data area of the table (not a field button or field heading).

2 Click the Field Settings button on the PivotTable toolbar.

3 In the PivotTable Field dialog box shown in Figure 27-16, click the Number button on the right side of the dialog box.

FIGURE 27-16.

Click Number in the PivotTable Field dialog box to apply a numeric format to all cells in the table.

Clicking Number takes you to a standard numeric formatting dialog box, just like the one you would see if you chose Cells from the Format menu.

Changing the Way a PivotTable Displays Empty Cells

Empty cells in a PivotTable are normally displayed as empty cells. For example, if cell F2 in Figure 27-1 on page 837 were empty, cell C7 in the PivotTable in Figure 27-2 on page 837 would also be empty, because it would have no data to report. If you prefer, you can have your PivotTable display 0 or some text value (for example, NA) in cells that would otherwise be empty. To do this, follow these steps:

1 Select any cell in the PivotTable.

2 Choose Table Options from the PivotTable menu on the PivotTable toolbar.

3 In the PivotTable Options dialog box, be sure that the check box labeled For Empty Cells, Show is selected. Then type a 0 or whatever other value you want to see in the edit box to the right of this check box.

Changing the Way a PivotTable Displays Error Values

As you may know, if a worksheet formula references a cell containing an error value, that formula returns the same error value (a formula that references a cell containing #N/A, for example, returns #N/A). The same is normally true in PivotTables. Error values in your source data generate the same error values in the PivotTable. If you prefer, you can have error values generate blank cells or text values.

To change the way a PivotTable responds to source-data error values, follow these steps:

1 Select any cell within the PivotTable.

2 Choose Table Options from the PivotTable menu on the PivotTable toolbar.

3 In the PivotTable Options dialog box, select the check box labeled For Error Values, Show. Then, if you want error values to generate blanks, leave the edit box empty. If you want them to generate a text value, type the text in the edit box.

Merging Labels

Figure 27-17 shows the same PivotTable as Figure 27-2, but with its outer field labels centered over (or beside) the corresponding inner field labels. The catalog number headings in column A of Figure 27-17 are centered vertically beside the channel headings in column B, and the year headings in row 4 are centered horizontally above the quarter headings in row 5. To achieve this effect, choose Table Options from the PivotTable menu on the PivotTable toolbar. Then, in the PivotTable Options dialog box, select the Merge Labels check box.

FIGURE 27-17.

You can use the Merge Labels option to center outer field headings beside and above corresponding inner field headings.

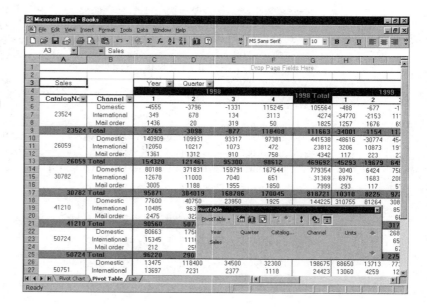

Using Multiple Data Fields

If you add a second field to the data area of your table, Excel displays subtotals for each field. Figure 27-18 on the next page shows an example.

Notice that the table now includes a new field heading called Data. As with other field headings, you can further rearrange the table layout by dragging the new field heading, as Figure 27-19 on the next page shows.

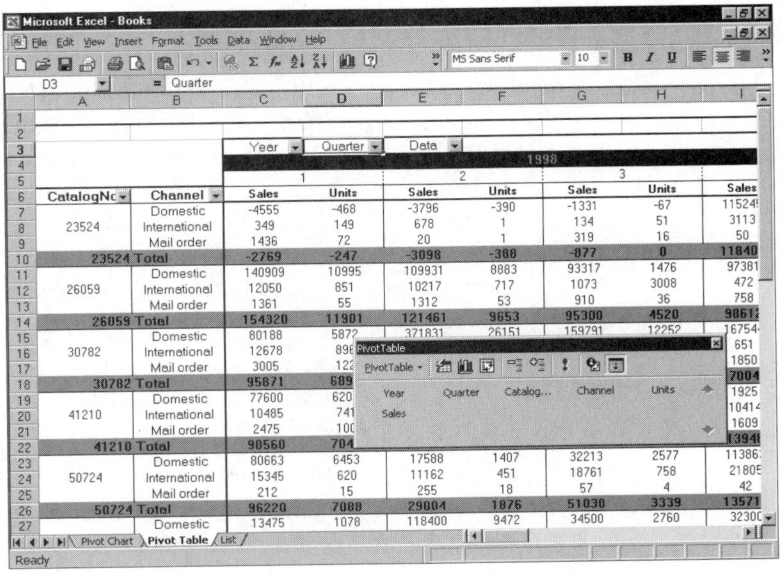

FIGURE 27-18.

You can add a second field, Units, to the data area.

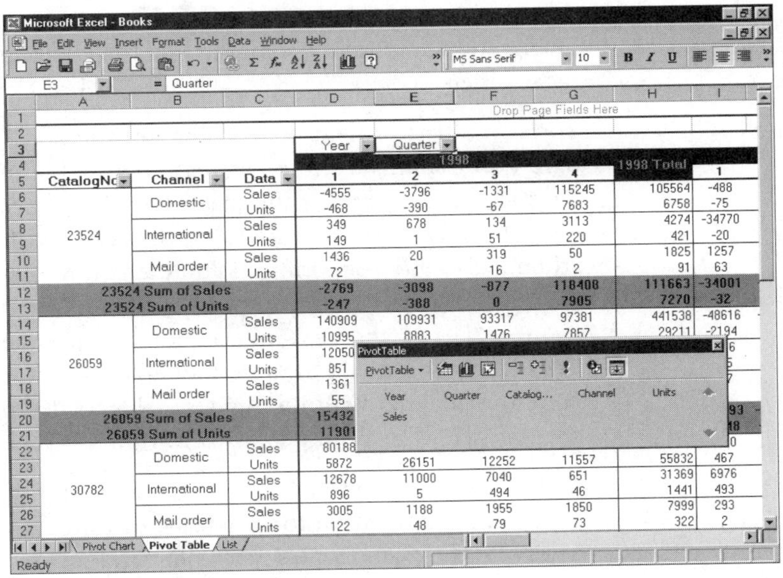

FIGURE 27-19.

The Data field heading, which appears whenever the data area has two or more fields, can be repositioned just as any other field heading can. Here we've moved it from the column axis to the row axis.

To remove a data field when you have more than one, drag the Data field button off the row, column, or page axis of the table. This clears all data items from the table. Then drag those fields that you want to restore from the PivotTable toolbar to the data area.

Renaming Fields and Items

Don't change a field heading in your pivot table to the name of another field in your data source. Doing so will have unintended consequences.

You don't have to use the field and item names supplied by the PivotTable and PivotChart Wizard. You can change these names by simply editing the field heading or any occurrence of the item in the PivotTable. When you change the name of an item in this manner, all other occurrences of the item are changed as well. For example, you can change the CatalogNo heading to Title in Figure 27-19 by selecting the heading in cell A5, typing *Title,* and then pressing Enter.

Sorting Items

If you sort field items using the standard Sort command on the Data menu, Excel will sort all instances of your field items and preserve the desired sort order when you rearrange your table. For example, to generate a descending sort of Channel items as shown in Figure 27-19 on the previous page—Domestic, International, and Mail Order—you could select cell B5, choose Sort from the Data menu, and specify a descending sort. Excel would then reverse the order of these labels, giving you Mail Order, Domestic, International, in every place where those labels occur.

You can also sort field items using an AutoSort feature. Like the standard Sort command, AutoSort rearranges table material across all instances and preserves the order you desire even when you move fields from axis to axis. However, the AutoSort feature gives you the additional option of sorting field items on the basis of their data values. For example, using AutoSort, you can sort the Channel items in Figure 27-19 on the basis of the Sum of Sales data or the Sum of Units data. You could arrange the table so that, for each CatalogNo item, the channel with the highest sales totals appears first and the channel with the lowest sales totals appears last.

AutoSort takes precedence over the standard Sort command. That is, if you turn AutoSort on for a field, you will not be able to sort that field with the Data menu's Sort command unless you subsequently turn AutoSort off.

Using AutoSort

To use AutoSort for a field, follow these steps:

1 Select any item or the field button of the field you want to sort. For example, to sort the Channel field items in Figure 27-19, you could select cell C6, C7, C8, or C5.

2 Click the Field Settings button on the PivotTable toolbar. (Alternatively, choose Field Settings from the PivotTable menu on the PivotTable toolbar.)

3 Click the Advanced button and the PivotTable Field Advanced Options dialog box shown in Figure 27-20 appears.

4 Choose the Ascending or Descending option, and then select the field you wish to sort from the Using Field drop-down list. For example, to sort Channel items on the basis of their sales values, with the highest grand-total values appearing first, you would choose the Descending option and Sum Of Sales.

FIGURE 27-20.

Use the PivotTable Field Advanced Options dialog box to choose sorting options.

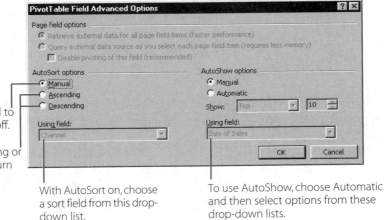

Choose Manual to turn AutoSort off.

Choose Ascending or Descending to turn AutoSort on.

With AutoSort on, choose a sort field from this drop-down list.

To use AutoShow, choose Automatic and then select options from these drop-down lists.

Using Nonstandard Sorting Orders

SEE ALSO

For more information about custom lists, see "Creating Custom Lists," page 245.

When neither an ascending nor a descending sort is exactly what you want, you can create a custom sort order by choosing Options from the Tools menu and then clicking the Custom Lists tab. You can then create a custom sort order by simply typing over your existing field labels. For example, to create the nonalphabetical sort order Domestic, Mail Order, International, you could select any International label in the table and then type *Mail Order*. When you overtype an existing item label with the name of another item label, Excel interprets your action as a command to swap the two labels. The program retains your nonstandard sort order when you refresh or pivot the table.

Showing the Top or Bottom Items in a Field

The AutoShow feature lets you display only the top or bottom *n* items in a field, based on values in the data area of your table. To use AutoShow, select the field you're interested in, then click the Field Settings button on the PivotTable toolbar. In the PivotTable Field dialog box, click the Advanced button to display the PivotTable Field Advanced Options dialog box, shown in Figure 27-20. Figure 27-21 shows an example of a PivotTable that uses AutoShow. To match this, rearrange the table so that the Quarter field appears on the row axis and the Channel field is on the column axis. Then apply AutoShow to the Quarter field, choosing to display only the top two quarters based on Sum of Sales.

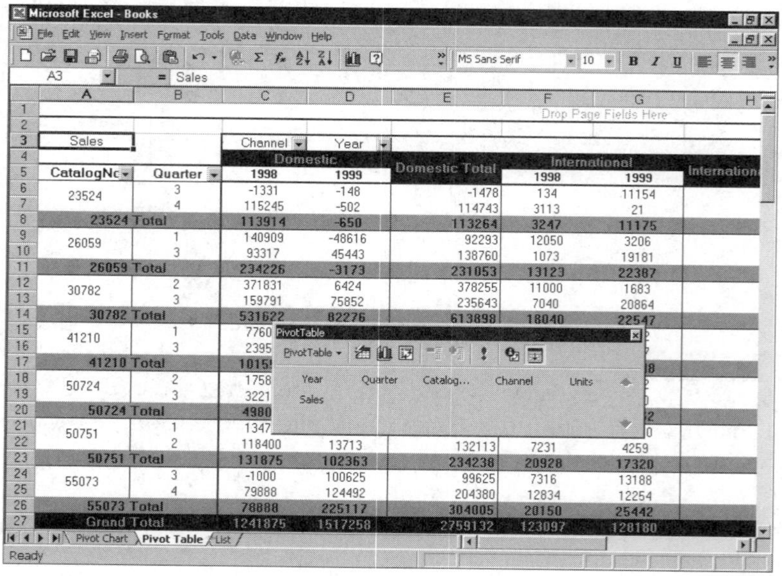

FIGURE 27-21.

You can use AutoShow to display only the top two quarters for each CatalogNo item, based on Sum of Sales.

Hiding and Showing Inner Field Items

In the PivotTable shown in Figure 27-2, CatalogNo and Year are *outer* fields, while Channel and Quarter are *inner* fields. The PivotTable repeats the items of the inner field for each item in the outer field. You can suppress a set of inner field items by double-clicking the associated outer field item.

For example, to hide the quarterly detail for 1998 in Figure 27-2, you can double-click the 1998 heading. Figure 27-22 shows the result. To redisplay the inner field detail, double-click the outer field heading a second time.

FIGURE 27-22.

You can hide the 1998 quarterly detail by double-clicking the 1998 heading.

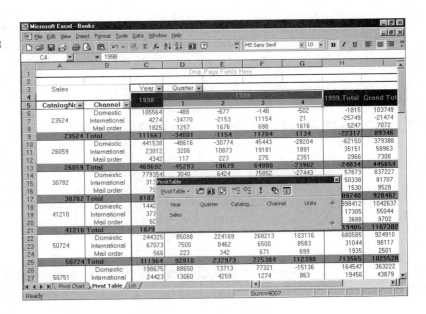

Displaying the Details Behind a Data Value

By double-clicking a data value, you "drill down" to the details behind the value. Excel copies the detail figures to a new workbook page.

Figure 27-23 shows an example of this process. Double-click the 1998 Total cell for catalog number 23524 (cell G9 in the table shown in Figure 27-2 on page 837). Excel responds by listing all the entries from the data source that contributed to that PivotTable value.

V

Database and List Management

FIGURE 27-23.

Double-clicking a value causes Excel to display the entries summarized by that value.

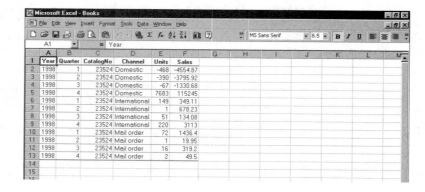

You can turn this capability off by opening the PivotTable Options dialog box (choose Table Options from the PivotTable menu on the PivotTable toolbar) and clearing the Enable Drilldown check box. If you do this, double-clicking a summary item has no effect.

Grouping and Ungrouping Data

The PivotTable facility automatically groups inner field items under each outer field heading and, if requested, creates subtotals for each group of inner field items. You might find it convenient to group items in additional ways—for example, to collect monthly items into quarterly groups, or sets of numbers into larger numeric categories. Excel provides several options for grouping items.

Creating Ad Hoc Item Groupings

Suppose that after looking at Figure 27-2 on page 837 you decide you'd like to see the Domestic and International sales figures grouped into a category called Retail. To create this group, follow these steps:

1 Select the Domestic and International headings anywhere in the table (for example, cells B6 and B7 in Figure 27-2).

2 Choose Group from the Group And Outline submenu of the Data menu.

Excel responds by creating a new field heading called Channel2 and grouping the selected items into a new item called Group1. Figure 27-24 on the next page illustrates these developments.

3 Select any cell that says Group1 and type the new name for Group1: *Retail*.

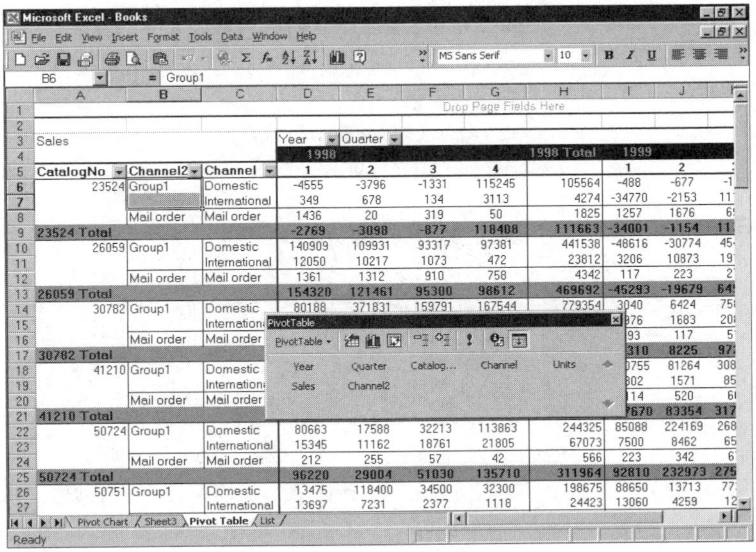

FIGURE 27-24.

You can create a group comprising the Domestic and International items in the Channel field.

At this point, the group is named appropriately, but the PivotTable still shows both the group and the items that comprise the group. You can suppress the detail behind the group by double-clicking the new group heading anywhere it appears in the table. To see the group's component values again, simply double-click the group heading a second time. If you want to eliminate the group's component values—in this case, Channel—from the table entirely, drag the innermost field heading off the table. Excel rebuilds the PivotTable as shown in Figure 27-25.

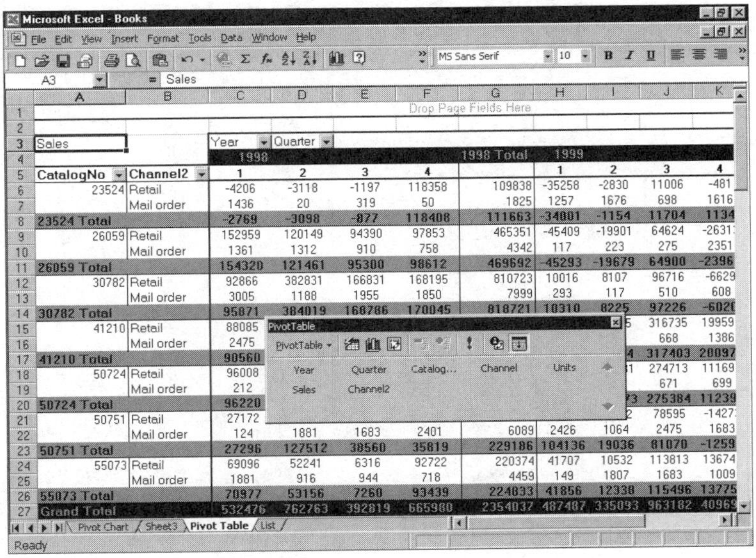

FIGURE 27-25.

We removed the original Channel grouping from the PivotTable shown in Figure 27-24.

V

Database and List Management

Grouping Numeric Items

To group numeric items in a field, such as the items in the Quarter field of Figure 27-2 on page 837, select any item in the field and choose Group from the Data menu's Group And Outline submenu. You'll see a dialog box similar to the one shown in Figure 27-26.

FIGURE 27-26.

Use this dialog box to group items in a field.

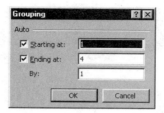

Fill in the Starting At, Ending At, and By values as appropriate. For example, to create two-quarter groups in Figure 27-2, you would enter 1 and 4 in the Starting At and Ending At edit boxes and then enter 2 in the By box.

Grouping Items in Date or Time Ranges

Figure 27-27 shows a PivotTable that summarizes daily transactions by Payee. As you can see, the data in this table is extremely sparse. Most intersections between a day item and a Payee item are blank.

FIGURE 27-27.

To make the data in this table more meaningful, you can group the date field.

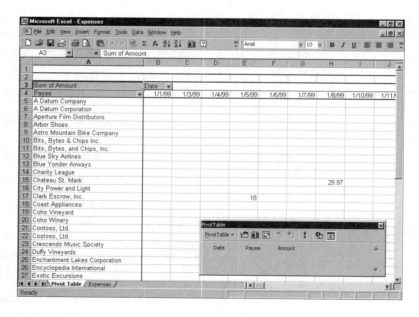

 **ON THE WEB**

You can find Expenses.xls used in Figure 27-27 on the Microsoft Press Web site at *http://mspress.microsoft.com/mspress/products/2050/*.

To make this kind of table more meaningful, you can group the date field. You do this by selecting an item in that field, choosing Group from the Data menu's Group And Outline submenu, and then filling out the dialog box shown in Figure 27-28.

FIGURE 27-28.

Fill out this dialog box to group a date field.

Excel gives you a great deal of flexibility in the way your date and time fields are grouped. In the By list, you can choose any common time interval from seconds to years, and if the standard time intervals don't meet your needs, you can select an ad hoc number of days. You can also create two or more groupings at the same time, as shown in Figure 27-29, by selecting more than one entry in the By list. To make a multiple selection—say, of Quarters and Months—hold down the Ctrl key while you click each component of your selection.

FIGURE 27-29.

Here is the table from Figure 27-27 with the date field grouped by months and quarters.

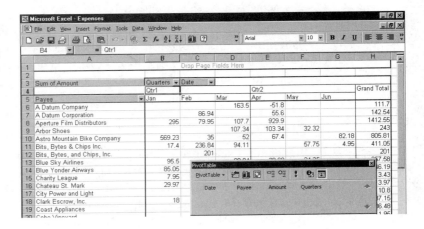

Database and List Management

Removing Groups (Ungrouping)

To remove any group and restore a field to its ungrouped state, select a grouped item and choose the Ungroup command from the Data menu's Group And Outline submenu.

> If one PivotTable serves as the data source for another, groups in either table affect the other.

Using Grand Totals and Subtotals

By default, Excel generates grand totals for all outer fields in your table and subtotals for all inner fields except the innermost field. You can suppress the default totals and also generate subtotals for the innermost fields.

Grand Totals

If you use more than one data field, the PivotTable and PivotChart Wizard generates separate grand totals for each data field. A grand total always uses the same summary function as the data field it totals. For example, if your PivotTable uses the Sum function, its grand totals are grand sums. If you use Average instead of Sum, you get grand averages, and so on.

> **Changing Summary Functions**
> To switch from one summary function to another, select an item in the data area of your PivotTable, click the Field Settings button on the PivotTable toolbar, and then choose then the function you want from the list that appears in the PivotTable Field dialog box.

To remove grand totals from a PivotTable, choose Table Option from the PivotTable menu on the PivotTable toolbar. Then clear the Grand Totals For Columns And/Or Grand Totals For Rows check boxes in the PivotTable Options dialog box.

Subtotals

By default, Excel creates subtotals for each field on the column and row axes of the PivotTable, with the exception of the innermost fields. For example, in Figure 27-2 on page 837, column G displays subtotals for the items in the Year field, and rows 9, 13, 17, and 21 display subtotals for the items in the CatalogNo field. Excel does not create subtotals for the items in the Channel and Quarter fields because these are the innermost fields on their respective axes.

As with grand totals, Excel generates one subtotal line for each data field in the table, and the subtotals, by default, use the same summary function as the associated data field. The subtotals that appear in Figure 27-2 on page 837 were calculated using the Sum function because the Sum function was used to calculate the numbers in the data area of the table.

In the case of subtotals, however, you can override the default summary function, and you can use more than one summary function. You can also suppress the generation of subtotals for particular fields. The steps for each of these actions follow.

To override the default summary function or use multiple functions, follow these steps:

1 Double-click the field button (not an item in the field) and the PivotTable Field dialog box appears.

   Alternatively, you can select the field button and then click the Field Settings button on the PivotTable toolbar.

2 Select one function or hold down Ctrl while you click to make multiple selections. When you are finished, click OK.

To remove subtotals for a field, follow these steps:

1 Double-click the field button (not an item in the field) and the PivotTable Field dialog appears.

   Alternatively, you can select the field button and then click the Field Settings button on the PivotTable toolbar.

2 Select the None option and then click OK.

If you decide later that you want the subtotals to appear after all, you can redisplay them. Follow these steps:

1 Double-click the field button (not an item in the field) and the PivotTable Field dialog box appears.

   Alternatively, you can select the field button and then click the Field Settings button on the PivotTable toolbar.

2 Select the Automatic option and then click OK.

Subtotals for Innermost Fields

Although Excel does not automatically generate subtotals for innermost fields, you can specify as many as you like, and you can use multiple summary functions. Such subtotals appear at the bottom or right edge of the PivotTable, just above or to the left of the grand totals. Figure 27-30 shows an example of innermost field subtotals (the subtotals appear in rows 34 through 39).

FIGURE 27-30.

You can add subtotals to the Channel field (an innermost field) using the Sum and Average functions.

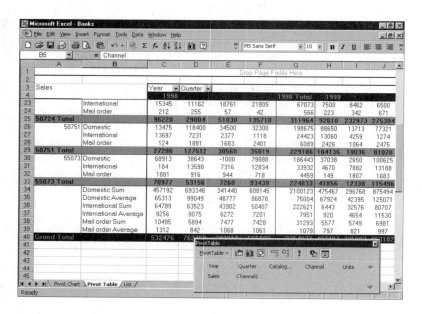

To add subtotals for an innermost field, follow these steps:

1 Double-click an innermost field button (not an item in the field) and the PivotTable Field dialog box appears.

Alternatively, select the field button and then click the Field Settings button on the PivotTable toolbar.

2 Select one or more functions and then click OK.

Changing a PivotTable's Calculations

By default, Excel populates the data area of your PivotTable by applying the Sum function to any numeric field you put in the data area or the Count function to any nonnumeric field. But you can choose from many alternative forms of calculation, and you can add your own calculated fields to the table.

Using a Different Summary Function

To switch to a different summary function, select any cell in the data area of your PivotTable. Then click the Field Settings button on the PivotTable toolbar. Excel displays the PivotTable Field dialog box, shown in Figure 27-16 on page 852. Select the function you want to use, and then click OK.

Applying Multiple Summary Functions to the Same Field

You can apply as many summary functions as you want to a field. To use a second or subsequent function with a field that's already in the data area of your PivotTable, simply drag another copy of the field button into the data area of your table. Then select a data cell, click the Field Options button on the PivotTable toolbar, choose the summary function you want to use, then click OK to return to your PivotTable. The available summary functions are Sum, Count, Average, Max, Min, Product, Count Nums, StdDev, StdDevp, Var, and Varp.

Using Custom Calculations

In addition to the standard summary functions enumerated in the previous paragraph, Excel also offers a set of custom calculations. With these you can do such things as have each item in the data area of your table report its value as a percentage of the total values in the same row or column, create running totals, or show each value as a percentage of some base value.

To apply a custom calculation, select any item in the data area of your table and then click the Field Options button on the PivotTable toolbar. Then, in the PivotTable Field dialog box (shown in Figure 27-16 on page 852), click Options. The dialog box expands to reveal additional options as shown in Figure 27-31.

FIGURE 27-31.

Use the Show Data As drop-down list to apply a custom calculation.

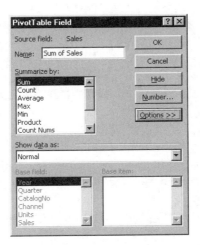

The default calculation is Normal (shown in the Show Data As drop-down list.) To apply a custom calculation, open this drop-down list, choose the calculation you want, and then select options from the Base Field and Base Item lists as appropriate. Here are your choices:

Custom Calculation	Does This
Difference From	Displays data as a difference from a specified base field and base item.
% Of	Displays data as a percentage of the value of a specified base field and base item.
% Difference From	Displays data as a percentage difference from a specified base field and base item.
Running Total In	Displays data as a running total.
% Of Row	Displays each data item as a percentage of the total of the items in its row.
% Of Column	Displays each data item as a percentage of the total of the items in its column.
% Of Total	Displays each data item as a percentage of the grand total of all items in its field.
Index	Uses the formula: ((value in cell) x (Grand Total of Grand Totals)) / (((Grand Row Total) x (Grand Column Total))

When you select a member of the Base Field list, the items in the selected field appear in the Base Item list. The Base Item list also includes special items identified as (Previous) and (Next). So, for example, to have your table report Sum of Sales as a difference from the previous Quarter, you would choose Difference From in the Show Data As drop-down list, Quarter in the Base Field list, and (Previous) in the Base Item list.

Using Calculated Fields and Items

In case custom calculations don't meet all your analytic needs, Excel allows you to add calculated fields and calculated items to your PivotTables. A calculated field is a new field, derived from calculations performed on existing fields in your table. A calculated item is a new item in an existing field, derived from calculations performed on other items that are already in the field. Once you create a custom field or item, Excel lets you use it in your table, as though it were part of your data source.

Custom fields and items can apply arithmetic operations to any data already in your PivotTable (including data generated by other custom fields or items), but they cannot reference worksheet data outside the PivotTable.

Creating a Calculated Field

To create a calculated field, select any cell in the PivotTable. Then choose Formulas from the PivotTable menu on the PivotTable toolbar. From the Formulas submenu, choose Calculated Field, and the Insert Calculated Field dialog box shown in Figure 27-32 appears.

FIGURE 27-32.

Create a calculated field in this dialog box.

1 Name your calculated field here.

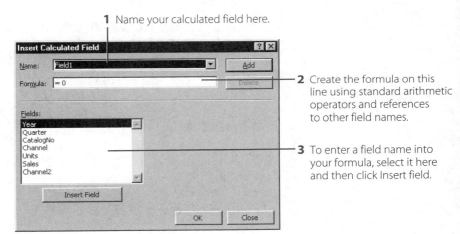

2 Create the formula on this line using standard arithmetic operators and references to other field names.

3 To enter a field name into your formula, select it here and then click Insert field.

Figure 27-33 shows an example of a calculated field.

FIGURE 27-33.

This calculated field multiplies an existing field by a constant.

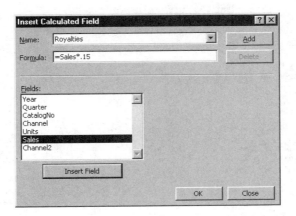

Excel automatically adds a new calculated field to your PivotTable when you click either Add or OK. You can then work with the new field using the same techniques you use to work with existing fields.

Creating a Calculated Item

To create a calculated item for a field, select any existing item in that field or the field heading. Then choose Formulas from the PivotTable menu on the PivotTable toolbar. In the Formulas submenu, choose Calculated Item. Excel displays the dialog box shown in Figure 27-34. Figure 27-35 shows an example created using the Calculated Item dialog box.

FIGURE 27-34.

Use this dialog box to create a calculated item for a field.

1 Type a unique name for the calculated item here.

2 Enter its formula here, using arithmetic operators and references to existing items.

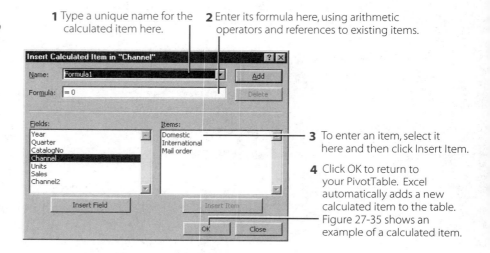

3 To enter an item, select it here and then click Insert Item.

4 Click OK to return to your PivotTable. Excel automatically adds a new calculated item to the table. Figure 27-35 shows an example of a calculated item.

FIGURE 27-35.

This calculated item will appear by default whenever the Channel field is included in the PivotTable.

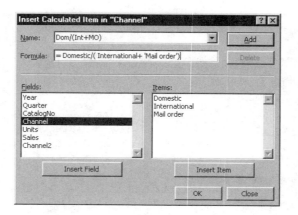

 NOTE

If one PivotTable serves as the data source for another, calculated fields and calculated items that have the same names in both tables affect each other.

Referencing PivotTable Data from Worksheet Cells

If a worksheet formula uses an ordinary cell reference to get data from a PivotTable, the formula will work fine as long as the referenced cell stays where it is. But the formula will "break" (return invalid data) when the table is pivoted. To avoid this problem, use the GETPIVOTDATA function when you want to reference PivotTable data in a worksheet formula.

GETPIVOTDATA takes two arguments. The first is a reference to the PivotTable itself. The second tells Excel what kind of data you want. The first argument can be any cell within the PivotTable, a range name assigned to the PivotTable, or a label stored in the cell above the upper left corner of the table. The second argument, contained within quote marks, names the fields from the intersection of which you want to retrieve data. Use spaces to separate field names in the second argument.

> **NOTE**
>
> The data retrieved by GETPIVOTDATA must be visible in the PivotTable.

For example, to get the Quarter 1 1998 domestic sales figures for title 23524 in Figure 27-2 on page 837, you could type:

    =GETPIVOTDATA(A1,"1998 1 23524 Domestic")

To get a row total from a PivotTable, specify all row fields and no column fields in GETPIVOTDATA's second argument. For example, to get the total domestic sales for title 23524 in Figure 27-2, type:

    =GETPIVOTDATA(A1,"23524 Domestic")

To get a column total, include all the column fields and no row fields. To get a grand total, specify "Grand Total" as the second argument.

Using a PivotTable to Consolidate Ranges

You can use the PivotTable And PivotChart Report command to consolidate data in separate Excel ranges. In the resulting PivotTable, each source range can be displayed as an item on the page axis. By using the drop-down list on the page axis, you can see each source range at a glance, as well as the table that consolidates the ranges. For example,

Figure 27-36 shows quarterly examination scores. The data is stored in four separate worksheets, Exams 1, Exams 2, Exams 3, and Exams 4.

W ON THE WEB

You can find the Consolidated Exam Scores.xls used in the following example at *http://mspress.microsoft.com/mspress/products/2050/*.

FIGURE 27-36.

Use the PivotTable And PivotChart Report command to consolidate the four worksheets in this workbook.

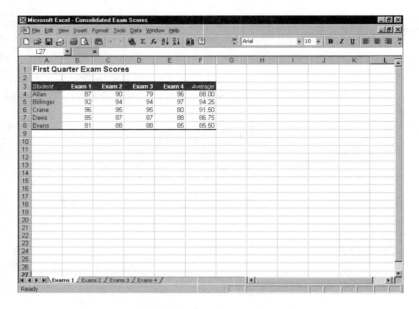

To generate a consolidation PivotTable from these worksheets, follow these steps:

1   Choose the PivotTable And PivotChart Report command from the Data menu.

2   When the Step 1 dialog box appears, select the Multiple Consolidation Ranges option and then click Next.

3   When the Step 2a dialog box appears, accept the Create A Single Page Field For Me option (the default option).

    Click Next and Excel displays the Step 2b dialog box, shown in Figure 27-37.

★ TIP

Include Column and Row Headings
When specifying ranges to consolidate, include column and row headings, but do not include summary columns and rows. In other words, do not include in the source range columns and rows that calculate totals or averages.

FIGURE 27-37.

In the Step 2b dialog box, specify each data range that you want your PivotTable to consolidate.

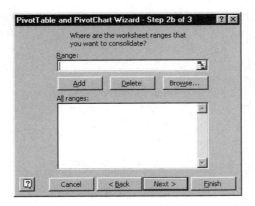

4   Select the first data range that you want the PivotTable to consolidate, then click the Add button. You may find it easier to use the Collapse Dialog button to select the data. In this example, the first range you'll want to consolidate is 'Exams 1'!A3:E8. You'll also want to consolidate 'Exams 2'!A3:E8, 'Exams 3'!A3:E9, and 'Exams 4'!A3:E7.

5   Repeat step 4 for each additional source range. When you have specified all your source ranges, click Next, tell Excel where you want the new PivotTable, and then click Finish.

6   Excel totals the values in your source ranges by default. If you want to use a different summary function, double-click the Sum Of Value heading, select the function you want, and then click OK.

Figure 27-38 on the next page shows the finished PivotTable. Notice that the current page-axis item is (All). This page shows the consolidated exam scores. Every other item on the page axis displays an unconsolidated source range, in effect duplicating the four source ranges within the PivotTable. If your source ranges are in separate workbook files, you can see these ranges much more easily by stepping through the page axis of the PivotTable than by opening each source file.

In this example, we selected the Create A Single Page Field For Me option in the PivotTable and PivotChart Wizard's Step 2a dialog box. Let's look now at an example in which you might want to select the I Will Create The Page Fields option.

V

Database and List Management

FIGURE 27-38.

The (All) item on the page axis displays the consolidated exam scores.

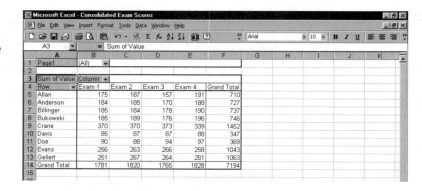

Figure 27-39 shows a workbook in which each of eight worksheets displays unit and sales figures for a particular year and quarter, broken out by catalog number. In consolidating these eight worksheets you'll want to have two page-axis fields, Year and Quarter.

ON THE WEB

You can find the Books by Quarter.xls used in the following example at *http://mspress.microsoft.com/mspress/products/2050/*.

FIGURE 27-39.

Each of the worksheets in this workbook displays quarterly unit and sales figures for each book in the catalog.

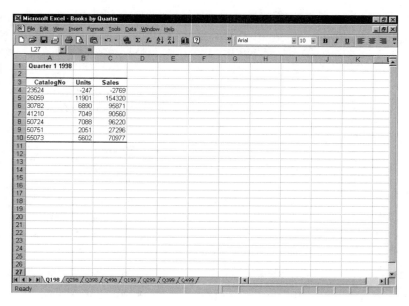

To create this PivotTable, follow these steps:

1 Choose the PivotTable And PivotChart Report command from the Data menu, and when the Step 1 dialog box appears, select the Multiple Consolidation Ranges option and then click Next.

2 When the Step 2a dialog box appears, select the I Will Create The Page Fields option, and then click Next.

Excel displays the Step 2b dialog box, shown in Figure 27-40. Because you selected the I Will Create Page Fields option, this version of the Step 2b dialog box is slightly more complex than the one shown in Figure 27-37 on page 873.

FIGURE 27-40.

When you create your own page fields, the Step 2b dialog box requires some additional information from you.

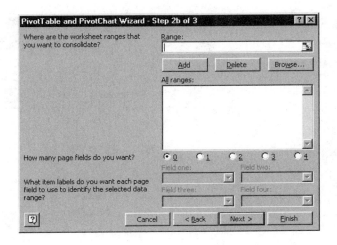

3 In the Step 2b dialog box, select the first data range that you want the PivotTable to consolidate and then click the Add button. You may find it easier to use the Collapse Dialog button to select the data.

4 Repeat step 3 for each additional source range.

5 When you have identified all your source ranges, select the 2 Page Fields option.

You select 2 in this case because you want to create two page-axis fields. You are allowed to create as many as four page-axis fields. Figure 27-41 on the following page shows the Step 2b dialog box after you have identified your data sources and selected the 2 Page Fields option.

6 Select the first range in the All Ranges list. Then enter *1998* in the Field One box. Next enter *Q1* in the Field Two box.

7 Select the second range in the All Ranges list. Enter *1999* and *Q1* in the Field One and Field Two boxes. Continue in this manner until you have identified each range specified in the All Ranges list box. Click Next and tell Excel where you want your PivotTable.

FIGURE 27-41.

After you identify your data sources and specify how many page-axis fields you want, complete the Step 2b dialog box by telling Excel which source ranges should be associated with which page-axis fields.

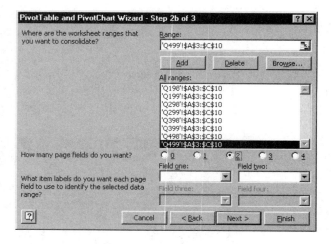

 TIP

Identifying Source Ranges

You will find it much easier to identify your source ranges if they are stored on separate named worksheets. In Figure 27-41, for example, the worksheet names Q198, Q298, and so on make it easy to tell which worksheets store which source ranges.

8 If you want to use a summary function other than SUM, double-click the Sum Of Value heading in the resulting PivotTable, select the function you want, and then click OK.

Figure 27-42 shows the completed PivotTable. By working with the drop-down lists beside the two page-axis field headings, you can make the table show various perspectives on your data.

FIGURE 27-42.

This consolidation PivotTable has two page-axis fields.

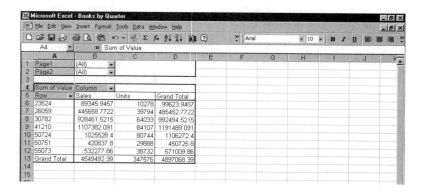

PART VII

Macros and Visual Basic

CHAPTER 28

Creating Macros

A macro is a set of instructions that tells Microsoft Excel 2000 to perform an action for you. Macros are like computer programs, but they run completely within Excel. You can use them to automate tedious or frequently repeated tasks.

Macros can carry out sequences of actions much more quickly than you could yourself. For example, you can create a macro that enters a series of dates across one row of a worksheet, centers the date in each cell, and then applies a border format to the row. Or you can create a macro that defines special print settings in the Page Setup dialog box and then prints the document. Macros can be very simple or extremely complex. They can even be interactive; that is, you can write macros that request information from the user and then act upon that information.

SEE ALSO
For more information about Microsoft Visual Basic, see Chapter 30, "A Sample Visual Basic Application."

There are two ways to create a macro: you can record it, or you can build it by entering instructions in an Excel sheet called a module. To enter instructions in a module, you use a special programming language called Microsoft Visual Basic. Visual Basic is a powerful language that has become increasingly common in Microsoft Windows and Macintosh applications, and it offers some definite advantages over other macro programming languages. For example, with Visual Basic, you have to learn only one language to control many different applications, and you can develop macros that work with more than one application. Using Visual Basic, you can write a series of macros that extracts stock price data from an information service, imports the data into an Excel worksheet, applies a series of special calculations to the data, prepares a stock price chart, and then moves the chart to a report in Microsoft Word.

NOTE

> The version of Visual Basic used in Excel is actually called Visual Basic for Applications (VBA), because it can only operate from within another application like Excel or Word. For brevity's sake, I use the term *Visual Basic* throughout.

In this chapter, we'll show you how to record a simple macro, and we'll introduce you to Visual Basic along the way. Next, we'll show you how to view the recorded macro and make it more useful by doing some simple editing. Finally, we'll discuss using absolute and relative references and subroutines in your macros as well as various ways to activate macros.

Recording Macros

Rather than type macros character by character, you can have Excel create a macro by recording the menu commands, keystrokes, and other actions needed to accomplish a task.

After you've recorded a series of actions, you can run the macro to perform the task again. As you might expect, this playback capability is most useful with macros that automate long or repetitive processes, such as entering and formatting tables or printing a certain section of a worksheet.

The overall process for recording a macro consists of three steps. First, you start the macro recorder and supply a name for the macro. Next, you perform the actions you want to record, such as choosing menu commands, selecting cells, and entering data. Finally, you stop the macro recorder.

Let's investigate this process by creating a simple macro that inserts a company name and address in a worksheet. Begin by saving and closing all open workbooks, and then open a new workbook. Choose Options from the Tools menu, click the Edit tab, and make sure the Move Selection After Enter option is cleared. Next, follow these steps:

1   Choose Macro and then Record New Macro from the Tools menu. (The Macro command does not normally appear on shortened menus. Click the downward-pointing double arrow at the bottom of the Tools menu to display the Macro command.) Excel displays the Record Macro dialog box shown in Figure 28-1.

FIGURE 28-1.

The Record Macro dialog box.

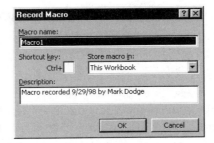

2   Assign a name to the macro. You can accept Excel's suggestion (Macro1) or enter your own name—let's use *CompanyAddress*. Note that this name cannot have any spaces.

3   Assign a key combination to the macro by entering a letter—in this case, uppercase *A*—in the Shortcut Key edit box.

4   Store the macro in the currently active workbook by making sure the This Workbook option is selected.

A macro stored in the Personal Macro Workbook is available when you start Excel; one stored in another workbook requires that that workbook be opened before the macro can be used. There are advantages to each method, discussed later in this chapter.

5   Enter a description for the macro in the Description box; in this case, type *Enter company address*.

6 To begin recording, click OK. Excel displays the message *Recording* in the status bar, and the Stop Recording Macro button appears on the Stop Recording toolbar, shown in Figure 28-2 below.

FIGURE 28-2.

The Stop Recording toolbar.

— Relative Reference

Stop Recording Macro

7 Select cell A6 and type

Consolidated Confetti Co.

Press the Down arrow key to select cell A7 and type

3012 West Beaujolais St.

Press the Down arrow key to select cell A8 and type

Walla Walla, WA 98107

Then press Enter.

8 Click the Stop Recording Macro button on the Stop Recording toolbar, or from the Tools menu choose Macro and then Stop Recording. This step is important; if you don't stop the macro recorder, Excel continues to record your actions indefinitely.

To test the new macro, clear the worksheet and then press Ctrl+Shift+A. Excel runs the macro and performs the sequence of actions in the same way you recorded them.

Quality Control

In some spreadsheet programs, if you type a word incorrectly or choose the wrong command, both the mistake and your efforts to correct it are recorded. Excel's macro recorder does not record an action until you complete it.

For example, the macro recorder does not record a cell as selected until you perform some action in the cell, such as choosing a formatting or editing command. Similarly, the macro recorder does not record a menu command that calls up a dialog box until you click OK in the dialog box. If you click Cancel instead, the macro recorder does not include the command in the macro.

Using the Macro Dialog Box

You don't have to know a macro's key combination to run the macro. Instead, you can use the Macro dialog box, like this:

1   From the Tools menu, choose Macro and then Macros to display the dialog box shown in Figure 28-3.

FIGURE 28-3.

You can run macros from the Macro dialog box.

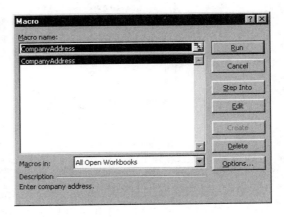

2   Select the name of the macro and click the Run button.

You can also use the Macro dialog box to view and edit macros, as you'll see in the next section.

Behind the Scenes: The Visual Basic Environment

Now that you've recorded your macro, let's find out what Excel did. When you clicked OK in the Record Macro dialog box, Excel created something called a *module* in the active workbook. As you entered the company name and address in the worksheet, Excel recorded your actions and inserted the corresponding Visual Basic code in the module.

The new module doesn't appear with the other sheets in the workbook; to view the module, from the Tools menu choose Macro and then Macros. Next, select the CompanyAddress macro we just created and click the Edit button. The Visual Basic Editor—a programming application that is independent from Excel—starts up, and the module that contains the CompanyAddress macro appears, as shown in Figure 28-4 on the next page.

FIGURE 28-4.

After translating each action you performed into Visual Basic code, Excel stores the code in the module.

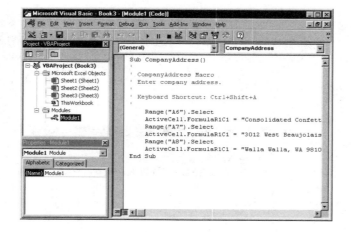

As you can see, a module doesn't look like a worksheet. Instead of a grid of columns and rows, you see a window much like the one you might see in a word processing program. The menu bar above the module includes menus for editing, debugging, and running Visual Basic code. In the module you can review, enter, copy, move, insert, and delete Visual Basic statements and comments using techniques that are similar to those you use in a word processing program. Of course, since the Visual Basic Editor is a separate application, you can switch back and forth between your Excel workbook and the Visual Basic Editor by clicking the appropriate button in the Windows taskbar.

The Microsoft Visual Basic environment is a big place, full of interesting details, but for now let's focus only on the code we've recorded. On the right of the Visual Basic Editor is a window displaying the module containing the code.

The first and last lines of the code act as the beginning and end points for the macro you've recorded; a Sub statement starts the macro and names it, and an End Sub statement ends the macro. You'll notice that special Visual Basic terms, called *keywords,* are displayed in blue. (You can view the colors assigned to various elements of a Visual Basic macro by choosing Options from the Tools menu and selecting the Editor Format tab.)

Getting Help on Visual Basic Keywords

You can get detailed information about a keyword by clicking the word and pressing F1. In Figure 28-4, if you place the insertion point in the keyword Sub and press F1, Excel presents a Help screen containing an entry for the Sub statement, as shown in Figure 28-5.

FIGURE 28-5.

The Help reference for the Sub statement.

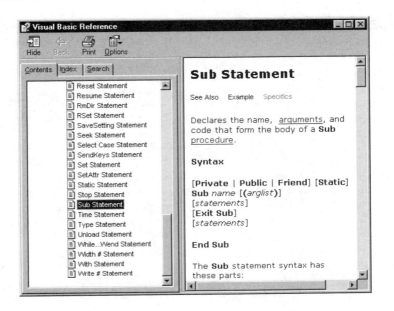

Many Help topics for Visual Basic keywords include a link that, when clicked, displays another Help screen containing one or more examples of the keyword as it might be used in working Visual Basic code. (In Figure 28-5, for instance, you can click the word Example just under the Sub Statement title.) You can copy this code, paste it into a module, and edit the resulting text to meet your needs.

Objects, Methods, and Properties

To Visual Basic, every item in the Excel environment is considered an object rather than an abstract set of data structures or an arrangement of pixels on the screen. As shown in Figure 28-6 on the next page, each object is a container for the objects within it (if any). The largest object is the Excel application itself; it contains all other objects.

? SEE ALSO

For information about working with comments, see "Documenting Macros and Custom Functions," page 909.

The first Visual Basic statement in the CompanyAddress macro after the Sub statement (that is, not including the comments that begin with the single quote (') character),

```
Range("A6").Select
```

illustrates an important characteristic of Visual Basic code: the syntax of many statements first specifies an *object* and then an action upon that object. An object can be a range, a worksheet, a graphic object, a workbook, or any of the more than 100 types of objects in Excel. Here, we specify a *Range* object—the absolute cell reference A6—and an action to perform—*select the range*.

You can find CocoStock.xls used in the following example on the Microsoft Press Web site at *http://mspress.microsoft.com/mspress/products/2050/*.

FIGURE 28-6.

Each labeled object is a container for any object within it.

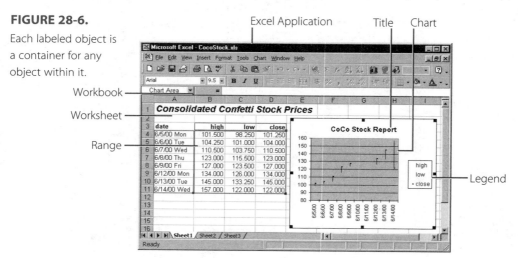

The behaviors, or sets of actions, that an object "knows" how to perform are called the *methods* of the object. Methods are like verbs. To understand this concept, let's say we are programming a robotic dog through Visual Basic. To cause the dog to bark, we might use the "statement"

```
Dog.Bark
```

Robotic dogs, however, are (or ought to be) capable of more than just barking. For example, you might want the dog to understand

```
Dog.Sit
Dog.RollOver
Dog.Fetch
```

The tricks our robodog can perform, such as barking, rolling over, fetching, and so on, are its methods. The list of methods an object can perform depends on the object. A Range object, for example, supports almost 80 different methods that you can use to copy and paste cells, sort, add formatting, and so on.

Like objects in the "real" world, objects in Visual Basic also have *properties*. If you think of objects as the nouns of Visual Basic and methods as its verbs, properties are its adjectives. A property is a quality, characteristic, or attribute of the object, such as its color or pattern.

Characteristics such as our robodog's color, the number of spots on its back, the length of its tinny tail, and the loudness of its bark might be its properties.

You set a property by following the name of the property with an equal sign and a value. Continuing our robotic dog example, we could set the length of the dog's tail with

```
Dog.TailLength = 10
```

where TailLength is a property of the Dog object.

For example, the third executable statement in our CompanyAddress macro,

```
ActiveCell.FormulaR1C1 = "Consolidated Confetti Co."
```

takes the active cell and changes one of its properties. The FormulaR1C1 property consists of the contents of the active cell, which we set to the name of the company, *Consolidated Confetti Co.*

The remaining statements in the CompanyAddress macro consist of two more cell-selection and text-entry couplets: the macro selects cells A7 and A8 and then enters text into each cell.

The Object Browser

You can view the various types of objects, methods, and properties available to Excel by switching to the Visual Basic Editor. To do so, select Macro from the Tools menu and then select Visual Basic Editor. Then choose Object Browser from the View menu. The window displayed on the right of the screen shown in Figure 28-7 appears.

FIGURE 28-7.

The Object Browser, showing the classes of objects belonging to the Excel application.

Project/Library
Drop-down List

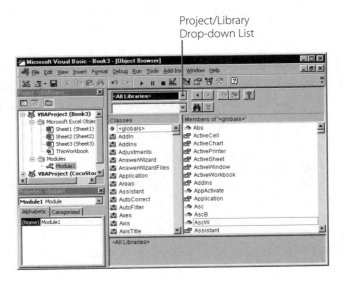

On the left is a scroll box that lists the various *classes* of objects available to Excel. You can think of a class as a template or description for a type of object; a specific chart, for example, would be an object that is an instance of the Chart class. In Visual Basic, classes belong to a project or library; if you select Excel from the Project/Library drop-down list, the object classes belonging to Excel are displayed in the Classes scroll box, as shown in the figure.

If you scroll down the classes and select the Range class, for example, the scroll box on the right side of the Object Browser lists the properties and methods (that is, the *members* of the class) belonging to the Range object, as shown in Figure 28-8.

 You can find Coco2.xls used in the following example on the Microsoft Press Web site at *http://mspress.microsoft.com/mspress/products/2050/*.

FIGURE 28-8.

The Object Browser, showing the Range object and a few of its methods.

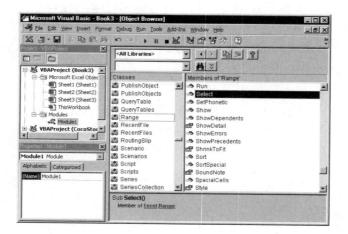

Collections of Objects

You can have more than one instance of the same Visual Basic object; together, these instances comprise a *collection*. Each instance in a collection of objects can be identified either by its index or its name. For example, the collection of all sheets in a workbook is

```
Sheets ( )
```

and a specific instance of a sheet might be either

```
Sheets(3) 'The third sheet in the collection.
```

or

```
Sheets ("Summary") 'A named instance of a sheet.
```

In Visual Basic, each item in a collection has its own index, but the range of index numbers might have gaps because if you delete one instance of an object, the indexes of the other instances might not be renumbered. For example, if you delete Sheets(3) from a collection of 12 sheets in a workbook, there's no guarantee that Excel will renumber Sheets(4) through Sheets(12) to fill the gap.

In other programming languages, you might use a For . . . Next construction, such as

```
For n = 1 to 12 'Activate each sheet
    Sheets(n).Activate
Next n
```

to repeat an operation many times. If you run this code after deleting Sheets(3), Visual Basic displays an error dialog box and stops the macro because Sheets(3) no longer exists. To allow for nonconsecutive indexes, Visual Basic offers the For Each . . . Next statement, a control structure that applies a series of statements to each item in a collection, regardless of the index numbers. For example, suppose you'd like to label each sheet in the active workbook by entering the text *Sheet 1, Sheet 2,* and so on, in cell A1 of each sheet. As you won't, in general, know how many sheets there are in any given workbook, you might use the following Visual Basic macro:

```
Sub EnterSheetNum()
    n = 0
    For Each Sheet In Sheets()
        n = n + 1
        Sheet Active
        Range("A1").Select
        ActiveCell.FormulaR1C1 = "Sheet" + Str(n)
    Next
End Sub
```

You can send a message to or set a property of an object contained in another object by specifying the "subobject" as a series of nested objects. For example, we can make the EnterSheetNum macro run faster by setting the FormulaR1C1 property of cell A1 on each sheet without activating the sheet first. To do this, you simply replace

```
Sheet.Activate
Range("A1").Select
ActiveCell.FormulaR1C1 = "Sheet" + Str(n)
```

with one line:

```
Sheet.Range("A1").FormulaR1C1 = "Sheet" + Str(n)
```

You can read this statement as *Set the FormulaR1C1 property of cell A1 of each to "Sheet n."* The main benefit of this change is that the new form of the macro runs faster because it doesn't make Excel activate each sheet before entering the text.

Naming Arguments to Methods

Many methods in Visual Basic have arguments that let you specify options for the action to be performed. If the Wag method of the Tail object of our mythical robodog has arguments (for example, *wagRate*, the number of wags per second; *wagTime*, the duration of wagging in seconds; and *wagArc*, the number of degrees of arc in each wag), you can specify them using one of two syntaxes.

In the first syntax, which is often called the *by-name syntax,* you name each argument you use, in any order; for example, the statement

```
Robodogs("Fido").Tail.Wag
    wagRate:= 3, _
    wagTime:= 3600, _
    wagArc:= 180
```

wags the tail three times per second for an hour, over an arc of 180 degrees. You assign a value to an argument by using a colon and an equal sign, and you separate arguments by using commas.

> **NOTE**
>
> The underscore at the end of the first and second lines of code tells Visual Basic that the following line is part of the same statement. Using this symbol makes the list of supplied arguments easier to read and allows you to document individual arguments, if needed.

In the second syntax, which is often called the *by-position syntax,* you enter arguments in a prescribed order. (The order of arguments for each method is listed in the Microsoft Visual Basic online Help.) For example, the preceding statement expressed in the by-position syntax looks like this:

```
Robodogs("Fido").Tail.Wag(3,3600,180)
```

Notice that the list of arguments is surrounded by parentheses. The by-position syntax isn't as easy to read as the by-name syntax because you have to remember the order of arguments, and when you review the code at a later date, you won't have the argument names to refresh your memory about their settings.

> **NOTE**

Excel's macro recorder records arguments by position rather than by name, which can make it more difficult to understand recorded macros than manually created macros in which you've named the arguments. Similarly, when you select a Visual Basic keyword and press the F1 key, Excel displays a Help topic describing the by-position syntax for the keyword.

Adding Code to an Existing Macro

Suppose you've recorded a macro that enters a series of labels, sets their font, and draws a border around them. Then you discover that you forgot a step or that you recorded a step incorrectly—you chose the wrong border format, for example. What do you do?

Earlier versions of Excel provided a built-in way to edit an existing macro by recording your subsequent actions at a location you specify in the macro, through the Mark Position For Recording and the Record At Mark commands. The current version of the Visual Basic environment does not support these features, however. To add code to an existing macro, you can record actions in a temporary macro, and then transfer the code into the macro you want to change.

For example, to add to the CompanyAddress macro a step that sets font options for the company's name, follow these steps:

1 Switch to the worksheet containing the address you entered earlier and select cell A6, which contains the name of the company.

2 From the Tools menu, choose Macro and then Record New Macro. Excel presents the Record Macro dialog box. In the Macro Name box, enter *MacroTemp* and then click OK. Excel displays the Stop Recording toolbar.

3 Choose the Cells command from the Format menu and click the Font tab. On the Font tab, select Arial (or any other installed font), 14-point font size, and the Bold Italic font style. Then click OK to apply the formats.

4 Click the Stop Recording button on the Stop Recording toolbar.

5 From the Tools menu, choose Macro and then Visual Basic Editor. If the Project Explorer window isn't visible from the View menu of the Visual Basic Editor, choose Project Explorer. If the

Object Browser is visible but the code isn't, choose the workbook name from the Window menu. In this example, choose *Book1 – Module1 (Code)* on the Window menu.

The Project Window lists the objects that belong to the Book1.xls workbook—three sheets, an object that represents the workbook as a whole, and one module.

6 Double-click Module1. A window appears that contains the original macro we recorded, plus the MacroTemp macro, as shown in Figure 28-9. Scroll down so that you can view all the MacroTemp code.

FIGURE 28-9.

The MacroTemp macro, containing the formatting code we've recorded.

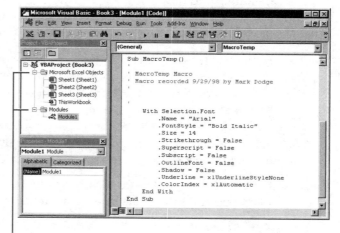

Click to display more detail.

7 Select all the code inside the macro—from the line beginning With through the line beginning End With—and then choose Copy from the Edit menu.

8 Scroll up to display the CompanyAddress macro.

9 Click at the beginning of the line containing the statement

```
Range("A7").Select
```

and press Enter to create a blank line, then position the insertion point at the beginning of the blank line.

10 From the Edit menu, choose Paste.

11 Scroll back down and delete the entire MacroTemp macro, from the Sub statement to the End Sub statement.

12 Finally, choose Microsoft Excel from the View menu to switch back to Excel.

You can test the edited macro by pressing Ctrl+Shift+A. When you run the macro this time, Excel not only enters the address but also applies the font formats you specified. Note that the address should already be there properly formatted as a result of creating this macro. To test it, select the cells, then from the Edit menu choose Clear and then All. The CompanyAddress macro should now look like this:

```
Sub CompanyAddress( )
Range("A6").Select
ActiveCell.FormulaR1C1 = "Consolidated Confetti Co."
With Selection.Font
    .Name = "Arial"
    .FontStyle = "Bold Italic"
    .Size = 14
    .Strikethrough = False
    .Superscript = False
    .Subscript = False
    .OutlineFont = False
    .Shadow = False
    .Underline = xlUnderlineStyleNone
    .ColorIndex = xlAutomatic
End With
Range("A7""").Select
ActiveCell.FormulaR1C1 = "3012 West Beaujolais St."
Range("A8").Select
ActiveCell.FormulaR1C1 = "Walla Walla, WA 98107"
End Sub
```

The With and End With statements specify a series of properties belonging to an object—in this case, the font of the current selection. The two statements provide a kind of shorthand for a series of Visual Basic statements that would look like

```
Selection.Font.Name = "Arial"
Selection.Font.FontStyle = "Bold Italic"
Selection.Font.Size = 14
Selection.Font.Strikethrough = False
Selection.Font.Superscript = False
```

and so on. In the CompanyAddress macro, the ActiveCell object and the Selection object both refer to the same range on the worksheet—cell A6. Because you can apply a series of font formatting options to an entire range, Excel records the action with Selection rather than ActiveCell.

Using Absolute and Relative References

In the CompanyAddress macro, Excel recorded references as absolute references in the A1 format (as opposed to R1C1 format); the CompanyAddress macro always enters the formatted version of the address in Cell A6. In Visual Basic, cell selections are recorded as absolute references unless you click the Relative Reference button on the Stop Recording toolbar. If you click this button, the button appears depressed to show that the command is active—that is, that you're recording relative cell references. You can toggle back and forth between relative and absolute references at any time while recording a macro.

Suppose that instead of inserting the company's name and address in cells A6:A8 of the active worksheet, you'd like to insert the address in whichever cell happens to be active when you run the macro. In order to do this, you need to create a new CompanyAddress macro—let's call it CompanyAddressRel—that uses relative references instead of absolute references:

1   Make sure you're on Sheet1 of the Book1 workbook. Select cells A6:A8 and from the Edit menu, choose Clear and then All. Next select cell A6.

2   From the Tools menu, choose Macro and then choose Record New Macro. In the Record Macro dialog box, enter *CompanyAddressRel* for the macro's name, lowercase *a* for the shortcut key, and in the Description box type *Enter company address in any cell.* Click OK. Excel displays the same Stop Recording toolbar shown in Figure 28-2 on page 6.

3   Click the Relative Reference button on the Stop Recording toolbar; when you do this, the button appears depressed, indicating that you will be recording relative references.

4   Choose Cells from the Format menu, select 14-point Arial Bold Italic, and then click OK.

5   Enter the text

    Consolidated Confetti Co.

Then press the Down arrow key once and type

    3012 West Beaujolais St.

Press the Down arrow key again and type

Walla Walla, WA 98107

Then press Enter.

6 Click the Stop Recording button.

Test this macro by clicking in various cells and pressing Ctrl+a (lowercase this time—no Shift key). If you switch back to the Visual Basic environment, open Module1, and look for the new CompanyAddressRel macro, you'll see the following listing:

```
Sub CompanyAddress( )
' CompanyAddressRel Macro
' Enter company address in any cell.
' Keyboard Shortcut: Ctrl+a
With Selection.Font
    .Name = "Arial"
    .FontStyle = "Bold Italic"
    .Size = 14
    .Strikethrough = False
    .Superscript = False
    .Subscript = False
    .OutlineFont = False
    .Shadow = False
    .Underline = xlUnderlineStyleNone
    .ColorIndex = xlAutomatic
End With
ActiveCell.FormulaR1C1 = "Consolidated Confetti Co."
ActiveCell.Offset(1, 0).Range("A1").Select
ActiveCell.FormulaR1C1 = "3012 West Beaujolais St."
ActiveCell.Offset(1, 0).Range("A1").Select
ActiveCell.FormulaR1C1 = "Walla Walla, WA 98107"
End Sub
```

The original macro enters the address in the range A6:A8, regardless of which cell is active when you start the macro. The new macro, on the other hand, enters the address starting in the active cell, no matter where that cell is located.

If you compare the two versions of the macro, you'll see that the only difference between them lies in the statements used to select cells. For example, the new version of the macro does not include a statement for selecting the first cell because it uses relative references and the first cell is already selected.

In addition, to select the second cell, the original macro uses the statement

```
Range("A7").Select
```

whereas the new version uses

```
ActiveCell.Offset(1,0).Range("A1").Select
```

To move from the active cell to the cell below it in the new macro, Visual Basic starts with the ActiveCell object, to which it applies the Offset method with two arguments for the number or rows and columns to offset. The Range keyword then returns a range with the same dimensions as its argument. In this case, the argument "A1" specifies that we want a range consisting of a single cell. Finally, the Select method selects the range, as in the original macro.

Obviously, the position of the active cell makes a great deal of difference when you use a macro that was recorded with relative references. Before you run the macro, be sure to select the cell in which you want to enter the address. Otherwise, the macro enters the address wherever the active cell happens to be.

The major difference between using cell references in a worksheet and in a module is this: in a worksheet, you use the dollar sign symbol ($) to indicate that a column or row reference is absolute, but in a Visual Basic module, all references are absolute. As a result, relative references in modules can be constructed only by using the Offset method on an absolute Range object.

Which form is better—absolute or relative? It depends. Absolute references are useful when you want to perform the same action in the same spot in several worksheets, or when you want to perform the same action repeatedly in the same part of one worksheet. Relative references are useful when you want to perform an action anywhere in a worksheet.

Macro Subroutines

Suppose you're creating a complex macro and you discover that, among other things, you want the macro to perform a task you've already recorded under a different name. Or suppose you discover that a task you've recorded as part of a macro is actually something you'd like to use by itself. In our CompanyAddress macro, for example, it might be nice if we could quickly and easily apply the font formats of the company name to other items in a worksheet.

With Visual Basic, you can conveniently divide large macros into a series of smaller macros, and you can easily string together a series of small macros to create one large macro. A macro procedure that is used by another macro is called a *subroutine*. Macro subroutines can simplify your macros because you have to write only one set of instructions rather than repeat the instructions over and over again. To use a macro subroutine in another macro, you call the subroutine by using its name in the other macro.

To demonstrate, let's split the CompanyAddressRel macro (the one that uses relative addressing) into two parts:

1   Switch to the CompanyAddressRel macro and select the statements that format the font of the company's name:

```
With Selection.Font
    .Name = "Arial"
    .FontStyle = "Bold Italic"
    .Size = 14
    .Strikethrough = False
    .Superscript = False
    .Subscript = False
    .OutlineFont = False
    .Shadow = False
    .Underline = xlUnderlineStyleName
    .ColorIndex = xlAutomatic
End With
```

2   Choose Cut from the Edit menu.

3   Click an insertion point below the End Sub statement at the end of the CompanyAddressRel macro, type

```
Sub CompanyFont( )
```

and press Enter to start a new line.

4   Choose Paste from the Edit menu to insert the font formatting code.

You've created a new CompanyFont macro by moving the font formatting codes from the CompanyAddress macro into the new CompanyFont macro. As mentioned, to run one macro from within another, you must use the name of the second macro in the first. To update the Company Address macro so it uses the CompanyFont macro, follow these steps:

1   Click an insertion point at the end of the statement

```
ActiveCell.FormulaR1C1 = "Consolidated Confetti Co."
```

and press Enter to insert a new line.

2   Type *CompanyFont*.

When you've finished, the two macros should look like the ones in the following listing:

```
Sub CompanyAddress()
ActiveCell.FormulaR1C1 = "Consolidated Confetti Co."
CompanyFont
ActiveCell.Offset(1, 0).Range("A1").Select
ActiveCell.FormulaR1C1 = "3012 West Beaujolais St."
ActiveCell.Offset(1, 0).Range("A1").Select
ActiveCell.FormulaR1C1 = "Walla Walla, WA 98107"
End Sub

Sub CompanyFont()
With Selection.Font
    .Name = "Arial"
    .FontStyle = "Bold Italic"
    .Size = 14
    .Strikethrough = False
    .Superscript = False
    .Subscript = False
    .OutlineFont = False
    .Shadow = False
    .Underline = xlNone
    .ColorIndex = xlAutomatic
End With
End Sub
```

When you activate the CompanyAddressRel macro by pressing Ctrl+a, Excel runs the first statement in the macro. When Excel reaches the statement that calls the CompanyFont macro, it switches to the first line of CompanyFont. When Excel reaches the End Sub Statement at the end of CompanyFont, it returns to the statement in CompanyAddress below the one that called CompanyFont and continues until it reaches the End Sub statement at the end of CompanyAddress.

Other Ways to Run Macros

Earlier in this chapter we assigned the CompanyAddress macro to the Ctrl+Shift+A key combination. Excel offers other ways to run macros: You can assign a macro to a command that appears on one of Excel's menus, to a button on a toolbar, and to a drawing object. You can also assign a macro to a button on a worksheet or chart. *See Chapter 30, "A Sample Visual Basic Application," for more information about these shortcuts. For more information about customizing menus and commands, see Chapter 3, "Toolbars and Menus."*

> **TIP**
>
> **Using a Drawing Object**
>
> You can also assign a macro to any drawing object. First, position the mouse pointer over any displayed toolbar, press the right mouse button, and then choose Drawing to display the Drawing toolbar. Next, click an object and drag in the worksheet to create an object of the dimensions you want. Finally, click the right button with the mouse pointer over the object, and from the object's shortcut menu, choose Assign Macro. When Excel displays the Assign Macro dialog box, select the name of the macro you want to assign to the object and then click OK. *For more information about using the Drawing toolbar, see "Creating Graphic Objects," page 346.*

Using the Personal Macro Workbook

When you recorded the CompanyAddress macro earlier in this chapter, we instructed you to place the macro in a module that belongs to the active workbook. A macro that has been placed in a module becomes available only when the workbook containing the macro is open.

To make a macro available at all times, store it in the Personal Macro Workbook. The Personal Macro Workbook is normally hidden; you can unhide it by choosing the Unhide command from the Window menu and double-clicking Personal in the Unhide dialog box. If you have not yet recorded a macro in the Personal Macro Workbook, however, the Unhide command is dimmed, and the Personal file is not listed in the Unhide dialog box. To get around this problem, record a simple macro, as described earlier, and then select the Personal Macro Workbook option in the Record New Macro dialog box. Excel creates the Personal Macro Workbook and places its file (Personal) in the main Excel directory.

The Personal Macro Workbook initially contains only one module, but you can add other modules—or even worksheets—to it. For example, you can use it to store modules that contain general-purpose macros, such as macros that enter company and client addresses.

To transfer an existing macro to an unhidden Personal Macro Workbook, follow these steps:

1   In the Visual Basic Editor, choose Project Explorer from the View menu and open the module containing the macro you want to move.

2   Select the macro (be sure to include the final End Sub statement and any statements that appear before the initial Sub statement) and then choose Cut from the Edit menu.

3   Use the Project Explorer to open the Personal Macro Workbook, Personal.xls, and open a module in it.

4   Click an insertion point in the module where you want to insert the macro and then choose Paste from the Edit menu.

5   Finally, switch back to Excel and choose Exit from the File menu. When you quit the current work session, Excel asks whether you want to save changes to the Personal Macro Workbook. Click Yes to save the hidden workbook. (You can unhide the Personal Macro Workbook, but be sure to hide it again before you save; otherwise, the workbook will appear each time you start Excel.)

Custom Functions

Although Microsoft Excel 2000 includes a multitude of built-in worksheet functions, you probably perform calculations for which no function is available. Suppose your company uses a special mathematical formula for computing discounts for buyers of your product. Wouldn't it be convenient if you had a function named Discount that could compute the discount for you on any order? In this chapter, we'll show you how to create such custom functions.

Custom functions, also known as *user-defined functions,* are one of the most innovative and exciting features of Microsoft Excel. To create a custom function, you must write a special Microsoft Visual Basic procedure, called a *function procedure,* that accepts information from the worksheet, performs calculations, and then returns a result to the worksheet. The types of information-handling and calculation tasks that you can simplify, generalize, or streamline with custom functions are virtually unlimited.

Like built-in functions, custom functions are initiated when Excel recalculates the formulas in a worksheet or macro sheet. Custom functions make calculations and return values without performing actions in the workspace; because they don't perform actions, you cannot record a custom function as you can a macro. The value returned to the worksheet is typically numeric but could also be a text value, a logical value, an error value, or an array of values.

After you create a custom function, you can use it the way you use any built-in function (except for the minor differences discussed in "Custom Function Rules," page 908). For example, you can create a custom function that computes the interest paid to date on a loan or one that computes a weighted average for a range of numbers. Often, custom functions let you condense into one cell calculations that would otherwise occupy a large amount of space in a worksheet.

SEE ALSO

For more information about add-ins, see "Converting to an Add-In Application," page 942.

You can also add custom functions to Excel and use them in exactly the same way you would any of the built-in functions, by saving the workbook containing the custom function in the special Add-In format.

Creating a Custom Function

Creating a custom function is a two-step process. First, create a new module or open an existing module to hold the Visual Basic code that defines the custom function. Second, type the Visual Basic statements that calculate the result you want to return to the worksheet.

In many spreadsheet programs, macros are stored in the cells of the related worksheet, but in Excel you create and store macros and custom functions in modules. Because the macros and custom functions are independent of a specific worksheet, you can use them with many worksheets. In fact, you can collect several macros and custom functions in one module and use it as a library.

To illustrate, let's build a simple custom function. Suppose your company offers a discount of 10 percent on the sale of a product, but only if the order is for more than 100 units. The worksheet in Figure 29-1 shows an order form that lists each item, the quantity, the price, the discount (if any), and the resulting charge.

ON THE WEB

You can find TreeOrders.xls found in the following example on the Microsoft Press Web site at *http://mspress.microsoft.com/mspress/products/2050/*.

FIGURE 29-1.

We want to calculate the discount for each item ordered.

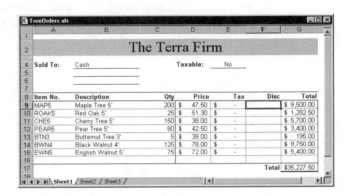

To create a custom function—in this case, one that computes each discount—perform the following steps:

1   Create a new module in the TreeOrders workbook by choosing Macro from the Tools menu and then choosing Visual Basic Editor. Excel starts the Visual Basic environment. Next choose Module from the Insert menu. (The Macro command does not normally appear on shortened menus. Click the downward-pointing double arrow at the bottom of the Tools menu to display the Macro command.) Excel opens a blank module, as shown in Figure 29-2.

FIGURE 29-2.

Choosing Module from the Insert menu adds a module to the workbook.

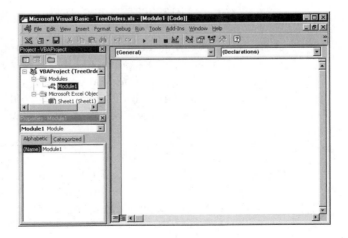

2 To give the module a name, first click the Module1 entry in the Project Explorer window. In the Properties window, double-click the entry in the Name field to select it, enter *SalesFncs,* and then press Enter. The name of the module changes to SalesFncs, as shown in Figure 29-3.

FIGURE 29-3.

Change the name of the module you've inserted into the active workbook.

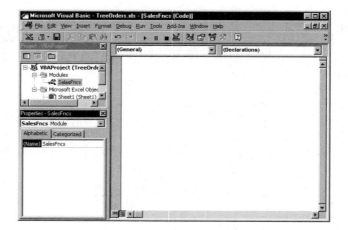

3 Switch back to the newly renamed module and enter Visual Basic statements that define the custom function. For this example, enter the following code, using the Tab key to indent lines:

```
Function Discount(quantity, price)
    If quantity >= 100 Then
        Discount = quantity * price * 0.1
    Else
        Discount = 0
    End If
    Discount = Application.Round(Discount,2)
End Function
```

The act of entering the function in a module defines the function's name (in this case, Discount) and makes it available to any open worksheet. You'll notice as you enter the Visual Basic code that Excel displays certain terms in different colors so that the purposes of the various parts of the code or function are easier to understand.

When you press Enter at the end of a line of code, Excel checks the new code for simple errors in syntax. If you make a typing error or misuse a Visual Basic keyword, Excel might display a message box telling you the nature of the error. At this point, you might not understand many of these messages; instead of trying to figure out the problem, compare what you typed with the example code and enter the text exactly. Figure 29-4 shows the module at this point.

FIGURE 29-4.

This custom function calculates the discount on a sales order.

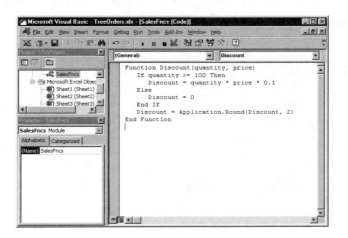

```
Function Discount(quantity, price)
    If quantity >= 100 Then
        Discount = quantity * price * 0.1
    Else
        Discount = 0
    End If
    Discount = Application.Round(Discount, 2)
End Function
```

Using Custom Functions

Now you're ready to use the new Discount function. Choose Microsoft Excel from the View menu to switch to the worksheet shown in Figure 29-1 on page 903. Next select cell F9, and enter

=Discount (C9,D9)

Notice that you don't have to identify the module containing the function procedure. The function's first argument, C9, identifies the cell that contains the quantity that corresponds to the function's *quantity* argument. The second argument, D9, identifies the cell that contains the price that corresponds to the function's *price* argument. When you press Enter, Excel calculates and returns the correct discount for the arguments supplied: $950.00.

You can now assign a dollar format to cell F9 and copy the formula from cell F9 to cells F9:F15, as shown in Figure 29-5 on the next page. To copy the formula, drag the AutoFill handle down six more cells. Because the references to cells C9 and D9 in the original formula are relative references, they change as the formula is copied to the new cells. For example, the formula in cell F14 is

=Discount(C14,D14)

If you change the values in cells C9:D15, the custom function immediately updates the discount calculations in cells F9:F15.

Macros and Visual Basic

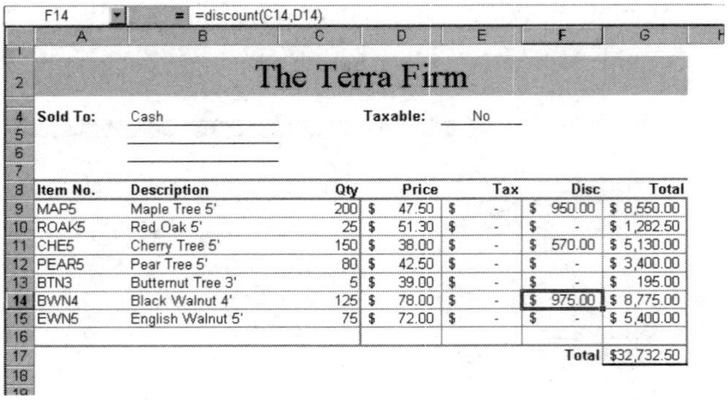
F14 = =discount(C14,D14)

The Terra Firm

Sold To: Cash   Taxable: No

Item No.	Description	Qty	Price	Tax	Disc	Total
MAP5	Maple Tree 5'	200	$ 47.50	$ -	$ 950.00	$ 8,550.00
ROAK5	Red Oak 5'	25	$ 51.30	$ -	$ -	$ 1,282.50
CHE5	Cherry Tree 5'	150	$ 38.00	$ -	$ 570.00	$ 5,130.00
PEAR5	Pear Tree 5'	80	$ 42.50	$ -	$ -	$ 3,400.00
BTN3	Butternut Tree 3'	5	$ 39.00	$ -	$ -	$ 195.00
BWN4	Black Walnut 4'	125	$ 78.00	$ -	$ 975.00	$ 8,775.00
EWN5	English Walnut 5'	75	$ 72.00	$ -	$ -	$ 5,400.00
					Total	$32,732.50

FIGURE 29-5.
This worksheet shows the result of the Discount custom function.

What's Happening

Let's consider how Excel interprets this function procedure. When you press Enter to lock in the formula in the worksheet, Excel looks for the name Discount in the current workbook and finds that it is a procedure in the SalesFncs module. The argument names enclosed in parentheses—*quantity* and *price*—are placeholders for the values upon which the calculation of the discount is based.

The If statement in the block of code

```
If quantity >= 100 Then
   Discount = quantity * price * 0.1
Else
   Discount = 0
End If
```

examines the *quantity* argument and determines whether the number of items sold is either greater than or equal to 100. If it is, Excel executes the statement

```
Discount = quantity * price * 0.1
```

which multiplies the *quantity* value by the *price* value and then multiplies the result by 0.1 (the numerical equivalent of a 10 percent discount). The final result is stored as the variable *Discount.* A Visual Basic statement that stores a value in a variable is often called an *assignment statement,* because it evaluates the expression on the right of the equal sign and assigns the result to the variable name on the left. Because the variable *Discount* has the same name as the function procedure itself, the value stored in the variable is returned to the formula in cell F9 of the worksheet.

Notice that formulas entered in a worksheet and Visual Basic statements entered in a module are different in several ways. In a worksheet, a formula always begins with an equal sign, and the result of the formula is stored in the cell containing the formula. You can use the Define Name dialog box to assign a name to a cell containing a formula, thereby creating a *named reference*. You can also enter a formula in the Define Name dialog box to assign a name to the formula without storing the formula in a cell, thereby creating a *named formula*. (The simplest case of a named formula is when the formula is a constant; for example, you might assign the name *Pi* to the formula =3.14159.) Depending on how you have set up your worksheet, you can use a value elsewhere in the worksheet by entering the reference of the cell containing the formula that produces the value, the named reference of that cell, or the named formula (or constant). When Excel encounters a named formula, it evaluates the associated formula and uses the result.

In a Visual Basic module, values are stored in variables, which are never coupled with locations on a worksheet. In this sense, a variable in a module is similar to a named constant in a worksheet; when Excel encounters an assignment statement such as *Discount = quantity * price * 0.1*, it doesn't store the expression *quantity * price * 0.1* in the variable, as you would expect if this were a worksheet. Instead, Excel evaluates the expression and stores only the result in the variable. If you use the variable name elsewhere in the function procedure, Excel uses the last value stored in the variable.

If *quantity* is less than 100, no discount is offered, and Excel executes the statement

```
Discount = 0
```

which simply sets *Discount* to 0.

The If...Else...End If sequence is called a *control structure*; If is a Visual Basic keyword that is analogous to the IF worksheet function. Control structures such as If...Else...End If let your macros and custom functions test for specific conditions on a worksheet or in the Excel environment and change the behavior of the procedure accordingly.

 NOTE

> Control structures cannot be recorded. Being able to use them in macros and custom functions is one of the primary reasons to learn to write and edit Visual Basic procedures.

Finally, the statement

```
Discount = Application.Round(Discount,2)
```

rounds the value that represents the amount of the discount to two decimal places. Notice that Visual Basic has no Round function, but Excel does. Therefore, to use Round in this statement, you tell Visual Basic to "look for the Round method (function) in the Application object (Excel)" by adding *Application* before the word *Round*. Use this syntax whenever you need to access an Excel function from a Visual Basic module.

Custom Function Rules

Our example illustrates many of the characteristics of custom functions. First, a custom function must start with a Function statement and end with an End Function statement. You need not explicitly specify that a macro is a custom function and define its name. With Visual Basic, the act of typing the name of the custom function in a Function statement in a module defines it. In addition to the function name, the initial Function statement almost always specifies at least one argument, enclosed in parentheses. You can specify up to 29 arguments, using commas to separate them. (Technically, you can create a custom function that uses no data from a worksheet but returns a value; for example, you could create a function that takes no argument but returns the current time and date as a specially formatted text string.)

Second, custom functions include one or more statements in Visual Basic that make decisions and perform calculations using the arguments passed to the function. To return the result of a calculation to a worksheet formula that uses the custom function, you assign the result to a variable that has the same name as the custom function itself.

Third, you can use only the custom functions that are located in the modules of open workbooks. If you close a workbook that contains a custom function used in a formula in an open worksheet, the value returned by the function changes to the #REF! error value. To regenerate the correct value, reopen the workbook containing the module in which the custom function is defined.

Visual Basic Keywords Available to Custom Functions

The number of Visual Basic keywords you can use in custom functions is smaller than the number you can use in macros. This is because custom functions are not allowed to do anything other than return a value to a formula in a worksheet or to an expression used in another Visual Basic macro or function. For example, custom functions cannot resize windows, edit a formula in a cell, or change the font, color, or pattern options for the text in a cell or the cell itself. As a result, the Visual Basic keywords that change these options cannot be used in a custom function.

Documenting Macros and Custom Functions

Even simple macros and custom functions can be difficult to read. You can make them easier to understand by entering explanatory text in the form of comments. You add comments by preceding the explanatory text with a single quotation mark. For example, Figure 29-6 shows the *Discount* function with comments. Adding comments like these will enhance your understanding should you have to change the *Discount* procedure in the future and will allow others who might inherit your work to understand the procedure.

FIGURE 29-6.

The Discount custom function now includes comments.

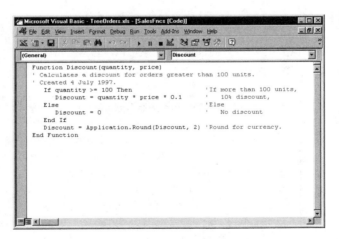

A single quotation mark tells Excel to ignore everything to the right on the same line, so you can place a comment to the right of a Visual Basic statement. You can also insert comments between the statements in a macro or custom function. For example, you might begin a relatively lengthy block of code with a comment that identifies its overall purpose and then use inline comments to document individual statements.

Another way to document your macros and custom functions is to give them descriptive names. For example, rather than name a macro Labels, you could name it RelMonthLabels, where *Rel* indicates that the macro uses relative references and *MonthLabels* describes the type of label the macro creates. Using descriptive names for macros and custom functions is essential when you've created many procedures, particularly if you create procedures that have similar, but not identical, purposes.

As a rule, you should give a custom function the shortest name that describes its purpose and yet sets it apart from other functions and Visual Basic keywords. For example, you might name a function that computes federal income taxes FederalIncomeTax, but it would be better to shorten that name to FedIncTax or FedTax. On the other hand, don't make the names of your custom functions so short that they aren't descriptive. For example, you probably wouldn't want to call your federal income tax function Tax because this name doesn't tell you what kind of tax the function computes. In addition, don't give your functions names that conflict with Visual Basic keywords such as End and Function.

How you document your macros and custom functions is a matter of personal preference. It doesn't matter which method you select, as long as you document them somehow. Documentation is most important for long and complex procedures, for procedures that you look at only once in a while, and for procedures that will be maintained by other people.

Deactivating Statements in Custom Functions

The essential difference between a statement in the Visual Basic programming language (which is executed) and a comment (which isn't) is that a comment is always preceded by a single quotation mark. Therefore, if you're building a macro or custom function and enter a statement that you don't want to be executed when you run the procedure, simply insert a single quotation mark before the statement to convert the statement into a comment. When you run the macro, Excel skips past the deactivated, or *commented*, statement as if it weren't there. So, for example, if you are developing a macro that formats your worksheet and then prints it, you can comment out the print statement during development to save a few trees.

Designing Flexible Custom Functions

Let's create another custom function to gain some experience with editing procedures in a Visual Basic module.

Some of Excel's built-in worksheet functions let you omit certain arguments. For example, if you omit the *type* and *future value* arguments from the PV function, Excel still computes the result. However, if you omit an argument from a custom function, Excel displays an error message unless you've specified that the argument is optional (by using the Optional keyword) and you have designed your function procedure to test whether the argument has been supplied.

For example, suppose you want to create a simple custom function, called Triangle, that uses the Pythagorean theorem to compute the length of any side of a right triangle, given the lengths of the other two sides, as illustrated here:

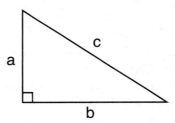

The equation that expresses the Pythagorean theorem is

$$a^2 + b^2 = c^2$$

where *a* and *b* are the short sides and *c* is the hypotenuse (the longest side).

Given any two sides, you can rewrite the equation in these three ways so that the unknown variable is always on the left of the equal sign:

$$a = \sqrt{c^2 - b^2}$$

$$b = \sqrt{c^2 - a^2}$$

$$c = \sqrt{a^2 + b^2}$$

The following custom function uses these three versions of the equation to return the length of the missing side:

```
Function Triangle(Optional short1, Optional short2,_
Optional longside)

If Not (IsMissing(short1)) _
And Not (IsMissing(short2)) Then
    Triangle = Sqr(short1 ^ 2 + short2 ^ 2)
Else
    If Not (IsMissing(short1)) _
    And Not (IsMissing(longside)) Then
        Triangle = Sqr(longside ^ 2 - short1 ^ 2)
    Else
        If Not (IsMissing(short2)) _
        And Not (IsMissing(longside)) Then
            Triangle = Sqr(longside ^ 2 - short2 ^ 2)
        Else
            Triangle = Null
        End If
    End If
End If
End Function
```

The first statement names the custom function and the optional arguments *short1*, *short2*, and *longside*. (Note that in this function we cannot use the word *long* as an argument name because *long* is a reserved word in Visual Basic.) The following block of code contains a series of If statements that use the Visual Basic IsMissing function to test whether each possible pair of arguments has been supplied and to calculate and return the length of the third side.

For example, the statement

```
If Not (IsMissing(short1)) _
And Not (IsMissing(short2)) Then
    Triangle = Sqr(short1 ^ 2 + short2 ^ 2)
```

tests for the presence of *short1* and *short2;* the IsMissing function returns True if the argument has not been supplied. If *short1* is not missing and *short2* is not missing, Excel computes the square root of the sum of the squares of the lengths of the two short sides and returns the length of the hypotenuse to the worksheet.

If fewer than two arguments are supplied, none of the If statements evaluates to True, and the statement

```
Triangle = Null
```

is executed. This statement returns the Visual Basic value Null, which becomes the #N/A error value in the worksheet.

Now let's see what happens when we use this custom function in a worksheet. The formula

> =Triangle(,4,5)

returns the value 3, the length of the missing short side. Similarly, the formula

> =Triangle(3,,5)

returns 4, the length of the other missing short side. And finally, the formula

> =Triangle(3,4,)

returns 5, the length of the hypotenuse. If the lengths of the two short sides, 3 and 4, are stored in cells A4 and B4, and you enter the formula

> =Triangle(A4,B4,)

in cell C4, Excel displays the result 5 in that cell.

If values for all three arguments are supplied, the first of the If statements evaluates to True, and the custom function acts as if the value for the hypotenuse were not supplied. But what if you enter cell references for all three arguments? For example, suppose you enter the following function in cell D4 of a worksheet:

> =Triangle(A4,B4,C4)

intending that the lengths of two of the triangle's sides will be entered in the referenced cells instead of in the function directly. If cells A4 and C4 contain the lengths of one short side and the hypotenuse, but cell B4 is empty, you might expect Triangle to return the length of the other short side. However, the reference to the empty cell B4 evaluates to 0, not #N/A. Because the first two arguments have numeric values, the function attempts to calculate the hypotenuse of a right triangle in which one of the short sides has zero length and returns the square root of the sums of the squares of the short sides as usual. The result is the length of the short side you supplied in the worksheet, not the length of the missing side.

One way to deal with this potential problem is to change the If statements so that they test for zero values as well as #N/A error values. A right triangle cannot have a side of zero length, so if an argument evaluates to zero, that argument wasn't supplied.

This problem highlights one of the major issues that faces the designer of custom functions: you must design custom functions so that they work even when used in unexpected ways.

A Sample Visual Basic Application

In the preceding two chapters, we covered the elements of recording macros and editing them, and creating custom functions and using them in a workbook. We've also presented enough of the Visual Basic programming language to get the job done, in as easy-to-digest a way as possible in the space allotted. In this way we hoped to demonstrate that working with Visual Basic in Microsoft Excel 2000 isn't arcane and that you don't have to belong to the secret society of those fluent in programming esoterica to get started with the language.

Perhaps the best way to begin learning a programming language, or any language, is to simply jump in and start reading it. Visual Basic is no exception. By analyzing Visual Basic code that has already been written or recorded, in the context of a well-defined task, you can more easily understand the correspondence between the code and the task.

In this chapter, we'll take a high-speed reconnaissance flight over the terrain. As examples, we'll use a few macros and custom functions that together attempt to solve a problem—transferring data to an Excel worksheet, formatting the resulting data, plotting a chart from the data, and finally preparing and printing a report in Microsoft Word. Along the way, the examples will illustrate the range and power of the Visual Basic language for formatting worksheets and charts, working with files, and modifying the user interface in various ways.

In many cases, we'll start with macros we've recorded and adapt them so they'll work better with the other macros presented in this chapter. Because we have a lot of ground to cover, we won't explain every line of every macro, relying instead on commented code and the self-documenting nature typical of Visual Basic to outline the steps involved. Upon occasion we will dig a little deeper to uncover a few programming tricks along the way.

Don't think, however, that working through this chapter will give you a complete understanding of Visual Basic. Just as in any language, it's comparatively easy to teach a few handy phrases—enough to help you find a bookstore, for example—but, given a phrasebook, you shouldn't expect to be able to write a sonnet. If you'd like to get more than just your feet wet, we recommend working through *Microsoft® Excel97/Visual Basic® Step by Step,* by Reed Jacobson, from Microsoft Press.

A Visual Basic Application

This chapter presents a series of sample macros and custom functions used to provide an Excel solution to a spreadsheet problem. Let's say you are measuring the amount of water flowing in the Skagit River in Western Washington, as part of a larger study among people collaborating to develop a model for flood control in the Skagit River Watershed. Others in your group are measuring river depth daily and publishing the data as a file at an FTP site. The file, RivrData.txt, contains the dates of the measurements at four sites along the Skagit River. Your Excel application transfers this data from the FTP site to your computer, appends it to a list of preexisting measurements, creates a new chart from the data, and uses Word to prepare and print a report that contains the data and chart. This all happens at a predetermined time, say 2:00 AM, so the printed report is ready for you when you come into the office in the morning.

We'll call this solution the RiverReport project, which is a collection of worksheets, a custom-defined dialog box (in Visual Basic, called a *userform*), macros, and functions, all contained in one workbook.

W ON THE WEB

This may be a relatively complicated project to create from scratch when you're first learning Visual Basic. If you'd rather start with the finished project and follow along in the text, you can download the RiverReport.xls project from the Microsoft Press Web site at *http://mspress.microsoft.com/mspress/ products/2050/*. For more information about using Excel to access remote FTP sites, see "Working with FTP Sites in Excel," page 619.

Loading a Workbook Automatically

You can specify that a certain workbook, such as one that contains a library of macros, be opened automatically each time Excel starts. To do this, put the workbook in Excel's XLStart folder, which is located in the C:\Windows\Application Data\Microsoft\Excel folder.

For example, to ensure that the RiverReport project workbook is loaded automatically when you start Excel, do the following:

1   Choose New from the File menu, select Workbook, and then click OK.

2   With the workbook active, choose Save from the File menu.

3   Go to C:\Windows\Application Data\Microsoft\Excel\XLStart folder.

4   Type the name of the workbook file—in this case, *RiverReport.xls*—in the File Name edit box.

5   Click Save.

? SEE ALSO

For more information about custom menus and commands, see "Creating New Menus," page 54.

Opening the workbook on startup ensures that the menu command for starting the RiverReport project (which we have not yet created) appears automatically when the user starts Excel.

Next, select Sheet1, rename it Data, and then create a table that contains the information shown in Figure 30-1 on the next page.

FIGURE 30-1.

The Data sheet in RiverReport.xls contains information returned from remote measurement sites.

RiverReport.xls								
	A	B	C	D	E	F	G	H
1	**Skagit River Depth Data**							
2	Depth data, in feet, returned from measurement points along the Skagit river.							
3	Name 'tableRange' is the entire area of the table.							
4								
5	Depth at bank:	5.50	7.25	12.50	21.50			
6								
7	date	site1	site2	site3	site4			
8	6/5/00 Mon	3.25	4.47	8.12	12.78			
9	6/6/00 Tue	3.33	4.59	8.76	14.05			
10	6/7/00 Wed	3.34	4.67	9.23	14.36			
11	6/8/00 Thu	3.43	5.10	9.46	15.44			
12	6/9/00 Fri	3.60	5.47	9.50	16.11			
13	6/10/00 Sat	3.70	5.84	10.12	16.21			
14	6/11/00 Sun	3.97	6.13	10.63	17.36			
15	6/12/00 Mon	4.10	6.68	11.42	18.80			
16	6/13/00 Tue	4.50	7.10	11.70	19.20			
17								

Data / AppOptions /

Finally, you need to ensure that the RiverReport folder will be there when you need it. (The sample application saves the finished Word report in this folder, located in the root directory of your C: drive. You can use another location for the report, but you'll need to specify this on the AppOptions sheet, described later in this chapter.) Open Windows Explorer, select the icon for the C drive, choose New and then Folder from the File menu, and change the folder name to RiverReport. Close Windows Explorer to return to Excel.

> **NOTE**
>
> When this application runs, it saves a copy of RivrData.txt in the specified folder on your hard drive. The next time you run the application, it will attempt to save another copy in the same location. If the file already exists there, a dialog box appears asking whether you want to overwrite the existing copy. You will need to first delete the local copy to avoid getting this dialog box if you want the application to run unattended.

Declaring Public Variables

The RiverReport project uses seven variables that contain information needed by the macros in order to remember the location of its files, the location of the remote FTP site, and so on. First, you need to create a module to contain our code. Choose Visual Basic Editor from the Macros submenu on the Tools menu.

In the Visual Basic Editor, from the Insert menu choose Module; the Module1 module appears. Select the Module1 module and in the Properties window, change the name of the module to AMainCode. In the

Project Explorer window the modules are listed in alphabetical order, and it will be clearer to have our modules listed in the order their component macros will be executed.

Next, in the AMainCode module, enter these variable declarations:

```
Public localPath 'Where to store downloaded data
Public docName 'Name of file to download
Public ftpPath 'Pathname to remote FTP site
Public wordDocPath 'Path to Word report doc
Public startTime 'When to download data
Public MyAppVersion 'RiverReport version number
Public chartSheetName 'Name of sheet created in table
```

Using the Public keyword in Visual Basic establishes the listed variables as *public variables* (often called global variables) that are available to all procedures in all modules in the workbook. Unless you declare a variable as public, the variable "belongs" only to the macro or custom function in which you use it, and no other procedure can access the value stored in that variable. In the case of the *docName* variable, for example, any procedure in the RiverReport project can determine the name of the file downloaded from the remote FTP site stored in the variable *ftpPath*.

The Main Sequence

The following procedures make up the main tasks in the RiverReport project, in order of execution:

1 Transfer a text file, called RivrData.txt, containing a series of recent river depth measurements from a directory at a remote FTP site to a directory on your computer.

2 Open the text file from a macro, select its contents, copy them, and then paste them at the end of a preexisting series of measurements in the sheet called Data.

3 Format the table containing the data.

4 Create a chart from the table containing the data.

5 Control Word from Excel to create a new report to receive the table and chart.

6 Copy the table and chart in Excel, switch to Word, and then paste them into the new report.

7 Save and print the new report.

To begin programming these tasks, enter the following routine a few lines below the area where you declared the public variables:

```
Sub MainProc()
    LoadVariables 'Load public variables.
    GetRemoteData 'Download file from remote FTP site.
    ImportData 'Import and convert data.
    FormatData 'Format the resulting table.
    CreateChart 'Create a new chart.
    GenWordReport 'Create a new Word doc for report.
End Sub
```

This routine calls nine procedures to perform the seven tasks. Of these, only a few can be recorded; for the others, you must enter the code for the necessary Sub and Function procedures. Of course, none of these procedures in the RiverReport project exist yet—you'll create them as you go through this chapter.

To allow the user to run these procedures by choosing a command from a menu, you'll add a menu item associated with a "master-control" procedure that manages the RiverReport project. When you're done, you'll package the group of routines as an add-in application that can be distributed to others.

Of course, you could adapt this project to track other information besides river depth data, such as stock prices, or to track progress in any project in which the participants are not in immediate communication with each other. However you use it, the project converts the information and inserts the data either in a separate worksheet in a single workbook or in separate columns in a single common worksheet.

Running a Macro Automatically

To run a macro automatically whenever the workbook that contains the macro is opened, all you need to do is name the macro Auto_Open. As an example of an auto-open macro, the next procedure runs a startup procedure called StartMyApp automatically whenever the RiverReport.xls file is opened. To begin, open the AMainCode module, if necessary, and enter the following auto-open procedure just after the public declarations:

```
Sub Auto_Open()
    StartMyApp
End Sub
```

TIP

> To open a workbook that contains a macro named Auto_Open and bypass the auto-open macro, choose Open from the File menu, select the filename from the list box, and then hold down the Shift key while you click Open.

Similarly, to run a macro whenever a workbook is closed, all you need to do is name the macro Auto_Close. Auto-close macros are useful for cleaning up after a system of macros has run its course, returning menu bars and toolbars to their original state, ensuring that the relevant files are closed, and so on.

 **TIP**

> To close a workbook that contains a macro named Auto_Close and bypass the auto-close macro, hold down the Shift key and choose Close from the File menu.

Waiting for an Event

 SEE ALSO

For more information about calling one procedure from another, see "Macro Subroutines," page 896.

Sometimes you'd like a macro to run, not at the moment the user initiates the macro (for example, by choosing a menu command, clicking a toolbar button, or pressing a key combination associated with the macro), but when a specific event occurs in the Excel environment. Examples of these events are:

- When the user presses a particular key combination

- When a worksheet is recalculated

- When a particular sheet or window is activated or deactivated

- When the user chooses the Undo or Repeat command from the Edit menu

- At a particular time or on a particular date

In the case of the RiverReport project, suppose you want Excel to wait until a predetermined time, say 2:00 AM, before downloading the river depth data from the remote FTP site. The StartMyApp procedure accomplishes this task. Enter it in the AMainCode module just after the Auto_Open macro.

```
Sub StartMyApp()
'Make sure we want the report.
answer = Notify("Download data tonight?")
```

```
'If user clicks OK, start MainProc at startTime.
If answer = vbOK Then
    RiverReportOptions 'Dialog box to verify settings.
    Application.OnTime _
      EarliestTime:=startTime, _
      Procedure:="MainProc"
End If
End Sub

Function Notify(msg)
'Standard message box for RiverReport project.
    btns = vbOKCancel + vbQuestion + vbDefaultButton1
    msgboxTitle = "River Depth Data Reporting System"
    Notify = MsgBox(CStr(msg), btns, msgboxTitle)
End Function
```

The StartMyApp procedure calls the Notify function, which in turn uses the MsgBox function to ask the user whether to go ahead with the request. The MsgBox function creates simple dialog boxes. The first argument in the MsgBox function specifies the message to display. The *btns* variable stores a series of Excel constants (beginning with the text *vb*) that specify the type of buttons to display, an icon, and which of the buttons to choose if the user presses Enter. The last argument specifies the title to use on the title bar of the dialog box. (In this case, via the variable *msgboxTitle*.)

For example, the MsgBox statement in the Notify procedure displays the dialog box shown in Figure 30-2. Clicking OK causes the MsgBox function to return TRUE. Clicking Cancel causes the function to return FALSE. These logical results are then used to branch to different parts of the macro, either ending or continuing the task.

FIGURE 30-2.

The Notify procedure displays this alert box.

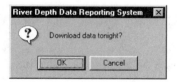

If the user clicks OK or presses Enter, the If...End If structure in the StartMyApp procedure calls the RiverReportOptions procedure (created in the next section), which presents the dialog box shown in Figure 30-3 so the user can enter or verify settings for the project.

The OnTime method posts a request to wait until the time value stored in *startTime* is reached, at which time Excel is to execute the MainProc macro, which calls the various procedures in the project, one by one.

The OnTime method runs a macro at a specified date and time. The *earliestTime* argument supplies a serial date value that represents the date and time at which you want the macro to run. If the value is less than one, the specified macro runs every day.

FIGURE 30-3.

The dialog box presented by the RiverReportOptions routine.

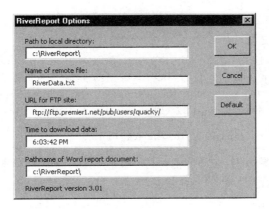

Under some circumstances, Excel does not respond to the OnTime method as expected. If the module that contains the macro isn't open when the correct time arrives, Excel ignores the request. Similarly, if Excel isn't in Ready mode at the specified time or during the tolerance period, it waits until the tolerance period elapses and then cancels the macro's execution. And (of course) Excel must be running at the specified time in order for the event to be trapped.

If you want to download the file every evening, you can add the StartMyApp routine to the auto-open procedure described in "Running a Macro Automatically," page 920. As long as the workbook that contains this auto-open procedure is in the Excel XLStart folder, all you need to do is start Excel. The workbook opens automatically, and Excel runs the procedure.

Using a Custom Dialog Box to Load and Save Options

When the user clicks OK in the little dialog box presented by the Notify function, the RiverReport project presents the RiverReport Options dialog box shown in Figure 30-3. This dialog box requests verification of settings for the project. Both the current and default settings for the project are stored on the AppOptions sheet in the

RiverReport workbook, and they are transferred to the custom dialog box you will create in the next section. You will also develop several Visual Basic routines that manage the process of transferring values back and forth between the sheet, the dialog box, and the Visual Basic code being executed.

Creating an Options Sheet

First, create a sheet in the RiverReport.xls workbook to store the current settings. This sheet will also store a set of default settings, so when the user clicks the Default button in the RiverReport Options dialog box, a routine will make the default settings the current settings.

To accomplish this, do the following:

1   Switch to Sheet2 in the RiverReport workbook and change its name to AppOptions.

2   In the sheet, enter the data shown in Figure 30-4.

FIGURE 30-4.

The AppOptions sheet, storing the current and default settings.

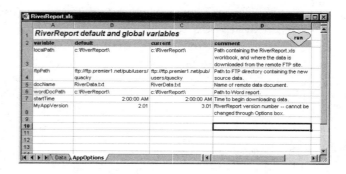

3   Next define range names on the sheet. Select range A3:C8 and choose Name and then Create from the Insert menu. In the Create Names dialog box, make sure only the Left Column option is selected, and then click OK.

This creates a series of names that refer to horizontal two-cell ranges on the AppOptions sheet. For example, if you choose Name and then Define from the Insert menu, and then select the *localPath* name, you see that *localPath* refers to the two-cell range $B$3:$C$3.

4   Select cells B2:C8 and choose Name and then Create from the Insert menu. In the Create Names dialog box make sure only the Top Row option is selected and then click OK.

This creates a pair of names that refer to vertical ranges on the AppOptions sheet. For example, if you choose Name and then Define from the Insert menu and select the *default* name, you see that *default* refers to the range $B$3:$B$8.

Now, to find a current or default setting for the project, you need only use Excel's *intersection operator* to find the value at the intersection of the relevant horizontal and vertical ranges. The intersection operator is a space character—that is, you press the Spacebar between the two range entries. For example, to find the default starting time for downloading the remote FTP file, you would enter the following formula in a cell on any worksheet in RiverReport.xls:

    =startTime default

This formula returns the value in cell B7, which should contain the time value 2:00:00 AM. (Note that the time may be formatted as a number. To display it in time format, right-click to display the shortcut menu and select Format Cells. Select the Number tab, click Time in the Categories list, select a type, and then click OK.)

Using the intersection operator to find range values is a very handy programming technique when you'd like to look up values in a rectangular array of cells using a method that is intrinsically self-documenting.

Creating a UserForm

Now that you have a place to store RiverReport settings from one session to the next, you need a way to present the settings to the user so they can be checked or changed, as needed. To do this, use the Visual Basic editing environment to create an object called a *form* (or sometimes, a *userform*). When displayed to the user, the form appears as the RiverReport Options dialog box. To create the form, do the following:

1 From the Tools menu choose Macro and Visual Basic Editor to switch to the Visual Basic Editor.

2 From the Insert menu choose UserForm to create a new form. Excel inserts a new userform and displays the Toolbox shown in Figure 30-5 on the next page.

Figure 30-5 shows the completed form, which you can recreate as you work through this section. Forms are containers for *controls*; you click a control in the Toolbox and drag it to the UserForm1 object to create a control on the form.

3 Click the Label tool (the large letter A in the Toolbox), and for each label shown in Figure 30-5, drag a rectangle, select the text in the rectangle, and then enter the text shown in Figure 30-5.

4 Click the TextBox tool and drag in UserForm1 to create the five text boxes shown in Figure 30-5.

5 Click the CommandButton tool and drag in UserForm1 to create the three buttons shown in Figure 30-5. Select the text in each button and then enter *OK*, *Cancel*, and *Default*, respectively.

6 For each item indicated in Figure 30-5, select the item, click the Properties window, and then change the (Name) property for the item to the name listed here.

Item	Name
Path to local directory:	localPathTextBox
Name of remote file:	docNameTextBox
URL for FTP site:	ftpPathTextBox
Time to download data:	startTimeTextBox
Path name of Word report document:	wordDocPathTextBox
RiverReport version:	MyAppVersionLabel

Step 6 is very important—the routines in the RiverReport project use the name given each text box to record the information entered and transfer it to the public variables and to the AppOptions sheet in the RiverReport workbook.

FIGURE 30-5.

Create a new userform that will become the RiverReport Options dialog box and name the items in it as shown.

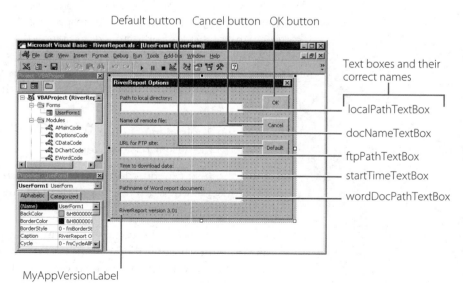

Default button   Cancel button   OK button

Text boxes and their correct names

localPathTextBox

docNameTextBox

ftpPathTextBox

startTimeTextBox

wordDocPathTextBox

MyAppVersionLabel

Displaying the UserForm

Now that you have both the AppOptions sheet and a dialog box for presenting options to the user, you need to develop routines for transferring values from the AppOptions sheet to the dialog box, displaying the dialog box, and then transferring values back to the AppOptions sheet.

1   In the Visual Basic Editor, choose Module from the Insert menu. Excel inserts a module called Module2 in the RiverReport project.

2   In the Project Explorer window, select the Module2 module, and in the Properties window, change the module's name from Module2 to BOptionsCode.

In the BOptionsCode window, enter the following routine:

```
Sub RiverReportOptions()
'Set RiverReport options, stored in sheet AppOptions.
'Code for OK, Cancel, and Default are in UserForm1

   Load UserForm1
   'Get & set public variables, declared in AMainCode.
   'Path to directory for downloading data.
   With Worksheets("AppOptions")
      localPath = .Range("localPath current").Value
      UserForm1.localPathTextBox.Value = localPath

      'Set path for FTP site.
      ftpPath = .Range("ftpPath current").Value
      UserForm1.ftpPathTextBox.Value = ftpPath

      'Name of remote document.
      docName = .Range("docName current").Value
      UserForm1.docNameTextBox.Value = docName

      'Path to Word report.
      wordDocPath = .Range("wordDocPath current").Value
      UserForm1.wordDocPathTextBox.Value = wordDocPath

      'Time to get data - uses Text property to
      'get the displayed date rather than
      'the underlying date value.
      startTime = .Range("startTime current").Text
      UserForm1.startTimeTextBox.Value = startTime

      'MyApp version number, put into
      'MyAppVersionLabel at the bottom of the form.
      MyAppVersion =.Range("MyAppVersion current").Text
      UserForm1.MyAppVersionLabel.Caption = _
         "RiverReport version" + CStr(MyAppVersion)
   End With

   'Present the dialog box.
   UserForm1.Show
End Sub
```

The first instruction in the routine,

```
Load UserForm1
```

loads the userform object into memory prior to actually displaying it to the user. The statement

```
UserForm1.Show
```

displays the userform object to the user.

The statements between these two lines of code use the With...End With construct in Visual Basic to apply a series of statements to the AppOptions worksheet object, to "preload" the userform with values transferred from the AppOptions sheet. This code appears in the routine as couplets. In the first couplet,

```
localPath = .Range("localPath current").Value
UserForm1.localPathTextBox.Value = localPath
```

the first line of code uses the intersection operator discussed earlier in this chapter to get the value from the cell that is the intersection of the *localPath* and *current* ranges on the AppOptions worksheet, and store that value in the public variable *localPath*.

The second line of code takes this value and puts it in the text box named *localPathTextBox* in UserForm1.

A Minor Problem

As long as you're in the BOptionsCode module, you need to solve one minor problem: when Excel encounters the OnTime statement in the StartMyApp routine and begins waiting for the appointed hour to retrieve the data at the remote FTP site, it "forgets" the values of the public variables you have set. To fix this, you need to add a routine called LoadVariables that reads the current settings from the AppOptions sheet into the public variables you have declared. LoadVariables is called as the first line of executable code in the MainProc routine described on page 920. To implement this routine, place the insertion point at the end of the RiverReportOptions routine and enter the following code:

```
Sub LoadVariables()
'Get RiverReport options, stored in sheet AppOptions.

  With Worksheets("AppOptions")
    'Path for downloading data.
    localPath = .Range("localPath current").Value
    'Path for FTP site.
    ftpPath = .Range("ftpPath current").Value
```

```
    'Name of remote doc.
    docName = Range("docName current").Value
    'Path to Word report.
    wordDocPath = .Range("wordDocPath current").Value
    'Time to get data - uses Text property to
    'get the displayed date rather than the
    'underlying date value.
    startTime = .Range("startTime current").Text
    'RiverReport version number.
    MyAppVersion = _
        .Range("MyAppVersion current").Text
  End With

End Sub
```

UserForm Code

1 Double click UserForm1 in the Project Explorer window to display the RiverReport Options dialog box code. You need to implement three routines that are activated when the user clicks the OK, Cancel, or Default buttons on the form. Click the right mouse button on the UserForm1 item in the Project Explorer window. Excel displays the shortcut menu for the item. Choose View Code.

2 In the window that appears, enter the following routines.

```
Private Sub OKButton_Click()
'Transfer info from dialog box to sheet and global
'vars. Get whatever's entered in the text boxes
'and store in worksheet as globals.
'Get and set global variables, declared in AMainCode.
'No validation of user entry in this routine.

  With Worksheets("AppOptions")
    'Path to directory for downloading data.
    localPath = UserForm1.localPathTextBox.Text
    .Range("localPath current").Formula = localPath

    'Set path for FTP site.
    ftpPath = UserForm1.ftpPathTextBox.Text
    .Range("ftpPath current").Formula = ftpPath

    'Name of remote document.
    docName = UserForm1.docNameTextBox.Text
    .Range("docName current").Formula = docName

    'Path to Word report.
    wordDocPath = UserForm1.wordDocPathTextBox.Text
    .Range("wordDocPath current").Formula = _
      wordDocPath
```

```
        'Time to get data. Could add error checking here
        'to see if the text entered can be converted
        'into a date, using IsDate().
        startTime = CDate(UserForm1.startTimeTextBox.Text)
        .Range("startTime current").Formula = startTime
    End With

    'Hide UserForm1 dialog box.
    UserForm1.Hide

End Sub


Private Sub CancelButton_Click()
'Just hide the UserForm1 dialog without
'updating sheet or global variables.
'Global variables remain as set in
'ASetOptions.RiverReportOptions

    UserForm1.Hide

End Sub


Private Sub DefaultButton_Click()
'Transfer default settings from AppOptions sheet
'to UserForm1 dialog box entries.

    'Get and set global variables,
    'declared in AMainCode.
    With Worksheets("AppOptions")
        'Path to directory for downloading data.
        localPath = .Range("localPath default").Text
        UserForm1.localPathTextBox.Text = localPath

        'Set path for FTP site.
        ftpPath = .Range("ftpPath default").Text
        UserForm1.ftpPathTextBox.Text = ftpPath

        'Name of remote document.
        docName = .Range("docName default").Text
        UserForm1.docNameTextBox.Text = docName

        'Path to Word report.
        wordDocPath = .Range("wordDocPath default").Text
        UserForm1.wordDocPathTextBox.Text = wordDocPath

        'Time to get data - uses Text property to
        'get the displayed date
        'rather than the underlying date value.
        startTime = .Range("startTime default").Text
        UserForm1.startTimeTextBox.Value = startTime
    End With

End Sub
```

As you can see, these three routines are very similar to the RiverReportOptions routine. When the user clicks the OK button, the OKButton_Click routine is run, the first couplet of which (for example)

```
localPath = UserForm1.localPathTextBox.Text
.Range("localPath current").Formula = localPath
```

takes the value entered in the dialog box and transfers it to the cell at the intersection of the range names *localPath* and *current* on the AppOptions worksheet. When all values have been transferred to the worksheet, OKButton_Click hides the form.

The CancelButton_Click routine is much simpler: it simply hides the form without updating the AppOptions worksheet.

The third routine, DefaultButton_Click, is similar to RiverReportOptions but loads the form with values from the *default* column of the AppOptions worksheet rather than the *current* column.

Downloading Data via the Internet

So far in the execution of the RiverReport project, the project has interrogated the user for the correct settings and waited for the time specified in the startTime public variable. Once the time specified in the OnTime statement of the StartMyApp procedure has been completed, the MainProc routine begins calling its subroutines, one after another: downloading data, updating the table, creating the chart, and so on.

The first subroutine, GetRemoteData, downloads the file stored in the *docName* variable (that is, RivrData.txt) from the public FTP site stored in *ftpPath,* which usually contains the default value

ftp://ftp.premier1.net/pub/users/quacky/.

This application does not include code to make a connection to your Internet service provider, so you will need to connect manually in order for this application to run unattended.

First choose Module from the Insert menu, rename the module CDataCode as before, and then enter the following routine:

```
Sub GetRemoteData()
'Open file at remote FTP site,
'and save in local directory. Mostly recorded -
'edited ftp pathname + doc name.
```

```
        Workbooks.Open FileName:=ftpPath + docName
        'Change to local directory.
        ChDir localPath
        'Save workbook in local directory.
        ActiveWorkbook.SaveAs _
          FileName:=localPath + docName, _
          FileFormat:=xlExcel5, _
          Password:="", _
          WriteResPassword:="", _
          ReadOnlyRecommended:=False, _
          CreateBackup:=False
        'Could add something here to shut down
        'the Internet connection.
        End Sub
```

? SEE ALSO

For more information about accessing remote FTP sites, see "Working with FTP Sites in Excel," page 619.

This routine, incidentally, was first recorded by opening an Internet connection and choosing a directory on the local hard disk; doing this "hard-wires" the directory choices into the recorded macro. After it was recorded, the routine was changed so the public variables *ftpPath*, *localPath*, and *docName* were used instead.

Working with Text Files

Excel's Text Import Wizard does an admirable job of importing files with formats other than those native to the Excel environment. For example, the text file of river depth measurements downloaded from the remote FTP site looks like this:

6/10/00   4.5   7.1   11.7   19.2

Each time the RivrData.txt file is accessed, there could be one or more lines of data in the form of text. Each line of text consists of the date and the measurements from each of the four sites along the river. Each item is separated from the next by a tab character.

For the RiverReport project, you need a procedure that can open and read the text for each day of data and transfer each item of data to the correct location at the end of the database that contains previously captured measurements. Figure 30-1 on page 918 shows the database as it looks when we start recording the macro. Notice that data for a few days was already entered.

After the macro was recorded, it was edited to replace hard-wired file and path names with the public variables and to add comments that describe the actions taken to create the macro.

Now enter the ImportData procedure just after the GetRemoteData procedure in the CDataCode module. This procedure was recorded using the steps described in the internal comments.

```
Sub ImportData()
'Import text file downloaded from remote FTP site.
'Select entire table, then go to next row.
  Windows("RiverReport.xls").Activate
  'Choose Edit>Goto, and double-click tableRange.
  Application.Goto Reference:="tableRange"
  'Relative reference: press Down arrow once.
  ActiveCell.Offset(1, 0).Range("A1").Select
  'Go to end of first column
  Selection.End(xlDown).Select
  'Relative reference: press Down arrow once.
  ActiveCell.Offset(1, 0).Range("A1").Select

  'Text Import Wizard options, reformatted a bit.
  'Changed FileName to point to localPath directory.
  Workbooks.OpenText _
    FileName:=localPath + docName, _
    Origin:=xlWindows, _
    StartRow:=1, _
    DataType:=xlDelimited, _
    TextQualifier:=xlDoubleQuote, _
    ConsecutiveDelimiter:=False, _
    Tab:=True, _
    Semicolon:=False, _
    Comma:=False, _
    Space:=False, _
    Other:=False, _
    FieldInfo:=Array(Array(1, 3), Array(2, 1), _
    Array(3, 1), Array(4, 1), Array(5, 1))

  'Select all the new data in the sheet, copy it,
  'switch to RiverReport.xls, and paste in new row.
  Range("A1").Select
  Selection.CurrentRegion.Select
  Selection.Copy
  Windows("RiverReport.xls").Activate
  ActiveSheet.Paste

  'Redefine tableRange to include new data,
  'so that Chart code can find it.
  Application.Goto Reference:="tableRange"
  Selection.CurrentRegion.Select
  Selection.Name = "tableRange"
  'This was not recorded.

  'Close source data file--added docName.
  Windows(docName).Activate
  ActiveWorkbook.Close

End Sub
```

Formatting a Worksheet

The simplest way to format a worksheet table from within a procedure is to turn on the Macro Recorder and use the Cells command on the Format menu, like this:

1   From the Tools menu, choose Macro and then Record New Macro. In the Record Macro dialog box, enter *FormatData* as the name of the macro and select This Workbook from the Store Macro In drop-down box. Click OK.

2   In the RiverReport.xls workbook, activate the Data sheet, select column A, and then choose Cells from the Format menu.

3   Click the Number tab. From the Category list, select Date, and then select the *m/d/yy ddd* format.

4   Click the Alignment tab. In the Horizontal group, select the Left alignment option and then click OK.

5   Select columns B through E and again choose Cells from the Format menu.

6   Click the Number tab. From the Category list, select Number and then specify two decimal places.

7   Click OK to close the Format Cells dialog box.

8   Click the Stop Recording toolbar button.

9   Activate the Visual Basic Editor and move the recorded macro from the module in which it was recorded to the end of the CDataCode module.

Here is the resulting code, with comments added to indicate the various formats selected:

```
Sub FormatData()
'Reformat the table.

    'Select Column A and apply date, alignment formats.
    Columns("A:A").Select
    Selection.NumberFormat = "m/d/yy ddd"
    With Selection
        .HorizontalAlignment = xlLeft
        .VerticalAlignment = xlBottom
        .WrapText = False
        .Orientation = xlHorizontal
        .AddIndent = False
    End With
```

```
      'Select cols B through E and apply number format.
      Columns("B:E").Select
      Selection.NumberFormat = "0.00"
   End Sub
```

Notice that Excel recorded every option set on the Alignment tab of the Format Cells dialog box. If you want, you can delete these lines in the With Selection-End With block, leaving only the specific options you want the procedure to set.

Creating a Chart

You may find it easiest to record the ChartWizard steps necessary to create and format a chart. For example, the following code is a series of statements recorded using the ChartWizard that charts the daily depths generated by the RiverReport project. The code was edited a bit; comments and edited code were added to mark the various actions taken.

Before you enter the code, create a new module in the RiverReport.xls workbook called DChartCode. Here's the CreateChart routine:

```
   Sub CreateChart()
   'Creates chart from data in Data!tableRange.

     Charts.Add
     ActiveChart.ChartType = xlLineMarkers
     'Store name of chart created--not recorded.
     chartSheetName = ActiveChart.Name

     'Establish source data for chart.
     'Replaced absolute cell range with tableRange.
     ActiveChart.SetSourceData _
       Source:=Sheets("Data").Range("tableRange"), _
       PlotBy:=xlColumns
     ActiveChart.Location Where:=xlLocationAsNewSheet

     With ActiveChart
       .HasTitle = True
       .ChartTitle.Characters.Text = _
         "Skagit River Depth Data"
       .Axes(xlCategory, xlPrimary).HasTitle = False
       .Axes(xlValue, xlPrimary).HasTitle = True
       .Axes(xlValue, xlPrimary).AxisTitle _
         .Characters.Text = "Depth, in feet"
       .HasAxis(xlCategory, xlPrimary) = True
       .HasAxis(xlValue, xlPrimary) = True
     End With
```

```
    ActiveChart.Axes(xlCategory, xlPrimary) _
      .CategoryType = xlAutomatic
    With ActiveChart.Axes(xlCategory)
      .HasMajorGridlines = False
      .HasMinorGridlines = False
    End With

    With ActiveChart.Axes(xlValue)
      .HasMajorGridlines = True
      .HasMinorGridlines = False
    End With

    ActiveChart.ApplyDataLabels _
      Type:=xlDataLabelsShowNone, _
      LegendKey:=False

    'Format y-axis
    ActiveChart.Axes(xlValue).AxisTitle.Select
    Selection.AutoScaleFont = True
    With Selection.Font
      .Name = "Arial"
      .FontStyle = "Bold"
      .Size = 14
    End With

    'Format chart title.
    ActiveChart.ChartTitle.Select
    Selection.AutoScaleFont = True
    With Selection.Font
      .Name = "Arial"
      .FontStyle = "Bold"
      .Size = 16
    End With

    'Format x-axis.
    ActiveChart.Axes(xlCategory).Select
    With Selection.Border
      .Weight = xlHairline
      .LineStyle = xlAutomatic
    End With

    With Selection
      .MajorTickMark = xlNone
      .MinorTickMark = xlNone
      .TickLabelPosition = xlNextToAxis
    End With

    Selection.TickLabels.AutoScaleFont = True
    With Selection.TickLabels.Font
      .Name = "Arial"
      .FontStyle = "Regular"
      .Size = 12
    End With
```

```
'Format chart legend
ActiveChart.Legend.Select
Selection.AutoScaleFont = True
With Selection.Font
  .Name = "Arial"
  .FontStyle = "Regular"
  .Size = 12
End With

'Set border and marker formats for each series.
'For Each...End With structure not recorded.
For Each Series In ActiveChart.SeriesCollection
  Series.Select
  With Selection.Border
    .Weight = xlThin
    .LineStyle = xlAutomatic
  End With

  With Selection
    .MarkerBackgroundColorIndex = 1
    .MarkerForegroundColorIndex = 1
    .MarkerStyle = xlDiamond
    .Smooth = False
    .MarkerSize = 7
    .Shadow = False
  End With
  Next
End Sub
```

The major edit in this mostly recorded macro is the last block enclosed with

```
For Each Series In ActiveChart.SeriesCollection
.
.
.
Next
```

We used this construction because we wanted to apply the same line weight and marker options to each of the four series in the chart, since Excel records the actions as four independent blocks of code.

The resulting chart looks like the one shown in Figure 30-6 at the top of the next page. (When running the application yourself, choose Sized With Window from the View menu to make the chart easier to see.)

FIGURE 30-6.

The chart of river depth data is created by the CreateChart routine.

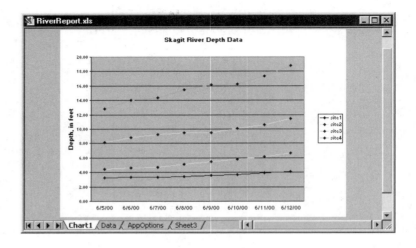

Controlling Word from an Excel Macro

You can use Visual Basic's support of Automation to directly access an object in another application. With Automation, you can act upon any object that is listed in the application's object library, such as windows, toolbars, documents, or data. For example, you could transfer text from an Excel worksheet to Word, make use of Word's search and replace features, and transfer the text back to an Excel worksheet without the user knowing that Word was used. This is the technique we'll use to control Word 2000 from Excel.

The GenWordReport Routine

This macro was created using Word 2000. If you're using an earlier version of Word, your results may vary.

This routine was created in an interesting way; instead of writing the code by hand, line by line, it was recorded as a Word macro! After recording it, the text of the macro was copied and pasted into an Excel module. Then each Word Visual Basic statement was transformed into a command from Excel Visual Basic to control Word externally.

For example, to create a new document in Word, you could turn on Word's macro recorder and then choose New from the File menu, resulting in the following Word Visual Basic code:

```
Documents.Add Template:="", NewTemplate:=False
```

To transform this into a command in Excel, you need to launch Word and store the name of the application object created in a variable. You do this with the CreateObject method, as follows:

```
Dim wordApp As Object
Set wordApp = CreateObject("word.application")
```

CreateObject launches Word and returns the name of the application object created, which is stored in the variable wordApp. Any Word Visual Basic command you've recorded can then be made a submethod or subproperty of the Word application object, as in

```
Documents.Add Template:= "C:\Windows\_
    Application Data\ Microsoft\Templates\Normal.dot",_
    NewTemplate:=False, Document Type=0
```

This is the approach we've used throughout the GenWordReport routine—any instruction that begins with wordApp was recorded first in Word and then moved to Excel.

Before entering the code, create a new module in the RiverReport project and name it EWordCode. Next, enter the last routine in the RiverReport application—the GenWordReport routine:

```
'Control Word from Excel, creating new report
'for Excel table and chart. Macro recorded
'mostly in Word, and transferred to Excel

Dim wordApp As Object
set wordApp = CreateObject("word.application")

'Make Word visible for debugging.
wordApp.Visible = True
```

We added the last instruction in this group so that you can watch Word create the new document; after you've debugged the GenWordReport routine, you could change True to False.

> **NOTE**
>
> Even though we're jumping in here to explain various aspects of tricky code, keep typing the Visual Basic code you see in the rest of this chapter as part of the GenWordReport routine.

```
'Create a new Word document.
wordApp.Documents.Add Template:="C:\Windows\_
    Application Data\Microsoft\Templates\Normal.dot", _
    NewTemplate:=False, Document Type=0

'Enter document title.
wordApp.Selection.TypeText _
    Text:="Data Collection Report"
wordApp.Selection.Style = _
    wordApp.ActiveDocument.Styles("Heading 1")
wordApp.Selection.TypeParagraph

'Enter creation date of document.
wordApp.Selection.TypeText Text:="Received "
```

```
wordApp.Selection.InsertDateTime _
  DateTimeFormat:="dddd, MMMM dd, yyyy", _
  InsertAsField:=False, _
  DateLanguage:=wdEnglishUS, CalendarType:= _
  wdCalendarWestern, InsertAsFullWidth:=False
wordApp.Selection.TypeParagraph
```

Here we enter in the new Word document the date the data was received, by concatenating the text Received with the date the report was created, formatted in the form Friday, January 01, 2000.

```
'Enter heading for raw data, in Heading 2 style
wordApp.Selection.TypeText Text:="The Data"
wordApp.Selection.Style = _
   wordApp.ActiveDocument.Styles("Heading 2")
wordApp.Selection.TypeParagraph

' Create bookmark for raw data table.
With wordApp.ActiveDocument.Bookmarks
  .Add Range:=wordApp.Selection.Range, _
    Name:="dataTable"
  .DefaultSorting = wdSortByName
  .ShowHidden = False
End With
```

Here we create a bookmark called dataTable, so we can find the correct place to insert the table of river depth data from the Excel worksheet.

```
'Down two lines, and enter heading for charted data.
wordApp.Selection.TypeParagraph
wordApp.Selection.TypeParagraph
wordApp.Selection.TypeText Text:="Charted Data"
wordApp.Selection.Style = _
   wordApp.ActiveDocument.Styles("Heading 2")
wordApp.Selection.TypeParagraph

'Create bookmark for data chart.
With wordApp.ActiveDocument.Bookmarks
  .Add Range:=wordApp.Selection.Range, _
    Name:="dataChart"
  .DefaultSorting = wdSortByName
  .ShowHidden = False
End With
```

In the following section of code, we move the table and chart created in Excel to the report created in Word. However, creating a routine for transferring material between Excel and Word requires another little trick. Neither Excel's nor Word's macro recorder can record actions in an application other than the application in which the macro is being recorded. Because of this, if you record the selection of the data table in RiverReport in Excel, copy it, switch to Word, and then paste the table into the new report, the resulting macro will contain only the actions performed in Excel. To get around this, simply record the sequence of actions twice—once while recording from Excel, and once while recording from Word—and then mesh the two recorded macros into one.

There are two main sequences in the following section of code. Each sequence finds an object in Excel, copies it as a picture, and then finds a bookmark in the Word document and pastes the object. Copying each object as a picture preserves the formatting of the object, makes it easy to paste the object into Word in line with text, and isolates the resulting Word document completely from the Excel workbook whose data was used to create the report.

```
'Switch to Excel, copy table as picture.
AppActivate "Microsoft Excel", False
Application.Goto Reference:="tableRange"

Selection.CopyPicture Appearance:=xlScreen, _
    Format:=xlPicture

'Switch to Word.
AppActivate "Microsoft Word", False

'Go to bookmark "dataTable"
wordApp.Selection.Goto Name:="dataTable"

'Paste table.
wordApp.Selection.Paste

'Select chart and copy as picture.
'Recorded, but replaced with global chart name.
Sheets(chartSheetName).Select
ActiveChart.ChartArea.Select
ActiveChart.CopyPicture Appearance:=xlScreen, _
    Format:=xlPicture

'Go to bookmark "dataChart"
wordApp.Selection.Goto Name:="dataChart"

'Paste chart.
wordApp.Selection.Paste
```

Finally, we want the routine to save the report to disk and print it, as shown in the final passage in the GenWordReport routine.

Printing a document in Word involves the Visual Basic equivalent of choosing Page Setup from the File menu, setting a series of printing options, clicking the Print button, and then clicking OK to print the document. As before, the macro was created by recording actions in Word and then the resulting macro was moved to Excel, as follows:

```
'Change to the directory specified.
wordApp.ChangeFileOpenDirectory localPath
```

Here the public variable localPath is used to set the directory where the new Word report is saved.

```
'Save report to the local directory.
wordApp.ActiveDocument.SaveAs _
   FileName:="Data Collection Report.doc", _
   FileFormat:=wdFormatDocument, _
   LockComments:=False, Password:="", _
   AddToRecentFiles:=True, _
   WritePassword:="", _
   ReadOnlyRecommended:=False, _
   EmbedTrueTypeFonts:=False, _
   SaveNativePictureFormat:=False, _
   SaveFormsData:=False, _
   SaveAsAOCELetter:=False

End Sub
```

Figure 30-7 shows a sample of the Word document generated by the GenWordReport routine.

FIGURE 30-7.

The Word document created by GenWordReport.

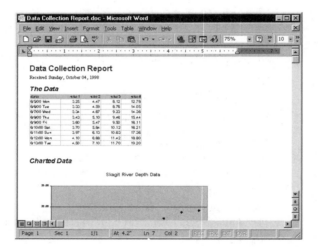

Converting to an Add-In Application

After you create and thoroughly debug a series of command and function macros that work well as a system, you can convert them to a format that makes them appear as if they are part of Microsoft Excel itself. To save the active workbook in add-in format, choose Save As from the File menu and then select Microsoft Excel Add-In from the Save As Type drop-down list. When you open the resulting add-in file, it is hidden and cannot be displayed with the Unhide command.

To protect the intellectual property of a developer of Excel macro applications, a workbook saved as an add-in is unreadable by anyone—even the developer. There are no passwords, and the data in the resulting file is stored in an unreadable format (unreadable by people, at least). It's a good idea to save a backup copy of the workbook that contains your modules before you convert it to an add-in, just in case you need to make modifications in the future.

You can put an auto-open procedure in a workbook destined to become an add-in, and you can put the add-in itself in the XLStart folder so Excel opens the add-in automatically. By careful use of an auto-open procedure in an add-in, you can even create an application that completely changes the standard appearance of Excel, replacing all the built-in menus and toolbars with those of your own design.

WARNING

Some sets of procedures work in a workbook but do not work when saved as an add-in. For example, RiverReport.xls does not work as an add-in. You cannot add data to an add-in file as you would to a normal workbook because add-ins are hidden and don't have windows. Instead, you could adapt the macro so the code is separate from the data, storing the data in a regular workbook and then creating the chart in that workbook.

To save a workbook as an add-in, perform the following steps:

1 With the workbook active, choose Save As from the File menu.

2 In the Save As dialog box, enter the name you want to give the add-in file. Be careful to give the file a different name from that of the workbook itself; if you use the same name, Excel will overwrite the readable workbook with the unreadable add-in, and you'll have to reconstruct the workbook from scratch if you ever need to change it.

3 Select Microsoft Excel Add-In from the Save As Type drop-down list.

4 Click Save.

Index

Note to the reader: Italicized page numbers refer to figures, tables, and illustrations.

About the Authors

Mark Dodge was still a professional musician in 1982 when he bought his first "computer," a tiny Timex-Sinclair ZX-1000. Within two years, he was off the road and using his Compaq luggable on a daily basis running spreadsheets in a corporate accounting office. Three years later Mark began working for Microsoft Press, and over the past 12 years has co-authored seven editions of Windows and Mac books on Microsoft Excel, was the technical editor for over a dozen other Microsoft Press titles, served as a staff Senior Technical Writer for the Microsoft Office User Education department, and was the humble recipient of five awards from the Society for Technical Communication for writing and editing. Mark and his wife Vicki enjoy a nice contrast to the high-tech lifestyle as owners and operators of a small alpaca ranch in Western Washington.

Craig Stinson has been an industry journalist since 1981. He is currently a contributing editor of PC Magazine and formerly was the editor of *Softtalk for the IBM Personal Computer.* Craig is the author of

Running Windows 98 and coauthor of *Running Windows NT,* both published by Microsoft Press. In addition to his numerous computer publications, Craig has written music reviews for *Billboard* magazine, the *Boston Globe,* the *Christian Science Monitor, Musical America,* as well as many other publications. He lives with his wife and children in Colorado.

Colophon

The manuscript for this book was prepared and submitted to Microsoft Press in electronic form. Text files were prepared using Microsoft Word 97 for Windows. Pages were composed by nSight, Inc., using Adobe PageMaker 6.5 for Windows, with text in Garamond Light and display type in Myriad Black. Composed pages were delivered to the printer as electronic prepress files.

Cover Designer

Tim Girvin Design, Inc.

Interior Graphics Specialists

Vanessa White, Samantha Stanko

Principal Compositors

Tara Murray, Angela Montoya

Principal Proofreaders

Rachel Fischer Alberts, William Oppenheimer, Rebecca Merz

Indexer

Rebecca Plunkett

up! Step

STEP BY STEP books provide quick and easy self-training—to help you learn to use the powerful word processing, spreadsheet, database, presentation, communication, and Internet components of Microsoft® Office 2000—both individually and together. The easy-to-follow lessons present clear objectives and real-world business examples, with numerous screen shots and illustrations. Put Office 2000 to work today, with STEP BY STEP learning solutions, made by Microsoft.

- MICROSOFT OFFICE PROFESSIONAL 8-IN-1 STEP BY STEP
- MICROSOFT WORD 2000 STEP BY STEP
- MICROSOFT EXCEL 2000 STEP BY STEP
- MICROSOFT POWERPOINT® 2000 STEP BY STEP
- MICROSOFT INTERNET EXPLORER 5 STEP BY STEP
- MICROSOFT PUBLISHER 2000 STEP BY STEP
- MICROSOFT ACCESS 2000 STEP BY STEP
- MICROSOFT FRONTPAGE 2000 STEP BY STEP
- MICROSOFT OUTLOOK 2000 STEP BY STEP

Microsoft Press® products are available worldwide wherever quality computer books are sold. For more information, contact your book or computer retailer, software reseller, or local Microsoft Sales Office, or visit our Web site at mspress.microsoft.com. To locate your nearest source for Microsoft Press products, or to order directly, call 1-800-MSPRESS in the U.S. (in Canada, call 1-800-268-2222).

Prices and availability dates are subject to change.

mspress.microsoft.com

Microsoft Press offers *comprehensive* learning solutions to help new users, power users, and professionals get the most from *Microsoft technology.*

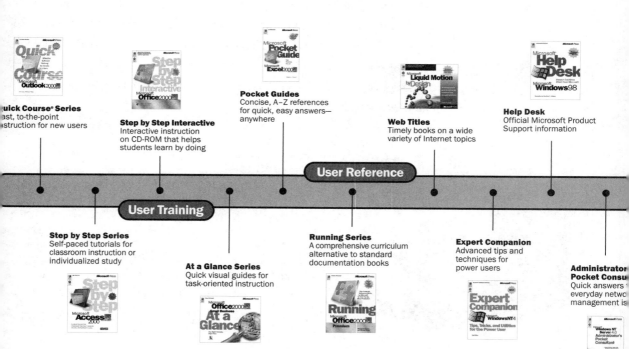

Quick Course® Series
Fast, to-the-point instruction for new users

Step by Step Interactive
Interactive instruction on CD-ROM that helps students learn by doing

Pocket Guides
Concise, A–Z references for quick, easy answers— anywhere

Web Titles
Timely books on a wide variety of Internet topics

Help Desk
Official Microsoft Product Support information

User Reference

User Training

Step by Step Series
Self-paced tutorials for classroom instruction or individualized study

At a Glance Series
Quick visual guides for task-oriented instruction

Running Series
A comprehensive curriculum alternative to standard documentation books

Expert Companion
Advanced tips and techniques for power users

Administrator Pocket Consu
Quick answers everyday netwo management is

Microsoft Press® products are available worldwide wherever quality computer books are sold. For more information, contact your book or computer retailer, software reseller, or local Microsoft Sales Office, or visit our Web site at mspress.microsoft.com. To locate your nearest source for Microsoft Press products, or to order directly, call 1-800-MSPRESS in the U.S. (in Canada, call 1-800-268-2222).

Prices and availability dates are subject to change.

With **over 200** *print,*
multimedia, and online resources—
whatever your information
need or learning style,
we've got a solution to help
you *start faster and go farther.*

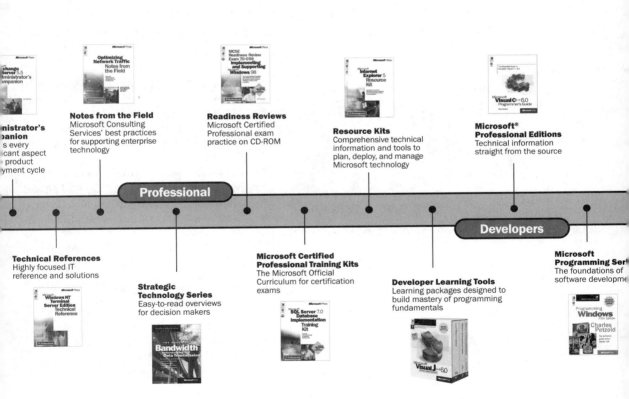

Exchange Server 5.5 Administrator's Companion

Notes from the Field
Microsoft Consulting Services' best practices for supporting enterprise technology

Readiness Reviews
Microsoft Certified Professional exam practice on CD-ROM

Resource Kits
Comprehensive technical information and tools to plan, deploy, and manage Microsoft technology

Microsoft® Professional Editions
Technical information straight from the source

Administrator's Companion
covers every significant aspect of the product deployment cycle

Professional

Technical References
Highly focused IT reference and solutions

Strategic Technology Series
Easy-to-read overviews for decision makers

Microsoft Certified Professional Training Kits
The Microsoft Official Curriculum for certification exams

Developer Learning Tools
Learning packages designed to build mastery of programming fundamentals

Developers

Microsoft Programming Series
The foundations of software development

Look for them at your bookstore
or computer store today!

mspress.microsoft.com

See clearly—
now!

Here's the remarkable, *visual* way to quickly find answers about the power-fully integrated features of the Microsoft® Office 2000 applications. Microsoft Press AT A GLANCE books let you focus on particular tasks and show you, with clear, numbered steps, the easiest way to get them done right now. Put Office 2000 to work today, with AT A GLANCE learning solutions, made by Microsoft.

- MICROSOFT OFFICE 2000 PROFESSIONAL AT A GLANCE
- MICROSOFT WORD 2000 AT A GLANCE
- MICROSOFT EXCEL 2000 AT A GLANCE
- MICROSOFT POWERPOINT® 2000 AT A GLANCE
- MICROSOFT ACCESS 2000 AT A GLANCE
- MICROSOFT FRONTPAGE® 2000 AT A GLANCE
- MICROSOFT PUBLISHER 2000 AT A GLANCE
- MICROSOFT OFFICE 2000 SMALL BUSINESS AT A GLANCE
- MICROSOFT PHOTODRAW® 2000 AT A GLANCE
- MICROSOFT INTERNET EXPLORER 5 AT A GLANCE
- MICROSOFT OUTLOOK® 2000 AT A GLANCE

Microsoft Press products are available worldwide wherever quality computer books are sold. For more information, contact your book or computer retailer, software reseller, or local Microsoft Sales Office, or visit our Web site at mspress.microsoft.com. To locate your nearest source for Microsoft Press products, or to order directly, call 1-800-MSPRESS in the U.S. (in Canada, call 1-800-268-2222).

Prices and availability dates are subject to change.

Microsoft®

mspress.microsoft.com

Register Today!

Return this
Running Microsoft® Excel 2000
registration card today

Microsoft®Press
mspress.microsoft.com

OWNER REGISTRATION CARD

1-57231-

Running Microsoft® Excel 2000

_____ _____ _____
FIRST NAME   **MIDDLE INITIAL**   **LAST NAME**

_____
INSTITUTION OR COMPANY NAME

_____
ADDRESS

_____

_____ _____ _____
CITY   **STATE**   **ZIP**

_____ **(   )**_____
E-MAIL ADDRESS   **PHONE NUMBER**

U.S. and Canada addresses only. Fill in information above and mail postage-free.
Please mail only the bottom half of this page.

For information about Microsoft Press®
products, visit our Web site at
mspress.microsoft.com

BUSINESS REPLY MAIL
FIRST-CLASS MAIL   PERMIT NO. 108   REDMOND WA

POSTAGE WILL BE PAID BY ADDRESSEE

MICROSOFT PRESS
PO BOX 97017
REDMOND, WA 98073-9830

NO POSTAGE
NECESSARY
IF MAILED
IN THE
UNITED STATES